NAVAL POLICY BETWEEN THE WARS

II: The Period of Reluctant Rearmament
1930–1939

Naval Policy Between the Wars

II: The Period of Reluctant Rearmament

1930-1939

STEPHEN ROSKILL

COLLINS

St James's Place, London

1976

William Collins Sons & Co Ltd
London · Glasgow · Sydney · Auckland
Toronto · Johannesburg

First published 1976
© S. W. Roskill, 1976
ISBN 0 00 211561 1
Set in Monotype Bembo
Made and Printed in Great Britain by
William Collins Sons & Co Ltd Glasgow

THIS BOOK IS DEDICATED TO THE
OFFICERS AND MEN OF THE ROYAL NAVY
WHO FOUGHT IN THE SECOND WORLD WAR,
AND IN MEMORY OF THOSE WHO GAVE
THEIR LIVES.

Illustrations

Contents

Contents

Glossary of Abbreviations

(British except where otherwise stated)

A-A	Anti-Aircraft (sometimes H/A for High Angle).
ABE	Aircraft Bomb Experiments Committee (1937).
ACAS	Assistant Chief of Air Staff.
ACHQ	Area Combined Headquarters.
ACNB	Australian Commonwealth Navy Board.
AC(Q)	Admiral Commanding Battle Cruiser Squadron.
Adm.	Admiralty paper in PRO followed by suffix indicated.
Admy.	Admiralty.
AFC	Anglo-French Conversations, 1939.
AFO	Admiralty Fleet Order.
Air	Air Ministry paper in PRO followed by suffix indicated.
AL	Admiralty letter followed by suffix indicated.
Air Min.	Air Ministry.
AM	Admiralty Message.
AMP	Air Member for Personnel, Air Council.
AOC	Air Officer Commanding, Royal Air Force.
AO, C-in-C	Air Officer Commanding-in-Chief, Royal Air Force.
A/S	Anti-Submarine.
ATB	Advisory Committee on Trade Defence (1938).
AWO	Admiralty Weekly Order.
BOT	Board of Trade.
Cab.	Cabinet Document in PRO followed by suffix giving series indicated.
CAFO	Confidential Admiralty Fleet Order.
CB	Confidential Book (Admiralty).
CE	Civil Establishments Branch, Admiralty.
CID	Committee of Imperial Defence or paper in PRO followed by suffix giving the series indicated.
C-in-C	Commander-in-Chief, Royal Navy.
Cmd.	Command Paper.
CNO	Chief of Naval Operations, US Navy.
CNS	Chief of Naval Staff, Admiralty.

Glossary of Abbreviations

COS	Chief of Staff or Chiefs of Staff Committee.
CP	Cabinet Paper followed by suffix giving number and year.
CS	Cruiser Squadron.
CW	Commissioned and Warrant Branch, Admiralty.
CZ	Czechoslovak Crisis, 1938.
DBFP	Documents on British Foreign Policy, followed by volume indicated.
DCAS	Deputy Chief of Air Staff, Royal Air Force.
DCM	Ministerial Disarmament Committee (1932–34).
DCNS	Deputy Chief of Naval Staff, Admiralty.
DEMS	Defensively Equipped Merchant Ship.
DM	Defence Preparedness Committee (1939).
DNAD	Director of Naval Air Division, Admiralty.
DNC	Director of Naval Construction, Admiralty.
DNE	Director of Naval Equipment, Admiralty.
DNI	Director of Naval Intelligence, Admiralty.
DNR	Director of Naval Recruiting, Admiralty.
DOD	Director of Operations Division, Admiralty.
D of P	Director of Plans Division, Admiralty.
DP	Defence Programmes Acceleration Committee (1939).
DP(P)	Defence Plans (Policy) Committee (1935).
DPRC	Defence Policy and Requirements Committee (1935).
DPS	Director of Personal Services, Admiralty.
DRC	Defence Requirements Committee (1933–35).
DSR	Director of Scientific Research, Admiralty.
DTD	Director of Trade Division, Admiralty.
EAC	Economic Advisory Council (1930), later Committee.
FAA	Fleet Air Arm, Royal Navy.
FDR	Franklin Delano Roosevelt, President of USA.
,,	Dep. Corresp. Roosevelt Papers, Departmental Correspondence.
,,	OF Roosevelt Papers, Official File.
,,	PPF Roosevelt Papers, President's Personal File.
,,	PSF Roosevelt Papers, President's Secretary's File.
FO	Foreign Office.
FP	Foreign Policy Committee of Cabinet.
F/R	Fighter Reconnaissance Aircraft.
FS	Fighting Services Committee (1929–30).
FRUS	Foreign Relations of the USA, followed by volume indicated.
GB	General Board, US Navy Department.
GCCS	Government Code and Cypher School.
GOC	General Officer Commanding.
GO, C-in-C	General Officer Commanding-in-Chief.
HDC	Home Defence Committee.

Glossary of Abbreviations

HR	House of Representatives, US Congress.
IC	Imperial Conference of year indicated.
IDC	Imperial Defence College.
JDC	Joint Home and Overseas Defence Committee.
JIC	Joint Intelligence Committee.
JPC	Joint Planning Committee.
LNC	London Naval Conference (1930).
L of N	League of Nations.
M	Military Branch, Admiralty.
MLC	Motor Landing Craft.
MP	Member of Parliament.
N	Naval Branch, Admiralty.
NA	Naval Attaché.
NC	London Naval Conference (1935–36) with suffix indicating series.
NC(M)	Ministerial Committee on above.
NCSO	Naval Control Service Officer.
NE	National Economy Committee, 1931.
NIRA	National Industrial Recovery Act, USA.
NL	Naval Law Branch, Admiralty.
NMM	National Maritime Museum, Greenwich.
NS	National Service Committee, 1936.
NZNB	New Zealand Naval Board.
ODC	Overseas Defence Committee.
OIC	Operational Intelligence Centre, Admiralty.
O-in-C	Order in Council.
ONI	Office of Naval Intelligence, USA.
Parl. Deb.	Parliamentary Debates (Hansard), Lords or Commons as indicated.
PD	Plans Division, Admiralty.
Premier	Prime Minister's Private Office correspondence in PRO.
PRO	Public Record Office, London.
PWA	Public Works Administration, USA.
RA	Royal Archives, Windsor (Also used for Rear-Admiral and for Reduction of Armaments Committee, 1929–31).
RAA	Rear-Admiral, Aircraft Carriers.
RABCS	Rear-Admiral Commanding Battle Cruiser Squadron.
RAF	Royal Air Force.
RAN	Royal Australian Navy.
RAOB	Royal and Antediluvian Order of Buffaloes.
RA(S)	Rear-Admiral, Submarines.
RCN	Royal Canadian Navy.
RG	Record Group in US National Archives.
RN	Royal Navy.
RNR	Royal Naval Reserve.

Glossary of Abbreviations

RNVSR	Royal Naval Volunteer Supplementary Reserve.
RNVR	Royal Naval Volunteer Reserve.
R of P	Report of Proceedings by HM Ships.
SDAC	Shipping Defence Advisory Committee (1936).
SOAF	Senior Officer, Atlantic Fleet.
SNO	Senior Naval Officer.
SNOA	Senior Naval Officer Afloat.
TD	Tactical Division, Admiralty.
TOO	Time of Origin (of message).
TSR	Torpedo-Spotter-Reconnaissance Aircraft.
UP	University Press indicated.
USN	United States Navy.
USNA	United States National Archives, followed by RG indicated.
VCS	Vulnerability of Capital Ships Committee (1937–39).
WPA	Works Progress Administration, USA.

Foreword

I FEEL THAT some explanation is necessary regarding the long interval between the publication of the first volume of this work in 1968 and the appearance of this one. The first volume, covering the years 1919–1929, was written under the rules incorporated in the 1958 Public Record Act (6 and 7 Eliz. ii, ch. 51) whereby 'authorised officers' of government departments were allowed to open official records before the expiration of the Fifty Year 'closed period' then in force. In my case the 'authorised officers' were at the time Sir John Lang, Permanent Secretary of the Admiralty, Sir Maurice Dean, Permanent Secretary of the Air Ministry and Sir Burke Trend, Secretary of the Cabinet and they all readily agreed to granting me that privilege provided that I submitted my typescript for scrutiny. That I did, and I was not required to delete or amend a single word.

I had originally intended to carry on immediately with this second volume, but when my research had progressed as far as about 1935 I found that the records I needed had not yet reached the Public Record Office. Though the departments concerned offered to allow me to carry on my research in their own Record Offices I was aware from my work on the maritime side of World War II (*The War at Sea 1939–1945*) that it would involve me in going through a vast mass of papers many of which were irrelevant to my purposes. Furthermore I was told that Xerox copying or microfilming of documents would not be possible, which would have been a considerable handicap. While I was deliberating on the problem facing me I was asked if I would write the authorised biography of the first Lord Hankey; and as I found that his large collection of papers and diaries had been left untouched since his death in 1963, I decided to undertake that work first and then return to *Naval Policy between the Wars*. This led to the production of the three volumes entitled *Hankey. Man of Secrets* (Collins, 1970–74).

By the time I had completed the Hankey biography the 1967 Public Record Act (15–16 Eliz. II, ch. 44) had been passed, reducing the 'closed period' for some but not all official records from 50 to 30 years. This change was obviously of great advantage to me, since it eliminated all question of obtaining special access to records or of submitting my typescript. But on resuming the research for this volume in 1973 I found that the departments had re-scrutinised their records and had imposed, as was permitted by the new Act, a longer 'closed period' than 30 years on many documents. I also found that some which I had used, and even quoted from, in my first volume, were now 'closed'. I was thus faced by the possible anomaly that my second volume would be written under more restrictive conditions than the first one; and when I pointed out the absurdity of this state of affairs the Department of the Navy agreed to open a large number of the closed papers to me, thus bringing the conditions to which both volumes were subject more or less into line. I am very grateful to Mr. D. R. J. Stephen, Deputy Under-Secretary of State (Navy) for the great trouble he took to achieve this desirable uniformity.

The main sources used for this volume are the Cabinet, Foreign Office, Treasury, Admiralty and Air Ministry papers in the Public Record Office, and I wish to thank Mr. J. R. Ede, the Keeper of Records, and his staff in Chancery Lane and Portugal Street for the efficiency and constant kindness shown in helping me to find what I needed and in answering my many importunities. All quotations from official documents are Crown Copyright and are reproduced by courtesy of The Controller, HM Stationery Office. I have made every endeavour to trace the ownership of copyright in other documents quoted, and to obtain permission to publish them. If I have inadvertently failed in any case to obtain permission I trust that the owner of the copyright will accept my apologies. Quotations from documents in the Royal Archives are reproduced by kind permission of HM The Queen.

In the Historical Branch of the Department of the Navy Rear-Admiral P. N. Buckley and his successor Commander R. C. Burton have been most generous in supplying answers to my questions, as has been Mr. Louis Jackets, Head of the Air Ministry's Historical Branch and his successor Group-Captain E. B. Haslam. Mr. Basil Greenhill, Director of the National Maritime Museum, Mr. David Proctor the Head of Education and Research Facilities and Mr. M. W. B. Sanderson, the Librarian, and his staff have all of them contributed substantially to the completion of this work.

For access to documents held in libraries and institutions I am indebted to the following:

HM The Queen—Papers of King George V.

Library of the University of Cambridge—Papers of 1st Earl Baldwin and 1st Viscount Templewood.

Library of the University of Birmingham—Papers of Sir Austen Chamberlain.

The Beaverbrook Library—Papers of 1st Earl Lloyd-George and 1st Viscount Davidson.

The National Maritime Museum—Papers of Admiral of the Fleet Baron Chatfield, Admiral of the Fleet Sir John Kelly and Admiral Sir Louis Hamilton.

Churchill College Archive Centre, Cambridge—Papers of Admiral of the Fleet Lord Keyes, 1st Viscount Weir, Earl Alexander of Hillsborough, 1st Earl of Swinton, General Sir Charles Bonham Carter, Captain J. Cresswell, Admiral Sir Reginald Plunkett-Ernle-Erle-Drax, Admiral Sir John Edelsten, Admiral J. H. Godfrey, Captain Russell Grenfell, Admiral Sir Reginald Hall, Captain A. R. Henderson, Admiral Sir Francis Pridham, Admiral Sir James Somerville, Admiral Wilfred Tomkinson and Professor A. V. Hill.

The British Museum—Papers of Admiral of the Fleet Viscount Cunningham of Hyndhope.

The Military Archive Centre, King's College, London University and Lady Liddell Hart—Papers of Sir Basil Liddell Hart.

For access to papers still in private hands I am indebted to:

The 2nd Earl Beatty—Papers of Admiral of the Fleet Earl Beatty.
Viscount Bridgeman—Papers of 1st Viscount Bridgeman.
Lady Lambe—Papers of Admiral of the Fleet Sir Charles Lambe.
Mrs. Stephen Lloyd—Papers of Mr. Neville Chamberlain.
Commander H. Pursey—His own papers.

I have had much correspondence with retired naval officers who had special experience of my period, and many of them were good enough to grant me interviews as well. Though nearly all of them are now navigating the seas of a higher realm I must record my particular debt to Admiral of the Fleet Sir Algernon Willis, Admirals Sir William James, Sir William Davis, Sir James Troup, Sir Reginald Plunkett-

Ernle-Erle-Drax and Sir Geoffrey Miles and Captain John Cresswell, whose work at the Staff College in the 1930s has been very valuable to me, as has Admiral J. H. F. Crombie's knowledge of naval communications. A particular debt is owed to Commander H. Pursey for allowing me to exploit his unrivalled knowledge of the Invergordon Mutiny of 1931 and his recollections of the Spanish Civil War of 1937–39. Admiral Sir Peter Gretton has also generously allowed me to exploit the fruits of his research on the Royal Navy's work in the Spanish Civil War.

Though my concern is of course chiefly with British Naval Policy it was so influenced by and intertwined with that of the other naval powers, and particularly the United States, that it would have been ridiculous to ignore the latter. A generous grant from the American Philosophical Society enabled me to pay a fairly long visit to the USA in 1969 to research in official archives and many private collections. While there I was once again treated most handsomely by my comrade of wartime and colleague of peace time years Rear-Admiral Ernest M. Eller, the head of the US Navy's Historical Branch. Dr. Dean Allard, with his intimate knowledge of that service's Operational Archives once again proved a staunch and invaluable friend and adviser. In recent times Vice-Admiral Edwin B. Hooper has carried on the tradition of helpful interchange of information established by Admiral Eller. I must also acknowledge my debt to the staff of the Manuscripts Division of the Library of Congress and of the US National Archives in Washington, and to Mr. William J. Stewart, then Acting Director of the Franklin D. Roosevelt Library at Hyde Park and his staff, whose hospitality and kindness made my stay by the banks of the Hudson River as enjoyable as it was profitable.

For information on the rebuilding of the German Navy in the 1930s I am greatly indebted to Professor Jürgen Rohwer of the Bibliothek für Zeitgeschichte, Stuttgart, but Kapitän zur See Heinz Bonatz, who served in the German Wireless Intelligence Service (*B-Dienst*) from the earliest times and again during World War II has given me invaluable information of the work of that service in studying British wireless traffic and so contributing to the efforts of the highly skilled German cryptanalysts to break our naval codes and cyphers.

For the Italian Navy the Defence and Naval Attaché in London, Capitano F. Mottolese has been good enough to obtain information I needed from the Ufficio storico della marina militare (the equivalent to our Naval Historical Branch) in Rome. That information has been amplified by the research which Signorina Rosaria Quarteraro, a research student at the London School of Economics and Political Science, has undertaken on my behalf, and I am deeply grateful for her help.

For information on the French Navy I am indebted to Monsieur Henri le Masson, formerly Président de L'Académie de Marine, and to Médecin de Ière Classe (Surgeon-Captain) Hervé Cras, whose writings on the French Navy under the pseudonym of 'Jacques Mordal' are well known. Both have been good enough to respond quickly and efficiently to my requests for information.

The Japanese side of the story was a serious difficulty, as I know no Japanese and have not been able to revisit that country. But I have been fortunate in gaining the friendship and help of Professor Stephen E. Pelz of the University of Massachusetts who has done so and has published the results in his admirable book *Race to Pearl Harbor* (Harvard UP, 1974). Professor Pelz has been good enough to pass to me information which he had collected in Japan.

Having passed the retiring age of my University some years ago I owe the completion of this task to the generosity of the Trustees of the Leverhulme Foundation for endowing a Research Fellowship and to Admiral Sir Charles Madden, the chairman of the Trustees of the National Maritime Museum, and his colleagues for electing me into that Fellowship at the Museum for 1974–76.

Once again I have to thank Commander Geoffrey Hare for continuing his most loyal and efficient work as my Research Assistant, a task he has now carried on for 20 years and nearly as many books. Without his help my progress through the enormous mass of documents in the Public Record Office would have been far slower.

Miss E. V. Eales, my secretary for seventeen years, has typed almost the whole manuscript with all her customary care and accuracy, and I cannot adequately express my debt to her. Miss Elizabeth Hunt (now Mrs. Peter Atkins), Miss Patricia O'Brien and Mrs. Rosemary Gooch have all helped me to deal with the large correspondence in which this work has involved me. Miss Angela Raspin and Mrs. Patricia Bradford, successively Chief Archivist at my college, have helped me greatly by drawing my attention to papers and letters which they had found while sorting and cataloguing the many collections in the Churchill College Archives Centre.

I must here repeat what I have said in all my earlier books about the many benefits I have drawn from the wisdom, experience and historical knowledge of my Publisher's Editor Mr. Richard Ollard. My debt to my wife for her toleration of my idiosyncratic habits and hours also remains immeasurable.

I must say a few words about the usages I have employed in this book. I almost always refer to Flag Officers merely as 'Admiral' since it would be tedious and could be confusing, to follow the ascent of each from Rear-Admiral to the higher ranks; and the dates of their promotions can, if required, easily be found in Navy Lists or other works of reference. Specific ranks are therefore given only where the seniority of an officer was important. In citing source references I usually give the original departmental number (e.g. Cabinet 21(36)) followed by the reference under which it will now be found in the PRO (e.g. Cab. 23/83). This has not been done for the sake of pedantry but because it follows the practice I have adopted in earlier books, and which students have told me they have found helpful in locating documents.

I have reproduced here the same Appendices D and E as were printed in my first volume, incorporating a few corrections. For reasons of economy I have not reproduced Appendices A, B and C of Volume I, and I trust that readers will not find it excessively tedious to refer to that book for details of the appointments of the principal Flag Officers, and the naval strength and building programmes of the chief naval powers. As regards the Bibliography I have in general only added books which have been published since the appearance of my first volume.

I must also acknowledge my debt to Mr. P. W. Ratcliffe, Honorary Secretary of the Naval Photograph Club, for help in identifying the ships shown in various illustrations and to the Rev. S. B-R Poole for the exemplary thoroughness with which he has once again compiled an index for me.

Finally I must thank my colleagues at Churchill College not only for the constant stimulus of their company but for their generosity in electing me into a Life Fellowship when I passed the University retiring age in 1970.

STEPHEN ROSKILL

Frostlake Cottage   *Churchill College*
Malting Lane   *Cambridge*
Cambridge
1973–1976

CHAPTER I

Setting the Stage

1929-1930

IN THE British General Election held on 30th May 1929 the Labour Party won 287 seats and was for the first time the largest party; but as the Conservatives held 261 seats and the Liberals 59 Ramsay MacDonald found himself, as in 1924, in a minority—if the other two parties combined against him. None the less when Baldwin resigned on 4th June and the King sent for MacDonald he accepted the invitation to form a government. Though unemployment was slightly lower than a year earlier, and continued to fall until December, the Labour Party had the misfortune to resume office just before the whole structure of post-war international economy collapsed. The crisis began with the crash on the American Stock Exchange at the end of October.

In the United States Herbert Hoover took over the Presidency from Calvin Coolidge on 4th March 1929 and appointed as his ambassador to London General Charles G. Dawes, whose name had previously been connected with the 1924 'Dawes Plan' for the restoration of economic stability in Germany and the resolution of the Reparations issue which had bedevilled European economic and political relations ever since the signature of the Versailles Treaty.[1]

At the end of May 1929, shortly before the General Election, Admiral W. W. Fisher, the Deputy Chief of Naval Staff, circulated a comprehensive 'Summary of Admiralty Policy'. It began with a re-statement of the principle of the 'One Power Standard', which he defined as the maintenance of 'such strength as will ensure adequate security for British territory, together with freedom of sea passage to and from all parts of the Empire'. As war with the USA was not considered a possibility and Japan was the next strongest naval power 'war

[1] See Stephen Roskill, *Hankey: Man of Secrets*, vol. II (Collins, 1972), pp. 371-2 regarding the Dawes Plan. Henceforth cited as Roskill, *Hankey*.

in the Far East', he continued, '[must] form the general basis on which preparations are made'. Thus the development of the Singapore base, even on the 'truncated scheme' approved in 1926,[1] which should be completed by 1937, assumed great importance, as did the building up of the oil reserves which were essential to enable a major fleet to proceed to the Far East and operate there. As regards building programmes the Admiralty aimed to obtain approval for steady and continuous replacements within the terms of the Washington Treaty of 1922, so that specialised manufacturing equipment did not become obsolete or skilled workmen lost to the industries concerned. As seventy cruisers, ten of which could be over the twenty-year age limit, were necessary 'to meet Empire requirements' three such ships should be laid down yearly. Taking account of the submarine strength of other powers a total of 144 flotilla leaders and destroyers was considered necessary, to meet which total nine 'must be laid down annually'. 'War requirements' of submarines were assessed at sixty large ones for overseas patrol and fleet work, to achieve which six must be included in each year's programme. Finally fifty-three sloops were needed for the variety of duties likely to fall to that class, including minesweeping; and that meant that seven should be built each year.

Regarding the reduction of armaments the Admiralty reiterated their preference for limitation by 'categories' rather than by 'global tonnage', and for limitation of displacement and calibre of main armaments within each category.

Policy concerning the Fleet Air Arm was governed by the Trenchard-Keyes agreement of 1924;[2] but the Admiralty planned to keep five aircraft carriers in full commission and one in reserve. The new ship of that class, provision for which had originally been included in the 1929–30 estimates,[3] had been 'deferred', but the Admiralty planned a steady increase of carrier aircraft from the 141 in service in 1929 to 251 in 1938—plus 50% reserves of aircraft and 150% of engines.[4]

In July Sir Oswyn Murray, the Permanent Secretary, circulated another paper by the DCNS on 'Redistribution of the Fleet'. Admiral Fisher drew attention to the fact that this matter had been under discussion since 1924, and that the congestion prevailing in Malta's har-

[1] See vol. I, pp. 463–4. [2] See vol. I, pp. 393–8.
[3] *ibid*, p. 561. This ship finally became the famous *Ark Royal* of World War II, completed in 1938.
[4] Memo. by DCNS of 21st June circulated by Sir Oswyn Murray on 4th June 1929. Adm. 167/80.

bours when the whole Mediterranean Fleet was concentrated there, together with the problems produced by the large proportion of naval personnel on foreign service, made it desirable to undertake a fundamental review of policy. The proposals put forward came under two headings. The first was to combine the Atlantic and Mediterranean Fleets under one C-in-C, while the second was to transfer certain ships from the Mediterranean to the Atlantic Fleet. As opposition to the first alternative by the Cs-in-C concerned was apparent Fisher suggested that the only solution was to transfer the *Queen Elizabeth* class battleships, except for the name ship which would stay on as Mediterranean fleet flagship, to the Atlantic Fleet. Admiral Sir Charles Madden, the First Sea Lord, concurred and the redistribution was in fact gradually carried out.[1]

To turn to the US Navy's policy at the opening of our period it was governed, firstly, by the basic principles of the achievement of parity with Britain—the 'navy second to none' of the Paris Peace Conference[2]—which in fact corresponded exactly to the Admiralty's 'one Power Standard'. Second came the maintenance of the Monroe Doctrine, which at this time was still regarded as having authority approaching that of holy writ.[3] The third principle was support for the 'Open Door' for trade with China. In addition the General Board remained anxious regarding the strategic weakness of the US Navy's position vis à vis that of Japan in the western Pacific which resulted from the Four Power Pact signed at Washington in 1922, and of the difficulty of defending the Philippines and other American possessions or dependencies in that area with no properly equipped base west of Hawaii. As regards the composition of the fleet the General Board strongly disliked any reduction of capital ship displacement and armament below the 35,000 tons and 16-inch guns agreed as the upper limits in the Washington Treaty.

The General Board still stood firmly by the view that 'the battleship is the ultimate measure of strength of the Navy'[4]—as indeed did the British Sea Lords. None the less Admiral W. A. Moffett, still Chief of the Bureau of Aeronautics,[5] remained a staunch supporter of the

[1] Memo. by same of 21st July 1929. *ibid.*

[2] See vol. I, p. 20 and *passim.*   [3] *ibid*, pp. 501–2.

[4] GB. 438–1, Serial 1385 of 11th Aug. 1928 and Serial 1408 of 28th Feb. 1929. See vol. I, pp. 59, 64 and 433–4 regarding the composition and functions of this body. All General Board (GB.) papers are in the US Navy's Operational Archives, Naval Historical Center, Washington. Their location will not henceforth be repeated here.

[5] See vol. I, pp. 57–8 and *passim.*

carrier-borne strike aircraft as the primary offensive weapon of the future; and it was perhaps his influence that led to President Hoover's acceptance of the view that the end of the period of dominance by the big gun battleship was approaching.

As regards cruisers the US Navy was still inferior to the British both in numbers and in tonnage, which rankled with the General Board. But the Act of 13th February 1929 authorised the building of fifteen cruisers (five in each year 1929–31) and one aircraft carrier.[1] The General Board was always insistent that their country's needs in relation to Japan made large numbers of 10,000-ton long-endurance Washington Treaty cruisers essential.

In meeting the difficulties produced for naval architects by the need to design the completely new class of cruiser permitted by the Washington Treaty the US Navy was markedly more successful than the British Navy, whose *Kent* and *London* classes of 1924–26 (10,000-ton, eight or six 8-inch guns), comprising fifteen ships in all,[2] were poorly protected and had the disadvantage of very high silhouettes. The Japanese too produced better treaty cruisers than the British, but in their case the superiority was we now know achieved by disregarding the displacement limitation in the case of their later ships.[3]

In April 1929 the US Navy's General Board produced its programme for the Fiscal Year 1931, in which they reaffirmed the large five-year programme first put forward in 1927 and approved by the President except for the five battleships proposed and nine flotilla leaders;[4] but as that programme was subject to substantial alteration we need not consider it in detail here.

The basic organisation of the US Navy established in 1922—namely a Battle Fleet, a Scouting Fleet, a Control Force and a Fleet Base

[1] The first five and three of the second five (*New Orleans* and *Tuscaloosa* classes) were 10,000-ton ships armed with nine 8-inch guns. The last two of the second five (*Brooklyn* and *Philadelphia*) were also 10,000-ton ships but armed with fifteen 6-inch guns. The aircraft carrier became the *Ranger* (completed 1933). Of the fifteen cruisers authorised the 70th Congress only appropriated funds to build ten.

[2] Including two for the Australian Navy and the smaller *York* and *Exeter* (six 8-inch).

[3] The *Furutaka* class (two ships of 1925) displaced only 9,150 tons and had six 8-inch guns as well as quite good protection. The US Navy's first treaty cruisers (*Pensacola* class) had ten 8-inch guns on a displacement of only 9,100 tons, and the six *Northampton* class which followed had nine 8-inch guns on about the same displacement.

[4] The original programme was for 5 battleships, 25 cruisers, 40 flotilla leaders and destroyers, 35 submarines and 5 carriers spread over 1929–33. GB. 420–2, Serial 1415 of 4th April 1929.

Force[1]—was still in being in 1929; but at the end of the following year the Control Force disappeared and a Submarine Force was added.[2] Prior to 1931 the Battle Fleet and the Base Force normally operated in the Pacific and the Scouting Fleet and Control Force in the Atlantic. In May 1932, as a result of Japanese aggression in Manchuria and at Shanghai, the Scouting Fleet remained in the Pacific, and the main strength of the US Navy stayed in that ocean until early in 1941 when a separate Atlantic Fleet was created.[3]

As regards British-American relations, on the naval level there had certainly been a marked improvement since the disastrous Geneva Conference of 1927;[4] and on the American side much of the credit for the change of outlook must be accorded to Admiral W. V. Pratt, who succeeded Admiral Charles F. Hughes as Chief of Naval Operations (the equivalent to the British First Sea Lord) on 17th September 1930. Though not an extreme Anglophile like Admiral W. S. Sims, who had thereby brought violent criticism and even obloquy on his head,[5] Pratt was a very fair and level-headed man whom members of the Board of Admiralty soon began to like and to trust, and with whom they never got seriously at loggerheads during negotiations on naval limitation—as had happened with Admiral W. S. Benson at the Paris Peace Conference of 1919.[6] Such coolness as still existed was on the British rather than the American side, the former still regarding the US Navy as something of a *parvenu* from whom they had little or nothing to learn. In contrast to British naval *hauteur*, when American officers visited their former ally's ships and establishments the Americans appear to have shown commendable open-mindedness and readiness to learn. For example when Captain W. D. Puleston, the future biographer of Alfred Thayer Mahan,[7] toured the British naval and military staff colleges and the Imperial Defence College in 1930 he reported very favourably on our instructional methods and wanted

[1] General Order No. 94 of 6th Dec. 1922. The US Navy Department records contain a valuable monograph produced in 1945 by Lieutenant R. W. Leopold entitled *Fleet Organisation 1919–1941*. Henceforth cited as *Leopold*.

[2] General Order No. 211 of 10th Dec. 1930, effective from 1st April 1931.

[3] *Leopold*, p. 4. On the outbreak of war in 1939 there were three independent fleets—Atlantic, Pacific and Asiatic.

[4] See vol. I, ch. 14. [5] *ibid.* pp. 51–3.

[6] *ibid.* pp. 51–4. Gerald E. Wheeler, *Admiral William Veazey Pratt: A Sailor's Life.* (US Department of the Navy, Historical Section, 1974) gives an excellent account of Pratt's career.

[7] Cape, 1939.

his own service to copy the IDC.[1] One may find in his report a contribution to the establishment of the US National War College, which was to undertake the higher education of senior officers of all three American services in World War II and afterwards.

To turn to the third of the major naval powers, Japan, the political trend remained on the whole liberal—despite a strong and murderous minority of extreme right-wingers—until the end of 1930. But the relegation of her navy to a status inferior to that of the USA and Britain by the 5:5:3 ratio for battleships and aircraft carriers agreed at Washington in 1922 rankled in naval circles; and the American Immigration Act of 1924, an overtly racialist measure comparable to the 'White Australia' policy, combined with the high US tariff wall and the British preferential trade measures introduced at the Imperial Economic Conference held at Ottawa in 1932,[2] produced strong resentment.[3] Furthermore the economic depression of 1929 hit Japan's export trade very hard, and lent impetus to the move away from democratic government and towards militarism. At the end of the first post-war decade Japanese foreign and economic policy was directed towards the consolidation and expansion of her interests on the Asiatic mainland, and especially in Manchuria. The concept of a southward drive to gain access to the wealth and raw materials of South-East Asia and Indonesia was not yet seriously envisaged.

As regards forward naval planning Japan, like Britain and the USA, was considering the design of the new battleships which it might be possible to build when the Washington Treaty expired at the end of 1931. Their first intention was to replace the *Kongo* class (1913–15) by 35,000-ton ships armed with 16-inch guns; but those plans were finally dropped in favour of the giant *Yamato* class which were not completed until 1941–42. Like the US Navy a small aircraft carrier (*Ryujo*, 10,600 tons, 36–48 aircraft) was projected, and completed in 1933. Japan's principal carrier strength still lay with the *Akagi* and *Kaga*

[1] US NA, RG 80, Box 171.

[2] See C. L. Mowat *Britain Between the Wars*, Methuen (Revised Ed., 1962, pp. 417–18 and 436–7. Henceforth cited as *Mowat*.

[3] See A. Iriye, *Across the Pacific* (Cambridge, Mass. 1965) for a study of American-Japanese-Chinese relations in the 20th century. J. Crowley, *Japan's Quest for Autonomy* (Princeton, 1966) is a useful 'revisionist' survey of Japanese policy and purposes in the 1930s, and R. A. Scalapino, *Democracy and the Party Movement in Pre-War Japan* (Berkeley, USA, 1962) is valuable for the growth of the movement towards military dictatorship.

of 1927–28 (36,500 and 38,200 tons and about 66–90 aircraft respectively).

To turn to cruisers, Japan laid down four *Nachi* class in 1924–25 and four *Atago* class in 1927–28. These eight ships were all armed with ten 8-inch guns and actually exceeded the Washington Treaty 10,000 limit by some 3,000 tons. Japan also had the two smaller *Aoba* class (1926–27) of some 9,000 tons with only six 8-inch guns, thus making a total of twelve 8-inch gun ships in addition to fifteen smaller cruisers of about 5,700 tons with five to seven 6-inch guns built in the 1920s.

As regards the two lesser European naval powers, France and Italy, our period opened at a time of marked mistrust in the political area and intense naval rivalry. France was obsessed by the need to secure herself against renewed aggression by Germany. The corner-stone of her policy was the treaties made with Belgium (1920), Poland (1921) and Czechoslovakia (1924), which were tenuously linked with the 'Little Entente' (Czechoslovakia, Yugoslavia and Roumania) initiated by M. Beneš of Czechoslovakia in 1920. In addition France repeatedly sought some form of commitment for military aid from Britain in the event of renewed aggression by Germany; but memories of 1914–18 made successive British governments very reluctant to accept a firm 'Continental Commitment'.[1]

The French Navy had not distinguished itself particularly in World War I, but under the energetic direction of Georges Leygues as Minister of Marine 1925–30 and 1932–33 and of Admiral François Darlan, his principal naval colleague, it had staged a marked recovery. In the 1920s eight Washington Treaty cruisers (*Tourville*, *Duquesne* and *Suffren* classes) were laid down and four smaller cruisers as well. But it was submarines, of which over 50 were launched by the French in the 1920s,[2] that they regarded as the principal weapon of the weaker power; and therein lay the seeds of a clash with Britain, which wanted such vessels strictly limited and was prepared to support their abolition. With the experiences of 1917 in mind the Admiralty could not view with equanimity the creation of a large submarine fleet so close to the British Isles and within easy striking distance of the Atlantic trade routes. In 1929 the Germans laid down the *Deutschland*, the first of their three 10,000-ton 'Pocket Battleships', and launched her in May 1931 with a great flourish of revived navalism. With their powerful arma-

---

[1] See the book of that title by Michael Howard (Temple Smith, 1972).
[2] *Les Flottes de Combat*, 1929 and 1931 (Paris).

ments[1] and long endurance they were plainly superior to all existing cruisers, and their possible use as commerce raiders caused the French Admiralty as much concern as the British; but it was not until 1932 that France laid down the first of her replies to this new class—the 26,500-ton battle-cruiser *Dunkerque*.[2]

French naval eyes were always concentrated on the Mediterranean as much as on the outer oceans, since it was in her North African possessions, and especially Algeria, that they had organised the colonial troops whose rapid transport to France would be essential in the event of renewed German aggression, and on which they relied to remedy the discrepancy in military strength brought about by their smaller, and declining population. It was the importance of the trans-Mediterranean routes to France that brought her into conflict with the aims of the revived Italian Navy. A further cause of tension between the two countries existed in the dispute over the boundary between their North African colonies of Tunisia and Tripolitania.

Under Mussolini the revival of the navy played an important part in Italian plans for overseas expansion; and it was watched with anxious eyes both in Paris and in London. Although at the Washington Conference Italy, like France had accepted a 1.75 ratio in total displacement of capital ships and of carriers to the 5 of Britain and USA and the 3 of Japan, the Italians were not prepared to extend such a low ratio to smaller warships, in which they insistently demanded parity with France—a proposal which the latter country was determined not to accept. At the beginning of our period the old battleships (*Giulio Cesare* class, 1911–13) had been modernised but no new ones were built until the *Italias* of 1937–39.[3] Six Washington Treaty cruisers were authorised or approaching completion in 1929,[4] and the Italian navy had six smaller ships of that class built or building. In destroyers the Italian navy was little inferior to the French, and although they had built or projected a dozen submarines since 1926 the Italian govern-

---

[1] The *Deutschland* (renamed *Lützow* 1939) and her two sister ships mounted six 11-inch and eight 5.9-inch guns. The two later ships of her class (*Admiral Graf Spee* and *Admiral Scheer*) were launched in 1933 and '34. Their true displacement was about 12,000 tons.

[2] Her sister ship the *Strasbourg* was laid down in 1934. They mounted eight 13-inch and sixteen 5.1-inch guns.

[3] Originally four of this class were planned but only three, the *Italia*, *Vittorio Veneto* and *Roma* were completed.

[4] These were the two *Trento* class laid down in 1925 and the four *Zara* class of 1929–31.

ment declared itself, at any rate in principle, to be ready to go along with Britain and the USA—if an agreement to abolish them were achieved.

Such, then was the general background to the naval plans, policy and strength of the principal powers when the second Labour government took office. The Admiralty was of course well aware of its commitment to disarmament—especially in the naval field—and prepared itself for a tussle to preserve the 1928–29 new construction programme,[1] and to prevent a drastic reduction in the estimates for 1929–30, which had been presented to Parliament in March 1929 by W. C. Bridgeman before he left the office of First Lord. They totalled just under £56 millions, which was a reduction of nearly £1½ millions on the previous year. The saving was chiefly achieved through cancellation of three cruisers of the 1927 and 1928 programmes.[2] The debate on the last estimates presented to Parliament by Bridgeman produced the customary protests about the continuation of the Singapore base from the Labour benches; while the Liberals argued that the Pact of Paris (or Kellogg Pact)[3] provided grounds for 'a large reduction of the Navy'.[4] The outgoing government thus ended its period of office on a very quiet note as regards the navy, and without fulfilling the steady programme of construction put forward in the White Paper of 1925.[5] We will defer consideration of the following year's estimates (1930–31) for the present since they were drastically affected by the Naval Conference to be described in the next chapter. It should however be mentioned here that in September 1929 the Naval Staff considered in detail the possibility of meeting British cruiser needs as regards numbers within a restricted total tonnage for that category by building smaller ships. Though no firm decision was reached, except that the one cruiser of the 1929 programme (*Leander*) should be a 7,000-ton ship with eight 6-inch guns, the papers produced show that Admiralty thinking was moving in the direction of getting more ships of the class within a restricted tonnage by reducing individual displacement even further.[6]

[1] Originally two cruisers, one submarine depot ship, one leader and eight destroyers, six submarines, four sloops and a river gunboat. The cruisers, the depot ship and two submarines were later cancelled. Cmd. 3052.

[2] Cmd. 3283 of 4th March 1929.   [3] See vol. I, pp. 552–3.

[4] Parl. Deb., Commons, vol. 226, cols. 1301–1420 and 1625–1708.

[5] Cmd. 2366. See vol. I, pp. 445–54 regarding the battle over the 1925–26 Navy Estimates.

[6] Paper entitled 'Smaller Cruisers' by Madden of 27th Sept. 1929 with comments

Approval of the 1929 naval estimates had, however, been made conditional on the prompt and detailed examination by the Naval Programme Committee of the Cabinet, a body which was continued after the Labour government took office as the Fighting Services Committee, and in July A. V. Alexander, the new First Lord, wrote to Snowden, the Chancellor of the Exchequer, pointing out that this review had not yet taken place. 'Uncertainty as to policy', declared the First Lord, 'tends to be injurious both to efficiency and economy', and he therefore pressed for the promised enquiry to take place as soon as possible. The firm tone of this letter certainly suggests that Alexander was prepared to stand up to the all-powerful Treasury on behalf of the department and service which he represented.[1] The gambit adopted by the Treasury in their counter-attack was described, probably by Murray, as 'their favourite manœuvre'—namely that because the Admiralty had included the modest total of twelve extra aircraft in their programme, the Treasury had replied 'let us know your whole programme over a series of years'. Such a guess, he continued, 'must either be based on the Naval situation as it exists', taking account of the treaties in force, or 'on an entirely imaginary situation based on the assumption that Naval reductions will advance by huge strides in the next few years'.[2] But the reply sent by the Admiralty did include the Naval Staff's long-term plans for 'a steady development of the Fleet Air Arm', taking account of American and Japanese strength at the present time and as it was likely to be in 1938. By that date the US Navy's total of aircraft might be as high as 477 and Japan's 176, compared to the British Empire's 251—if the steady expansion programme was approved.[3] In fact the estimates for 1929–30 included no provision for the 1931 building programme, because the London Naval Conference was in progress at the time. The result was that a Supplementary Estimate for nearly £½ million had to be presented to Parliament in July 1930.[4]

On the last day of 1929 MacDonald circulated a survey of the

by Admiral R. R. C. Backhouse (Controller), and paper by Captain B. A. Fraser, head of Tactical Section, on same subject. Adm. 1/8765.

[1] Alexander to Snowden 1st July 1929. Adm. 1/8733–38/1929.

[2] Memo. dated 28th Oct. 1929. The file copy, though unsigned, bears all the marks of Murray's style. *ibid.*

[3] The Staff paper of February 1929 had in fact already been sent to the Chancellor on 7th of that month. Murray repeated the same arguments and statistics in late October. *ibid.*

[4] See Cmd. 3799 of 2nd March 1931.

position regarding the 1929 building programme, which had been under consideration by the Fighting Services Committee.[1] The decision taken by the government was that the Admiralty's long-term programme would probably have to be postponed until after the forthcoming naval conference. For 1929 one cruiser (*Leander* class), a leader and four destroyers, four sloops and three submarines were approved, but the submarines were not to be laid down until after the conference —because we were proposing their abolition. This meant a substantial reduction in the programme originally approved, but was 'the minimum construction necessary to avoid heavy discharges in dockyard labour'—a statement which at any rate made the government's priorities clear, especially as MacDonald went on to admit that the Sea Lords were 'not satisfied that this programme provides the minimum of naval construction essential for national security'.[2] However in the following May the Cabinet approved that the three submarines should be laid down, since abolition was plainly ruled out owing to French opposition.[3]

If Alexander's support in the annual battle with the Treasury came as something of a surprise to the Sea Lords they can hardly have been taken unawares by the social and disciplinary reforms which he soon made clear as his aim. The most important of these was widening the field from which the Navy drew its officers, the great majority of whom were still selected at the age of thirteen for training at Dartmouth College, and came from middle or upper class families who were able to afford the fees. A much smaller entry, taken almost entirely from the independent Public Schools, came in at eighteen and did their preliminary training in not very satisfactory conditions on board the monitor *Erebus* moored in Devonport harbour. Promotion from the lower deck was only possible under the 'Mate Scheme' introduced as long ago as 1912;[4] and the chief handicap of that scheme was that ratings promoted under it were likely to be too old to have a good prospect of achieving even Commander's rank, let alone Post or Flag rank. In October 1929 the Second Sea Lord, Admiral Sir Michael Hodges, surveyed the problem for the benefit of the Board. 'Although the Mate Scheme has produced a number of useful officers', he wrote,

---

[1] FS(29) 18 and 19.

[2] CP.2(30) of 31st Dec. 1929. Cab. 24/209. Taken by Cabinet on 14th Jan. 1930. Cabinet 1(30). Cab. 23/63.

[3] Cabinet 27(30) of 14th May 1930. Cab. 23/64.

[4] See vol. I, p. 120 *note*.

'it has so far produced none of outstanding ability[1] and as a means of providing Commissioned Officers for the Navy promotion from the Lower Deck cannot be regarded as a substitute for the normal method of entry and training'.[2] If the Sea Lords were obviously unenthusiastic about increasing promotion from the lower deck allowance must be made for the fact that, after the London Conference, the same problem that had plagued the Board soon after World War I—namely an excess of officers of Lieutenant's and Lieutenant-Commander's rank, arose again in acute form.[3] A whole succession of schemes had to be devised and Treasury approval obtained in order to clear the blockage on the road to promotion to the higher ranks.[4] It is an ironical fact that many of the officers got rid of in the early 1930s had to be hastily recalled in the crises of 1938-39, by which time rapid expansion of the fleet was again in progress.

In March 1930 Alexander circulated to his naval colleagues a paper entitled, perhaps a little provocatively, 'Democratisation'. In eight cogently argued and moderately worded pages the First Lord stated the case for widening the scope of the Cadet Entry by tapping a more representative cross section of the population.[5] The reaction of the Sea Lords was far from favourable. The Second Sea Lord (Sir Michael Hodges) argued strongly against the whole principle of 'democratisation', while the First Sea Lord (Sir Charles Madden) concluded his counter-attack by stating 'To sum up, there appears to be no advantage to the Navy if [? in] introducing a large number of Secondary School boys by Special Entry [i.e. with the Public School boys at eighteen years old] and a glance at contemporary Navies warns us to be cautious. Such a system, however, applied in moderation, say 5-7% of entries

[1] Hodges was to be proved wrong here. Three former Mates achieved Flag Rank during World War II or later. See vol. I, p. 120 *note*.

[2] Memo of 26th Oct. 1929. Adm. 167/80.

[3] The matter was first discussed by the Board on 6th Nov. 1930. Adm. 167/81.

[4] Initially only a pension was offered (AFO. 289/31), but so few officers volunteered to accept it that the scheme was cancelled early in 1934. Compulsory retirement was first brought up in July 1932 and by the end of that year a list of officers for whom no further employment could be envisaged, totalling nearly 200, was drawn up by the Second Sea Lord. In January 1933, the month when Hitler achieved supreme power, the number to be got rid of was estimated to have increased from 175 to 235. The compulsory retirements aroused hostile reactions in the Press. At the end of 1933 the retirement scheme was extended to junior officers who were offered a £500 gratuity. For the whole story of the retirement schemes see Adm. 1/8817–193/35, 116/2719 and 2720, and Board Minutes in 167/88 and 89.

[5] Minute of 25th March 1930 by Alexander. Adm. 1/8740–53/1930.

will probably give better results than an extension of the Mate Scheme, which is, in the Executive line a failure'.[1] Alexander however, presumably as a result of the opposition his ideas had encountered, took steps to have the whole issue thoroughly investigated, and by educational experts as well as senior naval officers. At the end of October a committee was appointed under the Chairmanship of Sir Ernest Bennett, a distinguished academic and a Labour MP, to review whether the present system gave boys 'belonging to all classes of the community a fair opportunity' of gaining cadetships.[2] The committee reported that although in theory the Dartmouth and *Erebus* entries were 'widely democratic' in fact money (or the lack of it) did discourage applications from the sons of less affluent parents. In order to eliminate that undesirable feature they recommended that the fees payable by parents of boys sent to Dartmouth (which averaged £854 spread over 11 terms) 'should be reviewed'—which of course meant getting more money from the Treasury. As regards the Special Entry at eighteen the committee recommended approaching Local Education Authorities with a view to getting them to establish 'major scholarships'—presumably meaning free education for the one year spent in the *Erebus* (which cost £210) followed by 28 months afloat as Midshipmen. The committee studied carefully the origins of boys 'Qualified for Entry' from June 1925 to November 1929 and found that they did show 'a predominantly Middle Class background'.[3]

The second committee set up by Alexander was predominantly naval, and was chaired by Admiral Sir Frank Larken.[4] It was charged with reviewing the working of the Mate Scheme and the possibility of increasing promotion from the lower deck. The First Lord, in commenting on the prevailing paucity of such promotions drew his col-

[1] Memo. by First Lord of 25th March 1930 and replies by Second and First Sea Lords. Adm. 167/82.

[2] Terms of Reference approved 30th Oct. 1930. Adm. 167/84. The other members of the Bennett Committee were Admiral O. de B. Brock, Admiral Reginald P-E-E-Drax, Sir Edmund Phipps, a distinguished Civil Servant from the Board of Education and Mr. F. R. Dale, Headmaster of the City of London School. The secretary was H. V. Markham, later Permanent Secretary of the Admiralty.

[3] Report of Bennett Committee dated 29th June 1931. For the full record of its deliberations see Adm. 116/2779 and 2880.

[4] The other members were Sir Charles Walker, Deputy Secretary of the Admiralty, Engineer Rear-Admiral H. L. Perry, Captain A. T. B. Curteis and Commander (later Rear-Admiral) J. Figgins, the senior executive ex-Mate officer. Commander H. Pursey, the ex-Lower Deck officer referred to above (page 17), was specially recalled from the Mediterranean to give evidence to the Larken Committee. Adm. 167/84.

leagues' attention to Lord Justice Darling's quip that 'Justice is open to all—like the Ritz'.[1] Obviously the same principle applied in his view to the road from forecastle to quarter deck. The First and Second Sea Lords however declared, before the Larken Committee had reported, that 'It is not Officers who exhibit any snobbish traits in regard to Lower Deck promotion, but the men of the Lower Deck who give greater respect to what is known as the Officer Class than to other officers drawn from their own ranks'. Madden urged that it was 'a mistake to risk the impairment of the efficiency of an officer *cadres* [*sic*] and the service by a considerable democratisation', while Hodges assured Alexander that the Admiralty's Interview Board was 'not swayed by any question of class distinction . . . but is solely concerned in choosing . . . those boys whom it is considered are best fitted to become Naval Officers'. 'Have the present Naval Officers failed in any way?' he asked somewhat rhetorically. If not the proposal to increase the Direct Entry to about half the total, using government grants and bursaries 'to widen the sources' must be considered 'a most unsound experiment'. He wanted to continue the system of 'catching them young' as had been done 'since time immemorial'.[2]

The Larken Committee studied the results produced by the Mate Scheme ever since its inception in 1912[3] very thoroughly. The original scheme had produced 371 officers for the Executive, Signal and Wireless Telegraphy branches, 161 for the Engineering branch and 12 for the Royal Marines between 1913 and 1918. In 1920 a revised scheme was announced to try and reduce the age at which Mates reached Lieutenant's rank (about 28–29 as compared to 22 for ex-Dartmouth officers); but the next five years' experience proved that, as regards Executive Officers, it was not producing the desired results, though the Engineer Branch had benefited substantially from it. The Larken Committee reported on 24th February 1931,[4] and in the following May Alexander told the House of Commons that, as a result of its report the title of Mate, which had come to carry a stigma both forward and aft, would be abolished and that of Acting Sub-Lieutenant substituted. A new scheme, he continued, was to be introduced with the object of overcoming the age disparity on reaching Lieutenant's

[1] Remarks by Alexander of 25th March 1930. Adm. 1/8740–53/1930.
[2] Remarks by Madden and Hodges on above. *ibid*. See also Board Minute 2728 of 11th July 1930. Copy in Adm. 116/2791.
[3] See vol. I, p. 120 *note*.   [4] Adm. 167/84.

rank between ex-Lower Deck and ex-Cadet Entry Officers.[1] We will recount the results produced by the new scheme later.

Looking back today it is plain that Alexander's broad purposes were fully justified. His mistake was to try and attract 16-year-old boys holding the School Leaving Certificate from Secondary Schools to Dartmouth. This idea found no support among the Board, except from C. G. Ammon the Parliamentary Secretary;[2] and it is a fact that when, in September 1948, another Labour Government did introduce such an entry the number of candidates presenting themselves proved wholly inadequate. This led to the age of the Dartmouth entry being changed to eighteen in May 1955—in other words to a combination of the earlier systems. That Alexander's Conservative successors as First Lord, and the Navy as a whole, benefited from the efforts he made in 1930–31 to increase the opportunities for promotion from the lower deck now seems indisputable.

Another reform that Alexander endeavoured to introduce was the reduction of corporal punishment inflicted on Seaman Boys (ages fifteen to eighteen) which he 'viewed with considerable concern'.[3] A committee was appointed to investigate the matter, and came to the conclusion that 'caning is by far the most suitable punishment for boys'.[4] Bearing in mind that in 1917 the Board of Admiralty had seriously considered the re-introduction of flogging men 'who deliberately tried to avoid service'[5]—though the proposal was, fortunately, dropped—the belief of senior officers in the efficacy of corporal punishment in the early 1930s is not surprising. Alexander could well have turned his attention to its excessive use at Dartmouth as well as in the Seaman Boy training establishments; since the extent to which cadets were subjected to the indignity of caning—and by Cadet Captains only a year or two older than themselves—was probably greater than in the case of Boys.[6] But it was to take another World

[1] Promulgated in AFOS 2473 of 16th Oct. 1931 and 2945 of 23rd Dec. 1932. Parl. Deb., Commons, vol. 252, cols. 1950–54.
[2] Report of conference held on 29th July 1931. Adm. 1/8747–81/1931.
[3] Memos. of 6th and 29th July 1931. Adm. 167/83.
[4] Report dated 10th July 1931. Adm. 167/84.
[5] Adm. 1/8479.
[6] Two naval memoirs are revealing about corporal punishment in the Cadet Training Establishments—Commander William King, *The Stick and the Stars* (Hutchinson, 1958), pp. 12–14 and Captain Eric Bush, *Bless Our Ship* (Allen and Unwin, 1958) pp. 17–18. On the possible effects of similar treatment of a cadet (actually the son of the Captain of Osborne College) on the future King Edward VIII

War, and far-reaching educational and social reforms, to abolish the infliction of corporal punishment on junior officers and ratings; and the Labour Government of 1929–31 was not in office long enough to achieve any significant changes in the disciplinary customs and social outlook of the navy as a whole.

---

see Frances Donaldson, *Edward VIII* (Weidenfeld and Nicolson, 1974), pp. 28–9. This author's experience of the RN Colleges 1917–20 fully confirms the views and experiences recorded in the above books. That Alexander did not take up the question of corporal punishment in the Cadet Colleges is probably explained by the fact that, unlike the Boys' Training Establishments, they did not have to render regular 'punishment returns' to the Admiralty, and so he was probably unaware of what went on.

CHAPTER II

The London Naval Conference

1929-1930

━━━━━━━━━━◆━━━━━━━━━━

ALTHOUGH ECONOMIC problems and social reform stood high on the agenda of MacDonald's second Labour Government, it was disarmament that took up the greatest part of his and Alexander's energy; and, as in 1921, it was once again on the navies of the five principal powers that efforts were almost exclusively concentrated. In the United States President Hoover, whose background was Quaker and whose experience of organising the relief of the distressed populations of European countries after World War I had made him deeply conscious of the suffering produced by war, was as deeply committed to the principle that reduction of armaments was the surest way to achieve peace as was MacDonald. The broad purposes of both were to stimulate the work of the Preparatory Commission for the General Disarmament Conference, which the League Council had appointed in December 1925 and whose progress had so far been anything but rapid;[1] and to extend the provisions of the Washington Naval Treaty, which could be terminated at the end of 1936 and covered only the largest warships, to cruisers and smaller ships.[2] The preliminary negotiations—on both the politico-diplomatic and naval levels—were protracted; and if we here are chiefly concerned with the latter the two were so intertwined that we cannot ignore the former.

At the sixth session of the Preparatory Commission in April 1929 the American representative Hugh Gibson, who had led his country's delegation at the abortive Geneva Naval Conference of 1927,[3] made

[1] See vol. I, pp. 498 and 544-5.
[2] *ibid.* Ch. VIII regarding the Washington Treaty.　　　[3] *ibid.* Ch. XIV.

it clear that, although the United States favoured limitation in each category of warship, as had been accomplished at the Washington Conference for capital ships and aircraft carriers, he was aware that this was unacceptable to some powers. He was therefore prepared to accept an earlier proposal put forward by the French—that the total tonnage assigned to each nation should be agreed, and that total divided between the various categories of warships in specified tonnages. It should here be remarked that these two basic principles were always referred to respectively as 'limitation by categories' and 'global limitation', and the same terminology will be followed here. Gibson proposed that a formula should be invented to arrive at 'equivalent tonnage' of different classes, taking account of displacement, age, calibre of guns and perhaps 'speed and other factors'. This was the well known 'yardstick' formula, whose first use probably originated from Charles Evans Hughes when he was Secretary of State in President Harding's administration early in 1921, and to which Austen Chamberlain gave renewed currency in 1929, so placing it in the forefront of the negotiations.[1]

On 10th June the US Navy's General Board put forward recommendations which corresponded generally to Gibson's proposals but included two possible variations in the 'yardstick' formula.[2] Next H. L. Stimson, the Secretary of State, asked the General Board for a comparison of American and British naval strengths assuming that cruisers of less than 5,000 tons displacement were 8/10 or 9/10 the value of ships above that displacement. The tabulated reply showed that the result would be to produce a large disparity in the British favour, and the General Board therefore recommended dropping that tentative 'yardstick'. Meanwhile Admiral Hilary P. Jones a former Chairman of the General Board and a notorious 'hard-liner' towards British naval claims and interests,[3] drew the attention of the Chief of Naval Operations, Admiral Charles F. Hughes, to the disadvantageous position of his service due to the fact that so many of its cruisers were obsolescent. At the beginning of 1929 the US Navy possessed only ten modern cruisers (the *Omaha* class of 7,050 tons, twelve 6-inch guns)

---

[1] See Allen W. Dulles, article in *Foreign Affairs*, vol. VIII (1929) p. 180. Chamberlain did not actually use the word 'yardstick' but repeated the idea of a compensatory formula in a speech. See *The Times*, 28th Jan. 1929.

[2] The first was to take account of displacement and age of ships only, while the second was to add gun calibre as well. GB. 438–1.

[3] See vol. 1, pp. 59, 433–4 and 503–18.

though eight 'Washington Treaty' cruisers were building, and 15 more had been authorised for the years 1929–31. Thus was restated the US Navy's long-standing requirement for a total of 23 heavy cruisers armed with 8-inch guns.[1]

On 18th July Dawes telegraphed to Stimson about a letter received that day from MacDonald referring to Hoover's recent pronouncements. There appeared to be agreement, said Dawes, that the Washington Treaty ratios should not be disturbed; that parity between Britain and the USA should be achieved in cruisers, destroyers and submarines, and that an appropriate 'yardstick' should be devised to reconcile the difference in classes of cruisers already referred to. MacDonald, reported Dawes, had 'slowed up preparations for laying down two cruisers of [the] 1928 Programme',[2] and would propose again that submarines should be totally abolished—as indeed the British had proposed at Washington in 1921.[3] It is interesting to find that at this time King George V urged on MacDonald the need to abolish what he called 'this terrible weapon'.[4] The Admiralty drafted the reply, and said that they 'would gladly do so in conjunction with all the nations of the world', but that the French would never give up 'what they consider their primary arm of naval defence', and as long as they took that line it was impossible for other nations to abolish them.[5] To that the King replied that he was well aware of such considerations but none the less hoped that 'his present government will not be content with the *non possumus* attitude of France and will endeavour, in co-operation with the Americans, to overcome the opposition from our friends across the Channel';[6] to which the Prime Minister answered that he had 'the subject much in mind and does intend to take the steps desired by the King', though without any great hope of success;[7] and there the interchange ended.

---

[1] Memos. of 7th June, 1st Aug. and 14th Aug. 1929. GB. 438–1. Raymond G. O'Connor, *Perilous Equilibrium: The United States and the London Naval Conference 1930* (Kansas UP, 1962) is an admirable study based chiefly on American sources. Henceforth cited as *O'Connor*.

[2] These ships were to have been the 10,000-ton, 8-inch gun *Surrey* and *Northumberland*. See Memo. by Madden of 5th March 1929. Adm. 167/80. They were cancelled as a result of the naval conference.

[3] Dawes to Stimson no. 197 of 18th July 1929.

[4] Stamfordham to MacDonald 10th July 1929. Premier 1/71.

[5] MacDonald to Stamfordham 12th July 1929. *ibid.*

[6] Stamfordham to MacDonald 15th July 1929. *ibid.*

[7] MacDonald to Stamfordham 16th July 1929. *ibid.*

Six days after Dawes sent the optimistic forecast quoted above MacDonald spoke on the same theme in the House of Commons.[1] Dawes at once reported that his speech had received 'a fine reception', and that 'the few questions it evoked were well handled by him'. Dawes had also exchanged views with his Japanese colleague Tsuneo Matsudaira, whose mind, he reported 'runs parallel to ours' except as regards the abolition of submarines and for 'a slight increase for Japan' in the 5:5:3 ratio for classes other than capital ships.[2] If these reservations portended one cloud on the horizon MacDonald's letter to Dawes, written on the same day as his speech in the Commons, portended another; for MacDonald not only concentrated on the need to reach an acceptable 'yardstick' formula but entered into detailed and technical discussion regarding the discrepancy between the American assessment of British cruiser numbers, tonnage and gunpower and the data provided to him (presumably by the Admiralty) on the same subject.[3] Though MacDonald admitted that this problem was 'a somewhat complicated tangle to unravel' he was optimistic about accomplishing that purpose provided that 'we keep political and not service hands in control'—doubtless a reference to the failure at Geneva in 1927. He proposed therefore that 'we begin by assuming that our countries each has an absolute minimum enforced upon it by the present state of the world and that the settlement of details must conform to that general requirement'. 'As we are both determined to agree', he concluded, 'I feel pretty strongly that that is both the surest and the quickest way to set to work'.[4] Next day Stimson telegraphed to Dawes setting out the general principles which should guide him and Gibson in their negotiations with MacDonald and A. V. Alexander, whom Dawes had described as having 'the qualities of loyalty and trustworthiness of Gibson but not his technical competence'.[5] The principal points were

[1] Parl. Deb., Commons, vol. 230, cols. 1304–7. It was in this statement that MacDonald announced the cancellations and slowing down of the 1928 naval building programme.

[2] Dawes to Stimson no. 204 of 25th July 1929.

[3] MacDonald to Dawes, letter received by latter 25th July and reproduced verbatim in above message. The chief differences arose over whether the four British *Hawkins* class ships of 1916 design (about 9,800 tons with seven 7.5-inch guns) approximated more closely to Washington Treaty 10,000-ton 8-inch cruisers or to 6-inch cruisers; also whether the British C Class (averaging 4,200 tons, with four or five 6-inch guns) could be equated to the American *Omahas* (7,050 tons, ten 6-inch guns).

[4] MacDonald to Dawes, quoted in Dawes to Stimson no. 204 of 25th July 1929.

[5] Dawes to Stimson 23rd July 1929. No. 202.

that the conference should be regarded as a follow-up to the Pact of Paris;[1] that parity 'in combatant strength' was agreed; and that it should be settled on the basis of five *categories* of warship—not on 'global' tonnage. Stimson was fully in accord with Dawes on preserving the Washington Treaty ratios for capital ships and aircraft carriers, and also supported the concept of a 'yardstick' to arrive at the equivalent value of ships of different classes. He also telegraphed that, subject to agreement on other questions, the Americans would scrap destroyers (of which they possessed 284 as against Britain's 152 including 20 under construction) and submarines to bring their tonnage in those categories down to the British level 'either at present or by 1936'. He also agreed that submarines should if possible be abolished; and, lastly, that capital ship replacement under the Washington Treaty should be postponed until after 1936—in other words a five year extension of the ten year 'naval holiday' agreed at Washington.[2] The favourable auguries for agreement were enhanced by a report from Tokyo that the British-American proposals had been well received in Japan;[3] but that assessment was soon to prove optimistic.

On 29th July Dawes and Gibson reported to Stimson the result of their meeting with MacDonald and Alexander, before whom they had laid the broad American proposals referred to above. The seven main points were, they said, entirely agreed and only minor amendments had been suggested to the subsidiary proposals. MacDonald had however stressed the British need for a minimum of forty-five 6-inch cruisers to defend their world-wide trade, but would be satisfied with only fifteen of the big Washington Treaty class, and would accept the USA having eighteen of that type. To achieve the desired parity the British had proposed that America should be allowed to build ten big cruisers with 6-inch guns.[4] On the same day Dawes forwarded MacDonald's letter in which he had set out British needs in cruisers. Dawes said that he would work to reduce them below the totals of 45 and 15 in the two classes—if an agreement could be reached with France, Italy and Japan.[5] This message produced a strong reaction from the Secretary of State, who declared that the British proposals, which

[1] 'The International Treaty for the Renunciation of War', usually referred to as the Kellogg Pact. See vol. I, pp. 552–3.

[2] Stimson to Dawes 26th July 1929. No. 192.

[3] US Embassy, Tokyo to Stimson 27th July 1929. No. 80.

[4] Dawes and Gibson to Stimson 29th July 1929. No. 209.

[5] Dawes to Stimson 30th July 1929. No. 211.

gave them a total of over 376,000 tons of cruisers, had 'keenly disappointed' him and the President. They amounted, said Stimson, to abandonment of both the principle of *decreasing* armaments and of achieving parity in that class of ship, since the American tonnage would only amount to some 250,500 plus the ten unbuilt 6-inch ships. 'It is our belief', continued Stimson, 'that he [MacDonald] has been won over by the Admiralty'. If Britain needed a large preponderance in small cruisers she must surely, he continued, concede American preponderance in the big 10,000-ton class.[1] When MacDonald received this rebuff he expressed his disappointment, and explained his need to take account of 'popular feeling' and of the outlook, needs and fears of the Dominions. He admitted that the British figures were high, but declared—with less than complete regard for the truth—that 'they have been put in under no Admiralty pressure'.[2]

Dawes tried to reassure Stimson that MacDonald was not trying 'to put anything on [? over] us' on the Admiralty's behalf, and pointed out, correctly, that the new British claim was far lower than that put forward at Geneva in 1927.[3] The problem, as he saw it, was 'to discover some means of reducing the cruiser strength of Great Britain in co-operation with a man who . . . is honestly willing to carry it out'. He recommended a personal meeting between MacDonald and Hoover to try and achieve that purpose.[4] On 6th August he reported the result of a further conference with the two British Ministers at which MacDonald had made 'a very helpful approach', and had conceded that the American navy should have 'a material preponderance' in big cruisers; but he could not ignore the building of such ships by other nations—and especially by Japan, whose number would of course increase on the 5:5:3 ratio proportionately to American numbers. MacDonald, reported Dawes, was anxious to meet the Secretary of State's views but did not want to visit Hoover 'until a practical agreement is reached'.[5]

In his next communication on the subject Dawes reported that the Prime Minister had now proposed that Britain should reduce her total cruiser strength to 50 ships by 1936.[6] Dawes again stressed the need to establish the elusive 'yardstick', and said they were examining the

[1] Stimson to Dawes 31st July 1929. Nos. 195 and 196.
[2] Quoted Dawes to Stimson 1st Aug. 1929. No. 216.
[3] See vol. I, ch. xiv.   [4] Dawes to Stimson 4th Aug. 1929. No. 220.
[5] Same to same 6th Aug. 1929. No. 223.
[6] The letter MacDonald to Dawes was dated 8th Aug. from Lossiemouth.

possibility of introducing a much smaller class of ship for imperial services, generically described as 'police craft'.[1] To that message Stimson replied that 'we think we see daylight', and that the 'friendly frankness of the Prime Minister deserves to be met in a similarly sincere spirit'.[2]

Towards the end of August MacDonald wrote again to Dawes, and he sent the letter on to Stimson. In it the Prime Minister stood by his acceptance for Britain of 50 cruisers totalling some 339,000 tons, but pointed out that if he referred to the American superiority in 10,000-ton cruisers as coming within the definition of parity 'the people would turn round and rend us'. He admitted in a somewhat abrupt change from his earlier optimism that he was 'more depressed than since we began our conversations'.[3] In his reply Stimson produced a somewhat sophistical statement on the American view regarding what would constitute parity in cruisers but declined to produce any indication of what 'yardstick' formula he was working to.[4]

Next MacDonald asked for details of the American cruiser strength in the same format as they had recently been produced for British strength. Since no one could build a 6-inch ship on 4,000 tons displacement (the upper limit suggested for the 'police craft' class) MacDonald said he had been reluctantly compelled to increase the British total requirements by 9,000 tons. Furthermore if the USA built twenty-three 10,000-ton ships and Japan was allowed a 3·5 ratio she could claim to have sixteen, which was one more than the British Commonwealth possessed. If on the other hand the Americans reduced their number to twenty-one and the 5:3·5 ratio were maintained Japan could only claim 12·6 such ships; and Britain would accept her having twelve.[5] Dawes evidently felt some sympathy with MacDonald over Washington's reluctance to produce either their own cruiser strength or the 'yardstick' formula, since on the last day of August he pressed Stimson to meet MacDonald's requests.[6] He did not, however, elicit a clear and unequivocal reply from the Secretary of State, who emphasised instead that it was 'practically hopeless to present to

[1] Dawes to Stimson 9th Aug. 1929. No. 228.

[2] Stimson to Dawes 15th Aug. 1929. No number.

[3] MacDonald's letter, again from Lossiemouth, is undated but Dawes to Stimson 24th Aug. 1929. no. 242 repeats it verbatim.

[4] Stimson to Dawes 28th Aug. 1929. No. 226. Dawes to Stimson 30th Aug. 1929. No. 252.

[5] MacDonald's letter to Stimson of 30th Aug. Transmitted in Dawes to Stimson 31st Aug. 1929. No. 254.   [6] Dawes to Stimson 31st Aug. 1929. No. 255.

Congress proposals which would give Britain 50 cruisers but allow the USA only 28'.[1] The influence of the General Board is to be detected in this reply as clearly as the Admiralty's influence over MacDonald's attitude. In fact the General Board next accepted that the level of parity should be 50 ships totalling 339,000 tons for Britain and 315,500 tons for the USA, the difference being compensated for by a 'yardstick' factor based on displacement and age. The full General Board with Charles F. Adams (Secretary of the Navy) met the President and Stimson at the White House on 11th September when the foregoing proposals 'were confirmed as meaning parity with Great Britain'.[2] Thus was eliminated perhaps the greatest cause of rancour and ill-feeling in American naval circles towards their British counterparts—namely the superiority of the Royal Navy in cruisers.

Another possible source of Anglo-American friction arose from the British claim to exercise 'Belligerent Rights' at sea in time of war,[3] which ran entirely counter to the principle of 'Freedom of the Seas'—one of President Wilson's famous 'Fourteen Points' of January 1918, to which many Americans remained wholly committed. Soon after MacDonald took office in June 1929 he told Sir Maurice Hankey, the influential Secretary of the CID and the Cabinet, that he intended to take 'a personal interest in the question of relations with the USA'. Hankey evidently scented danger in this seemingly innocent proposition, because it could lead to pressure on Britain to relax her claim to Belligerent Rights—a development against which Hankey had thrown all his weight when the issue was raised in 1928.[4] To forestall any such move Hankey sent MacDonald the earlier CID reports on the subject[5] and warned him that 'the subject is one which arouses strong feelings'.[6]

[1] Stimson to Dawes 3rd Sept. 1929. No. 237.

[2] GB. 438-1. Serial no. 1444A of 11th Sept. 1929. A manuscript note on the original by Admiral Hughes says however that it was '*not delivered* to the Secretary of the Navy' but the greater part of it was 'read to the President, the Secretary of State and the Secretary of the Navy at the White House 11th Sept. 1929 a.m.'. So the contents obviously at once reached the addressees for whom it was intended. It was circulated officially to Stimson and Adams in May 1930.

[3] This included the right to stop neutral vessels suspected of carrying contraband goods, to 'visit and search' them, and to seize such ships and their cargoes if condemned before a nationally constituted Prize Court.   [4] See vol. I, pp. 549–51.

[5] CID. 943B and 944B. First and Second Reports of the Sub-Committee on Belligerent Rights of 13th Feb. and 6th March 1929. Cab. 16/79.

[6] Hankey to MacDonald 13th June 1929. Premier 1/99.

The ground was now clear enough for MacDonald to pay his visit to the USA, and on 28th September he and his advisers (who did not include any Admiralty representative[1]) sailed from Southampton in the *Berengaria*. He received an extremely warm welcome in New York and Washington, and from 4th to 10th October he and Hoover held informal talks at the President's holiday 'camp' on the Rapidan River in Virginia and in Washington.[2]

The outcome of the Hoover-MacDonald meeting may be summarised under the heading of each class of warship considered. With regard to battleships the Prime Minister pressed for reduction of displacement from 35,000 to 25,000 tons, and of their main armament from 16-inch to 12-inch guns—which the Admiralty had accepted as a measure of economy. Replacement should, he proposed, be deferred by increasing their age limit from 20 to 26 years. To these proposals Hoover replied that the USA did not wish to build any more battleships before 1936 because many naval officers held the belief 'that owing to the development of aircraft the days of the battleship were numbered'. When MacDonald expressed the Admiralty's dislike for a total cessation of construction, because of its effect on the supply of specialised machinery and skilled men, Hoover replied that when the ships in service became too old for use 'he did not wish to replace them at all', and asked if Britain would agree to a reduction in the number allowed under the Washington Treaty. MacDonald, again speaking to the Admiralty's brief, pressed for a reduction of size rather than of number. It became apparent later in the talks that the Americans might accept the 25,000-ton limit 'in the last resort'—provided that they were allowed to build one 35,000-ton ship to compensate for Britain's possession of the *Hood* (1918), *Nelson* and *Rodney* (1925). Construction of the last two in the 1920s, as permitted by the Washington Treaty, was a source of continuing resentment in the General Board and Navy Department; and Hoover was certain that his advisers would not yield on the 16-inch gun question.

[1] MacDonald's party consisted of Sir Robert Vansittart (Principal Private Secretary), Dr. Thomas Jones (Deputy Secretary of the Cabinet), R. L. Craigie (Head of American Department, Foreign Office) and Miss Rosenberg (Private Secretary). Lord Arnold (Paymaster-General) accompanied the party 'in an unofficial capacity' and so did MacDonald's daughter Ishbel. Thomas Jones, *Whitehall Diary*, vol. II, ed. Keith Middlemas (OUP, 1969) pp. 189 and 210–15 has an interesting inside account of the visit.

[2] DBFP, Second Series, vol. I, pp. 106–16. FRUS, 1929 vol. II, pp. 3–33 have respectively the British and American official records of the conversations.

The discussions on cruisers revolved largely around the 'yardstick' question whereby the gap between British and American total tonnage might be bridged. Hoover emphasised that the Americans attached more importance to age than to any other factor in arriving at the formula, and was as anxious as his visitor to bring the American total of 8-inch cruisers down from twenty-three to eighteen.[1] Though the high British total tonnage (339,000) and the proposed replacement programme of fourteen new ships presented difficulties he none the less made it clear that he would meet the British 'at least half way'.

Turning to destroyers MacDonald declared his willingness to reduce the British total to 150,000 tons—if other powers reduced their strength in submarines sufficiently 'to make this possible'; and Hoover said that such a figure 'would be acceptable to the United States'. But MacDonald added a caveat that if France insisted on retaining the 90,000 tons of submarines given in her current programme the British would have to increase their destroyer total by 50,000 tons.[2] As to American submarine tonnage Hoover was prepared to come down to the British total of 50,000, and perhaps allow Japan 70,000 tons—though that concession was to be held in reserve for possible use in persuading Japan to come to an agreement on the cruiser issue.

The Americans, reported MacDonald, suggested a reduction in the Washington Treaty aircraft carrier tonnage from 135,000 to about 120,000, and also wanted to fix a minimum displacement for this class 'to prevent them dropping down into the cruiser class' and so upsetting the 'delicate adjustments' in that class which the British and Americans were trying to achieve. Here it should be mentioned that Admiral Moffett and the General Board repeatedly harped on the handicap allegedly imposed on their service by the great size of the *Lexington* and *Saratoga* (some 36,000 tons each).[3] Those two ships absorbed so great a proportion of the permitted tonnage that the USA could not achieve parity in numbers with the six British carriers. The General Board proposed to get out of the difficulty by classifying the two big ships as 'experimental', which would result in their exclusion from the authorised total tonnage.[4] Moffett repeatedly returned to the

[1] Hoover suggested a 'discount' perhaps as high as 50% for ships over twenty years old. In other words a 5,000-ton ship would count as only 2,500.

[2] The French 'Statut Naval' of Dec. 1924 forecast a total of 96,000 tons of submarines by 1943. *Les Flottes de Combat* (Paris),

[3] See vol. I, p. 334. Though always shown in the official records as displacing 33,000 tons these two ships were about 3,000 tons larger.

[4] GB. 438–1, Serial 1464 of 3rd Jan. 1930.

charge on this issue, and wanted to build two 10,000 ton carriers if the total tonnage was reduced as proposed. His dislike of the large size, and so of the big aircraft complements, of the *Lexington* and *Saratoga* was one of the few issues concerned with naval aviation on which he showed less than his normal foresight.[1] It is not surprising that the British naval staff later took much the same line as the General Board by pressing that the carrier *Furious*, which was to be reconstructed, should also be classed as 'experimental'.[2] Finally, on the tricky question of the transfer of tonnage from one category to another MacDonald and Hoover agreed that 10% transfer might 'go some way towards meeting the difficulties of the Italians and French', though the latter would probably ask for a higher percentage.[3]

Though the Admiralty was probably well satisfied by the exclusion of the controversial issue of Belligerent Rights and Freedom of the Seas from the agenda for the conference the decision was a severe disappointment for Hoover and Stimson, who had hoped at least to get food ships exempted from the British claim. They were equally firmly, but tactfully rebuffed when they raised to MacDonald the desirability of Britain demilitarising her naval and military bases in the western hemisphere. This was an old sore which had been periodically reinflamed by anti-British elements in the USA—notably by the General Board, which refused to subscribe to the view 'that the existing military and naval stations of Great Britain in the Western Hemisphere are not in a condition to be a menace to the United States'.[4] As the garrisons of the bases were in fact tiny and their defences almost negligible this line was, to put it mildly, somewhat xenophobic. Perhaps as a result of the General Board's apprehension Hoover offered

[1] Moffet to Pratt 19th Feb. and 31st March 1930. Pratt papers.

[2] Director of Plans Memo. of 13th May 1931. LNC(E)10. Cab. 29/149.

[3] This summary of the MacDonald-Hoover conversations is based on Circular Telegram B.180 of 22nd Nov. 1929 to Dominion Prime Ministers and all quotations are taken from that source. Copy in Adm. 116/2717. The full record of the Mac-Donald-Hoover conversations of 4th–10th Oct. 1929 in Washington and of the MacDonald-Mackenzie-King conversations held in Ottawa 17th–20th Oct. 1929 is in CP. 312(29), undated but circulated on about 10th Nov. 1929.

[4] GB. 438-1, Serial 1453 of 8th Oct. 1929. The General Board actually included the bases on both the east and west coasts of Canada, as well as those in the Caribbean, as part of the 'menace' to the USA. However in August of that year the US Navy had opened tentative negotiations to lease sites for seaplane bases in Bermuda and Trinidad—thereby foreshadowing Churchill's famous 'destroyers for bases' deal of 1940. USNA, RG 80, Box 171. The CID frequently considered the defence of West Indian bases in the 1920s e.g. those at Jamaica and Bermuda in CID 325C. Cab. 5/7.

to divide the world into eastern and western hemispheres, and to maintain no bases in the latter if Britain gave up hers in the former. This suggestion, reminiscent of Pope Alexander VI's famous Bull *Inter Caetera* of 1493 dividing the Atlantic Ocean between Spain and Portugal on a line arbitrarily drawn 100 leagues to the west of the Azores,[1] was finally rejected by the British Chiefs of Staff on the grounds that freedom to refortify bases such as Bermuda, Trinidad and Kingston (Jamaica) and increase their garrisons in emergency was essential to the defence of the Caribbean trade routes.[2]

At the end of the Hoover-MacDonald conversations a joint communiqué was issued in which they said that 'In view of the security afforded by the Peace Pact [the Kellogg-Briand Pact of 1928] we have been able to end, we trust for ever, all competitive building between ourselves, with the risk of war and the waste of public money involved, by agreeing to a parity of fleets category by category'; and, probably due to Hankey's pressure,[3] no mention was made of Belligerent Rights or of Freedom of the Seas.

Shortly after MacDonald had returned to London he directed that the CID Sub-Committee's report on Belligerent Rights, which had been produced while the Baldwin government was still in office,[4] should be circulated to all members of his Cabinet.[5] The reaction of Lord Parmoor, the Lord President of the Council, was vigorous. The CID report was, he wrote, 'based on assumptions which the Labour Party and Labour Government have publicly rejected, and its conclusions are such as my colleagues could not well accept, at least until the whole subject has been thoroughly considered afresh . . .'; and in the reappraisal of the issue he urged that 'Service representatives should attend only in [the] capacity of advisers to their political colleagues . . .'[6] MacDonald does not seem to have answered this attack, but a short time later he wrote to Hoover that a Cabinet committee had been appointed to examine 'the various problems and considerations involved in the Freedom of the Seas including your own contribution regarding food ships'. He went on however to warn the President not to expect too much because 'our people have a deep sentimental regard

[1] See J. H. Parry, *The Spanish Seaborne Empire* (Hutchinson, 1966), pp. 45-6.

[2] See for example CID. 325, 356, 363, 376 and 390C regarding the garrison of Bermuda. Many other papers in the same CID series refer to this subject. Cab. 5/7.

[3] See for example Hankey to MacDonald 11th Oct. 1929. Premier 1/99.

[4] CP. 304(29) of 6th March 1929. Cab. 24/206.

[5] On 4th Nov. 1929. *ibid.*

[6] CP. 310(29) of 6th Nov. 1929. *ibid.*

for their historical position on the sea and . . . the simple fact of a re-examination is apt to unsettle and stampede them'.[1] Thus MacDonald held out no strong hopes that the purposes which he and Hoover had discussed could be brought to early fruition, and the dilemma in which life-long pacifists like himself and Parmoor were placed when they came face to face with the realities of nationalist rivalries became cruelly apparent.

Early in 1930 the Admiralty reviewed the question whether the rules regarding 'visit and search' of merchant ships, particularly with regard to submarines and aircraft, should be raised at the conference.[2] As it was plainly impossible for submarines and aircraft to conform to the Hague Conventions applicable to surface warships this now appears to be an example of legalistic considerations obscuring practical realities. However the Naval Staff view was that prohibition of attacks by submarines on merchant ships would not be accepted by the conference, though submarines probably would be required to conform to the rules governing surface warships—as in the amorphous Root Resolutions of 1922.[3] The Staff proposed that aircraft should be treated in the same manner. Madden, the First Sea Lord, sensibly concluded that it was best not to raise these complicated issues at all. He told Alexander so, and the First Lord passed this recommendation on to the Prime Minister.[4] None the less the issue was revived in the following year—partly as a result of a public lecture given by Admiral Richmond,[5] who saw the realities clearly though he much underestimated the influence of aircraft. Admiral Backhouse, the Third Sea Lord, now repeated the desirability of aircraft being made subject to the same rules as submarines (which, as already remarked, were themselves impracticable). 'If in another war', he wrote, 'aircraft are to be allowed a free run all this [i.e. the experience of the submarine crisis of 1917] is likely to happen again';[6] which was true enough though one may feel that concentration on practical methods of defence would have offered better prospects than trying to apply unrealistic rules.

Almost simultaneously with the announcement of the outcome of the Hoover-MacDonald talks the Board of Admiralty reviewed the

[1] MacDonald to Hoover 19th Nov. 1929. Premier 1/99.

[2] Adm. 1/8786–101/35.   [3] See vol. I, pp. 327–8.

[4] Madden to Alexander 19th Feb. and Alexander to MacDonald 1st March 1930. Adm. 1/8786–101/35.

[5] On Empire Defence Problems at the Caxton Hall, Westminster. Reprinted in *The Navy*, the journal of the Navy League of August 1931.

[6] Minute by Backhouse of 14th Aug. 1931. Adm. 1/8786–101/35.

building programme which might be undertaken during the period when a new naval treaty would remain in force—that is to say until the end of 1936. These deliberations were of course part of the process of framing the proposals which the British government would place before the conference, to which further reference will be made shortly. Madden asked for an estimate of the cost of a programme consisting of one battleship (25,000 tons displacement armed with 12-inch guns) yearly starting in 1931, two 6-inch cruisers in 1929 and thereafter three per year until 1933, a flotilla of destroyers (one leader and eight) and six submarines yearly.[1] Murray, the Permanent Secretary, put the cost at nearly £60 millions in 1929 rising to a peak of £63 millions in 1936. 'In my opinion', he wrote, 'these figures are both politically and financially impossible of realisation';[2] and that was, temporarily, the end of such ambitious hopes, though a few weeks later the Sea Lords decided to hold out at the forthcoming conference for the 25,000-ton, 12-inch capital ship and, for the sake of economy, to extend their useful life from 20 to 26 years.[3]

Soon after MacDonald reached home he became involved in talks with the representatives of France, Italy and Japan with the object of reconciling their differences of outlook and purpose, and bringing them into line with the broad principles which he and Hoover had agreed. For France Aristide Briand, the Foreign Minister, at once made it plain that acceptance of parity with Italy was out of the question, and that his country 'was specially interested in submarines'. The Italian ambassador Antonio Bordonaro was equally insistent on parity with France but was 'not much interested in submarines if an agreement could be arrived at'. The Japanese ambassador Tsuneo Matsudaira stressed that British-American agreement on heavy cruisers at eighteen and fifteen respectively would force his country to build more than their present or projected twelve ships of that class, and asked for a 70% ratio applicable to all categories to be substituted for the Washington 5:5:3 ratio. MacDonald pressed Matsudaira strongly not to disturb what he regarded as 'a state of equilibrium'; but the latter claimed that the security of his country was at stake, and cited the identical argument used earlier by British and American naval authorities about the length of coastline to be defended and the nation's dependence on imported food and raw materials. In addition

[1] Minute dated 2nd Oct. 1929. Adm. 116/3372.
[2] Minute of 15th Oct. 1929. *ibid.*
[3] Sea Lords' meeting of 20th Dec. 1929. *ibid.*

Matsudaira claimed that there was a 'large number of his countrymen living in China who had to be protected'.[1]

More or less simultaneously with these exchanges in London Stimson was exerting similar pressure on the Japanese representative in Washington.[2] The Admiralty was satisfied by the 'strong and sound line' both President and Prime Minister had taken, and hoped that it would be 'staunchly maintained'. Their view on the heavy cruiser question was that Britain should certainly not accede to the 70% ratio demanded by Japan. The real difficulty, they truthfully remarked, lay in the undefined 'yardstick' arrangement between Britain and the USA.[3] By the end of November it was abundantly plain that a Five Power naval limitation agreement was not going to be easily arrived at. However the invitations sent on 7th October to attend the conference, which was to open towards the end of January 1930, were accepted by all five powers, and discussions on the agenda and procedure at once began in London.

On 11th December the Dominions were given an outline of the arrangements made. After the opening public session in the House of Lords on 23rd January, at which the Chairman and Secretary-General were to be elected, a private Plenary Session would immediately follow, and other similar sessions would be held periodically. At the first of these a key body, to be known as the First Committee and consisting of the principal delegates, would be formed. It would be empowered to appoint sub-committees either of the same general character as the First Committee or to deal with technical questions. Another committee would work in parallel with the First Committee throughout the conference to handle all questions of procedure. When its work was completed the First Committee would report to the conference, which would then reassemble in Plenary Session. The aim of the conference was defined as 'to attain agreement on the reduction of existing naval strengths and programmes and on the limitation of war vessels on the basis of mutually accepted strengths'; and the suggested date by

[1] These conversations are summarised in Circular Telegram B.182 of 22nd Nov. 1929 to the Dominions. Adm. 116/2689.

[2] State Department Aide Memoire of 12th Nov. 1929. Copy in Adm. 116/2689. Presumably supplied to the British Embassy in Washington.

[3] A. Flint (Admy) to R. L. Craigie (FO) 17th Nov. 1929. Endorsed 'Approved' by A. V. Alexander. Henderson to Sir John Tilley (Tokyo) of 18th Nov. 1929 gives the Foreign Office's summary of the MacDonald-Matsudaira talks in very similar terms to the Circular Telegram cited above. Both in Adm. 116/2689.

which this 'equilibrium' was to be reached was to be the last day of 1936.[1]

The replies received from Italy and France were entirely predictable, since both countries held fast to the conditions and reservations communicated to MacDonald by their ambassadors in the preliminary talks. But the nomination by Italy of two Admirals as delegates (Admirals Acton and Sirianni) and by Japan of one Admiral (Takeshi Takarabe) infringed the MacDonald-Hoover plan to keep the negotiations out of the hands of naval 'experts'. Though the Italian nominations produced a protest from the British ambassador in Rome[2] both they and the Japanese admiral were accepted by Britain and the USA because they held civilian posts.[3] The French in their reply refused to accept that Italy should be granted parity with themselves or to abolish submarines. They stressed once again that a security guarantee must precede disarmament, and that they preferred 'global' limitation to limitation by categories. They also sought a Mediterranean pact analogous to the Locarno Treaty, and a settlement of colonial frontiers in North Africa.[4]

Meanwhile the Cabinet had appointed a committee from among its members to plan the arrangements for the conference and consider the memoranda submitted from the departments concerned.[5] From our point of view the most important memorandum was that submitted by Madden, who had been asked by MacDonald to make a comprehensive statement of the problems which the Admiralty had to face in connection with the conference. It reflected the serious misgivings felt in the Admiralty over some of the proposals put forward by MacDonald and accepted in principle by him and Hoover—especially with regard to the arbitrary reduction of the number of cruisers from the 70 stated at Geneva in 1927 to 50.[6] The New Zealand government had decided not to send a special representative to the

---

[1] Circular Telegram B.202 of 11th Dec. 1929. Adm. 116/2690.

[2] *O'Connor* (p. 64) is not right to say that 'no objection [to the nomination of Admirals as delegates] was made by the other nations'. The Italian reply to Sir R. Graham's protest is in Graham to Henderson no. 838 of 13th Dec. 1929. Grandi defended Acton's appointment on the grounds that he came as a Senator and not as a naval 'expert'. Copy in Adm. 116/2690.

[3] Admiral Takarabe was Minister of Marine.

[4] The French reply is in Tyrrell to Henderson no. 1748 of 27th Dec. 1929. Copy in Adm. 116/2690.

[5] Cab. 29/117.

[6] LNC(29) 4th meeting of 13th Dec. 1929. Cab. 29/117.

conference but to rely on Admiral Lord Jellicoe, who had been Governor-General of that Dominion 1920-24 and its chief delegate at the abortive conference of 1927.[1] The Admiralty took advantage of this arrangement to enlist Jellicoe's support on the cruiser issue, and he represented that to have only 50 cruisers by the end of 1936 was 'inadequate for the security of our sea communications'.[2] A climax came on 15th January 1930 when Madden wrote to Alexander in his capacity of 'Principal Naval Adviser' protesting that the policy decided on by the government was 'in direct opposition to the advice of the Admiralty'—by which he presumably meant the Sea Lords. As regards battleships, the First Sea Lord objected to the postponement of all replacements until after the next conference in 1935, and to the reduction of the numbers agreed in the Washington Treaty. On the issue of cruisers he reiterated that the absolute need was 70, and that the figure of 50 could only be considered provided that other powers limited their cruiser strength commensurately, that the agreement was 'for a strictly limited period', and that 'a steady replacement programme of 3 ships a year' of adequate size was approved. The file copy of this paper is endorsed 'Handed to PM 15th January 1930'; but it obviously did not deflect him an inch from his purposes.[3]

The short-circuiting of naval advice was not confined to the British. At about the same time as Madden made his protest on behalf of the Sea Lords the American General Board objected to the reduction of the US Navy's heavy cruisers to 18, which they described as 'a radical step' demanding reconsideration in the light of 'decidedly well-considered opinion'. They were, however, prepared to accept that the level of parity in cruiser tonnage should be 280,500 or even 250,500; and if the latter were agreed the total of eighteen heavy cruisers would be acceptable.[4]

In mid-January the Cabinet took at one session all the papers produced by the Admiralty and COSs on the policy to be adopted at the forthcoming conference.[5] MacDonald spoke at length on the outcome of the preliminary conversations and the announcements made by participating powers. He read out a letter received from Snowden, the Chancellor of the Exchequer, who was absent at the second Hague

[1] See vol. I, p. 503.
[2] LNC(29)3 of 6th Jan. 1930. Cab. 29/117 and Adm. 116/2747.
[3] Memo. by Madden of 15th Jan. 1930. Became CP. 1(30). Cab. 24/209.
[4] GB. 438-1. Memo. of 7th Jan. 1930.
[5] CP. 2(30), 5(30), 12(30), 13(30) and 14(30). Cab. 24/209.

conference on Reparations,[1] and the draft of a memorandum on the government's policy. Snowden's letter reflected of course the views of the Treasury, which were that whereas the Foreign Office wanted *agreement* and the Admiralty *limitation*, only they wanted *reduction* of naval forces. They therefore urged that 'the Admiralty be instructed immediately to prepare . . . an alternative plan . . . in conformity with the general principles indicated'—which were to effect a saving of £4 millions.[2] This bombshell drew a strong riposte from the Admiralty, who pointed out that the current estimates were based on a level of parity agreed between the Prime Minister and the President, and to scrap them would mean the loss 'of four months of endeavour'. The Treasury's proposals, declared the Admiralty, would also 'undermine the naval position of the British Empire', and the parity level agreed with the Americans 'must stand as the proposals with which we enter the conference'.[3] This was strong stuff, and one cannot but admire the way Alexander supported his colleagues and stood up to the all-powerful Chancellor and his Treasury team.

In their Conclusions the Cabinet took each class of warship in turn. 'The battleship', they stated, 'is simply and solely a ship of war, and as political security is strengthened it must stand [sic. ? tend] to disappear'. The line to be taken was that all replacements should be postponed until after the next conference in 1935, and that if a 'transition period' came to pass before the class disappeared the numbers agreed at the Washington Conference and the size and armaments of any new ships built should be reduced and their effective life lengthened. As to cruisers, the Cabinet 'believed that the number of 50 is amply adequate' to fulfil the purposes of that class; and efforts should be made 'to induce the conference' that the size of individual ships should be fixed at the 'lowest possible limits'.

Turning to submarines they had already announced their support of abolition, which would produce great economies; but as France and Japan were opposed to such a measure 'there is very little chance of our success'. We would therefore have 'to fall back on reductions', and would 'use all the pressure we can to bring submarine strengths down to the utmost [degree]'. Destroyers, the Cabinet stated, should also be subject to 'a maximum individual tonnage . . . with a total gross tonnage which we should try to keep to not more than 150,000'. In the

[1] See Roskill, *Hankey*, II, pp. 502–8.
[2] CP. 12(30) of 16th Dec. 1929. Cab. 24/209.
[3] CP. 13(30) of 20th Dec. 1929. *ibid.*

next section the Cabinet declared that 'we must see that the Agreement puts an end to competitive building', and they would therefore strongly resist the principle of making up a deficiency of tonnage in one class by increasing that of another class—generally referred to as the 'transfer principle'. They wanted if possible to avoid discussion of 'political matters such as a Mediterranean agreement', for which the French were likely to press; but as that might prove impossible they would 'make it clear that this country will refuse to take upon itself any obligations over and above those which it has already undertaken under the Covenant of the League of Nations, the Locarno agreement etc.'. Finally Alexander was given the difficult task of 'informing the Board of Admiralty of the foregoing conclusions'. He was to 'indicate that they were based on political grounds', and that 'the most careful consideration had been given to the views of the Admiralty throughout'— an assurance which was likely to ring a little hollow in the ears of the Sea Lords. The Prime Minister was to make 'the main declaration' in a Plenary Session at a time decided by him.[1]

To return to American preparations, towards the end of January 1930 a 'Tentative Plan' was produced by their delegation—apparently without consulting the General Board.[2] It reduced the number of 8-inch cruisers to eighteen—contrary to Admiral Jones's frequently reiterated demand for 23, and allowed Japan a total of twelve such ships. Early in February Jones protested vigorously to Pratt on this score; but the latter defended the proposal with equal vigour to Stimson.[3] The American plan proposed that Britain and USA should have parity in destroyers and submarines, and Japan have 60% and 66.7% of the tonnage allowed to the two major powers in those classes respectively. The number of capital ships was to be reduced from the Washington Treaty totals to 15, 15 and 9; but America was to be allowed to build one new battleship—for reasons mentioned earlier.[4] What the American plan made absolutely clear was that the Japanese demand for a 70% ration in all classes was far from met; and when its contents became known in part their reaction was predictably hostile.[5]

[1] Cabinet 1(30) of 14th Jan. 1930. Cab. 23/63.

[2] Revised Edition, dated 28th Jan. 1930. GB. 438–1.

[3] Jones to Pratt 5th Feb. and Pratt to Stimson ('with utmost secrecy') 13th Feb. 1930. Pratt papers. His acceptance of 18 big cruisers was conditional on America being allowed to build five additional 6-inch gun cruisers. *O'Connor*, p. 70.

[4] The General Board had originally asked for two new battleships for USA and one for Japan by 1934. GB. 438–1. Memo. of 6th Jan. 1930.

[5] *O'Connor* pp. 71–2. The figures of 60,000 tons of submarines for Britain and USA

Nor were internal difficulties and differences confined to the American delegation. Their British counterparts began a series of meetings designed to arrive at an agreed policy in December 1929, and early in the following month they refused to revise the 18-15-12 total for heavy cruisers or to allow Japan the 70% in that class which she demanded.[1] Henderson, the Foreign Secretary, wanted a big reduction in the maximum tonnage of capital ships; but Madden declared that such ideas derived from Admiral Richmond's campaign in favour of smaller capital ships, and that he 'lacked experience' of the constructional side.[2] Alexander remarked that the Americans were unlikely to come down to the 25,000-ton maximum which the Admiralty favoured, and would want to retain the 16-inch gun; while Japan would demand 70% of the larger navies' tonnage in that class; and France would insist on a larger permissible 'transfer' of tonnage between the various categories than the 10% which the British and Americans were prepared to allow. MacDonald considered a higher transfer allowance 'quite unacceptable'. As regards submarines, the British noted that Italy as well as USA was likely to accept abolition, but Japan and France were unlikely to do so. On 9th February the British delegates discussed the American 'Tentative Plan', and noted with satisfaction the reduction of their big cruiser total from 21 to 18. Madden then described Pratt as being 'of the younger school of thought', and coming round to the British view on the value of smaller cruisers. He also believed that Pratt would be prepared to reduce capital ship maximum tonnage to 27,000, probably with 14-inch

---

and 40,000 for Japan given here do not correspond with those in the Revised Edition of the 'Tentative Plan' of Jan. 1930 which shows 90,000 tons for the first two countries and 60,000 for Japan. Pratt personally 'wanted submarine tonnage abolished' but was prepared to allow Japan a ratio 'agreeable to Britain'—even amounting to 70%. Pratt papers.

[1] There were two sets of meetings by British delegates—one with only the British representatives present and the other with those of the Commonwealth nations as well. The papers submitted to the two were given respectively LNC(B) and LNC(E) numbers. In Cab. 29/128 and 29/133.

[2] Richmond, a very original thinker on naval policy, had been favoured for the post of First Sea Lord by the Labour Party when it came to power in 1929. But he had brought extreme unpopularity on himself among senior admirals by his advocacy of smaller capital ships in articles in *The Times* of 21st and 22nd Nov. 1929. See A. J. Marder, *Portrait of an Admiral* (Cape, 1952), pp. 29–30. Also LNC(29) 5th meeting of 9th Jan. 1930. Adm. 116/2747 and Cab. 29/117.

guns.[1] MacDonald was strongly opposed to allowing 6-inch cruisers of tonnage as large as 10,000, and against the proposed new American battleship; nor would he accept the American 'yardstick' for the future —should that long gestating concept materialise.[2]

By the middle of January the British Commonwealth delegates had reached sufficient unanimity to issue a long paper, on MacDonald's instructions, setting out the proposals which the British government would place before the conference;[3] but as the views it contained with regard to general questions, such as limitation by 'global tonnage' or by 'categories', the Empire's requirements in each class of ship, and the Admiralty's attitude to the proposals put forward by the other four nations had become plain during the preliminary talks, already described, there is no need to recapitulate them.

The first Plenary Session of this enormous conference, in which the delegates, expert advisers, technical staff and secretaries totalled over 150, took place in the Royal Gallery of the House of Lords on 21st January when the King made the opening speech. MacDonald was then unanimously elected chairman.[4] The second Plenary Session took place in St. James's Palace two days later, and Sir Maurice Hankey, whose experience of organising big international conferences went back as far as 1916 and was unrivalled, was appointed Secretary-General on the proposal of Dino Grandi.[5] The chief delegates of France and Italy—but not Stimson—then made statements which revealed the wide divergence in their outlook and purposes. MacDonald summed up, truthfully if somewhat apprehensively, that 'the problem

[1] Madden met Pratt again on 17th Feb. 1930 when they discussed in a most friendly manner the cruiser needs of their respective countries. Pratt showed understanding with regard to the British need for a large number of cruisers for trade defence, provided that the principle of parity with his country was maintained. As to the much discussed Washington Treaty ships, according to Madden he 'does not like the 8″ class', and would be prepared to settle for 15 for each country instead of the 23 on which his own General Board was so keen. 'He is a great believer in the air,' wrote Madden, and wanted 'as much aircraft carrier tonnage as they could get'. He also advocated battleships of not *less* than 27,500 tons with 12-inch guns—which was not very far above the Admiralty's desire. Pratt also 'considered the importance of submarines would diminish' as they could be 'largely controlled by good air work'. Memo. by Madden of 18th Feb. 1930. Adm. 116/3624, which contains A. V. Alexander's papers on the 1930 London Conference.

[2] Adm. 116/2747.

[3] LNC(E)7 of 14th Jan. 1930. Became CP. 5(30). Cab. 24/209. Copy in Adm. 116/2746.

[4] LNC 1st Meeting. Cab. 29/119. Also in Adm. 116/2741.

[5] Roskill, *Hankey*, vol. II, pp. 512-15.

that now faces us is how to get at the details [and] . . . the difficulties'.[1]
At the third Plenary Session a week later the agenda was circulated.
Three points of importance were raised by the French, two by the
Italians and one by the British; and the French and British points
related to 'global' limitation or limitation by categories. Gibson then
referred to the French proposal for limitation by four categories—
capital ships, aircraft carriers and 'auxiliary vessels' of 600–1,850 tons
and 1,850–10,000 tons, which was reminiscent of the unhappy story
of the Anglo-French compromise proposal put forward to the great
annoyance of the Americans after the 1927 *débâcle* at Geneva.[2] André
Tardieu, the French Premier supported Gibson on limitation by
categories, and Alexander, after stressing the vital importance of sea
power to Britain, agreed—subject to the cruiser class being divided
into two categories, namely ships armed with 6-inch or smaller guns
and those with guns larger than 6-inch. He was prepared to accept
transfer between categories only in the case of the less powerful ships.
On a resolution proposed by Stimson the issue was referred to the First
Committee,[3] and it is to the deliberations of that body that we must
therefore now turn. It met eight times between 31st January and 12th
April and produced six reports, all of which were sent to the Plenary
Sessions of the conference.[4] The discussions in the First Committee were
lengthy and detailed and need not be quoted, but the reports it produced merit attention. The first of them dealt with the various means
whereby limitation might be applied; the second covered the categories of 'special vessels' which would not be subject to limitation; the
third dealt with the abolition of submarines or, alternatively, regulations regarding their size and methods of use—notably the prohibition
of 'unrestricted warfare' against merchant shipping; in the fourth
report the committee dealt with the disposal of vessels of war with the
object of preventing their sale to non-signatories of the treaty; the
fifth proposed rules for the replacement of warships and the age limits
which should be applied to each class; while the last report dealt with a
'holiday' in capital ship construction until the next conference was
convened in 1935.[5] A Committee of Experts acted as an advisory body

[1] LNC 2nd Meeting. Cab. 29/119. Also in Adm. 116/2741.
[2] See vol. I, pp. 545–9.
[3] LNC 3rd Meeting of 30th Jan. 1930. Cab. 29/119 and Adm. 116/2741.
[4] Cab. 29/123.
[5] LNC. 9, 13, 14, 15, 16 and 17 of 20th Feb., 15th March, 12th April (the last three
reports). Cab. 29/120.

to the First Committee and produced reports on such matters as global limitation or limitation by categories, and on the size and employment of submarines.[1]

More important were the many meetings of Heads of Delegations, since it was at them that most of the bargaining took place.[2] For example the seventh and eighth meetings were entirely taken up by discussions on the French proposals between Tardieu, Henderson and MacDonald, and it was probably at these sessions that MacDonald developed strong feelings about the way the French were obstructing progress in the main conference. In addition to the Heads of Delegations' meetings a great many private conversations took place between the British and foreign delegates.[3] Many of them dealt with French and Italian problems, such as the desire of the former for a Mediterranean Pact, and the refusal of the latter to produce any figures at all showing their strength until 'certain outstanding difficulties', notably the claim of the Italians to Tunisia, had been settled. The delegations of Britain and the Commonwealth countries met together nine times between 15th January and 13th March, chiefly with the object of keeping the Commonwealth delegates informed about what was going on in the many bilateral or trilateral conversations.[4]

The fourth Plenary Session took place on 11th February, and MacDonald then said that, while awaiting the report of the First Committee, he would raise the issue of submarines. Alexander spoke out strongly for abolition, and was supported by Stimson and by the delegates from Australia and New Zealand. For France Georges Leygues, the Minister of Marine, refused to consider abolition on the well-known grounds that 'the submarine is the defensive weapon of the lesser navies'; but he wanted the 'illegal' use of submarines to be 'outlawed', and so get rid of the idea that such vessels were 'a barbarous instrument of war'.[5] For Italy Grandi declared himself 'perplexed' about the issue of abolition, but he would not 'object to the principle' involved. The outcome was that the French and American Resolutions were referred to the First Committee, which in turn passed the issue to the Committee of Experts, whose chairman was R. L. Craigie of

---

[1] Cab. 29/124.

[2] LNC(D)1 to 28 between 23rd Jan. and 8th April 1930. Cab. 29/121.

[3] Between 13th Feb. and 14th April there were 28 such conversations. Cab. 29/129.

[4] LNC(E) series. Cab. 29/133.

[5] LNC 4th Meeting. Cab. 29/119. See also statements by French and Italian Delegations of 12th and 19th Feb. 1930. Cab. 29/130. Copy in Adm. 116/2741.

the Foreign Office. That body decided however, that as abolition was a policy issue it lay outside their jurisdiction. They therefore returned it to the First Committee, which failed to reach agreement on it.[1]

The Committee of Jurists handled the legal aspects, and on 19th March a British revision of the relevant part of the Washington Treaties (the so-called 'Root Resolution')[2] was adopted by that body and finally approved in formal session. In effect it maintained that submarines must conform to the same rules of International Law as surface warships—which was in fact a highly unrealistic proposition, though it did overcome the objections of France, which had never ratified the Root Resolution. On reading the report of the deliberations of the legal experts Madden commented to Alexander 'ist Lord. I am strongly in favour of supporting the French view. We will *certainly* wish one day to use submarines in a legitimate way against commerce.'[3] Agreement was also reached limiting the displacement of submarines to 2,000 tons and 5.1-inch guns, though again it was necessary to introduce qualifications to satisfy the French desire for bigger vessels. Destroyers were to be limited to 1,500 tons and 5-inch guns, but a proportion was allowed to go up to 1,850 tons as 'flotilla leaders'.

Despite the concessions made to France in several respects her insistence on the inclusion of a security guarantee, such as America could never accept, combined with Italian insistence on parity with France, not only made a Five Power Treaty impossible but in March came near to bringing about failure of the conference—because the Anglo-American agreement was contingent on a settlement with France.

An interval of more than two months took place between the fourth and fifth Plenary Sessions; but during that period the First Committee and the Committee of Experts held many meetings, and a great many informal conversations and negotiations took place behind the scenes.[4] We will therefore briefly review the latter.

On 11th February MacDonald met Stimson and his principal colleagues. The Secretary of State then emphasised the trouble he had

[1] Adm. 116/2743 and Cab. 29/123.   [2] See vol. I, pp. 326–8.

[3] Madden to Alexander 26th Feb. 1930. Adm. 1/8741–88/30.

[4] Minutes and Memoranda of First Committee (A. V. Alexander chairman) are in Cab. 29/123 and Adm. 116/2742. Those of the Committee of Experts (R. L. Craigie chairman) are in Cab. 29/124 and Adm. 116/2743. The issues of abolition of submarines and regulation of their use were discussed at the 13th, 14th and 15th meetings of the latter on 5th, 6th and 7th March. A maximum displacement of 2,000 tons was agreed on 6th and next day the Committee's report was approved.

experienced with Admiral Jones over reducing the total of American 8-inch cruisers, and said he could not accept the British figure of 100,0C0 tons for aircraft carriers—because of the deleterious effect of the two 'monster' ships *Lexington* and *Saratoga* on American numbers in that class.[1] Next day the British delegates discussed among themselves the proposal received from the French that they should have ten 8-inch cruisers and a 'global' tonnage of 800,000—about two-thirds of the British total. MacDonald then remarked that all the powers except Britain appeared to be planning to increase their navies.[2] That same evening the British and French delegates met together, and Tardieu then said he was prepared to reduce his country's 'global' figure to 725,000 tons, but his greatest difficulty arose from the new German 'pocket battleship'[3] to which his country would have to build a reply. He was, however, prepared to accept a substantial reduction in the size of capital ships—coming down as low as 17,500 tons if all the powers agreed to such a limitation. None the less MacDonald expressed his concern over 'this very ambitious French programme'.[4]

The next step was for the British delegates to consider the Japanese and French proposals simultaneously.[5] They decided to discuss the former with the American delegates, and try and get their agreement to Japan having no more than twelve big cruisers while the French should be restricted to half that number. The French demand for nearly 100,000 tons of submarines by 1936 they described as 'impossible'; and if all that country's demands were met it would inevitably lead to large building programmes by ourselves and the Italians.[6] Three days later the British delegates met again, and R. L. Craigie, the chairman of the Committee of Experts, then said that he was fully aware of what France really wanted—namely a treaty of guarantee against aggression on the lines of the Four Power Pact signed at Washington in 1921.

Towards the end of February MacDonald raised to the British delegates the question of modernising older battleships, which the

[1] Adm. 116/2747 and Cab. 29/121.

[2] Meeting of 12th Feb. 1930. *ibid.* The French proposals are in Adm. 116/2741 and Cab. 29/127.

[3] See pp. 27-8.

[4] Meeting of MacDonald and Alexander with French delegates, 11th Feb. 1930. Adm. 116/2747.

[5] The Japanese proposals are in LNC(E)17 and those of the French in LNC(E)18. Cab. 29/134. Copies in Adm. 116/2747.

[6] Meeting of 13th Feb. 1930. Adm. 116/2747 and Cab. 29/128.

Americans had put forward. He was prepared to accept this proposal provided that Britain could do the same. MacDonald also reported on a talk he had held with Grandi, whose country's attitude he mildly described as 'rather negative'. The Italian Foreign Minister had admitted that he could not 'induce his naval advisers to produce a programme'; and that of course 'greatly influenced the attitude of the French'. MacDonald said he was still aiming to achieve a Five Power Treaty, and insisted that none of his colleagues should admit that we might be prepared to settle for less.[1]

At the meetings of the British and Commonwealth delegates between mid-January and mid-March the discussions followed the same lines as those held by the British delegates alone, and there is no need to recapitulate them in detail. The most interesting development was the clash between Henderson and the Treasury on the one side and the Admiralty on the other. The navy, declared Henderson, was costing 25/– per head of population per year, which he regarded as far too high; but Alexander fought back on the 'absolute' needs of Britain for Imperial defence and trade protection, which in his view were different in principle from the 'relative' needs of other countries.[2] At the next meeting MacDonald protested, with good reason, that 'the work of the conference was going far too slowly', that there had been no progress in the First Committee, and that he must soon call another Plenary Session.[3] Despite continued pressure from Henderson the Admiralty's representatives, having reluctantly accepted a total of only 50 cruisers by 1936, refused to accept a capital ship total of less than 15 or to reduce the total aircraft carrier tonnage permitted by the Washington Treaty (135,000 tons).[4] Next MacDonald reverted to the question of big cruisers, and even suggested a 'yardstick' of one 8-inch cruiser ton being treated as equivalent to 2.37 6-inch cruiser tons as a means of bridging the 30,000-ton gap between British and

[1] Meeting of 28th Feb. 1930. *ibid.*

[2] 3rd meeting of British Empire delegates on 31st Jan. 1930. *ibid.*

[3] 4th meeting of same on 5th Feb. 1930. *ibid.* The First Committee actually rendered its first report (Paper no. 9) on 10th Feb., with the first report of the Committee of Experts attached as Appendix III. Neither achieved any real progress towards the solution of the 'global' or 'categories' limitation issue or the permissible transfer percentage. Adm. 116/2744 and Cab. 29/128.

[4] 5th meeting of British Empire delegates on 6th Feb. 1930. Cab. 29/128 and Adm. 116/2747. Discussion of the British proposals (LNC(E)12 of 7th Feb.) referred to above took place at this meeting and the next one.

American cruiser tonnage in order to achieve a figurative 'parity'.[1] It is interesting to find that the British delegation thus came closer to producing an actual figure for the 'yardstick' than the Americans ever did—despite the fact that the idea had been originated by the latter.

Next political issues bedevilled the conference's progress. Japanese elections were to be held on 20th February, and MacDonald believed that if the government won them, as it did, they might modify their demand for 70% of heavy cruisers. Then, on 17th, a financial crisis brought down the government of France, and the formal conference had to adjourn to allow the delegates to return to Paris. However Tardieu soon returned to office, and on 6th March a new delegation, in which Briand was again included, arrived in London. During the interval T. M. Wilford of New Zealand warned the British Empire delegates of the danger of Japanese southward expansion, which he did not consider adequately appreciated in Britain; but J. E. Fenton of Australia was less apprehensive, and expressed faith in the fact that the Pacific Islands, in which the 'magnificent harbour' of Truk was situated, were only held by Japan under a League Mandate.[2] According to American records the two antipodean Dominions threatened to build their own ships if the British-Japanese ratio was unsatisfactory;[3] but no such threat appears in the British records; and if it was in fact made it cannot have carried much weight, since the authorities in London were well aware that the industrial and shipbuilding capacity of the two Dominions was quite inadequate to fulfil it.

Despite all these troubles some progress was made. The Americans dropped their demand for a new battleship, agreement was reached that the older ones could be modernised, and the cruiser tonnage of USA was settled at 323,500 tons with only eighteen ships of the Washington Treaty class. The elimination of the chief cause of bad Anglo-American relations, which had reached their nadir at the 1927 Geneva Conference, was perhaps the greatest accomplishment of the 1930 conference.[4]

With Britain and USA brought into accord it remained for the latter to find an acceptable compromise with the Japanese; and that was not easily accomplished with the Americans adamantly opposed to granting an increase in the cruiser ratio. Moreover the American

[1] 6th meeting of same on 10th Feb. 1930. *ibid.* The British 'yardstick' proposals are in LNC(E)12, part II, paras. 2–20.

[2] 7th meeting of same on 17th Feb. 1930. Adm. 116/2747.

[3] *O'Connor*, p. 73.   [4] See vol. I, ch. XIV.

Immigration Act of 1924, mentioned earlier, had deeply offended Japanese sensibilities and dissipated much of the goodwill generated by the Washington Conference.[1] On 17th February the British, American and Japanese delegates met to explore the ground—despite the fact that it had already been thoroughly covered. The chief credit for breaking the deadlock—after the election of 20th had strengthened the Japanese government's hand—must be accorded to the American Senator D. A. Reed and Mr. Matsudaira, the ambassador in London. Although by 12th March Stimson and MacDonald were preparing to downgrade their hopes to a Two Power Treaty between Britain and America a settlement was in fact quickly reached, and perhaps stimulated, by that threat. Mr. Wakatsuki, the chief Japanese delegate, and a majority of his team accepted a 60% ratio in 8-inch cruisers, 70% in 6-inch cruisers and destroyers, and parity in submarines. Both sides accepted qualifications to this agreement—namely that Japan could demand the right to replace her smaller 8-inch ships (the *Furutaka* class) by larger ships in 1943; while the USA reserved the right to contest this claim but agreed to delay construction of the last three ships of their heavy cruiser programme. Japan was thus restricted to the 12 heavy cruisers already built or under construction, was only allowed a small increase in 6-inch cruiser tonnage, and accepted a substantial reduction in destroyer and submarine tonnage. The compromise was at once agreed to by Hoover; but the Japanese government, under pressure from the big navy lobby, hesitated for so long that doubts about the achievement of a Three Power Treaty continued until Premier Hamaguchi broke the deadlock on 2nd April.[2]

We must now return to the Plenary Sessions. On 14th April MacDonald took the chair at the fifth Session, which had the reports of the First Committee and the Committee of Experts before it. MacDonald said that the former contained so many reservations (especially by France and Italy) that it should not be accepted but merely be 'noted'. None the less a measure of accord on various issues had been reached in the informal discussions. The Japanese had withdrawn their proposal for a 'non-construction zone' between the lower limit for cruisers and the upper limit for destroyers; characteristics for the latter

[1] O'Connor, p. 13. The possibility of amending the Act was raised unofficially by the Americans at the end of January, but neither President Hoover nor Congress would have accepted such a proposal. *ibid.* pp. 77–8.

[2] O'Connor, pp. 81–3.

The Mediterranean Fleet in Grand Harbour, Malta c.1935. Left to right *Royal Sovereign*, *Queen Elizabeth* (Fleet Flagship), *Revenge* all of First Battle Squadron, *London* and a sister ship of First Cruiser Squadron.

Part of Mediterranean Fleet in Alexandria at time of Abyssinian crisis 1935-36. Left to right—destroyers of 'E' and 'R' classes from Home Fleet; unidentified merchant ship; repair ship *Resource;* two heavy cruisers of *London* class; British India steamship (possibly *Nuddea* with MNBDO equipment); destroyer depot ship *Woolwich; Exeter,* heavy cruiser from South American station. Singapore type RAF flying boats nearer to shore. Ras-el-Tin palace in foreground. The aircraft carrier *Glorious* can just be seen alongside behind the *London* class cruisers.

Pomp and Circumstance. Men of the Mediterranean Fleet led by the massed bands of the Royal Marines march through Alexandria during the Abyssinian crisis 1935-36.

Types of British service men in the Fleet Club (formerly Claridge's Hotel), Alexandria during the Abyssinian crisis 1935-36.

class had been agreed, as had the lists of 'special vessels' not subject to limitation. There was no agreement on the abolition of submarines, but the application of International Law to their use represented some advance. The rules governing retention of over-age vessels and for replacements had been defined, and an extension of the 'capital ship holiday' accepted. These agreements provided, MacDonald said, 'the raw material for the drafting of a [Three Power] treaty', and the delegates agreed that the work should at once be taken in hand by a committee of legal experts.[1] At the sixth and final Plenary Session on 22nd April the title of the treaty was agreed, Part II of it was to be sent to the Secretary-General of the League of Nations, and the treaty was actually signed. Much mutual self-congratulation by the principal delegates followed, and warm tributes were paid to MacDonald and to his right hand man Sir Maurice Hankey; but the fundamental disagreements between France and Italy were entirely glossed over.[2]

As soon as success, limited though it was, became apparent MacDonald wrote to the King from Chequers 'with his humble duty' saying that the conference had ended 'with a Five Power agreement on certain important general points which had hitherto defied settlement', which was in truth a considerable overstatement. He continued, more accurately, that 'the attitude of the French and Italians was deplorable and required much patience and delicate handling to prevent an angry and an open rupture'; and he also reported, correctly, on how the progress of the conference had been greatly delayed by the French political crisis, and the Three Power Treaty jeopardised by the last minute troubles of the Japanese 'who had a stiff struggle with their Naval Board'. As regards the French demand for a treaty of guarantee he was insistent that 'one rule must be firmly observed'—namely that 'Great Britain must not take on further responsibilities, and must not be put in the position of having to act mechanically and without freedom of judgement should trouble arise in Europe'. France, he declared, was 'trying hard to get us into that position'. 'The results of the Conference', he concluded, 'will be of great benefit, if they are allowed to mature, and one of the greatest of these will be our improved relations with the United States. From beginning to end the two delegations worked in complete harmony. To all intents and purposes they were one team . . . The mischief maker [presumably France] is not silenced, but he has become, for the moment at any rate,

[1] 5th Plenary Session of 14th April 1930. Cab. 29/119. Copy in Adm. 116/2741.
[2] 6th Plenary Session of 22nd April 1930. *ibid.*

something of an Ishmael'[1]. If MacDonald's description of Anglo-American team work was somewhat hyperbolical his broad conclusion regarding the effect of the conference on relations between the two countries was certainly justified. Much of the credit for that accomplishment is attributable to the broad-mindedness of Admiral W. V. Pratt, which contrasted so markedly with the anglophobia of Admiral H. P. Jones, his predecessor as chief American naval 'expert'. Jones actually returned home to USA a sick and disgruntled man before the end of the conference. The King replied very warmly to MacDonald's letter, rejoicing in 'the good news that . . . a partial Five Powers Agreement and a complete Three Powers Settlement have been secured'. He attributed these results to the Prime Minister's 'untiring labours, patience and tact'.[2]

MacDonald was not alone in glossing the disagreements which had simmered beneath the surface throughout the conference. After it was all over A. V. Alexander told the Board of Admiralty that he 'wished to place on record on behalf of the Government and himself personally their appreciation of the valuable assistance rendered by the Admiralty', and referred particularly 'to the services of the First Sea Lord, the Controller, the DCNS and Naval Staff';[3] which, considering that Madden and the Naval Staff had repeatedly, and on at least one occasion formally represented their disagreement with the government's policy, was a considerable euphemism.

Soon after the end of the conference the Sea Lords reviewed the effect of the treaty on the Dominion Navies and on their relation with the Royal Navy. The British government was in their view bound to encourage the Dominions to build all classes of ship, so relieving Britain of a proportion of the cost of 'the Empire Fleet'. But in twenty years' time that fleet might well consist of ships provided by five different Dominions and 'could not be compared in efficiency with the United States fleet, which would be trained and operated as one unit'. Furthermore the larger the Dominion Navies became the greater would be 'the dispersion of the Empire Fleet, and the resulting weakness'; and as the Dominions were completely free to pay off ships as they desired Britain could 'only partially mobilise the Empire Fleet on

---

[1] MacDonald to George V. Holograph from Chequers 12th April 1930. RA GV G2258. The results of the conference are well summarised in Cmd. 3547 of 15th April 1930.

[2] George V to MacDonald 18th April 1930 from Windsor Castle. *ibid*.

[3] Board Minute of 1st May 1930. Adm. 167/81.

the declaration of war', and 'the first shock . . . will have to be met by the Royal Navy'. The First Sea Lord urged that such matters should be 'carefully considered at the [1930] Imperial Conference, and the Admiralty position safeguarded as much as possible'; also that when the 1935 Naval Limitation Conference took place 'an allowance [should be] claimed for the dispersion of the Empire Fleet on declaration of war';[1] but in fact such considerations did not play a prominent part in the Imperial or international discussions of the 1930s.

Looking back today, and endeavouring not to exploit the wisdom derived from our knowledge of later events, it seems that, apart from the improvement in Anglo-American relations already referred to, the conclusion reached by Raymond O'Connor—namely that 'the sacrifice of national autonomy' by the three principal naval powers in order to reach an international agreement 'was misplaced'—can hardly be refuted. The apparent equilibrium reached in 1930 was, he continues, 'not only deceptive but it was erected on an illusory foundation'— because it 'put the control of weapons in the wrong sequence on the road to security'.[2]

If the Board of Admiralty derived little comfort from the 1930 London Treaty, especially with regard to the arbitrary reduction of cruisers from 70 to 50, when Pratt returned to the USA he found himself so unpopular with the General Board and senior naval officers that he offered to resign but was talked out of doing so by Adams.[3] In Japan the treaty produced a nationalistic outburst leading to the resignation of the Chief of the Naval Staff and the assassination of Premier Hamaguchi. From the point of view of the British Empire and the USA the treaty certainly helped to make rearmament slower and more difficult when, in the mid-1930s the need for it was becoming ever plainer. In Japan reactionary and xenophobic elements were already gaining ground, and it is likely that the treaty lent impetus to such movements, and so contributed to the overt aggression in Manchuria in

[1] Memo. by Madden of 17th June 1930. Adm. 1/8744–125/30.

[2] *O'Connor*, p. 128.

[3] I am indebted to Professor Clark G. Reynolds of the University of Maine for this anecdote, which derives from Pratt's son. In 1932 Adams incurred Hoover's wrath over naval appropriations and offered to resign. He in turn was talked out of it by Pratt. Letter from Professor Reynolds of 7th April 1975. Other authorities however consider the anecdote dubious. It is not mentioned in Gerald E. Wheeler's biography of Pratt (Annapolis, 1974) though he does quote (pp. 308–9) a letter he wrote to his wife expressing his discouragement that 'so many of the older officers have turned against me'.

September 1931 and at Shanghai in the following January. And as it was those events which made the impotence of the League of Nations in face of a determined aggressor clear beyond any possible doubt the long-term results of the London Conference of 1930 can hardly be described as having contributed to world peace.

In the autumn of 1930 A. V. Alexander and Arthur Henderson, the Foreign Secretary, set off on a mission to Paris and Rome in order to try and bring Italy and France into accord with the terms agreed at the London Conference. Alexander was of course also concerned to eliminate naval disagreements before the General Disarmament Conference met at Geneva early in 1932. However he found Jacques Dumesnil, the French Minister of Marine in the Tardieu government, 'very rigid', and was alarmed by his country's claim to possess some 83,000 tons of submarines, as compared with the British total of 52,700 tons.[1] Admiral Field, now First Sea Lord, remarked that if the French adhered to that figure we would have to increase our destroyer strength.[2] In Rome Alexander found Admiral Sirianni, the Minister of Marine, and his principal colleague Admiral Burzagli far more conciliatory than the French. Indeed the Minister stressed his country's desire for conciliation, and wanted a ratio established between French and Italian strength on Washington Treaty lines; but the Italians did not believe that the French would reduce their demand for ten big 'Treaty' cruisers or their submarine tonnage; nor, in his opinion, would they be prepared to grant Italy parity.

At the end of March 1931 the Cabinet reviewed the 'serious position' reached in the Franco-Italian talks as set out by Alexander and Henderson;[3] but no solution could be suggested. In May Field and Alexander met Craigie of the Foreign Office, and the First Sea Lord then remarked that the French attitude 'had resulted in largely upsetting what was done in London'.[4] If that was something of an exaggeration so was Alexander's commendation of the final compromise tentatively reached between France and Italy but which was never ratified.[5] It is interesting to find the Admiralty a short time later praising German 'forbearance'

[1] Telegram Alexander to Admiralty of 16th Sept. 1930. Adm. 116/3624.

[2] Memo. to Alexander of 22nd Feb. 1931. *ibid.*

[3] Cabinet 21(31) of 31st March 1931. Cab. 23/66. The French statement of their position and the British reply is in CP. 106(31) of 23rd April 1931. CP. 64(31), undated, is the report by Alexander and Henderson on their visit to Paris and Rome. Cab. 24/220.

[4] Record of meeting on 11th May 1931. Adm. 116/3624.

[5] Board Minute 2807 of 5th March 1931. Adm. 167/83.

for not building right up to the limits allowed by the Versailles Treaty or replacing old ships as was permitted;[1] but that forbearance was not to last much longer.

In the autumn of 1930 the renewal of the Anglo-American arbitration treaty[2] and the old issue of Freedom of the Seas came before the Cabinet, as MacDonald had foretold in his letter of November 1929 to Hoover. The two subjects were linked together because in some quarters in London it was thought that the USA might refuse to renew the arbitration treaty unless Britain modified her stand on Belligerent Rights. Hankey sent MacDonald papers on these subjects by the Foreign Office and Admiralty,[3] and himself supported the Admiralty view that 'to expose Belligerent Rights to the hazards of arbitration' would be dangerous. If the issue had to be discussed he would prefer a special conference to be convened for the purpose. 'But', he concluded, 'instinct and reason convince me that it is best to let sleeping dogs lie'.[4] MacDonald wrote on Hankey's note that Hoover had said he would not raise the issue 'as he understood that it involved very difficult matters'. Doubtless it was for that reason that Stimson had kept off the subject at the naval conference; and there the matter rested—for the time being.

At the end of July 1930, some three months after the signature of the London Treaty, Admiral Madden handed over the office of First Sea Lord to Sir Frederick Field. Madden's selection for that post in succession to Beatty owed a good deal to the desire to heal the schism between the Jellicoe and Beatty factions, which had arisen out of the indecisive outcome of the Battle of Jutland; for Madden had been Chief of Staff to Jellicoe as C-in-C, Grand Fleet 1914–16. His three years of office were not distinguished by any important developments in the fields of material or personnel, and his personal outlook was very conservative on nearly every issue. Yet the criticism to which he was subjected now seems to have been unfair, since, with a Labour Government committed to economy in the fighting services in power, it is difficult to see how any First Sea Lord could have done much more. Had Sir Roger Keyes succeeded to the office on Beatty's retirement, as

---

[1] Admiralty to Foreign Office 17th July 1931. *ibid.*

[2] This was the Root-Bryce Treaty of 1908. See vol. I, p. 549.

[3] CP. 331(30) and 342(30). Cab. 24/215.

[4] Hankey to MacDonald 10th Oct. 1930. Premier 1/99. For the Admiralty's view that 'naval opinion remained strongly against allowing the question of Belligerent Rights to be a matter for arbitration' see Board Minute no. 2751, 7th Oct. 1930. Adm. 167/81.

he and some senior officers desired, a major crisis between the Sea Lords and the politicians would almost certainly have occurred; and that would hardly have benefited the navy. If Madden's term as First Sea Lord was undistinguished the selection of Field as his successor was to prove disastrous—partly because his health was not really up to the strains of that office. Furthermore Hodges the Second Sea Lord was succeeded in May 1930 by Admiral Sir Cyril Fuller, who was anything but a success in that post; and in the following month Admiral F. C. Dreyer took over as DCNS from the highly intelligent and politically sophisticated William Fisher. The officers who assembled in the historic Board Room in the early 1930s were certainly not likely to gain the confidence of the navy as a whole.

CHAPTER III

Financial Stringency and Disarmament

1929-1931

———◆———

THE STORY of the British naval estimates for 1930–31 actually begins some six weeks before the London Conference opened, when the Admiralty and Treasury representatives forwarded a joint report to the Cabinet Fighting Services Committee which, although signed by both, showed that the views of the two departments were in fact irreconcilable. The Sketch Estimates for the new financial year had come to nearly £54 millions; but Snowden, the Chancellor of the Exchequer, was pressing very hard for a reduction of £5 millions on the total of nearly £56 millions approved for 1929–30. The two departments agreed that a cut of the order demanded by Snowden could only be achieved if the whole 1929 building programme (except two sloops which had already been started) was cancelled. If the government was not prepared to go to such extreme lengths it was plainly desirable to establish an order of priority in the programme—despite the fact that in the Admiralty's view 'there is an unanswerable case for each item', and that 'omission or suspension' of any part of the programme must mean either a decline in British strength proportionate to that of other powers or a heavy increase of expenditure later on 'in order to overtake arrears'. The Treasury however refused to accept the premise on which the Admiralty's case was based—namely 'that the fleet must consist of a given number of ships of a given size to be decided at the present juncture'; and they particularly objected to the inclusion of six submarines in the programme when we were about to propose to the London Conference the abolition of that class. The conclusion reached was that the estimates should be fixed provisionally at

£50.9 millions (i.e. the Chancellor's £5 million reduction) and a Supplementary Estimate presented later should that prove necessary—as in fact it did.[1]

Early in the New Year the Board of Admiralty met to consider the Fighting Services Committee's recommendation that, of the 1929 building programme, only one light cruiser (*Leander*) instead of three, one leader and four destroyers instead of eight, four sloops and three submarines should be proceeded with; and construction of the submarines was to be suspended until the outcome of the London Conference was known. No addition was to be made to fuel reserves and no new flights provided for the Fleet Air Arm—economies which the Sea Lords described as 'undesirable in the extreme'. They gave Alexander a strongly worded memorandum on these matters and on 'the inadequacy of the reduced shipbuilding programme'; and he agreed to circulate it to the Prime Minister and Cabinet.[2]

Despite the Sea Lords' vigorous objections Snowden held firmly to the sum he was prepared to find. On 2nd February 1930 he wrote to Alexander that he approved Parliament being asked to vote £51¾ millions; and when on 3rd March the new construction programme was announced it corresponded exactly to the proposals made by the Fighting Services Committee—except that all submarines were omitted. Thus the final outcome of the long debate was the imposition of almost as big a reduction as the Chancellor had demanded; and Vote A (personnel) was to be reduced from nearly 100,000 officers and men to 97,300 by 1st April 1930 and to 94,000 a year later. These were indeed slashing cuts on a service which had for many years been under heavy pressure to economise.[3] Furthermore, as Murray pointed out, the cancellation of two cruisers from the 1928 and 1929 programmes had produced heavy claims for compensation from the building firms.[4]

Soon after the results of the London Conference were known the Board began to frame the Sketch Estimates for 1931–32 and the building programme for 1931—with every prospect of another severe fight ahead of them. Battleship replacement was of course now postponed for at least five years; and the Admiralty had to scrap three of the

[1] Memo. by Admiral W. W. Fisher (DCNS) and G. C. Upcott (Treasury) of 13th Dec. 1929. Adm. 1/8739–40/1930 and 116/3389.

[2] Board Minute 2676 of 9th Jan. 1930. Adm. 167/81.

[3] Cmd. 3506 of 3rd March 1930.

[4] Memo. by Murray of 3rd May 1930. Vickers-Armstrong were claiming £800,000 compensation for the 8-inch gun mountings for the cancelled *Surrey* and *Northumberland* of the 1928 programme. Adm. 1/8739–41/30.

Emperor of India class and the battle-cruiser *Tiger* (all of 1912–13) in order to bring their number of capital ships down to the total of 15 which had been made the agreed level of 'parity' with the USA.[1] As the old British battleships were in service as a training squadron their loss produced difficult problems over giving young ratings adequate sea experience before they were drafted to fully commissioned ships.

The Admiralty's discussions on the building programmes for the period of the London Treaty (1930–36) naturally revolved chiefly around the question of what cruisers should be built within the 339,000-ton total and fifty ships permitted by the treaty, of which the existing fifteen 8-inch ships absorbed nearly 149,000 tons and 6-inch cruisers some 100,000 tons. The recommendation finally arrived at was to use the surplus 90,000 tons by building ten 7,000-ton and four 5,000-ton 6-inch cruisers, and to ask for three of the former to be included in the 1930 programme and the remainder spread over the following three years, after which replacement of nineteen ships over sixteen years old (totalling some 86,000 tons) would arise. The Naval Staff considered that no 'useful purpose would be served by forecasting the pro-grammes' after 1933. As to the 150,000 tons of destroyers allowed by the treaty, if Britain was to have all its allowance in modern ships by the time the treaty expired over two flotillas per year would have to be laid down between 1930 and 1933. But as the Admiralty considered it hopeless to ask for such large programmes they decided to try and get one leader and a flotilla of eight ships every year up to 1936. Much the same argument applied in the case of sloops, and they recom-mended that authority should be sought to build four every year. Submarines of three types (fast patrol, small patrol and combined minelaying and patrol types) were envisaged, and from 1930–1933 five of the first and second types and two of the third type were put in the programme.[2] The 1930 instalment of those proposals was sent to the Fighting Services Committee early in May 1930. It consisted of three 6-inch cruisers, nine destroyers, three submarines, four sloops and a

[1] The treaty provided for the USA scrapping the *Florida*, *Utah* and either the *Arkansas* or *Wyoming* (1911–12). The *Wyoming* was actually retained in demilitarised state as allowed. The British were similarly allowed to retain the *Iron Duke*, which was never remilitarised; but the Japanese battleship *Hiyei*, which was their equivalent ship, was extensively modernised and remilitarised 1936–40. Her final statistics were 31,980 tons (eight 14-inch guns).

[2] This programme appears in identical form as an Appendix to Board Memo. of 24th Oct. 1930 and Board Minute 2891 of 10th Dec. 1931. Adm. 167/84.

netlayer, and the total cost was given as £9.6 millions.[1] In the following month the proposed White Paper was redrafted as required by Alexander 'to meet criticisms from the Left Wingers [J. M.] Kenworthy and party' as the Naval Staff put it.

Soon after the end of the London Conference, and probably to help overcome the expected opposition to building up to the limits permitted by the treaty, the Admiralty wrote to the Foreign Office to seek their view on the continued validity of the 'Ten Year Rule' instituted in 1919 and made self-perpetuating by Churchill as Chancellor of the Exchequer in 1928.[2] This approach was almost certainly initiated by Hankey who had come to dislike the rigidity of the rule strongly and was preparing to launch a campaign to get it rescinded.[3] In May 1930, when Admiral Madden brought that year's building programme before the Board, he reported that a reply had been received from Sir Robert Vansittart, Permanent Secretary of the Foreign Office, to the effect that while it was 'in our interests and policy to maintain the League and all it stands for' the European continent was 'riddled with pre-war thought' and 'the Old Man Adam [i.e. warlike propensities] still remains'.[4] Our difficulties and dangers, Vansittart continued, would be enormously increased if we adopted a policy of 'undue enfeeblement economically or navally', and so led the world to assume that we were somnolent. With this powerful support in his hand Madden told the Board that 'The Admiralty have made exceptional efforts and accepted grave responsibility in order to meet the government's policy of securing a naval understanding with the United States . . . I trust the Cabinet will not press on the Admiralty any reductions below their official programme, and I could not accept any additional responsibility in this respect.' He went on to criticise severely the proposals received from the Fighting Services Committee to build only an average of $2\frac{1}{2}$ cruisers a year for four years, of which three would be of the small 5,000-ton (*Arethusa*) type, and only $3\frac{1}{2}$ flotillas of destroyers in the same period. Such slow replacement would, he pointed out, mean that we would not reach the strength permitted by the treaty until long after it had expired—in fact not until 1942 or '43. The adoption of such a policy would, moreover, in his view con-

[1] FS. 29(26) of 9th May 1930. Adm. 116/2606.

[2] See vol. I, p. 215 and *passim*.

[3] See Roskill, *Hankey*, vol. II, pp. 521–2 and 535–8.

[4] Hankey often referred to this paper by Vansittart as his 'Old Man Adam' paper. *op. cit.*, pp. 521–2 and 529.

stitute 'a grave breach of faith with the Sea Lords', who had made the conditions on which they had accepted the London Treaty absolutely plain.

Madden and his colleagues won that battle, and on 5th June the Board noted 'with satisfaction' that the full instalment of the first of the four year programme had been agreed.[1] None the less in October Snowden sent a personal appeal to Alexander 'to make an altogether exceptional effort to economise' in order to help him produce a balanced budget. He urged that the Sketch Estimates should be scrutinised again with that object in view.[2] But, as Murray remarked a little later, 'The Chancellor strongly deprecated any cuts which would mean dockyard discharges.'[3] Alexander replied at length defending the Sketch Estimates but offering the Chancellor various olive branches, including a fairly high 'shadow cut' (i.e. the estimated under-expenditure for the year)[4] of over a million, and various minor economies which would enable a small overall reduction to be claimed when the estimates were presented to Parliament. He also forecast a further drop in personnel from 93,650 in April 1931 to 91,840 a year later.[5] Despite the First Lord's co-operative endeavours Snowden wrote again saying 'how greatly disappointed I am at the nature of your proposals', and asking for a new scrutiny of the estimates;[6] but Alexander must have known that he had gone as far as he could carry his naval colleagues with him and stood firm.

Alexander actually presented the estimates on 2nd March 1931 at £51.6 millions, which was some £350,000 less than the previous year's. In the ensuing debate he enlarged on the attempts he had made to bring France and Italy 'to reconcile their aspirations within the London Naval Treaty'; but his self-congratulation on what he described as the agreement reached rings a little hollow, since it was in effect no more than an agreement to differ. Leo Amery from the Conservative benches said that the submarine tonnage allowed (81,900 to Italy and 52,700 to France) was, as compared with Britain's, 'ridiculously high', and deplored the state of the country's cruiser and destroyer forces as well as the cut in personnel. But Alexander may well

[1] Board Minute of 5th June 1930. Adm. 167/81.

[2] Snowden to Alexander 27th Oct. 1930. Adm. 1/8747–82/1931.

[3] Minute by Murray to Board of 2nd Feb. 1931. *ibid.*

[4] See vol. 1, pp. 206–7 regarding the principle of the 'shadow cut' in each year's Navy Estimates.

[5] Alexander to Snowden 15th Dec. 1930 and 3rd Feb. 1931. Adm. 1/8474–82/1931.

[6] Snowden to Alexander 14th Jan. and 5th Feb. 1931. Adm. 116/3389.

have felt that he got away with surprisingly little criticism of the building programme from his own party.[1] Nor did Ammon, the Parliamentary Secretary, have a rough passage when in March he had to present the expected Supplementary Estimate for nearly £½ million to provide money to start building the ships of the 1930 programme which had been postponed pending the outcome of the London Conference.[2]

Planning for the 1930 Imperial Conference started towards the end of February of that year, when MacDonald formed a Policy Committee under his own chairmanship to decide in broad outline the subjects to be discussed.[3] At the second meeting on 7th May the Service Ministers were present, and it was decided that, as at the 1926 Conference,[4] the subject of Defence should be covered initially by statements made by the Chairman of the CID and of the COS Sub-Committee. The Annual Review of the Chiefs of Staff, which was actually circulated at the end of July, was not to be sent to the Dominions prior to the conference, and the whole question of the Singapore base was held up pending a Cabinet decision on the future of the scheme. Meanwhile a Foreign Policy and Defence Sub-Committee, of which Hankey was chairman, was set up to prepare memoranda on such subjects for the conference. This body produced eighteen papers which, taken together, provided a mine of information on subjects ranging from Industrial Mobilisation to the 'Single Budgetary' principle for the limitation of armaments.[5] From the point of view of our subject the most important paper was that entitled 'The British Commonwealth of Nations—Naval Policy 1930'. It started with a historical survey, went on to discuss the types of warship of the carrier class and below needed for Imperial Defence, oil storage throughout the

---

[1] Parl. Deb., Commons, vol. 249, cols. 1205-1354.

[2] Parl. Deb., Commons, vol. 250, cols. 305-8 (18th March 1931).

[3] The other members were A. Henderson (Foreign Secretary), W. Wedgwood Benn (India), Lord Passfield (Dominions) and W. Graham (Board of Trade), but Lord Sankey (Lord Chancellor) attended when legal or constitutional issues were to be discussed. The minutes of the 13 meetings held by this body between 24th Feb. and 3rd Oct. 1930 are in Cab. 32/70. Sir Maurice Hankey acted as secretary throughout.

[4] See vol. I, pp. 464-6.

[5] The papers are the IC(FD) series in Cab. 32/77. They were mostly also printed in the CID. B or C series. For example IC(FD)4, the sub-committee's Interim Report, is also CID. 344C which came before the CID at its 248th meeting on 29th May 1930. Cab. 2/5.

Empire and kindred subjects;[1] but as the COSs' Annual Review dealt with the same matters it will be more convenient to summarise the latter. The COSs stressed that the total of 50 cruisers had only been accepted 'for the strictly limited period up to 31st December 1936', and that 70 were 'necessary to meet Imperial Defence requirements'— as they had stated in their 1928 Annual Review. 'It is pertinent', they continued, 'to emphasise that in agreeing to 50 cruisers and 150,000 tons of destroyers, the Admiralty have accepted a risk for a limited period as these numbers are inadequate relatively to the projected continental building programmes . . .' which, if adhered to, might involve invoking the 'escape clause' (Article 21) of the London Treaty. They went on to stress 'the increasing importance of the Fleet Air Arm', for which 'a steady programme of two flights *per annum* is considered necessary', and also the inadequacy of the defences of the overseas bases on which the Navy must depend in war. They held that the London Treaty 'introduces no new factors tending to diminish the strategic importance of the Singapore base, and that $7\frac{1}{2}$ million tons of oil were needed in reserve as against the four million tons then held in stock.[2] These issues became, as we shall see, a constantly repeated refrain in the Admiralty's statements of policy throughout the 1930s. At about the same time the COSs circulated their comprehensive study of 'Imperial Defence Policy', in which they reviewed British relations with France, Germany, Italy, Japan and the USA. Perhaps the most interesting passages of this voluminous document are those in which 'the re-establishment of Germany as a world power' and the 'Anschluss' with Austria were regarded as likely developments. On the other hand 'the likelihood of this country being drawn into hostility with Italy' was, except possibly in fulfilment of obligations under the League Covenant, considered 'remote'; and the signature of the London Treaty, they concluded on a happier note, 'may be said to mark the end of a difficult phase in Anglo-US relations'.[3] Such was the broad survey of Defence problems prepared as a brief for the British spokesmen at the Imperial Conference.

The conference opened on 1st October with MacDonald in the chair. With the exception of the Irish Free State all the Dominions were represented by their Prime Ministers, and its deliberations were very

[1] IC (FD)12 of 24th May 1930. Cab. 32/77. Copy in Adm. 116/3372. Also CID. 997B.

[2] CID. 1009B of 29th July 1930. Cab. 4/20.

[3] CID. 1008B of 29th July 1930. *ibid.*

protracted—no less than twenty-eight meetings being held. The chief emphasis was from the start, not on greater preparedness for war, but on disarmament and the settlement of disputes by arbitration, to study which a special committee was appointed under the chairmanship of Mr. Dupré of Canada. That body supported the draft Disarmament Convention which had been prepared for the forthcoming conference at Geneva.[1] The committee also considered the various schemes for limitation of armaments, such as Budgetary Limitation or restriction of the total effectives in the defence services.[2]

The Fighting Services were given a comparatively subordinate place in the conference, merely providing a Committee of Experts under the chairmanship of Admiral Field. It met for the first time on 21st October (Trafalgar Day!) when Field raised the disproportionate cost of Imperial Defence borne by Britain (a subject on which the Dominions had been fully informed at earlier conferences),[3] and stressed the importance of the naval requirements with which the reader is already familiar. He looked for help from the Dominions especially in the field of establishing larger oil reserves, improving Imperial communications, minesweeping and the defence of ports and bases;[4] but the response was not enthusiastic.

At the seventeenth meeting of the main conference the report of the Singapore Base Committee, of which Snowden was chairman was discussed,[5] and the Chancellor of the Exchequer said that there had been no change in the policy announced a year earlier—namely that all work which could be suspended should be suspended and that no new contracts would be placed.[6] The protests of J. H. Scullin and J. W. Forbes, Prime Ministers of Australia and New Zealand respectively, were of no avail. Although the policy of 'ultimately establishing a naval base at Singapore' still held good, as the dour Chancellor was not prepared to provide any money for it no progress could be made.

Without doubt the most important outcome of that conference, and the one by which the Dominion representatives set the greatest store, was the acceptance at the end of October of the draft Statute of Westminster, by which the evolution of Empire into Commonwealth

[1] E(30) 26 and 27. Also CID. 1025, 1026 and 1027B. *ibid.*

[2] CID. 1025B of 12th Nov. 1930. *ibid.*

[3] See vol. I, pp. 297–8 and 465–6.

[4] Adm. 116/2788.

[5] 17th meeting of Imperial Conference on 17th Nov. 1930. Cab. 32/79.

[6] On 16th Oct. 1930. The report of the Singapore Base Committee is E(30)36 of 27th Oct. 1930. Cab. 32/91.

was carried a stage further, and the complete autonomy of the Dominions given statutory recognition.[1] The question of a new Arbitration Treaty with the USA, to replace the Root-Bryce Treaty of 1908, which had expired in June 1928, was raised at the conference, and that led inevitably to the question whether we should offer a *quid pro quo* in the form of some relaxation of our claim to Belligerent Rights at sea in order to satisfy American susceptibilities. Although the issue had been thoroughly thrashed out as recently as 1928, and a decision had then been taken to make no such overture,[2] Arthur Henderson appears to have been attracted by the idea two years later. At any rate his attitude provoked Hankey into sending him a lengthy history of the subject and a letter urging him not to bring the matter up at the Imperial Conference.[3] The Admiralty certainly supported, and possibly inspired Hankey's strong line. At any rate between them they succeeded in persuading Henderson to hold his hand.

As regards integration of Commonwealth defence policy with that of the Mother Country, or even acceptance of the principle of 'collective responsibility' for defence, which the British Chiefs of Staff desired, the outcome of the conference was wholly nugatory; and Hankey was justified in protesting to MacDonald over the vast amount of rather futile discussion, involving the accumulation of a mountain of paper in order to produce such small results.[4]

Meanwhile Alexander, who had already refused to have Sir Roger Keyes as First Sea Lord,[5] was having trouble over the succession to the office of Second Sea Lord, who was responsible for all personnel problems. In June 1931 Field, the First Sea Lord, wrote to Sir John Kelly that Alexander would not appoint him to that office. The reason given was that Kelly was too senior, and to have given him the post would have blocked the promotion of younger men;[6] but one may feel that, as with Keyes, the Labour First Lord wanted to keep strong personalities off the Board of which he was head. Be that as it may Kelly protested vigorously that he had been promised either the post of Second Sea Lord or command of the Atlantic Fleet, and accused the unfortunate Field of having broken his spoken and written word.[7] Then Keyes weighed in on behalf of Kelly; but an angry interview with

---

[1] 12th meeting of Imperial Conference on 31st Oct. 1930. *ibid.*
[2] See vol. I, p. 549.   [3] Hankey to Henderson 21st Oct. 1930. Cab. 63/43.
[4] Roskill, *Hankey*, vol. II, pp. 528-9.   [5] See vol. I, pp. 46-8.
[6] Field to Kelly 12th June 1931. Kelly Papers KEL/109.
[7] Kelly to Field 22nd June 1931. *ibid.*

Alexander produced no result.[1] If Alexander thus disembarrassed himself of two potentially difficult colleagues the result was to produce perhaps the weakest Board of Admiralty of all time;[2] and it is ironical that, as will be told in the next chapter, Sir John Kelly had to be recalled to restore the Atlantic Fleet's morale only three months after Alexander had refused him employment in Whitehall or afloat.

The darkening of the Far Eastern horizon produced by the Japanese aggression in Manchuria in September 1931 naturally brought about a gradual shift of emphasis in British naval policy. In June of that year the Admiralty had set up a high-level Naval Planning Committee,[3] and although at its first meeting it approved a 'Naval Appreciation of a war against Russia' it switched to Far Eastern problems later in that month, and reviewed the effects of the government's decision to defer for five years all expenditure on the defence of the Singapore base.[4] In the event of war with Japan the intention was to send out a fleet including eleven capital ships, but a second base was, the committee pointed out, essential if such a fleet was to operate effectively, and although the security of Hong Kong still enjoyed first priority the committee seems to have doubted whether it could in fact be achieved. At any rate they considered sending one or both of the World War I 15-inch gun monitors (*Erebus* and *Terror*) to Singapore as a stop gap.[5] In the following year the Planning Committee reviewed the possibility of a 'Locarno War' against France—that is to say a war in which France was the aggressor (presumably against Germany) and our obligations under the Locarno Treaty of 1925 were invoked. They concluded that the 50 cruisers agreed at the recent London Conference would be 'quite inadequate' to meet such a contingency, and that the seaward defences of Freetown, Sierra Leone, which was uncomfortably close to the

---

[1] Keyes to Kelly 2nd July 1931. *ibid.*

[2] This was the view of Lord Stanhope who became Parliamentary Secretary of the Admiralty in Sept. 1931 and was First Lord Oct. 1938–Sept. 1939.

[3] The First Sea Lord was chairman, and the other members were the DCNS, ACNS and Director of Plans. Adm. 1/8765-313/32.

[4] Third meeting of above on 16th June 1931. *ibid.*

[5] The *Terror* (two 15-inch guns) recommissioned on 12th Sept. 1933, and in mid-November the Admiralty announced that she would serve as a 'base ship' at Singapore. *The Times*, 15th Nov. 1933. She was recalled to the Mediterranean when war with Italy appeared likely, and was sunk off the Libyan coast by German bombers on 24th Feb. 1941. When the Japanese launched their attack on 7th Dec. 1941 the fixed defences of Singapore included five 15-inch (the same calibre as the *Terror*'s), six 9.2-inch and sixteen 6-inch guns. See S. W. Kirby and others, *The War Against Japan*, vol. I, Map 21 for details of where they were sited.

French bases at Casablanca and Dakar, should be strengthened.[1] In fact the possibility of such a war receded as the years passed, and in 1939 Freetown was still virtually defenceless.

While the Admiralty was coping with the adjustment of its programmes and policy to comply with the government's decisions about Singapore and the terms of the London Treaty, and planning for the five years of its duration, the US Navy's General Board was undergoing very much the same process, and in October 1930 they put forward their proposals for the 1932 Fiscal Year.[2] Battleship replacement being altogether eliminated until the end of 1936 they merely 'took note' of the fact; but with some 55,000 tons of carrier displacement in hand they proposed to build one fairly small ship of that type each year from 1931 to '35. Three 8-inch cruisers were included for 1933–35 to bring the total up to the permitted eighteen of that class, and five 6-inch cruisers were proposed for the first three years of the quinquennium in order to achieve parity with Britain. The General Board reserved the question of the design of the next ships of that class because Admiral Moffett was pressing for flying deck cruisers to be built. Though the Board approved that a design study of such a type should be made they felt no enthusiasm for Moffett's proposal;[3] and when he suggested that all the permissible tonnage of 6-inch cruisers should have flying decks his letter was endorsed with a peremptory 'No'.[4] Three years later the same proposal was turned down equally emphatically.[5]

As regards destroyers and flotilla leaders the General Board proposed to replace thirty-eight of the US Navy's old ships between 1932 and '36, which corresponded closely in numbers to the Admiralty's programme of nine per year. Twenty-four of the older submarines were also to be replaced. But it was in the provision of additional naval aircraft that the General Board far exceeded the Admiralty's modest proposal for two additional flights. Over 500 new ship-borne aircraft were asked for by the Board, and production was to be at a rate of some 120 per year for each of the last four years of the treaty's duration. If Moffett was wrong in his dislike of the big *Lexington* and *Saratoga*

[1] 4th meeting of above on 14th July 1932. Adm. 1/8765–313/32.

[2] GB. 420–2, Serial 1473 of 16th Oct. 1930. The American Fiscal Year, unlike the British one, which ran from 6th April to 5th April, ran from 1st July to the following 30th June. See vol. 1, p. 209.

[3] GB. 420–2, Serial 1507 of 21st Nov. 1930.

[4] Bu.Aer. letter of 23rd March 1931. GB. 420–2.

[5] GB. 420–8 of 20th Feb. 1934.

and in his staunch advocacy of the rigid airship, and his flying deck cruisers would probably have proved unsuccessful hybrids, his insistence on providing large numbers of new types of strike aircraft for the US Navy's carriers was to give that service an enviable advantage over the Royal Navy when the clash came.

Incidentally it may be remarked here that, although the American Bureau of the Budget established in 1921[1] possessed theoretical power over the appropriation of funds for the navy analogous to those of the British Treasury, it seems never to have submitted the General Board or the Navy Department to the persistent and often petty inquisitorial interrogations with which the Treasury constantly persecuted the Admiralty, and which on occasion provoked the balanced and even-tempered Murray to protest. Rather does the Bureau of the Budget appear to have helped the Navy Department in the preparation of Appropriation Bills, and when D. W. Bell was Acting Director of the Bureau in the 1930s a satisfactory compromise or solution was nearly always reached between the two departments. Though this did not necessarily result in Congress passing the Bills it must have been encouraging to the General Board and to the Chiefs of the Navy Department's Bureaux, who had to justify them before the Naval Affairs Committees.[2] This feature of the financing of naval needs becomes more marked after Roosevelt had settled in as President—though he could, as we shall see, sometimes did criticise the Navy Department quite sharply. Perhaps the generally helpful attitude of the Bureau of the Budget owed a good deal to the fact that Roosevelt, having served as Assistant Secretary of the Navy from 1913 to 1920 always regarded himself, in Churchill's terminology of 1940, as something of a 'Former Naval Person'.

Though it was probably no more than a coincidence Secretary Adams asked the General Board at the very time when they were considering the building programmes for 1930–35 for their 'Estimate of the Situation and Navy Basic Plan for Orange War' (i.e. war with Japan).[3] In their reply the General Board first recapitulated the views expressed when the issue had been considered early in 1929. They had

---

[1] See vol. I, pp. 210–14.

[2] General Board records. The Bureau of the Budget's remarks and recommendations are always to be found with the proposals to appropriate funds for building, personnel, shore establishments, etc. Copies in Roosevelt Library, official files, Hyde Park.

[3] Adams to General Board 2nd Oct. 1930. (SC)A16(0), Op-12–CD.

then reported that 'Our superiority will . . . be sufficient to enable us to advance into the Western Pacific at an early date and to establish there an advance fleet base from which to operate against Orange, while at the same time denying to Orange the establishment of an advance base in waters near to the continental United States'. The assumption was then made that, within thirty days of the outbreak of war, 'the main combatant strength of the Navy, in strength at least 25% greater than the entire Japanese Navy' could be assembled in Hawaiian waters. One is reminded of the Admiralty's 'ninety days to Singapore' for the British fleet in the same circumstances. Taking account of the difference in distance (some 3,000 miles from the west coast of America to Hawaii as against 8,100 miles from Portsmouth to Singapore) the two assumptions were remarkably alike.[1] But, continued the General Board, the London Treaty had fundamentally altered the basis on which the foregoing plans had been framed. Japan was now allowed an increased ratio in 'auxiliary vessels' (cruisers and below) and parity with the USA in submarines. Furthermore she was maintaining 'a progressive and balanced building programme' which would soon bring her navy fully up to treaty strength.[2] The final conclusion reached was that 'the estimate of the situation should immediately be revised to date'.[3] It seems probable that stimulation of the Navy Department's plans 'to have the Fleet self-supporting during manœuvre periods through its Train service', which dated back as far as 1921 and in which the origins of the famous Fleet Train of World War II are certainly to be found, owes a good deal to the review of the 'Orange War' undertaken in 1932.[4]

Here we must retrace our steps and review the measures taken by the Labour government soon after it took office to expedite the work of the League of Nations' Preparatory Commission for the General Disarmament Conference, which had been engaged in rather futile

[1] See vol. I, pp. 282–3 and *passim*. In September 1939 the time required for the main fleet to reach Singapore and be fully operational was re-assessed at 180 days. See S. Woodburn Kirby, *Singapore: the Chain of Disaster* (Cassell, 1971), p. 35 and *passim*.

[2] This was true. The Japanese launched the carrier *Ryujo* (10,600 tons, 48 aircraft) in April 1931; the four cruisers of the *Takao* class (13,160 tons, ten 8-inch guns) were launched in 1930–31 and the four *Mogami* class (12,400 tons, ten 8-inch guns) were projected. Sixteen destroyers and four submarines were also included in the 1931 programme. See A. J. Watts, *Japanese Warships of World War II* (Ian Allan, 1966) for details.

[3] General Board reply to Adams of 4th May 1932. GB. 425, Serial 1502.

[4] GB. 420–2, Serial 1509 of 7th May 1931.

negotiations ever since 1926,[1] and so bring about the long-awaited agreement on large scale disarmament. In December 1929 the Cabinet set up a Sub-Committee of the CID under Arthur Henderson, the Foreign Secretary, 'to study the various problems which will arise in the near future in connection with proposals for land and air disarmament . . .'[2] The Commonwealth statesmen present in London for the forthcoming Imperial Conference were members, but the service departments were only allowed to nominate officers and officials who might be 'co-opted in an advisory capacity'. This committee threw off a subordinate body under Viscount Cecil 'to examine the whole question of Budgetary Limitations', and on that body the three service departments were allowed representation. Its conclusion, obviously inspired by Cecil, was that 'Budgetary Limitation is the only way in which armaments as a whole can be limited', and the committee recommended that it should be included in the draft treaty.[3] However the Admiralty representative (Mr. A. Flint) managed to include a qualification that, as regards naval forces, 'limitation of expenditure cannot be accepted for us unless it is accepted by other naval powers';[4] while the Air Ministry representative (Air Vice-Marshal Sir Cyril Newall) refused to sign the report. Meanwhile the draft of a 'Model Treaty to Strengthen the Means of Preventing War' had been prepared, and the government had signed the so-called 'Optional Clause' accepting that all disputes which might lead to conflict should be referred to the International Court of Justice at The Hague—subject on the part of Britain to certain reservations.[5] The chief of these concerned the maintenance of Belligerent Rights at sea, which, as already mentioned, had for many years been a cardinal point of British naval policy.[6] On 29th November 1929 Alexander sent Henderson his department's reservations, and the Foreign Secretary accepted them—doubtless to the relief of the Naval Staff.[7]

It is interesting to find that a little later Admiral Pratt proposed that the US Navy should 'depart from its position as a great neutral', and adopt the British view of Belligerent Rights; which of course was a complete reversal of the doctrine of 'Freedom of the Seas', the long-

---

[1] See vol. I, p. 498ff.   [2] RA. 9 of 19th Dec. 1929. Became CID. 976B.

[3] RA. 30 of 22nd Sept. 1930, Appendix III, para. 10 (D). Copy in Adm. 116/2610.

[4] RA. 27A of 26th May 1930.

[5] CID. 966B has the Optional Clause and the British reservations. It was signed by the British government on 19th Sept. 1929 Cab. 4/19.

[6] Memo. by First Sea Lord of 11th Nov. 1929. Became CID. 966B. *ibid.*

[7] 246th CID meeting of 5th Dec. 1929. Cab. 2/5. Copy in Adm. 116/2716.

standing American axiom which had been so strenuously advocated by President Wilson, Secretary Daniels and Admiral Benson at the Paris Peace Conference of 1919.[1] Pratt had consulted Dr. A. Pearce Higgins of Trinity College, Cambridge on this issue, and the well-known international lawyer declared that he found himself 'much in harmony' with the American Admiral's outlook and purpose.[2] This *volte-face* by the Chief of Naval Operations must have delighted the Admiralty— after the many years of conflict waged with anglophobe American Admirals such as W. S. Benson and H. P. Jones on this very issue. Furthermore Pratt declared himself willing to go along with the British so far as to reduce the maximum displacement of battleships to 27,500 tons and their guns to 12-inch, and to accept a 'building truce' up to the next conference in 1935—if other powers would do the same. But he admitted that he was 'at odds with most naval men' on the size and armament of battleships.[3] Taken with the cordial attitude adopted by Adams and Pratt at the London Conference these developments must have seemed to the Admiralty and Foreign Office to promise a new era in Anglo-American relations—as indeed they did.

In the autumn of 1930 the British Naval Staff expended a great effort on preparing the details of a draft Disarmament Convention. It comprised sixteen headings, ranging from the long-standing pre-ference for limitation by global tonnage through reduction in the size of capital ships and carriers to comparatively minor matters such as what training vessels could be retained and limitation of the size of torpedo tubes. The implications of all forms of limitation were worked out in full detail.[4] On 28th October the draft was sent to the Foreign Office, and in the following month it was given to the American, French, Italian and Japanese delegations to the Disarmament Con-ference. Fundamental disagreement on many of the British proposals at once became apparent; but the Admiralty, having recently been the target for a good deal of criticism over the London Conference decisions, and especially the arbitrary reduction of the Royal Navy's cruisers from 70 to 50, was not in the mood to give further ground.

[1] GB. 438–2, Serial 1521U. Pratt to Adams 8th Aug. 1932. It was chiefly the American advocacy of 'Freedom of the Seas' at the Paris Conference which produced the notorious 'Naval Battle of Paris' (Josephus Daniels's epigram). See vol. 1, pp. 53–4 and 80–2.

[2] Higgins to Pratt 28th Jan. and 1st April 1931. Pratt papers.

[3] Pratt to Adams. Op. 10 Hu. of 12th Oct. 1931. Pratt papers.

[4] Adm. 116/2826. The draft British Convention as finally approved by the govern-ment was published as Cmd. 4122, *Declaration of British Disarmament Policy* (1932).

In the following spring Admiral Field produced an 'Appreciation of the Naval Situation' which Alexander approved. In it Field restated the British case in terms very similar to those used by his predecessor at the London Conference, ending with the statement 'Finally it must be emphasised that the whole history of Naval Armaments since the war has been one of unilateral reduction by this country', with the result that our strength relative to that of other countries was much reduced, and our 'absolute strength was far below requirements'.[1] Field also reminded the government that the Board had only accepted the terms of the London Treaty 'for a strictly limited period', and refused to consider any further limitation measure except reduction in the displacement and gun calibre of future capital ships.[2] The other service departments, especially the Air Ministry, were equally firm; but we are not here concerned with their views.[3] None the less the government continued to press ahead with preparations for the Disarmament Conference, and in October 1931 appointed another CID Sub-Committee, this time under the chairmanship of A. G. M. Cadogan of the Foreign Office, to continue the work.[4] The principal recommendations produced were that Budgetary Limitation should only be accepted if all the major naval powers agreed to it, that the Washington and London treaties should form 'the starting point' of the Disarmament Conference, that the naval forces of the British Commonwealth should be regarded as a single entity and that the 'escalation clause' in the London Treaty 'must be included in the Disarmament Convention'.[5] The most discordant note in these inter-departmental deliberations was introduced by Lord Amulree, the Secretary of State for Air, and Sir John Salmond the Chief of the Air Staff. The latter urged that 'expansion in seaborne air forces is proceeding at a rapid rate, and that the need for its limitation is urgent'; while Amulree pressed for limitation of such forces 'on a parity basis' with the USA[6]—a proposal which was not likely to appeal to Moffett and the rising generation of American naval aviators. Furthermore, coming as it did so soon after the Air Ministry had refused to sign the report on Budgetary Limitation, it was ob-

---

[1] Dated 16th April 1931. *ibid.*

[2] Memo. of 14th April. Became CID. 1047B. Cab. 4/21. Also CP. 100(31).

[3] CID. 1046B of 31st March and 1048B of 27th April are corresponding memos. by the CIGS and CAS. Cab. 4/21.

[4] RA. 1–1 of 8th Oct. 1931. Copy in Adm. 116/2611.

[5] RA. 1–3 of 30th Sept. 1931. *ibid.*

[6] RA. 4 of 2nd and 6th Oct. 1931. *ibid.* Became CP. 259(31). Cab. 24/214.

viously an oblique attack by the Air Staff on the Fleet Air Arm—an ancient feud dating back to 1919.[1]

At the end of July 1931 Hankey wrote to MacDonald urging that during the talks which he was to have with Stimson he should 'make an attempt . . . to ride President Hoover off bringing up at the Disarmament Conference his [Hoover's] proposal that food ships should be declared free from interference in time of war'. He went fully into the reasons why, with a blockade declared, it would be impossible to treat food ships differently from other vessels; while to grant them immunity would not only deprive us of a very potent weapon but would open a simple means of shipping contraband goods through the blockade. Hankey argued, with Admiralty support, that it would be a cardinal error to mix up the *use* of armaments with their *reduction*, which was the purpose of the conference. He said that the Admiralty, which had deferred to MacDonald's wishes at the Naval Conference, would become 'extremely restive' if this proposal went forward. Public opinion, which was strongly in favour of disarmament, would in his opinion split on the issue; and he feared that 'Anglo-American relations at the [Disarmament] conference may become less intimate' when 'the close working of the two countries is vital to the success of the conference'.[2] This cleverly argued letter was of course all part of the long campaign waged by the Admiralty and Hankey against any emasculation of Belligerent Rights. Though MacDonald does not appear to have answered Hankey's letter in fact the exclusion of food ships from the exercise of Belligerent Rights was never considered at Geneva.

Meanwhile a somewhat academic attempt was being made to distinguish between 'offensive and defensive armaments'; but the Chiefs of Staff, for once in unanimity, agreed that 'it is virtually impossible to draw any hard and fast distinctions . . . no matter what type of weapon is selected'.[3] Perhaps the most outstanding feature of the preliminaries to the Disarmament Conference is the vast accumulation of paper produced by consideration of the various schemes, such as limitation of 'Effectives', Budgetary Limitation and the precise strength of existing forces.[4] Plainly the time and effort of the service staffs and their civilian colleagues were so taken up by the preparation of these

[1] See vol. I, chs. VI, X and XIII.
[2] Hankey to MacDonald 31st July 1931. Premier 1/99. A full discussion of the Admiralty's views on this matter is in Adm. 116/3621.
[3] RA. 1–9 of 24th Sept. 1931. Became CID. 1064B. Cab. 4/21.
[4] Adm. 116/3203–4 consists of large volumes on these subjects.

highly involved statements that their proper functions, such as the welfare and service conditions of personnel, the development of new material, and deliberation on strategic issues faded into the background. Indeed it may not go too far to suggest that the disaster which overtook the Navy in the autumn of 1931, to be described in the next chapter, owed something to the Board of Admiralty having to devote its attention mainly to the intricacies of disarmament during the preceding year.

In November 1931 the Inter-departmental Committee reported—very much on the lines taken in the papers and discussions already outlined,[1] and by the end of the year the proposals which the British government intended to place before the conference when it assembled at Geneva early in February 1932 were ready. But cataclysmic events occurred at home before that date, and it was actually a Liberal-National Foreign Secretary (Sir John Simon) in a National government who presented them. We will therefore leave the subject of the search for disarmament for the present.

---

[1] RA. 1–16 (Revise) of Nov. 1931. Copy in Adm. 116/2611.

CHAPTER IV

Invergordon, September 1931, and the Aftermath

◆

THE FATEFUL year 1931 was only a few days old when there took place in the submarine depot ship *Lucia* at Devonport a case of 'mass indiscipline' amounting to mutiny. The subsequent inquiry proved that the basic causes were excessive hours of work combined with curtailment of leave on a Sunday in order to paint the ship's side just before she sailed; and, perhaps above all, the shortcomings of the Captain, First Lieutenant and a Divisional Officer—all of whom were placed on half pay. The ship was paid off and of the 31 men involved four were tried by Court Martial and 27 punished summarily with varying degrees of severity. All the Court Martial sentences were reduced on review by the Admiralty, as were the heavier of the summary punishments.[1] This was beyond question a case of an 'unhappy ship' in which the handling of the men was seriously mismanaged. Questions of pay did not arise and as it had no connection with the far more serious indiscipline which shook the Navy, and indeed the whole country, most severely nine months later it need detain us no longer.

The Economy Committee under Sir George May, which had been set up in March 1931 to put forward wide-ranging measures to balance the Budget and stop the run on the pound reported on 24th July.[2] At the end of April the Board of Admiralty sent to the May Committee a memorandum in which they stated that 'All the departments agreed

[1] Of the Court Martialled men two were sentenced to imprisonment with hard labour (6 and 3 months respectively) and dismissal from the service. The former was reduced to 3 months' imprisonment and the latter had 2 months' detention substituted for imprisonment. Two men were sentenced to 6 months' detention, reduced to 4 months. Of the summary punishments the heaviest (78 days' detention) were reduced to 52.

[2] Cmd. 3920. Published on 31st July.

that men in the fighting services in 1919, or who had since entered, had a moral claim *up to a point* and in certain cases . . . there would have been a contractual obligation, *had it not been for the Crown's privilege*' (italics supplied).[1] They went on to quote the statements issued on the subject in 1924 and 1925, and in particular the Fleet Order of 1925 which had said that, although the government had no legal obligations men on the 1919 rates 'will continue to be paid under the existing scales until discharged'.[2] This was not perhaps a very convincing paper to put to a body whose charter was to effect drastic economies; and the italicised words plainly offered a loophole to the May Committee by admitting that the moral claim to retain the 1919 rates was not absolute. However the Board did mention that in 1925 answers to Parliamentary Questions which aimed to clear up a plainly ambiguous situation had stated that no reduction to the 1919 rates was contemplated 'so far as the present Parliament is concerned'. But the refusal to commit future Parliaments, though understandable, must surely have appeared to the May Committee as another loophole.

In August the May Committee's report was discussed many times by the Cabinet Committee appointed to review its recommendations —which were drastic. But the economic situation continued to deteriorate, and on 25th MacDonald's Labour government resigned and an all-party National government was formed with him still Prime Minister but supported by only three members of his former Cabinet. Austen Chamberlain replaced A. V. Alexander as First Lord, and the Labour Parliamentary and Financial Secretary and Civil Lord were replaced by Conservatives a little later.[3] It was an unfortunate moment to make a clean sweep of the civilian members of the Board. Furthermore when, on 9th August, the Treasury declared that it was 'imperative' that departmental observations on the May Committee's proposals should reach the Cabinet Committee which was to review them by 11th only three members of the Board, Admirals R. R. C. Backhouse and L. G. Preston (Third and Fourth Sea Lords) and Mr. C. G. Ammon (Parliamentary Secretary) were available. Alexander was abroad in Germany from the last day of July and was not recalled

---

[1] Dated 29th April 1931. Adm. 116/3396.   [2] AFO. 2859 of 3rd Oct. 1925.

[3] G. H. Hall, the Labour Civil Lord, resigned on 26th Aug. and no successor was appointed until 11th Nov. Sir Bolton Eyres Monsell succeeded Chamberlain as First Lord on 9th Nov. and took with him from the Conservative Party Whips' Office Captain D. Euan Wallace as Civil Lord. Earl Stanhope replaced C. G. Ammon, the Labour Parliamentary and Financial Secretary, on 7th Sept. and on 11th Nov. Lord Stanley was appointed in Stanhope's place.

until 18th August; his principal naval colleague Admiral Field, who had been unwell for some time, was on leave throughout the early period of the crisis; the Second Sea Lord, Admiral Fuller, whose special responsibility was for the Navy's personnel, and the Deputy Chief of Naval Staff Admiral F. C. Dreyer both went on leave in August.[1] Furthermore the very experienced Permanent Secretary Sir Oswyn Murray was away from 10th August to 5th September. The result was that such members of the Board as were available were not in full touch with the cataclysmic events which burst upon them suddenly; and action to reassemble the full Board, was to put it mildly, tardy.[2] On 14th the three available members of the Board told the Treasury that they were not prepared to accept the May Committee's recommendations on pay cuts until the Cabinet had decided that 'on principle these and other reductions affecting other classes of the community are to be adopted in order to meet the national emergency'.[3]

Four days before the change of government took place Alexander told the Cabinet 'I think the personnel of the Navy as a whole will loyally accept the sacrifice that is demanded of them in pay if equivalent reductions are made throughout the Public Service and if the unemployment rates are reduced'.[4] One must presume that Alexander's memorandum represented the view of the Board, though it is known that Admiral Preston protested vigorously against acceptance of the application of the 1925 scale of pay to men who had entered the service on the substantially higher 1919 rates.[5]

---

[1] The exact dates when Admirals Fuller and Dreyer went on leave and returned to London are difficult to establish. Both were present at the Board Meeting held on 29th July, Fuller next appears at the meeting held on 27th Aug., and both Admirals were present when the Board met again on 3rd Sept. It is therefore probable that they were on leave for the greater part, and possibly the whole of August. Adm. 167/83.

[2] Minute by Sir Vincent Baddeley, Deputy Secretary, of 13th July 1932. Adm. 178/79.

[3] 'Admiralty Narrative of Events Connected with the Reduction of Naval Pay and the resulting Unrest in the Atlantic Fleet.' Copy in Royal Archives RA GV K2330(3)/20, /34 and /36. Henceforth cited as *Narrative*.

[4] CP. 205/31 of 20th Aug. 1931. Adm. 167/84 and Cab. 24/223.

[5] See vol. 1, pp. 117–18 regarding the introduction of the 1919 rates and pp. 401–2 regarding Treasury pressure to reduce that scale and the Admiralty's very sharp reaction to the proposal that men on the 1919 scale should be put on the lower rate of pay. The *Narrative* remarks that as there was 'no difficulty in recruiting or retaining men ... it is reasonable to infer that it [the 1925 scale] is a fair scale'—which totally ignored the fact that there were about 2 million unemployed at the time.

On the last day of the month Chamberlain, the new First Lord, represented his department's views to the Cabinet. He expressed opposition to allowing men to take free discharge from the Navy rather than be put on the 1925 rates of pay—as the May Committee had recommended—but accepted that body's proposed cut in dock-yard workmen's wages; and he concluded by protesting about the general condition of the Navy's ageing ships and the service's inadequate logistics support. He did not apparently raise the very serious issue of the effect of placing the 1919 men on the 1925 rates of pay—though previous Boards had always resisted such a measure as being 'a breach of contract on an unprecedented scale'.[1] Two days after the Cabinet discussion civil service representatives of all three defence departments met to consider the detailed arrangements for bringing the cuts into force and co-ordinating their action 'so that inconsistencies should be avoided'. The note by Sir Vincent Baddeley, the Admiralty representative, ends by stating 'In regard to the reduction of the pay of ratings to the 1925 scale it was agreed that there were no particular questions requiring consideration, the Cabinet having decided that the men affected were not to be released from their engagements . . .'[2] It is hard to believe that if Murray had been available he would have accepted that complacent statement.

There exists, however, an undated but scathing draft of the Admiralty's 'observations' on the report of the Cabinet Committee which reviewed the May Committee's proposals in which it was stated that men on the 1919 rates could not be put on the lower scale 'without breaking pledges given both by past Labour and Unionist governments, each of whom recognised that . . . the men who were in the service in 1919 and those who entered between 1919 and 1925 in the belief that the 1919 rates were permanent have a moral claim to retain them throughout their service'; and again that 'the Admiralty have no doubt whatever that such action would be regarded by the whole Navy as a breach of faith, and that any attempt to justify it officially by such arguments as the [Cabinet] Committee advance would merely add to the resentment felt'.[3] Unhappily such views, though sent to the

---

[1] Sir Oswyn Murray frequently expressed this view in the 1920s, and always had the support of the Board.

[2] Minute of 2nd Sept. 1931 by Baddeley. Adm. 167/84.

[3] Draft Memo. NE(31)22, undated, paras. 21 and 38. Adm. 167/84. As the *Narrative* states that the 'Admiralty's observations were prepared by the Permanent Secretary [Murray] by Saturday 8th August' this seems to fix both the date and the authorship

Cabinet on 11th August, were not firmly represented by Chamberlain, and when on 3rd September he reported to the full Board he said that the Cabinet had been 'induced to override public pledges given to the Naval Service in the matter of pay and pensions'. Not only were the May Committee's recommendations to be accepted, subject only to minor modifications, but a further cut of £2 millions was to be made in the 1932–33 estimates; and 1st October was fixed as the date when the pay reductions were to come into force.[1] The situation was, moreover, aggravated by the fact that men under 25 years old then received no marriage allowance. Thus although the younger men, being already on the 1925 scale of pay, were not directly affected by the cuts they were all too likely to make common cause with the more seriously affected older ratings who were on the 1919 scales.[2] In sum it would have been hard to conceive a scheme more calculated to unite the whole lower deck in opposition to the cuts.

The Board also decided to send a cypher message to Commanders-in-Chief telling them of the decision regarding men on the 1919 rates and about the other cuts intended.[3] They said that they hoped that Vote A (approved total of personnel) and the money approved for new construction would not be affected—which suggests that the pay and pensions of men actually serving were not the first of the Board's priorities.[4] The Cs-in-C were invited to forward proposals for other economies; but although Admiral Sir Hubert Brand (C-in-C, Plymouth) replied that the cuts appeared to fall more heavily on junior than senior officers and ratings none of them remarked on the effects of the universal application of the 1925 rates.

The copy of the cypher message referred to above addressed to the C-in-C, Atlantic Fleet, Admiral Sir Michael Hodges, was, very

of the 'observations'. The *Narrative* repeats verbatim the argument about putting men on the 1919 rates on to the 1925 rates used in the 'observations', which certainly bear many marks suggesting Murray's authorship. RA GV K2330(3)/20, /34 and /36.

[1] Board Minute 2848 of 3rd Sept. 1931. Adm. 167/83 and 116/2864. This meeting was attended by Admirals Field, Fuller and Backhouse, all of whom had been on leave earlier.

[2] The Army and RAF were much less seriously affected by the pay cuts than the Navy. Whereas 72.1% of naval men, and 94% of its Chief and Petty Officers, were on the 1919 rates only 31% of the Army (excluding the Indian Army) and 40% of the RAF were similarly affected. Adm. 178/79.

[3] Board Minute 2848 of 3rd Sept. 1931. Adm. 167/83.

[4] AM. 1738 of 3rd Sept. 1931. This message is often, if somewhat erroneously, described as the 'Warning Telegram'.

naturally, sent to the fleet flagship *Nelson* at Portsmouth, and a draft reply was prepared by his Chief of Staff Admiral R. M. Colvin to await the return of Hodges from leave on 7th September. That the message was not distributed to the senior officers of the fleet may reasonably be attributed to the fact that it was addressed to the C-in-C; yet the contents were potentially so serious that it seems surprising that Colvin did little or nothing about it for three days. However it is almost certain that Admiral Wilfred Tomkinson, who was in command of the Battle Cruiser Squadron with his flag in the *Hood* and second-in-command of the fleet, saw the telegram on board the *Nelson* on Monday 7th September. If that is so he appears not to have appreciated the full significance of its contents. At any rate he did not ask for a copy.

At its meeting on 3rd September the Board decided that a Fleet Order should be issued on Monday 7th September, when the other Service Departments would take parallel action. But on the 4th the Treasury intervened objecting to any notice being sent out until after the Chancellor of the Exchequer (Philip Snowden) had made his Budget speech on Thursday 10th. Though Chamberlain wanted the fleet to be told at once he deferred to the First Sea Lord's view that the Treasury's request should be complied with.[1] The White Paper explaining the 'National Economies' which were to be imposed was issued shortly after Snowden's Budget speech and received wide publicity in the Press. Meanwhile a letter had been prepared by the Accountant-General, Sir Conrad Naef, and the letter as finally despatched to all Cs-in-C and Commanding Officers of ships and establishments on 10th did not differ materially from the draft.[2] A series of administrative blunders delayed receipt of this letter by some ships and authorities at home, and several writers on the Invergordon mutiny have made a great deal of the effects of this delay.[3] As however the Devonport ships sailed for the autumn cruise and exercises on 7th and

---

[1] Adm. 178/79.

[2] AL. CW. 8284 of 10th Sept. 1931. Endorsed 'Confidential until Friday 11th Sept.' Adm. 1/8747. The draft is in Adm. 116/2864.

[3] K. Edwards, *The Mutiny at Invergordon* (Putnam, 1937) and David Divine, *Mutiny at Invergordon* (MacDonald, 1970). Henceforth cited as *Edwards* and *Divine* respectively. Edwards is however wrong to write (pp. 165–6) that the above Admiralty letter was sent 'two days after . . . the Economy Bill . . . was introduced to Parliament'. It was introduced on 9th and released on Thursday 10th Sept.

the Portsmouth and Chatham ships on 8th they could not have received the letter before they arrived at Invergordon on 11th. The only way in which the contents could have been made widely known in the fleet at the earliest possible moment was for the Admiralty to send a summary by wireless. But such action seems never to have been considered.

When Admiral Hodges returned from leave on 7th September he was at once discharged to Haslar Hospital at Gosport, where a thrombosis was diagnosed. The departure of his flagship was held up and command of the fleet automatically devolved on Admiral Tomkinson. The Admiralty decided to give him the somewhat equivocal title of Senior Officer, Atlantic Fleet (SOAF); but the administration of the fleet was to remain in the hands of the C-in-C's staff in the *Nelson*—an arrangement which certainly contained plentiful seeds of muddle and confusion. Tomkinson thus found himself suddenly propelled into a position of great responsibility in a fleet which contained two officers of his own rank (Rear-Admirals E. A. Astley-Rushton, commanding 2nd Cruiser Squadron and W. F. French, commanding 2nd Division of 2nd Battle Squadron), and without the rank or appointment appropriate to his responsibility. It seems plain that Tomkinson should at least have been made an Acting Vice-Admiral. As *locum tenens* for whoever might eventually replace Hodges his position was unenviable.[1]

As the May Committee's proposals had been published on 31st July and the September issue of the naval periodical *The Fleet*, which Lionel Yexley[2] had started in 1905, carried a letter signed 'Neutralis' revealing that a general reduction to the 1925 scale of pay was being discussed in August, it is a reasonable assumption that the men of the lower deck were alive to what was in the wind.[3]

---

[1] Though Tomkinson had been with the fleet during the preceding summer cruise he was not at all well known outside his own flag ship.

[2] 1862–1933. Joined Navy 1878 as a Seaman Boy resigning from Coastguard 1897 to take up journalism, and especially to attack abuses in victualling and canteen systems. Started *The Bluejacket* 1898 and edited it until 1904. Founded *The Fleet* 1905 and *The Fleet Annual* 1906. A friend and adviser of Admiral Sir John ('Jacky') Fisher as First Sea Lord until his death, and of Churchill as First Lord 1911–15. Author of many books on naval affairs, particularly on improvement of conditions of service on lower deck. Lectured at RN Staff College on lower deck welfare 1919–27. Several incorrect dates about Yexley are printed in *Who Was Who*.

[3] The author of the letter was apparently a seaman serving in the destroyer *Acasta* in the Mediterranean.

The Atlantic Fleet exercised while on passage north and on Friday 11th September ten big ships berthed in two lines off Invergordon with the six capital ships and two cruisers in the northern line—the one nearer to the shore—and two cruisers in the southern line. Meanwhile the Fleet Orders giving full details of the new rates of pay had been prepared by the Admiralty.[1] They were despatched to the squadron flagships (*Hood*, *Warspite* and *Dorsetshire*) on Saturday 12th, but distribution throughout the fleet was not completed until some 24 hours later.

The Admiralty were also concerned about ships on foreign stations, and on 12th they therefore wirelessed to all Cs-in-C abroad.[2] A few hours later they sent a further message whose wording certainly now seems singularly ill-chosen. 'Their Lordships do not doubt', it read, 'that reductions decided upon by HM Government in the national interest will be loyally accepted by all ranks and ratings'. Senior officers were told that in case they encountered the argument that the men were being asked for greater sacrifices than the officers they should bear in mind that the government's policy was 'to take account of [the] more favourable treatment received by some classes [presumably a reference to those on the 1919 rates of pay]', and 'to re-establish fair relativities for all Government servants and with wage-earners generally'.[3]

At Invergordon the Admiralty letter of 10th September referred to above had definitely been received on 11th by Admirals Astley-Rushton and French and by the Captains of three other big ships— namely the *Nelson* (at Portsmouth), *Rodney* and *Adventure*; and as the last two were among the worst affected in the mutiny the delay in other ships receiving it can hardly have been an important factor. When the *Nelson*, now a 'private ship', arrived at Invergordon on the evening of Sunday 13th she brought a copy of the letter with her,[4] and Tomkinson got his first sight of it when he signalled for the C-in-C's copy. He did not receive his personal copy until next day because the Admiralty had addressed it to the *Renown*, which he had left in the previous July and

---

[1] AFOS. 2238 and 2239/31 dated 12th Sept. 1931. The file copy has the date amended to 11th Sept. in pencil. Adm. 116/2864.

[2] AM. 1321 of 12th Sept. 1931. Copy in Adm. 116/2864.

[3] AM. 1652 of 12th Sept. 1931. *ibid.*

[4] The *Nelson* berthed at the eastern end of the northern line. The *Rodney* was at the western end. The matter is only of importance because it has been alleged that the *Rodney*'s company encouraged the *Nelson*'s in the mutiny. The distance between them makes this impossible.

Destroyers of the Home Fleet at high speed. Osprey fighters overhead. March 1935.

The era of the big gun. Rodney's nine 16-inch at sunset, July 1937.

The sinking of the Nationalist heavy cruiser *Baleares* after being torpedoed by the Government destroyer *Lepanto* off Cartagena during the Spanish civil war. Taken from H.M.S. *Kempenfelt* at about 2 a.m. on 6th March 1938. Note survivors (left) in the water. Over 400 were rescued by British warships.

H.M.S. *Shropshire's* seaboat about to be lowered to pick up survivors from the Danish merchant ship *Bodil* which had been bombed and sunk, probably by German aircraft, off Minorca on 23rd July 1938 during the Spanish civil war.

which was refitting at Portsmouth.[1] Tomkinson ordered the first four paragraphs of the letter, which gave the reasons for the pay cuts and the history of the introduction of the 1925 scales of pay, to be explained to ships' companies—only to be told that four ships had not received copies of the letter. He at once ordered copies to be made and distributed; but some ships did not receive their Admiralty copies until Tuesday 15th.

The Admiralty letter of 10th September was not happily worded, and in ships whose Captains tried to use it, in conjunction with the Fleet Orders, to explain the cuts the effect produced on the men was not persuasive or tranquillising. Though the Fleet Orders were extremely complicated, taken with the Admiralty letter of 10th they did make it plain that the cuts would fall very heavily indeed on some men; for example an Able Seaman on the 1919 rate was to have his basic pay reduced from 4/- to 3/- per day. Though it is true that a cut of such dimensions was mitigated in the case of some men by 'non-substantive' (i.e. specialist) pay, and by various allowances, it was the heavy cut in basic pay on which attention was chiefly concentrated.

At Invergordon shore leave was available to men of each 'watch' (half the ship's company) in turn from 1.0 p.m. on Saturdays and Sundays and from 4.30 on other days; but as there were few attractions there except recreation grounds and the canteen, leave expired at 8.30 p.m. (9.0 p.m. for Chief and Petty Officers).

Here it is desirable to say a few words about the system of shore patrols used to maintain order when leave was given at Invergordon. There was a Town Patrol and a Canteen Patrol, both of about half a dozen reliable men with a Commissioned Gunner or Lieutenant in charge;[2] and the senior officer had authority to employ them separately or together as he might judge necessary.[3] Two smaller Pier Patrols would be landed at about 7.0 p.m. to keep order while the libertymen were embarking in drifters or boats to return to their ships. On the present occasion the Sunday and Monday Patrol Officers were warned that meetings of a subversive character might take place in the canteen,

---

[1] Endorsement in Tomkinson's hand on his copy of the letter, and his letter to Admiralty of 14th Sept. 1931. Tomkinson papers. Churchill College, Cambridge.

[2] The exact strength of the patrols is not known.

[3] Atlantic Fleet General Orders. Quoted in report by Lieutenant R. F. Elkins of *Valiant* dated 25th Sept. 1931 from Sheerness. Henceforth cited as *Elkins, Report*. He also kept a detailed diary of events from 14th to 16th Sept. Henceforth cited as *Elkins, Diary*. I am indebted to Admiral Sir Robert Elkins for copies of both documents. The originals are now in the NMM.

and they were therefore at hand and, with little trouble, stopped the speech making. Nothing of note happened on the Friday or Saturday evening.

At about noon on Sunday 13th Lieutenant-Commander H. Pursey,[1] himself a former rating, who was serving as Commander's Assistant in the *Hood*, was given a newspaper in which the pay cuts were headlined. He went to the Executive Officer, Commander C. R. McCrum, and said words to the effect that 'If the cuts are not reduced there will be trouble . . . If there is trouble it will be on Tuesday (15th) at 8.0 a.m.' The situation, he contended, would then be tailor-made for a mass protest—because it was the end of the breakfast hour and four of the capital ships (*Valiant, Nelson, Hood* and *Rodney*) would be sailing or preparing to sail for exercises. But the Commander disagreed, and the warning was ignored.[2] That afternoon it seemed at first that McCrum's confidence was justified, since he and his Captain (J. F. C. Patterson) went ashore soon after the libertymen landed, walked past the canteen on their way back to the ship and noted that everything appeared to be quiet. However Admiral Astley-Rushton also passed that way a little later and heard a speech being made to a crowd of men. He warned the Officer of the Patrol and then went on board the *Hood* to inform Tomkinson.[3]

The *Warspite* was 'Guardship' on 13th, and it therefore fell to her to provide the patrols. At about 7.30 p.m. a message was received on board from the Patrol Officer 'Trouble at the Canteen. Request larger patrol'. Reinforcements were landed from the *Hood* and *Warspite*, but order was restored before they reached the canteen and the bar was closed at 8.0 p.m. By about 9.30 all libertymen had returned to their ships, and although some were noisy on the pier or in the drifters and boats it seemed no more than was to be expected from men some of whom had imbibed rather too freely. Tomkinson received reports from the *Hood*'s Captain and *Warspite*'s Commander, who had landed

[1] 1891– . Joined RN as Seaman Boy 1907. Commissioned 1917. Retired 1936 and took up journalism. War correspondent in Spain during Civil War 1937. MP (Lab.) for East Hull 1945–70. A prolific writer and lecturer, especially on naval affairs from lower deck point of view. See for example his letter in the RUSI Journal, vol. CXVI, no. 661 (March 1971) for a succinct account of the long history of the pay of the lower deck.

[2] Pursey to the author 16th Jan. and 22nd Feb. 1974. Confirmed by interviews 1974–75.

[3] R of P Rear-Admiral Commanding 2nd Cruiser Squadron, para. 3. Adm. 178/110.

with the reinforcing patrol from his ship, consulted Admirals Astley-Rushton and French and concluded that the incident had no serious implications.[1] Next day, Monday 14th, he signalled to the Admiralty 'Slight disturbance in canteen yesterday . . . I attach no importance to the incident'.[2]

It would be unfair to make any criticism of Tomkinson, bearing the difficulty of his position in mind, before Sunday 13th, especially as an endorsement in his hand on his copy of *Warspite*'s patrol report states that he did not receive it 'before late in the afternoon of Tuesday 15th September', presumably because the *Warspite* was at sea for exercises on the Monday.[3] On the other hand receipt of the Fleet Orders and a sight of the Admiralty letter of 10th September must have put him in possession of full information regarding the pay cuts by Sunday evening. In retrospect it does seem that he ought then to have *signalled* to Flag and Commanding Officers telling them to draw the attention of ships' companies to paragraphs 1 and 4 of that letter, in which the reasons for the pay cuts and the decision to abolish the 1919 rates of pay were set out, instead of waiting until next morning. In fact he did not meet the senior officers who had so suddenly been placed under him until a formal dinner party took place in the *Hood* on the Monday evening; and that party had nothing to do with the pay cuts.

As to what actually took place in the canteen on the Sunday evening the various accounts recollected and written up long afterwards conflict and are unlikely ever to be reconciled. Probably the report of *Warspite*'s Patrol Officer is the most reliable, and he stated that 'the cause of the disturbance was due to a few men who were making speeches about their reduction in pay, and so causing a crowd to gather around, who commenced to shout and cheer and throw glasses about'. He identified men from the *Norfolk*, *Rodney* and *Warspite* among the speakers, but in his covering letter the Captain of the *Warspite* wrote that the three men identified as coming from his ship had been interviewed on returning aboard, and as far as he could tell 'their remarks were quite harmless and stupid'.[4]

---

[1] *ibid.*   [2] RABCS to Admy 1025 of 14th Sept. 1930.

[3] Copy in Tomkinson papers.

[4] Report by Mr. F. J. Wood, Commissioned Gunner (T) of 13th Sept. and covering letter by Captain St. A. B. Wake to SOAF of 14th Sept. 1930. Copy in Tomkinson papers. The three men from *Warspite* identified were Stoker T. A. Winstanley, Marine C. Hill and Telegraphist C. Bousfield; but it seems possible that Bousfield was a Security Service agent. See p. 115 below.

In 1931 a pamphlet was published under Communist Party imprimatur and using the name of Leonard Wincott, an Able Seaman from the *Norfolk* as author.[1] It gives a very different version of the events of Sunday evening but is highly unreliable. Wincott was unquestionably involved in the mutiny but claims far too much for himself.[2] After being discharged from the navy he emigrated to the USSR in 1934 and was sentenced to a long term in a labour camp during the Stalinist repression. In 1974 he published a book which was apparently 'ghosted' for him to a great extent, and which, as regards the events at Invergordon in 1931 is also unreliable.[3] Unfortunately the 1931 pamphlet, which Wincott publicly disowned when in England in 1974,[4] was treated as authoritative not only in two earlier books on the mutiny[5] but in the official account originally produced in confidential print for the Admiralty.[6] Though Wincott was unquestionably in the canteen on the Sunday evening,[7] and probably took some part in the speech making and disturbance, his claim to have been the chief organiser of the mutiny is palpably absurd. The fact that so much weight has been given to Wincott's story is probably explained by it being the only lower deck account available when Edwards and Owen produced their works; and Divine merely followed them. Between them they provide an excellent example of 'historians repeating each other'. A much later

---

[1] Entitled *The Spirit of Invergordon*. It is riddled with falsehoods.

[2] In the typescript entitled *I Was There. The Only Authentic Account of Invergordon*, a copy of which was sent to the author by Mr. Wincott from Moscow in 1974 and is still in his possession. Also in *Invergordon Mutineer* (Weidenfeld and Nicolson, 1974). Henceforth cited as *Wincott*.

[3] In fairness to Wincott it should be stated that he not only paid to the RN Benevolent Trust 10% of a legacy which he received from his sister in 1972 but in November 1974 he contributed to the same good cause 50% of the profits on this book less his expenses while in England. These donations amounted to £160 and £150 respectively. Admiral Sir Desmond Dreyer, Chairman of the RNBT, to author 13th Dec. 1974.

[4] In a television confrontation with Commander Pursey on 25th July 1974.

[5] See *Edwards*, pp. 205–6 and *Divine*, pp. 113–14.

[6] *Mutiny in the Royal Navy*, vol. II by Commander J. H. Owen. The typescript is in Adm. 178/135 with many minutes on whether it should be printed and issued confidentially to the fleet.

[7] Both the *Norfolk*'s R of P (Adm. 178/110, Enclosure) and Wincott's own account say that he obtained a 'turn of leave out of watch with substitute' to enable him to go ashore two days running. The *Norfolk*'s Captain described him as 'one of the principals' in the mutiny according to reports from senior ratings and Marines.

work by a lower deck rating Frederick Copeman, an Able Seaman who like Wincott was serving in the *Norfolk*, need not detain us.[1]

To turn from unreliable or fictitious statements to facts, on Sunday evening 13th, Astley-Rushton signalled to the Captains of ships of his squadron to report on board his flagship at 11.0 a.m. next day, and he then informed them of the previous evening's events and discussed the effects of the pay cuts and the best course of action to take; but his report gives no details on the point.[2]

On Monday 14th the *Valiant*, now having 'the Guard', landed the usual patrols under Lieutenant R. F. Elkins. But the *Hood* had quietly prepared a reinforcing patrol in case a call similar to that made the previous evening was received. Since much of Elkins's report has already been published it will merely be summarised here.[3] On arriving at the canteen he found the doors locked on the inside and courageously forced his way in alone in order to stop the speech making, which could clearly be heard from the outside; but after a glass had been thrown in his direction some of the men linked arms and pushed him out, though without violence against his person. Most of the crowd then left the canteen and reassembled on the nearby football field, where more speeches were made.

Elkins hovered on the outskirts of the crowd on the recreation ground endeavouring to identify the speakers; but that proved difficult as most of them had removed their caps with their ships' names on them. Elkins noted however that nearly all the speakers were long-service men wearing several Good Conduct badges,[4] which of course meant that they were on the higher 1919 rates of pay. At about the time when the reinforcing patrol from the *Hood* arrived and was met by Elkins the crowd on the football field broke up and some of the men

---

[1] See F. Copeman, *Reason in Revolt* (Blandford Press, 1948). After being discharged from the navy Copeman worked for the National Unemployed Workers' Union, which was controlled by the Communist Party. Fought on the Republican Government side in the Spanish Civil War 1936–38 and commanded British Battalion of the International Brigade. Became completely disillusioned with Communist Party by 1939, and did excellent work in Civil Defence organisation for London, receiving the OBE for his services. Later received into Roman Catholic Church and became a leader of Moral Rearmament movement. Councillor for Borough of Lewisham and Chairman of Housing Committee 1945.

[2] R of P Rear-Admiral 2nd Cruiser Squadron, paras. 4 and 5. Adm. 178/110.

[3] See *Edwards*, pp. 236–9 and *Divine*, ch. 12.

[4] Good Conduct badges were awarded after 3, 8 and 13 years' service in those days.

returned to the canteen.[1] The doors were once again locked on the inside, but the three officers made their way in by a back entrance, leaving the men of both patrols outside. Pack-Beresford recalls that some men were standing on the tables making speeches, and tells how he was approached by men who had recently served with him on the East Indies Station. 'They', writes Beresford, 'promised they would stand by me whatever happened';[2] which must have been a heartening experience, and confirms what other men had told Elkins earlier in the evening—that they felt no animosity towards their officers. The best account of the events in the canteen that evening is, expectedly the report of the senior officer of the reinforcing patrol from the *Hood*.[3] He wrote that there were about 300 men present 'and many of them were drunk'. Speeches 'of a mutinous nature such as "Are we going to take our pay cuts lying down? *NO*" and "Shall the Fleet go to sea tomorrow? *NO*"' were being made. Robinson blew a whistle for silence and stood up on the bar to talk to the men. For some minutes he was 'shouted down', but a proportion of the men urged that he should be given 'a fair hearing'. Eventually he obtained silence, and told the men 'they were going the wrong way about things', that complaints should be brought up 'in the Service manner', and that he would 'permit of no more speeches'. This had 'the desired effect' except for one man whose name the Patrol Officer took. He then closed the bar and cleared the canteen, after which he 'marched with my Patrol down to the pier', where the men were 'very noisy' while embarking and some speech making continued.

[1] The *Hood*'s patrol was under Lieutenant-Commander L. G. E. Robinson with Lieutenant T. A. Pack-Beresford as his assistant. As an example of Wincott's unreliability he states that 'Lieutenant-Commander Beresford' was in charge, and that it was he who addressed the men in the canteen. *Wincott*, pp. 109–10. Actually it is doubtful whether Wincott was even present in the canteen on the Monday evening.

[2] Pack-Beresford's letter to the author of 16th Dec. 1973.

[3] The only copy of this report to survive appears to be the one in the Tomkinson papers. It is endorsed in Tomkinson's hand 'This is as near as possible a copy of Lt.-Cdr. Robinson's report dated 15th Sept. 1931, which was in original only and was taken to Adty the same day by the C[hief] of S[taff]'. It appears to be in Robinson's hand. He was killed in London by enemy action in World War II. Elkins (*Report*, para. 23) is surely wrong about who spoke to the men in the canteen. *Edwards*, though he makes several mistakes in his account, is correct on this point (p. 245). *Divine* (p. 143) is wrong in attributing the pacifying speech to Pack-Beresford, though *Wincott* says the same (pp. 109–10). Pack-Beresford's memory is unsure on this matter, but he recalls 'persuading Robinson to get up on the Bar and talk to the chaps'. Letter to the author of 16th Dec. 1973.

It was probably Robinson's report that caused Tomkinson to write that the libertymen had returned to their ships 'in a very disorderly manner'.[1] In some ships numbers of men then gathered on the forecastles, though the reports of Captains state that no disorder or objectionable conduct took place. By 10.0 p.m. all men had gone below and appeared to have turned into their hammocks.

Meanwhile Tomkinson's dinner party had broken up prematurely at about 9.30 p.m. and the senior officers returned to their own ships. Bearing in mind that the Captains of the ships due to sail for exercises early next morning were present at the party it seems clear that this was the moment when Tomkinson should have cancelled the programme. At 11.15 p.m. he signalled to the Admiralty 'Further disturbance this evening . . . considerable unrest among a proportion of lower ratings'[2] —which hardly conveyed the strength of feeling against the pay cuts on the lower deck.

The decision whether to allow the exercise programme to stand or to cancel it was certainly a difficult one. But after interviewing the officers who had been in charge of the patrols, and consulting Admirals Astley-Rushton and Colvin (Chief of Staff to the absent C-in-C) and his own Flag Captain (J. F. C. Patterson) Tomkinson decided to adhere to the programme. Astley-Rushton definitely came on board the *Hood* at about midnight on 14th–15th and was met by Pursey.[3] The signal sent about an hour later must surely therefore have been his as much as Tomkinson's. It said that it might be difficult to get the ships to sea, and that he had ordered a thorough investigation of cases of hardship caused by the pay cuts.[4] This passing of the responsibility to the Admiralty instead of taking an initiative himself was Tomkinson's second mistake. But none of the three Admirals and ten Captains who had attended Tomkinson's dinner party appear to have felt or expressed any doubts about whether their ships would sail in the morning.

Tuesday 15th was the fatal day when the mutiny broke out. At 6.30 a.m. the *Repulse*, which was lying further down the Firth off Cromarty, sailed according to orders. The *Warspite* and *Malaya* were at anchor off

---

[1] SOAF report of 19th Sept. 1931. Adm. 178/110. This document was produced as Part II of the Admiralty 'Narrative' of the mutiny. Copies are in RA GV K2330(3) and in Tomkinson papers.

[2] SOAF. 2315 of 14th Sept. 1931.

[3] Pursey to the author 20th Jan. 1975.

[4] SOAF. 0120 of 15th Sept. 1931.

Lossiemouth and Nairn respectively. Of the ships off Invergordon the *Valiant* was to sail at 8.0 a.m.; but only a few senior ratings, young seamen and most of the Royal Marines fell in to prepare for sea; and her stokers prevented the ship sailing. In the *Rodney* also there was a general stoppage of work from 6.0 a.m. The *Nelson's* and *Hood's* men worked normally until 7.0 a.m., when the breakfast hour began. Then large numbers gathered on the forecastles of all eight ships—as they were perfectly entitled to do during 'their own time'. The next order —for Quarters Clean Guns at 7.55 a.m.—was largely ignored. The hoisting of 'Colours' at 8.0 was carried out with the usual formality, but after it was over general cheering took place, and the order to fall in for work at 8.30 was extensively disobeyed. It was now obvious that the *Nelson*, *Hood* and *Rodney*, which were due to sail at 10 o'clock in that order, would not go to sea. It should be made plain that of the capital ships those three and the *Valiant* (which was already in a state of mutiny) were the only ones affected. There was no serious trouble in the *Warspite*, *Malaya* and *Repulse*—despite the last two being subjected to considerable barracking when they rejoined the main body later in the day.

To turn to the cruisers, the day began normally with 'scrub decks' at 6.0 a.m., and the Marines also turned to. The first overt indiscipline took place at 8.0 a.m. on board the *Norfolk* and came from the stokers. The seamen and Marines followed their example, and only senior ratings continued their duties. At 8.30 a.m. 'hands fall in' the *Dorsetshire* (Astley-Rushton's flagship) had a number of absentees (not including any Marines), but by 10 o'clock the firm persuasiveness of the Captain and officers had restored discipline. In the *York* there was only slight trouble on the Tuesday, but it became more serious next day, when she had a mutiny of her own.[1] The minelaying cruiser *Adventure* was among the worst affected; but in the *Exeter*, which only arrived late on Tuesday 15th, there was hardly any trouble. Thus the impression sometimes given that the whole fleet was in a state of mutiny for two complete days is false. The *Valiant* and *Rodney* were the only ships in that condition from 6.0 a.m. Tuesday to 5.0 p.m. Wednesday. It is however fair to mention that the cruiser Captains had an easier task than those of the capital ships because they were not under orders to sail on Tuesday.

[1] See *Edwards*, pp. 249–50 regarding the effect of the *York's* Commander (C. Coppinger) diving overboard to rescue a man who had fallen into the sea when libertymen were returning on Monday 14th Sept. Edwards is, however, wrong to say there was no trouble in the *York*.

Thus no question of weighing anchor or raising steam for sea arose in those ships.[1]

Soon after 9.0 a.m. on Tuesday Tomkinson cancelled the exercises and recalled the ships already at sea (*Warspite, Malaya* and *Repulse*), informing the Admiralty of what had happened.[2] His 1.20 a.m. message had been the first intimation received in Whitehall that trouble in the fleet was likely to prove serious. Admiral F. C. Dreyer, the DCNS, definitely saw this message; but he took no action. It was while the Sea Lords were discussing the implications that the far worse news in Tomkinson's 9.16 a.m. message reached them.

At about that time Chamberlain, the First Lord, was on his way to the Admiralty when he met Sir Samuel Hoare, the Foreign Secretary, in Hyde Park. Chamberlain had himself wanted the Foreign Office and membership of the Cabinet, and it may have been knowledge of this that caused Hoare to remark to him 'What a delightful office. Unlike the Foreign Office, the Admiralty runs itself and the First Lord need not worry about it'.[3] Within 24 hours Chamberlain was shown Tomkinson's signal that some ships of the Atlantic Fleet had mutinied.

Tomkinson next told the Admiralty that he was sending Hodges's Chief of Staff (Admiral Colvin) and his secretary by the night train to London to report personally to the Board. By that time (around 10.0 a.m.) only four of the eight big ships (*Valiant, Rodney, Norfolk* and *Adventure*) were still in a state of mutiny. The other four ships' companies had resumed duty between 8.30 (*York*) and 10.10 (*Dorsetshire*). Thus if the Admiralty had forthwith ordered the ships to return to their home ports the mutiny would probably have ended after about two hours instead of it going on for nearly two whole days.

During the second half of the forenoon watch (10 a.m. to 12 noon) a document usually referred to as a 'Manifesto' but better described as a 'Petition' was produced in the *Norfolk*—about two hours after the start of the mutiny and some time after half the affected ships had resumed duty. It began 'We the loyal subjects of HM the King' and ended 'The men are quite willing to accept a cut which they, the men, consider reasonable'. Though Wincott claims to have been the author it was more probably a co-operative effort. It was typed by the Commander's

[1] This and the preceding paragraphs are based on the Rs of P of individual ships in Adm. 178/110.
[2] SOAF. 0916 of 15th Sept. 1931.
[3] Viscount Templewood, *Nine Troubled Years* (Collins, 1954), p. 23.

writer,[1] according to Wincott's 1971 account without any undue pressure being placed on him,[2] and about half a dozen copies were produced. One was certainly sent ashore and reached London. It was published two days later in the *Daily Herald* and quoted in the House of Commons. Though Wincott claims that others were distributed around the fleet by boat we have no proof of this. What is certain is that the document, of which a good deal has been made, had negligible influence in the fleet.[3]

Although the Admiralty can as yet have had only a very vague idea of the trend of events off Invergordon they now signalled to Tomkinson 'Their Lordships entirely approve of the action you have taken'[4]— a commendation which was to produce lengthy recriminations and controversy. Furthermore this message did not give the slightest assistance to the officers of the fleet, who were waiting all day for the Admiralty to help them in coping with the reaction to the pay cuts. During the afternoon the *Repulse* returned to Cromarty, the *Warspite* and *Malaya* rejoined the main fleet and the cruiser *Exeter* arrived. In none of these ships was there serious trouble. Nor was there any in the training battleship *Iron Duke* and the destroyer and submarine flotilla at Rosyth; but they had the advantage of the Admiralty letter of 10th September being received in time for explanation of the cuts to be made and investigation of cases of hardship to be begun at once.

That evening came the first prospect of trouble for Tomkinson, and of the Admiralty starting a campaign of self-exculpation, when he received a message that his earlier reports 'had failed to convey to Their Lordships a true picture of the situation'.[5] Not unnaturally this suggestion caused the Admiral 'some concern'—presumably a euphemism for 'considerable indignation'.[6] Yet it now seems clear that Tomkinson was either inadequately informed or took the whole issue of the pay cuts insufficiently seriously in the early stages.

No helpful action having been taken by the Admiralty for some

[1] This was George Hill, Able Seaman, who later achieved Warrant Rank and retired as a Lieutenant-Commander.

[2] cf. Wincott's earlier account quoted in *Divine*, p. 158.

[3] *Edwards*, pp. 269-70. *Divine*, pp. 158-9. Both print the same parts of the 'Manifesto'. The full text is included as Enclosure 3 to *Norfolk's* R of P (Adm. 178/110). As it has not been reproduced before it is printed as an appendix to this chapter.

[4] AM. 1205 of 15th Sept. 1931.

[5] AM. 1910 of 15th Sept. no. 913. Received at 2000.

[6] SOAF report. Adm. 178/110.

twenty hours, by 'turn-to' at 6.0 a.m. on Wednesday 16th the situation was plainly deteriorating. No work was done in *Valiant*, *Rodney*, *Norfolk* and *Adventure*. At about 10 a.m. the situation in the *Hood*, whose company had withstood abuse from the *Rodney*, was aggravated by the arrival of the morning papers with the Admiralty's Press statement that 'the reduced rates of pay has led to unrest among a proportion of the lower ratings . . .'[1] The result of this flagrant understatement was that the men refused to work during the second half of the forenoon—so increasing from 2 to 4 hours the period during which the *Hood* was in a state of mutiny.[2] Soon after 9.0 a.m. Tomkinson signalled to Astley-Rushton and French 'I should like to see you at 1100'.[3] His reason undoubtedly was that, having received no help from the Admiralty, he wanted to discuss what could be done—such as forming a committee of senior officers to interview lower deck representatives with the object of ascertaining the feelings of the men. The chief difficulties facing the three Admirals were how to select the lower deck representatives and how to inform the fleet—signalling having become unreliable. The committee could not in any case start work before the afternoon, by which time some action should surely have been taken by the Admiralty; furthermore the men might refuse to nominate representatives. The decision taken was therefore not to adopt such a course, but to send another message to the Admiralty.[4] Accordingly a few minutes before noon Tomkinson telegraphed 'I am of the opinion the situation will get entirely out of control unless an immediate concession is made'. He suggested that the cut in pay for junior ratings should be made proportional to that suffered by senior ratings, and that a representative of the Board should at once come north 'to discuss matters on the spot'.[5] One may, however, doubt whether the latter

---

[1] The statement is quoted in full in *Edwards*, pp. 285–6.

[2] The statement in the typescript of Commander J. H. Owen's work *Mutiny in the Royal Navy*, vol. II (Adm. 178/133) that the *Hood*'s men stopped work when the turn of the tide brought her temporarily parallel with the *Rodney* in the middle of the forenoon and abuse was shouted at the former from the latter is based on *Hood*'s R of P of 21st Sept. but does not appear in SOAF's report or in *Rodney*'s R of P (Adm. 178/110). Commander Pursey is certain that it is untrue. To the author 22nd Feb. 1974.

[3] AC(Q) 0917 to CS2 and RA2 of 16th Sept. 1931. Note Tomkinson's use of his former title 'Admiral Commanding Battle-Cruisers' and not SOAF.

[4] I am indebted to Commander Pursey for this information, which is not recorded in any of the reports sent in by the three Admirals concerned.

[5] SOAF. 1148 of 16th September 1931.

proposal would have had any effect, since no member of the Board possessed authority to modify the cuts. Such action rested of course with the Cabinet.

On 16th Chamberlain gave the Cabinet a summary of what had happened in the fleet during the preceding two days. But although his colleagues admitted that 'grievances of a specially onerous kind might exist in the fleet', they were 'deeply concerned' about the effect that concessions to the navy would have 'on the whole scheme of Government economies'. The Secretary of the Cabinet, Sir Maurice Hankey, recorded that 'doubts were felt as to whether it was expedient . . . to withdraw the ships to the home ports as desired by the Sea Lords'; but the proposal 'was eventually agreed to on the understanding that it was clear that this was done in obedience to an order from the Admiralty'.[1] It therefore seems absolutely clear that the delay over recalling ships to their home ports was chiefly the fault of the Cabinet and not of the Admiralty, though the latter might have pressed for such a measure at least 24 hours earlier.

When the Cabinet met at noon on 16th[2] the situation at Invergordon was that five ships, now including the *Hood*, were in a state of mutiny and seven were not. Everyone—officers and men—was waiting for action by the Admiralty. But the question of the moment was—what would happen at 1.15 p.m. when the men's dinner hour would be over? Had a C-in-C been in command it seems very likely that a signal to 'Make and Mend Clothes' (naval terminology for a half day's holiday) would have been made—in order to avoid provoking further refusals of duty and play for time; since it must have been obvious that the Admiralty would have to take action soon.[3] Even though the fleet was without a C-in-C either Tomkinson should have given a general order or Astley-Rushton and French have given one to their own squadrons.

According to Tomkinson reports were now reaching him which indicated a rapidly deteriorating situation in the worst ships—including interference with running machinery, breaking out of their ships by parties of mutineers, and organising visits to those which had not

---

[1] Cab. 56(31) of 16th Sept. 1931, conclusion 3. Cab. 23/68.

[2] See SOAF to AF in company 1320 of 16th Sept. 1931.

[3] Pursey suggested to his Commander that the *Hood* should 'Make and Mend Clothes', and McCrum gave the necessary order. Three other ships—*Repulse*, *Malaya* and *Dorsetshire*—took similar action, thereby probably avoiding aggravation of the trouble. Pursey to the author 22nd Feb. and 23rd April 1974.

joined in the mutiny or had returned to work.[1] Such rumours must have increased his anxiety; but shortly after 3.0 p.m. it was alleviated by the receipt of orders for all ships to return to their home ports. The Admiralty also said that the Board was 'fully alive to the fact that amongst certain classes of ratings special hardship will result' from the pay cuts, and that such cases of hardship would be fully investigated.[2]

It took about ten minutes to decode and distribute the Admiralty's signal, which was received in the *Hood* at 3.10 p.m. As soon as Tomkinson read it he signalled to Astley-Rushton and French 'I should like to see you now'.[3] The three Admirals decided the time at which squadrons should sail, which depended on the time required to raise steam (about four hours) and, in the case of the capital ships, on high tide slack water. It appears that the resultant orders were distributed to individual Captains orally or by boat message. In fact Tomkinson ordered the squadrons to sail independently, starting with the cruisers at 9.30 p.m. —some 5 hours after receipt of the Admiralty signal. Thus there was no need to prepare for sea in the men's leisure time. But in some ships (notably *Valiant* and *Nelson*) measures which savour of panic were discussed—such as going ahead and parting the cables if the men refused to unmoor the ship (*Nelson*), and even using force to suppress further mutiny (*Valiant*).[4] She was the only ship in which such action was seriously considered. We may be thankful that it was never applied, since the first shot fired would undoubtedly have converted the mutiny from a 'sit down strike' into an orgy of violence.

As late as 7.45 p.m. Tomkinson felt obliged to report 'I am not sure that all ships will leave as ordered [the cruisers at 9.30 and the capital ships at 10.0 p.m.] but some will go'.[5] It now seems clear that this was an unnecessarily pessimistic view, probably conveyed earlier to Tomkinson by Astley-Rushton's report on *Norfolk* and French's report

[1] SOAF report. Adm. 178/110. It seems clear that these rumours produced exaggerated pessimism. The ships had few boats out, and inter-ship visiting on a large scale was scarcely feasible.

[2] AM. 1445 of 16th Sept. 1931.

[3] AC(Q) to CS2 and RA2 1523 of 16th Sept. 1931.

[4] Rs of P *Nelson* and *Valiant*. Adm. 178/110. Also *Elkins, Diary*. In this author's opinion *Edwards*, ch. XVII gives a better account of this period than *Divine*, pp. 168–77, though *Edwards*, pp. 344–6 is wrong about the *Nelson* still being in a state of mutiny when the cruisers steamed past her. Edwards plainly had access to *some* Captains' reports.

[5] SOAF. 1947 of 16th Sept. 1931. *Divine*, p. 174 gives the TOO of this message wrongly as 1917.

on *Valiant*; but the reports sent in by the Captains of those ships, perhaps understandably, do not provide evidence to support Tomkinson's pessimism.[1] A general survey of the situation indicates that, after the Admiralty's signal ordering the fleet back to its home ports had been read to the ships' companies, six ships (*Warspite, Malaya, Repulse, Dorsetshire, York* and *Exeter*) were in normal condition. Between 5.0 p.m. and 7.0 p.m. the other six ships' companies returned to duty and prepared for sea correctly when the time to do so came. It is therefore true to say that 7.0 p.m. on 16th September marked the definitive end of the mutiny.

In retrospect it seems a pity that Tomkinson did not send a positive signal to the Admiralty by 8.0 p.m. at the latest, instead of the dubious and pessimistic one he did send; for the condition of the fleet certainly justified a positive message. One can only assume that the one he sent was based on earlier information received from some of the worst affected ships; and if that is so by 8.0 p.m. it was certainly out of date. Not until shortly before midnight, and in answer to an anxious enquiry from the Admiralty, did he signal that all ships had sailed.[2]

In this short account of a very complicated story the actions of Flag Officers (except Tomkinson) and of individual Captains have been largely ignored—partly for reasons of space and partly because a good deal has already been published about them. Yet study of their reports, and of such impartial evidence as has survived, must lead any fair-minded person to the conclusion that nearly all of them kept their heads and acted sensibly on most occasions. The only possible exceptions were Astley-Rushton, whose angry speech to the *Norfolk*'s company calling them 'bloody fools' and 'bloody hooligans' was, if Wincott quotes him correctly,[3] not calculated to pacify mutinous men, Captain C. A. Scott of the *Valiant* who apparently seriously considered the use of strong-arm methods, and Captain A. D. H. Dibben of the *Adventure*, of whose conduct the Naval Secretary later expressed a poor opinion.[4] As regards the remainder one feels that few if any

[1] Rs of P *Norfolk* and *Valiant*. Adm. 178/110.

[2] SOAF. 2345 of 16th Sept. 1931. The target ship *Centurion* which was boiler cleaning, and her attendant destroyer were left behind. They sailed on 17th.

[3] *Edwards*, p. 301. *Divine*, p. 172 mentions his visit to *Norfolk* but does not quote from his speech. *Wincott*, however, declares that the words quoted were used (p. 122). As Edwards got the story from Wincott's 1931 pamphlet *The Spirit of Invergordon* it can hardly be accepted as proven.

[4] Comments by Rear-Admiral G. K. Chetwode on the senior officers concerned. Adm. 178/120.

other Post Captains who found themselves in the position of those commanding the worst ships would have done any better; yet they, and in some cases their Commanders as well, were to suffer for the unhappy chance of being placed where they were.

After it was all over Tomkinson wrote to the Admiralty that 'For two days ships at Invergordon . . . were in a state of open mutiny'—which was true only of the four ships named earlier. He was confident that there had been 'organisation in the actual outbreak', and believed 'that preparation must have been made over a considerable period'. The first statement was correct only in the sense that the mutiny was organised on ships' mess decks on Sunday and Monday 13th and 14th September. The second statement, implying that outside influences like the Communist Party had been at work for some time, is not supported by any acceptable evidence. More correctly Tomkinson considered the prime causes to have been 'the disproportionate reduction [of pay] of the lower ratings entered before 1925', its unexpectedness, the suddenness with which it was announced, the short interval before the cuts were to take effect (1st October), and the feeling of breach of faith among men on the 1919 rates. 'In my opinion', he concluded, with candour which was not likely to endear him in Whitehall, 'the cause of complaint was well-founded'.[1]

With the Atlantic Fleet steaming south from Invergordon we may turn to the effects of the pay cuts on men serving on foreign stations. Though the large Mediterranean Fleet probably reaped considerable advantage through being widely dispersed on its autumn cruise and not reassembling until after the cuts had been limited to 10%, there was no trouble at all; and all cases of hardship were carefully investigated and reported to the Admiralty after the fleet had returned to Malta in October.[2] The China Fleet was able to report an equally clean bill of health.[3] Only in the light cruiser *Delhi* on the North America and West Indies Station did refusal of duty on a scale comparable to that in some Atlantic Fleet ships take place.[4] Though there are certainly no grounds for supposing that the officers of ships on foreign stations

[1] SOAF report. Adm. 178/110.

[2] Personal experience of author, who was serving in *Royal Sovereign* in the Mediterranean Fleet at the time and report by C-in-C, Mediterranean in Adm. 1/8761–240/32.

[3] Adm. 178/111.

[4] Adm. 178/73. The trouble in *Delhi* took place while at St. Andrew's, New Brunswick. Her visit to New York was cancelled and she was recalled to Bermuda. On 9th Nov. the Admiralty approved the manner in which the C-in-C (Admiral V. H. Haggard) and the ship's Captain had handled the situation.

were better than their counterparts in the Atlantic Fleet they did enjoy the advantage of continuity of service throughout a commission (2 to 2½ years); and that enabled them to get to know their men better than was possible in the Atlantic Fleet, in which a large proportion of every ship's company was changed each time the ships returned to their home ports—usually to enable men to undergo courses of one type or another.[1] Another handicap under which the Atlantic Fleet laboured was the effect of long leave periods three times a year, which meant that something like a new start had to be made after the end of each such period. This was particularly important in 1931, since the men had five weeks (1st August–7th September) in which to discuss the effects of the threatened pay cuts.

When Tomkinson sailed from Invergordon he took with him the Battle Cruiser Squadron (*Hood* and *Repulse*) and the 1st Division of the 2nd Battle Squadron (*Nelson* and *Rodney*). While these ships and the other squadrons were steaming south the Admiralty, which had preserved a deafening silence regarding modification of the pay cuts during the critical period, sent out a stream of signals which were mostly irrelevant to that issue. Though the long silence of the Admiralty during the vital period is probably attributable to the difficulty of getting a quick decision from the Cabinet, which of course had to consult Departmental Ministers and get their views, it undoubtedly aggravated the difficulties facing the senior officers in the fleet.

After the fleet had sailed the main object in the minds of senior officers was to get their ships to the home ports *and* up harbour by noon on Saturday 19th in order that the maximum week-end leave should be granted; and to accomplish that purpose with the big ships bound for Portsmouth and Devonport it was essential to arrive before high tide slack water.

On Thursday 17th September, the day after the fleet had sailed, Chamberlain made the expected statement in the House of Commons on an Adjournment Motion. He then said that 'The past is past. It is in the interest of everyone in the Navy or out of it to forget [the mutiny]. I am not going to look back. I am going to look forward . . .'[2] The First

[1] Admiral Elkins, letter to the author of 11th May 1972, stresses the effect of the frequent changes. So does Admiral Kelly in several places in his official report of 9th Nov. 1931, referred to below.

[2] Parl. Deb., Commons, vol. 256, cols. 1104–22. The Adjournment was moved by Captain W. G. Hall (a former *Army* officer and Labour MP for Portsmouth Central), who quoted the *Norfolk*'s 'Petition' (col. 1107). Chamberlain's remarks are in col. 1120.

Lord's attitude at least made it certain that there would be no Courts Martial, which was fortunate as they would have involved the public washing of dirty naval linen to an extent which would have made even the notorious *Royal Oak* affair of 1928 appear insignificant.[1] But, as we shall see, it also produced acutely difficult problems concerning the future of men identified as ringleaders of the mutiny.

That same forenoon Tomkinson took the initiative about the leave question by signalling that '. . . usual week-end leave [was to be granted] . . . to one watch and night leave to part [i.e. half] of . . . other watch'.[2] Shortly before this message was sent the Admiralty came up, somewhat unnecessarily, with a signal that 'usual leave' was to be granted.[3] Tomkinson then made a long reply quoting his earlier message and adding that with '. . . ordinary leave . . . a part [i.e. half] one watch would not get on shore on Saturday or Sunday'.[4] The Admiralty's reply approving his first proposal took 24 hours to reach him.[5] Next Tomkinson asked the C-in-C, Devonport, whether the *Rodney* could be taken up harbour on the Saturday morning,[6] to which the answer was that this could be done provided that she reached Plymouth Sound by 10.25 a.m. Tomkinson at once detached the *Rodney* to go ahead on her own. Meanwhile he had told the C-in-C, Portsmouth that the *Nelson* would arrive early on Saturday morning and asked what time those ships could be taken up harbour;[7] but when the *Warspite* had to reduce speed to 5 knots that forenoon because of boiler trouble it seemed unlikely that she would get to her home port in time.

On the evening of 17th, the Admiralty addressed all the ships of the Atlantic Fleet in terms which, apart from their pomposity, look very much like an attempt to restore the Board's authority. 'The Lords Commissioners of the Admiralty', they signalled, '. . . view with the greatest concern the injury which the prestige of the British Navy has suffered . . . The Board rely on the personnel of the fleet to do their utmost to restore the confidence of the country by their future be-

[1] See vol. I, pp. 559–60.

[2] SNOA. [Senior Naval Officer Afloat] 1155 of 17th Sept. The originals of this message and of the 1205 of 17th to C-in-C, Portsmouth (see below) are in the same hand. It is therefore possible that the same signal rating made the same mistake twice in ten minutes, writing down SNOA when he should have written SOAF.

[3] AM. 1147 of 17th Sept.   [4] SOAF. 1358 of 17th Sept.

[5] AM. 1350 of 17th Sept. Time of Receipt 1402 of 18th Sept.

[6] SOAF. 1841 of 17th Sept.

[7] SNOA. 1205 of 17th Sept.

haviour'.[1] Angry men who were thinking of the security of their homes and families rather than their service's prestige were not likely to take being scolded like school children very kindly. No reactions to this message are on record.

Shortly before the Admiralty's admonition was received Tomkinson asked what speed the four ships which had sailed with him could steam 'with present . . . boilers without pressing', and on learning that the *Hood* could steam 12½ knots, which was higher than the 'economical speed' normally used when cruising in peace time, he ordered an increase to the higher speed.[2] But when early on 18th the ships ran into thick fog and had to reduce speed the odds against getting up harbour on time lengthened. As soon as the weather cleared sufficiently Tomkinson increased speed to fourteen knots, lighting up more boilers to do so. At 5.35 a.m. on Saturday 19th September the *Hood* stopped in Spithead to pick up a pilot, and about an hour later she and the *Nelson* were safely berthed up harbour.[3] The *Warspite* got in late that evening, and the *Rodney* reached Plymouth on time, as did the five cruisers at the three home ports. Tomkinson left by train for London soon after the *Hood* had berthed,[4] and probably read in *The Times* that the three Cs-in-C, Admirals Sir Hubert Brand (Plymouth), Sir Arthur Waistell (Portsmouth) and Sir Reginald Tyrwhitt (The Nore) had been called into conference at the Admiralty the previous day. The *post mortem* had evidently begun.

We may here turn to the question whether the Communist Party or any other subversive organisation played a part in organising the mutiny, or took any effective steps to foment trouble after the ships had returned to their home ports. As to the former no reliable evidence indicating that the mutiny was other than spontaneous has ever come

---

[1] AM. 1910 of 17th Sept. Six days later the Admiralty informed the senior officers of the destroyer and submarine flotillas that this message did not apply to them—a somewhat belated recognition of the fact that they had taken no part in the mutiny. AM. 1553 of 23rd Sept.

[2] AC(Q) to Battle Cruiser Squadron and 1st Division, 2nd Battle Squadron 1820 and 1840 of 17th Sept. The appearance of so many different titles for the same originator of messages at this time (AC(Q), SNOA and SOAF) makes it appear that there was considerable confusion in the signal department.

[3] The *Malaya* did not arrive at Plymouth until 2.0 a.m. on Sunday, 20th Sept., having carried out some exercises after leaving Invergordon. Her ship's company did not therefore receive week-end leave. *Naval and Military Record*, 23rd Sept. 1931, p. 607.

[4] Pursey to the author 22nd Feb. 1974. I am also indebted to him for copies of the signals passed while at sea, some of which do not exist in the Admiralty's records.

to light.[1] After the ships had reached their home ports a few Communists were sent down to Portsmouth—presumably in the hope of fomenting further trouble; but they appear to have been singularly ill fitted to play the part assigned to them.[2] Special Branch detectives and MI5 agents were undoubtedly sent to Portsmouth and Plymouth to try and identify ringleaders; and some men of the fleet apparently amused themselves by leading them along false trails. As a generalisation the reports sent to London by such agents must be regarded as unreliable, and they were by no means entirely accepted by the DNI when he submitted his 'final report on the origin of the Invergordon incident'. Though he declared that neither the Third International nor

[1] A good deal has been made of a signal alleged to have been passed from *Rodney* to *Nelson* during the passage south. The C-in-C, Plymouth reported as 'definite information received' and gave the wording as '*Nelson* will now take over pivotal ship. Keep your end up and do not forget 0800 next Tuesday' (C-in-C, Plymouth to Admiralty 1849 of 19th Sept.). Though the wording is slightly different the message appears in the typescript of vol. II of Commander Owen's *Mutiny in the Royal Navy* (ch. III, p. 45. Adm. 178/133). See also *Divine*, p. 191 and Copeman, *Reason in Revolt*, p. 50. None the less the passing of this message can be regarded as no more than dubious. The only evidence the author has found of Communist Party links with the Navy in between the wars was at the time of the prolonged miners' strike of 1926, when a number of ratings in uniform attended CP meetings in Hyde Park 'in support of the miners'. Such incidents were reported to the Admiralty several times in 1926 and '27, and there was discussion about initiating a Naval Patrol in London to stop them. Adm. 178/66. Between 1933 and 1936 there were six fairly serious cases of sabotage to ships' machinery while in dockyard hands, and the Admiralty and MI5 investigated the question of the employment of members of the Communist Party in the Royal Dockyards. The outcome was the dismissal of five workmen (four of them employed at Devonport where five of the six sabotage cases had occurred). The matter was raised in the House of Commons by Attlee on a Private Notice Question to the First Lord on 19th January 1937. Hoare defended the Admiralty's action vigorously and it was not pressed; but the Admiralty was bombarded with protests from Trade Unions. Adm. 178/64.

[2] Wincott to the author 24th Jan. and 6th March 1972. As Wincott was at Devonport and the Communist agents were sent to Portsmouth it is likely that Wincott's knowledge of them was obtained at second hand. He names George Allison, a miner, and William Shepherd, a woodworker. Those two and two others were prosecuted for 'Incitement to Mutiny' in November 1931 at Winchester Assizes, and Telegraphist S. Bousfield (see p. 99) was an important witness for the Prosecution. Allison was sentenced to three years' penal servitude and Shepherd to 20 months' imprisonment. *The Times* 27th Nov. 1931. For an account by the officer sent to Invergordon by the Director of Naval Intelligence to investigate subversive activities, and later involved in the tracing of Communist Party agents at Portsmouth, see Colonel S. Bassett, *Royal Marine* (Peter Davies, 1962), ch. v. As however it was written long after the event, and without access to documents it must be treated with caution.

the Communist Party of Great Britain 'can be held directly responsible' for the outbreak, and indeed asserted that the latter was 'completely taken by surprise', he did state that group meetings had been held in many ships *before* they sailed on the autumn cruise, and that the Lodges of the Royal and Antediluvian Order of Buffalos (RAOB) had been used as cover for secret meetings ashore and afloat.[1] Incidentally the fact that the Admiralty did at this time employ secret agents on board ships of the fleet is proved by a later decision to abandon such practices when they were away from their home ports.[2]

On the afternoon of Monday 21st September MacDonald announced in the House of Commons that pay cuts were to be limited to 10% except for higher ranking officers, and that men on the 1919 rates of pay were to receive their current rates less 10%. The Fleet Orders explaining the original pay cuts were cancelled.[3] Furthermore a special fund was to be set up and administered by the RN Benevolent Trust to alleviate hardship among married men under 25;[4] but as this was in fact a 'charity scheme' and those applying for help under it were subject to a 'means test' it had very little appeal to the men. What it does show is that the pay of married men under 25 was, judged by any reasonable standard, inadequate; and that must go a long way towards explaining why the men on the 1925 rates made common cause with the much more seriously affected men on the 1919 rates. At any rate the decision of 21st September involved a complete climb-down by the government. The tragedy was that it had taken a mutiny to accomplish it. The Fleet Orders setting out the revised pay cuts were received on the forenoon of Saturday 3rd October, and Captains at once explained

---

[1] Report by the DNI dated 20th June 1932. Adm. 178/110. Commander Pursey, who has consulted RAOB Headquarters, is certain that only one Lodge (*Rodney*'s) was suspect, and that the procedure regularly adopted at meetings made it impossible for discussion of pay or any matter not on the agenda to take place. However the Admiralty ordered that no private meetings of societies were henceforth to be allowed in ships or establishments—including the Anglican Church's religious organisation 'Toc H'. Note by Naval Law Branch of 7th Feb. 1934. Adm. 1/8774–115/34. Also AL N. 1269 of 27th April 1934. *ibid.* Much ironically humorous correspondence passed between The Rev. P. B. ('Tubby') Clayton, the founder of Toc H, and Admiral Kelly over the banning of the organisation's meetings.

[2] Board Minute 2974 of 30th June 1932 mentions the activities of a security service agent who had visited Invergordon at the time of the mutiny. The Board decided that agents should not in future go on board ships or 'undertake espionage work' away from home ports. Adm. 178/50.

[3] Admy. A. Message 1618 of 21st Sept. 1931.

[4] AM. 1901 of 1st Oct. 1931.

them to their ships' companies. In truth little or no explanation was necessary, as the orders were simplicity itself—namely that no one was to lose more than 10% and men on the 1925 rates nothing. On 5th Tomkinson signalled the orders for all Atlantic Fleet ships to resume their rudely interrupted autumn cruise—probably his last action in the unenviable capacity of its temporary senior officer.[1]

The most important issue which had to be decided after Admiral Hodges had been invalided was who should take over command in succession to him and replace the temporary incumbent Tomkinson. J. C. C. Davidson, a former Parliamentary Secretary, considered that there were only two possible candidates—Sir Reginald Tyrwhitt and Sir John Kelly; and as the health of the former was reported to be 'not very good', he favoured the latter. However Chamberlain, according to Davidson, had no intention of appointing either. Davidson therefore 'made his views known to the Court', probably acting through Sir Clive Wigram, the King's private secretary who kept the Monarch informed on all aspects of the naval unrest,[2] and also drew Baldwin's attention to the matter.[3] Whether Davidson's influence was actually as great as he implied cannot be said; but the Cabinet and the King both did approve Kelly's appointment and on 26th September he was called to the Admiralty and Chamberlain personally offered him the post for a year.[4] Kelly was of course in a position to make his own terms. He insisted that all discharges of men involved in the mutiny should be completed before he took over, and that he should only do so shortly before the fleet sailed. In other words he claimed, and obtained, a free hand to make an absolutely fresh start.[5] Accordingly for 12 days the ships of the Atlantic Fleet remained under the Cs-in-C of the home ports, with Tomkinson still as its 'senior officer'. On 6th October Kelly hoisted his flag in the *Nelson*.

Next day Parliament was prorogued for the General Election to be held on 27th October. During the nineteen days the fleet had been in

[1] SOAF. 1201 of 5th Oct. 1931.

[2] Rear-Admiral G. K. Chetwode, Naval Secretary to the First Lord, corresponded frequently with Wigram about the mutiny and its aftermath. See Adm. 178/129 for example; also RA GV K2330(3)/13, /17 and /19.

[3] R. R. James, *Memoirs of a Conservative* (Weidenfeld and Nicolson, 1969), pp. 374–5.

[4] On 28th Sept. Chamberlain, in answer to a Parliamentary Question by Alexander, said that Hodges's health would prevent him resuming command of the fleet. He had therefore asked to be relieved and the King had approved Sir John Kelly's appointment as his successor. Parl. Deb., Commons, vol. 257, col. 35.

[5] Kelly papers, KEL/109–111.

its home ports there had been no trouble; nor was any to arise in the future. On 16th October Field wrote to Kelly—only ten days after he had assumed command 'My dear Joe, I am glad to hear that you find the spirit of the Fleet reassuring . . .'[1]

Inside the Admiralty the *post mortem* and aftermath to the mutiny were very prolonged. On 4th October Chamberlain wrote, cautiously but candidly that, regarding the Board Minutes on Tomkinson's Report of Proceedings, he 'reserved any expression of opinion as to responsibilities . . . In these matters I think that we of the Board of Admiralty must accept some measure of blame . . . [We did not show all the foresight that might have been expected of us'—which was perhaps a considerable understatement.[2] He was less candid, and certainly less accurate, in the apologia he sent to the King; for he wrote that 'All the evidence goes to show that the men affected expected, and were prepared to accept without murmuring, a moderate cut in their rates of pay . . . but that the severity of the cuts, particularly on the lower ratings, burst upon them like a thunderclap and swept them off their feet . . . The lesson to be drawn from these happenings is clear. If at any future time it is necessary to ask a similar sacrifice of men actually serving, explanation, enquiry and consultation must take place before, and not after the decision is taken . . . Sir Austen Chamberlain . . . feels deeply indebted to his Naval colleagues from whom he has received invaluable guidance and help throughout the crisis . . . Sir Austen concludes . . . that this was no mutiny as the word is generally understood . . .'[3] When the first draft of the 'Admiralty Narrative' was before him he expressed reluctance to send it even to Cs-in-C 'as appearing to justify ourselves' and revealing 'our relations with the Treasury, Cabinet, etc.' Excisions were made to avoid giving the impression that the whole blame should be placed on the late or present Cabinet, or that the Board refused 'unconditionally and to the end to accept the cuts . . . and definitely dissociated itself from that decision', or that the Cabinet was 'actuated by financial panic and stampeded by the Board', or 'any suggestion of difficulty caused by [the] absence . . . of any member of the Board'.[4] In fact the Narrative underwent considerable revision, and the final document is far less open to the criticism

---

[1] Field to Kelly. Kelly papers, KEL/109.   [2] Adm. 178/110.

[3] RA GV K2330(3) dated 25th Sept. 1931.

[4] Minute by C. B. Coxwell, Principal Assistant Secretary (Staff) of 21st October 1931. Adm. 178/110.

Chamberlain made of the draft.[1] None the less the Narrative was given no circulation, but was passed to Chamberlain's successor, Sir Bolton Eyres Monsell, early in November; and he merely noted it.

The departure of Austen Chamberlain from the Admiralty after what Murray, the Permanent Secretary, described as 'one of the shortest if not actually the shortest [terms of office] in the whole history of the Board' provides the opportunity to survey his part in what was certainly a most difficult and unhappy period. He took over at a time when his predecessor A. V. Alexander had already told the Cabinet that the Navy would accept the pay cuts—provided that they were uniformly applied throughout the government services and to unemployment benefit; but he made no protest to the new Cabinet over the application of the 1925 rates to men paid on the 1919 scale. A generous interpretation of his failure is that his naval colleagues did not adequately emphasise the 'breach of contract' aspect of this decision, and that in the short time available Chamberlain could not master the long and complicated history of that proposal. At any rate he made no bones about the Board's share in the responsibility for the disaster that followed. Murray, who was not given to exaggeration or adulation of his colleagues, wrote to him that 'the universal feeling' was that 'we have lost the greatest First Lord that anyone now connected with the Department has had experience of'; while Hankey sent him a warmly appreciative letter about his handling of the crisis.[2] If one accepts those sentiments at their face value the conclusion must surely be that the Sea Lords bear a greater share of the responsibility for the *débâcle* than the First Lord, since it was their duty to brief the First Lord adequately. Chamberlain, perhaps embittered by the experiences of 1931, never took office again, but thereafter played the part of a respected Elder Statesman; but when the threat from Hitler's Germany began to look ominous in 1936 he emerged from retirement to throw his weight and influence on the side of those who were urging faster rearmament.

Perhaps the least attractive feature of the Admiralty end of the *post mortem* is the self-appointment of Admiral F. C. Dreyer, the DCNS, as chief counsel for the Board's defence—and at almost any cost to others. Dreyer was an extremely ambitious man with a marked streak of ruthlessness in his character. He unquestionably had his eye on the

---

[1] The final draft is dated 28th Sept. The final revised draft, a copy of which was sent to the King, is dated 22nd Oct. 1931.

[2] Murray to Chamberlain 19th April 1932 and Hankey to Chamberlain 4th Nov. 1931. Chamberlain papers AC. 39/4/55 and 39/4/19 respectively.

office of First Sea Lord, to attain which he had to be given command of one of the two major fleets (Home or Mediterranean). He was able but extremely prolix on paper, and his hand is to be detected not only in the minutes which he actually signed about responsibility for the events here described but in a large number of documents on the subject circulated within the Admiralty—probably including the original draft of the Narrative. We will quote but one example of his efforts to exculpate the Board, and himself, and lay the blame elsewhere. On the final report of the DNI on the origin of the mutiny he minuted 'Of one thing I have no doubt whatsoever—that if the situation at Invergordon had been properly handled there would never have been any outbreak'.[1] Moreover there is a marked contrast between the tone of the letters Dreyer wrote personally to Tomkinson during the aftermath, all of which begin 'My dear Tommy', and the criticism of that same officer's conduct which he was promulgating within the Admiralty.[2]

If the campaign of self-exculpation within the Admiralty's walls leaves an unpleasant taste so does the treatment of the men chiefly involved—or believed to have been involved. Chamberlain's amnesty announcement made it impossible to take disciplinary action—except in cases where it could be shown that subversive activities were continued after the fleet had returned to its home ports. In mid-October Murray wrote to Chamberlain in some alarm that the situation regarding the 121 men removed from their ships and sent into Barracks before the fleet sailed again was 'so serious and difficult' that the Sea Lords felt they *must* discuss the matter with the First Lord. 'One cannot doubt', continued Murray, 'that if the men are discharged [from the Navy] the first inference drawn, in the Navy and out of it, will be that they have been dealt with for their complicity in the events at Invergordon and contrary to your promise'.[3] Two days later the Board decided that discharges were not to take place during the General Election fixed for 27th October because such action 'would be misrepresented and could

---

[1] Dated 30th June 1932. Adm. 178/110.

[2] Dreyer to Tomkinson letter of 1932. Tomkinson papers.

[3] Murray to Chamberlain 15th Oct. 1931. Adm. 178/114. The total of men taken out of Atlantic Fleet ships and sent into Barracks was:—
Chatham—*Valiant* 30, *York* 8, *Wessex* 1.
Portsmouth—*Nelson* 14, *Hood* 10, *Warspite* 6.
Devonport—*Rodney* 30 (including 15 Marines), *Dorsetshire* 8, *Norfolk* 9, *Adventure* 5.
In addition 20 Marines from the *Norfolk* were divided up between a number of different ships. AL of 4th Dec. 1931. Adm. 178/112.

not be explained'; but the Sea Lords argued strongly that men who had
continued subversive activities after reaching the home ports should be
discharged.[1] The final decision taken was that 27, all Devonport men,
would be discharged; but as one had already left the service by free
discharge, another by purchase, and one had 'under his wife's influence
expressed contrition' his discharge was cancelled 'as an act of mercy'.[2]
On 2nd November Chamberlain obtained the authority of Mac-
Donald to discharge the remaining 24 under the regulation which permitted the service to get rid of 'unsuitable or incompetent men' without
formal trial.[3] Though the Admiralty acted wholly within its rights,
and the need for a fighting service to be able to cleanse itself of dis-
affected or inefficient officers and men is obvious, they did not wholly
avert Parliamentary hostility. On 23rd November the discharge of the
24 men was raised—again on an Adjournment Motion.[4]

Actually, if one accepts as reliable the evidence from Special Branch
detectives and MI5 agents, the Admiralty does appear to have acted
with reasonable humanity and fairness. By the beginning of December
most of the men held in Barracks since they were discharged from their
ships were declared available for draft in the ordinary way but prefer-
ably abroad. Despite understandable misgivings some of the black-
listed men were allowed to re-engage for pension; and to try and give
those drafted to the China station a fresh start the Admiralty refused to
give the C-in-C their names.[5] On the other hand letters, often from
wives, relating to the hardships suffered by long-service men who had
been discharged failed to produce a change of heart in Whitehall.[6]
Apart from the fact that the men discharged to Devonport Barracks
were subjected to a very severe course of disciplinary training, which
amounted in fact though not in name to harsh and unauthorised
punishment, the ratings earmarked for discharge appear to have been
reasonably treated;[7] and over the next year or so the Navy, which was
in any case being pressed to reduce its numbers, got rid of several

---

[1] Board minute 2860 of 17th Oct. 1931. Adm. 178/114.

[2] Board Minute 2863 of 19th Oct. 1931. *ibid.*

[3] King's Regulations and Admiralty Instructions, Article 420.

[4] Parl. Deb., Commons, vol. 260, cols. 174–84. Also Parliamentary Questions on
12th and 18th Nov. *ibid.*

[5] Admiralty letters, minutes and discussions with Cs-in-C on all these matters are
in Adm. 178/112.

[6] Adm. 178/113 contains several such letters.

[7] Wincott in his *Authentic Story* writes that he 'went through Hell' after being discharged to Devonport Barracks. See also *Invergordon Mutineer*, pp. 141–2. *Copeman,*

hundred men on the principle put forward by Admiral Tyrwhitt that the only acceptable alternatives were either 'serve loyally or get out'.[1]

As part of the aftermath Field, the First Sea Lord, formed a sort of Elder Statesmen's committee consisting of the three Cs-in-C of the home ports to advise on immediate measures, such as relief for cases of extreme hardship resulting from pay cuts, the identification and treatment of ringleaders, and longer term measures to rectify defects and failings revealed, and reduce the possibility of a repetition of the mutiny. But some very senior officers brought little comfort to the harassed First Sea Lord. Admiral Sir Stanley Colville[2] left with him 'a very scathing and wholesale condemnation of the Board of Admiralty' which Field rebutted vigorously;[3] while Sir Reginald Tyrwhitt (C-in-C, Nore) represented that 'the men do not regret Invergordon, nor are they ashamed of themselves'. Their chief grievance was, he continued, against the Board of Admiralty 'in whom the men have lost confidence'[4]—a view which corresponded closely to that held by the King, who told the former First Lord, Bridgeman, that 'it would have been a good thing if all the Sea Lords had been made to retire'.[5] Field also sent a lengthy defence of the Board to Lord Beatty—another Elder Naval Statesman—in which he reiterated his department's principal complaint, namely that they had only accepted the May Committee cuts on the understanding that those applied to teachers, police and the unemployed would be on a comparable scale; and that the government had ameliorated the latter and announced their decision in Parliament without giving the service departments prior warning. As the Atlantic Fleet had at the time already sailed for Invergordon the Board was, according to Field, faced with a very different situation from that envisaged when they had accepted the

---

p. 51 confirms Wincott's account, but *Edwards*, p. 377, remarks that 'In some ways it is undoubtedly an exaggeration'; with which view this historian is disposed to agree.

[1] C-in-C, Nore letter of 9th Jan. 1933. Adm. 1/8769–127/33.

[2] Colville, who had been C-in-C, Portsmouth 1916–19 had retired in 1922. In 1931 he held the somewhat honorific titles of Vice-Admiral of the United Kingdom and Lieutenant of the Admiralty. Presumably it was in those capacities that he took it on himself to berate the Board.

[3] Colville's paper is dated 15th Oct. and Field's rebuttal 21st Oct. 1931. Adm. 178/129.

[4] Murray's summary of Cs-in-C's replies to AL of 30th Dec. 1932. Adm. 167/89.

[5] Bridgeman diary. (Ms.), p. 253.

May Committee cuts.[1] Though there was some substance in this complaint it still remains true that the full impact of the proposed cuts on the 1919 men was not appreciated in the Admiralty.

On 8th October the fleet sailed for Rosyth, and on 17th the Admiralty sent Kelly a letter directing him to 'make a careful examination of the state of discipline in the ships of that Fleet', and to 'undertake inquiries into the whole circumstances of the recent failure of discipline'.[2] The answer was probably a good deal more forthright and condemnatory of themselves than Their Lordships had anticipated; for Kelly wrote to Field that, having drawn 'on every possible source . . . one thing stands out beyond everything else: that Officers and Men alike, from the highest to the lowest, appear to attribute the Mutiny . . . directly to the action of the Admiralty in accepting the "Cuts" as at first promulgated'. Furthermore his inquiries had led him to believe 'that complete confidence in the Administrative authority will not be restored so long as the present Board of Admiralty remain in office'.[3] On 9th November he followed up this initial salvo with a long official letter covering the whole range of the subjects he had been asked to report on, repeating verbatim his opinion of the basic cause of the mutiny as expressed to Field but omitting his view that the Board should resign—probably because he realised that this letter would receive wide circulation within the Admiralty. The report is too long even to summarise here, and moreover extensive extracts from it have already been published.[4] On two points, however, the report is open to serious criticism. The first is Kelly's statement that the Petty Officers of the fleet 'failed deplorably, miserably'[5]—which was an unjustified libel on a loyal and efficient body of men. Several Captains in fact went out of their way to praise the conduct of their Petty Officers in their reports;[6] while other reports suggest that the real fault lay in the failure

[1] Field to Beatty 22nd and 28th Sept. Holograph with typed 'Brief Narrative of Cause of Naval Unrest'. Beatty papers.

[2] Adm. 1/8761–240/32. Also in RA GV K2330(3). This letter is misdated 17th *Sept.* in *Divine*, p. 221.

[3] Kelly to Field 22nd Oct. 1931. Adm. 178/89.

[4] See *Divine*, pp. 227–30. However confusion may result from the report being here given 'Sections' with Roman numbers. In fact it is divided into 64 paragraphs with consecutive Arabic numbers. Adm. 1/8761–240/32. Copy in RA GV K2330(3).

[5] C-in-C, Atlantic Fleet, report of 9th Nov. 1931, para. 39. Adm. 1/8761–240/32.

[6] The *Malaya* reported that 'the example set by Chief and Petty Officers and Leading Rates was magnificent'. In the *Nelson* the Petty Officers were sent around the mess

of the officers to make clear what was required of the POs. Indeed there were some cases of senior POs actually seeking orders from their officers and being rebuffed. The truth is that on 'Mutiny Day' (15th September) most officers remained sublimely confident until almost the last moment that their ships would sail. The second point on which Kelly's report may be criticised was described by the usually cool and temperate Murray as his 'extraordinary attack on the Admiralty organisation', which he considered 'totally irrelevant to the Invergordon incident';[1] for the C-in-C considered that 'a much larger admixture of Naval Officers in the Civilian Departments of the Admiralty, and in particular those of the Accountant-General of the Navy and the Director of Victualling, would lead to a more sympathetic attitude and to a closer understanding of the relative importance and urgency of matters connected with Personnel'.[2] Bearing in mind that naval officers rarely served for much over two years on end at the Admiralty it is difficult to understand how Kelly could have supposed that they could have mastered all the intricacies of the work of civil departments such as those he singled out for attack. But in other respects, such as his analysis of the causes of the mutiny, his conclusions regarding errors made by officers, notably Tomkinson, and his recommendations to put matters right in the future his report stands up well to scrutiny—even 40 and more years on. But the Admiralty, and especially Admiral Dreyer, viewed matters quite differently; and in 29 pages of somewhat intemperate comment Dreyer sought to place the blame chiefly on Tomkinson—and to exculpate the Board. He even asserted 'I have no hesitation in saying that if I had been in command of the ships at Ivergordon I should have taken action as above'—namely to prevent further meetings and agitation on Sunday 13th, and not to have ordered ships to sea for exercises on the 15th 'so depriving the agitators of initiative'.[3] Though Murray declined to go all the way with Dreyer, and rejected Kelly's placing of the responsibility on the government and Admiralty, he too was critical of Tomkinson's actions (or inaction) on 13th and 14th September.

Meanwhile Kelly had carried out the King's command to write to him personally 'as soon as I had been able to form a reasonable opinion

---

decks 'intensively', and soon afterwards the Commander reported 'ready for sea'. Rs of P Adm. 178/110.

[1] Minute of 1st Jan. 1932. Adm. 178/111.

[2] C-in-C, AF report para. 56. Adm. 1/8761–240/32.

[3] Minute of 9th Dec. 1931. Adm. 178/111.

as to the state of this fleet'; and he did so in his own hand. Here he repeated 'the complete unanimity of conviction that there appears to be in the minds of Officers and Men alike . . . that the Board of Admiralty—in accepting the cuts as originally promulgated—were directly responsible for the Mutiny', and that confidence 'will never be completely restored while the present Board . . . remains in Office'. He also told the King that he had 'written this and much more to Field . . . though at present he obviously holds the view that the Admiralty's yard-arm is clear'. He then outlined the main features of his official report, including the need to make 'drastic alterations in the present system of appointing and employing officers of Commander's rank and above'. Finally he hoped that the reconstituted Board would be headed by a First Lord 'of David Beatty's kidney: strong, fearless—and human'.[1]

When Monsell took over as First Lord on 9th November he inherited a sea of troubles such as can rarely if ever have beset the political head of the Navy—at any rate in peace time. Fortunately his experience of the service, combined with parliamentary skill, tact and patience were such that, after hearing his admission that 'The Navy realises that today we no longer occupy that very high opinion in the hearts of the British people that for centuries we have held', Parliament was prepared to accept his plea that its former position 'will be regained all the more quickly if the House of Commons and the country will leave the Navy alone, to deal with its own special interests'.[2]

Not least of Monsell's troubles must have been the very strained relations which developed between Field and Kelly because the former was extremely resentful of the criticisms of the Board's handling of the pay cuts and the mutiny made by the latter.[3] Field told Kelly that he had 'offered to resign' but had been told, presumably by Chamberlain, that 'it would be quixotic [and] neglecting my duty to do so'.[4] Kelly also sent his criticisms of the Board to Chatfield, the C-in-C, Mediterranean,[5] who did his best to smooth things over by telling Kelly how much he deplored 'such a rather strained ['very acute' deleted] feeling

[1] Kelly to George V 1st Nov. 1931. RA GV K2330(3).

[2] Parl. Deb., Commons, vol. 260, col. 182. The debate was on 23rd Nov. 1931 on an Adjournment Motion.

[3] Field to Kelly 27th Oct. 1931. Kelly papers, KEL/109, answering the criticisms in Kelly's letters of 22nd and 24th Oct.

[4] Same to same 30th Oct. 1931. *ibid.*

[5] Kelly to Chatfield 16th May 1932. Chatfield papers, CHT/2/2.

between you and Field'.[1] There is in fact a great deal of evidence of strained relations among the top Admirals at this time[2]—which is not altogether surprising. Early in 1932 Field, whose health had for a long time been indifferent, was evidently afflicted by a perforated stomach ulcer, no doubt brought on by worry; for he wrote to Chatfield that he had suffered 'an internal haemorrhage . . . [and was] down and out from loss of blood';[3] but a full year was to elapse between that collapse and Chatfield taking over as First Sea Lord—a change which certainly expedited the naval regeneration initiated by Kelly.

While these clashes were in progress at the very top of the Navy List the Board of Admiralty took action on the lines of the Kelly report to investigate and remedy the deficiencies and defects exposed by the mutiny, and enlarged upon in the many reports which had reached it from a wide variety of sources. The principal decisions were to form a Fleet Committee under the First Sea Lord which would handle the disposition of ships and the organisation of the fleet, and two ancillary bodies called the Personnel (Officers and Ratings) Committee and the Disciplinary and Welfare Committee, both under the Second Sea Lord, whose functions are indicated by their titles.[4] These latter threw off no less than nine sub-committees (lettered A to I) which were to report on the problems peculiar to officers and ratings of every branch, including their entry and training. We cannot here go into the lengthy deliberations of all those bodies and the detailed recommendations they made,[5] but a few of the more important results may be mentioned. Thus the Board took early action to reduce complements of officers—because the presence of too many officers tended to detract from the status and authority of the Petty Officers. They also ordered that 'changes of personnel were to cease immediately as far as possible'.[6] Everything possible was to be done to improve the standing and responsibilities of Divisional Officers and the training of Petty Officers

---

[1] Chatfield to Kelly 26th May 1932. *ibid.*

[2] In the Chatfield and Kelly papers as well as in the Admiralty's records.

[3] Field to Chatfield 17th Jan. 1932. Chatfield papers, CHT/2/2,

[4] Confidential Office Acquaint of 21st Oct. 1931. The Terms of Reference of the three main committees are in Board Memo. of same date. Adm. 167/86. Promulgated in CAFO. 2572/31.

[5] Adm. 116/2861, 2893, 2895, 2896 and 2897 contain the transcripts of the committee's meetings and their reports.

[6] Board Minute 2937 of 9th May 1932. Adm. 167/86. Sub-Committee F drew attention strongly to the fact that 47% of the *Royal Sovereign's* seamen had changed in $11\frac{1}{2}$ months and 56% of the *Rodney's* in 20 months.

and Leading Rates in 'initiative and power of command'.[1] As regards the welfare of the men and the representation of grievances it was recognised that the Welfare Conferences, which dated to 1919,[2] had proved irritatingly ineffective and the decision was taken to abolish them—as indeed Admiral Kelly had recommended. That measure could not, however, be instituted until the Admiralty had a substitute ready, and as the biennial Welfare Conference was due to take place in 1932 it went ahead as planned.[3] It had 111 representations to deal with.

The Admiralty then decided to replace the Welfare Conference with an 'Admiralty Review of Service Conditions' by which they hoped to show that grievances put forward through the proper channels would be dealt with promptly by the authority on whom responsibility for the discipline, welfare and morale of the fleet rested. The Admiralty order instituting the reviews stated that they 'would be held from time to time', and that they contemplated the first one taking place 'about the end of 1935'.[4] Because of the deteriorating international situation that was the only Review of Service Conditions ever held.[5] More successful administrative innovations were the institution in the Admiralty of a Director of Personal Services as the Board's adviser on all matters affecting the men's welfare and service conditions, and the amendment of King's Regulations to make Divisional Officers the persons to whom grievances and complaints should initially be represented. Measures were also taken to make Petty Officers more aware of the need to keep themselves informed about 'complaints or dissatisfaction among the men', and of their responsibility for 'preserving order and regularity wherever the crew . . . may be employed'[6]—which doubtless was a reflection of Kelly's criticism of the Petty Officers.

No matter how much substance there may have been in the Kelly report, and how necessary or effective the measures recommended by the pyramid of committees set up in the Admiralty may have been, after wading through the avalanche of paper produced by the Invergordon mutiny one returns to an indisputable fact—namely that Kelly reported, without doubt correctly, that 'When ships of the Atlantic

---

[1] Board Minute 2970 of 30th June 1932. Adm. 167/86.   [2] See vol. I, p. 119.

[3] See *Brassey's Naval Annual*, 1937 'From Petitions to Reviews' by H. P. (Commander Harry Pursey), p. 109.

[4] AWO(N. 2500) of 23rd Sept. 1932. An edited version is given in *Brassey's Naval Annual*, 1933, p. 23.

[5] *Brassey's Naval Annual*, 1937, pp. 109–10.   [6] Adm. 178/89.

Fleet returned to Home Ports in July 1931 . . . at the end of the summer cruise I have every reason to believe that the state of discipline was excellent, and that . . . the relations between Officers and Men appear to have been entirely satisfactory';[1] and as early as 24th September of that year (nine days after the mutiny) Sir Clive Wigram reported to the King that 'Sir Austen Chamberlain . . . wished me to let Your Majesty know that all was now well in the Navy'.[2] Though the latter statement was somewhat premature it remains beyond dispute that the cause of the mutiny was the severity of the pay cuts as first announced and the inept manner in which the Admiralty presented them to the fleet.

Perhaps the most difficult issue which Monsell's Board had to face revolved around the future of the naval members who had been in office at the time of Invergordon, and of the unfortunate Tomkinson. The Sea Lords had met on 1st January to consider the future of the latter. Taking account of Kelly's view of his conduct they finally approved a letter stating that Their Lordships were 'unable to relieve you of responsibility for a serious error of judgement in omitting to take decided action on 13th and 14th September . . .'[3] Though Tomkinson had been re-appointed in command of the Battle Cruiser Squadron on promotion to Vice-Admiral in February he was now told that he was to be relieved in August—despite the fact that he had been 'definitely offered the appointment for a period of two years'.[4]

Tomkinson protested at once about being censured for action which had gained him the Admiralty's commendation at the time when he had first reported on the trouble in the fleet,[5] and while still in the West Indies he considered applying for a Court Martial or for an inquiry to be held into his actions.[6] But after returning to England in

[1] Kelly report para. 5. Adm. 1/8761-240/32. Copies in Royal Archives and Kelly papers.

[2] Wigram to George V 24th Sept. 1931. RA GV K2330(3)/13.

[3] AL to Tomkinson of 2nd Feb. 1932. *ibid.* Copies in Keyes papers (7/37) and Captain A. R. Henderson papers (File 8), Churchill College. Henderson had been Tomkinson's secretary, and his papers were deposited by his daughter Mrs. Anthea Trenchard in 1972, with her own very interesting recollections of her father's service and his part in the Invergordon affair. Another copy, and much interesting correspondence on the subject, is in the Tomkinson papers, also deposited at Churchill College.

[4] Telegram to Admy. from Trinidad of 17th Feb. 1932. Adm. 178/111.

[5] Namely the Admiralty message of 15th Sept. See p. 106.

[6] Tomkinson to Admiralty, letter of 13th March 1932. Copy in Tomkinson papers.

mid-March he declared with dignity that he would take no such steps lest they should cause 'further injury to the Navy in the eyes of the public'.[1] It is justifiable here to record that when W. M. James relieved Tomkinson in command of the Battle Cruiser Squadron, an appointment which he says 'was entirely due to Kelly', he found the condition of the flagship, the *Hood*, far from satisfactory. 'I never met a more unhappy party', writes James; 'Tomkinson had been told he would be relieved. He and his Flag Captain Patterson were at daggers drawn, and the Commander, McCrum, had lost all interest through being "hunted" by Tomkinson, whose habit it was to find fault with everything'. Tomkinson had apparently recommended that, because of her part in the mutiny, the *Hood* should be paid off; but James says he got that proposal cancelled and, with a first class new Flag Captain (T. H. Binney), the morale of the ship was quickly restored.[2]

Nearly a year after Tomkinson had decided not to seek any redress for himself he was told that he would not be employed again. He then changed his mind and asked for 'a thorough and impartial inquiry'.[3] This second change of mind was doubtless influenced by Admiral Keyes, who was greatly incensed by the treatment meted out to his former Chief of Staff.[4] But so much time had elapsed since the events about which Tomkinson wanted an inquiry, and witnesses had become so widely scattered, that it would certainly have proved very difficult to meet his request—even if the Admiralty had been prepared to countenance it. As it was they sent a very carefully worded reply rejecting his request and claimed that 'the Board is the final authority in such matters'.[5] In July 1934—nearly three years after the mutiny—Keyes was still resolved to take up the cudgels on Tomkinson's behalf before he was placed on half-pay after two years without an appointment. Accordingly he sent strongly-worded letters to Monsell[6] and, having become an MP, he also reopened the matter in the House of Commons; but his speech contained so many inaccuracies and glosses that Monsell had little difficulty in rebutting his allegations.[7]

[1] Letter of 2nd May 1932. Adm. 178/111.
[2] Letter to the author of 15th May 1964.
[3] Tomkinson to Admiralty, letter of 14th March 1933. Copy in Tomkinson papers.
[4] Evidence in Keyes and Tomkinson papers.
[5] Admiralty to Tomkinson, letter of 27th March 1933. *ibid.*
[6] Keyes to Monsell, letters of 4th and 11th July 1934. Copies in Tomkinson papers.
[7] Parl. Deb., Commons, vol. 292, cols. 2557-65. The copy of Hansard in the Keyes papers is heavily amended in an unknown hand. In replying to Keyes Monsell was able to quote a letter in which Keyes had written to him that 'after my talk with

The Admiralty's review of the handling of the mutiny in each individual ship ended with the decision that seven Captains should be relieved of their commands. These were the Captains of the four capital ships which had refused to sail—*Valiant, Nelson, Hood* and *Rodney*—and three of the four cruisers whose companies had in varying degree refused duty—*Norfolk, York* and *Adventure*. The only Captain of one of the eight big ships present when the mutiny started at 8.0 a.m. on Tuesday 15th September who was not relieved was A. J. Power of the *Dorsetshire*, Astley-Rushton's flagship; and he rose to be an Admiral of the Fleet after giving very distinguished service in World War II. It is fair to mention that when war came all the officers who had suffered through their involvement in the Invergordon mutiny and were still available returned to the service of their country in some capacity—including Tomkinson.

Five days after the decision on Tomkinson was taken Field again met the Elder Naval Statesmen to consider the future of the junior Sea Lords and whether Kelly's command should be extended beyond the year originally promised him. The opinion of the meeting was unanimous on many points—namely that Kelly's appointment should be extended, that Tomkinson should be relieved, that Fuller should be given no further appointment on completion of his time as Second Sea Lord, and that Dreyer should not become C-in-C, Atlantic Fleet,[1] which decision barred the road to his becoming First Sea Lord.

Tomkinson I am content, as he is, to leave his future in the hands of Chatfield and your new Board'. *ibid*. Col. 2570. When Tomkinson died in 1971 at the age of 93 the obituary in *The Times* produced a flood of letters from Commander Pursey, Mrs. Trenchard, 2nd Lord Keyes and this author (correcting Wincott). Expectedly the question of Tomkinson's culpability remained undecided. See *The Times* Oct. 9th–28th 1971.

[1] Meeting of 6th Jan. 1932. Adm. 178/129. Dreyer actually became C-in-C, China 1933–35 and fully lived up to his reputation (the author was serving in that fleet at the time). It is only fair to record that he made something of a come-back in World War II. After a period in the hazardous job of Commodore of Convoys Admiral Pound, the First Sea Lord, recalled him to the Admiralty, where he did excellent work in training Merchant Navy crews to deal with air attacks, and in getting armaments for their ships. However in July 1942 Pound made the extraordinary mis-judgement of appointing him Chief of Naval Air Services—a subject about which he had no knowledge or experience. When this nearly caused a mutiny among Fleet Air Arm Officers and he was relieved Dreyer returned to his previous form, and the First Sea Lord's papers of the period are full of lengthy letters of self-justification to Pound (now in Adm. 205/12). Dreyer even asked to be allowed to state his case to Churchill. One would very much like to know what his reaction would have been if that request had been granted.

Looking back at the whole unhappy story today, and bearing in mind that the cloud produced by Hitler's megalomania was in 1932 no bigger than a man's hand, it does seem that the Monsell-Chatfield Board of 1933–36 handled these very tricky issues with sensibility and fairness. After all their primary task was to restore the standing of the service for which they were responsible in the public eye; and that they certainly did accomplish—in a remarkably short time. To fulfill that purpose it was probably inevitable that some officers, as with the 24 discharged men, should have received less than completely just treatment.

The attitude of the Board, on which Field and Dreyer continued to serve until January 1933, towards a possible recrudescence of 'mass indiscipline' is a good deal less commendable than the longer term policy of the Monsell-Chatfield régime. In April 1932 a letter was sent to all Commanding Officers telling them that they were 'expected to put down any further disturbances . . . with a strong hand'.[1] In the following August the Admiralty's 'Notes on Dealing with Insubordination' were widely distributed. One passage reads 'Should there be any evidence of general discontent which might develop into massed disobedience, or if such disobedience occurs, the *action of all officers must be such as to indicate unmistakably that they intend to retain or regain control and to uphold discipline*' (italics as printed). The letter continued by emphasising that although 'prompt action must be taken', it should at the same time be made clear to the men that grievances will be investigated, and 'if found genuine' [? by whom] remedied with as little delay as possible. Eight 'broad principles' were laid down for application 'when massed disobedience is suspected or occurs'—some of which would certainly not have proved easy to put into practice. The final principle dealt with the use of force, which, not very helpfully, the Admiralty declared 'must depend on circumstances'. However 'shooting to kill should', it concluded, 'only be resorted to as a last extremity'; and it is good to record that since those days it has never come near to being employed in the Navy.[2]

If good can ever be said to have been the produce of evil the Invergordon mutiny did make the Admiralty far more conscious of the needs and outlook of the lower deck; and that the Board could not win, let alone retain, the confidence of the men if it remained an aloof,

[1] Board Minute 2834 of 11th April 1932.
[2] AL NL 1201/32 of 12th Aug. 1932. Though classified 'Secret' 700 copies were made. Adm. 178/133.

Olympian body. Doubtless this explains the frequent visits paid later to ships and naval establishments by Monsell, Chatfield and their colleagues on the Board—and in uniform instead of in frock coats and top hats.[1] As to the officers of the fleet, the best of them, of which there were many, certainly worked hard to bridge the gulf which had existed between the wardroom and the mess decks; and the prolonged and vital struggle for control of the seas and oceans of the world between 1939 and 1945 amply demonstrates the degree of success achieved. The victory at sea in World War II also confirms the view that the lamentable and tragic events of September 1931 in only nine ships of the Royal Navy,[2] and in some of them for only two hours of the four days of unrest and trouble at Invergordon, should never have occurred.

To end on a more congenial note, in the middle of 1936 the King proposed that Admiral Kelly should be specially promoted to Admiral of the Fleet. The Chancellor of the Exchequer did not demur, and the appointment was made by Order-in-Council on 3rd July. As however Kelly died on the following 4th November he did not enjoy his new rank and status for long.[3]

APPENDIX

The Norfolk*'s* '*Petition*'[4]

'We the loyal subjects of His Majesty the King do hereby represent to My Lords Commissioners of the Admiralty our representations to implore them to amend the drastic cuts in pay that have been inflicted upon the lowest paid man [sic] of the lower deck.

'It is evident to all concerned that this cut is the forerunner of tragedy, misery and immorality amongst the families of the lower deck, and unless we can be guaranteed a written agreement from Admiralty confirmed by parliament stating that our pay will be revised

---

[1] See Lord Chatfield, *It Might Happen Again* (Heinemann, 1947), ch. v regarding his efforts as First Sea Lord to bring the Board of Admiralty closer to the men of the fleet, and on the wearing of uniform by the Board when making official visits.

[2] The figure nine includes the *Delhi*. Only eight ships at Invergordon were affected.

[3] Adm. 1/9043-136/36.

[4] Enclosure No. 3 to *Norfolk*'s R of P of 18th Sept. 1931. Adm. 178/110.

we are still to remain as one unit, refusing to serve under the new rate of pay.

'Men are quite willing to accept a cut which they, the men consider in reason.'

The above was placed in the cabin of one of *Norfolk*'s Divisional Officers on Tuesday 15th September.

CHAPTER V

The Failure of the Search
for Disarmament

1932-1933

———◆———

PREPARATIONS FOR the General Disarmament Conference continued throughout 1931, with the debate in London centering on the question of the basis on which Budgetary Limitation and limitation of 'Naval Effectives' should be calculated. The Board of Admiralty was determined that 'limitation of personnel must not impose additional limitation to that already effected by limitation of tonnage', wanted the same principle applied to Budgetary Limitation[1], and sought the agreement of the other Service Departments and of the Colonial, Dominions and India Offices to these principles.[2] The Admiralty next recapitulated their long-held view that limitation should be by size and tonnage, as in the Washington and London treaties, and not by any new-fangled and complicated devices such as the two referred to above; and they sought the views of Dominion and Colonial governments on these matters—presumably hoping for their support.[3]

The General Disarmament Conference opened at Geneva on 2nd February 1932. In the previous May Arthur Henderson had agreed to accept the chairmanship—despite the fact that MacDonald, who was never on very good terms with his Foreign Secretary, had preferred Smuts.[4] The chief item on the agenda was consideration of the draft convention produced by the League's Preparatory Commission.

[1] Adm. 116/3616.   [2] Letter of 20th Aug. 1931. *ibid.*

[3] Memo. by A. V. Alexander of 1st July 1931. *ibid.* See also his memo. RA1(3), reprinted as CP. 258(31) of 30th Sept. 1931.

[4] See David Carlton, *MacDonald versus Henderson* (Macmillan, 1970) for a study of the relations between these two.

Though the auguries for the conference were far from good, especially with regard to bridging the wide gulf between French determination to uphold the Versailles Treaty and German determination to achieve equality in armaments, at the opening meeting Henderson declared that he refused 'even to contemplate the possibility of failure'. In London the issues at stake were placed in the hands of a Disarmament Committee set up on 5th March 1931 on which all three political parties agreed to serve; and at the end of July at its tenth and final meeting that body approved the Resolutions which the British delegation should place before the Geneva Conference.[1]

In August the text of the Resolution was telegraphed to the Dominions, who were told that, while the British government adhered to the principle that armaments should be reduced 'to the lowest point consistent with national safety', they also intended to emphasise the reductions already made by Britain—which of course had chiefly affected the navy—and to insist that any further reductions 'must be part of an international agreement'. Contrary to the view expressed by the Admiralty Budgetary Limitation was named as a possible line of approach, and 'the specific character of the armaments'—a reference to the distinction between 'offensive' and 'defensive' weapons—was to be taken into account. The British delegates were also to 'reaffirm our desire to see conscription abolished', a proposal which was bound to arouse French antagonism. If, as was likely, this aim proved unacceptable the Dominions were told that other methods must be found 'for the limitation of effective strength of land and air personnel'.[2] As regards naval disarmament British policy was not to introduce any new initiative but to concentrate on maintaining intact the Washington and London treaties, extending the provisions of the latter to France and Italy, and negotiating the strength to be allowed to other countries on the basis of the figures agreed between the five principal naval powers. In the opening stages of the conference it appeared to the British delegates that the Americans would take a similar line.[3]

In February 1932 Admiral Field set out in concise form the limitations in size and armament which the Admiralty was prepared to accept after the expiration of the London Treaty. Capital ships could, he wrote, come down to 25,000 tons if the main armament was limited

---

[1] CP. 195(31) of 27th July 1931. The deliberations of the Three Party Committee are in the DPC. Series. Cab. 21/344.

[2] Circular Telegram no. 99 of 10th Aug. 1931. Cab. 21/346.

[3] Paper entitled 'Naval Disarmament' of 11th Jan. 1933. Adm. 116/2827.

to 12-inch guns, but proportionately higher displacements would be necessary if the guns were larger. Aircraft carriers could be limited to 22,000 tons, and we were prepared to reduce the Washington total of 135,000 tons for that class of ship to 110,000. Cruisers armed with 6.1-inch or smaller guns could be limited to 7,000 or at most 8,000 tons, and the number of ships in that category could be restricted. The First Sea Lord also proposed that we should firmly declare that we needed a total of 70 cruisers (60 under the age limit of 16 years)—so getting rid of the figure of 50 enshrined in the London Treaty.[1]

The chief naval delegate nominated for the Geneva Conference was Admiral A. D. P. R. Pound who, having served as ACNS 1927–29 and being about to return to the Board as Second Sea Lord, had the whole previous history of naval limitation at his finger tips. His earliest report indicated that the Italians favoured limitation in the size of 6-inch cruisers;[2] but at about the same time Craigie of the Foreign Office reported that Senator Swanson, the American delegate who, though nearly 71 years old, was to be chosen by President Roosevelt to become Secretary of the Navy in 1933, was strongly opposed to any reduction in the size or armament of capital ships at this conference. Swanson also told Craigie 'very confidentially' that future American cruisers were more likely to be 6-inch than 8-inch ships, with displacement nearer to 8,000 than 10,000 tons—a change of policy of which the Admiralty was in fact well aware. Swanson was prepared to accept the reduction of total carrier tonnage proposed by the Admiralty.[3]

As was anticipated one of the most serious stumbling blocks at this stage arose over the French attitude about submarines. They were only prepared to accept a maximum tonnage of 1,200, which was far higher than the Admiralty wanted, and Pound reported that our proposal to abolish them altogether 'will not meet with much support'.[4] In truth the Admiralty, while constantly putting forward this drastic idea, had never expected it to prove acceptable by the other powers—especially France.

In June 1932 that naval *enfant terrible* Admiral Richmond proposed in a letter to *The Times* that the abolition of the 'locomotive torpedo' would achieve vast savings;[5] but that idea attracted little support—

---

[1] Memo. by Field of 11th Feb. 1932. Adm. 116/3617.
[2] Record of Pound-Captain Maroni conversation 25th Feb. 1932. *ibid.*
[3] Report of Craigie-Swanson conversation on 28th Feb. 1932. *ibid.*
[4] Pound to Admiralty 22nd Feb. and Admiralty to Pound 2nd April 1932. *ibid.*
[5] *The Times* 18th June 1932.

chiefly on the grounds that it was impossible to distinguish between such weapons and fixed or floating mines, whose purpose was much the same. In that same month the abolition of air bombing was raised, which of course affected the design and employment of naval aircraft.[1] This proposal gave the Air Ministry an opportunity to propose 'the drastic reduction and limitation of the aircraft carrying capacity of fleets'[2]—an overt attack on the Fleet Air Arm which was bound to re-open the long-standing feud between the two departments over naval aviation. It produced later the statement from the Admiralty that 'Aircraft are essential for the efficiency of the British fleet', and that its minimum needs were 210 aircraft and 60,000 tons of carriers.[3] The Japanese, with some logic, refused to accept abolition of bombing unless aircraft carriers were also abolished.[4]

The months of February to June 1932 marked the first phase of what was to prove a very prolonged conference, and during that period the French put forward their plan. As had been expected in London it comprised an endeavour to enhance French security by increasing the power of the League, including the provision of international forces for use by it against an aggressor. But the real difficulty lay of course in arriving at an agreed definition of an aggressor. Though the French plan was shelved discussion on security remained in the forefront of the conference's deliberations, and the idea of achieving a measure of security through strengthening the power of defence and weakening that of attack gained some support. This gave rise to what became known as the 'qualitative' and 'quantitative' principles of disarmament. Under the former heading certain types of weapon would be prohibited absolutely and others severely restricted in size or other characteristics; while under the latter heading the aim would be to reduce the quantity of those types of weapons which were to be allowed for defensive purposes. On 22nd April 1932 the General Commission of the Conference adopted a Resolution that 'in seeking to apply the principle of qualitative disarmament . . . the range of land, sea and air armaments should be examined by the competent special commissions', which bodies were to be charged with the intractable, even impossible task of deciding which weapons were the most 'specifically offensive or those most efficacious against national defence, or most threatening to civilians'. The attempt to comply with this Resolution involved the

[1] Adm. 116/3618. [2] Air Ministry memo. of 12th Sept. 1932. *ibid.*
[3] Memo. by Chatfield of 31st March 1933. DC(M)(32)42. Copy in *ibid.*
[4] DC(O)151 of 8th June 1933. Copy in *ibid.*

special commissions in protracted and unprofitable arguments, during which each country tried to prove that the weapons they favoured were defensive and those they disliked were offensive.[1]

While these negotiations were in progress Heinrich Brüning's Centrist government, which had taken office in Germany in March 1930 at the height of the economic crisis, found its position becoming steadily weakened by the nefarious activities of the right wing parties and the failure to gain any appreciable concessions at Geneva on the issue of equality in armaments. In May 1932 the Brüning government fell, and he was replaced as Chancellor first by the wily Franz von Papen, and, in November, by General Kurt von Schleicher—who was to be a victim of the Nazi purge of 30th June 1934.[2]

Meanwhile by June 1932 the British government realised that, if the conference was to be saved, a new initiative was essential. After prolonged deliberation it was agreed that this should take the form of supporting the total abolition of naval and military aircraft. The Admiralty was prepared to support this proposal—provided that civil aviation was brought under some form of international control, because of the ease with which civil aircraft could be converted to military use. However it was agreed that MacDonald and Sir John Simon, the Foreign Secretary, should sound the French government on the matter when they passed through Paris on their way to Geneva. The French were, however, prepared to go no further than the prohibition of bombardment of civilian targets from the air—and even that was to be made dependent on a satisfactory system of international control.

But it was not only in Paris and Geneva that the possible abolition of military aircraft produced friction. We saw earlier how, when limitation of aircraft numbers came up for discussion, the Air Ministry used the proposal as a weapon with which to attack the Admiralty's programme to increase the Fleet Air Arm. In 1932 Monsell, the First Lord, complained to Baldwin that Lord Londonderry, the Secretary of State for Air, wanted 'to make the world safe for bombers', and that he 'trembled to think of the consequences'.[3] Plainly the old Admiralty-

---

[1] The report of the Naval Commission is in League of Nations Document D. 121 of 28th May 1932.

[2] For an admirable study of this critical period in German politics, which culminated in Hitler's accession to power at the end of January 1933, see Joachim C. Fest, *Hitler* (Weidenfeld and Nicolson, Eng. Trans., 1974), Book IV.

[3] Monsell to Baldwin 9th May 1932. Baldwin papers, vol. 118.

Air Ministry feud over naval aviation, which Hankey had long been trying to damp down, was likely to break out again at any moment.

While the departmental discussions on disarmament were in progress in London in the spring of 1932 the question of limiting the displacement of individual warships to the 10,000 tons to which Germany was restricted by the Versailles Treaty was considered unofficially as a possible step towards granting Germany a measure of 'equality'.[1] Norman Davis, an American delegate to the Geneva Conference, who was in London at the time, evidently communicated the reports on this matter which had reached him to Washington. The result, according to British contemporary records, was that the Americans 'determined to forestall us with proposals of their own'.[2] Though no confirmation of such a purpose exists in the American records on 22nd June Hugh Gibson, the chief American delegate, placed President Hoover's proposals before the General Commission of the conference.[3] After enunciating five principles which 'should be our guide' he made the sweeping proposal that 'the arms of the world should be reduced by nearly one third'. As regards land forces 'all tanks, all chemical warfare and all large mobile guns' were to be abolished, and 'the strength of all land armies over and above the so-called police component' should be reduced to one third. As Germany's 65 million people were allowed 100,000 soldiers by the Versailles Treaty he proposed that all nations should accept 'a basic police component of soldiers proportionate to the average which was thus allowed Germany . . .' Turning to air forces Hoover proposed, *tout court*, that 'all bombing planes be abolished'. The naval proposals, with which we here are primarily concerned, were far more complicated. The number and tonnage of battleships were both to be reduced by one third, and those of aircraft carriers by one fourth. The treaty tonnage of submarines was to be reduced by one third and no nation allowed more than 35,000 tons of such vessels. As Britain, the USA and Japan had accepted capital ship, carrier, cruiser, destroyer and submarine limitations under the Washington and London treaties Hoover proposed that French and Italian strength in cruisers and destroyers, which had of course been the chief bone of contention at the 1930 conference and afterwards, 'should be

---

[1] See p. 56 regarding Admiral Richmond's advocacy of smaller capital ships in 1929.

[2] Adm. 116/2827 of 11th Jan. 1933.

[3] Copy in GB. 438–2, Serial 1521–w of 23rd June 1932. See also Simon's telegram no. 257 of 22nd June 1932 to FO. Copy in Adm. 116/2827.

calculated as though they had joined in the Treaty of London on a basis approximating the so-called accord of March 1st 1931'[1]—which of course the two countries had not ratified. Hoover's description of these proposals as 'simple and direct' was perhaps a little naïve, but Gibson supported them enthusiastically and urged that the other powers should make sacrifices comparable to those America was prepared to make—which he summed up as scrapping 300,000 tons of warships and foregoing the right to build a further 50,000 tons.

In London the Hoover proposals aroused profound disquiet. Not only did they take no account of Britain's special needs, but they raised 'in an acute form' the very issue which had brought about the breakdown at Geneva in 1927—namely American preference for limitation by numbers of ships as against British preference for limitation by size.[2] Yet the British delegates were well aware that 'we could not simply return a blank negative' to the President's proposals.[3] So they set about framing 'constructive suggestions' which, while rejecting much that had been proposed in the American plan, 'would meet our own requirements'. Thus were born the proposals placed by Simon before the conference on 7th July. The most important measures were to reduce battleship displacement at least to 25,000 tons, and to 22,000 tons if agreement to abolish the 8-inch cruiser could be achieved; to limit cruisers to 7,000 tons, prohibit the construction of submarines, and accept 'an attendant reduction of one third in destroyer tonnage'.[4] Obviously there was a great deal in those proposals to which the General Board and the US Navy would object very strongly. Yet it was plainly desirable that before the conference adjourned for the summer recess towards the end of July it should 'at least give the appearance of some measure of accomplishment'. In consequence a somewhat hectic round of discussions took place with the object of producing a Resolution setting out the points on which agreement had been reached and 'principles to guide the work of the future'. The result was made public on 23rd July.[5] The chief points were that 'a substantial reduction of world armaments should be effected', and should be applied to land, sea and air forces alike. Secondly that 'the

[1] Set out in Cmd. 3812 of 1931. But agreement between France and Italy on the lines set out in that document had broken down when it came to drafting the actual accord.

[2] The Naval Staff's detailed critique of the American proposals is in Plans Division Memo. of 23rd June 1932. Adm. 116/2827.

[3] *ibid.*   [4] Cmd. 4122 of 1932.

[5] League of Nations paper, Official Number Conf. D. 136.

primary objective shall be to reduce the means of attack', including 'absolute prohibition of air attack against civil population'. Thirdly, as regards land armaments, the method of limitation was accepted, and 'chemical, bacteriological and incendiary warfare' was to be 'absolutely prohibited'. The second part of the Resolution merely invited the signatories of the Washington and London treaties to confer together regarding the Hoover proposals, and to report to the General Commission 'as to the further measures of naval reduction which might be feasible'. The various delegations then departed from Geneva, but in September Allen Dulles and Admiral A. J. Hepburn of the American delegation came to London to confer with their British counterparts from the Foreign Office and Admiralty—R. L. Craigie and Admiral R. M. Bellairs.

The British Cabinet tried to stimulate progress towards agreement with the Americans by instructing the defence departments 'to examine and advise as to the Resolutions of the Disarmament Conference in a constructive spirit . . .'; and that 'the Admiralty should prepare a full statement of the British attitude towards the Hoover proposals and Naval Disarmament generally'.[1] The British record of the ensuing Anglo-American conversations states that 'it was soon seen that the object of the United States representatives was to do their best to work with us', and that they considered publication of the Hoover proposals 'without previous consultation with us was a mistake'.[2] A position was soon reached where the gap between the British proposals and Hoover's had, in respect of most classes of ship, been 'very considerably narrowed', and both sides' negotiators reported accordingly to their superiors. While the Americans showed greater flexibility than in 1930 over reducing the size and gun calibre of capital ships the British forebore to press the point that, if an agreement extending beyond 1936 was envisaged, they would have to increase cruiser and destroyer construction above the London Treaty figures. Both parties agreed that the fundamental difficulty lay in the Franco-Italian impasse, and that before cruiser and destroyer totals could be realistically discussed it was essential to bring those two nations into accord—as indeed had been contemplated in the Hoover proposals.[3] Meanwhile on 16th September, shortly before the start of the Anglo-American conversa-

---

[1] Cabinet meeting of 4th Aug. 1932. Quoted in Monsell's memo. of 24th Aug. Adm. 116/2827.

[2] Adm. 116/2827.

[3] The American record of the conversations is in USNA, RG. 80, File A 19, Box 97.

tions the Germans announced their withdrawal from the Disarmament Conference on the grounds that no progress had been made towards meeting their claim to equality.

Despite this serious setback the British and Americans persevered. While Davis, Hepburn and Dulles travelled assiduously between Paris, Rome and Geneva the British delegates got into touch with the Italian and French representatives. But neither party succeeded in bringing the two recalcitrants closer to agreement; nor did a new French plan, put forward by Joseph Paul-Boncour, now Prime Minister, have significantly greater appeal to the British than the many earlier plans to achieve greater security for that country. On the naval side the French proposed that the strengths published by each nation in the League's *Armaments Year Book* for 1932 should be accepted as the basis on which a percentage reduction should be made—which certainly appeared to be an attractively logical piece of reasoning.

On 17th November Simon produced the British reaction to the German demand for equality of rights ('Gleichberichtigung'). On the naval side the general idea was that she should be allowed to possess ships of those types permitted to other nations, but that any new construction should not increase the total tonnage in any category to which she was already restricted.[1] Plainly there was no chance of this echo of Versailles proving acceptable to the increasingly vocal—and violent—nationalist elements in that country. None the less conversations about ways and means of bringing Germany back to the conference table were put in hand, and on 11th December a formula was produced granting Germany equality of rights in a system providing (so it was hoped) security for France. The five nations concerned (Britain, USA, France, Italy and Germany) declared their intention to produce forthwith a Convention effecting a substantial reduction of armaments immediately, with provision for further reductions in the future. Despite Norman Davis's urging that the Convention should be produced by Christmas this proved impossible; so the naval powers reverted yet again to the attempt to bring France and Italy within the scope of the London Treaty.

Next the Japanese delegation chose this inopportune moment to produce their own plan for naval disarmament.[2] Its broad purpose

[1] Cmd. 4189 *Declaration of the Policy of His Majesty's Government in the United Kingdom on Disarmament in Connexion with Germany's claim to Equality of Rights* (1932).
[2] League of Nations Document **D. 150.**

was all too plain—to increase her own relative power and to alter the existing ratios in her favour. But as the Japanese included the abolition of aircraft carriers—surely in full awareness of the importance Britain and the USA attached to that class of ship—they gave the Air Ministry an opening to attack the Fleet Air Arm again, by proposing that aircraft carrier tonnage should be reduced 'to the lowest possible limit'.

Looking back today at the prolonged and fruitless deliberations of 1932 it is of course plain that all the naval powers sought to gain advantages for themselves and to maintain what they regarded as their own special needs. In Germany the Nazis read the situation accurately in discounting the possibility of any really effective agreement being reached. Moreover they were able to profit from the discord between the naval powers to take what in any case they were determined to have—namely such weapons as *they* deemed necessary. Certainly MacDonald did not exaggerate when, towards the end of the year, he told Baldwin that 'There is no doubt a great deterioration in the disarmament position . . .'[1] As regards the British plans and proposals, though the particular problems posed by the need to defend a world-wide trade must surely be admitted, in other nations' eyes it seemed that they were as insistent as everyone else on furthering their own interests; and on a more parochial level their proposals also now seem to make it plain how both the Admiralty and Air Ministry could and did seize every opportunity to gain an advantage at each other's expense.[2]

As regards the proposal to abolish air bombardment, and possibly all bomber aircraft, which at one time appeared the most promising move at Geneva, there was in truth no more likelihood of it being accepted than the abolition of submarines—indeed probably less, since whereas civil aircraft could be converted to military use quite easily surface warships could hardly be turned into submarines. The pity of it was that the politicians allowed the possibility of air bombardment to produce what Hankey aptly described as 'a fear complex' in the democracies; and such a complex is not the ideal psychological equipment wherewith to withstand the purposes of utterly ruthless dictators. Furthermore Baldwin himself undoubtedly encouraged that

[1] MacDonald to Baldwin 3rd Dec. 1932. Baldwin papers, vol. 118.

[2] Sir Edward (later Lord) Bridges who was serving in the Treasury at the time and became Secretary of the Cabinet in succession to Hankey in 1938 expressed this opinion to the author. Interview 15th Aug. 1968.

complex by the lugubrious forecast he made at this time in Parliament that 'the bomber will always get through'.[1]

With the Disarmament Conference bogged down we will turn to the first and tentative British steps towards rearmament in the naval field. Japanese aggression in Manchuria in September 1931 and at Shanghai just before the Disarmament Conference opened had made it abundantly plain that the League of Nations was incapable of deterring a determined aggressor, that the British Navy was far too weak to oppose Japan in that remote theatre—especially when trouble was looming ahead with Italy in the Mediterranean—and that no effective help could be looked for from the USA. In such circumstances rearmament up to the limits allowed by the London Treaty, and perhaps invocation of the 'Escalator Clause' incorporated in it[2] plainly had to be considered by the Naval Staff. Furthermore abolition of the 'Ten Year Rule' was obviously the first step which had to be taken to meet the new situation produced by German determination to rearm and Italian and Japanese expansionist policies. It was the influential Hankey, backed by the Admiralty, who first went into action with that object in view; and he had behind him the Cabinet decision of 15th July 1931 that the rule should be 'thoroughly examined in the light of developments in 1932'.[3] He had actually tried to get the issue opened early in 1931 by urging MacDonald that the rule should be re-examined; but, with the Disarmament Conference about to resume its efforts, the Prime Minister had declined to make any move in that direction.[4] In March 1932, by which time the stalemate at Geneva was plain, the Cabinet took the Chiefs of Staff's and CID's papers recommending that the rule should be cancelled.[5] Though the COSs pointed out that Hong

---

[1] Parl. Deb., Commons, vol. 270, cols. 630–8. Speech of 10th Nov. 1932.

[2] Article 21 specifically permitted the signatories 'to make a proportionate increase in the category or categories specified' if 'the requirements of national security' of one signatory 'are *in the opinion of that party* (italics supplied) materially affected by new construction of any Power other than those who have joined in Part III of this Treaty'—that is to say the limitation clauses. Italy and Germany were of course not parties to the Treaty.

[3] 254th CID Meeting of 7th Dec. 1931. Cab. 2/5.

[4] Memo. by Hankey of 9th Jan. 1931 and reply by Sir Geoffrey Fry (Private Secretary) of 28th. Cab. 63/44.

[5] Cabinet 19(32) of 23rd March 1932. Cab. 23/70. The papers before the Cabinet were the COSs' Annual Review of 23rd Feb. 1932, circulated as CID. 1082B, a note by the Treasury CP. 105(32) circulated at the Chancellor's request, and the draft minutes of the 255th CID meeting held on 22nd March. There is no doubt that the CID then

Kong was virtually defenceless and Singapore little better, and that the warships sent to Shanghai were hostages to the greatly superior Japanese Fleet, the Treasury argued that 'the fact is that in present circumstances we are no more in a position financially and economically to engage in a major war in the Far East than we are militarily'. The Ten Year Rule they described as 'an essay in prophecy', and 'no more than a working hypothesis intended to relieve the COSs from the responsibility of preparing for contingencies which the Government believe to be either remote or *beyond the financial capacity of the country to provide against*' (italics in original). 'What we need above all', the Treasury concluded, 'is a period of recuperation, diminishing taxes, increased trade and employment . . . It is not surprising if our people are anxious to avoid heavy expenditure on armaments; and that such is the attitude of the nation is undoubted'.[1] Obviously it was going to be no easy matter to get the rule rescinded.

At the same Cabinet the reports prepared by departments for use by the COSs in preparing their Annual Review for 1933 were considered, and the decision was taken that they should be referred, somewhat inappropriately, to the Ministerial Disarmament Committee—the body which had originally been set up under Henderson in February 1931 to prepare the British proposals for the General Disarmament Conference.[2] The Cabinet Conclusion recorded that 'in considering the Reports, the [Ministerial Disarmament] Committee *could assume* [italics supplied] the abandonment of the assumptions governing the estimates of the Defence Services during the last years that there will be no major war for ten years'.[3] This was certainly not a clear-cut decision by the Cabinet that the rule had been abolished; and the fact that it had not been cancelled is brought out by a letter Hankey sent MacDonald

accepted the recommendation in the COSs' Review that the Ten Year Rule should be cancelled. (Conclusion I(a) of 255th Meeting.) But when the matter came before the Cabinet the outcome is less clear cut, since Hankey merely recorded that '*no dissent was expressed* from acceptance by the CID of the COSs' recommendation . . .' (italics supplied). That conclusion is surely very different from approving it; and the Cabinet also agreed that 'the whole of the above reports should be referred for early consideration by the Disarmament Conference Ministerial Committee'—which again does not imply approval of them. Historians have stated again and again that the Ten Year Rule was dropped in March 1932; but this one, after a great deal of deliberation and examination of the records, has come to the firm conclusion that it was not formally cancelled until 15th Nov. 1933. (Roskill, *Hankey, III*, p. 537.)

[1] CID. 1087B of 11th March 1932.
[2] Cabinet 19(32) of 23rd March 1932. Cab. 23/70.
[3] *ibid.*, and note by Hankey on CID. 1112B of 30th June 1933.

early in 1933. He then wrote that the position regarding the Ten Year Rule was 'in an unsatisfactory state', and 'at present no one quite knows whether the rule stands or not . . .'[1] Yet in the following March he wrote to Neville Chamberlain, the Chancellor of the Exchequer, that 'the ten years assumption has been abolished'.[2] The only reasonable conclusion surely is that the Cabinet Secretary himself was among those who did not know 'whether the rule stands or not'; and if that is so the Service chiefs and their staffs must indeed have found themselves in a perplexing situation. It was not cleared up until the middle of November 1933, when the Cabinet had before it the draft of the COSs' Annual Review for 1933, and the CID's Conclusions on it. The most important of the latter was that the COSs, Foreign Office and Treasury 'should prepare a programme for meeting our worst deficiencies [in the defence services] for transmission to the Cabinet'; and in that decision the origin of the Defence Requirements Committee (DRC), to which we will revert shortly, is to be found.[3] With the setting up of that body the Ten Year Rule was quietly allowed to lapse. No Cabinet Conclusion exists recording its final demise.

Here we must retrace our steps to review the preparation and consummation of the Navy Estimates for the 1932–33 Financial Year. The Sketch Estimates had, after the usual prolonged deliberations, arrived at a figure of £51¾ millions, but Monsell, the First Lord, finally only asked the Chancellor for £50½ millions.[4] The reduction was accomplished chiefly by bringing into force the May Committee's proposals for economy (which of course had caused the Invergordon mutiny) and by postponing the start of the 1931 building programme—despite the fact that this measure made, in Monsell's view, 'serious inroads on the efficiency of the fleet'.[5] The Chancellor's initial reply was a flat refusal to find any money for new construction;[6] but in the end Monsell was able to ask for a token sum to start the 1932 building

---

[1] Hankey to MacDonald 16th Jan. 1933. Cab. 63/46.

[2] Hankey to Chamberlain 2nd March 1933. *ibid.*

[3] Cabinet 62(33) of 15th Nov. 1933. Cab. 23/77. That the end of 1933 is the correct date for the end of the Ten Year Rule is confirmed by a brief Hankey produced for the Prime Minister's use in a Parliamentary debate on Defence Co-ordination in Oct. 1936. He then wrote 'In 1934 we escaped from the hampering chains of a rule laid down for us in pre-war years . . . that there would be no major war for 10 years . . .' Cab. 21/736, p. 183. Dated 26th Oct. 1936.

[4] Adm. 116/3389.

[5] Monsell to Chamberlain 14th Jan. 1932. Adm. 116/3389.

[6] Chamberlain to Monsell 26th Jan. 1932. *ibid.*

programme when, on 7th March, he presented the estimates to Parliament.

Meanwhile the design of the long-debated small (5,000-ton) cruisers of the *Arethusa* class had been approved.[1] The first one was included in the 1931 programme and another was added in each of the three following years. The 1932 programme was, in essentials, a repetition of the previous year's programme.[2] In the debate on the estimates Monsell, who had just returned from the Geneva Disarmament Conference, again demonstrated his Parliamentary skill, and even the chief Opposition speaker G. H. Hall, congratulated him on 'the lucid and interesting manner' in which he had explained the estimates; but Hall did conclude by emphasising that the Labour party would 'support any proposal for a drastic and universal reduction of naval and all other armaments'. The only serious charge made by the Opposition was that the economies reported to the House were 'almost wholly due to savings in wages, clothing and victualling'; but the First Lord was able to rebut the accusation by pointing out that a greater proportion of the savings had accrued from postponing the laying down of the 1931 programme, the cancellation of a new flight for the Fleet Air Arm and economies in fuel and ammunition expenditure.[3]

At about the time the estimates were presented the Board considered whether the displacement of the *Leander* class cruisers should be increased from 7,000 to 7,500 tons, which would in their view make them much better ships, but which would absorb so much of the tonnage permitted by the London Treaty that the number of ships which could be built by the end of 1936 would have to be reduced from 14 to 13. The proposed change was influenced by the fact that most of the other naval powers were building or had projected more powerful and better protected 6-inch cruisers—notably the US Navy's *Brooklyn* class.[4] The Board finally ordered sketch designs for 'improved

---

[1] Board Minute 2906 of 14th Jan. 1932. Adm. 167/85. The *Arethusas*, of which four were completed 1934–36, had six 6-inch guns. Their displacement actually came out at about 5,250 tons.

[2] Memo. by Sea Lords of 11th Sept. 1932. Adm. 116/2606. The two *Leander* class cruisers, *Apollo* and *Phaeton*, were transferred to the RAN in 1938 and renamed *Hobart* and *Sydney*. The *Arethusa* class ship became the *Galatea*.

[3] Parl. Deb., Commons, vol. 262. cols. 1493–1608.

[4] The nine ships of this class (launched 1936–37) displaced about 10,000 tons and mounted fifteen 6-inch guns. The six *Gloire* class (1935–36) displaced 7,600 tons and mounted nine 6-inch guns, while the Italian *Garibaldi* and *Emmanuele* classes (four ships, 1934–36) displaced 7,300 to 7,900 tons and mounted eight or ten 6-inch guns.

Leanders' with nine or ten 6-inch guns to be prepared and a triple 6-inch mounting to be designed.[1] This was to prove a far-sighted decision, since it took much longer to design and produce in quantity a new power-operated gun mounting than to build the ships in which it was to be installed. It seems certain that the Board's decision was inspired by the current trend towards larger and more heavily armed 6-inch cruisers, and by the increasingly probable failure of the Disarmament Conference to restrict the size of such ships. Be that as it may the triple 6-inch mounting became the main armament of the bigger cruisers of the 1933 and later programmes, which we will encounter shortly. The final decision was that one *Leander* was to be omitted and the permissible tonnage devoted to nine ships of that class and five *Arethusas*.[2]

While the foregoing negotiations were in progress the Admiralty was not ignoring Far Eastern problems in general and the defence of the Singapore base in particular. Late in 1931 they received from Admiral W. H. Kelly,[3] the C-in-C, China, a report on a combined exercise in which the attackers had carried out a successful night landing on Singapore Island itself. Apparently the defenders had relied on air reconnaissance to give adequate warning of the 'enemy's' approach; but the air crews were inexperienced, 'the results obtained were poor', and the 'enemy' vessels were never sighted.[4] Kelly followed up this ominous report with a full account of an inter-service conference held early in 1932. His conclusions were that 'the present situation at Singapore from the point of view of defence can only be described as deplorable'. All the fixed defences (five old 9.2-inch and six 6-inch guns) were obsolete, the RAF had only six flying boats and eight antiquated Horsley torpedo-bombers. There were no fighter aircraft, and the eight 3-inch A-A guns were as inadequate as the coastal defences. 'It can therefore be said', Kelly concluded, 'that in so far as Naval interests are

The Admiralty also had a report that the Japanese had recently laid down two 6-inch cruisers of about 8,500 tons and had two more projected. (Adm. 116/2918). These were undoubtedly the *Mogami* class of 1934–36, whose turrets were specially designed for the rapid mounting of 8-inch guns—as was actually done later. Their true displacement was about 12,400 tons instead of the 10,000 permitted by the Washington and London Treaties.

[1] Board Memo. of 25th Feb. and Board Minute 2928 of 17th March 1932. Adm. 167/86 and 85 respectively.

[2] Board Minute 2818 of 31st March 1931 and 2906 of 14th Jan. 1932. Adm. 1/9336.

[3] 1873–1952. Brother of Admiral Sir John Kelly who took over the Atlantic Fleet after the Invergordon mutiny.

[4] The exercise took place early in Oct. 1931. Adm. 116/2862.

concerned, there are no defences'; and 'air defences unsupported by fixed defences can never suffice'—partly because, especially in the monsoon season, the weather was often unsuitable for flying. Kelly enclosed the reports of the GOC, Malaya and of the AOC, Far East, which were quite as depressing as his own. Meanwhile the US Navy Department had received, quite independently, a report of a Japanese Fleet exercise obviously designed to test the capacity of the Americans to defend the Philippine Islands. The attackers were as successful against Manila as they had been at Singapore. The umpires decided that the defending fleet was 'completely destroyed' and, prophetically, that 'air forces have a great effect on the outcome of a fleet action'.[1]

In February 1932 the COSs discussed the question of the Singapore base, and Hankey gave them cautious encouragement by suggesting that the Cabinet was well aware of their anxiety and would probably prove sympathetic towards proposals such as they desired.[2] A telegram from the Governor of Singapore expressing the strength of feeling aroused in Malaya by the fact that, after contributing £2 millions, the purpose of the gift was not being carried out possibly helped to get things moving.[3] At any rate in July Monsell evidently thought that the time had come to open the issue of reversing the 1929 decision to suspend all possible work on the base. Whilst admitting that financial considerations might preclude the full reinstatement of even the 'truncated scheme', he stressed that the prevailing state of affairs was 'most unsatisfactory'. He urged that at least the graving dock, which lacked a caisson and so was useless, should be completed; and that the Cabinet should approve in principle the modernisation of the defences 'as finance allows', leaving it to the Admiralty to fight the inevitable battle with the Treasury.[4] Despite these hopeful auguries October had come before the issue was actually raised in Cabinet. Broadly speaking the decision then taken was to restart work on the base, though no active steps were to be taken while the Disarmament Conference's 'truce' was in operation.[5]

Towards the end of 1932 the Naval Intelligence Division produced 'an exhaustive analysis of Japanese naval activities', stressing in particular the big increases in oil fuel storage provided and the expansion

---

[1] ONI Monthly Bulletin, vol. xii, nos. 6 and 7. The exercise took place in 1930.
[2] 102nd COS meeting on 28th Feb. 1932. Cab. 53/4.
[3] Governor, Malaya, telegram 152 of 26th Aug. 1932. Copy in Adm. 116/3615.
[4] Memo. by Monsell of 11th July 1932. Became CP. 252(32). Adm. 116/3615.
[5] Cabinet 50(32) Conclusion 9 of 11th Oct. 1932. Cab. 23/72.

of their naval air arm. The true state of affairs, the DNI insisted, was totally different from the Japanese attitude at Geneva, which was designed to show 'how they have been disarming'. In fact their expenditure for 1933 was more than a third greater than in the previous year (372 million yen as against 224 plus 67 million for the Manchurian operations).[1] Murray commented on this report 'As long as the League of Nations Union and the like go on demanding the coercion of Japan it will not be surprising if she shows "activity" '.[2] However on reading the Foreign Office telegrams a short time later, and admitting that 'Japan knows both what she wants and what she is doing', he strongly questioned the need for Britain to oppose her. 'Is it not possible', he asked, '. . . that our true policy would be to keep on the best of terms with Japan, to exert a moderating influence on her in the *means* she employs, but not to oppose her *ends*?' Such a policy would undoubtedly be the most economical, and Murray did not believe that it had ever been 'fairly considered'. The other members of the Board were in general sympathy with the Secretary, but as the policy of the Foreign Office was to support the League, despite its obvious impotence over Manchuria, the real issue was, in the DCNS's view 'how can we in the Admiralty influence such a policy?'[3] The answer to that question was of course to plague successive governments throughout the 1930s; and as it lay, at any rate in part, in hastening rearmament it is to the 1933 estimates that we must now turn.

While the Sketch Estimates were making their usual progress around the Admiralty departments, Admiral Field had a comprehensive 'Review of the Present Conditions of the Navy and General Remarks on Future Policy' prepared. He probably intended this document to be his 'Swan Song' and a guide to his successor, since he knew that he was to hand over his office to Admiral Chatfield early in 1933. But his survey appears not to have been well received by his colleagues, since the original was heavily amended after two discussions by the full Board, and no fair copy appears ever to have been made or circulated.[4] That being so we need say no more than that Field included a table showing the building programmes he considered necessary for the

---

[1] Memo. of 18th Nov. 1932 by DNI. Adm. 116/3116.

[2] Minute dated 15th Dec. 1932. *ibid*.

[3] Minutes by Murray of 1st Feb. and by Admiral Little, the DCNS, of 4th Feb. 1933. *ibid*.

[4] Original in Adm. 116/3434 dated 14th Nov. 1932. Another copy in Adm. 167/87. It was discussed by the full Board on 8th and 9th Dec. Board Minute 3022.

whole decade 1933–42.[1] In the main these were carried out for the first five years, but after rearmament began in earnest in 1937 Field's proposals were greatly altered.

Towards the end of 1932 Monsell wrote at length to the Chancellor about the Sketch Estimates for the following Financial Year. He opened his case with a complaint about the difficulties caused by the Ten Year Rule, and of the 'severe pruning' to which each year's estimates had been subjected in recent times—particularly with regard to the long desired building up of oil fuel reserves and other essential stores. To eliminate all those deficiencies would, he wrote, cost £22–23 millions, of which £9½ millions were needed for oil reserves. To spread the load he proposed to ask for £2¼ millions yearly for the next decade, but for the 1933–34 Financial Year he was prepared, in view of 'the serious financial situation still existing', to limit expenditure to a much smaller sum. As regards the Fleet Air Arm, in 1931 only one new flight had been provided for and in 1932 none at all. Monsell now asked for two new flights for 1933 and re-equipment of two obsolescent torpedo-bomber flights as well.[2] Though he argued his case with great skill his proposals were not likely to appeal to Chamberlain or the Treasury. None the less the Chancellor's reply was not wholly unsympathetic—except as regards the long-sought new flights for the FAA, which he asked to be deferred. Expenditure should, he wrote, be limited to £53½ millions.[3] The First Lord, however, returned to the attack, and Chamberlain finally agreed to a compromise by which the Fleet Air Arm received a small sum for re-equipment.[4] The Chancellor, however, reminded the First Lord of the views expressed by the Treasury when the COSs' last Annual Review came before the CID 'that financial and economic risks are by far the most serious that the country has to face . . .'[5]

The estimates were finally presented to Parliament at the figure of £53½ millions agreed by Chamberlain,[6] and in the subsequent debate the increase of about £3 millions aroused little opposition. Indeed George Hall once again complimented Monsell on the clarity and tact

[1] Section X of Appendix to above.

[2] Monsell to Chamberlain 14th Dec. 1932. Adm. 167/87 and 116/3390.

[3] Chamberlain to Monsell 10th Jan. 1933. Adm. 167/89 and 116/3390. Also Board Minute 3046 of 19th Jan. 1933. Adm. 167/88.

[4] Monsell to Chamberlain 21st Jan. and Chamberlain to Monsell 2nd Feb. 1933. Adm. 116/3390.

[5] CID. 1087B of 11th March 1932.

[6] Cmd. 4266 of 28th Feb. 1933.

shown in his presentation of the estimates.[1] In the Admiralty it is a fair assumption that there must have been considerable relief over the comparatively easy passage given to them.

Almost simultaneously with the passing of the Navy Estimates for 1933–34 the storm clouds over Europe and the Far East, which the Geneva Conference had been trying to disperse, became more threatening than ever. On 30th January 1933 President Hindenburg appointed Adolf Hitler Chancellor of Germany—despite the fact that in the elections of the previous November the Nazi Party's representation in the Reichstag had fallen from 230 to 196. On 24th February Japan gave notice to leave the League—in protest against the opposition to her aggressive policy on the Asiatic mainland. Small wonder that on 3rd March Eden reported to London that the situation at Geneva was 'critical', and urged that MacDonald should make a new initiative in an effort to avert the threatened breakdown of the Disarmament Conference.[2]

Across the Atlantic President Roosevelt actually assumed office on 4th March 1933, so ending the period of uncertainty about who would represent the USA when the Disarmament Conference resumed its deliberations. But if that seemed a hopeful augury the new German elections held that same month were the reverse; for the Nazis, by exploiting to the limit the alleged Communist conspiracy to set fire to the Reichstag building, increased their representation in the Reichstag to 288. Although still in a minority in the 584-member chamber the support of the Nationalists enabled the Nazis to obtain dictatorial powers on 23rd March—though by highly dubious constitutional means. That date may be taken to mark the achievement of Hitler's supremacy.

Despite these highly unfavourable developments MacDonald persevered in his efforts to instil new life into the moribund Disarmament Conference by producing a new draft Convention which included all the proposals which appeared, from the earlier discussions, to stand the best chance of acceptance.[3] The British Cabinet insisted that this document 'represents not only a balanced plan but also the maximum

---

[1] Parl. Deb., Commons, vol. 275, cols. 2159–2260. The debate took place on 16th March 1933.

[2] DC(M)(32) 13th Meeting of 3rd March 1933. Cab. 21/379.

[3] DC(M)(32)42. The draft Convention was presented by MacDonald at Geneva on 16th March 1933. Cab. 21/379.

distance to which HM government are prepared to go . . .'[1] From the German point of view the most attractive feature of the plan was that it replaced the disarmament clauses of the Versailles Treaty—to which they had so long and so strenuously objected. But if, as is plainly the case, the British government hoped by this means to entice the Germans into renewing negotiations on disarmament such hopes were soon shown to be vain. The weakest point in the British plan lay in the fact that it exempted 'police bombing' in 'outlying regions' (which obviously meant the parts of the Empire where the RAF had assumed responsibility for internal security by the euphemistically described system called 'air control') from the general abolition of air bombardment.[2]

In May 1932 Monsell wrote to Baldwin from Geneva that he was going to Mentone to meet Admiral Sir Ernle Chatfield, the C-in-C, Mediterranean, who was coming there from Malta. 'I think it is generally admitted, in the Navy', wrote Monsell, 'that he should be the next First Sea Lord, but as I have not yet seen him I think it is of the greatest importance that I should discover his views as to the proposed changes etc. before he is definitely offered the post'.[3] Precisely what Monsell meant by the 'proposed changes' is not clear, but he may have been referring to the internal changes in the Admiralty which were part of the outcome of the prolonged heart-searching which had followed on the Invergordon mutiny. If that is so Monsell probably had in mind the decision to merge the Accountant-General's Department (on which a share of the blame for the inept handling of the 1931 pay cuts could justly be placed) with the Secretariat,[4] and the re-inclusion of the Assistant Chief of Naval Staff as a full member of the Board, which he had not been since 1929.[5]

Monsell's meeting with Chatfield evidently went well, since he was offered the post of First Sea Lord shortly afterwards and accepted it. The First Lord told him that one reason for making the change as soon

[1] DC(M)(32) 17th Meeting of 19th June 1933. *ibid.*
[2] On British policy with regard to this issue see DC(M)(32) 8th and 10th Meetings of 17th and 22nd March 1933 and Eden to Simon 12th June 1933 in DC(M)(32)49. All in Cab. 21/379.
[3] Monsell to Baldwin 9th May 1932. Baldwin papers vol. 118, pp. 174–6.
[4] The move to amalgamate the two was initiated by Murray on 19th Nov. 1931, only two months after the mutiny. It was approved on 22nd Jan. 1932. Adm. 116/3344 and 167/86.
[5] Adm. 1/8785–152/1935.

as possible was 'to endeavour to stop the intrigue now proceeding';[1] and a letter from Field makes it plain that the chief intriguer was Keyes, who had been attacking Field ever since Invergordon and 'has been on the warpath again'.[2] Keyes's description of a letter he had received from Monsell at this time as 'so intolerably insolent' surely makes his highly intemperate approach to the problems of the day clear;[3] while his attempts a few years later to get himself kept on as an Admiral of the Fleet up to the age of 65 by the Admiralty seeking approval for an additional appointment in that rank suggests that self-interest and vanity were not absent from his character and purposes.[4] Monsell told Chatfield that the end of January 1933 was the latest date he should take over (Field had suggested the end of February), and Chatfield agreed with Monsell that a completely new Board was desirable.[5] He actually took up the appointment on 21st January. In the Navy as a whole the change was welcomed very warmly, since Chatfield's experience at sea and on both the staff and material sides of naval administration, was unrivalled—Chief of Staff to Beatty in World War I, ACNS 1920–22, Third Sea Lord and Controller 1925–28, C-in-C, Atlantic Fleet 1929–30 and of the Mediterranean Fleet 1930–33. Small of stature and very quiet-spoken his personality might at first encounter seem unimpressive; but his gentle manner concealed a steely determination; and in negotiations he could and did show unbreakable patience while giving away nothing that he regarded as essential. His mind worked quickly and with crystal clarity, and on paper he was never discursive or indecisive. The whole navy knew that with his appointment it had got the finest leader at the top since Beatty. As for the unfortunate Field, he disappeared from the scene unlamented, and it is difficult not to feel that he was never a big enough man for the job. Though it would be unfair to lay the blame for everything that went wrong at Field's door it is undeniable that his régime saw the nadir of

[1] Holograph postscript to Monsell to Chatfield letter of 14th June 1932. Chatfield papers CHT/2/1. Also same to same 26th June 1932 stressing the need for Chatfield to take over as soon as possible 'to get rid of the intrigue and criticism that is going on'. *ibid.*

[2] Field to Chatfield 10th June 1932. *ibid.*

[3] Keyes to Chatfield 26th July 1932 referring to Monsell's letter to him of 21st July. *ibid.*

[4] Admiral Royle (Naval Secretary to First Lord) to Chatfield 25th April 1935. *ibid.*

[5] Letter to Monsell of 3rd July 1932. Draft in *ibid.*

the navy's spiritual and material fortunes during the interlude between the two world wars.

To return to Geneva, though Paul-Boncour for France made it plain that his country's search for security was far from met by the MacDonald plan, and the pronouncements of leading Germans varied from the intransigent to the conciliatory,[1] early in June the British proposals were accepted as a basis for further progress, and the conference adjourned until the autumn. Arthur Henderson then set out on a 'disarmament pilgrimage' around the capital cities of Europe; but in Paris he found no hope of France reducing her forces unless an effective system of supervision had been devised. Whatever hopes Henderson may have entertained about German intentions were rudely shattered when, on 14th October, a telegram announcing their withdrawal from the conference reached him at Geneva; and Germany's notice to resign from the League soon followed. Though the conference dragged on into the spring of 1934 it became increasingly plain that the likelihood of agreement was remote; and in June the decision was reached to adjourn the conference but preserve it in a state of suspended animation.

All that it had in fact achieved was to reveal the wide gulf between British aspirations for disarmament and French insistence on security; while the Germans had gained nearly two years in which to progress their plans for rearmament virtually unimpeded. In London one man at any rate saw the truth. Early in April 1934 Hankey told MacDonald that he was increasingly convinced 'that the present Disarmament Conference should be liquidated, as it is only making international friction'. In the meantime he urged that we should put our own defences in order, and try to keep the peace by 'a purely opportunist policy, avoiding heroic remedies'—by which he was plainly referring to draft Conventions such as had been produced at Geneva.[2] Here at least was a whiff of realism; and it is therefore to the start of the rearmament of Britain that we must now turn.

Soon after the Navy Estimates for 1933–34 had been approved the COSs began work on their Annual Review for 1933. An enormous

[1] On 11th May Constantin von Neurath, the Foreign Minister, published an article spelling out Germany's intention to rearm without regard to whatever recommendations Geneva might produce, but on 17th Hitler himself made an unexpectedly conciliatory declaration of policy. It now seems likely that his purpose was to maintain discord among the other powers and produce uncertainty about Germany's real intentions.

[2] Hankey to MacDonald 6th April 1934. Cab. 21/388.

dossier (120 printed pages) containing the views of all the departments was accumulated, and in the final report the COSs reviewed 'Naval Responsibilities' in the light of the situation prevailing in Europe, the Mediterranean and the Far East. They defined the 'dominating factors' as capital ship and cruiser strength, and the omission of any mention of the aircraft carrier is surely significant. Oil fuel reserves were less than half the amount needed, and serious deficiencies existed in virtually all reserves of ammunition and weapons. The 'seaward defences' (i.e. heavy coast defence guns) of Singapore were still inadequate but 'progress is now being made'. They stated that in a war against Germany with France as ally 'our naval forces would be adequate'; and we should be capable of simultaneously fighting Japan provided that the two capital ships likely to be undergoing modernisation at the time could be brought back into service quickly, and the deficiencies in oil and stores were rectified. Finally the Navy would be able to safeguard the sea routes which played an essential part in the 'Defence of India Plan'. The first priority for expenditure should, the COSs concluded, be given to defence of our 'possessions and interests in the Far East'. Second came 'European Commitments', and third 'the defence of India against Soviet aggression'.[1] If these priorities now seem to have a nineteenth-century ring about them it must be recalled that Hitler had only achieved power six months earlier, Italy's aggressive plans against Abyssinia had not yet darkened the Mediterranean horizon, and that the Japanese had just agreed to an armistice at Shanghai, and soon began to withdraw their troops from the city.[2]

Here we may cross the Atlantic to review the problems which beset the Roosevelt administration during its first months of office and developments in Anglo-American relations. As regards the latter we have seen how the 1930 London Conference produced a substantial improvement; and during the discussions on the DRC Programme the effect of it on the USA was constantly in the Naval Staff's mind. The broad British policy seems to have been to keep relations on a friendly though rather distant basis, but not to yield on any point which would increase the US Navy's relative strength. As to exchange of information the Admiralty did not believe that there was anything of importance to be learnt from the other service, and when in August 1933 the US Naval Attaché raised the possibility their reaction was cautious in

[1] CID. 1112 and 1113B of 30th June and 12th Oct. 1933. Cab. 4/22.

[2] See C. Thorne, *The Limits of Foreign Policy: The West, the League and the Far Eastern Crisis of 1913–1933* (Hamish Hamilton, 1972), pp. 203–10 and 273–4.

the extreme. The Admiralty did however consider that it would 'be politic to accede to the request', but wished to restrict discussions to 'general lines' and avoid going into 'points of detail'.[1] There matters rested for the time being.

In fact in the early 1930s there existed a number of potential sources of irritation between the RN and USN, which could be and sometimes were stridently exploited by the anti-British interests in America. The activities of the Irish lobby were incessant, and anti-imperialism was widespread among American 'Liberals'—who found it convenient to ignore the USA's own imperialist and colonialist activities in the Philippines, Guam, the Panama Canal Zone, the central American republics, and Caribbean islands such as Cuba and Puerto Rico.[2] President Roosevelt and his Secretary of State Cordell Hull were themselves strongly unsympathetic towards European imperialism, and there was no likelihood at all of American power and influence being exerted anywhere in the world in the British interest. Furthermore in the spring of 1934, after Britain had ceased war debt repayments, Congress passed the Johnson Act prohibiting American loans being made to any country in default to the USA. This Act was a serious blow to Britain should she become involved in a new conflict.[3] The acquisition by American oil companies (notably Standard Oil) of a substantial interest, amounting to control through a subsidiary company, of the production of the Bahrein oil fields also aroused the antagonism of the British, who had long regarded Persian Gulf oil as their private preserve. After the C-in-C, East Indies, had reported his concern over this matter the Admiralty reviewed the whole problem. The Secretariat considered that Andrew W. Mellon, the immensely wealthy banker and industrialist, who was American Ambassador in

[1] Naval Attaché, Washington to DNI 25th Aug. 1933 and US Naval Attaché, London, to same. Board Minute 3108 of 1st Nov. 1933. Adm. 1/8766–43/33.

[2] Prem. 4–42/9 contains interesting papers of 1942 regarding British resentment of what was regarded as 'widespread ignorance' in USA about our Colonial Empire, as evidenced by a recent speech by Wendell Wilkie and an article in *Life* magazine. On 16th June 1942 Attlee, Secretary of State for Dominion Affairs and leader of the Labour Party, told Churchill that 'The High Commissioners [of the Commonwealth Countries] are also disturbed by the economic imperialism of the American business interests—under the cloak of a benevolent and avuncular internationalism'. He cited Pan-American Airways and US Radio firms as 'staking out post-war claims'. At about the same time (16th June) Eden, the Foreign Secretary, protested to Churchill that, in this matter 'The American position is becoming highly absurd'.

[3] See Stephen E. Pelz, *Race to Pearl Harbor* (Harvard UP, 1974), pp. 71 and 117. Henceforth cited as *Pelz*.

London 1932–33, 'seems to have made very improper use of his position'; but Chatfield held that the situation was not as bad as it looked since Britain would in all probability be able to pre-empt the purchase of all Gulf oil in war, even if it were American-controlled.[1] None the less the British continued to take a very strong interest in Middle East Oil and in the rulers of the countries which produced it. For example when King Feisal of Iraq paid a state visit to England in June 1933 special naval exercises and demonstrations of new equipment were laid on for his benefit by the Home Fleet.[2] In the following September Feisal died suddenly in Switzerland, and a cruiser was sent to Brindisi to pick up his body and carry it to Haifa, whence the RAF flew it to Baghdad. With Feisal's death Britain lost a firm friend in this critically important area.[3]

To return to the prospects for a new agreement on naval limitation, British-American relations still remained in a delicate condition and plentiful causes of friction existed. Thus a visit by US warships to British ports in return for one paid by units of the Home Fleet to Balboa in 1931 was first repeatedly postponed and finally declared by Monsell to be 'quite impossible' in July 1934 in view of the approaching naval conference and the need not to give the Japanese the impression that Britain and the USA were acting in collusion.[4] In fact no substantial rapprochement between the British and American navies took

---

[1] Report of 11th Dec. 1933 by C-in-C, East Indies (Admiral Sir M. Dunbar-Nasmith). Summary of oil situation in Persian Gulf, Jan. 1934 and letter Chatfield to Nasmith of 5th Feb. 1934. Adm. 1/8773–57/34.

[2] Adm. 1/8769–133/33. Report by Admiral Commanding Battle Cruiser Squadron of 14th July 1933.

[3] Adm. 1/8769–135/33. The British High Commissioners in Iraq and Palestine (Sir F. Humphreys and Sir A.Wauchope) reported that the honours paid to the defunct monarch had produced an excellent effect on the Arab people; but that view was, as regards Palestine, certainly exaggerated since a serious Arab revolt, directed chiefly against Jewish immigration, broke out in April 1936. Feisal was succeeded by King Ghazi, who was killed in an accident in 1939. British-Iraqi relations became very difficult thereafter, culminating in the bloody riots and revolution of July 1958, when Feisal II, the Regent and Nuri-es-Said the Prime Minister were murdered and a Republic under General Kassem was established. It only lasted until 1962 when Kassem was killed.

[4] The proposal had been put up by the C-in-C, America and West Indies Station (Admiral Sir V. Haggard) in 1930 but was dropped because of the economic crisis. The *Nelson*, flying the flag of the C-in-C, Home Fleet, visited Balboa in March 1931. Minute by Monsell of 19th July 1934. Adm. 116/3292.

place until 1938—by which time the international situation had deteriorated alarmingly.

To turn to the problems which beset President Roosevelt during his first term of office, his predecessor had drastically cut funds for naval construction in 1931 and had eliminated them completely for the following year. Roosevelt himself had been elected on a programme which placed economic recovery as the first priority, and was committed against involvement in anything resembling 'entangling alliances'. Thence arose his opposition to the USA joining the League of Nations, which dated to 1928. Pacifist and isolationist organisations were strong and vociferous; Roosevelt was pledged to make the Geneva Disarmament Conference a success, and if he showed any incaution over naval rearmament Congress was certain to pull him up short. That he himself wholly mistrusted the Japanese and Germans for their militaristic attitude and expansionist policies is certain; and in his disapproval of Japan's aggressions on the Asiatic mainland he was in complete accord with Cordell Hull, whose strong sense of moral rights and wrongs had thereby been outraged. In London Japan's policy caused far greater anxiety; but British interests in the Far East were much greater than those of the USA. Roosevelt and his advisers believed that, if war with Japan should come, she might well achieve early and quick successes, but her ultimate defeat was certain because of her economic weakness, her vulnerability to blockade, and above all her need to import almost all the oil she consumed.[1]

As regards the member of the Roosevelt administration with whom we here are chiefly concerned, the choice of Claude Swanson as Secretary of the Navy is difficult to explain except on the grounds that the President, having been Assistant Secretary of the Navy in the Wilson administration of 1913–20, regarded himself as an expert in naval affairs and did not want a man of strong and independent views as head of the service. Be that as it may Swanson was 71 years old on taking office and far from being a fit man.[2] In those circumstances a great deal of the responsibility for naval policy devolved on Henry L.

[1] *Pelz*, pp. 73–6.

[2] See Hugh L'Etang, *The Pathology of Leadership* (Heinemann Medical Press, 1969). The author cites the 'appalling saga' of Swanson as a case study of the effects of a sick man being placed in a position of high responsibility. Because of high blood pressure he was admitted to hospital in December 1933, and when he next attended a Cabinet in March 1934 he had difficulty in holding a cigarette. By March 1939 he was virtually incapable of speech yet remained in office until he died of a stroke on 7th July 1939.

Roosevelt the Assistant Secretary; but he died, while still in office, less than three years later. With weak and ailing civil leadership it was fortunate for the US Navy that in Admirals William V. Pratt and William H. Standley it had two able and broad-minded officers as Chiefs of Naval Operations (September 1930 to June 1933 and July 1933 to January 1937 respectively). By comparison with them most of the successive Chairmen of the General Board, of which there were no less than eight between 1930 and 1939, appear undistinguished—which probably accounts for the conservatism of outlook of that body;[1] but as it had purely advisory functions one must not exaggerate its influence.[2]

Before President Roosevelt had actually assumed office the General Board had been considering the building programme for 1933, and Pratt approved putting forward proposals to ask for one 10,000-ton 8-inch cruiser and two 6-inch cruisers (one of 10,000 tons with a flight deck and one of slightly less displacement without one), two carriers of 13,800 tons (which became the *Yorktown* and *Enterprise*, laid down in May and July 1934, but finally displaced some 20,000 tons), a leader and three destroyers and six submarines. No less than 390 aircraft for carriers were included in the programme, the cost of which was estimated at nearly $400 millions. But when these ambitious proposals reached Roosevelt he told the Secretary of the Navy that they were 'not in accordance with the President's financial programme'.[3] Far from embarking on large new expenditure the Navy Department was ordered to make a cut in its appropriations of $50–60 millions. This meant that one third of the fleet would have to be paid off, and Pratt loyally prepared a scheme to introduce such a measure on a rotational basis. Fortunately the march of events overtook this crippling blow.

[1] See vol. I, pp. 26–7 regarding the history and functions of the General Board.

[2] *Pelz*, 86–8 may be justified in attacking the US naval hierarchy as 'a self-perpetuating group' of rigid outlook, and the same criticism could be made of the British Sea Lords. But to this historian the pejorative description cannot justly be applied to Admirals Pratt and Standley; and, after all, the naval hierarchy was no more 'self-perpetuating' than that of any other government department, since the outgoing heads normally recommend their successors. Furthermore a great deal of admirably far-sighted work, notably in the field of naval aviation, was done by the Navy Department in the 1930s.

[3] GB. 420–2, Serial 1523 of 20th April 1931 and Serial 1568 of 13th April 1932. The pros and cons of the flight deck cruiser were re-opened early in 1934 (GB. 420–8) which was sent on to the President on 8th March. Navy Department opinion was strongly opposed to this type but it was decided that the fleet should investigate its possible value. Roosevelt papers, PSF. Box 25.

A situation which had looked extremely gloomy for the navy was saved by Congress passing the National Industrial Recovery Act (NIRA) on 16th June 1933. That measure and other 'New Deal' legislation, such as the creation of the Public Works Administration and Work Progress Administration (PWA and WPA), enabled the President to authorise large expenditure for naval purposes as 'relief' measures.[1] Important though the appropriations under NIRA were it was clear that, if the USA was to overtake all accumulated deficits and have a real 'treaty navy' by 1942 additional funds would be essential. However, Roosevelt and Swanson moved very cautiously, and early in 1934 the latter asked Congress for no more than the money needed to start four cruisers. None the less this modest proposal produced difficulties later, because having asked for no destroyers or submarines it became inevitable that only the Japanese should be asked to scrap such ships in order to achieve a new treaty; and they were most unlikely to agree to such an inequitable proposal. Had the USA started a destroyer and submarine programme between 1934 and 1936 they would have been in the much stronger position of being able themselves to offer cancellations during the treaty discussions. Pratt diagnosed the problem accurately when he told Swanson that 'The country is reasonably safe defensively on both oceans for the time being'; but the next two or three years would 'constitute the period of greatest danger for the Navy'.[2] None the less by June 1933, when Pratt handed over the office of Chief of Naval Operations to Standley, a substantial new building programme had been approved—although an order was given to cut the normal appropriations for 1934 by $266 millions 'in order to help balance the national budget'.[3] Despite this unfavourable portent on 3rd August Swanson was able to announce that no less than $238

---

[1] Roosevelt papers, Official Files, Box 27. The 'Oral History' of Vice-Admiral G. F. Hussey, Jr., Chief of the Bureau of Ordnance Dec. 1943 to Sept. 1947, the typescript of which he kindly allowed the author to study, fully confirms the enormous benefits derived by the US Navy from funds appropriated for New Deal agencies and especially NIRA. A valuable study of the relation between American national recovery and naval rearmament is the unpublished thesis by Robert H. Levine entitled *The Politics of American Naval Rearmament 1930–1938* (Harvard University, 1972).

[2] Pratt to Swanson 12th April 1933. Pratt papers.

[3] Roosevelt papers, Official File 18, Box 27. The same file contains a delightful example of Roosevelt's acceptance of the use of New Deal agencies for defence purposes. 'Please remind me', he wrote to the Director of the Bureau of the Budget on 22nd Dec. 1933, 'to take some $500,000 out of PWA or some other fund for anchorage basin for the Fleet in the Bay of Panama'.

millions had been provided under the NIRA programme to start 32 ships; and five more were included under the regular 'Increase of the Navy' programme. They included the last of the Washington Treaty cruisers, already authorised, and three of the new 10,000-ton 6-inch *Brooklyn* class—which caused so much concern in London; and it was all done at a stroke of the pen by Executive Order.[1] Roosevelt himself seems to have been surprised at the ease with which this large increase went through, remarking to Swanson 'Claude, we got away with murder that time'.[2]

Towards the end of 1933 and early in the following year Swanson and H. L. Roosevelt wrote to the President pressing for large amounts of money ($100 millions was mentioned) to be provided either by normal Appropriations or under New Deal legislation to continue the Navy Department's eight-year programme.[3] In general these proposals followed the arguments for expansion previously put up by the General Board;[4] and the Appropriations Act for the 1934 Fiscal Year made nearly $50 millions available 'for increase of the Navy'.

Shortly before he left office Pratt wrote a long paper entitled 'For the Equalization and Limitations of Armaments' and sent a copy to Hull as well as Swanson. In it he reviewed the aims and aspirations of the major naval powers, and the prospects for further agreement on limitation in every class of ship. After describing Japan as adopting 'a truly aggressive attitude', and Germany much the same, he came to the conclusion that in 'the final analysis the best hope of peace . . . is that the United States and the United Kingdom must stand firmly side by side, shoulder to shoulder, 50–50 in all things'; and 'in the case of a break [i.e. war] the mutual interests of Great Britain and ourselves in sea power will draw us inevitably closer together, provided we take care not to let economic and other matters drive a rift between us'. However, for reasons already discussed, neither Roosevelt nor his Secretary of State were prepared to advance along the road of Anglo-American co-operation as rapidly as the far-sighted Pratt wished.

[1] The 1933 programme and appropriations, together with the contracts awarded, are summarised in Swanson's letter of 6th Nov. 1934 to FDR. Roosevelt Papers, PSF, Box 28. (Swanson file).

[2] Quoted *Pelz*, p. 79.

[3] Swanson to FDR. 22nd Dec. 1933, and H. L. Roosevelt to same 5th Jan. 1934. Roosevelt papers, PSF, Dept. Corresp., Box 28.

[4] GB. 420–2, Serial 1568 of 13th April 1932, revised by Serial 1578 of 16th Sept. 1932.

None the less on leaving office he wrote to Roosevelt as his C-in-C 'Especially do I want to tell you what a pleasure it is to me to know that the fate of the Navy lies in the hands of a man who loves it as you do'.[1] Fortunately for Britain Admiral Standley proved as staunch a friend as his predecessor—if a somewhat more cautious one.

[1] Pratt to Secretary of Navy and Secretary of State 19th May and to President Roosevelt 9th June 1933. He retired on 30th June. Pratt's outlook is admirably expressed in his article 'Our Naval Policy', US Naval Institute Proceedings, vol. 58, no. 7 (July 1932).

CHAPTER VI

The First Moves for
Rearmament
1933-1934

———————◆———————

THE COLLAPSE of the General Disarmament Conference, though long
expected, can be dated to 14th October 1933 when Hitler gave notice
of Germany's withdrawal and of her intention to leave the League of
Nations; but it was not in fact formally adjourned *sine die* until May
1934. Plainly the period of hopefulness for a new era of international
accord initiated by the Locarno agreement of 1925 had ended, and
Hitler had won his first diplomatic success. In the Admiralty this
development had long been anticipated, and a competition in cruiser
construction was expected. Although hopes were still entertained that
agreement to limit the size and armament, and so the cost, of such ships
might be achieved on 20th September Monsell ordered that the design
of the new and larger 6-inch cruisers already mentioned should 'be
pressed on at all possible speed'.[1] Accordingly the 1933 building programme was reviewed and, MacDonald having accepted in principle
the change in cruiser policy,[2] the revised programme was circulated to
the Cabinet. Its principal features were the substitution of three M
(or *Minotaur*) class cruisers of nearly 9,000 tons and armed with twelve
6-inch guns for the *Leanders*; but the programme was finally reduced
to two such ships and one of the small *Arethusa* class—presumably to
obtain the greatest possible number of cruisers within the tonnage
permitted by the 1930 London Treaty.[3] The Naval Staff admitted that

---

[1] Board Minute 3110 of 27th July 1933 (Adm. 167/88) and Memo. of 20th Sept.
1933. Adm. 116/2998.

[2] Letter J. A. Barlow to 1st Lord of 2nd Aug. 1933. Adm. 167/89.

[3] The first two M class (later renamed 'Town' class) cruisers became the *South-*

the bigger cruisers had been designed 'in reply to the large 6-inch cruisers now being built by USA and Japan'—that is to say the *Brooklyn* and *Mogami* classes; but they still hoped that it would prove possible to 'isolate' these ships (i.e. treat them as special cases outside the general question of cruiser construction) as had been done with the Washington Treaty 8-inch cruisers.[1] Chatfield told Sir William Fisher, the C-in-C, Mediterranean, that he was stopping the building of the *Leander* class at once, and regretted that we had built as many as eight of that type. Our initiative in trying to reduce the size of cruisers had, he wrote, been 'flouted' by the other powers, and designs for bigger ships were therefore being prepared.[2] A little later he briefed Beatty for the debate on the Navy Estimates in the House of Lords, explaining not only the Admiralty's cruiser policy but why more money was needed for defence of bases, building up oil reserves and so on. He told his former C-in-C in strict confidence about the M class design, and that he was determined that at the 1935 conference Britain should free herself of the 50 cruiser total imposed in 1930.[3] In addition to the three new cruisers the 1933 programme included a flotilla of nine destroyers (the G class), three submarines, five sloops of three different types for convoy work and minesweeping,[4] and various small craft.

Shortly after the foregoing revised programme for 1933 had been agreed Monsell circulated his proposals for the following year.[5] They included the long-deferred aircraft carrier which had first been proposed in 1929 and finally became the *Ark Royal*,[6] four cruisers (three *Town* class and the last of the four *Arethusas*), another flotilla of destroyers (the H class), and a fairly close repetition of the previous

---

ampton and *Newcastle*. The name *Minotaur* was probably dropped because the armoured cruisers of 1904–7, the previous class to bear the name, were not successful ships and suffered heavy losses at Jutland. For discussion on the building of larger cruisers see Adm. 1/9427, 9355 and 9360.

[1] Board Minute 3246 of 25th Oct. 1934. Adm. 167/90 and Adm. 1/9364.

[2] Chatfield to Fisher 9th Aug. 1933. Chatfield papers CHT/4/5.

[3] Chatfield to Beatty 10th Oct. 1933. *ibid.*

[4] The long-term programme for sloop construction was drastically revised in July 1931 when the total needs were calculated at 51—of which 21 were to be Patrol type and 30 minesweepers. The three classes, designed to replace the obsolescent *Flower* class of World War I, were then known as Convoy Sloops, Sloop Minesweepers and Coastal Sloops. Adm. 116/2607.

[5] Board Minutes 3104 of 9th Oct. and 3106 of 1st Nov. 1933. Adm. 167/88.

[6] See vol. I, p. 561.

year's provision of submarines and sloops.[1] We will return in a later chapter to the effects of the proposal to build a new carrier on Admiralty-Air Ministry relations.

While the foregoing programmes were being formulated the Sea Lords and the Naval Staff were also reviewing the question of modernising the older capital ships and the design of new ones—if and when the treaty restrictions were removed. The engines of all five *Queen Elizabeth* class ships had been found to be in bad order, and in addition there was the need to increase the elevation, and so the range, of their main armament, as the Americans and Japanese were doing, to strengthen deck armour against air attacks, increase A-A armaments, and improve underwater protection. Plainly these measures would be costly and take a long time to complete; and the international situation, especially in the Far East, was such that the Board viewed with concern the prospect of having two or three capital ships laid up for long periods. No decisions were taken in late 1933 and early 1934, but the implications of the whole problem were thoroughly surveyed.[2] As regards restarting capital ship construction, which would only be permissible after the expiration of the London Treaty at the end of 1936, Chatfield jibbed against waiting so long because by 1937 no less than nine of the fifteen British capital ships would be over 26 years old.[3] The Staff accordingly prepared 'characteristics' for new battleships, taking account of those built or projected by all foreign powers. In fact the design followed closely that of the successful *Queen Elizabeth* class of 1913-15 but with improved armour protection and A-A armaments. The staff did not specify the calibre of the main armament, but as both the USA and Japan had 16-inch ships built or projected it must have been obvious that those countries would be reluctant to accept smaller weapons. Though the Admiralty was prepared, and even anxious, to reduce the displacement and armament of capital ships[4] the 1937 ships were in truth almost certain to be no smaller than the Washington Treaty's 35,000 tons.[5] The other dominant consideration in the Admiralty's planning was still that a minimum of 70

[1] Memo. by Monsell of 21st Dec. 1933. Adm. 167/89. Became CP. 311/33. Cab. 24/245.

[2] Memo. by Chatfield of 29th June 1933. Adm. 1/8774. Board Minutes 3177 and 3182 of 8th and 15th March 1934 (Adm. 167/90) and Memos. of 6th March and 11th July 1934. Adm. 167/91.

[3] Memo. of 29th June 1933. Adm. 1/8774.

[4] See vol. 1, pp. 498-500.

[5] Memos. (undated but probably late 1933) in Adm. 1/8766 and 9354.

cruisers was needed for fleet work and trade defence. But as the London Treaty limited total cruiser tonnage, and the decision had been taken to build bigger cruisers, the only way the required number could be achieved was by retaining over-age ships in service. In the autumn of 1934 Chatfield accordingly brought this matter before the Board,[1] which approved reducing the number of World War I ships to be scrapped in order to fill the gap of 20 ships. The cost was estimated at nearly £2 millions.[2]

The broad outcome of the deliberations discussed above was that the Sketch Estimates for 1934 came out at £57.4 millions and Vote A (personnel) rose to 92,300—the first increase since 1931.[3] Three new flights were to be provided for the Fleet Air Arm and eight other flights re-equipped.[4] Expectedly the Chancellor of the Exchequer demurred; but the cuts demanded were fairly moderate and a settlement was quickly reached at just over £56½ millions—with which Monsell and the Sea Lords were probably satisfied.[5] Monsell again showed great skill and tact in presenting the estimates to Parliament[6] —so much so that G. H. Hall, who again led for the Opposition, described him as 'the most dangerous occupant which that position [First Lord] has had for some time', because he was so businesslike and so able in disarming critics.[7] In his opening speech Monsell pre-empted attack by the air lobby and by those who held the 'heresy' that the battleship was obsolete by declaring that 'I do not believe that it would be possible to find a Board of Admiralty who would not say that the battleship is, and must remain, the backbone of our fleet'.[8]

Meanwhile the Foreign Office had given warning that the Japanese aggressions in Manchuria and North China, combined with 'the threatening and provocative attitude of Germany', pointed unmistakably to a serious deterioration in the international situation, and Hankey therefore brought together in one comprehensive paper the views and opinions needed for the COSs to prepare their Annual Review for 1933.[9] Both papers made depressing reading—especially

---

[1] Memo. of 6th Oct. 1934. Adm. 167/91.

[2] Board Minute 3246 of 25th Oct. 1934. Adm. 167/90. [3] See Appendix D.

[4] Board Minute 3150 of 12th Dec. 1933. Adm. 167/88.

[5] Chamberlain to Monsell 22nd Jan., Monsell to Chamberlain 26th Jan. and reply by latter of 30th Jan. 1934. Adm. 167/91.

[6] Cmd. 4523 of 1st March 1934 and Parl. Deb., Commons, vol. 287, cols. 41–158.

[7] *ibid.*, cols. 58–61. [8] *ibid.*, cols. 49–52.

[9] CID. 1112B of 30th June and 1113B of 12th Oct. 1933. The latter is the Annual Review. Cab. 4/22.

with regard to Britain's capacity to defend her possessions and interests in the Far East. The CID took them simultaneously on 9th November with MacDonald in the chair.[1] Chamberlain, the Chancellor, proposed that, as a substitute for the defunct Ten Year Rule, the likelihood of war with the USA, France and Italy should be wholly discounted—which went no way to reduce the anxieties of the COSs. The CID agreed to send the COSs' Review, the principal points of which have already been given, to the Cabinet and gave the Far East first priority. No expenditure was to be incurred 'to provide exclusively against attack by the USA, France or Italy'; and, most importantly, that 'the COS Committee with the representatives of the Treasury, the Foreign Office and the Secretary of the CID, should prepare a programme for meeting our worst deficiencies . . .' This was the origin of the Defence Requirements Committee (DRC), which met for the first time only six days later. Apart from the COSs the members were Sir Warren Fisher and Sir Robert Vansittart, the Permanent Secretaries of the Treasury and Foreign Office respectively, and Hankey; and at the first meeting on 15th November Hankey was unanimously elected chairman. It is hard to conceive a better selected body than the DRC, since all three principal interests—Defence, Finance and Foreign Policy—were represented by men of outstanding experience and influence. Yet it is not surprising that the difference of outlook and purpose of the three leading members quickly became apparent. While Fisher mistrusted Germany, in which sentiment he had a powerful ally in Vansittart, he also favoured a rapprochement with Japan, in which purpose he enjoyed Chamberlain's support; and of course he gave high priority to the limitation of expenditure to what was possible within the need for a balanced budget—which was already endangered by the government's pledges to reduce taxation and restore the 1931 pay cuts. Fisher viewed the Admiralty's pressure to build a fleet capable of fighting at any rate a defensive war with Japan and to complete the Singapore base with distaste—chiefly because he considered a two-ocean navy beyond the country's economic resources.[2] Vansittart went much further than Fisher in wanting to treat Germany as the greatest danger; and for that reason he wanted such money as could be provided to go to the RAF rather than to the Navy. Montgomery-Massingberd, the CIGS, and Ellington, the CAS, supported this view —the former in order to prepare an Expeditionary Force to send to the

[1] 261st CID meeting. Cab. 2/6.
[2] Fisher to Hankey 26th Jan. 1934. Cab. 21/434.

continent and the latter to gain higher priority for his service.[1] Against them stood Chatfield, who enjoyed the tactfully expressed but none the less firm support of Hankey. At the end of November Chatfield circulated to the Board a paper which was in fact an extension and revision of his predecessor's paper of November 1932 on naval policy, mentioned earlier.[2] He included a statement of 'the total amount necessary to meet our general requirements' and, secondly, 'the amount necessary to meet the maximum requirements for an emergency in the Far East'; but the DRC's instructions necessitated the addition of a third statement setting out 'Special Items for European Commitments'. Originally the policy had been to rectify the 'worst deficiencies' by 1942 (about a decade after the abandonment of the Ten Year Rule); but the DRC had decided at its first meeting that a five-year programme should be put forward by all three services, and Chatfield had adjusted the Admiralty's requirements accordingly.[3] The DRC took the Admiralty's paper at its 4th, 5th and 6th meetings in January 1934.[4] The total cost of the new construction proposed was estimated at nearly £107 millions; and in addition the Singapore base would require £4½ millions between 1934 and 1940, while the Fleet Air Arm needed £6½ millions for the expansion proposed up to 1941.[5]

We need not here follow the deliberations of the DRC in detail. Its report was circulated on 28th February 1934 and was unanimous—though Vansittart did informally protest that the committee was asking for 'too little Air'. Considering the complexity of the issues raised the production of this comprehensive survey in just over three months was a remarkable accomplishment, and a tribute to the efficiency of the CID secretariat.[6] The DRC report naturally reflected the difference of opinion and outlook of its members. For example the committee recorded that 'we cannot over-state the importance we

---

[1] Meeting of DRC on 14th Nov. 1933 and Vansittart to Hankey 24th Feb. 1934. Cab. 16/109.

[2] See pp. 150-1.

[3] Memo. by Chatfield of 30th Nov. 1933 and Appendices I, II and III. Adm. 116/3434 and 167/89. Became DRC. 6 of 20th Dec. 1933.

[4] Minutes in Cab. 16/109. Copies in Adm. 116/3434.

[5] Appendix II to DRC. 6 (Revised). *ibid.*

[6] DRC. 14 of 28th Feb. 1934. Adm. 116/3434 and Cab. 16/109. The Admiralty put forward a large number of amendments to the draft report when first circulated and most of them appear to have been accepted. Undated paper (c. Feb. 1934) in Adm. 116/3434. For details of the DRC's deliberations see Roskill, *Hankey*, III, ch. 2 and *passim*.

attach to getting back, not to an alliance . . . but at least to our old terms of cordiality and mutual respect with Japan'; and 'There is much to be said for the view that our subservience to the United States of America in past years has been one of the principal factors in the deterioration of our former good relations with Japan . . .'; which statements can confidently be attributed to Fisher. On the other hand the statement 'that danger to us in Europe will only come from Germany', and the assumption that 'we take Germany as the ultimate potential enemy against whom our "long range" defence policy must be directed' equally certainly reflected Vansittart's views.[1]

The total sum asked for to make good the five-year Deficiency Programme of all three services was £71.3 millions, but a further £11 millions would be needed thereafter to complete the programme. For the Navy the principal items were:

1. Fleet Air Arm £1.9 millions to make up the shortage of 51 aircraft and associated equipment spread over 5 to 6 years.
2. Modernisation of capital ships £1.9 millions spread over 6 years.
3. Personnel £8 millions spread over 9 years.
4. Anti-submarine equipment £¼ million spread over 5 years.
5. Local Seaward Defences £0.6 million spread over 5 years and £1 million over 9 or more years.
6. Fuel reserves (oil and storage) £6.7 millions spread over 6 years.
7. Ammunition, torpedoes, mines and depth charges £1.7 millions spread over 2 to 9 years.
8. Stores of various classes and storage £4.3 millions spread over 9 years.
9. Singapore Base £4.4 millions spread over 5 years.

In addition, and dependent on the result of the forthcoming naval conference, the Admiralty's Sketch Estimates indicated an average annual expenditure on new construction of some £13.4 millions for 5 years.[2]

In the Admiralty, though its official records give little sign of it, the signature of the DRC report must have been viewed with relief, and

[1] *ibid.*, paras. 8, 9, 11 and 12.
[2] The long-term building programme originally in the DRC report provided for 3 battleships, 12 cruisers (6 large and 6 small), 4 destroyer flotillas, 12 submarines and 2 submarine depot ships, one aircraft carrier, 17 sloops of various types and 21 trawlers and small craft. Adm. 116/3436.

regarded as the start of a new era. At any rate Chatfield wrote to Hankey in his own hand to tell him 'how much I feel we all owe to you . . . your guiding hand on the tiller kept us to a correct and steady course'.[1]

Unfortunately the response to the DRC's proposals in ministerial circles was both slow and inadequate. In the Cabinet, MacDonald was by no means pleased with the committee's recommendations, and considered that to attempt a rapprochement with Japan would have disastrous repercussions in the USA, Canada and China. Simon, the Foreign Secretary, was also lukewarm about reaching an accord with Japan; but as he always trimmed his sails to the strongest wind his views probably carried little weight. Chamberlain on the other hand favoured a non-aggression pact with Japan, chiefly to achieve a reduction in expenditure on defence by concentrating on the German threat and ignoring the remoter one—in distance though not in time—from Japan.[2]

The Cabinet decided to refer the report to the Ministerial Committee which had been brought into existence to frame British policy for the Geneva Disarmament Conference—though Hankey protested about the illogicality of a Disarmament Committee deliberating a rearmament report. Chamberlain pre-judged the issue by writing that 'to put it bluntly we are presented with proposals impossible to carry out', and proposed to cut the DRC programme to £50.3 millions spread over five years. The Army was to receive £20 millions—about half the sum recommended by the DRC, while the RAF was to receive about the same sum to complete the 52 squadron air defence scheme approved as long ago as 1923—which was nearly double the sum recommended by the DRC. While the Ministerial Committee paid lip service to 'the paramount importance of the Navy as the shield of the whole Empire and of its vital seaborne communications' they flatly refused to commit themselves to the long-term building programme put forward by the Admiralty, and even cut the sum required to make good naval deficiencies to £13 millions.[3]

The deliberations of the Ministerial Committee produced rising concern in the Admiralty as it became clear that there was no possibility

[1] Chatfield to Hankey. Holograph, 28th Feb. 1934. Cab. 21/434.

[2] Minutes of Ministerial Disarmament Committee's 13 meetings. DC(M)(32) series. Cab. 16/110.

[3] CP. 204(34) of 31st July 1934 signed by Baldwin. Cab. 24/250. Taken by Cabinet on same day. Cabinet 31(34). Cab. 23/79.

of the whole of their deficiencies, let alone the long-term building programme, being met. In its final stages of these protracted deliberations the Admiralty's concern rose to anger, and even the customarily quiet-spoken Chatfield told Monsell that 'The Chancellor has invented an entirely new Imperial Defence policy, a somewhat bold step, as the new policy is not based on the solid reasoning which has determined our Imperial policy in the past, but upon the question "what is the cheapest way in which we can keep face with the world?" '[1] For the final meeting of the Ministerial Committee he gave Monsell a clear and precise brief of sixteen points, the last of which was 'Is the Cabinet aware that the Navy is seriously unprepared for war both in material and personnel, [and] what is their policy to put things right?'[2] But it was to no avail.

Looking back today, and bearing in mind that the money asked for by the DRC was about one tenth of the sum which the government had to find three years later, which in turn proved totally inadequate to meet the situation, it does seem that a great opportunity was lost in the early months of 1934 when full acceptance of the DRC programme could well have provided the means to enable our statesmen to 'face the dictators' from a position of some strength when the deepening crisis made negotiation from weakness certain to fail.

The debates in the Ministerial Committee which took the DRC report were often acrimonious, especially regarding Far Eastern strategy and the oft-repeated promise made to Australia and New Zealand that their security would be provided by a strong fleet sent to Singapore. Chamberlain's proposal that we should 'postpone the idea of sending out . . . a fleet of capital ships', and confine the use of the base to submarines and light craft horrified Monsell; and he was supported by J. H. Thomas, the Dominions Secretary, who considered that such a proposal could lead to the antipodean Dominions charging us with a breach of faith. MacDonald finally came down in favour of maintaining 'the continuity of Imperial strategy which has been carried on by every Government since the war'.[3] Presumably he had forgotten his own governments' action in cancelling the base in 1924 and slowing down work on it in 1929.

[1] Chatfield to Monsell 21st June 1934. Adm. 116/3436.

[2] Same to same 27th July 1934. *ibid.*

[3] Proceedings of Ministerial Committee of the Disarmament Committee of 1932, which took the DRC's First Report DRC. 14 and CP. 64(34). See DC(M)(32) series.

After some hesitation the CID recommended that the DRC's and the Ministerial Committee's reports should not be sent to the Dominions—at any rate immediately.[1] But as Hankey was about to set off on an Empire tour, ostensibly to attend the Melbourne Centenary celebrations but actually to explain to the Dominions that the British government had, albeit reluctantly, decided to embark on a programme of rearmament, he took with him a brief prepared by himself and containing the essential features of the two reports. His celebrated tact, wisdom and experience stood him in good stead, and even in South Africa and Canada, the two Dominions most likely to resent any hint of an infringement of their political independence, he achieved a large degree of success.[2] If no very rapid results in the form of increased expenditure on defence were to be expected, the Dominions were at any rate made aware of the fact that Britain had begun to take the threat of the dictatorships seriously.

While Hankey was abroad the Naval Staff set to work to trim their programmes to keep them within the total sum Chamberlain was prepared to find.

The US Navy's plans were at this time still concentrated chiefly, both on paper and in fleet exercises, on the 'Orange Plan' for war with Japan,[3] and the naval planners repeatedly expressed grave concern over the difficulty and danger of sending their main fleet west from Hawaii to the relief of the Philippines in face of Japanese submarine and air attacks while lacking any bases west of Pearl Harbour. In fact the Japanese plans were to fight an 'attrition' campaign of that very nature

---

Cab. 16/110. Chamberlain's Note on the DRC report is DC(M)(32)120 of 20th June 1934.

[1] 266th CID meeting on 22nd Nov. 1934. Cab. 2/6.

[2] Roskill, *Hankey*, III, ch. 3. Hankey reported on his return that he had discussed the two reports with all the Dominion Prime Ministers (Cabinet 4(35) of 16th Jan. 1935. Cab. 23/81). While in Australia he wrote a report on 'Certain Aspects of Australian Defence'. See unpublished Doctoral Thesis *Australian Naval Policy 1919–42* by B. N. Primrose (1974) pp. 202–4 (typescript). The chief sources for Hankey's Empire Tour are the Hankey Papers in Churchill College, Cambridge, the Cab. 63 series in the PRO (Hankey's official papers and correspondence) and Adm. 1/8825–126/35.

The Australian Defence Committee's minutes in CRS. A2031 give that body's reactions to Hankey's proposals, and indicate the strength of feeling in favour of Australia concentrating on local air and military defence as opposed to contributing to the 'Empire Fleet' concept favoured by Hankey. Australian Archives, Kingston, ACT.

[3] See vol. I, pp. 541–3. Records of Fleet Problems X and XI (May and July 1930), XIII (n.d. but probably 1932), XIV (Jan. 1933) and XV (April 1934). US National Archives, Record Group 80, Boxes 65–68. Also GB. 434 for 1931–33 exercises.

in order to reduce American superiority before the anticipated fleet action took place in the western Pacific.[1] But in addition to the 'Orange Plan', which was revised again in 1934 by the Joint Planning Committee,[2] the Americans also kept in being plans for a 'Red' war against Britain, a 'Red–Orange' war against Britain and Japan in alliance, and also plans for conflict with Mexico and Cuba—all of which were revised at various dates during our period.

The main concerns of the US Navy's General Board and of the planners in 1933–34 were the relative weakness of the navy, which was still far below treaty strength *vis à vis* Japan, and the strategic and logistic problems involved in a westward movement made in sufficient time and strength to save Guam and the Philippines.[3] It should however here be remarked that the US Navy, like the British and Japanese, still gave considerable weight to the concept of a Jutland-type fleet action in which the battleship would prove, as in earlier times, the dominant weapon. It seems probable that in all three nations the influence of the American naval theorist Captain Alfred T. Mahan, whose philosophy was derived mainly from British experience and strategy in the Napoleonic War, was still strong.[4] For example in the autumn of 1934 Admiral J. M. Reeves, the C-in-C, US Fleet, sent President Roosevelt his proposals for an exercise in the Pacific culminating in 'a fleet engagement involving all types of vessels, including shore-based aircraft, simulating the type of engagement which would occur in the Western Pacific'—that is to say a fleet action of the Jutland type.[5] As regards building programmes, there is a remarkable similarity between the eight year programme proposed by Admiral Pratt, the Chief of Naval Operations, entitled 'The Navy's Needs' of July 1933 (including the

[1] *Pelz*, pp. 34–9.

[2] See Louis Morton, *The War in the Pacific: Strategy and Command: The First Two Years* (Washington, 1962), pp. 37–9. The 1934 discussions revealed a cleavage between the Army, which wished to wage a defensive campaign and to keep the main US Fleet east of Hawaii, and the Navy which insisted that the war could only be won by an offensive movement into the western Pacific.

[3] GB. 425 Serial 1502 of 4th May 1932. 'Estimate of the Situation and Navy Basic Plan for Orange War.' This review gave the US Navy only 50% of the permitted treaty tonnage whereas Japan had 88%.

[4] *Pelz, passim* strongly argues that this was the case.

[5] Reeves to Roosevelt 27th Oct. 1934. Roosevelt Papers, Official File 18. Reeves did however also state that he wanted to investigate both 'the possibility of basing the entire fleet at Honolulu' and at Midway Island 'which may prove a most important strategical outpost for the Hawaiian Islands'. The latter hypothesis was to be amply substantiated in June 1942.

dominance of the battleship) and the 5–9 year programme put up by the Admiralty to the DRC.[1]

Although President Roosevelt had to proceed with extreme caution and to show great political acumen in putting forward proposals for rearmament during his first term he did give Carl Vinson, Chairman of the House Naval Affairs Committee, strong encouragement to ask Congress to authorise a programme to bring the US Navy up to treaty strength. The resultant Vinson-Trammell Act (named also for Senator Park Trammell, Vinson's colleague as Chairman of the Senate Naval Affairs Committee), was signed by the President on 27th March 1934.[2] Vinson soon followed it up with proposals for further legislation to provide the personnel needed to man the larger navy.[3] The Act of 1934 did not of itself add a single ship to the navy; since that process could not begin until either Congress had passed the necessary Appropriation Act or the President had, by Executive Order, provided funds for naval construction from the New Deal agencies referred to earlier. None the less the Vinson-Trammell Act was a significant milestone in the history of the long-starved US Navy. When Roosevelt encouraged its introduction in Congress he undoubtedly had in mind not only the wide gap between the existing navy and what it was entitled to possess under the treaties, but that all the signs were that Japanese policy was veering away from co-operation with the western democracies, and

[1] Pratt to Swanson 24th March 1933. Op-10. Also Roosevelt Papers, Official File 18, Box 21. The 'needs' included 3 aircraft carriers, 8 large cruisers (one with 8-inch, seven with 6-inch guns), 85 destroyers and 23 submarines. The cost was estimated at $944 millions. On the dominance of the battleship as 'our most useful type' in terms of what is now known as 'costs-efficiency' see Pratt to Swanson 27th March 1933. For example the 'defensive life' of the battleship was estimated at 10 to the aircraft carrier's 5.7, and the striking power of the former at $20 per ton displacement to $87 for the latter. Roosevelt papers, Special File 18, Box 27.

[2] For a detailed discussion on the Vinson–Trammell Act (HR. 6604) see article by Charles F. Elliott *The Genesis of the Modern US Navy* in US Naval Institute Proceedings, vol. 92, no. 3 (March 1966). Although as finally passed the Act rigidly limited the profits made by shipbuilding and armament firms Senator Trammell remained highly suspicious of their activities. On 1st Aug. 1933 he wrote to the President that he was sure there had been collusion over the bids put in by the four firms which were to build some of the *Brooklyn* class cruisers, in order to 'protect' each other. Roosevelt sent the complaint on to Swanson who assured Trammell that, after 'full examination', he was satisfied that the allegedly competitive bids were genuine. Roosevelt Papers, Official File 18. Box 21.

[3] Swanson to FDR 21st Nov. 1934 enclosing Vinson's proposals. *ibid.*, Roosevelt papers, PSF, Dept. Corresp., Box 28 (Swanson file).

that militaristic elements were in the ascendant in that country. Though the Japanese military and naval leaders were by no means unanimous on future policy—notably on the issue whether preparations should be made for a new war with Russia or whether a drive should be made to the south to secure the raw materials of the French, British and Dutch colonies, none of them had the slightest intention of modifying, let alone abandoning, the expansionist campaign on the Asiatic mainland. Moreover the Japanese admirals were most unwilling that their navy should continue in the inferior ratio of Britain and American's strength incorporated in the treaties of 1922 and 1930. Yet, despite the President's cautious and astute handling of the naval problem, he was subjected to a storm of protest over the Vinson-Trammell Act from those who regarded any measure of rearmament as evil by definition; and the fact that much of the protest came from the President's political supporters meant that he could only ignore it at his peril.[1] In July Roosevelt endeavoured to explain his policy to the nation; but as he made his speech from the cruiser *Houston* while on passage in the Pacific from Panama to Hawaii—possibly as a warning to Japan—its effect on the home audience was by no means what he had probably hoped for.[2]

Early in September the British Cabinet asked for a study to be made of the American programme, and especially of the big 6-inch cruisers.[3] The Naval Staff replied that the construction in question, and also the recent Japanese programme, were 'strictly within the provisions of the London Treaty', though the large size of the American cruisers was 'a disappointment to us', and would probably cause the Japanese to hasten their 'replenishment programmes' and step up the size of their new cruisers. 'We are now witnessing', the staff correctly concluded, 'the first steps in competitive building of a new type . . . [and] we shall inevitably have to follow suit'. Prospects for a new limitation agreement were, they considered, 'gloomy in the extreme'.[4] The British government made a forlorn attempt to stem the tide by offering to

[1] Roosevelt Papers. PPF. 5901 contains many letters and telegrams of protest against the Act.

[2] *ibid.*, Official File 18, Box 21. The Navy League of the USA expectedly gave Roosevelt's speech of 22nd July a very warm welcome. 'Release' of 30th July 1934, copy in Roosevelt papers. But the isolationist and pacifist lobbies and press were extremely hostile.

[3] Cabinet 50(33) of 5th Sept. 1933. Cab. 23/77.

[4] Naval Staff memo. of 7th Sept. 1933. Adm. 116/2998.

suspend building larger 6-inch cruisers if the USA and Japan would do the same; but the Washington embassy reported that Cordell Hull, the Secretary of State, had 'evinced slight enthusiasm' for the proposal, which was in fact quickly rejected.[1]

Meanwhile the General Board had framed its recommendations for the 1935 Fiscal Year. With the 1934 programme well under way they asked for two aircraft carriers, seven more of the big 6-inch cruisers, 47 destroyers and 18 submarines. If approved and carried out the deficiency remaining to bring the US Navy up to treaty strength by the end of 1936 would be comparatively small. In other words the Navy Department saw the target towards which it had so long striven at last within sight.[2] The extent of the US Navy's first steps towards recovery is perhaps best illustrated by a report sent to the President by the Navy Department early in 1935 listing all the ships building and appropriated for from NIRA funds. The principal ones were three aircraft carriers (*Yorktown*, *Enterprise* and *Wasp*[3]), three 8-inch cruisers of the *Vincennes* class, nine 6-inch cruisers, 13 large and 40 small destroyers and 16 submarines.[4] In addition to the foregoing in the spring of 1935 Swanson sent to Roosevelt proposals for modernising older warships and building more 'auxiliary vessels' (i.e. destroyers and smaller ships) at respective costs of $27 and $158 millions. The Director of the Bureau of the Budget remarked that 'If it is decided that the Navy should be built up to treaty strength in all respects as soon as practicable, the need for the legislation . . . is not questioned'; otherwise he considered the moment 'inopportune' to present such proposals to Congress. Roosevelt asked the Director to speak to him on the subject, but no record of the outcome has been found.[5] However in November Swanson wrote again pressing for modernisation of the older battleships, including increasing the elevation of their main armament guns; and the Navy Department also wanted to modernise the big carriers *Lexington* and *Saratoga*, which they now described as 'ships of great

---

[1] British *aide mémoire* of 14th Sept. to Washington, and telegram 510(R) of 23rd Sept. 1933 reporting its rejection. Sir Ronald Lindsay's despatch of 8th Dec. 1933 no. 1572 described accurately Swanson's attitude and policy and also the probable Japanese reaction. See also report by Naval Attaché, Washington of 25th Jan. 1934 on appropriations and contracts for 1934 programme. All in Adm. 116/2998.

[2] GB. 420–2, serial 1619 of 10th May 1933.

[3] Laid down respectively on 21st May 1934, 16th July 1934 and 4th Jan. 1936.

[4] Bureau of Construction and Repair, Navy Dept. to FDR. Roosevelt papers, PSF, Dept. Corresp., Box 25.

[5] Bureau of Budget to FDR 27th April 1935. *ibid.*, Official File 18, Box 2A.

value'.[1] In fact appropriations were gradually approved to carry out this work.

Although the Bureau of the Budget appears to have been helpful in general over the financing of the first steps towards US naval re-armament the opposition of the groups and interests mentioned earlier became so vociferous that, in September 1935, the President felt obliged to make a public announcement that 'American naval building policy is precisely and without change what it has been during the last $2\frac{1}{2}$ years; to bring the Navy up to the strength provided for in the Washington and London treaties'; and that purpose would be accomplished by 1942.[2] However the President firmly declined to answer his critics in greater detail, holding that it was 'far better not to answer the professional pacifist'. To hit back, he continued, would 'only create controversy'[3]—a policy which the Admiralty also consistently maintained.

An interesting point is that in the early 1930s the British Admiralty and the US Navy Department were both plagued by congestion in the lower ranks of their officers, which tended to make promotion far too slow, and produced excessively old senior officers. The steps taken by the Admiralty between 1929 and 1933, culminating in compulsory retirement of officers with indifferent records, have already been re-counted.[4] In America H. L. Roosevelt wrote to the President early in 1934 that it was 'essential to reduce [the] congestion' caused by the entry of large numbers in 1919–21 before the fleet had been reduced by the Washington Treaty; but the expansion of the navy after 1934 appears to have saved the US Navy from adopting such drastic measures as the Admiralty, and in fact Vinson was soon sending Roosevelt proposals to *increase* the number of 'Line' (i.e. executive) officers.[5] The US Navy

[1] Swanson to FDR 2nd Nov. 1935. Roosevelt Papers, Dept. Corresp., Box 28. Cf. Moffet's view of these ships. See pp. 46-7.

[2] Statement of 27th Sept. 1935. Roosevelt Papers, Official File, Box 2A. The flood of protest against the naval building programme is well illustrated by the letters and telegrams in File 18, Box 21.

[3] To H. L. Roosevelt 2nd Feb. 1934. *ibid.*, Official File, Box 2A.

[4] See p. 32.

[5] Forwarded by Swanson to FDR 21st Nov. 1934. Vinson's draft Bill asked for a total of 7,012 Line officers (5.1% of enlisted strength), but neither the President nor the Bureau of the Budget liked it, the latter amending it substantially because the total of officers named would only be reached in 1948. The increase required was in the main met by gradually raising the number of entries to the US Naval Academy and from the organisation of the Reserve of Officers, of which more later.

however suffered from a problem which never at this time afflicted the Admiralty—namely shortage of enlisted men. In late 1934 Swanson told Roosevelt that 'a very unsatisfactory condition' prevailed because the whole fleet except its submarines was undermanned. He was in conflict with the Bureau of the Budget over the numbers to be authorised for the Fiscal Year 1936, and asked for 88,000 enlisted men.[1] At about the same time the British Navy's Vote A amounted to over 94,000.

Study of the President's papers leaves one in no doubt about his strong interest in even the *minutiae* of naval policy, and his extreme confidence in his own judgement. For example when answering a question from H. L. Roosevelt about the functions of the Chief of Naval Operations in relation to the Chiefs of the Bureaux and the Secretary of the Navy he cited the knowledge acquired through 'my somewhat long experience in the Department';[2] and when in the following year he received a large file of papers on naval reserves he sent them back 'with some comments which may sound harsh but which are called forth by my general feeling that once more the Navy Department has dropped the ball . . . this time, after 22 years of effort I intend to get results'. Yet if the senior officers of the Navy Department were sometimes resentful of the President's incursions into their field, and of his occasional forthright criticisms of their actions, the broad picture of Roosevelt's first term provides convincing evidence of the benefits then gained by the navy.

As regards the naval policy of the other powers during the period covered by this chapter, on 27th March 1933 Japan, having been condemned at Geneva for her aggression against China, gave notice of her intention to leave the League of Nations—which in theory required two years to take effect. In August of the following year the decision was taken, after a period of intense pressure by the extreme

[1] Swanson to FDR 2nd Nov. 1934. Roosevelt papers, PSF, Dept. Corresp., Box 28 (Swanson file). The US Navy's statutory number of officers was 5% of the total of enlisted men.

[2] FDR to H. L. Roosevelt 2nd March 1934. On the 1934 H. L. Roosevelt Board's review of the duties of the Chiefs of Bureaux, the CNO and the Secretary, and the President's reactions, see article by Thomas W. Ray, *The Bureaus Go On Forever*, in US Naval Institute Proceedings, vol. 94, no. 1 (Jan. 1968). The Bureau system actually endured until May 1966, though there was often friction between their Chiefs and the CNO—especially during Admiral E. J. King's time as CNO (March 1942–Dec. 1945). The author of this history had first-hand experience of this friction while serving in the British Admiralty Delegation, Washington 1944–45.

naval interests on the Prime Minister, Admiral Keisuki Okada, and the Foreign Minister Kōki Hirota, to abrogate the Washington Treaty and achieve parity with Britain and the USA.[1] That year the Japanese Navy began to build the giant *Yamato* class battleships (64,170 tons, nine 18.1-inch guns), on which work was carried out in the utmost secrecy.[2] Thus the years 1933–34 marked a climacteric in Japanese foreign and naval policy, by refusing further co-operation in naval limitation; and if this change resulted in a building race, as the Japanese admirals realised was likely, they were confident that they would win it. Such in brief was the background to the euphemistically named 'First Replenishment Programme', which was to be completed between 1931 and 1935. It consisted of four heavy cruisers (*Mogami* class), twelve destroyers and four torpedo-boats, nine submarines and a number of minelayers and minesweepers. In 1934, before that programme had been completed, the Japanese framed a far more ambitious 'Second Replenishment Programme'. It comprised two aircraft carriers (*Soryu* and *Hiryu*) and three seaplane carriers (which were later converted into light fleet carriers), two 'light' cruisers (*Tone* class, actually of 11,200 tons with eight 8-inch guns), fourteen destroyers and eight torpedo-boats, four submarines, plus the usual auxiliary and minor warships; all to be completed by 1937.[3]

Though the Japanese admirals realised that in the long run the United States was fully capable of outbuilding them, they had great confidence in the advantages they would derive from certain technical developments, by means of which they expected to reduce the possible superiority of the US fleet during its long passage from Hawaii westwards to the Philippines. The chief weapons in question were, firstly, the 2,000-ton Fleet Type 6 submarines, which carried a reconnaissance aircraft by which they hoped to gain early knowledge of the enemy's movements. Eight of those were built between 1931 and 1934 (the I.5, I.168 and I.6 classes) under the First Replenishment Programme. The second new weapon was the high-speed reconnaissance aircraft which became the Mitsubishi Type 96 shore-based bomber, which was in 1932 the fastest aircraft in the world. In 1932–33 they also built new and successful carrier-borne fighters and dive-bombers, and in 1933

---

[1] For an excellent account of the events leading to this decision see *Pelz*, chs. 3 and 4.

[2] Only two of the five projected ships of this class were completed as battleships— *Yamato*, completed 1941, and *Musashi*, completed 1942. A third one, *Shinano*, was converted to aircraft carrier. All three were sunk in World War II.

[3] See *Pelz*, pp. 174, 196–7 and 216–17.

they began work very secretly on midget submarines (Types A and Ha) which were the forerunners of a large number of similar craft. They were to be used as part of the 'ambush' strategy designed to reduce American surface ship superiority, but were in fact never very successful. By contrast the big Type 95 long-range, high speed torpedo (known as 'Long Lance') developed at this time proved a deadly weapon and superior to the torpedoes of any other power. All in all Japanese technical developments in the early 1930s were more advanced and sophisticated than either the Admiralty or the US Navy Department appreciated. Only in Radar development did the Japanese lag seriously behind Britain and the USA; and that deficiency was in the long run to offset the advantages gained by their other developments.[1]

Apart from the issue of parity between the British and American navies and the refusal of Japan to continue the Washington ratios, rivalry was increasing at this time between France and Italy, and the latter was insisting on parity with the former—despite the French claim that, because they had Mediterranean and Atlantic sea frontiers to guard, they needed the greater strength. Nor in the prevailing political climate could the British Admiralty disregard either the potential threat of a revivified French navy mostly based on the flank of the principal British trade routes and particularly strong in submarines, or the threat posed by a powerful Italian navy to our Mediterranean traffic and to control of the sea routes to the Far East. Such fears were aggravated when in June 1934 the Paris Embassy reported that the French Chamber had approved laying down another *Dunkerque* class battle-cruiser. Furthermore, continued the Ambassador, if Italy went ahead with her two projected 35,000-ton battleships France would lay down similar ships in 1935 and '36.[2] At about the same time the Naval Attaché, Paris reported that France would indeed go ahead with the above ships (which finally became the *Richelieu* and *Jean Bart* of 1939-40), but the Minister of Marine, François Piétri, was prepared to accept smaller ships of 27,000 tons if—as was most unlikely—his naval advisers agreed. The Attaché also reported that he had told Piétri that France had 'more submarines than she needs', since about 80 were completed or building at the time; and the Minister did not disagree.[3] The Foreign Office had meanwhile instructed the Ambassador in Rome to

[1] See *Pelz*, pp. 30-2 for details regarding Japanese technical developments.
[2] Sir George Clerk to FO no. 187 of 30th June 1934. Copy in Adm. 116/2998.
[3] Naval Attaché letter to Sir E. Drummond, Ambassador in Rome, of 28th June 1934. *ibid.*

represent to Mussolini the British government's concern over the building of two big battleships at a moment when a new naval limitation conference was in the offing, and we were hoping to reach agreement to reduce the size of such ships. But London had to admit that Italy was acting within treaty rights,[1] and the departments cannot have been surprised when the Ambassador replied that, although he had stated the British case to Mussolini, he had made 'little impression'.[2] Further pressure would, he reported, produce no result except to irritate the Italian dictator.[3] The interchange was ended by the despatch of a *Note Verbale* expressing regret at the Italian decision—to which the reply was totally negative despite a somewhat hypocritical reference to 'the spirit of friendly frankness which characterises Italo-British relations'.[4] The fact that the ships (which became the *Littorio* and *Vittorio Veneto*, completed in 1940) were to be laid down on the anniversary of the Fascist 'March on Rome' in October 1922 probably added insult to the British sense of injury.[5]

As regards cruisers and submarines, the two classes of ship with which the Admiralty was most concerned, between the signature of the Washington Treaty in 1922 and 1934 the Italians had built or authorised nineteen of the former (seven of them allegedly of Treaty tonnage, but actually a good deal larger) and 55 of the latter (mostly of about 800 tons surface displacement).[6] Thus Italy was still a good way behind France in both classes, but by 1934 was showing very evident determination to achieve 'parity'. One may describe Italo-French rivalry as a lesser building race taking place simultaneously with the greater building race between the three major powers.

Possibly to help Hankey in his conversations with the Commonwealth countries on the need for British rearmament, mentioned earlier, a telegram was sent to all Commonwealth Prime Ministers telling them of Italy's intentions as regards battleships.[7] But if the British Admiralty hoped for more concrete help in naval defence from

---

[1] FO to Drummond no. 198 of 13th June 1934. *ibid.*

[2] Drummond to FO no. 189 of 22nd June 1934. *ibid.*

[3] Same to same no. 206 of 7th July 1934. *ibid.*

[4] *Note Verbale* of 19th July and Italian reply of 25th July 1934. *ibid.*

[5] Drummond to FO 27th Oct. 1934. *ibid.*

[6] These figures are based on A. Fraccaroli, *Italian Warships of World War II* (Ian Allan, 3rd Imp., 1974) and on information kindly supplied by the Directiore Ufficio Storico Della Marina, Rome. See also Cmd. 5038, *Fleets of the British Commonwealth of Nations and Foreign Countries* of Dec. 1935.

[7] Circular Telegram no. 72 of 5th July 1934.

the Commonwealth, as appears to be the case, their hopes were, in the short term, to prove optimistic. Not only were all the countries still gravely affected by the aftermath of the world economic crisis and afflicted by high unemployment and acute budgetary problems, but except in the case of Australia and New Zealand, their political leaders would not look beyond their own local defence problems, and continued to rely on the Royal Navy for the protection of British imperia interests as a whole. As long ago as 1926 the Imperial Conference had agreed that the Dominions' naval policy should be based on four progressive phases. The first was to be provision of local naval defence, the second to take steps towards creation of a 'High Seas Force', the third was to be provision of a sea-going squadron additional to local defence vessels, and in the final phase that force would be increased by the addition of further squadrons.[1]

Despite these good intentions, by the early 1930s only Australia had reached the third phase; but her estimates for 1933–34 recognised 'the urgent need for certain extensions of our defence activities' and allotted £280,000 for naval construction. In 1934 she decided also to modernise her cruisers, with the result that by 1937 she possessed three comparatively new ships of that class as well as a half flotilla of destroyers. New Zealand, though still regarded in London as being in the second phase in 1930, obtained two modern cruisers from Britain in 1924–25, and by 1934 was plainly moving into the third phase— albeit in a small way.[2] The situation was worst in South Africa, Canada and India. Canada had not gone far to fulfil the first phase, and the RCN was only beginning to recover from the severe cuts of the 1920s—which had amounted almost to abolition. As to South Africa, in 1933 Oswald Pirow, who had pronounced pro-Nazi leanings,

---

[1] Adm. 116/2797 contains an analysis of the Commonwealth countries' naval defences in the early 1930s in the light of the policy adopted in 1926. G. Hermon Gill, *Royal Australian Navy 1939–1942*, vol. I, ch. I (Canberra. Australian War Memorial, 1957) has an admirable account of Australian naval policy in between the wars. For the parallel Canadian story see G. N. Tucker *The Naval Service of Canada*, vol. I (King's Printer, Ottawa, 1952). The *History of the New Zealand Navy* is by S. D. Waters (Department of Internal Affairs, Wellington, 1956) and his Chapter I describes the genesis of the RNZN. L. C. F. Turner, H. R. Gordon-Cumming and J. E. Betzler in *War in the Southern Oceans* (OUP, 1961), Chapter I does the same for the South African Naval Service.

[2] The *Dunedin* and *Diomede*, which joined the NZ Division of the Royal Navy in 1924–25, were replaced by the *Achilles* and *Leander* in 1936–37. The NZ Division did not become the Royal New Zealand Navy until Sept. 1941. Waters, *op. cit.*, pp. 13–14.

declared that 'the land and air services have first claim [for money] over the Navy';[1] while India, which had of course not yet achieved Dominion status and was not visited by Hankey on his Empire tour, was chiefly concerned with the nineteenth-century concept of defence of the north-west frontier, and although represented by a somewhat second-class membership at the Imperial Conferences since 1923, had shown little concern over the defence of her huge coastline or of the oceans which washed her shores.[2] The Admiralty was well informed about the lack of naval interest in Canada, South Africa and India by the reports received from the naval Cs-in-C on those stations.

With Japan plainly determined to set out on a new course, even if it meant starting a naval race, France and Italy viewing each other with persistent hostility and embarking on new battleship construction, the anxieties felt in Whitehall as 1934 drew to a close can easily be understood. They were greatly aggravated by Germany's very evident intention to shake off all the shackles of the Versailles Treaty. Although Hitler's unilateral repudiation of it did not take place until 21st May 1935, the Naval Staff began to review the possible implications six months earlier by producing forecasts of what Germany's naval strength might be in 1939 and 1942, and what could be regarded as the basis for an acceptable agreement on limitation with that country.[3] The prospect of Germany possessing eight or nine battleships (four *Deutschlands* and four or five much larger ships), one or two aircraft carriers, ten to fourteen cruisers and 28 to 30 submarines by 1942 was, when the situation in the Far East and tension with Italy were taken into account, alarming; and although a German programme which followed the Naval Staff's forecasts very closely was not announced until early in July 1935,[4] by the end of the previous year the spectre of a simultaneously hostile Germany, Italy and Japan, which was to condition all British naval thinking and planning for the next five years, had begun to haunt the corridors of Whitehall.

The worsening crisis in the Far East naturally produced a change of

[1] Report by Vice-Admiral Sir H. Tweedie, C-in-C, South Africa, of 21st June 1933. Adm. 116/2878.

[2] See vol. I, pp. 459–60 and 538–40.

[3] Adm. 116/3373. Both Plans and Intelligence Divisions produced forecasts of German strength—the latter being in most classes of ship slightly the higher.

[4] NCM(35)59. Cab. 29/148. The announcement was made on 9th July 1935, and the new programme comprised two battleships, two heavy cruisers, 16 large and heavily armed destroyers, and 28 submarines of three different sizes, including the first two of the big 'Atlantic' boats (to be known as Type VII).

emphasis in the deliberations of the Naval Staff and of the COS Committee in 1933, and the latter repeatedly emphasised the weakness of the British position.[1] Though Neville Chamberlain, the Chancellor of the Exchequer, said that 'the risks of the financial situation were perhaps more pressing than the risks from Japanese aggression' he admitted that the COSs had good cause for anxiety. In consequence the CID approved expediting work on the fixed defences of Singapore so as to complete them by mid-1936, and decided that plans should be made to take certain 'immediate measures' to send out short-term reinforcements for the garrison and air defences. Larger reinforcements were to be prepared for despatch in the event of an emergency arising before the fixed defences were completed. The Cabinet, perhaps encouraged by the strong support given to these measures in the CID by S. M. Bruce, Prime Minister of Australia, gave them their approval.[2]

While these deliberations were in progress in London the C-in-C, China, Admiral Sir Frederic Dreyer was considering the same problems from the local point of view and in the light of his predecessor's report on the inadequacy of the Singapore defences.[3] Prior to 1928 the defence of Hong Kong had been given priority on the assumption that the defences of Singapore would be proceeded with 'on a steady programme'. However the 'premises on which that decision was based did not materialise', and Dreyer was told that, in the light of the new situation 'the first duty of the forces under your command will therefore be to make certain that no expedition can reach Singapore from Japan unlocated and unhindered', thus ensuring the safe arrival of reinforcements from India.[4] Approval was given to a conference being held at Singapore early in the following year with all the interested parties, including Australia and New Zealand, represented. The Admiralty followed up their signalled instructions with a letter analysing the current situation and setting out their views and policy. Singapore was, they wrote, 'the pivot of our whole naval strategical position in the Far East'; but until adequate defences had been provided it was 'liable to capture or destruction by a *coup de main* before our Main Fleet can arrive on the scene'. Such a disaster would, they

[1] See especially CID. 1103B of 31st March 1933. Report by COS Committee on 'The Situation in the Far East'. Cab. 4/22. Taken by CID at 258th meeting on 6th April 1933. Cab. 2/5.

[2] *ibid.* The Cabinet approved these recommendations on 12th April 1933. Cab. 23/75.

[3] See pp. 148-9.

[4] AM. 1222 of 25th April 1933. Adm. 116/3472.

realistically continued, be followed by the disintegration of our entire position in the Far East; and the inevitable conclusion was therefore that 'the present strategical position in the Far East is fundamentally unsound'.[1] Dreyer was pressing for the battle-cruisers (of which we possessed three World War I specimens) to be sent out; but the Admiralty told him that such a proposal was 'open to serious political objections'—presumably meaning that the Japanese would regard it as provocative.[2] However the monitor *Terror* and a second torpedo-bomber squadron were being despatched, more A-A guns and search-lights provided, and modest military reinforcements were being sent. Finally they told the C-in-C about the recent Cabinet decision to complete the first stage of the fixed defences of Singapore by mid-1936.[3]

Throughout the summer of 1933 Dreyer continued to bombard the Admiralty with a barrage of lengthy letters on the same subject, and from the marginal comments these evidently irritated the Naval Staff.[4] The Admiralty replied with restraint that 'The Naval Staff is now fully apprised and you will be informed when decisions in regard to our combined strategy have been approved'; and the C-in-C was told to be more economical in the use of land cablegrams and not to use the prefix 'Immediate' unless it was essential.[5] A few months later Chatfield sent him a stiff reprimand about the length, and in some cases the sub-ject matter of his numerous letters and cypher signals;[6] but neither the collective displeasure of the Board nor the personal reprobation of the First Sea Lord seem to have had much effect on the voluble and ambitious Admiral.

The projected conference, attended by the Cs-in-C, China and East Indies, the First Member of the Australian Navy Board and the Commodore, New Zealand Division, took place at Singapore between 23rd and 27th January 1934.[7] The Admiralty's War Memorandum (Eastern) in which the navy's broad plans were set out, was agreed;[8] and the forces likely to join a new and greatly expanded 'Eastern Command', which included virtually the whole Australian Navy and the existing East Indies station ships, were set out. The Main Fleet was

---

[1] AL. M. 00505/33 of 26th April 1933. *ibid.*
[2] AL. M. 00509/33 of 8th July 1933. *ibid.*   [3] AM. 1654 of 25th April 1933. *ibid.*
[4] The letter of 18th July is typical. Adm. 116/3471.
[5] Letter of 4th April 1933. *ibid.*
[6] Chatfield to Dreyer 15th Nov. 1933. Chatfield papers CHT/4/4.
[7] C-in-C, China's report. Adm. 116/3121.   [8] M. 00518/33. Adm. 116/3467.

expected to come out by the Suez Canal, and the time between 'Zero Hour' and its arrival at Singapore still stood at 38 days, as had been estimated in 1932.[1] The capacity of the Singapore base to supply all the forces envisaged was reviewed, and Dreyer reported large deficiencies in virtually every department—which the Admiralty did not altogether view with favour.[2] The areas of concentration for the forces available before the arrival of the Main Fleet were to be to the north of Java and at the northern entrance to the Malacca Straits.[3] Trade defence measures were reviewed, and the Intelligence system throughout the Far East given a much-needed overhaul. Finally plans were made on the basis that operations would pass through three phases, starting with 'The Period before Relief' and ending with 'The Period of Advance' to the north. These somewhat optimistic hopes were based on Dreyer's ambitious aim 'to deprive the Japanese of all access to the sea south of a line Malaya to Fiji'.[4]

Towards the end of 1934 the C-in-C, China, paid a visit to Japan in his flagship, after receiving instructions to avoid the month of October, when the Japanese would be carrying out their big naval exercises, and to exclude all naval bases. He reported that the visit was very successful and that he had been 'shown much kindness and friendship';[5] but we now know that the Japanese navy had not at that time come to a decision to drive to the south, and that their army, already deeply involved in North China, was still primarily concerned about war with Russia.[6]

Looking back today at the measures taken to meet the Far Eastern crisis in 1933–34 it is plain that, although the Cabinet, the Chiefs of Staff and the Admiralty were all fully alive to the dangers, and a great deal of sound and realistic thinking was put on paper about them, very little was actually done. True the completion of the Singapore base had been expedited; but that still lay some three years ahead. Though the possibility of trouble in Europe—especially with Germany—had become a reality it had not yet reached a point where it would make the long-planned despatch of a large fleet to the Far East impossible. Thus it is understandable that the Naval Staff and Admiralty, who were

[1] Note by Hankey covering COS review of 23rd Feb. 1932 and Report on Situation in the Far East of 22nd Feb. 1932. CID. 1082B and 1084B respectively. Hankey's note became CP. 104(32). Cab. 24/229.
[2] AL. M. 0831/34 of 1st Feb. 1935. Adm. 116/3466.
[3] Adm. 116/3466 and 3467.   [4] Letter of 12th Nov. 1934. Adm. 116/3471.
[5] Letter of 12th Nov. 1934. *ibid.*   [6] See *Pelz*, chs. 3, 4 and 12.

deeply conscious of the dependence of Australia and New Zealand on the deployment of adequate British naval strength on their northern flank, should have adhered to that plan; since there really was no alternative except to abandon those countries to their fate and give up the attempt to safeguard the huge British interests in the whole area— which was of course unthinkable. As regards looking for help from other nations, the USA was still largely unarmed and much influenced by isolationist sentiment; France was an uncertain ally and in any case regarded Germany and Italy as far greater threats to her security than Japan; Holland was incapable of defending her rich Far Eastern possessions; and Russia was still ostracised on account of western fears of 'Bolshevism', the avowed aim of the Third International to achieve world-wide revolution, and knowledge, though far from complete, regarding the repression that was going on behind Stalin's tightly closed frontiers.

Where British naval authorities went avoidably wrong was, we now know, in their under-estimate of Japanese skill and prowess and their ability to produce armaments at least as good as, and in some cases markedly better than those of the western nations. It seems likely that this misjudgement derived from Japan's long period of tutelage under British advisers. Perhaps the best example of this under-estimation of a potential enemy is to be found in a report from the Naval Attaché, Tokyo, to which the Admiralty gave wide circulation in 1935. 'The Japanese', wrote Captain G. Vivian, 'have peculiarly slow brains. Teachers . . . have assured me that this is fundamentally due to the strain put on the child's brain in learning some 6,000 Chinese characters before any real education can start . . . The inertia shows itself by an inherent disability to switch the mind from one subject to another with rapidity . . . I am convinced that it is for this reason that the Japanese people are a race of specialists . . . An English master at the Naval College has described the training there as a system of over-training the boys physically [and] over-cramming them mentally, the finished product being a thoroughly over-tired human being . . . All the other foreign Naval Attachés are firmly convinced that the unwillingness of the authorities to show more [i.e. of their ships and weapons] is due rather to the barrenness of the cupboard than to any secrets it may contain'.[1] When this paper was circulated Admiral R. G. H. Henderson, the Controller, one of the most brilliant officers of his generation and a staunch advocate of naval aviation, was almost the only person to

[1] Report by Captain G. Vivian to DNI of 18th Feb. 1935. Adm. 116/3862.

sound a note of warning. 'I think one must be careful', he wrote, 'not to belittle the general efficiency of a possible enemy . . .'; but the Admiralty sent the report on to the Staff College, where presumably it was given close attention by the cream of the officer corps.

Though preparation of the naval estimates and building programmes and the strategic problems produced by the Far Eastern crisis took up the major part of the Admiralty's time and thought in 1933–34—as indeed they did in the US Navy Department—the entry, training and welfare of officers and men continued to figure largely in its deliberations. This was of course, at any rate in part, a by-product of the Invergordon mutiny. The revival of sail training was actually first raised by Admiral R. R. C. Backhouse, when Controller in September 1930, as a result of a visit by the Greek barquentine *Ares* to Portsmouth. He considered it 'remarkable that so many Foreign Navies are reverting to sailing vessels for training of cadets'.[1] In 1932, after Invergordon, the Sea Lords several times discussed whether the Royal Navy should follow suit. The decision was to build a special sailing ship to give cadets that type of training, and when Monsell introduced the 1932 Estimates he told the House of the intention—about which he himself was enthusiastic.[2]

Chatfield evidently heard of this intention before he took over as First Sea Lord, since in May 1932 he wrote apprehensively to Monsell about such vessels being used in winter when 'amateur knowledge and inexperienced Officers and Petty Officers' could lead to a disaster if gales were encountered—as was very likely. He considered that sail training ships should only be used in the summer, and was not prepared to carry the responsibility for endangering 'so many valuable young lives', which was bound to fall on the First Sea Lord of the day, if they were sent out in winter.[3] Though Chatfield's fears were not to be fully realised for 25 years, as he had served in sail and knew the risks his misgivings were surely justified.[4] None the less when he took over as

---

[1] Minute by Backhouse of 18th Sept. 1930. Adm. 116/3283. Actually Argentina, Chile, France, Germany, Greece, Italy, Portugal, Spain, Sweden and Yugoslavia all had sailing vessels in service or projected for training purposes at that time.

[2] Meetings of 19th and 29th April 1932. Adm. 116/3283. Board Minute 2943 of 26th May 1932. Adm. 116/2893. See also Adm. 1/8756–150/1932 and 1/8761–246/1932 for details of the scheme.

[3] Chatfield to Monsell 2nd Feb. 1933. Chatfield papers, CHT/3/3.

[4] In September 1957 the four-masted barque *Pamir* (3,103 tons, built in 1905 and used to train officers and men for the German mercantile marine) was overwhelmed

First Sea Lord early in 1933 he found that the design of the ship had been approved. She was to be named *Wanderer*—presumably in compliment to John Masefield, the Poet Laureate, and to the ship of that name whose story he had told in prose and in a long ballad.[1] But Chatfield also learnt that the Board intended to build four barque-rigged sailing vessels to train some 130 boys and a few midshipmen by making four-month cruises in them, and had begun to collect names of officers with experience in sail. Chatfield felt the strongest misgivings about both proposals, on the grounds that such training was anachronistic in an increasingly technological age, the money required would be substantial and could be better expended, and the likelihood of serious accidents was too great to contemplate with equanimity.[2] Though the Sea Lords were equally divided in opinion Chatfield enlisted the support of many experienced senior officers, and he finally got his way.[3] Instead the decision was taken to revert to the earlier practice of converting an old cruiser (the *Frobisher*) to a cadet training ship. In retrospect it seems clear that Chatfield was right.

The Board also issued to the fleet a long and rather platitudinous statement on the principles on which the fleet should train its men as seamen, in the use of weapons, and in the employment of small arms— which was to be chiefly the Royal Marines' responsibility. Emphasis was placed on the importance of boat work (under oars and sail), and on giving junior officers and senior ratings 'every opportunity' of being put 'in charge of parties'. Finally the Divisional System was to be overhauled to make sure that senior ratings 'are playing their proper part in the organisation . . .'[4] These exhortations were obviously inspired by the Kelly report on Invergordon;[5] but one may doubt whether they had any substantial effect in the fleet because they said nothing that was new, and there was no hard evidence that failure of training methods had been a contributory cause of the mutiny.

---

by a hurricane off the Azores with the loss of 80 lives. See *Der Untergang der Pamir* (Horst Hamacher, Kassel, 1973).

[1] *The Wanderer* (Heinemann, 1930).

[2] Paper by Chatfield of 31st Jan. and Sea Lords' meeting of 2nd Feb. 1933. Adm. 1/9086–61/1937. Also Chatfield to Sir John Kelly 13th Feb. 1933. Kelly papers, KEL/III.

[3] The Deputy and Assistant Chiefs of Naval Staff supported Chatfield, but the 2nd, 3rd and 4th Sea Lords (Admirals Pound, Forbes and Blake) wanted to go ahead with the scheme. Adm. 1/9086–61/1937. There is no Board Minute recording its demise, but see Lord Chatfield, *It Might Happen Again* (Heinemann, 1947), ch. VI.

[4] Board Minute 3073 of 1st June 1933. Adm. 167/88.   [5] See pp. 123–6.

We saw earlier how the ineffective Welfare Conferences were abolished as a result of Invergordon, and a periodical 'Review of Service Conditions' substituted. The principle was that representations by the men should be made to their Divisional Officers in the first instance. 'Ship Committees' under the Captains of ships and establishments would then consider them. From that body the representations would go to a 'Fleet Committee', whence they would ultimately reach the Admiralty.[1] The first review was to be held in October 1935;[2] but this procedure was little less clumsy and slow than that of the Welfare Conferences; and it was, partly through circumstances totally outside the Admiralty's control, no more successful. For one thing there were almost as many 'excluded subjects' as under the old system, which caused Monsell concern and led to Murray endeavouring to cut them down.[3] In September 1935 the Admiralty was forced by the Abyssinian crisis to postpone the Review,[4] and it was in fact begun a year later. But as by that time over 4,000 requests had been received, and early in 1937 decisions were promulgated on only 29 of them,[5] the mountain had indeed given birth to a very insignificant mouse.[6]

If the attempt to handle welfare questions by means of a pyramid of committees was not a success the new scheme for promotion of able men from the lower deck, which came into full operation in 1933 in place of the unlamented 'Mate Scheme' mentioned earlier,[7] did in the end achieve an improvement. The number of officers commissioned during the first five years (1932–36) were eighteen Executives, fifteen Engineers and two Marines. Though some of those officers did well in their later examinations for Lieutenant's rank the number recruited from the lower deck thus continued to be very small compared with those entered as cadets. The chief reason for there being so few candidates gradually became apparent—namely that to a great extent they

[1] Board Minute 3255 of 13th Dec. 1934. Adm. 167/90. See also Adm. 116/3748, 3749, 3750 and 3751 in which a vast amount of paper on the proposed Review is collected.

[2] Adm. 116/3748 and AFO. 1672/35.

[3] Murray to Pound, 2nd Sea Lord, 13th Feb. and minute by latter of 14th Feb. 1935. Adm. 116/3748.

[4] AM. 2145 of 12th Sept. 1935 and AFO. 1801/36. *ibid.*

[5] AFO. 274/37.

[6] Adm. 116/3596. For a concise history of the presentation of Lower Deck grievances up to 1937 see article by 'H.P.' (Commander Harry Pursey) in *Brassey's Naval Annual* for 1937.

[7] See pp. 32-5.

had to prepare for the preliminary professional and educational examinations in their own time, a truly formidable task. New regulations were accordingly introduced in 1937.[1] They included a special professional and educational course of 8–9 months' duration, and in its first year 31 candidates went through it. The number promoted to commissioned rank increased to 22 that year, and thereafter the improvement was maintained. Promotions to the higher ranks (Commander and Captain) also increased, and by 1937, 79 Commanders or Majors RM had come in 'through the hawse pipe'; but the weak point was that of that total 64 were Engineers and only 15 Executive Officers. None the less the fact that between 1913 and 1937 no less than 783 ratings or RM 'other ranks' were promoted shows that opportunities for able men on the lower deck to achieve commissioned rank did steadily improve—especially after the reforms of 1933.[2]

As regards the pay of officers and men the Board devoted much time to considering what could be done to ameliorate the worst hardships produced by the 1931 cuts, and how complete restoration of the cuts, to which the government was pledged though no date had been settled, could best be handled. The problem was greatly complicated by the fact that men could come within no less than four different categories for pay and pensions, according to the dates of entry or re-engagement.[3] The Board also considered what the effect in the fleet would be as, with the passage of time, an increasing number of men would inevitably be on the lower 1925 scale of pay.[4] The issue was regarded as so important that Monsell took it to the Cabinet, which decided that he and the Chancellor should try and reach agreement.[5] That was accomplished in a few days, evidently to the pleasurable surprise of the Board; and they had no hesitation in accepting the compromise offered, which, although it fell short of full restoration of

[1] AFO. 1864/37.

[2] I am indebted to Commander H. Pursey for the analysis of lower deck promotions in his article 'Lower Deck to Quarter Deck', signed 'Historicus', in *Brassey's Naval Annual* for 1938 and for many helpful letters and interviews on the subject.

[3] Board Minute 3042 of 13th Jan. 1933. Adm. 167/88.

[4] Memo. for Board by Murray of 14th March 1934. Adm. 167/91.

[5] Cabinet 10(33) of 22nd Feb. 1933, Item 5. Cab. 23/75. Monsell stressed that very few Army and Air Force men were affected, because they had far fewer than the Navy on the 1919 rates of pay; nor would the police and teachers, who had also suffered cuts in 1931, be affected. Some opposition was however expressed in Cabinet on the grounds of the principle involved; but the general view was sympathetic to the 1st Lord, who as always, presented his case persuasively.

the 1931 cuts, ensured that no man should suffer a reduction of pay on re-engagement and also provided some improvement in pensions.[1] A General Message was accordingly sent to the fleet telling of these good tidings; but its effects may well have been somewhat vitiated by the unctuous statement that the Board 'wish to observe that these adjustments . . . are the direct result of representations made through the proper Service channels'.[2] As regards the officers' pay, which had recently fluctuated repeatedly, and in the downward direction as the cost of living index fell, the Board pressed that it should be stabilised once and for all by March 1934; and they also reopened their long-standing complaint about naval officers, unlike those in the Army and Air Force, receiving no marriage allowance.[3]

While dealing with the intricate question of pay it is amusing, and in the light of Invergordon ironical, to learn that in 1933 the Board discovered that, although an Order in Council was required 'for settling the manner and conditions' of making payments to personnel, the right 'to issue orders fixing rates of pay and emoluments' rested with themselves under the Letters Patent appointing them. The views of the Treasury Solicitor were sought, and his opinion confirmed that 'complete power derived from their Patent'. The Board thereupon decided to consult the Law Officers.[4] However the Treasury Solicitor, in which office a change had recently taken place, then apparently got cold feet and told the Admiralty that reference to the Law Officers, if officially delivered, 'might prove embarrassing';[5] so the Board decided to leave matters where they were. One would like to know what the outcome would have been had the latter fought the case with the Law Officers—and won! However it was at least satisfactory that by 1934 the first steps had been taken to restore the pay cuts imposed with such disastrous results three years earlier.

[1] Board Minute 3055 of 25th Feb. 1933. Adm. 167/88.

[2] Admiralty 'A' Message of 13th March 1933. Adm. 116/3390 and AFO. 643/33.

[3] Memo. of 20th July 1932 by Murray. Adm. 167/87. See vol. I, pp. 118, 418–19 and 449–50 regarding the earlier fight for officers' marriage allowance.

[4] Board Minutes 3095 and 3098 of 13th and 27th July 1933. Adm. 167/88.

[5] Board Minute 3193 of 3rd May 1934. Sir Thomas Barnes had succeeded Sir Maurice Gower, who had given the original opinion, as Treasury Solicitor.

CHAPTER VII

The Naval Aviation Controversy
1930-1935

ONE OF Churchill's last acts as Chancellor of the Exchequer was to launch a strong attack on the Admiralty's proposals for expanding the Fleet Air Arm. He wanted the whole programme to be referred to a Cabinet Committee.[1] The reply sent by Bridgeman, the First Lord, was that 'A new branch such as the FAA must be built up by regular entries of personnel, concurrently with a regular increase in the number of aircraft'. Because it took eleven months to train a pilot 'it is', he continued, 'imperative that sudden fluctuations should be avoided'. Next the Treasury asked the Admiralty for a breakdown of the cost of the FAA, and the Air Ministry for a statement of the cost of its shore accommodation.[2] 'It appears', commented Admiral Pound the ACNS, 'that the Treasury line of attack will be that keeping carriers in commission is so expensive that in peacetime any air co-operation should be produced by aircraft flown from shore stations . . .';[3] which was probably close to the mark and certainly accorded with the Air Ministry's view. When in June 1929 the second Labour government took office and Philip Snowden became Chancellor he followed his predecessor's intentions very closely.

At the beginning of our period the perennial feud between the Admiralty and Air Ministry over control of the Fleet Air Arm was about to be reopened by the proposals prepared for the 1930 London

[1] Churchill to Bridgeman 31st Jan. 1929. Adm. 116/2551.

[2] Treasury letters of 26th Feb. 1929. *ibid.*

[3] Minute of 6th March 1929. *ibid.* In fact the cost to Navy Votes of the FAA was £3.2 millions—about 7% of the total Navy Estimates.

Naval Conference and, later, for the Geneva Disarmament Conference. In April 1929 the Admiralty told the Air Ministry about the cancellation of the new carrier which had been included in the programme for that year. In consequence the total number of aircraft needed was reduced to 176 for the five carriers in service,[1] and about 75 for catapults fitted in battleships and cruisers. As the navy only had 141 aircraft approval for the increase had to be sought, and the Admiralty proposed that the gap should gradually be filled during the period ending in 1938.[2] The first move was to ask the Treasury for approval to add the two new flights of torpedo-bombers required for the recently refitted *Glorious*. By July no answer had been received except that the Air Ministry, touchy as ever, had protested that *they* and not the Admiralty should have approached the Treasury. Then Snowden, the Chancellor, passed the matter to the Fighting Services Committee of the Cabinet. The Admiralty, in presenting their case, pointed out that the USA had 229 naval aircraft in service and Japan 118, and that the former figure would be increased to 400 by 1938. What the Japanese increase would be they did not know.

In November Snowden sent Alexander a stalling letter, in consequence of which the First Lord agreed to hold the long-term increase 'in suspense'.[3] Then the Treasury proposed that no new flights should be added in 1929 or 1930,[4] which produced a vigorous protest from Madden, the First Sea Lord, to the effect that the result would be that, in naval aviation, the Royal Navy would soon fall far behind the other powers.[5] After discussion the Sea Lords agreed, under protest, to drop the two 1929 flights but adhered to the hope that the two 1930 ones should stand.[6] The outcome was that the Naval Staff produced a revised and more modest expansion programme, rising from 141 to 213 aircraft in 1935–36; but they stuck to the figure of 241 by 1938.[7] The two 1930 flights were approved in August, and the Sea Lords then decided to go for at least two more in 1933.[8]

[1] These were *Glorious* and *Courageous* (52 aircraft each), *Furious* (36 aircraft), *Eagle* (18 aircraft) and *Hermes* (15 aircraft). The *Vindictive* (then a seaplane carrier) required 3 aircraft.
[2] Admy. to Air Min. letter M. 0971/29 of 9th April 1929. Adm. 116/2551.
[3] Snowden to Alexander 18th Oct. and reply by latter of 31st Oct. 1929. *ibid*.
[4] Treasury to Murray 30th Nov. 1929. *ibid*.   [5] Minute of 12th Dec. 1929. *ibid*.
[6] Sea Lords' meeting of 19th Dec. 1929 and Board Minute 2676 of 9th Jan. 1930. *ibid*.
[7] FS(29)31 of 19th June and FS(29)33 of 11th July 1930. Cab. 27/407.
[8] Minutes by Backhouse of 18th Feb. and Field of 22nd Feb. 1932. Adm. 116/2551.

In 1930–31 the fitting of catapults in capital ships and cruisers went ahead slowly, and by mid-1932 fifteen ships were so equipped. In March 1931 Chatfield, then C-in-C, Mediterranean, forwarded proposals for a 'semi-aircraft carrier' to carry eighteen catapult-launched torpedo-bombers, and for the Washington Treaty cruisers to carry six similar aircraft.[1] It is interesting to remark that a few years later the US Navy's General Board also considered building a 'flight deck cruiser', as was mentioned earlier;[2] but it found hardly any supporters.[3] When Chatfield forwarded his proposal he made the unfortunate prophecy that 'attack of [? on] ships at sea by aircraft will be unremunerative in a few years'. Presumably this optimistic view was based on the anticipated but unproven effectiveness of the new multibarrel close-range A-A weapons and the new long-range A-A fire control system, which he had a large hand in producing as Controller 1925–28.[4] On the other hand Chatfield did think that air attacks on ships in their bases 'promises good results';[5] and that was amply confirmed at Taranto in November 1940 and at Pearl Harbour in December 1941.

A long interchange of opinions between the Cs-in-C, Atlantic and Mediterranean Fleets and the Admiralty on the functions of catapult aircraft followed. The general view was that reconnaissance work and spotting for the capital ships' gun fire were their most important functions; but naval aviators doubted whether it would be practicable to provide continuous air spotting in battle.[6] In both the main fleets serious doubts were entertained about whether the spotter-reconnaissance aircraft provided (the Fairey IIIF) was robust enough for the job. Indeed one Admiral described them as 'delicate and unreliable toys'.[7]

When in 1929 preparations for the first London Naval Conference were in train Lord Thomson, the Secretary of State for Air, wrote to MacDonald urging the need for revision of the Washington Treaty

---

[1] Chatfield to Admy. 29th March 1931. This proposal had been put up by the Rear-Admiral Commanding 1st Cruiser Squadron, but Chatfield extended his remarks to general considerations regarding the function of ship-borne aircraft and the effects of air attacks on warships. Adm. 116/2792.

[2] GB. 420–8 of 20th Feb. 1934. Forwarded to FDR on 3rd March.

[3] See p. 81.   [4] See vol. I, pp. 344–5.

[5] Chatfield to Admy. 29th March 1931. Adm. 116/2792.

[6] Letters from Kelly (C-in-C, Atlantic Fleet) of 3rd Dec. 1931 and 24th May 1932 and from Chatfield (C-in-C, Mediterranean Fleet) of 9th March 1932. *ibid.*

[7] Minute by Backhouse (Controller) of 9th Dec. 1931 and report by Admiral Commanding 2nd Cruiser Squadron (Rear-Admiral E. A. Astley-Rushton). *ibid.*

definition of the aircraft carrier as a vessel displacing over 10,000 tons,[1] because of the latitude it gave to 'competitive building' of small carriers, which he considered to be 'of a most undesirable character'.[2] The Naval Staff considered that Thomson had made 'suggestions which are not within his province', and declared that they were 'fully aware of the necessity of limiting by some means or other small aircraft carriers . . .'[3] Alexander, the First Lord, sent no reply to Thomson's letter, but early in the New Year the Air Minister wrote again to MacDonald urging that carriers of *all* sizes should be included in the new tonnage limitations which would, so it was hoped, replace the Washington Treaty figures for Britain, the USA and Japan. Though Thomson admitted, a trifle condescendingly, that 'The Navy of course needs some aircraft', he stressed that 'the Fleet Air Arm is an integral part of the RAF', and that every aircraft allocated to it must therefore reduce by one the total of aircraft 'immediately available for Home Defence'.[4]

This overt attack on the Fleet Air Arm did produce a reply from Alexander who wrote that the description of it as an integral part of the RAF was 'surely true only in a narrow technical sense'. 'The FAA', he continued, 'exists for the Navy. Its machines are designed to meet naval requirements and are paid for by naval vote . . . It will be required to operate with the Fleet in any part of the world in which the Fleet is needed. For all practical purposes therefore it is an integral part of the Navy'. Alexander also took exception to Thomson's statement that 'an adequate number of aircraft can always be made available [from the RAF] in case of emergency', because in his view, they 'would be very little use to the Navy'. Finally he claimed that whereas Thomson appeared to consider mainly Home Defence 'the Admiralty must be concerned with a broader aspect, namely Imperial Defence'.[5] The argument continued, and Thomson circulated two lengthy memoranda on 'Limitation of the Aircraft Carrier' and 'Limitation of Aircraft Carriers of under 10,000 tons and its reactions on the general limitation of Air Armaments',[6] in which he restated the case already made semi-officially to MacDonald. Alexander replied strongly disputing Thom-

[1] Washington Treaty, Section II, Part 4.
[2] Thomson to MacDonald 17th Dec. 1929. Adm. 116/3479 (A. V. Alexander's papers).
[3] Minute of 21st Dec. 1929 by Director of Plans. *ibid.*
[4] Thomson to MacDonald 13th Jan. 1930. *ibid.*
[5] Alexander to Thomson 20th Jan. 1930. *ibid.*
[6] LNC(E)14 and 15 of 1st Feb. 1930. *ibid.*

son's claim that the small carrier was 'incomparably more formidable' than the 8-inch cruiser, and claiming that 'just the reverse' was true; but the Admiralty had, he wrote, 'reluctantly agreed that all ship-borne aircraft should be included in the general limitation of aircraft, but it has never been accepted that there should be a general aircraft quota out of which the naval quota would have to be found'.[1] The exchange then continued on Secretary's level. Surprisingly Christopher Bullock,[2] the polemical and combative Permanent Secretary of the Air Ministry, told Alexander's secretary that 'we don't want avoidable controversy', and agreed to the papers being given a more restricted circulation than had been originally intended.[3] In fact the London Conference did not achieve any alteration of the Washington Treaty tonnage and displacement limits for aircraft carriers, and the issue was 'left over until a conference in 1935'; but the British proposal that carriers under 10,000 tons 'should be included in the aircraft carrier category', which Thomson had originated, was 'generally agreed to'.[4] However it never took effect because all naval powers built much bigger ships.

The next inter-departmental clash arose when the proposal to reduce the Washington Treaty tonnage of aircraft carriers for Britain and the USA from 135,000 to 110,000 was made in connection with the preparations for the General Disarmament Conference. The Admiralty was only prepared to accept such a cut 'by gradual stages and provided that no obligation to start reduction should become operative until after December 1936', when the Washington and London treaties expired. But Lord Londonderry, now Secretary of State for Air, took the offensive by writing to Simon, the Foreign Secretary, pressing for 'a more drastic limitation of ship-borne aircraft than could possibly be secured on the basis of the Admiralty's proposals', and put forward financial and political arguments in support of his case.[5] This renewed and opportunist attack on the Fleet Air Arm produced a moderate and reasoned reply from Monsell, pointing out that the Cabinet's

[1] Alexander to Thomson 21st Feb. 1930. *ibid.*

[2] See vol. I, p. 381, *note*; Roskill, *Hankey* II, pp. 417–18, and correspondence in *The Times* following on Bullock's death on 16th May 1972.

[3] Bullock to Fry 22nd Feb. 1930. Adm. 116/3479.

[4] Cmd. 3547 of 15th April 1930. Article 3 of the London Treaty of 1930 redefined aircraft carriers as any ship 'designed for the specific and exclusive purpose of carrying aircraft', and Article 9 continued the Washington Treaty rules regarding their replacement.

[5] Londonderry to Simon 5th Feb. 1932. Copy in Adm. 116/2792.

policy was to leave the treaty ratios and tonnage limitations intact, and that the principle of parity with the USA must surely include naval aircraft 'having regard to the very great importance known to be attached to the Fleet Air Arm by the other naval powers'. To Londonderry's argument that the British Draft Convention for the Disarmament Conference proposed 'global limitation on the *total* number of aircraft maintained in commission and in Immediate Reserve', and that reduction in the total must therefore fall on ship-borne aircraft, Monsell riposted that parity with France in shore-based aircraft was not, as the Air Ministry claimed, a vital consideration, but the Air Minister's proposals 'would place our fleet at a definite disadvantage . . . in the matter of Air equipment'. In the event the failure of the Disarmament Conference made the argument a dead issue; but the resurrection of what Monsell reasonably called 'this old controversy' was a bad augury for the future.[1]

Though relations between the two departments on the issue of principle remained strained and antagonistic in the early 1930s the Admiralty was able to make progress in fields where the Air Ministry could not claim a direct interest. Such was the appointment of a Flag Officer to command the fleet's carriers—which had actually first been made in 1917.[2] In May 1930 it was resurrected, and although fears were expressed in the Admiralty that such an appointment might be held to infringe the Balfour Report of 1923[3] and perhaps bring about a clash over the duties of the RAF's Coastal Area Command, the appointment was finally approved on 12th March 1931 to take effect in the autumn. The Air Ministry was informed accordingly.[4] The Admiralty decided, after a lot of argument, that the flag of the new Admiral Aircraft Carriers (RAA) should be flown in a carrier and not a cruiser as some senior officers preferred, and in June the announcement was made that the first holder would be Admiral R. G. H. Henderson. His flag was to be flown in the *Courageous*; he was to be responsible 'for the tactical operations of the carriers and of the carrier-borne aircraft in that [the Atlantic] Fleet', and 'the recognised Naval Adviser to other Fleets on all matters connected with the Fleet Air

---

[1] Monsell to Simon 11th Feb. 1932. *ibid.*

[2] See vol. I, p. 586.

[3] Cmd. 1938 and 2029. See vol. I, pp. 373–8.

[4] Admy. letter to Air Min. of 2nd April 1931. Adm. 116/2771, which contains the whole history of the appointment of the RAA and many letters on the subject from the Cs-in-C, Atlantic and Mediterranean Fleets.

Arm'.[1] Henderson was to prove an inspired selection for the new appointment, and much of the credit for the progress made in naval aviation in the 1930s and for improving the status and morale of the FAA should unquestionably go to him. Though he came on the scene much later, to the Royal Navy he was in many respects what Admiral W. A. Moffett had been to the US Navy.[2]

Also in 1931 the Mediterranean Fleet carried out a 'Strategical Investigation' into the employment of flying-boats for reconnaissance and trade defence. The conclusions were that, although such aircraft could not replace carriers they were very useful for reconnaissance, and that 'if aircraft accompany convoys the danger of submarine attack will be reduced'. The C-in-C (Chatfield) went on to declare that 'It is time that flying-boats formed part of the fleet'; but the Admiralty declined to raise such a potentially explosive issue.[3] However in the following year the Sea Lords reviewed the matter and recommended that 'Every possible effort should be made to get the Air Ministry to agree that Naval Co-operation should be considered the *primary* function of Flying Boats', and that naval Observer Officers should be lent to the RAF to help train their crews in navigation and in identification of ships.[4] Though the functions of Coastal Command aircraft were not finally agreed until five years later, in 1932 the Admiralty did take up with the Air Ministry the question of where the 'Coastal Reconnaissance Units' (as they were then called) should be stationed, and what co-operation they should provide for the navy in war. As flying-boats were very expensive the Admiralty proposed that a land plane should be developed. The total requirement was estimated at $29\frac{1}{2}$ flights, or $49\frac{1}{2}$ if convoy was adopted; and the Naval Staff was satisfied that these proposals were 'a satisfactory beginning' to what was to prove a vital need.[5]

While the Admiralty was striving to expand the Fleet Air Arm and to arrive at a working arrangement with the Air Ministry on the training and functions of the shore-based coastal squadrons they were in serious straits over the shortage of volunteers for training as Pilots and Observers. In 1932 they introduced a compulsory three-week course

[1] AM. 1634 of 20th March, letter to Cs-in-C of 11th June and Office Acquaint No. 99 of 24th Aug. 1931. *ibid.*

[2] See vol. I, *passim.*

[3] Report by C-in-C, Mediterranean, of 23rd Dec. 1931. Adm. 116/2862.

[4] Minutes by ACNS and DCNS of Oct. 1932. *ibid.*

[5] Air Min. to Admy. letter of 23rd Dec. 1933 and reply by latter of 23rd Feb. 1934. *ibid.*

in flying for all junior officers in the hope of encouraging more volunteers; but the results were not substantial.[1] The basic trouble lay in the dislike of junior officers for serving in a branch with divided allegiance, and in the belief that promotion prospects were better in the older specialist branches.[2] Moreover Pilots depended not only on promotion in their naval rank by the Admiralty but in their RAF rank by the Air Ministry. Negotiations on this tricky issue began in 1928 and dragged on throughout the next three years without reaching any satisfactory solution.[3] Whereas the Air Ministry was reluctant to fill higher ranks in the RAF (Wing-Commander and above) with naval officers the FAA pilots saw little future in their careers unless they received such promotion. Bullock's solution was the old one—that the number of naval pilots in the FAA should be reduced below the 70% agreed in 1924, and that the RAF should supply the deficiency;[4] but that the Admiralty was most reluctant to accept—despite the chronic shortage from which they were suffering.[5] By the end of 1931 *impasse* was reached, and Austen Chamberlain, then First Lord for a few months, proposed that application should be made to the Cabinet for a new arbitration by the Lord Chancellor, seeking amendment of the Trenchard-Keyes agreement to improve promotion of Pilots in their RAF ranks.[6] But the change of government and of First Lord in that year apparently stultified the proposal. Nor did a series of interdepartmental conferences on a fairly high level progress matters.[7]

[1] Adm. 116/2554 and AFO. 1927/32.

[2] The first Observer to be promoted to Commander, which of course was a purely Admiralty decision, was R. de H. Burton on 30th June 1929. The first Pilot to receive the same promotion was L. C. Sharman on 30th June 1930. No further promotions of Pilots took place until 1932, in which year there were two. In the following year there were three, which compared favourably with the older specialisations.

[3] Adm. 116/3002 and 3003.

[4] Letter by Bullock to Admy. of 5th March 1931. Adm. 116/3003. Though the Admiralty was reluctant to accept RAF *airman* pilots, especially while the Air Ministry refused to train naval ratings in that capacity, in mid-1933 five airman pilots were sent to the *Courageous* in substitution for Flying Officers RAF. In Sept. 1933 the RAA (Henderson) reported that they were satisfactory but he would only recommend them for fighter squadrons. The C-in-C, Home Fleet (Admiral Sir W. H. D. Boyle, later Earl of Cork and Orrery) thereupon re-opened the issue of naval rating pilots. Letter to Admy. of 22nd Sept. 1933. Adm. 116/3007.

[5] Plans Division minute of 5th June 1931. *ibid.*

[6] Minute by Chamberlain of 30th Oct. 1931. *ibid.*

[7] Three conferences between the Second Sea Lord and Air Member for Personnel took place in June and July 1932. *ibid.* See also Memo. (undated) for Board in Adm. 167/87 and Board Minute 2993 of 28th July 1932. Adm. 167/85.

The result was that, in the Naval Staff's despairing words 'no progress [had been] made . . . on the many outstanding questions, and the FAA will remain in its present unsatisfactory state'.[1] Thanks to pressure from Admiral Henderson, the recently appointed Rear-Admiral Aircraft Carriers, in 1933 a new squadron organisation was produced whereby carriers were to have 9 or 12 aircraft per squadron, with a Squadron-Leader in command and three Flight-Lieutenants to lead the flights;[2] and naval pilots' promotions in the RAF were slightly improved.[3] But the old problem of shortage of volunteers was not resolved, and early in 1934 the Admiralty again called for more from the fleet.[4] If the Admiralty was stubborn in its refusal to accept NCO pilots from the RAF the Air Ministry was equally so in refusing to train naval ratings as pilots, and in sticking firmly to their claim to provide more of the officers of Flight-Lieutenant's rank and above.[5] Furthermore the position regarding reserves of pilots, which had been in dispute since 1924, remained thoroughly unsatisfactory, and it was obvious that, if war came, their numbers would be totally inadequate.[6] To try and mitigate the shortage of reserve pilots the Admiralty resurrected a proposal to train RNR officers, which had first been put up as long ago as 1924; but the idea was turned down flat by the Treasury.[7] As a makeshift the Admiralty introduced a 14-day course in 'elementary aeronautics' for reserve officers; but that went no appreciable way towards solving the problem.[8]

What made the situation produced by these clashes especially galling for the Admiralty was that they were well aware that neither the Americans nor the Japanese suffered from comparable troubles—because the manning and operation of ship-borne aircraft was entirely in the hands of their navies. For example in mid-1933 the Naval Staff

[1] Minute on Ellington's letter of 26th July 1932. Adm. 116/3004.

[2] AFO. 1266/33.

[3] A total of 16 Squadron Leaders was agreed at a conference on 12th Jan. 1933. Adm. 116/3005.

[4] AM to Cs-in-C of 15th March 1934. There was a shortage of 6 officers for the next FAA course. *ibid.*

[5] On 12th July 1932 Admiral Henderson, the RAA, wrote to the Admiralty protesting that *not one* FAA pilot had yet been promoted to Flight Lieutenant RAF. Adm. 116/3004.

[6] Paper by the ACNS of 21st Jan. 1932. Adm. 116/3008. At the time the total of possible, though not certain, reserve pilots was only 69.

[7] Admy. letter to Air Min. of 18th Feb. 1929. Adm. 116/2422.

[8] AFO. 566/31.

drew attention urgently to the fact that the original programme for Japanese expansion had provided 17 shore-based squadrons by 1932, that their 'First Replenishment Programme' included 14 *more* squadrons (472 aircraft) by 1937, and their 1934–35 estimate provided for 8 more new squadrons. This made a total of 590 shore-based and 329 ship-borne aircraft (including reserves) by April 1937, and 400 ship-borne aircraft by 1938—including those for the two new carriers and two cruisers included in the 1934–35 estimates. 'The full measure of the weakness of our air power in the Far East', wrote the Naval Air Division, 'will be realised when it is pointed out that our one carrier in China [*Eagle*] has a capacity of 21 aircraft . . . If we do not expand the FAA, air superiority, with all its great advantages, will go to the Japanese Fleet. This will entail continuous torpedo-bombing and dive-bombing attacks, and uninterrupted air spotting [for the enemy's gun-fire] . . . day and night reconnaissance of our fleet and night attacks by air assisted by destroyers . . .' 'The need for a more adequate Fleet Air Arm is, therefore, sufficiently plain' they concluded.[1] All of which was a prophetic forecast of the events of December 1941 to March 1942. It is also interesting to find that, at about the same time as he wrote the above cogent minute, the Director of the Air Division reviewed the various possible forms of air attack on ships. His conclusion was that, although ships were most vulnerable below the water line, and attack by torpedo-bomber or by 'B Bombs' (delay-action underwater bombs) was therefore attractive, the magnetic torpedo pistol was so unreliable that priority should be given to dive-bombing.[2]

Such was the general position when Chatfield took over as First Sea Lord in January 1933, and in retrospect he wrote that 'Of all the battles with which I was faced . . . there was only one which gave me real anxiety,—namely control of the Fleet Air Arm'.[3] The sort of problem he was up against must quickly have been apparent to him, since early in 1934 Sir Philip Sassoon, the Under-Secretary for Air, wrote to Monsell objecting to the proposed new carrier in the 1934 programme (*Ark Royal*) on the grounds that considerable costs which would not be recoverable from the Admiralty would fall on the Air Votes (e.g. for providing shore accommodation for aircraft and aircrews).[4] He

---

[1] Minute by DNAD of 3rd Nov. 1933. Adm. 116/3007.
[2] Minute by same of 11th May 1933. Adm. 116/3473.
[3] Lord Chatfield, *It Might Happen Again* (Heinemann, 1947), ch. xv.
[4] Sassoon to Monsell 11th Jan. 1934. Adm. 116/2607. For the earlier use of these

also reopened the issue put forward by Lord Thomson in 1929 when the draft Convention for the Disarmament Conference was being considered, and which his successor Lord Londonderry had repeated in 1932—namely that expansion of the FAA was undesirable in principle because it would reduce the strength available for Home Defence and was also extravagant in money. It is not unreasonable to detect the hand of Sir Christopher Bullock in this revival of the earlier attacks on the FAA. Sassoon used the dislike of the American Admiral Moffett for the big carriers (*Lexington* and *Saratoga*) to bolster his argument; but that was in fact one of Moffett's comparatively rare misjudgements.

Monsell must already have been well briefed to answer the Air Ministry, and he flatly refused to accept the proposal that no money should be spent on the new carrier until the Defence Requirements Committee's report was received—because 'the new carrier is required by the Navy at the earliest possible date' in order to fill 'a glaring deficiency in the fleet which we were entitled by the treaties to fill, and because the aircraft which the new ship would carry were as essential as the ship itself' (which was something of a 'chicken and egg' argument). As to the cost of shore accommodation, Monsell pointed out that it was through no desire of the Admiralty's that this fell on the Air Votes, and that as long ago as the Salisbury Committee of 1923 they had made it clear that they were 'ready and anxious to meet our own requirements in such matters'; and he correctly drew Sassoon's attention to the fact that Moffett had argued that two small carriers were better than one large one. As Sassoon had sent a copy of his letter to the Chancellor of the Exchequer—presumably to enlist his support on the costs issue—Monsell did the same.[1] The paper warfare continued throughout the month of January 1934, and at great length. It ended when Monsell, carefully briefed by Chatfield,[2] stuck firmly to his guns, repeated that he was 'absolutely convinced that there should be no delay at all in building a new carrier', and asserted that no unbiased critic who viewed 'our present and prospective position in relation to Japan' could doubt 'not merely the wisdom but the necessity of building this carrier immediately'.[3] In fact Monsell won the argu-

---

arguments see Thomson to Alexander 17th Dec. 1929 (Adm. 116/3479) and Londonderry to Monsell 5th Feb. 1932. (Adm. 116/2792.)

[1] Monsell to Sassoon 17th Jan. 1934. Adm. 116/2607.
[2] Chatfield to Monsell 26th Jan. 1934. *ibid.*
[3] Sassoon to Monsell 23rd Jan. and reply by latter of 31st Jan. 1934. *ibid.*

ment fairly easily and the carrier was approved with the rest of the 1934–35 Estimates in March 1934.[1] Mention should here be made of the fact that nearly 20 years of experience, and the result of many experiments—and some failures—were put into the design of the *Ark Royal*, which proved a very successful ship.[2]

Though the Admiralty and Air Ministry were constantly at loggerheads over the expansion of the Fleet Air Arm and the provision of aircrews during the period covered by this chapter the records suggest that, on the technical level, relations were very much better. In the paper about the design of the *Ark Royal* mentioned above Sir Stanley Goodall, the Director of Naval Construction, paid a warm tribute to the assistance and advice received from the Air Ministry's Director of Technical Development, and described the whole project as 'a good example of co-ordinated defence'. Furthermore a Technical Sub-Committee of the Fleet Air Arm Advisory Committee was formed in 1932 with scientists and engineers from both departments serving as members under the chairmanship of an Air Commodore. It did not meet very often between 1932 and '35, but the fact that in 1937 and '38 it met over 30 times each year, and that it continued its work after the outbreak of war, surely suggests that it served a useful purpose.[3] The trouble was that war came before satisfactory designs of carrier aircraft had been put into production, and that in the later 1930s, after rearmament had started in earnest, naval aircraft received a lower priority for machine tools and scarce materials than those required for Bomber and Fighter Commands. It is of course impossible to say whether, had the Admiralty regained full control of the FAA earlier, it would have been better equipped than it was in 1939; but the troubles described in this chapter certainly suggest that this would have been the case.

Early in 1934 the Admiralty wrote at length to the Cs-in-C, Home

[1] See Cmd. 4523 of 1st March 1934.

[2] For an admirable account of her design and construction see paper by Sir Stanley V. Goodall read at the 80th Session of the Institution of Naval Architects on 29th March 1939. I am indebted to Mr. W. A. D. Forbes of the Royal Corps of Naval Constructors, who was one of the naval architects most intimately concerned with the design of the ship, for providing me with a copy of the paper and for many valuable letters about the ship. The hull and machinery were ordered from Cammell Laird, Birkenhead, on 17th April 1935, she was launched on 13th April 1937 and taken over after trials on 16th Nov. 1938. On her war service see Roskill, *The War at Sea*, vol. 1 (HMSO, 1954), *passim*. She was sunk by U81 off Gibraltar on 14th Nov. 1941.

[3] Minutes from 4th meeting on 3rd Feb. 1933 are in Adm. 116/4022.

and Mediterranean Fleets making 'a careful review of the policy to be followed in the aircraft equipment of the fleet' in the light of 'the active steps recently taken by the American and Japanese navies to increase it'—to totals estimated at 750 and 350 aircraft respectively by 1938–40, apart from shore-based naval co-operation squadrons. 'Both countries', they declared, 'are thus making determined efforts to dominate the air in naval warfare especially in their own waters'. The Admiralty's projected response was to build two new carriers of 22,000 tons to complete in 1938 and 1940, and to increase the total of all shipborne aircraft to 400 by the latter year. If however account was taken of catapult aircraft and of the fact that not all the six modern carriers would be available 'to accompany the fleet for service in distant waters' —by which they presumably meant the Far East—the real 'air strength of the fleet' was unlikely to exceed 300. 'The security of the British Fleet with regard to the air is thus', they continued, 'a matter for serious concern'. Turning to the question of tactics the Admiralty expressed the view that Flag Officers should aim primarily 'at so placing the battlefleet in action that Gunnery superiority is assured and the destruction of the enemy thereby achieved'. They also declared that while 'modern detection devices . . . can provide reasonable security from the submarine . . . defence against air attack is not yet secured and our measures to counteract it are incomplete'. Accordingly the Admiralty went on to seek the Cs-in-C's views on whether the proportion of two Torpedo-Spotter-Reconnaissance (TSR) squadrons to one Fighter-Reconnaissance (F/R) squadron required modification. Plainly the Admiralty was finding it difficult, if not impossible, to reconcile the old principle of victory by heavy gunfire with the new need to defend the fleet against air attack and launch effective attacks against the enemy fleet.[1]

In the Naval Staff the view was that 'One thing is perfectly certain, and that is that the greater the number of carriers in the fleet the easier will the solution of the problem become', and that the two-seater F/R aircraft was 'probably the correct fighter type for *all* Fleet work'.[2] Admiral Forbes, the Controller, who was responsible for the supply of equipment, wrote that 'the right place for aircraft is in aircraft carriers attached to the squadron or fleet'. Evidently he had little use for catapult aircraft, on which a considerable effort had recently been expended. Chatfield summed up by writing that 'a great carrier fleet'

[1] AL of 20th Feb. 1934. Adm. 1/9007.
[2] Minute by DNAD. Adm. 1/9007–79/34.

was gradually being built, and would eventually carry some 300 aircraft. For the Far East he envisaged a fleet of 10–12 capital ships and at least 4 carriers. As to the aircraft needed 'the type we cannot have too many of', he continued, 'is fighters';[1] and it was on these terms that the letter to the Cs-in-C was drafted.

The reply from the RAA, now The Hon. Sir Alexander Ramsay, argued that each carrier should be given a particular function, such as striking force or reconnaissance, and that the proportions of TSR to F/R aircraft should be decided by the parent ship's function. Plainly such an idea had much to commend it—once the navy had enough carriers. On the use of air striking forces as a decisive weapon in their own right Ramsay was disappointingly vague, merely declaring himself 'loath not to consider the potentialities of a weapon which may not only be effective against carriers but also by its use against a retiring fleet, make action possible'.[2] Nor did he challenge the Admiralty's view that the main function of the FAA was 'to defend the fleet against air attack whilst relying on the gunfire of the fleet to obtain a decision in action'. In retrospect this reply, coming from the principal sea-going authority on carrier aircraft, appears both timid and unimaginative. The C-in-C, Mediterranean (Admiral W. W. Fisher) did not take a clear and decided line, merely answering the Admiralty's questions about the proportions of each type of aircraft to be embarked in various classes of ship.[3] Obviously these replies went no way towards developing an efficient strike aircraft or encouraging their use as offensive weapons; and the big gun's dominance remained unquestioned and unchallenged; but as Chatfield, Fisher and Forbes were all former Gunnery Officers this is perhaps not surprising. It is at this stage that one feels the lack in the Royal Navy's counsels of one or two naval aviators with plenty of gold braid on their sleeves, which had arisen because almost all its experienced aviators had turned over to the RAF on its formation in 1918.

While the foregoing fundamental issues regarding the function and employment of ship-borne aircraft were being discussed the question of how the increased number of aircraft were to be manned was reopened inside the Admiralty with a justifiable sense of urgency. After a lot of debate they wrote to the Air Ministry pointing out that 452 pilots (excluding reserves) would be needed by 1940, and repeated the

[1] Minute of 6th Feb. 1934. *ibid.*
[2] Letter RAA to Admy. of 2nd March 1934. Adm. 1/9007.
[3] Letter C-in-C, Mediterranean to Admy. of 10th April 1934. *ibid.*

request first made in 1926 that naval ratings should fill the gap produced by the shortage of officer volunteers. They used the success of
the small number of RAF airman pilots recently appointed to the
Courageous to support their case that naval ratings would prove just as
good; and they now wanted to train naval ratings as Observers as well
as Pilots.[1] Unfortunately, and one may feel narrow-mindedly, the Air
Ministry refused to budge an inch from their earlier stand—that such
a step would be contrary to the Balfour Report of 1923 and the many
other investigations into the matter.[2] Faced by this renewed *impasse*
the Admiralty decided to try personal discussion with the Air Council,[3]
and early in 1935 the Second Sea Lord and ACNS accordingly faced
the Air Member for Personnel and the DCAS across a table.[4] Air
Vice-Marshal Bowhill, the AMP, then frankly admitted that his
department's 'objection to the Lower Deck pilots proposal was that it
struck at the root of the principle of the unified Air Force';[5] which
shows how deeply ingrained the Trenchard gospel still was more than
15 years after he had enunciated it.[6] In March the Air Ministry again
confirmed this stand in writing.[7] The result was, expectedly, that the
Admiralty's attitude hardened and they became more determined than
ever to regain complete control of the FAA.[8]

Meanwhile the Admiralty had set up a committee under Rear-
Admiral C. F. S. Danby, who had recently commanded the carrier
Furious, 'to report on the working of the Trenchard-Keyes agreement
[of 1924] . . .' 'whether the arrangements made by the Air Ministry for
providing RAF pilots are satisfactory . . .', and 'to make proposals for
re-organising the FAA in any respect which adverse reports on the

---

[1] Admy. to Air Min. letter of 31st March 1934. Adm. 116/3007 and Board Minute
3194 of 3rd May 1934, Adm. 167/90. Also Admy. letter of 23rd April 1934 on rating
Observers. Adm. 116/4025. The number of Observers at the time was 101 (all
officers) but by 1940 the requirement would rise to 351. Memo. (unsigned) for Board
of 7th Dec. 1934. Adm. 167/91.

[2] See vol. i, pp. 372–7 and 493–4.

[3] Board Minute 3221 of 12th July 1934. Adm. 116/3007.

[4] The representatives were Admirals Pound and Kennedy-Purvis for the Admiralty
and Air Marshals Bowhill and Ludlow-Hewitt for the Air Ministry.

[5] Record of meeting of 11th Jan. 1935. Adm. 116/3007.

[6] See vol. i, pp. 39, 253–4 and *passim*. Trenchard's famous paper on 'The Permanent
Organisation of the Royal Air Force' was circulated by Churchill, the Secretary of
State, on 11th Dec. 1919. Cmd. 467.

[7] Air Min. to Admy. letter of 7th March 1935. Adm. 116/3007.

[8] Board Minute 3289 of 9th May 1935. Adm. 1/9034.

above points may indicate'.[1] The Danby Committee rendered an Interim Report early in 1935, just after the abortive inter-departmental meeting referred to above, and a Final Report in the following April. The latter was a huge and comprehensive document, but we here need only concern ourselves with the principal recommendation. Rather surprisingly the Committee did not criticise the Trenchard-Keyes agreement and the subsequent modifications made to it. But they stated that 'The cause of the failure lies deeper . . . the majority of the Fleet Air Arm's difficulties are traceable ultimately to the existing policy of "dual control" '.[2] In May Chatfield produced a full statement for the Board in which he wrote that 'Consequent on the continued refusal of the Air Ministry to agree to the Admiralty proposal to employ Naval Rating Pilots, I have reviewed the whole position of the FAA in consultation with the Sea Lords'; and he continued on the general lines of the Danby Report.[3] Plainly the Admiralty could now only try and get the dispute considered by the Cabinet. Accordingly Monsell sent MacDonald a copy of a letter he had written to Londonderry enclosing the draft of a memorandum for the Cabinet, which he asked the Prime Minister's permission to circulate. He said that the *impasse* reached left him with no alternative but 'to submit the matter to the arbitrament of our colleagues'.[4] MacDonald however evidently jibbed at this proposal, since two months later Monsell wrote again to him (as Lord President of the Council by that time) pointing out that the alternative he (MacDonald) had proposed, namely direct consultation between the two of them, had not yet borne fruit. He pressed the view, as 'many important matters vitally affecting the Fleet Air Arm are in suspense' the promised discussion might take place either with MacDonald or with Baldwin, who had become Prime Minister on 7th June.[5] MacDonald sent this appeal on to Baldwin who asked Hankey for his views. In the draft reply to Monsell prepared by Hankey the Prime Minister was invited to say that he was 'wholly opposed to the reopening of the general question of the control of the FAA at the present time', because he was 'convinced that the mere fact of a fresh Inquiry would prove detrimental to the good relations now

---

[1] Terms of Reference dated 23rd Oct. 1934. Adm. 116/3723.
[2] The proceedings of the Danby Committee are in Adm. 116/3009. The Interim and Final Reports of 24th Jan. and 12th April 1935 are in Adm. 116/3008.
[3] Memo. by Chatfield and Board Minute 3289 of 9th May 1935. Adm. 1/9034.
[4] Monsell to MacDonald and Londonderry 20th May 1935. Premier 1/282.
[5] Monsell to MacDonald 19th July 1935. *ibid.*

existing between all three services'. Hankey went on to say that it might be possible to settle the questions regarding the terms of service of RAF officers in the FAA and the institution of naval rating pilots between the two departments, and suggested that Monsell should approach Cunliffe-Lister, who had just succeeded to the office of Secretary of State for Air, with that object. MacDonald 'fully concurred' with Hankey's proposed letter, and it was accordingly sent to Monsell.[1] Early in August Baldwin evidently saw the two contestants, and as the former's private secretary wrote 'We can put away' on the file the matter was evidently dropped.[2]

In the autumn of 1935 another attempt was made to arrive at a satisfactory *modus vivendi*. Hankey took the chair at a meeting at which Monsell and Chatfield for the Admiralty and Cunliffe-Lister and Ellington for the Air Ministry were present; but the deadlock was not broken.[3] Monsell therefore raised the whole issue to Sir Thomas Inskip, who was appointed Minister for Co-ordination of Defence in March 1936. Such was the chain of events leading to the Inskip Inquiries of 1936–37, to which we will revert in a later chapter.

While the Admiralty and Air Ministry were locked in internecine strife and, except for the ordering of the *Ark Royal*, little progress had been made in naval aviation—except to amass a mountain of paper—the US Navy was, thanks largely to Roosevelt's use of 'New Deal' agencies to provide funds, already recounted, making a steady advance in the same field. In May 1933 the General Board recommended the inclusion of two new carriers in the programme for the 1934 Fiscal Year, two more in that for 1935 and one for 1936;[4] and in July the CNO asked for 342 aircraft for the first three carriers and 78 for cruisers fitted with catapults.[5] A very ambitious programme for providing $13·870 millions for aircraft in the Fiscal Years 1938–40 was also put forward.[6] However, as with the Admiralty, the General Board still held to the concept that the battleship was the dominant instrument. Thus on 1st October 1934 they told Swanson that 'the capital ship force is the backbone of the modern Navy . . . the basic strength of the surface fleet is in its heaviest vessels . . .'; and they therefore

[1] Note by MacDonald's secretary of 24th July and Baldwin to Monsell of 25th July 1935. *ibid.*

[2] Note by H. G. Vincent of 7th Aug. 1935. *ibid.*

[3] Record of discussion of 1st Oct. 1935. Adm. 1/9034–33/36. A useful history of the dispute (unsigned and undated) is in Adm. 116/3721.

[4] GB. 420–2, serial 1819 of 10th May 1933 and serial 1659 of 9th May 1934.

[5] CNO Memo. 'The Navy's Needs' of 20th July 1933.   [6] *ibid.*

pressed for modernisation of the older vessels of that class and for construction of two 35,000-ton 16-inch vessels if other powers built such ships.[1]

Admiral W. A. Moffett was still, at the beginning of this period, the chief supporter of the development of US naval aviation;[2] but his enthusiasm for lighter-than-air craft was to prove misplaced and ended in tragedy. In March 1933 he christened the new airship *Macon*, and received President Roosevelt's congratulations;[3] but in April of that year Moffett's death in the disaster which overtook the *Akron* confirmed the views of Swanson and the Navy Department,[4] who did not share Moffett's enthusiasm for large rigid airships. In July the Secretary told the President that he could 'find no justification for recommending the construction of lighter-than-air ships',[5] and the possibility of restarting it was not raised for another five years. If Moffett's judgement was at fault over the usefulness of hydrogen-filled dirigibles and also over the size of future aircraft carriers, the US Navy none the less owes him a great debt for his steadfast support of naval aviation—especially in the 1920s when, but for his efforts, that service might well have found itself in the same predicament as the British.

As regards crews for the ship-borne aircraft and adequate reserves the US Navy was also more fortunate than the Royal Navy. Late in 1934 Swanson sought the President's approval to build up a reserve of naval aviators, and in April of the following year Roosevelt signed an Act 'to provide for aviation cadets in the Naval Reserve' to a total of about 350.[6]

Though the lack of internal minutes and letters in the US Navy Department's records to which this author has been allowed access may possibly have given him an over-optimistic impression it none the less seems clear that the US Navy suffered from far less acute difficulties over naval aviation than the Royal Navy. In fact the only serious complaint is contained in a letter from Swanson to Roosevelt of 1935 protesting about the delays between the placing of contracts for aircraft and the first deliveries, which, in the case of the new torpedo-bombers had amounted to 107 days. But as Swanson attached a table

---

[1] Recommendations of General Board for London Naval Conference of 1935, GB. 438-1, serial 1640, part VII, para. 12.

[2] See vol. I, pp, 57, 249–50 and *passim*.

[3] Roosevelt papers, Official File 18, Boxes 4 and 27.

[4] See vol. I, pp. 527–8.   [5] Swanson to FDR 21st July 1933. *ibid*.

[6] HR. 5577. Roosevelt papers, Official File, Boxes 2A and 27.

showing that, at the beginning of 1936, the US Navy would have 1,218 aircraft 'on hand' and the RN was still struggling to obtain 305 (204 TSR and 101 F/R[1]) by 1940 it is clear that the US Navy was far ahead.

As to Japan, the 1930 London Treaty had been very badly received because of its continuation of the Washington Treaty 5:5:3 ratio, and in the spring of 1934 they discarded for good the concept that agreement on naval strength should be achieved by negotiation. Excellent carrier-borne fighters and dive-bombers were already in production and, although the big-gun battleship still remained dominant, increasing funds were being allocated to building carriers and to providing both shore-based and ship-borne naval aircraft. Though the victory of the extreme 'Fleet Faction' of 8th June 1934 marked the beginning of a new era it was not until the 'Third Replenishment Programme' of 1936 was begun that Japan started building on an enormous scale and in utmost secrecy.[2] The Admiralty and the US Navy Department certainly knew in outline what the Japanese were doing, including the very rapid development of carrier-borne aircraft; but they greatly under-estimated both the power of their new weapons and the efficiency of their personnel. The disillusionment, when it came, was to be shattering.

---

[1] These are the figures given in Appendix II to Admy. letter to Cs-in-C of 20th Feb. 1934. Adm. 1/9007. In 1930 the total need was assessed at 241 aircraft by 1936. FS (29)31 of 19th June 1930. Adm. 116/2551.

[2] See *Pelz*, pp. 14–15, 32–4 and 55 regarding the composition and activities of the Japanese 'Fleet Faction'.

CHAPTER VIII

More Sealing Wax than Ships
1935-1936

———◆———

IN OCTOBER 1934 Monsell wrote to Chamberlain, the Chancellor of the Exchequer, about how they should handle the 1935 building programme and the 'naval deficiencies' tabulated in the first report of the DRC. The First Lord wanted them to be taken simultaneously and at the usual time, namely in the early autumn. He enclosed an advance copy of the building programme but stressed that he was asking for no more than a token sum to start it. Though he stressed the Admiralty's desire to get back to 'the old practice' of actually placing orders early in the Financial Year he accepted that, as other needs demanded higher priority, this practice could not be adopted at once. As the 'deficiencies' section of the Sketch Estimates totalled £3½ millions— excluding money needed for the expansion of the FAA and to restore in part the 1931 pay cuts—the First Lord was obviously trying not to open his mouth too widely. Furthermore there was, he argued, 'an entirely unavoidable increase' amounting to £¾ million for maintenance and repair of ageing vessels—of which the fleet had a plethora. The total of £61.3 millions asked for showed an increase over the 1934 estimates of £4¼ millions—which the Chancellor was not likely to accept without argument; but the First Lord gilded the pill by pointing out that the sale to Australia of a modified *Leander* class cruiser (*Phaeton*, later renamed *Sydney*) should bring in a substantial sum.[1]

Expectedly the Treasury came back at the Admiralty with a long string of questions which, in the aggregate, amounted to seeking a reduction of £½ million and an increase of the 'shadow cut';[2] but in the end Chamberlain agreed that a Supplementary Estimate should be put

[1] Monsell to Chamberlain 26th Oct. 1934. Adm. 116/3436.
[2] Bridges to Murray 29th Oct. 1934. Adm. 1/8800–78/35.

forward if the pace of expenditure justified it.[1] What worried the Admiralty was that the reductions asked for were bound to fall mainly on the 'deficiencies'—such as providing reserves of stores and defences for naval bases; and they were well aware that the position regarding such items had, through the forced economies of recent years, become far from satisfactory. In the end Monsell asked Parliament for just over £60 millions and for 2,000 more men for the fleet. This was the first rise in Vote A (personnel) since 1932.[2]

As to new construction, Chatfield told the Board that, apart from maintaining the strength of the fleet at a level no lower than in recent years, the chief needs were to start replacing the old ships of the Battle Fleet as soon as possible, and to increase the rate of replacement of the old cruisers. His aim was to lay down two new battleships early in 1937, immediately after the Washington and London treaties had expired and gradually to increase the number of cruisers and destroyers in each year's programme, accepting that in the cruiser class we would have to build some smaller ships than the *Southamptons* in order to keep within the total tonnage permitted by the London treaty. He also wanted a 'trade protection carrier' or aircraft depot ship to be included in the programme, and a similar ship for the Mobile Base organisation—about which more will be said later.[3] The building programme for 1935 was finally settled at three cruisers (*Southampton* class), a flotilla of nine destroyers (I class), three submarines and a submarine depot ship, four sloops and a number of smaller vessels which was in the aggregate a good deal smaller than the previous year's programme; but a second destroyer flotilla (seven ships of a larger type) was added later.

To return to the famous Defence White Paper of 1st March 1935, which Hankey had drafted on his way back from Canada early in the year, in its final form it first recapitulated Britain's obligations under the League Covenant, the Washington Treaties, the Locarno Pact of 1925 and the Kellogg-Briand Pact of 1928, and emphasised the lead we had given in the field of reduction and limitation of armaments. It then referred to the *impasse* reached at Geneva, and to 'the fact that Germany was not only re-arming openly on a large scale' and in defiance of the Versailles Treaty, but had given notice of her withdrawal from the League and the Disarmament Conference. Japan had done the same

---

[1] Chamberlain to Monsell 3rd Dec. 1934. *ibid.*

[2] Cmd. 4823 of 1st March 1935.

[3] Board Minute 3315 and Memo. of Chatfield of 28th Nov. 1935. Adm. 167/92.

with regard to the League; and 'all the larger Powers . . . were adding to their armed forces'.[1] Taking account of these facts and of 'the serious deficiencies that had accumulated in our defence forces and defences', the paper continued, 'His Majesty's Government felt that they would be failing in their responsibilities if . . . they delayed the initiation of steps to put our own armaments on a footing to safeguard us against potential dangers'. 'If peace should be broken the Navy is, as always, the first line of defence . . . of our essential sea communications', declared the paper; 'the Main Fleet is the basis upon which our naval strategy rests . . . [and] in the Main Fleet the capital ship remains the essential element upon which the whole structure of our naval strategy depends'. In those firm declarations of faith one can surely detect the hands of Hankey and Chatfield.[2] Most unusually the White Paper bore the initials of MacDonald; and thus 'by one of the many ironies in his life . . . the apostle of peace signed as one of his last state papers the announcement that Britain must rearm'.[3] His health had long been failing, and on the 7th June he was succeeded as Prime Minister by Baldwin.

The White Paper was laid before Parliament on 4th March, and four days later Hankey sent Baldwin an exhaustive brief for him to use when the first debate on it took place.[4] Expectedly the paper was greeted with extreme hostility by the Labour Party and the disarmament lobby, and also by the Left Wing Press;[5] while outside Parliament the League of Nations Union and other pacifist bodies threw the whole weight of their propaganda against it.[6] In the Commons the most

[1] Roskill, *Hankey*, III, pp. 140–1.
[2] Cmd. 4827 of 1st March 1935.   [3] *Mowat*, p. 479.
[4] A copy of the brief (30 quarto pages) is in the MacDonald Papers (Box 1/7, Brown) but I have not found the original in the Baldwin Papers. Possibly he destroyed it after the debate, in which MacDonald could not take part because of ill health.
[5] The debate in the House of Commons took place on 11th March, when Attlee moved that the policy of the government was 'completely at variance with the spirit in which the League of Nations was created to establish a collective world peace'. Parl. Deb., vol. 299, cols. 35–162. The Lords debated the same matter two days later (vol. 96, cols. 51–118) and on 22nd May a further debate on defence took place in the Commons, when Attlee moved to reduce the Treasury Vote by £100. Parl. Deb., vol. 302, cols. 359–482. Although the government obtained large majorities in both Commons debates press reports revealed widespread anxiety about rearmament and, in the Left Wing organs, total opposition to it.
[6] See David S. Birn, *The League of Nations Union and Collective Security*: Journal of Contemporary History, vol. 9, no. 3, for an excellent account of these bodies' activities. Though the inconsistency of the LNU's attitude in wanting to use 'the

effective attack came from Aneurin Bevan; but Attlee's motion against acceptance of the paper was defeated by a huge majority, and the Admiralty was probably well satisfied by the ease with which this important hurdle had been surmounted. In Germany Hitler's recovery from the notorious 'diplomatic cold' produced by the White Paper was sufficiently rapid for him to announce the introduction of conscription on 16th March.

The next step towards rearmament lay with the Defence Requirements Committee, which was given new Terms of Reference on 1st July. It was now required to make proposals 'to review the existing programme of Defence Requirements in the light of recent changes in the situation . . .';[1] by which the government obviously meant the increasingly plain Italian intention to attack Abyssinia and the rising hostility of Germany. The DRC worked fast and on 24th rendered an Interim Report. It was short and it only made two points of importance. The first was that, because the armaments industry had been so long neglected, it was not safe to assume that Britain could achieve 'a reasonable state of preparations' before the beginning of 1939—which left only three 'budget years' available for rearmament; while the second was that, as Parliament was about to go into recess, the committee should merely 'work out programmes on the basis that they are to be completed as soon as possible', and that financial considerations should at last give place to achieving 'the earliest possible security'.[2] The Ministerial Disarmament Committee which had reviewed the first DRC report had now been replaced by the Defence Policy and Requirements Committee (DPRC), and early in August that body gave a cautious and qualified approval to the DRC's proposals. It made plain that the Service Departments were by no means to receive a blank cheque for rearmament, and that emergency financing, such as the launching of a Defence Loan, was not yet on the cards.[3]

The foregoing decisions, though by no means as clear and unequivocal as the Admiralty must have hoped, provided grounds for the staff to prepare a new long-term building programme for the years 1936 (when the limitation treaties expired) to 1942. Though the staff opened its mouth pretty wide, and estimated the total cost at £193

whole force of the League' to curb aggressions while opposing rearmament is very plain it now seems likely that its influence was exaggerated by, among others, Chamberlain and Baldwin.

[1] DCM(32) 65th Meeting. Cab. 16/112. [2] DPR. 12 of 24th July 1935. *ibid.*
[3] 4th Meeting of DPRC on 29th July 1935 and DRC. 27 of 8th Aug. 1935. *ibid.*

millions, the Board revised the programme upwards.[1] As finally sent to the DRC it consisted of twelve battleships, four carriers, 23 cruisers of three different classes, five flotillas of destroyers (including two of a much larger type), 24 submarines, 37 sloops of three types and a host of auxiliary ships and minor war vessels. The cost was now estimated at £226 millions.[2] Although in the light of the parsimony of the last fifteen years these figures must have seemed staggering they were hardly questioned by the DRC, and when it produced its monumental final report in November the Admiralty's proposals reappeared almost intact.[3] The Board of Admiralty merely 'took note' of the report,[4] two words which probably concealed feelings of relief and satisfaction —even though they had not of course yet got any of the huge sum of money needed to convert the expression of needs into the concrete realities of ships, aircraft, weapons—and men.

A few of the chief points in the DRC report may here be mentioned. It first recapitulated the principles on which our naval strength had been based since 1932—namely that 'we should be able to send to the Far East a fleet sufficient to provide "cover" against the Japanese fleet . . . [and] at the same time we should be able to retain in European waters a force sufficient to act as a deterrent and to prevent the strongest European Naval Power from obtaining control of our vital Home terminal areas . . .' But, they continued, the recent resurgence of German naval power, the antagonism produced by Italian expansionist policy in Africa, and 'continuing anxiety for the safety of our possessions in the Far East' had led to the DRC accepting the concept of 'a new standard of naval strength'—which was in effect what the Admiralty had proposed.

Turning to the increases proposed in the various classes of warship the DRC accepted the need to build seven capital ships in 1937 to 1939, which would provide equality in new ships with Germany and Japan by 1942—provided that those countries did not further increase their building programmes. The four new carriers proposed by the Admiralty (some possibly of a smaller type) were accepted, as was the cruiser replacement programme of five ships per year—though the latter was to be treated as provisional and subject to later review. As to de-

[1] Director of Plans to First Sea Lord 20th July and 6th Aug. 1935. Adm. 116/3437.
[2] Memo. by Chatfield of 9th Oct. 1935, Appendix I, and DRC. 33 9th Oct. 1935. Cab. 29/112. Also in Adm. 116/3437.
[3] DRC. 37 of 21st Nov. 1935, vols. I and II.
[4] Board Minute 3316 of 28th Nov. 1935. Adm. 167/92.

stroyers, an additional flotilla of the larger type which the Admiralty was considering should be built in 1936–37, and a new flotilla in alternate years up to 1942. Submarine and sloop construction should continue at the rate of about three and five or six respectively in each year. Turning to deficiencies, the DRC recommended that the reserves of ammunition, anti-submarine equipment and many other stores for which the Admiralty had long been pressing should be made good, and that complete or partial modernisation of seven battleships should be put in hand.[1] The Fleet Air Arm should be increased from the 190 aircraft embarked in carriers and catapult ships in 1935 to 357 in 1939 and 504 in 1942.[2] To man the new ships the DRC calculated that 35,600 additional men would be needed between 1936 and 1942.

It will be convenient here to carry on the story of the DRC's final report to the end. The Ministerial (DPRC) Committee took it in February 1936.[3] It accepted the DRC's review of the worsening international situation as presenting 'a generally accurate picture', and 'fully associated' itself with the DRC's presentation of the four alternative policies which might be followed. These were, firstly, adherence to the time-worn principle of 'Collective Security'; secondly a more limited form of the same on the Locarno model; thirdly a return to the prewar system of alliances or *ententes*; and, finally, isolation. They also

---

[1] The *Warspite*, *Queen Elizabeth*, *Valiant* and *Renown* were to be completely reconstructed, and this was actually carried out. The *Malaya*, *Barham*, *Royal Oak* and *Repulse* were scheduled for partial modernisation, but the work was never completed. Reconstruction of the *Warspite*, the first of her class to be taken in hand, was considered by a Committee under the Controller appointed in June 1934. The elevation of her 15″ guns was increased and, with the supply of a new design of shell, gave much longer range. She was fitted with new engines and boilers, thicker deck armour, new fire control systems and greatly increased A-A armaments, and completed as an entirely new and very successful ship in 1937. The cost was about £2½ millions. Adm. 1/8779–190/34. The author of this history was her Gunnery Officer and First Lieutenant.

[2] The comparable figures for Japan and USA in 1938 were estimated at 374 and 670 aircraft respectively.

[3] DPR(DR9) of 12th Feb. 1936. This body was chaired by the Prime Minister and included ten other Cabinet Ministers, including the Foreign Secretary (Eden), the Ministry for League of Nations Affairs (Cranborne, later 5th Marquess of Salisbury), and the Ministers for the three Service Departments (Monsell, Duff Cooper and Cunliffe-Lister, later Earl of Swinton). The Chiefs of Staff attended its meetings as 'expert advisers'. The minutes of the DPR Committee for 1935–36 are in Cab. 16/136, and the memoranda circulated to it are in Cab. 16/138–140. Many COS papers were reprinted for the DPRC and given a DPR number.

accepted that 'a strong Britain is now clearly essential to the success of the [League] Covenant system', which other nations would only support if that state of affairs were evident. Isolation would, they considered, 'undoubtedly require the greatest strength of all'. Only such strength as would enable us 'to take our full share in maintaining the peace of the world' could, they predicted, lead to a time when 'reduction of armaments by consent may become possible'; but, they concluded, 'That time however is not yet'. In other words the era of naval limitation begun at Washington in 1922 was ended.

The Cabinet took the DRC and the DPRC reports together on 25th February 1936, and discussed the latter paragraph by paragraph. Their most important conclusion was 'to approve the Report generally and provisionally on the understanding that the programmes contained therein were liable to modification in the light of new considerations' —such as the increasing range and power of aircraft. The qualifications made to the Admiralty's proposals and programmes were not significant, except possibly that the building of the four new carriers might require reconsideration in the light of recent developments in air power—especially in the narrow seas.[1] The Cabinet decided that the possible adoption of a new standard of naval strength and of the capital ship building programme should be totally excluded from the next Defence White Paper, and that only the one carrier included in the 1936 programme should be mentioned.[2] These precautions were obviously inspired by the desire not to provoke the dictatorships into undertaking retaliatory building, and to avoid alarming the home population. In retrospect it is clear that the dictatorships would not have been induced to modify their intentions by full knowledge of British rearmament, and that it would have been far better to tell the British people the whole truth about the country's danger and the government's intentions. As soon as the Cabinet's decisions were known the Admiralty issued, for internal circulation, orders on how the remedying of deficiencies and the execution of the DRC report should be handled.[3]

[1] Cabinet 10(36) of 25th Feb. 1936. Cab. 23/133. The most convenient source for studying the DRC, and DPRC reports and the Cabinet Conclusions is perhaps CID. 1215B of 2nd March 1936 in Cab. 4/24. But the papers are there printed in reverse order to their production, i.e. the Cabinet Conclusions come first, then the DPRC report, and the DRC's original paper (DRC. 37) last.

[2] Cmd. 5107 of 3rd March 1936.

[3] Office Memos. of 14th March and 22nd April 1936. Adm. 1/9042.

While the high-level discussions on rearmament were in progress the Naval Staff and Supply Departments were devoting great attention to the design of the new ships which were now likely to be built, and it will be convenient to consider how each new design evolved.

The class initially called 'the 1937 Capital Ship' (i.e. the ships which could be built after the expiration of the Washington and London treaties) was first considered in 1928 and was to have been a repetition, with improvements, of the very successful *Queen Elizabeth* class (eight 15-inch guns in twin turrets). But the decision taken at the 1930 London Conference not to lay down any such ships between 1931 and 1936 had caused it to be put in cold storage.[1] When at the Geneva Disarmament Conference we had proposed to reduce the size and armament of capital ships four alternative designs with 12-inch guns in twin or triple mountings were produced.[2] But the problem was now complicated by the Germans producing the *Deutschland* class 'pocket battleships' (about 12,000 tons, six 11-inch guns) and the French building the *Dunkerque* (26,500 tons, eight 13-inch guns) in reply.[3] In 1935 four designs of battle-cruisers with eight, ten or twelve 14-inch or nine 16-inch guns, were prepared; and a fifth design, for a ship with twelve 14-inch in quadruple turrets was produced a little later.[4] In September 1935 the Sea Lords discussed the various alternatives. They were of course aware of American reluctance to accept smaller ships than the 35,000 tons permitted by treaty, and smaller guns than 16-inch; but they were far more concerned about the reports received regarding bigger Japanese ships, the German *Scharnhorst* class (32,000 tons, nine 11-inch guns), and Italy's first two *Littorio* class (about 42,000 tons, nine 15-inch) laid down in 1934, than with American preferences. In September 1935 Chatfield came down in favour of the first two new ships being of the 35,000-ton design and armed with 15-inch guns; but they were to be capable of 29 knots and well protected as in the earlier 14D design. Our policy remained, he wrote, to press for a lower tonnage and 14-inch gun limitation 'mainly for economical and political reasons'; and if international agreement was achieved the later ships in the DRC programme could be smaller.[5] The Staff, which had long expressed anxiety about the inadequate protection of our capital

[1] Adm. 1/9354.
[2] These were known as designs N, O, P and Q. Adm. 1/9371.
[3] Undated memo. by Naval Staff, c. March 1931. Adm. 1/8766–65/33.
[4] These were known as designs 14C, 14D, 14E, 16A and 14F. Adm. 1/9379.
[5] Memo. by Chatfield of 24th Sept. 1935. Adm. 1/9387.

ships and cruisers,[1] continued to press for thicker armour to be provided against both bombs and shells, and for better underwater protection; but as in all ship design a compromise had to be accepted between displacement, gunpower, speed and protection. We will return later to the design finally selected.

While the Board was pressing to restart capital ship construction in the mid-1930s the 'Bomb versus Battleship' controversy was raging furiously, and the CID had appointed a special sub-committee to investigate the 'Vulnerability of Capital Ships' (VCS Committee), under the chairmanship of Sir Thomas Inskip, the Minister for Co-ordination of Defence.[2] It would be tedious to go through the evidence taken by the many witnesses who gave evidence or submitted papers— much of which consisted of assertion and counter-assertion. For instance Sir Eustace Tennyson d'Eyncourt, a former Director of Naval Construction, declared that 'As the capital ship is the only one which can be made safe against modern attack of various kinds, the Capital Ship is an absolute necessity'.[3] Sir John Salmond, a former CAS, admitted that 'As far as I am aware the Capital Ship is the one remaining surface craft which, if severely hit, will not sink', and foretold that 'it should have a useful life for some time to come'; while Trenchard expended most of his argument in an attack on the plan to send a battle fleet to the Far East.[4] The committee reported on 30th July 1936, and its twelve recommendations were singularly anodyne[5]—as were the Conclusions of the CID itself when it took the report, approved it and sent it to the Cabinet 'for information'.[6] The truth was that the inquiry resolved nothing; but as it produced no evidence or conclusions which could have justified rejecting the Admiralty's building proposals Chatfield was probably satisfied by the outcome.

One development which arose out of the VCS investigation was that Chatfield and Ellington agreed that an impartial investigation into the

---

[1] A Tactical Division minute of 4th April 1933 stated that 'the great majority of our capital ships and all the 8-inch cruisers are inadequately protected'. Adm. 1/9354.

[2] The other members were Lord Halifax (Privy Seal), Malcolm MacDonald (Dominions), and Walter Runciman (Board of Trade). Chatfield (1st Sea Lord) and Ellington (Chief of Air Staff) were 'expert advisers', and the Terms of Reference were 'to consider the experiments that have taken place or are proposed in connection with the defence against aircraft and the vulnerability from the air of Capital Ships'.

[3] VCS. 21 of 29th June 1936. Copies in Adm. 116/4324.

[4] VCS. 22 of 30th June 1936. *ibid.*

[5] CID. 1258B. Cab. 4/24. Also VCS. 27 of 30th July 1936.

[6] 282nd CID meeting on 8th Oct. 1936. Cab. 4/264.

effectiveness of bombing and A-A gunfire should be carried out under the chairmanship of General Sir Hugh Elles assisted by the distinguished scientists Sir Henry Tizard and Sir Frank E. Smith, who were joined later by R. H. Fowler of Cambridge University.[1] By the beginning of 1937 however the service departments had got themselves tied into knots regarding what the Terms of Reference should be. After about six weeks of intermittent and sometimes acrimonious debate they finally agreed that their brief should be 'to consider the value of A-A fire as a protection against air attack' in various conditions, and 'the value of level and dive-bombing' in different circumstances.[2]

Perhaps the most useful experiment carried out during the great 'Bomb v Battleship' controversy was the construction by the Admiralty of a full-scale model representing in one part a section of a modern capital ship and in another part a section of a modern cruiser. It was used for trials in 1934-35 carried out in the Medway estuary. Explosives were attached to the outside of the hull and detonated electrically to represent hits by 'B bombs' (delay action underwater bombs) and torpedoes, and RAF aircraft attacked the model with 500- and 250-pound bombs.[3] Several interesting points were brought to light, notably that no bomb pierced four inches of armour. The committee appointed to conduct the trials and to make recommendations derived from their results reported in October 1936, and a copy was sent to the Air Ministry, which appears to have been disappointed by the results obtained by the bombers and asked for live (i.e. fused and filled) bombs to be used—which the Director of Naval Construction angrily described as 'butting in on ship design questions'.[4] Though these trials were a genuine attempt to reproduce the actual damage caused by various weapons the results were vitiated not only by unfilled bombs being used but by the fact that the model was not fitted with all the complicated and multifarious equipment installed in a modern ship, and did not of course have any personnel embarked.

---

[1] This body, set up as a result of 282nd CID meeting of 8th Oct. 1936, was at first called 'The Sub-Committee of Assessors on Bomb v Battleship Experiments', but in March 1938 it was changed to 'The Sub-Committee on Bombing and A-A Gunfire Experiments'. (ABE. 54). However it was always referred to as the 'ABE Committee', and its papers were given a series title with that heading. Cab. 16/178 and 179.

[2] Papers of 27th, 29th Oct., 27th Nov. and 8th Dec. 1936. Adm. 116/3732.

[3] The construction was known as 'Job 74', or colloquially as the 'Chatham Float'. Adm. 116/3500 and 3594.

[4] Minute by DNC of 1st May 1936. Adm. 116/3594.

Thus the results could hardly be said to reproduce actual action conditions.[1] However they did lead to the important decision to place the magazines (always the most dangerous spot) below the shell rooms in new ships in order to protect them better, and to strengthen the anti-torpedo 'bulges'.

In addition to studying the large number of alternative designs for capital ships, summarised above, the Admiralty carried out parallel investigations for every other class of warship asked for in the new DRC programme. In 1933–34 lengthy investigation of the design of the *Ark Royal* of the 1934 programme was carried out. The final decision was that she was to be an 'Island type' ship like the *Glorious, Courageous, Eagle* and *Hermes* and not a 'flush deck' ship like the *Furious*. She was to be capable of carrying and operating 72 aircraft (48 Torpedo-Spotter-Reconnaissance and 24 Dive-Bombers), to have two hangars, and be capable of 30 knots. Her flight deck (800 feet long) was divided into two parts by a crash barrier, the forward part being used for flying off and parking aircraft while the after part was the landing area. Two 'accelerators' (modified catapults) were to be fitted to facilitate launching aircraft, and by cutting down on ammunition storage the displacement was got down to 22,000 tons, which was well below the Washington Treaty limit of 27,000 but left us with a sufficient surplus of the permitted total tonnage (135,000 tons) to build more ships of moderate size when the older ships were due for replacement.[2] The RAA, Admiral Henderson, when consulted about the design, made the prophetic remark that carriers might well have to act as 'the advance guard of the Royal Air Force';[3] and so it proved in Norway 1940 and elsewhere. The design and legend were approved in June 1934 and January 1935 respectively.[4]

In 1936 the Admiralty turned their attention to the design of the four carriers included in the DRC programme and, as with the capital ships, many alternatives were considered.[5] Treaty limitations again

---

[1] Air Min. letter of 8th April and Admy. reply of 26th May 1936. *ibid.*

[2] Adm. 1/9330 and 9353.

[3] AL of 22nd Aug. and reply by RAA of 7th Sept. 1933. Adm. 1/9353.

[4] Board Minute 3207 of 21st June and 3271 of 31st Jan. 1935. Adm. 1/9369. The 'legend' of a class of warship comprised the constructional, engineering and armament specifications (e.g. length, beam and draught, horsepower of main engines, and calibre of all guns). It should not be confused with 'Staff Requirements', which were *desiderata* and often could not be met because of technical limitations. 'Legends' were prescribed on a standard Admiralty form.

[5] Designs X and Y were to carry 54 aircraft, Z and ZA 36. X and Z were both to

restricted the size which could be accepted, but Admiral Henderson, who had taken over as Third Sea Lord and Controller in April 1934, pointed out that 'It has been approved for some time to build large carriers', and proposed to keep the smallest of the alternatives offered (12,700 tons) 'in the bag'.[1] In July 1936 the Board took the plunge and decided to build the new ships with a 3-inch armoured flight deck and 4½-inch side armour—though it meant reducing the number of aircraft carried to 36 and increased the displacement to 23,000 tons.[2] The legend of the ships which were to become the *Illustrious* and *Victorious* (1936 programme) was approved at the end of the year, and so came to fruition a revolutionary change in carrier design which was to pay a very good dividend in war; for the armoured deck would be proof against 500-pound semi-armour-piercing (SAP) bombs dropped from 7,000 feet, while the side armour would defeat 6-inch shells.[3] Another important decision was to convert the old *Argus* (14,000 tons, converted in 1917) to a trade protection carrier capable also of operating the wireless-controlled 'Queen Bee' target aircraft.[4] This appears to be the first mention of the use of aircraft carriers for trade protection; but treaty limitations and the priority given to building other types of warship prevented any more being built or converted to such service until after the outbreak of war. This is surely a case where the Staff got its priorities wrong, doubtless due to the dominance of the 'battle fleet concept' over trade protection. The result was that various extemporised measures had to be adopted early in the war when the need for convoys to carry their own air defence with them became glaringly apparent.[5]

To turn to cruiser development, we have seen how treaty limitations, combined with the need for large numbers of such ships for trade defence purposes, forced the Admiralty to build the small *Arethusa*

---

have an armoured flight deck. A fifth design to carry 24 aircraft on a displacement of 12,700 tons was also produced. Adm. 1/9399.

[1] Minute by Henderson of 7th July 1936. *ibid.*

[2] Board Minute 3389 of 21st July 1936. Adm. 1/9399. The *Illustrious* and *Victorious* only had one aircraft hangar.

[3] Board Minute 3430 of 14th Dec. 1936. Adm. 1/9406.

[4] Approved by Board 7th April 1936. Adm. 1/9399.

[5] The extemporised measures were Catapult Aircraft Merchantmen (CAM) and Fighter Catapult Ships (FCS). See Roskill, *War at Sea*, I, p. 477. On escort carriers see *op. cit.*, I, pp. 478–9 and II, pp. 366–70.

class of the 1931 and '32 programmes,[1] and how they only adopted
the much larger *Southamptons* of the 1933–36 programmes reluctantly
and because the USA and Japan were building large cruisers.[2] In 1935
no less than five alternative designs for small cruisers (3,500 to 5,000
tons) were considered because the Staff wanted 'powerful general
purpose cruisers' armed with 6-inch guns—which was asking too much
on the displacement which could be afforded.[3] In the end the Board,
doubtless influenced by the increasing threat from the air, went for a
totally new class with five twin 5.25-inch HA/LA guns on a displacement of 5,300 tons.[4]

As to destroyer design, all the ships built between 1927 and 1935 had
been armed with four single 4.7-inch guns (except for the Flotilla
Leaders, which had five) and two quadruple torpedo tubes—increased
to quintuple tubes in one of the 1933 (G class) and all the 1934 (I class)
flotillas. Late in 1934 the Controller, Admiral Henderson, pointed out
that three twin 4.7-inch could be mounted instead of four singles for a
small increase in displacement and cost.[5] The arrival of the new twin
mounting appears to have triggered off the idea of building considerably larger destroyers with four such mountings. They would, in the
Admiralty's view, be the counterparts to the French *Fantasque* class
(about 2,600 tons, armed with five 5-inch guns and three triple 21.7-inch
torpedo tubes)[6] and the Japanese *Fubuki* class (about 2,090 tons, armed
with six 5-inch in twin mountings and nine 24-inch torpedo tubes).[7]

[1] Originally there were to have been eight *Arethusas*, working in two squadrons;
but only four were built. Adm. 1/9336 and 9427.

[2] The first and second groups of *Southamptons* consisted of eight ships (9,100–9,400
tons); the third group (1936 programme) of two ships (10,000 tons). One of the latter
the *Belfast*, possibly the most successful cruiser of the period, is now preserved off the
south bank of the Thames. The design of the 1936 ships was approved by Board
Minute 3374 of 28th May 1936. Adm. 1/9391.

[3] Adm. 1/8828–123/1935.

[4] The design actually came out at about 5,450 tons.

[5] Henderson to Chatfield 12th Nov. 1934. Adm. 1/8828–123/1935.

[6] For calculation of total tonnage under the treaties these French ships had to be
counted as cruisers. See Cmd. 5038, p. 18 *note*. In 1935 France had 32 vessels of displacement above the 1,850-ton limit in the London Treaty of 1930. The French did
not ratify that treaty and called the ships 'Contre-torpilleurs'.

[7] The Japanese completed twenty of this class in 1928–29. The gun armament of the
later ones was made dual purpose (HA/LA). They were good ships but tended, with
the addition of refinements, to be top-heavy and unstable. They were extensively
modernised in 1936, and it was then that their displacement increased from 1,680 to
2,090 tons and they lost 4 knots in speed.

The new British class, referred to initially as 'V Leaders', produced conflicting views from the Cs-in-C, Home and Mediterranean Fleets; but the Sea Lords finally came down in favour of them and proposed that seven should be added to the 1935 programme.[1] Thus was born the famous *Tribal* class destroyer, of which 16 were built for the RN under the 1935 and '36 programmes.[2] They were excellent ships, but suffered from their main gun armament (eight 4.7-inch in twin mountings) not being dual purpose.[3]

The reader will have remarked that in the Admiralty trade defence was regarded mainly as a cruiser function against surface raiders; and that state of affairs continued almost up to the outbreak of war. Although all destroyers were fitted with Asdics after 1932,[4] and so were capable of defending *mercantile* convoys against submarines, they received little or no training in that function.[5] Again and again does one find mention in exercise reports and correspondence of destroyer attacks on a *battle fleet*, by night as well as by day;[6] and such a function,

---

[1] Letters from Cs-in-C, Home and Mediterranean, minutes by members of Board and Sea Lords' meeting of 20th Feb. 1935. Adm. 1/8828-123/1935.

[2] During World War II Australia built three *Tribals*, four were built for Canada in Britain and four more in Canada. Thus the grand total in the Commonwealth navies became 27. The Australian and Canadian ships only had three twin 4.7-inch but also carried one twin 4-inch A-A mounting.

[3] The *Tribal*'s 4.7-inch guns only had 40 degrees elevation, but were sometimes referred to as 'dual purpose'—probably because a rudimentary A-A control system was fitted for them. Though they could be, and were, used in barrage fire against low-flying torpedo-bombers they were useless against high-level or dive-bombers and so were not 'dual purpose' in the commonly accepted sense of the definition. Letter to the author from Admiral Sir Richard Onslow (Captain of HMS *Ashanti* 1941–42) of 20th Jan. 1975.

[4] Adm. 1/8755-57/1932. The decision was taken on 17th June 1932.

[5] See for example Chatfield's report on the Atlantic Fleet's exercises of autumn 1929 (AF. 250/55).

p. 8 'The main object of the autumn period has been Gunnery and Torpedo training'. pp. 9–12 Description of day and night anti-submarine screening of Battle Fleet. pp. 15–16 Destroyer attacks on Battle Fleet by day and night. Chatfield papers, CHT/2/1.

Also Chatfield to Field 28th Oct. 1930. 'I intend in the winter cruise to have one exercise lasting two or three days with the whole fleet to develop air attack on the fleet in harbour and the defence problem'. In the Combined Fleet Exercises of March 1931 Chatfield intended to carry out 'a more prolonged strategic exercise . . . to test our day and night [fleet] organisations'. *ibid.*

[6] Some convoy exercises did take place in the 1930s, but they were concerned either with the defence of *military* as opposed to *mercantile* convoys or with defence against

combined with defence of heavy ships against submarine attack, continued to be regarded as the primary function of destroyers until the harsh lessons of experience taught us the truth. It is only fair to mention that the US Navy's exercises of the 1930s reveal the same fallacy;[1] and such evidence as has become available about the Japanese Fleet's training leaves little doubt that it too was obsessed by the battle fleet concept— and was moreover far slower than the British and American navies to accept the strategy of convoy and escort.

In 1936 an interesting exchange took place between Chatfield and Churchill on the defence of merchant shipping against air and submarine attacks. Chatfield did not at that time believe that air attacks were likely; but, he wrote, 'even one A-A gun in a merchant ship' would keep the aircraft at a height such that the chance of destroying the ship was 'very small'. As regards submarine attacks he wrote that 'our methods are now so efficient [he assessed them at 80% successful] that we will need fewer destroyers in the North Sea and Mediterranean'. But he qualified his confidence drastically by adding that 'Unless the Admiralty can ensure that our convoys can get through to this country despite air attack and submarine attack, then we are doomed'.[2] However a few weeks later he wrote that 'As regards the defence of our merchant ships against air attack, I have no doubt that we can do this. Our sloops will be given anti-aircraft as well as anti-submarine methods . . . Their main job is to protect the convoys against the insidious submarine and aircraft'.[3] Churchill, who had recently visited

---

surface forces as opposed to submarines. For example in the 1934 Combined Exercises the C-in-C, Home Fleet was escorting a convoy from the West Indies to a Spanish port *with his battle fleet*, while the C-in-C, Mediterranean endeavoured to intercept and destroy it. (Admiral Sir W. M. James to the author 15th May 1964 contains a description of this exercise.) A rather similar example is to be found in Serial 8 of the Combined Exercises of 1938, which was designed 'to exercise the protection of a large convoy when attacked by surface, submarine and air forces'. The speed of the convoy was 10 knots (slow SC convoys in World War II were in theory capable of 7 knots and 'fast' HX convoys of 9 knots), and its escort consisted of two battleships, two battlecruisers, a carrier, a cruiser squadron and three destroyer flotillas—which would of course be absurd for a mercantile convoy. See Adm. 116/3873. Arthur Marder in *From the Dardanelles to Oran* (Oxford UP, 1974) pp. 38–40 arrives at a wholly erroneous conclusion regarding the exercises of that period, in many of which the author of this history took part.

[1] Fleet Problems XIV to XVIII, carried out between Feb. 1933 and May 1937 all show this tendency. US Navy Operational Archives.

[2] Chatfield to Churchill 5th May 1936. Chatfield papers, CHT/4/3.

[3] Same to same 28th May 1936. *ibid.* CHT/3/1.

the anti-submarine school at Portland, replied that he had been very impressed by all that he had seen. 'The faithful effort has', he wrote in typically picturesque metaphor, 'relieved us of our great danger'.[1]

Although at this time the defence of merchant shipping against air and submarine attacks still played little part in British peacetime training the need for mercantile convoy escorts was not totally ignored in the building programmes of the 1930s. The Admiralty designed for that purpose a special 'Convoy Sloop', the first of which appeared in the 1933 programme. But as sloops of two other types were included in the same programme it is fairly plain that no one was very clear regarding their functions. This is confirmed by the next year's building programme including 'General Service Sloops', 'Sloop Minesweepers' and 'Coastal Sloops'; but in the following year a single 'Convoy Sloop' appears again (still with others of different functions). Not until the end of 1936 was the legend for new convoy sloops approved.[2]

Though the provision of small Asdic-fitted escort vessels undoubtedly took too lowly a place in the building programmes of the 1930s it should be mentioned that by 1934 the Admiralty had designed an anti-submarine trawler to their own specifications 'with a view to rapid construction in emergency'; and although approaches from trawler owners for subsidies to enable their ships to carry out escort duty were coolly received, the Admiralty did inspect and earmark certain trawlers (notably those of the Mac Line of Fleetwood) for requisitioning in war. Other fishing vessels, such as drifters, were earmarked for minesweeping; and steps were taken to provide the necessary anti-submarine and minesweeping equipment.[3] None the less the comparative neglect of escort vessels in between the wars surely indicates that the lessons of 1914–18 were ignored or misinterpreted. The euphoria aroused in the 1920s by the invention of the Asdic,[4] and failure to appreciate that it was useless against a surfaced submarine, certainly contributed to this neglect. As to the introduction of convoy one must surely take the words spoken in Parliament by Lord Stanley, Parliamentary Secretary to the Admiralty, on 15th March 1935 as expressing the views of the Naval Staff and Board. 'I can assure the House', said Stanley, 'that the convoy system would not be introduced at once on the outbreak of war'; and he went on to recount the

[1] Churchill to Chatfield 18th June 1936. *ibid.* CHT/4/3.

[2] On 1st Dec. 1936. Adm. 1/9410.

[3] Adm. 116/3367 and minute by Henderson of 18th Sept. 1937.

[4] See vol. 1, pp. 345–7 and 536.

oft-repeated but largely fallacious disadvantages of the convoy system. His conclusion was therefore that construction of sloops (or indeed any convoy escorts) must be put 'into its proper order of priority'; by which he obviously meant a low priority.[1]

A similar criticism to the relative neglect of escort vessels at this time can be made with regard to the design, equipment and training of minesweepers. Most of the training of such vessels as were built was carried out against moored mines, though experiments against Antenna mines (which the Italians were to use very successfully in the Mediterranean) were carried out. As regards a mine fitted with a magnetic pistol the senior officer concerned reported that 'the material proposed [by the Admiralty] . . . is not part of the equipment of a modern minesweeper'; nor would it be effective if, he continued, such a mine were produced by a foreign country.[2] On the other hand the Anti-Submarine school did report late in 1939 that an Acoustic mine was practicable and that a 'towed source' would be necessary to cope with it.[3]

As regards British submarine construction, we have seen how at the Washington and first London conferences, and again in the Draft Disarmament Convention put forward at Geneva in 1930, we proposed their total abolition, or failing that severe limitation in size and in numbers. But the truth was that we never entertained any serious expectation of abolition being accepted. In the 1920s we built a total of 19 submarines, and from 1930 to 1935 added three each year, after which building was increased to eight in 1936 and seven in the following year. By way of contrast France built 77 submarines between 1922 and 1930 and added ten more between 1931 and '37.[4]

The submarines built for the Royal Navy in the 1920s (O, P and R classes) were developments from the World War I L class, but proved unhandy vessels. The three *Thames* class of the 1929–1932 programmes (about 1,850 tons on surface and 2,700 submerged and capable of some

[1] Parl. Deb., Commons, vol. 199, cols. 674–7.

[2] Annual Report by Captain, Fishery Protection and Minesweeping for 1936–37. Adm. 1/9084–56/1937.

[3] Reports of 9th and 12th Dec. 1939. Adm. 1/9807. The 'towed source' mentioned here may be regarded as the genesis of the 'Foxer' device introduced in 1943 to cope with the German acoustic torpedo. See Roskill, *War at Sea*, vol. III, part I, pp. 40–41.

[4] From *Les Flottes de Combat* (Paris). I am indebted to Surgeon Captain (Retd.) Hervé Gras, well known as a writer on French naval affairs under the pseudonym 'Jacques Mordal', for this information and for many valuable letters on the French Navy.

22 knots when surfaced) were the last attempt to produce a fleet sub-marine; but the S and T classes and the *Porpoise* class minelayers of 1929 and later years can be described as successful.[1] Command of the submarines at home (two flotillas) was in the hands of a Rear-Admiral who flew his flag in the depot at Portsmouth; but in 1935 he proposed that he and his staff should move to the Admiralty to improve co-ordination. The Admiralty agreed in principle but declined to make a firm commitment until war experience had confirmed the necessity.[2] As regards training of submarines it seems true to say that they too suffered from the 'battle fleet concept', since in exercises both we and the Americans regarded attack on heavy ships as their primary function. But one has to remember that from the time of the Washington Conference of 1921–22 the signatories of the naval treaties were obliged only to employ submarines against merchant shipping in accordance with International Law as applicable to surface warships; and to train submarine crews for attacks on merchant shipping con-trary to the treaty provisions would have been too flagrant for any British or American government to countenance it.[3] Yet the fact is that the multifarious duties performed by our submarines in World War II (ultimately in disregard of all treaty obligations) bore little relation to their peacetime tactical training. However the fact that the submarine, like the convoy escort and the Fleet Air Arm, remained a poor relation of the big ship navy in between the wars was not entirely the fault of the 'battleship admirals'. For the submarine officers did conduct themselves too much in the spirit and guise of a 'private navy' whose arcane mysteries were not for communication to out-siders—who in any case would not understand them. This attitude probably both contributed to and was aggravated by the small number of submarine specialists on the Naval Staff proper, and to the failure to integrate their weapons into the fleet's strategy and tactics *as a whole*. And of course knowledge that their own government had several times offered totally to abolish them, combined with the lingering memory of the description of the submarine by an admiral at the

---

[1] Adm. 1/9373 has sketch designs of the classes which became the S and T.

[2] RA (S) to Admy. 11th Sept. 1935 and reply by Admy. of 8th Jan. 1936. Adm. 1/9039–118/1936. In fact the Submarine Command headquarters moved to Swiss Cottage in north London in 1939.

[3] As France and Italy never signed the London Treaty of 1930 they were not bound by part IV, article 22 regarding the use of submarines, which was extended by the Protocol of 1936, and to which Germany acceded.

beginning of the century as 'underhand, unfair and damned un-English'[1] were not exactly morale raisers for the latter day members of that branch of the naval service.

Though one cannot but regret, and without benefiting from the wisdom of hindsight, that a greater proportion of the Navy Votes was not devoted in the 1930s to escort vessels, minesweepers, submarines and the Fleet Air Arm (which, in the form of the RN Air Service had done great work in convoy defence in 1917–18) instead of to the battle fleet, in 1935–36 steps were initiated to organise—on paper—the creation of a world-wide convoy system. An attempt to preserve the experiences of 1914–18 had been made early in 1921, when a committee was formed to consider 'a peace organisation of Royal Navy Transport Service capable of rapid expansion in war';[2] but it was very short-lived, and not until 1928 was the question of training retired officers for such a service raised—by the Board of Trade. A dozen officers underwent a course in 1931 and a similar number were selected for the next year; but again the scheme seems to have died. Probably it was a casualty of the great depression.[3] It will be told later how it was energetically revived, and thoroughly organised shortly before World War II, by which time the likelihood of unrestricted submarine warfare being waged again had been accepted. Before that date a Naval Control Service Manual was however issued, and in it convoy was described as 'the ideal form of protection' for merchant shipping; but 'because of its well-known disadvantages' it was not to be introduced in the eastern trades 'until proved necessary'.[4] We have already seen how the 1934 Singapore Conference optimistically hoped to keep trade moving except to the north of Borneo, and without benefit of convoy.[5]

The emergency of 1935, to be discussed in the next chapter, caused the Naval Staff to review the arrangements necessary to bring a Contraband Control Service into force, and the recruitment of linguists from the universities to serve as interpreters at Contraband Control stations was organised on paper.[6] But when the possibility of

[1] Admiral Sir A. K. Wilson in 1902. Quoted A. J. Marder, *Fear God and Dread Nought*, vol. 1 (Oxford UP, 1961), p. 333. See also William Jameson, *The Most Formidable Thing* (Hart-Davis, 1965), pp. 75–76.

[2] Memo. of Feb. 1921. Adm. 1/8742–101/30.

[3] BOT to Admy. 6th Dec. 1928 and 22nd Jan. 1930. *ibid.*

[4] CB. 01764(26), pp. 18–19.

[5] Adm. 116/3121. Report of Singapore Conference 1934. See pp. 185-7.

[6] Secret Office Acquaint of 27th May 1935. Adm. 116/3866.

war with Italy faded the subject was allowed to lapse, and nothing more is recorded about it until July 1937, when the Staff agreed that the lists of men selected earlier should be brought up to date, and that officers of wider experience than ex-university linguists were needed.[1] We will return later to the structure of a full Contraband Control organisation, designed to enforce a blockade of the Axis powers, instituted shortly before the outbreak of war.

Meanwhile the Imperial Shipping Committee, first set up in 1920 but long inactive, was reconstituted in 1933. Four years later Lord Runciman, President of the Board of Trade, asked for a survey to be made of trade problems in the Far East; but the emphasis was on American and Japanese competition rather than on the defence of shipping.[2] None the less a large number of instructional handbooks on the duties of Reporting Officers, whose function it was to report all movements of enemy merchant shipping and kindred subjects, was issued in confidential print and by Fleet Orders between 1927 and 1937. The Naval Control Service Manual was also brought up to date, and arrangements were made for training Reporting Officers in their duties.[3]

Here we may review the developments in American naval policy which took place concurrently with those described for Britain. In May 1935 the General Board recommended that the programme for the 1937 Fiscal Year should comprise one 35,000-ton battleship (but the 'characteristics' were to be determined later), twelve destroyers, six submarines and various lesser ships—which was a fairly modest step towards fulfilment of the needs set out in the Vinson Act of 1934.[4] In June Swanson wrote to the President about this programme, and

[1] Office Acquaint of 12th July 1937. *ibid.* The Officer in charge of the Co-ordination of Contraband Control between the Admiralty, the Board of Trade and the Ministry of Labour was Rear-Admiral H. G. Thursfield (Retd.), one time Naval Correspondent of *The Times*; but he seems never to have been given an official title for this work.

[2] Adm. 1/9083–55/1937.

[3] The principal confidential books issued on this subject were:
CB. 3000A(27) Instructions for Reporting Officers abroad;
CB. 01764(36) Naval Control Service Manual (Revised Ed.);
CB. 01671, A, B and C, Secret charts and explanatory pamphlets on routeing of shipping.
Also CAFOS. 378 and 379/37. The former dealt with training of Reporting Officers. Adm. 1/9078–45/1937.

[4] GB. 420–2, serial 1886 of 24th May 1935.

he approved the destroyers and submarines which, he said, replaced obsolete tonnage; but he added that it was 'important that nothing be said in regard to this [the battleship] for a few months to come'—by which time the treaty situation should be clearer. However Roosevelt gave the Secretary authority to go ahead with the design, though with absolutely no publicity.[1] When the British Defence White Paper of March 1936 announced the intention to lay down two battleships early in 1937 and to continue modernising the older ones the Navy Department asked the President for a Supplemental Appropriation to enable them to do the same.[2] Roosevelt was, however, cool about the proposal—perhaps because he was in trouble with Congress and the Supreme Court over his New Deal legislation.[3] He told the Assistant Secretary of the Navy that he preferred to wait until early in 1937, when the intentions of the European powers would be clearer, rather than seek funds during the present session of Congress. When the proposal to build two new battleships became known a flood of telegrams and letters of protest descended on the President from religious and pacifist organisations.[4] In the end they did not appear in the 'Navy Budget Request Construction' until the 1938 Fiscal Year,[5] a delay which caused Swanson to press for approval to accelerate the modernisation of the navy's older ships of that class.[6]

The Navy Department, like the Admiralty, soon found it necessary

[1] Swanson to FDR 29th June 1935 and reply by latter of 2nd July. Roosevelt papers, PSF, Dept. Corresp., Box 28.

[2] Assistant Secretary to FDR 12th March 1936. Roosevelt papers, PSF, Dept. Corresp., Box 25. Also Admiral Standley's request of 20th April 1936. *ibid* Box 27. H. L. Roosevelt, the Under-Secretary had died in office on 22nd Feb. 1936 and Charles Edison was not appointed as his successor until 18th Jan. 1937. In the interim Assistant Secretary Andrews acted for Swanson.

[3] See *Roosevelt and Frankfurter*, annotated Max Freedman (Bodley Head, 1967), ch. 7 regarding the Supreme Court cases of 1935–36 which led to Roosevelt's unfortunate attempt to 'pack' the Supreme Court, and resulted in perhaps the worst defeat of his career.

[4] Roosevelt papers, Official File 18, Box 21.

[5] These became the *North Carolina* and *Washington*, the names being suggested by Swanson. Letter of FDR of 25th Feb. 1937. Roosevelt papers, Official File 18, Box 3A. The American Fiscal Year ran from 1st July to 30th June. See vol. 1, pp. 209–10.

[6] Swanson to FDR 2nd Nov. 1935 sets out the whole battleship modernisation programme desired by the Navy Dept. to increase main armament gun elevation, add new A-A batteries and instal new engines and boilers. The proposals were very similar to the British capital ship modernisation programme. Roosevelt papers, PSF, Dept. Corresp., Box 28.

to ask for more officers and men for the expanding fleet; but they seem to have had a harder struggle. For example in July 1935 the Under-Secretary wrote to the President that, although 7,000 additional enlisted men had been approved for 1937 the increase of 3,000 in the Marine Corps had been refused, and the Bureau of the Budget declined to recommend approval.[1]

As the US Navy was not involved in the Mediterranean crisis of 1935–36 those years were, compared with the immense strain placed on the British Navy, comparatively quiet for it. Apart from the battleships already mentioned the only new construction started was twelve destroyers and six submarines in 1936, and seven of the former and four of the latter in the following year. But steady progress on base facilities, dockyards, airfields and other shore facilities was made with money appropriated earlier for New Deal agencies; and, perhaps more important in the long view, the plans made in 1931 for Industrial Mobilisation, which had been placed in the hands of the War Policies Commission and included many highly important administrative organisations such as the War Reserves Administration and War Labour Administration, were revised and approved by the Secretaries of the Navy and War Department.[2] Equally important was the negotiation of a new treaty with the Republic of Panama, with which relations had long been very uneasy, over control of the Canal Zone and the presence in it of American forces, though it was not ratified until 1939.[3]

As regards War Plans, the American 'Orange Plan' for war against Japan had been revised in 1934, when a fundamental difference between the Army and Navy became apparent. Whereas the former wanted to keep the country's naval strength mainly between the east coast and the Hawaiian islands for defensive purposes, the latter were convinced that only an offensive move to the western Pacific could bring victory. In May 1936 the Joint Planning Committee wanted to reduce the American military commitment in the Philippines to merely holding the entrance to Manila harbour; and the Army admitted that the garrison of the islands could not hold out against a major Japanese assault.

To return to the European scene, the Admiralty was watching

[1] Reeves to FDR 17th July 1937. Roosevelt papers, PSF, Dept. Corresp., Box 28.
[2] GB. 425. Revised 1936 and again in 1939.
[3] Roosevelt papers, Official File, Box 2A has correspondence on the new treaty between FDR and the State, Navy and War Departments.

anxiously the building programmes of Germany and Italy, especially in capital ships, and was deeply disappointed when in 1934 the Italians insisted on going ahead with two 35,000-ton ships—alleging that they were compelled to do so to counter the French *Richelieus*. By the beginning of 1935 British hopes of reducing the size and armament of such ships had virtually disappeared; and it was chiefly the Americans and the French who frustrated such hopes, though the Japanese were certainly not far behind them. In May 1935 the Naval Staff reviewed the implications of allowing Germany to build up to 35% of our tonnage. Though the situation would, they considered, be precarious for some years as regards capital ships and cruisers—if the Germans built fast—their general conclusion was that 'we can face hostilities against Germany in Europe with France as our ally, and at the same time preserve a defensive position against Japan'.[1] However the Staff urged that the German percentage should be calculated on a basis of *numbers* of ships and not of *tonnage*; which would only allow them five capital ships.[2] The story of the Anglo-German naval negotiations of 1935 is told in a later chapter.

In May 1935 the Franco-Soviet treaty of mutual assistance was signed,[3] and in a speech on 21st Hitler used it to justify his repudiation of the Treaty of Versailles, giving at the same time an assurance that he would faithfully observe the Locarno Treaty, including its provisions regarding the Rhineland demilitarised zone. On 7th March 1936 German troops marched into the Rhineland—on the pretext that the Franco-Soviet treaty was incompatible with Locarno, and in the following November the 'Rome-Berlin Axis' was announced.

While the storm clouds were thus gathering over Europe the Admiralty adhered to their plan to send a major fleet to the Far East. Late in 1934 the intention was changed from sending out the Mediterranean Fleet via Suez to sailing it in three groups via the Cape. If the whole fleet sailed together unacceptable delays in refuelling would result, and proposals were therefore put forward to provide two 12,000 ton oil tanks at Sierra Leone and six at Cape Town. To expedite refuelling tankers were also to be sent to the two bases.[4] As to Singapore

---

[1] Memo. by D of P of 27th May 1935. Adm. 116/3373.
[2] Memo. by same of 12th June 1935. Adm. 116/3374.
[3] Ratifications were exchanged on 27th March 1936. *Gathorne-Hardy*, p. 373.
[4] The three groups planned for the Far East at this time were:
Group A Two *Nelson* class battleships, four 'Town' class, six *Leander* class and two *Arethusa* class cruisers.

itself, the policy decided on was that, when the base was completed, the dockyard should not be regarded in peacetime as comparable to the great dockyards at home and in Malta, but should 'be able to function reasonably' on arrival of the fleet, with the facilities and personnel already there. It was to be brought up to a fully operational dockyard within six months of the start of an emergency.[1]

Very naturally the Americans, as well as the Japanese, were watching British defence developments, at Hong Kong as well as Singapore. In August 1934 Swanson reported to Roosevelt that we were 'slowly but steadily strengthening the defences' of the former[2]—although in truth not much could be, or was done as long as the Washington Treaty non-fortification clause remained in force. In the following year the Secretary reported to the President that 'a complete study' had been made of the US Navy's Pacific bases. His department recommended that Kiska (Aleutians), Guam and Samoa should remain in 'status quo' (i.e. pre-Washington Treaty) condition, but that plans should be made to develop them for use as 'subsidiary bases' in emergency. If the treaties lapsed the navy would, he considered, need 'a main outlying fleet base in the Philippines' as well as the one at Pearl Harbour and the home bases at Puget Sound (in Washington State, just south of the Canadian border) and at San Francisco. These proposals, wrote Swanson, were made on the assumption that the USA 'will not initiate a naval race either in ships or bases'.[3] In the same month President Roosevelt asked the General Board for 'consideration and recommendation concerning retention of a base in the Philippines' if, as was intended, independence was granted to the islands.[4] The reply was that no base should be retained in that eventuality, as it would be 'a military-naval liability'; but as a general principle the Board laid down that 'the United States must take steps to ensure that its naval power can be made available in the area concerned—which means that a base capable

---

Group B Four *Queen Elizabeth* class and four R class battleships, the carrier *Courageous* and six destroyer flotillas.

Group C Three old C or D class cruisers and two destroyer flotillas.

By dividing refuelling between Sierra Leone and Cape Town the Staff estimated that only 68 hours would be needed at the former and 70 at the latter. Adm. 1/9530.

[1] Memo. by Murray of 7th Dec. 1934. Adm. 167/91 and Board Minute 3254 of 12th Dec. 1934. Adm. 167/90.

[2] Swanson to FDR 26th April 1934. Roosevelt papers. PSF, Dept. Corresp.

[3] Swanson to FDR 1st May 1935. Roosevelt papers, PSF, Dept. Corresp., Box 28.

[4] A constitution for the Philippines was approved on 8th Feb. 1935 but independence was not actually achieved until 1946.

of sustaining the Fleet must either be provided under American sovereignty or furnished by another nation in agreement'.[1] In truth the dilemma in which the Navy Department found itself over the provision of a secure base in the western Pacific did not differ materially from the Admiralty's problems over Alexandria and Singapore.

With another naval limitation conference in the offing and pacifist and isolationist sentiment still running high Roosevelt was having to tread very warily with Congress over such matters as providing funds for naval bases. Though there can be no questioning his personal desire to improve both the strength and the readiness of the US Fleet, in fact little was done regarding the bases referred to by Swanson until the world situation had deteriorated much further. For example a request for $1½ millions from PWA funds for Midway and Wake Islands was turned down with the order 'to put a smaller item in the next Budget'.[2] The Navy Department was also anxious about what developments were going on in the Japanese mandated Pacific islands, which lay along the southern flank of almost the whole of the western half of the 4,200 miles of sea between Pearl Harbour and Manila. In fact however it is now known that the Japanese did not violate the 'non-fortification clause' of the Washington Treaty in respect of those islands,[3] though they did of course contain numerous excellent harbours from which a large fleet could operate; and airfields could be constructed fairly quickly on them.

A plan for the concentration of the British China Fleet and ships from the East Indies station to the east of Singapore in the event of war with Japan had been approved in 1933;[4] but events nearer home then concentrated attention on the Mediterranean and Red Sea and it was not reviewed and revised until late in 1937. In the interim Admiral Dreyer continued to bombard the Admiralty with lengthy dissertations giving his ideas on how Singapore should be defended and a war

[1] Memo. of 21st May 1935, initialled J.W.G. US Navy Operational Archives, Misc. Corresp.

[2] Roosevelt papers, Official File, Box 4.

[3] In the article 'For Sugar Boats or Submarines?' published in *US Naval Institute Proceedings*, vol. 94, no. 8 (Aug., 1968) Lieutenant-General Masatake Okumiya produces evidence to this effect, and it is noteworthy that at the Tokyo War Crimes Trials none of the accused were convicted on the charge of having fortified the Mandated Islands. The best study of the subject is Thomas Wild's article 'How Japan Fortified the Mandated Islands' in *US Naval Institute Proceedings*, vol. 81, no. 4 (April 1955).

[4] AL. M. 00518/33. Referred to in Adm. 1/9767.

against Japan conducted.[1] The Admiralty was however very busy with other events, and Dreyer's ideas were not reconsidered until the summer of 1936. The Naval Staff then found itself in marked disagreement with the C-in-C, who was in consequence given highly optimistic instructions regarding how his forces should be employed. For example 'diversionary operations in Japanese waters' and attacks on Japanese trade and on their 'detached naval forces' can hardly be described as realistic.[2] In Whitehall there seems to have been at this time a blind faith that, somehow or other, a 'main fleet' could be conjured up for the Far East, when the truth was that, whatever the possibility of sending out such a fleet may have been in the 1920s, by 1935 it had become extremely remote. Yet the gospel of the previous decade was stoutly reaffirmed—as gospels usually are. Though one can readily appreciate the evident irritation of the Naval Staff with the loquacious and obstinate C-in-C, China it would surely have been wiser to consider whether the British plan was based on a firmer foundation than to send snubbing replies to Dreyer.[3]

In 1936 what appears to have been a sincere and genuine attempt to improve relations with the Japanese was made by approving a visit of one of her cruisers to Hong Kong—despite the fact that British warships and their crews had recently been received with overt hostility in Japan. The cruiser *Yubari* accordingly spent a fortnight there, and her crew took every possible opportunity to photograph our naval installations. As the C-in-C, China, now Admiral Sir Charles Little, put it 'their curiosity overwhelmed their good manners'.[4] The experiment was not repeated. As so often we find the US Navy Department taking a similar line to the Admiralty—by welcoming proposed Japanese warship visits to the Aleutians in the hope of obtaining reciprocity for visits to the mandated islands.[5] We will return later to the British 'Far East Appreciation' produced in May 1937; since it is necessary now to consider the development of two projects concerned with the application of sea power which were first to arise in connection with develop-

---

[1] 'Singapore Emergency Defence Scheme' of 31st Jan. 1934. Adm. 116/3862.

[2] AL M. 00570/35 of 6th Aug. 1936. *ibid.*

[3] Apart from the letter referred to above criticising his plans Dreyer was snubbed for exceeding his authority by opening the matter of co-operation with the Dutch, and for arranging a personal and private cypher between himself and Admiral Upham, the C-in-C of the US Asiatic Fleet. Adm. 116/3862.

[4] R of P by Admiral Little of 18th April 1936. Adm. 1/8861.

[5] Admiral Standley to Sec. Nav. 21st May 1936. GB. 438.

ments in the Mediterranean—namely Combined Operations and the necessity for a Mobile Naval Base and its defences.

As regards Combined Operations it has been mentioned that interest was stimulated by the efficiency shown by the Japanese at Shanghai in 1933, and that a big exercise was carried out on the Yorkshire coast in the autumn of the following year. But actual production of Motor Landing Craft (MLCs) was still proceeding at a snail's pace, since they were not given any priority for allocation of funds. However a 'Manual of Combined Operations' was produced by a joint service team in 1936,[1] and in the following year agreement was finally reached, after a long interchange of correspondence between the three Service Departments, that a properly equipped Headquarters Ship was essential to the successful conduct of this difficult and dangerous form of warfare—a proposal first put up by the Staff College in 1931.[2] War experience was to prove that the supporters of this proposal were absolutely right; but there is no mention of any funds for construction or conversion of such a vessel in the pre-war Navy Estimates.

We have so far considered only the material, strategical and tactical aspects of naval policy during the period covered by this chapter. But the Invergordon mutiny of 1931 continued to cast a dark shadow over many, perhaps most, of the Board of Admiralty's deliberations; and one finds personnel problems receiving far greater attention than had been the case in earlier years. Moreover the uncertainty about the distribution of the fleet to meet the successive crises in the Far East and Mediterranean, which inevitably affected the periods spent on foreign service and the granting of home leave to ships' companies, made it extraordinarily difficult to frame equitable plans to meet such needs, and to adhere to them as demands for the presence of warships constantly changed.

Throughout the 1930s the Admiralty showed extreme sensitivity about Press reports of disciplinary trouble in the fleet. For example in 1933 a rumour that there had been trouble in the *Hood* appeared in the *Daily Mail*, and a special investigation was made into its source. Though the paper published a retraction the Admiralty protested vigorously about the rumour having been printed *after* the paper had

---

[1] Letter Captain John Cresswell, who was the naval member of the team, to the author 1st Nov. 1968. Also Memo. of 22nd Feb. 1936 in Naval Staff College papers on 'The Naval Side of Combined Operations and the Necessity for its Development in Peace'.

[2] Adm. 116/3674.

been told it was false.[1] A year later greatly exaggerated reports appeared about trouble in the RAN destroyer *Stuart*, some of whose crew were from the RN, at Gibraltar on her way to Australia, and the Admiralty itself issued a denial.[2] In December 1934 a rather similar case, also at Gibraltar, occurred about the cruiser *Berwick*, and the DNI wrote semi-officially to the Newspaper Proprietors' Association, Reuters and to various news agencies asking them not to print unfounded rumours such as this one. The replies received were, in general, helpful; but the Proprietors' Association gave warning that in Fleet Street a suspicion always existed that a denial from Whitehall was 'a smoke screen' laid down to conceal the truth, and that such feelings were 'ineradicable'.[3]

The great economy campaign of 1931–32 necessitated, as was seen earlier, widespread changes in the distribution of the fleet, in the maintenance of ships' equipment, and in the conduct of exercises and training. In the aggregate these measures could not but militate against both fighting efficiency and the introduction of new techniques and weapons.[4] During the succeeding years the Admiralty had to expend a great deal of effort on endeavouring to mitigate these ill effects; but the shortage of money limited what could be done until the first DRC report of February 1934 produced signs of a change of climate, albeit initially only a slight and general one.[5] At the time of the DRC's deliberations a review was made of probable requirements for personnel (Vote A)—extending as far as 1937 and 1938 in the light of the new construction asked for; but such forecasts remained of course no more than crystal gazing until the time when rearmament started in earnest. Recruiting for the lower deck remained satisfactory as regards *numbers* of applicants—except in the Artificer branches and of technical personnel for the slowly expanding Fleet Air Arm.[6] In 1935, however, anxiety arose about the poor educational quality of many volunteers for the Seaman branch, which was found to produce a shortage of the 'Advanced Class Boys' needed chiefly for the Signal and Wireless specialisations. In March the Director of Naval Recruiting reported

---

[1] *Daily Mail* 11th and 12th Oct. 1933. Adm. 1/8770–139/33.

[2] The rumour appeared, with banner headlines, in the *Sunday Times of Malaya* of 3rd Dec. 1933 and in several Australian papers. Adm. 1/8777–159/34.

[3] *ibid.*

[4] The effects of these measures can be followed in Adm. 116/2798, 2860, 2884 and 2886, and in the many AFOs issued as a result of the deliberations conducted in those files.

[5] See pp. 168-72.   [6] Adm. 116/3986.

that out of 546 boys accepted during the current quarter over 300 had received no more than elementary school education.[1] The Director of Naval Education, Instructor Captain A. E. Hall, considered that even those figures were optimistic, because many boys coming from 'senior schools' were in truth no better educated than those from the elementary schools. He was doubtful whether the local education authorities would help the navy to procure better educated entrants because 'In these days of Peace Ballots and pacifist propaganda' they were frightened 'of being accused of militarism'.[2] In fact the adverse trend continued, and later in the year the Captain of the training establishment at Shotley reported a further decline in young entrants qualified to join the 'Advanced Class'.[3] The outcome was joint action by all three services to advertise by posters and other means the advantages of a career in the fighting services; but one may doubt whether in the prevailing climate it had much effect, because, as the Director of Recruiting put it, 'We have a political bogey to contend with'.[4]

In contrast to these difficulties competition for naval cadetships continued to be very satisfactory; but in 1933–34 a serious shortage of two classes of officer (apart from Fleet Air Arm pilots, referred to earlier) became apparent. The first was insufficient applications to specialise in the Torpedo Branch, and Chatfield considered that it arose from the Torpedo specialist's responsibility for electrical equipment. He wanted a separate specialist Electrical Branch to be formed to cope with the ever-increasing complexity of the new installations; but many years were to elapse before that measure actually came to fruition, and the interim scheme of transferring high power electrics to the Engineers whilst leaving low power with the Torpedo specialists was not a very satisfactory compromise.[5]

The second shortage among officers was for promotion from the lower deck to Warrant rank—which was the more worrying because the long experience, loyalty and deep understanding of the navy's ways characteristic of Warrant Officers (Gunners, Torpedo Gunners, Boat-

---

[1] Report of 1st March 1935 by DNR. Adm. 178/179.

[2] Minute by Hall of 27th May 1935. *ibid.*

[3] Report by Captain, HMS *Ganges* of 7th May 1935. He reported again on 10th March 1936 that the decline in unemployment was likely to lead to a decrease in applicants. *ibid.*

[4] DNR to DPS 3rd Aug. 1935. *ibid.*

[5] Adm. 1/8768–120/33. Chatfield's views are in his minute of 18th Dec. 1933.

swains, Signal Boatswains, Warrant Engineers, etc.) had for many years been a source of great technical and disciplinary strength to the Service. The issue was thoroughly ventilated in 1935–36, and a committee appointed to make recommendations to improve matters.[1] The basic trouble turned out, not unexpectedly, to be financial; since on moving into the Warrant Officers' Mess men found themselves without a marriage allowance and required to keep up a higher standard of living than as Petty or Chief Petty Officers. The Board decided that the whole subject of promotion from the lower deck, including selection of young ratings for commissions under the system which had replaced the Mate Scheme,[2] had to be treated comprehensively and as a first step they would renew the fifteen-year-old battle for marriage allowance for *all* officers.[3] A qualified success was achieved in that matter in the following year.

In 1935 a comprehensive review of the complements of all ships to meet the needs of what was described as 'the air age' took place. The object was not only to introduce a new class of trained men, but to keep down the number of junior officers needed—which was showing every sign of increasing as more and more A-A weapons were fitted.[4] Apart from recommending a substantial reduction in complements of junior officers, thereby placing greater responsibility on senior ratings,[5] probably the most important outcome of the inquiry was the institution of a branch of A-A gunnery rates to man the new weapons.

Nor was the education of officers neglected at this time of far-reaching change in every aspect of naval warfare, and in 1935 a high-powered committee of officers of proven intellectual capacity was appointed to survey the whole field of elementary and higher naval education—from Sub-Lieutenant's courses, through the Tactical and Staff Courses and the War Courses for junior and senior officers to the final laureate of the Imperial Defence College. Co-operation with the Army and Air Force through their own Staff Colleges and the IDC came within its terms of reference. Though the report is too detailed

---

[1] Adm. 116/3755. The Committee under Admiral T. F. P. Calvert was appointed in May 1936 and reported in July.

[2] See pp. 34–5 and 191–2.

[3] Board Minute 3454 of 16th March 1937. Adm. 116/3755 and 167/96.

[4] The Committee under Admiral T. H. Binney was 'to examine the peace and war complements of HM ships'. An Interim Report was rendered on 18th July 1935 and the Final Report in Feb. 1936. Adm. 1/8795–93/35 and Board Minute 3466 of 5th May 1937. Adm. 167/97.

[5] See p. 126.

even to summarise here it should be mentioned that it proposed a scheme of 'obligatory professional education' from Sub-Lieutenant right through to the attainment of Post Rank. Doubless this was a very desirable measure; but it was difficult to fulfil even in peacetime, when specialist training and sea appointments were bound to interfere with broad 'professional education'.[1]

In 1936, when expansion of the fleet was demanding substantial increases of men, the Board decided to close the gap between the 16½-year-old 'Continuous Service' and 18-year-old 'Special Service' entries for ratings by introducing a Short Service scheme of 12 years enlistment. Treasury approval was obtained without apparently much difficulty.[2] At about the same time, and also in connection with the increasing need for more men and the likelihood of war, the formation of a Royal Naval Supplementary Reserve of officers, composed of yachtsmen or other amateurs with seafaring experience, was proposed. It was not to be 'a legally constituted reserve' but 'a list of gentlemen who undertake to serve as RNVR officers if and when called upon to do so'. Again Treasury approval proved no obstacle, and many applications were soon received from all over the Empire.[3] In World War II the RNVSR officers performed outstanding service. One cannot but contrast these measures to obtain more officers and men with the drastic reductions of 1930–32 and the continuous pressure to clear the lists of 'surplus' officers in the early 1930s already described.[4]

The possibility of restarting a Women's branch of the naval service was first raised in 1934 in the form of a 'Women's Reserves Organisation'—which was a very different scheme from the WRNS or 'Wrens', which had been disbanded soon after World War I. The matter was referred to the Man Power Sub-Committee of the CID and to an

---

[1] The committee under Admiral W. M. James (C-in-C, Portsmouth 1939–42) took evidence from, among others, the future Admiral Sir Reginald Drax (C-in-C, The Nore in World War II), Admiral J. H. Godfrey (DNI 1939–1943) and Admiral of the Fleet Sir Arthur Power (C-in-C, East Indies Fleet 1944–45). All the foregoing were among the most intellectually distinguished officers of the period. Adm. 116/3060. The file 116/3059 which also dealt with this committee's deliberations is shown as 'missing' in the PRO's index.

[2] Adm. 1/8837–146/36. Treasury approval was obtained on 10th Feb. 1936 and an Order-in-Council issued on 3rd July.

[3] Adm. 116/3509, Board Minute 3402 of 15th Oct. 1936 and AFO. 2984/36. Adm. 167/94. Treasury approval was obtained on 21st Oct. and an Order-in-Council issued on 3rd Nov. 1936.

[4] See p. 32.

Admiralty Committee, the other Service Departments were consulted and an immense accumulation of paper resulted.[1] The only result was the conclusion 'that creation of a Women's Reserve is not desirable',[2] and not until 1938 was recruitment of 'Wrens' on the World War 1 model seriously reconsidered and ultimately adopted.[3] There is ample literature regarding the splendid service of the Wrens in many fields during World War II.[4]

While discussing the recruitment of reserves it is relevant to mention that the Admiralty appears to have been the first Service Ministry to appreciate that, if war came, a vast influx of scientists and technologists would be needed. As early as May 1935 an Office Acquaint asked for details of exactly what each Admiralty department would require by way of university graduates, and the moving spirit behind the scheme was F. C. (later Sir Frederick) Brundrett of the Department of Scientific Research.[5] This led to the Man Power Committee being brought in, and to the creation of the National Register of Scientific Personnel—which proved invaluable when war broke out, though the demand quickly outran the supply and necessitated emergency training measures.[6] As so often one finds the US Navy taking analogous steps to the Admiralty's at almost exactly the same date; for in mid-1935 the Bureaux, in response to a request from Admiral Standley, the CNO, produced 'plans for utilising available scientific research facilities in the United States'.[7]

To turn to the Naval Staff, in mid-1934 a revision of the confidential monograph 'The Naval Staff of the Admiralty—its Work and Development' was issued after some controversy regarding whether the Trade Section should be placed under Plans or Intelligence.[8] At the time of the

[1] Adm. 116/3701. The CID papers on the subject are in the NS(WR) series.

[2] NS(WR)8 of 12th May 1936.

[3] Meeting in Admiralty on 11th May 1938. Adm. 116/3701. Board Minute 3572 of 25th July 1938.

[4] See for example Dame Vera L. Mathews (Chief Superintendent, WRNS) *Blue Tapestry* (Hollis and Carter, 1948), Nancy Spain, *Thank You—Nelson* (Hutchinson, 1945), and J. Lennox Kerr and W. Granville, *The R.N.V.R.* (Harrap, 1957).

[5] Sir Frederick Brundrett to the author 22nd Sept. and 5th and 14th Dec. 1972 described the early steps to recruit scientists. The Admiralty side of the story is in Adm. 116/3974.

[6] See Roskill, *Hankey. Man of Secrets*, vol. III (Collins, 1974), ch. 13 regarding the war-time measures to supply scientists and technologists.

[7] USNA, RG. 80, Box 50. Standley to all Chiefs of Bureaux 11th March 1935 and replies by Bureaux.

[8] CB. 3013. Adm. 1/8760–217/32, 1/8766–66/33 and 1/8773–21/34.

Abyssinian crisis it was decided that Plans, Intelligence and Operations should come under the DCNS, while the ACNS, who was restored to full membership of the Board in June 1935, should be responsible for Training and Policy in so far as they affected the use of weapons. New Divisions were to be formed in due course for Trade (instead of it being a section of Plans Division), Economic Pressure (i.e. blockade) and Local Defence, while the Air Division was to assume 'full control of naval aviation'.[1] Some of those changes gradually came into force between 1936 and '37.[2]

A double misfortune befell the Admiralty just when the department was having to cope with the Abyssinian crisis and with all the problems concerned with the beginning of rearmament. The Board had, ever since the days of Samuel Pepys,[3] relied greatly on the continuity of experience and broad grasp of naval problems personified by the Secretary and his department. Early in 1936 Sir Vincent Baddeley retired after 36 years' service in the Admiralty, the last five of them as Deputy Secretary,[4] and in the following July Sir Oswyn Murray, described by Chatfield as 'a great Permanent Secretary' and 'for twenty years the wise and trusted counsellor' of the Board died.[5] The Board recorded their deep sense of loss,[6] which now seems the more severe since his successor Sir R. H. Archibald Carter does not appear to have been a man of Murray's character and intellect.

In 1935–36, when rearmament was beginning to get under way, pressure by pacifist organisations caused the government to agree to appoint a Royal Commission to investigate the alleged evils of the private manufacture of armaments—the so-called 'merchants of death'. There is no doubt that the widespread and often tendentious propaganda organised against such firms had produced strong popular feeling that it was wrong for armaments to be manufactured by private firms, which of course were concerned primarily to show a profit on their undertakings. Moreover the campaign enjoyed the support of the Left Wing Press and of the League of Nations under Article VIII of the Covenant, and so that of the influential League of Nations Union in

---

[1] Adm. 1/8531 contains Instructions for the Naval Staff from 1924 to 1937.

[2] Office Memo. G of 15th Dec. 1937. *ibid.*

[3] See Richard Ollard, *Pepys. A Biography* (Hodder and Stoughton, 1974).

[4] Board Minute 3331 of 3rd Jan. 1936. Adm. 167/94.

[5] See vol. I, p. 209 and Lord Chatfield, *The Navy and Defence* (Heinemann, 1942), p. 185 and *It Might Happen Again* (Heinemann, 1947), pp. 16 and 63.

[6] Board Minute 3385 of 21st July 1936. Adm. 167/94.

Britain;[1] while the League itself still had a committee considering the question as late as 1938.[2] It is interesting to find Norman Davis, President Roosevelt's chief delegate to the London Naval Conference of 1935–36 pressing his chief to give his full support to the British move against the alleged 'evils of the international traffic in arms'; but Roosevelt was evidently too wise to do any such thing.[3] In London Hankey appointed himself chief advocate for not disturbing the *status quo*, and went to enormous trouble to collect evidence in support of his case. Thus in February 1935 Murray sent Hankey, presumably at his request, a long paper on Admiralty policy regarding manufacture of arms for foreign countries,[4] and early in the following year the War Office and Admiralty joined hands in defence of inventors in the service of government departments.[5] The hearings by the Royal Commission were delayed by the Abyssinian crisis, though that event does not appear to have taken any of the steam out of the attack on the manufacturers. Although, with the help of Murray and of his opposite number in the War Office Sir Herbert Creedy, by May 1935 Hankey had assembled the evidence he intended to give, he did not actually appear before the Royal Commission until a year later.[6] On the same day that he took the witness stand Murray sent him a rebuttal of Lloyd George's evidence regarding the notorious Mulliner case of 1910.[7] The Royal Commission finally reported in September 1936;[8] but the CID made no recommendations that anything should be done about it.[9]

[1] See for example LNU Pamphlets 347 and 359 of July 1933 and Jan. 1934—described by the Director of Contracts, Admiralty, as 'full of inconsistencies and inaccuracies'. Copies in Adm. 116/3341.

[2] Adm. 116/3364 and 3365.

[3] Davis to FDR 19th Feb. 1935. Roosevelt papers, PPF, File 33. A manuscript note on Davis's letter makes it clear that Roosevelt did not follow up his proposal.

[4] Murray to Hankey 26th Feb. 1935. Adm. 116/3339.

[5] Memo. of 6th March 1936. *ibid.*

[6] Roskill, *Hankey*, III, pp. 228 and 246–9.

[7] The allegation was that H. H. Mulliner, Managing Director of Coventry Ordnance Works, had procured an increase of the 1909–10 British naval programme, to the advantage of his own firm, by producing evidence of German acceleration of building from a visit to Krupps. Mulliner blamed the Admiralty for his dismissal. Letter in *The Times* of 12th Dec. 1909. On 3rd Jan. 1910 *The Times* published an article on the case. Murray's evidence refuted the whole story as published by Mulliner. The 1906 file on his visit to Krupps is in Adm. 116/3340.

[8] Cmd. 5292.

[9] CID. 1299B, taken on 22nd Jan. 1937. Cab. 4/25.

The whole matter was soon quietly buried—after a vast expenditure of effort which could, at such a time of crisis, have been better devoted to the far more urgent matter of expediting rearmament in order that our diplomats and ministers might be able to negotiate with the dictators from a position of strength.[1]

---

[1] For a recent reappraisal of the allegations made against the arms manufacturers see Clive Trebilcock, *Legends of the British Armaments Industry 1890-1914. A Revision.* Journal of Contemporary History, vol. 5, no. 4 (1970). Many interesting papers on the attacks made in the 1930s are in Adm. 116/3339, 3340, 3341 and 3342.

CHAPTER IX

Crisis in the Middle East

1935-1936

—◆—

WE NOW know from Marshal de Bono's candid memoirs that as early as 1933 Mussolini was planning an assault on Abyssinia;[1] and despite the continued closure of British intelligence records it is hard to believe that London remained ignorant of his intentions. For example it was in 1933 that Admiral Sir William Fisher, the C-in-C, Mediterranean raised the question of strengthening the defences of the bases within his command, and especially the air defences of Malta. He considered it certain that in the event of war the fleet would want to use Malta 'frequently if not continuously', and he represented that making Malta 'as impregnable as Malta should be would have a wholesome effect in this island as well as elsewhere'—by which he must surely have meant in Italy.[2] The Naval Staff agreed, but considered it hopeless to ask for money for such a purpose at the time. So all Fisher got was the discouraging reply that there were 'even more serious defence commitments elsewhere'.[3] Presumably the Admiralty had Singapore chiefly in mind. In the autumn of 1933 Fisher returned to the charge in a personal letter telling Chatfield 'I do really feel that we are taking an unjustifiable risk about Malta', and claiming that the defences of that 'key position' could be put in order during two or three years at a cost of only some £150,000.[4] But Chatfield probably felt that, with so many demands being pressed and so many bases ill-defended, he could not make a special case for Malta.

At the time when these exchanges were in progress the Joint Over-

---

[1] *La Preparazione e le Prime Operazioni.* (Eng. Trans., 1967.)

[2] Letters C-in-C, Mediterranean to Admy. of 10th April and 20th June 1933. Adm. 116/3473.

[3] AL of 3rd Oct. 1933. *ibid.*

[4] Fisher to Chatfield 17th Nov. 1933. Chatfield papers, CHT/4/5.

seas and Home Defence Committee (JDC) reviewed the whole question
of base defences all over the world; but their report was little more
than a catalogue of deficiencies.[1] Equally important to Malta's defences
were those of the Suez Canal; but that question was complicated by
the fact that Egypt was, strictly speaking, a foreign country; and until
the new treaty of 1936 was signed she was not even an ally of Britain's.
The fact that the Suez Canal Company was a commercial concern
registered in Paris complicated the situation still further—despite the
purchase by Britain of the Khedive's shares (amounting to 7/16 of
the total) in 1875. In 1934 the Chiefs of Staff reviewed the means which
might be employed to prevent the canal being blocked, and produced
a report which went to the CID,[2] and in the same year the Admiralty
sent a memorandum on defence of the canal against blocking or
sabotage to the C-in-C, and asked for a plan to be prepared to put
their proposals into effect. They expected the Canal Company to
prove co-operative, since French as well as British interests were at
stake; but from Egypt no more than 'sulky acquiescence' could, they
wrote, be looked for.[3] Early in the following year the C-in-C was told
that the CID had approved that we should 'assume control of the Suez
Canal at any time at which the situation appeared to warrant such
action', and Chatfield added a paragraph making clear what Admiralty
policy was with regard to the despatch of the Mediterranean Fleet to
the Far East in the event of trouble with Japan, and of the Home Fleet
to the Mediterranean to replace it.[4] Fisher replied with details of the
'Control Force' (a cruiser squadron and a destroyer flotilla) which he
proposed to use to secure the Suez Canal, and in May of that year he
was told that the provisional Defence Plan had been approved by the
three services and was being sent out to him by hand.[5] The C-in-C
agreed to the plan 'in principle', and it was taken by the COSs in
October.[6] Such in brief outline was British policy regarding the Suez
Canal at the time the crisis with Italy blew up in 1935. It should be

---

[1] 25th to 27th Meetings of JDC 27th April 1933 to 12th April 1934 and CID. 402C
of 1st Oct. 1934. Cab. 5/8. This volume is 'closed' until 1989, but the deliberations on
base defences in Malta and Egypt will be found in Adm. 116/3473.
[2] COS. 333 of 2nd May (Cab. 53/23) and CID. 1141B of 4th Nov. 1934. Cab. 3/23.
[3] Admy. to C-in-C, Mediterranean 2nd Aug. 1934. Adm. 116/3489.
[4] AL of 24th Jan. 1935. *ibid.*
[5] C-in-C, Mediterranean, to Admy. 30th March 1935 and Admy. to same 22nd
May 1935. *ibid.*
[6] C-in-C, Mediterranean, to Admy. 28th June 1935 and 151st COS meeting of
4th Oct. 1935. Cab. 53/5.

made plain that closure of the canal by us did not depend merely on *force majeure*—despite Article 1 of the Convention of 1888 having stated that it 'shall always be free and open in time of war as in time of peace to every vessel of commerce or of war without distinction of flag'. Article 10 of the same convention allowed Turkey to close the canal for her own defence or if Egypt became involved in war, and that right was transferred to Britain in 1919. Under Article 4 it would have been perfectly legal for us to blockade the entrances to the canal—so long as it was done from outside the three mile limit of Egypt's territorial waters.

As early as mid-1932 the Admiralty had sent to the CID an appreciation of the measures which might be taken to apply economic pressure to Italy. Its principal points were that, with the greater part of her imports and power plants concentrated in the north, over half her industrial supplies coming in through her west coast ports and, perhaps above all, her well-known shortage of coal and raw materials, there was little doubt that she was very vulnerable to that form of pressure. But of course economic pressure (or blockade) always needs considerable time to take effect.[1]

To return to Mussolini's plans to seize the greater part of Abyssinia the 'border incident' needed to set a match to the carefully laid powder train was duly applied at Walwal on 5th December 1934, though no one knew whether the place was actually inside Abyssinia or not. Lives on both sides were lost, Italy protested, Abyssinia demanded arbitration, and when this was refused submitted the dispute to the League, firstly under Article 11 (threat of war) and, after incidents had continued, under Article 15 (mediation by the Council) in March 1935. The reader will note that this coincided exactly with Hitler's introduction of conscription in Germany,[2] which of course diverted attention from Abyssinia despite the continued despatch of Italian reinforcements to Eritrea. In July Hoare, the Foreign Secretary, described to Robert Bingham, the American ambassador in London, who was about to return home to prepare for the 1935 Naval Conference, the 'calamitous results' he anticipated from an Italo-Abyssinian war, and described the efforts his government was making to avert it. He asked Bingham to press the US administration to make parallel efforts; but with America outside the League and isolationist sentiment

[1] Appreciation of March 1931, sent to CID 31st May 1932. Adm. 1/8739-47/30.
[2] See pp. 214-6.

strong Hoare must have known that such a possibility was remote.[1]

Despite the storm clouds gathering in the Middle East the long-planned decision to hold a Fleet Review at Spithead in July 1935 as part of the celebrations organised to mark the Jubilee of the accession to the throne of King George V was not modified, and most of the Mediterranean Fleet came home to take part in it. The disruption to normal training brought about by the need for all ships to look their best was not negligible, and both before and after each ship or squadron arrived and took up its appointed place 'spit and polish' was the order of the day. The Review took place on 16th and was blessed by good weather. The assemblage of 160 warships looked impressive and included two aircraft carriers; but to the knowledgable it was painfully obvious that the proportion of new ships present was small, and that few of the older ones (many of which were of World War I vintage) had been fully modernised. In truth the shop window was mainly filled with obsolescent goods.[2] No foreign warships were present on this occasion, but the big German liner *Columbus* was crowded with sightseers, and it is a safe guess that among them were professionals from the German and Italian Intelligence services.

On 17th the King led the fleet to sea in the Royal Yacht and witnessed exercises and firing in the Channel. The anti-aircraft part of the programme caused a good deal of anxiety in the Admiralty, which had recently been making fervid declarations regarding the effectiveness of the new A-A armaments. Early in the year, when the exercise programme was being prepared, Chatfield wrote to Fisher asking whether he could 'more or less guarantee to bring down' the 'Queen Bee' wireless-controlled target aircraft. Fisher replied that he thought it 'reasonably certain' that it would be accomplished, though 'stage fright' was a handicap and success might not be achieved immediately.[3] The Queen Bee was of course a slow and vulnerable light

---

[1] Hoare-Bingham conversation of 29th July 1935. Cab. 29/149.

[2] *The Times* 16th, 17th, 18th July 1935. The paper's Special Correspondent remarked on the large proportion of small ships present, that 'the real strength of the Navy, which lies in its heavy ships, had been whittled to the bone', and that 'many of them are elderly veterans'; but he claimed that the 100 Fleet Air Arm aircraft which flew past showed that 'in all other respects' the Navy was 'truly up to date'. If there was some substance in the first part of his commentary the second part was nonsense. *The Times*, 16th July 1935.

[3] Chatfield to Fisher 23rd Jan. and reply by latter of 21st Feb. 1935. Adm. 1/8777-164/34. See also Chatfield to Dreyer 31st May 1935 'I am taking the King out . . . to see our gunnery practice including HA firing against the "Queen Bee" aeroplanes.

aircraft with no capacity for riposting against her tormentors. Nor does anyone appear to have remarked that Fisher apparently considered the presence of Royalty a greater handicap to A-A efficiency than that of enemy bombers. However the exercises went off satisfactorily, the first Queen Bee crashed on being catapulted and the second one was 'eventually' shot down by the *Rodney*.[1] The Mediterranean Fleet then went back to its proper station—where it was soon to have to take its vulnerability to air attack very seriously.

In the same month that the Fleet Review took place the COSs began deliberations which, with scarcely a break, were to last until the end of the crisis. At the first meeting Hankey reported that the Cabinet required a report on the application of Article 16 of the Covenant (the sanctions article) against Italy, and the possibility of exerting economic pressure on her. 'The COSs', warned Hankey, 'should bear in mind the military implication of sanctions'; while Chatfield stressed that it would be 'absolutely necessary for service preparations to be completed before sanctions were imposed'. For the Navy this meant, he continued, mobilisation and the calling up of reserves.[2]

The COSs continued their deliberations in late July and early August, and it seems clear that Chatfield dominated the committee. The broad outcome was that the COSs declared that the Prime Minister should be told that sanctions or the blockade of the Suez Canal would 'almost inevitably lead to war', and that far-reaching naval, military and air preparations were therefore essential before sanctions were imposed. Equally important was 'the active co-operation of at least the other principal naval participating powers'—by which they must chiefly have meant France.[3]

On 6th August the COSs met under the Prime Minister to examine 'what the position would be if Italy took the bit between her teeth' and whether 'there were any steps that ought to be taken at once to provide against it'.[4] A few days later Vansittart wrote to Admiral Little, the DCNS, that he considered 'that the odds were very long on *present form* [his italics] against the French being prepared to take any

The Press will be present and I hope we shall shoot down the "Queen Bee", as we usually do now, and thereby counter the insidious propaganda that battleships are defenceless against air attack'. Chatfield papers, CHT/4/4.

[1] *The Times*, 18th July 1935.

[2] 146th COS meeting on 5th July 1935. Cab. 53/5.

[3] COS 147th and 148th meetings of 30th July and 8th Aug. 1935. Cab. 53/5. COS. 388 reviewed the military implications of sanctions. Cab. 53/25.

[4] Adm. 116/3038.

strong line at Geneva', and that he anticipated that the League meeting of 4th December 'will end in fiasco' and so 'to the ultimate serious deterioration of the situation in Europe'.[1] Little replied emphasising the importance the COSs attached to the 'active co-operation of the French and other powers', and the need for 'postponing . . . any crisis so as to give a breathing space' to the services to enable them to prepare for war in earnest. The Admiralty was, he said 'pushing ahead with unobtrusive preparations', and most of the Home Fleet would be ready to sail by the end of August. Preliminary steps had also been made, he wrote, to send out the Mobile Naval Base Defence Organisation, about which more will be said shortly.[2]

On 28th August Admiral Fisher signalled ' . . . I feel content that on receiving suitable reinforcements from Home Fleet any situation at sea could be dealt with . . . provided France was friendly'. Hostile acts by Italy should, in his view 'be met by [the] strongest possible counter-offensive within hours if possible'.[3] Meanwhile an Admiralty 'Office Acquaint' had been issued saying that, by direction of the Cabinet, 'no action is to be taken by the Admiralty which might be interpreted by Italy as provocative'. The Home Fleet would have assembled at Portland by 30th August; the aircraft carrier *Courageous*, a flotilla and a half of destroyers and a submarine flotilla with its depot ship would then part company and proceed quietly to join the Mediterranean Fleet. In reply to any questions asked the answer was to be that these were 'routine movements', and that the Mediterranean Fleet was '*not being reinforced*'.[4] Belief in a remarkable degree of gullibility on the part of the Italians must have prevailed in Whitehall if the government thought that such prevarications carried conviction. A number of other preparatory measures were quietly taken on different stations at this time. For instance the C-in-C, China, was told to send the mine-laying cruiser *Adventure* to Singapore to complete with mines in order to be nearer the scene of possible 'hostilities'; while the Australian Navy Board was asked to move the heavy cruisers *Canberra* and *Sussex* to Port Darwin on the north coast, whence they could easily move into the Indian Ocean and thence to the Red Sea.[5] As in Septem-

[1] Vansittart to Little 9th Aug. 1935. *ibid.*
[2] Little to Vansittart 10th Aug. 1935. *ibid.*
[3] C-in-C, Med., to Admy. No. 426 of 20th Aug. 1935. *ibid.*
[4] Secret Office Acquaint of 16th Aug. 1935. *ibid.*
[5] Admy. to C-in-C, China 29th Aug. and Navy Board Melbourne to Admy. 13th Sept. 1935. *ibid.*

ber the Italians only had two cruisers (*Taranto* and *Bari*), two leaders
and three destroyers, two submarines and a small number of support
or auxiliary vessels in the Red Sea it seems likely that control of those
waters could have been wrested from them in the event of war.[1] However we now know that mobilisation of the Italian Navy was begun
on 1st July 1935, and not in October, the date officially given out by the
authorities, and that by mid-September it was almost completely
mobilised and deployed throughout the eastern Mediterranean and
Red Sea.[2] It was therefore in a far more advanced state of readiness than
the British, let alone the French Navy and a contest for control of the
disputed waters in the summer of that year would certainly not have
been a walk-over for Britain. The Admiralty seems not to have learnt
the true state of the Italian Fleet until late in October, when the Naval
Attaché, Rome, forwarded a full and accurate statement on it.[3]

On 21st August Fisher vigorously drew the Admiralty's attention to
the parlous state of Malta's defences. Guns and searchlights were, he
said, not manned, and the harbours were entirely open to surprise
attack. Anti-submarine booms could not be put in place because two
or three Italian merchant ships used the harbours almost daily. He was
therefore keeping the fleet at short notice to move to Alexandria.[4]
Another of his anxieties was the fleet's acute shortage of A-A ammunition, and on 2nd September the Admiralty told him that they were
sending out almost the whole of the stock held at home. At least half
the Malta stocks was, they said, to be put afloat.[5] On 5th September
Fisher reported that, when ordered to move east his fleet would
probably consist of three battleships, three heavy and four light
cruisers, two carriers and some two dozen destroyers—which made an
impressive array; and he hoped for reinforcements, including two
battle-cruisers, two more light cruisers and another destroyer flotilla
shortly.[6] But Fisher refused to accept the policy that Malta could not
be defended, and in mid-September he again urged that 'every avail-

[1] Adm. 116/3296.

[2] I am indebted to Dottore Rosaria Quarteraro for this information, culled from her
doctoral thesis *Y Rapporti Italo-Inglesi Fra Europa e Mediterraneo 1933–1936* (Rome
University), which I have been allowed to study in draft.

[3] Report of 29th Oct. 1935 by Captain H. Pott. Forwarded to FO by Sir E. Drummond, the ambassador on 5th Nov. However the DNI probably received a copy direct
from the attaché earlier than this official one. FO. 371/19158.

[4] C-in-C, Mediterranean, to Admy. 2241 of 21st Aug. 1935. *ibid.*

[5] Admy. to C-in-C, Med. 2nd and 4th Sept. 1935. *ibid.*

[6] C-in-C, Med., to Admy. 2113 of 4th Sept. 1935. *ibid*

able H-A gun should be sent . . . [and also the] despatch of fighters and bombers up to the limit that can be operated there'.[1] However the Admiralty over-rode Fisher's desire to have the battle-cruisers under his command, because it might 'provoke' the Italians, and also his earnest desire to have Malta properly defended.[2]

Between 29th August and mid-September the Mediterranean Fleet and a large supporting force of auxiliary vessels carrying stores, ammunition and fuel accordingly slipped unobtrusively out of Malta's harbours in penny numbers and gradually concentrated at Alexandria, while some units were detached to Port Said and Haifa. Two Admiralty letters to all Cs-in-C set out with admirable clarity the policy of the government and the naval measures taken at this time.[3] It seems clear that bringing the fleet to a high state of readiness without mobilisation, and moving it to what was in fact its war stations, was carried out with remarkable smoothness. Later in September the Admiralty followed up those letters with two more setting out in detail the dispositions made, the reinforcements expected from stations as distant as China, Australia and the West Indies, the arrangements for the supply of this big fleet, the institution of measures for contraband control and for the control of British shipping all over the world and its protection against surface raiders.

Submarine attack was considered by the Admiralty, but they did not expect the Italians to send them out into the Atlantic; which reduced the submarine threat to shipping to the minor one of two (later four) boats based on Massawa in Eritrea.[4] It seems likely that, in the conditions of 1935 and with the prospect of Italy being the only enemy, this playing down of the submarine threat was justifiable; for the German U-boat programme had not yet progressed very far, and in any case we were still hoping to prevent a German-Italian alliance. Be that as it may, by the middle of September all the draft messages for the Admiralty to assume world-wide control of merchant shipping were ready, and on 13th the preliminary one was despatched.[5] All Italian ports were closed to British shipping, all through-Mediterranean traffic was to be diverted via the Cape of Good Hope or the

---

[1] C-in-C., Med., to Admy. no. 382 of 16th Sept. 1935. *ibid.*
[2] Chatfield to Fisher 25th Aug. 1935. Chatfield papers, CHT/4/5.
[3] ALs of 24th Aug. to Cs-in-C of home ports and of same date to Cs-in-C, Home and Mediterranean Fleets of 24th Aug. 1935. Adm. 116/3049.
[4] ALs of 17th and 28th Sept. 1935. *ibid.*
[5] Admy. A Message 2237 of 13th Sept. 1935. Adm. 116/3353.

Panama Canal, and instructions to Consular Reporting Officers were prepared.[1] Intelligence Centres all over the world in British colonies, prepared long in advance, were activated, as were those under the control of the Commonwealth governments; while the Foreign Office arranged for the Reporting Officers sent to foreign ports, of which there were 37, to receive the necessary instructions.[2] The only serious difficulty in establishing control of shipping seems to have arisen over the undesirability of diverting ships to Spanish ports, because conditions in that country were very unsettled. In the end it was agreed that they should be sent to the nearest French, French North African, Greek or Yugoslav port.[3] The actual introduction of all these instructions was to be done by the broadcasting in plain language of a message known as the 'Funnel Telegram' beginning with the words 'Admiralty has assumed control of movements of British merchant ships';[4] but that was in fact never sent during the Abyssinian crisis.

The reader should not assume that all the foregoing precautionary moves and measures were taken by the Admiralty in isolation; for very close touch was maintained throughout the crisis with the Foreign Office, the CID, and through the latter with the Cabinet itself. The smooth working of the administrative machine on this occasion is a tribute to the organisation created by Hankey, and on 9th October he raised the whole issue of 'the Machinery of Sanctions' in the CID. He pointed out that, although it was his duty under the War Book to brief the Prime Minister on 'the Supreme Control in War', the prevailing situation was unprecedented in that 'the League as a whole is concerned' and 'we have no experience of the conduct of sanctions by the League'. He had therefore prepared, in consultation with the DRC, a memorandum on 'the Machinery of Sanctions in the event of their application to Italy by the League'.[5] When the CID took this paper MacDonald urged 'that the question of military sanctions should not be discussed'; and thus, almost from the beginning of the crisis, the full application of Article 16 of the Covenant was deleted from the British

[1] CB. 3000A(27) for Reporting Officers abroad and 3000B for those at home. The Naval Control Service Manual, which outlined the organisation of convoy if it was introduced, was CB. 01764. Intelligence Centres were established at Bermuda, Cape Town, Malta, Colombo, Singapore, Hong Kong, Shanghai, Gibraltar and Wellington. Also the DNIs at Ottawa and Melbourne were brought in to establish similar centres in Canadian and Australian ports. Adm. 116/3353.

[2] *ibid.*   [3] *ibid.*   [4] *ibid.*

[5] CID. 1192B of 9th Oct. 1935. Cab. 4/24.

Cabinet's agenda.[1] At about the same time Hankey circulated a 'Summary of Precautionary Measures taken since the Cabinet meeting of 22nd August 1935', when the Cabinet had placed on the DPRC the responsibility for providing it with the necessary advice.[2]

Meanwhile the Anglo-French conversations begun in Paris on 16th August had broken down, and the dispute had been referred to the Council of the League, which met on 4th September. The Italians then adopted what Hankey called 'a completely *non-possumus* attitude', though they did agree to a Conciliation Committee of five being set up, on which Eden and Laval represented Britain and France. But the build-up of Italian forces in East Africa and Libya continued to an alarming extent, and on 14th September Mussolini trumpeted his defiance by declaring 'in the most explicit manner that the Ethiopian problem does not admit of a compromise situation . . .' In other words he meant war. The League Assembly met on 9th September, and two days later Hoare delivered his strong affirmation of British support for 'the League and its ideals as the most effective way of ensuring peace'. This speech certainly made it appear that, despite the serious misgivings of the COSs and the justifiable doubts about whether France would go along with us, Britain was prepared to take strong action on behalf of the League—if necessary alone. But in truth it was a bluff designed to frighten Mussolini; for Hoare and Laval had secretly agreed a few days earlier that military sanctions would not be employed and economic sanctions only very cautiously—in which, as we have seen, Hoare was certainly not out of step with his chief Cabinet colleagues.

While the Home and Mediterranean Fleets were in effect mobilising and completing with war stores—whilst carefully avoiding calling the preparations by any such name—the security of the fleet's bases received renewed urgency. Chatfield can hardly have liked leaving Malta defenceless, but he told Fisher that the island 'is a minor matter in the long run', that 'if Italy is mad enough to challenge us . . . she will be defeated', and that Malta 'even if it is demolished, will [then] come [to us] again'.[3] There was certainly strategic logic in his reasoning. More urgent therefore than Malta was strengthening the defences of Alexandria, and solving the problem of finding an alternative if it should

---

[1] 271st CID meeting on 14th Oct. 1935. Cab. 2/6.

[2] CID. 1193B of 20th Sept. with covering note by Hankey of 8th Oct. 1935. Cab. 4/24.

[3] Chatfield to Fisher, 25th Aug. 1935. Chatfield papers, CHT/4/5.

prove impossible for the fleet to remain there in face of the powerful bomber force which the Italians had assembled in Libya. Moreover an advanced base nearer to Italy than Alexandria would plainly be a great advantage. Thence arose the plan to use Navarino Bay, the 'Port X' on the west coast of the Peloponnese—if necessary without Greek acquiescence.[1] We must therefore now turn to the despatch from England of the Mobile Naval Base Defence Organisation (MNBDO).

The need for a Mobile Naval Base arose from the air threat to fixed bases overseas, and to Malta and Alexandria in particular. The defence of such a base was placed under the Royal Marines in 1929, and two years later the weapons, equipment and personnel required were agreed.[2] The general idea was that within 48 hours of the fleet arriving at the selected harbour the MNBDO should be established on shore and rudimentary defences installed. Within a week the base should be 'moderately safe from attack by submarines, destroyers or from the air', and within a month it should be 'completely organised as far as defence measures are concerned'.[3] The next step was, very naturally, to write an MNBDO Manual,[4] and when one recalls the equipment which had to be provided for the Normandy landings of 1944 it is interesting to find that 100-foot-long piers, beach roadways and landing craft were included in the requirements.

At the end of August 1935 the naval staff prophesied that 'in the near future the MNBDO may be called on to furnish A-A defences for service overseas at short notice';[5] and such indeed proved to be the case. Two large merchantmen of good lifting capacity were requisitioned to take out the first flight of men and equipment,[6] which consisted of anti-torpedo baffles and anti-submarine nets, controlled mines, 22 A-A guns, six coast defence guns, 33 searchlights, moorings for big and little ships, a communications section and the headquarters staff. Early in September Fisher held discussions regarding whether Navarino or Suda Bay in Crete was the better suited for use as the fleet's advanced base, taking account of the greater air threat at the former. His final proposal was to use Navarino but not to commit

[1] 150th and 159th COS meetings of 13th Sept. and 13th Dec. 1935. Cab. 53/5. Also Chatfield to Fisher 19th Dec. 1935. Chatfield papers, CHT/4/5.

[2] Report of conference held on 12th Aug. 1931. Adm. 116/3386.

[3] Plans Division minute of 12th Dec. 1931. Adm. 116/3386.

[4] CB. 1936(34).

[5] Minute of 30th Aug. 1935. Adm. 116/3386.

[6] The ships were the *Bencruachan* (Ben Line) and *Bellerophon* (Alfred Holt, Blue Funnel Line).

himself completely to it until experience of the air threat had been gained. So the laying of the anti-submarine boom and installation of the coast defence guns would be held up for a time.[1]

In August and September a number of transports, fleet auxiliaries and requisitioned merchantmen left England with what was somewhat transparently designated 'the Malta A-A Reserve' and other equipment.[2] Actually they carried the MNBDO's A/S boom, controlled mining equipment and other stores, and on the way out they strengthened the underwater defences of Gibraltar. Next, on 7th October, the government decided not to approach the Greek government regarding the proposed use of Navarino; and finally at the end of November Fisher changed his policy completely. The MNBDO was not, he now proposed, to be established immediately on the outbreak of war, and Alexandria was to be the main fleet base.[3] The COSs approved the change, and it thus came to pass that all the equipment sent out was now to be used to make Alexandria more secure; and the MNBDO never got any further than that port.[4]

After it was all over the C-in-C reported that the MNBDO undertaking had passed through five distinct phases. These were, firstly, mobilisation (25th August to 16th September 1935), secondly the voyage out (16th to 26th September), thirdly concentration and reorganisation at Alexandria (26th September to 15th October), fourthly the period of waiting for developments to show whether a move should be made (15th October to 26th December), and finally from 26th December onwards diversion to the defence of Egypt.[5] At the end of his long report on the adventures of the MNBDO, Admiral Fisher remarked that 'Never has there been a better illustration of the dictum that it is always the unexpected that happens in war. The peace-time organisation and training of the MNBDO has been based on three major assumptions, all of which turned out to be wrong'.[6] Thereafter a Standing Committee was formed by the Admiralty to handle all questions of equipping and manning the organisation; but its first

[1] Adm. 116/3476.

[2] These ships were the *Benarty* (Ben Line), *Lancastria* (Cunard), *Neuralia* (troop transport), *Atreus* (Alfred Holt) and *Nuddea* (British India SS Co.). The *Benarty* carried A/S boom equipment, the *Atreus* controlled mining equipment, the *Bellerophon* and *Neuralia* Army A-A units, and the *Lancastria* headquarters units and military reinforcements. Adm. 116/3476 and 3050.

[3] C-in-C, Med. to Admy. 30th Nov. 1935. Adm. 116/3476.

[4] *ibid.*

[5] Report of 16th May 1936 on the MNBDO. Adm. 116/4186.   [6] *ibid.*

serious employment in World War II—at Suda Bay, Crete in 1941—proved no more successful than its non-employment at Port X in 1935. Whilst dealing with plans which went awry an instance of more accurate prophecy by a man of highly original mind may here be mentioned. At the time of the Abyssinian crisis Admiral Pratt, who had been the US Chief of Naval Operations from September 1930 to June 1933, received a copy of a letter by Admiral Sir Herbert Richmond (then Vere Harmsworth Professor of Naval History, Cambridge University). 'If we have war in the Mediterranean', wrote Richmond, 'the big ships of Italy will go to Venice and of England to Alexandria and Australia. And the fighting for the command of the sea will be between the small vessels who fear neither the submarine nor aircraft'.[1]

On 6th September Fisher telegraphed to the Admiralty his outline plan for operations if war broke out. He was then still expecting to set up the MNBDO at Navarino, and proposed to take the offensive at once against Taranto, the main Italian naval base in southern Italy, and other bases in that area and in Sicily.[2] The reply was that such plans were being discussed with the French Ministry of Marine, but 'In the meantime it is considered [that] if a war situation is reached we must be ready to act single-handed at any rate in the early stages';[3] but forces from Gibraltar, the Admiralty continued, 'will make concurrent sweeps off [the] west coast of Italy', and possibly the two British Fleets could meet in the Malta Channel. A little later the Colonial Office told the Governors of all Mediterranean and African colonies that war had started in Abyssinia without a declaration by either side, and tried to define what rules should be applied to Italian warships or merchantmen calling at British colonial ports—which produced highly intricate problems regarding the application of International Maritime Law.[4] However the Foreign Office expressed the emphatic view that Italy was not entitled to exercise Belligerent Rights—that is to say stop and search neutral vessels on the high seas—because she was not engaged 'in a lawful war'.[5] This theory provoked an enquiry from the Admiralty regarding what our position would be if, in a future conflict, rules such as we were applying to Italian ships were applied to us.[6] The

---

[1] Letter of 23rd Oct. 1935 from Jesus College, Cambridge. Copy in Pratt papers.
[2] C-in-C, Med. to Admy. no. 513. Adm. 116/3038.
[3] Admy. to Cs-in-C, Med. and HF 18th Sept. 1935. *ibid.*
[4] Colonial Office telegrams of 3rd and 10th Oct. 1935. *ibid.*
[5] FO to Paris no. 303 of 29th Oct. 1935. *ibid.*
[6] Admy. to FO and CO 8th Nov. 1935. *ibid.*

truth obviously was that the accepted rules of International law did not cater for the sort of problems which had arisen, and no one knew how to disentangle such labyrinthine complexities. It was however notice-able that the French were treating Italian shipping far more leniently than we were—for example by allowing them to take in fuel and car-goes at Djibouti which we had refused them at Aden.[1]

The Admiralty's views and purposes played such a large part in deciding the actions—or inaction—of the British government during the Abyssinian crisis that it is worth examining them a little more closely. Though Monsell had far more political experience than Chat-field, his principal naval colleague, it does seem that the latter played an unusually prominent role in framing policy and in getting it ac-cepted by the CID or Cabinet. Chatfield was of course a disciple of Beatty's and must have been aware how Beatty had dominated the Board during his long term of office as First Sea Lord (1919–1927). Though Chatfield did not possess anything like his mentor's charisma, and generally dealt with the politicians only through the First Lord— the constitutional channel which Beatty by no means always observed —it seems that his influence was little if at all inferior to Beatty's. Nor is there any sign of disagreements between Chatfield and Monsell or his successors Hoare and Duff Cooper. Chatfield took trouble to cultivate the friendship of the influential Hankey, and worked closely with him on all issues that came before the CID.[2] His views on the Abyssinian crisis are perhaps seen clearest in a letter he sent to Admiral Dreyer at this time. 'It is a disaster', he wrote, 'that our statesmen have got us into this quarrel with Italy, who ought to be our best friend because her position in the Mediterranean is a dominant one'. The 'miserable business of collective security', he continued, had 'run away with all our traditional interests and policies', with the result that 'we now have to be prepared . . . to fight any nation in the world at any moment'. And so it had come to pass that he was 'preparing for a war . . . which we have always been told could never happen'. As to the actual con-quest of Abyssinia, Chatfield had 'no objection to the Italians being established there', and believed it would prove 'a weakness rather than a strength' to them so long as we kept command of the sea—a prophecy which was to be wholly vindicated in 1940–41. Chatfield, like Hankey, held that a maritime colonial empire, as opposed to a continental one, depended wholly on maintaining command of the sea; and that

[1] Adm. 116/3088.
[2] See Roskill, *Hankey*, III, *passim*.

it was neglect of that principle ever since 1918 which had brought us to the sorry pass in which we found ourselves in the mid-1930s.[1]

In May Italy had told us she intended to declare a blockade of Abyssinia,[2] and the question arose whether we should make a proclamation of neutrality. The Foreign Office produced a statement on what they considered our position would be in various circumstances, and a somewhat heated interchange with the Admiralty ensued because the latter considered that, if war came, it would be mainly a naval war waged by us, and sanctions were bound to be ineffective unless we exercised Belligerent Rights against Italy. Furthermore the Admiralty considered that, if we exercised such rights, Italy was certain to retaliate with force, and that the Foreign Office line gave her all the advantages, such as declaring sanctions to be 'an unfriendly act' and choosing her own time to attack, say, Malta.[3] In the end the Admiralty told Fisher that if Italy declared war on Abyssinia she should be accorded Belligerent Rights unless or until she was deprived of them by the League; but no military measures were to be taken if she claimed such rights without declaring war.[4] As in the event Italy neither declared war nor claimed Belligerent Rights the issue did not arise, and the British departments wisely decided 'to let sleeping dogs lie'. But the interchange did emphasise the extraordinarily complex and novel problems produced by an undeclared war, a League decision to apply sanctions to the aggressor, and the certainty that if shooting began it would be directed mainly, and perhaps solely, at the British.

Those issues led naturally to the vital question of how far we could rely on French co-operation and support. In November the Naval Attaché, Paris, reported that Admiral Durand-Viel, the Chief of Naval Staff, wanted to communicate direct with the Admiralty about talks he had held with the Italians—a proposal which seems to have elicited no response. However in the same month the Naval Attaché sent over particulars of the disposition and condition of French warships in the Mediterranean, and details of their docks and oil reserves—which the Admiralty must in fact already have known fairly accurately. The particulars of the docks were signalled to Admiral Fisher,[5] and he proposed to send a destroyer to Bizerta as secretly as possible. This was

---

[1] Chatfield to Dreyer. Chatfield papers, CHT/4/4.
[2] FO to Admy. 9th May 1935. CP(98)35. Cab. 24/255.
[3] Admy. to FO 21st Sept. 1935. Adm. 116/3487.
[4] AM 2034 of 4th Oct. 1935 to C-in-C, Med. *ibid.*
[5] Admy. to C-in-C, Med. 1936 of 9th Dec. 1935. Adm. 116/3398.

done; but the arrival of the *Wishart* (Commander Lord Louis Mount-batten) caused the local French naval commander (Admiral Laborde) consternation, and produced little except an extremely witty report from Mountbatten.[1] Plainly co-operation with the French was not going to prove straightforward; and without a full and unequivocal assurance that such co-operation would be forthcoming the Admiralty, which to a great extent meant Chatfield, was markedly reluctant that the government should commit itself to the only sanction likely to prove effective—namely a complete embargo on oil imports. This view of the vital importance attached to full co-operation by the other League powers, and especially France, is very apparent in the deliberations of the DPR Committee in September.[2] Nor were doubts regarding French intentions allayed by the talks with the French naval staff which began in Paris on 18th September, against a background of constant evasion by Pierre Laval, the Foreign Minister.

The actual invasion of Abyssinia started on 3rd October and four days later the Council of the League condemned Italy's resort to war. This automatically brought into force Article 16 of the Covenant—the sanctions article. Although Admiral Fisher and all senior members of his staff and in the fleet were perfectly ready to fight, and confident of success if war came,[3] in London things looked differently—because of the likelihood of losses vitiating the plan to send a fleet to the Far East, and the probability that Japan would make the most of our consequential embarrassment.[4] In December the First Lord and Secretary of State for Air warned the Cabinet in very strong terms regarding the likely effect of Italy performing what was called at the time 'a mad dog act', and attacking us in reprisal for the application of oil sanctions.[5] It was perhaps now that the full effect of the long neglect of the navy, the Ten Year Rule and the limitation treaties first had a drastic impact on our foreign policy—despite the low opinion Chatfield held of the Italian navy.[6] In London pressure against sanctions was also being exerted, though for somewhat different reasons to those expressed by the COSs. Early in October for example L. S. Amery, whom no one

[1] *ibid.*

[2] 6th and 9rd Meetings of DPR Committee on 5th and 23rd Sept. 1935.

[3] See for example Lord Cunningham, *A Sailor's Odyssey* (Hutchinson, 1951) pp. 173-4. Cunningham was at the time Rear-Admiral (Destroyers).

[4] COS. 405 of 10th Oct. 1935 expresses those apprehensions strongly.

[5] Cabinet 50(35) of 2nd Dec. 1935. Cab. 23/82.

[6] Chatfield to Fisher 25th Aug. 1935. Chatfield papers, CHT/4/5. The COSs expressed similar views at their 150th meeting on 13th Sept. Cab. 53/5.

could accuse of lack of courage, wrote to Baldwin saying that he, supported by a number of other MPs, 'respectfully but earnestly appeal to HM government to reassure public anxiety by making it clear that it will not at Geneva advocate or be a party to any sanctions in any way likely to lead to war';[1] and a little later Baldwin met Amery and his group to hear their views on the danger incurred by the policy adopted at Geneva.[2]

The notorious Hoare–Laval plan was signed in Paris on 8th December, and perhaps Norman Davis, Roosevelt's principal delegate to the forthcoming naval limitation conference, summed up the position most accurately when he wrote to the President that 'Laval had told the British . . . [that] they [the French] could not be relied on to help in retaliation by Italy, and that Mussolini had threatened both England and France in case oil sanctions were imposed; also that Van Sittart [sic], who has become obsessed with fear of Germany and who has never cared much for the League but favours an Anglo-French alliance . . . helped to persuade Hoare to take the course that led to his downfall'. Davis went on to say that it was remarkable the way 'the moral consciousness of England has been aroused, and made itself felt'. He entertained high hopes for Eden as Foreign Secretary because 'he is really more friendly to the United States than the others'; which was perhaps less than fair to Hoare and Baldwin, and ignored the totally negative part that Davis's own country was playing in what was in fact a world crisis.[3]

In October, when the crisis was at its height and it seemed that war might come at any moment Admiral Fisher learnt that his elder son Neville, who had joined the RAF, had been killed in an air accident. The shock, coming on top of so many professional anxieties, must have been severe; but within a few days Fisher was able to tell Chatfield that 'I have weathered the storm', that as regards the fleet 'All is well— very well indeed I think'. Admiral Pound, the C-in-C designate, had arrived on the station and had remained to work as Fisher's unofficial deputy. Though Fisher wrote 'I get more glad every day that Dudley Pound came out', and that they 'never disagreed' the presence of two full Admirals working in tandem on the same job was, to say the least, unusual.[4]

---

[1] Amery to Baldwin 11th Oct. 1935. Premier 1/177.
[2] On 15th Oct. 1935. *ibid.*
[3] Davis to FDR. Roosevelt papers, PSF, folder 2.
[4] Fisher to Chatfield 25th Oct. 1935 (two letters). Chatfield papers, CHT/4/5.

Early in November the Admiralty, probably recalling the great benefits gained in the 1914–18 war from our having cut the trans-Atlantic cables, so enabling us to intercept German diplomatic telegrams, surveyed the security of our Mediterranean cables. Italy had three ships capable of cutting them, and they concluded that the most probable place for this to be attempted was in the Sicilian channel. We had four cable ships in or near the Mediterranean and a few more at home, and the conclusion reached was that the secrecy of our cable routes had been preserved and that to cut them would be difficult.[1] At about the same time as they reviewed security of cable communications the Admiralty considered the possibility of the Italians using poison gas, which they did do in the later phases of the Abyssinian war. If, they wrote, the government decided to retaliate the only means of delivery would probably be by aerial bombs; and steps were therefore being taken to charge bombs with gas.[2] Thus does one act of terrorism nearly always lead to escalation in warfare.

The partial, and disguised, mobilisation ordered late in August and the reinforcement of the Mediterranean Fleet totally disrupted the normal programme for training officers and men both in the home shore establishments and at sea—just at the time when expansion of the fleet was producing increased demands for trained men. Furthermore the Home Fleet ships concentrated at Portland in readiness to go out were unable to carry out a proper training programme because of the frequent autumnal gales. In September, Admiral Backhouse, who had taken over command of the Home Fleet from Lord Cork a month earlier, wrote to Chatfield about sending more Home Fleet ships to Gibraltar, where the weather was far less likely to hinder training. Furthermore such a move would be 'strategically advantageous' if war with Italy came.[3] In fact the government would not allow more than minor changes, or exchanges, between the Home Fleet and the forces assembled at Gibraltar because such action was regarded as 'politically unwise'.[4] In November Backhouse represented that the ships detached to the Mediterranean should come home in time to give Christmas leave, and in the same month the Admiralty began to work out a comprehensive plan whereby ships should be exchanged between the two fleets, so enabling men to get the leave to which they would have

[1] AL of 5th Nov. 1935 to Cs-in-C, Med. and E. Indies. Adm. 116/3050.
[2] Air Min. letter to Admy. of 24th Dec. 1935. Adm. 116/3050.
[3] Backhouse to Chatfield 9th Sept. 1935. Chatfield papers, CHT/4/1.
[4] Covering note to above by Little. *ibid.*

been entitled but for the crisis. 'In the interests of welfare', they wrote, perhaps again with the shadow of Invergordon in mind, it was essential to avoid all Home Fleet crews falling due for leave simultaneously; but the negotiations with Italy were making such slow progress that the battle-cruisers would either have to stay at Gibraltar or be relieved by Home Fleet battleships.[1]

Admiral Fisher, not surprisingly, saw the problem differently. 'As long as [the] emergency exists in present acute form when Italy is making every possible warlike disposition . . . consideration of leave', he signalled, 'should be disregarded', and his fleet kept at its present strength.[2] The Admiralty assured him that 'no weakening of forces in Eastern Mediterranean is contemplated unless situation improves';[3] but that still left the leave problem unsolved, and all that could be done was to assure all authorities of the Board's 'awareness of the disappointment of men of the Home Fleet' over the probable loss of their Christmas leave.[4] In mid-December the Admiralty told all concerned that it was 'the complete readiness' of our forces which provided the best guarantee that peace would be preserved, and Fisher replied that his fleet was absolutely ready and so contributing to that cause[5]—a statement which the unquestionable anxiety about the possible effects of the Italian air power on that same fleet makes dubiously valid.

Towards the end of the year the DPR Committee, with Baldwin in the chair, discussed the question of what objectives we should attack in the event of hostilities with Italy—a matter on which the COSs had already reported.[6] The DPR Committee decided that, for the guidance of the Cs-in-C concerned, five broad principles should be adhered to. Firstly we would not take the initiative in any naval or air bombardment 'directed against the civilian population'; secondly if the Italians attacked 'legitimate British naval, military or air objectives' we would reply on a tit-for-tat basis; thirdly that even if the Italians attacked 'non-military objectives' Cs-in-C were not to retaliate 'unless specific approval from Home is given'; fourthly authority was given to retaliate without higher authority in the event of attacks 'upon objectives . . . in the occupation of military forces'; and lastly, and somewhat

[1] AL of 20th Nov. 1935. Adm. 116/3046.
[2] C-in-C, Med. 1618 of 3rd Dec. 1935. *ibid.*
[3] AM. 1502 of 7th Dec. 1935. *ibid.*
[4] AM. 2001 of 18th Dec. 1935. *ibid.*
[5] AM. no. 398 of 18th Dec. 1935. Adm. 116/3468.
[6] DPR committee 16th meeting of 12th Dec. 1935. Adm. 116/4078.

contradictorily, the DPR Committee declared that, in the event of hostilities, nothing in these instructions should be taken as inhibiting 'the immediate commencement of military operations against military objectives . . .' It is not surprising that when draft instructions on the foregoing lines were prepared for despatch to the senior officers concerned the Admiralty and Air Ministry should have come into conflict over the precise meaning of 'military objectives' and 'legitimate targets'.[1] Whereas the Admiralty held that the Hague Convention of 1909 and the draft 'Rules for Aerial Warfare' drawn up in 1923[2] covered the problem adequately the Air Ministry argued that bombing was legitimate if a 'known military objective' which could be identified from the air existed in any area. If, as appears to be the case, the Air Ministry's assumption was that such targets could be attacked without causing civilian casualties they certainly showed great confidence in the accuracy of bombing—or perhaps a desire not to weaken the Trenchard gospel about its decisiveness. The argument continued throughout 1936, and was referred to the CID. That body held that British policy was 'to adhere to the general humanitarian principle inherent in the draft rules' of 1924.[3] But the truth was of course that, as 'Jacky' Fisher had remarked nearly half a century earlier, 'You can no more humanise war than you can humanise hell'; and the attempt to do so was bound to produce all sorts of contradictions and, if war came, to favour the belligerent which entertained the least scruples.

On New Year's Day 1936 Chatfield sent Eden a proposal that, as it was politically undesirable to strengthen Fisher's fleet a 'spring cruise' of Home Fleet ships to Gibraltar, Spanish ports and the Canary Islands should be permitted, after which some major units would be brought home from the Gibraltar force. Eden agreed, and replied that the Foreign Office would inform the Italian government that the movements were 'a normal cruise for training purposes'. The programme was announced on 7th January,[4] and next day the Admiralty promulgated the present and prospective world-wide dispositions of the whole navy, including the Australian and New Zealand ships which had moved to Aden or Alexandria as part of the preparations for war. There was no weakening of Fisher's fleet, but the chief anxiety still of

---

[1] Admy.-Air Min. correspondence Jan.–March 1936. Adm. 116/4078.
[2] Cmd. 2201 of 1924.   [3] CID. 1246B. Cab. 4/24.
[4] Chatfield to Eden 1st Jan. and reply by the latter of 3rd Jan. 1936. AM. 2055 of 7th Jan. and Branch Acquaint of 8th. *ibid.* After the spring cruise the *Hood, Ramillies, Orion* and *Neptune* were to come home from Gibraltar and give leave.

course concerned the effects of the large Italian bomber and submarine strength.[1] In February 1936 however they were worried to learn that ten small German U-boats had arrived at Trieste in sections—which could have increased the underwater threat appreciably.[2]

In March 1936 Fisher, who was about to haul down his flag as C-in-C, sent home a comprehensive survey of the problems which had arisen since the beginning of the crisis, and the steps taken to meet them. The broad objects had been 'the removal of the most important units [of the fleet] outside the range of air attack'; and 'to occupy a strategic position near the Suez Canal and to afford additional security to Egypt as a whole'. If war came his aim would be 'to obtain and maintain' control of the central area between Italy, Tripoli and Greece, attacking the enemy wherever he might be found at sea and where feasible in harbour. But the inadequacies of Alexandria as a main base had forced him to use Haifa 'as an overflow', which handicapped both training and the execution of his plan. He went on to describe the intensive programme of training against air, submarine and various forms of surprise attack; and the possibilities inherent in the latter had inevitably necessitated keeping the fleet at short notice for steam, so severely restricting shore leave. As to the defences of Alexandria and Haifa, they had been steadily developed, and Fisher now felt justified in describing them as 'formidable and, after many night exercises, efficient'. He concluded by paying a warm tribute to 'the unflagging zeal' of the officers of his staff, and of those not only in the warships but in all the multifarious auxiliaries which had joined his command.[3] Plainly under Fisher's strong and energetic leadership the fleet he commanded had become a superb instrument of war; and so it was to remain under his successors.

In the following month Chatfield sent the First Lord two notes in which he made the dubious claim that 'the Admiralty took action . . . which saved the League'; and, more justifiably, he drew attention to the mobility which had made it possible to fulfil strategic demands 'within a week', whereas the Army and RAF had, he said, taken 'many weeks if not months' to meet their roles in the emergency.[4] Chatfield

---

[1] Adm. 116/3041.

[2] Drummond to FO 11th Feb. 1936 enclosing report from British Consul, Trieste. FO. 371/19160. The U-boats were assembled at Spezia, but none was operational before the end of the crisis.

[3] C-in-C, Med. letter of 19th March 1936 to Admy. Adm. 116/3468.

[4] Notes of 27th and 28th April 1936. Adm. 116/3042.

urged the First Lord to impress on the Foreign Office the serious effects on the efficiency of the navy as a whole of keeping the fleet on a 'war footing' for eight months. Surely, he continued, Italy was unlikely to attack us now that victory in Abyssinia was 'within her grasp'; and he wanted the Cabinet to be pressed to allow the Mediterranean Fleet to go back to Malta and the Home Fleet ships to return.[1] But on 29th April the Cabinet decided that, pending the meeting of the Council of the League on 11th May, 'no major redistribution' was to take place, though 'some relaxation . . . and unostentatious movements' were permissible.[2] On 5th May Italian forces occupied Addis Ababa; but the League Council meeting referred to above did not in fact greatly change the situation. Although Admiral James, now DCNS, correctly remarked at the end of April that 'the sanctionist front is cracking',[3] the decision to abandon sanctions was not actually taken until 6th July. The desirable but untried ideal of 'collective security' had finally broken down; and today it seems undeniable that the reluctance of the COSs, and especially of the Admiralty, to risk armed conflict with Italy at a time when Japanese expansionist plans were rampant, Germany's intention to rearm was plain, the support of France was doubtful and our own rearmament had barely got off the ground, played a major part in bringing about that collapse.

On 19th June the Admiralty signalled to all Cs-in-C proposing that the ships at Alexandria and Aden should return to their normal stations, and two days later increased the notice at which the fleet stood ready for sea to 72 hours.[4] Admiral Pound, now C-in-C, proposed to hold the Fleet Regatta at Alexandria early in July in order to allow the ships from distant stations to participate, and also wanted to give a 'Fleet Ball' or 'other large official At Home' to return the cordial hospitality shown by the people of Alexandria'[5] The regatta was approved but not the social function—because of 'British and Egyptian court mourning' (for the death of King George V on 20th January and of King Fuad on 28th April); and on 18th July, just after the end of the regatta, the Mediterranean Fleet returned to Malta and Home Fleet ships to their home ports. On 9th Chatfield proposed to Sir Samuel Hoare, who had become First Lord in succession to Monsell on 6th June, that an expression of 'Their Lordships . . . high appreciation of the services

---

[1] Cabinet 31(36) Conclusion 9. Cab. 23/84.
[2] *ibid.*   [3] Minute of 22nd April 1936. Adm. 116/3042.
[4] AMS. 1759 of 19th June and 1634 of 21st June 1936. *ibid.*
[5] C-in-C, Med. 1408 of 22nd June 1936. *ibid.*

rendered' by all the officers and men throughout a period 'which has been arduous and has involved much hardship' should be sent; and Hoare was 'delighted to send this message'.[1] As a rather belated after-thought the appreciation was extended to 'the MNBDO personnel, civil staff, crews of supply ships, oilers and chartered vessels' three days later.[2]

The emergency of 1935–36 was of course a costly affair for the British taxpayer. Between September 1935 and March 1936 nearly 100 applications were made by the Admiralty to the Treasury for addi-tional expenditure, many of them for items—such as more aircraft for the FAA and larger ammunition reserves—for which the Admiralty had been pressing for years. By the end of 1935 nearly £10 millions additional expenditure for the Navy alone had been approved, but Parliamentary sanction was not obtained until four Supplementary Estimates to cover a substantial increase of personnel as well as a lot of money were presented in the 1935–36 and 1936–37 Financial Years.[3]

We have already seen how the inadequacies of the eastern Mediter-ranean bases worried both Admiral Fisher and the Admiralty as the crisis deepened. In September 1935 the Naval Staff reviewed the con-jectural problem that air power might render Malta 'untenable', and concluded that a base in Cyprus would be 'a great help in war with France or Italy'. The alternatives were to make Malta 'impregnable' if possible, or if that could not be done to abandon it as a 'main mainten-ance and repair base', to develop Gibraltar dockyard to take capital ships, to create a new base at Famagusta in Cyprus, or to enlarge the MNBDO to enable us 'to obtain a base quickly wherever needed'.[4] The technical departments worked out estimates and concluded that to make Famagusta adequate for the Mediterranean Fleet would cost over £22 millions plus £3.3 millions for defences—which was not a proposition likely to appeal to the Treasury. As the desirability of a Cyprus base was mentioned in the deliberations of the DRC[5] Chat-

---

[1] Admy. 'A. Message' 1156 of 11th July 1936. *ibid.*

[2] AM. 1600 of 14th July 1936. *ibid.*

[3] Details of the items approved are in Adm. 116/3465. The Supplementary Estimates are in Cmd. 5031 of Dec. 1935 (unnamed increase in Vote A numbers), *Accounts and Papers, 1935–36 Session*, vol. XVII of 12th Feb. 1936 (3,500 additional men and £4.85 millions), *ibid.*, of 28th April 1936 (2,036 additional men and £10.3 millions), *ibid.*, of 7th July 1936 (£1.1 millions). Also *loc. cit.*, 1936–37 Session, vol. XVIII of 1st March 1937 (1,000 additional men and £100—a token sum pending final calculations).

[4] Plans Div. memo. of 18th Sept. 1935. Adm. 1/9044–140/36.

[5] DRC. 33 of 9th Oct. 1935, appendix 5. Cab. 16/112.

field took the matter up with Hankey its chairman after the end of the Abyssinian crisis. He proposed a scheme rather like the 'truncated scheme' of 1926 for Singapore,[1] of which the first stage would cost about £7.4 millions.[2] Hankey appears to have been unenthusiastic— probably because, with Singapore far from completed, it would have been highly optimistic to open the question of building another major base, and partly because so many other high priority demands had been raised in the DRC's final report.[3] At any rate Chatfield told Pound that the Cyprus base was 'out of the question for the immediate needs of the moment', and that he preferred to develop Alexandria. In consequence nothing more was heard of the Cyprus scheme, and when war broke out there was still no naval base on the island.[4]

Instead of pursuing the Cyprus scheme attention returned to the defences of Malta in September 1936, now that the Cabinet decision of November 1933 that 'no expenditure should for the present be incurred on measures of defence required to provide exclusively against attack by USA, France or Italy' plainly required reconsideration with regard to the last named country.[5] The Governor of Malta, General Sir Charles Bonham Carter, had held 'full discussions' with the local naval and air authorities, and the conclusion reached was that, although the island could not be used as a fleet anchorage and dockyard in the event of war with Italy it could 'fulfill a very useful function' as a base for submarines and motor torpedo-boats, and as a supply base for refuelling and replenishing ships of the fleet. The considered opinion of the three services was, he continued, 'that Malta can be made almost impregnable', and that 'a properly defended Malta can act as a base for offensive action by sea and air . . .' He went on to list in detail the 'immediate requirements' and those which were 'desirable if sound strategy is to be observed'. For the Navy provision of minesweepers and formation of a Malta Reserve Force came in the former category, and 'bomb proof shelters for submarines' was the first item in the second category.[6] Nor did the Naval Staff disagree; but when

---

[1] See vol. I, pp. 463–4.
[2] Chatfield to Hankey 25th Nov. 1936. Adm. 1/9044.
[3] See pp. 216–19.
[4] Chatfield to Pound 23rd Nov. 1937. Chatfield papers, CHT/4/10.
[5] See p. 168.
[6] General Bonham Carter to Colonial Secretary, Malta Command Letter of 11th Sept. 1936. Copy forwarded to Admy. by C-in-C, Mediterranean 26th Sept. Adm. 116/4061. The Bonham Carter papers in Churchill College, Cambridge contain many interesting letters about the defence of Malta at this time.

the matter came before the JDC in July 1937 that body considered that execution of the Governor's full proposals was ruled out by the recent Cabinet decisions 'that priority in defensive preparations in Europe should be given to the provision of a deterrent to aggression by Germany', and that 'no very large expenditure should be incurred in increasing the defences of ports in the Mediterranean and Red Sea'.[1] The Admiralty considered that the provision of bomb-proof shelters for MTBs and submarines, and certain lesser proposals, fell within the limitations imposed by the first of the two JDC recommendations quoted above and so had to be ruled out.[2] Nor could they see their way to meet the demand for minesweeping drifters. Presumably the Admiralty's reluctance to fight for such proposals as the bomb-proof shelters derived from recent experience gained in the Abyssinian crisis; but seen in retrospect their view was wholly mistaken, and the submarines stationed in Malta during the long siege of 1941–43 suffered severely for lack of such shelters.[3] However early in 1938 the Governor reported that the construction of underground fuel storage and of a Combined Headquarters, involving the laying of buried telephone lines, had been begun, as had work on many lesser projects which were permitted by the rulings quoted. His report was sent to the JDC, who passed it on to the ODC;[4] but the truth is that too little was done too late to put Malta's defences into really good order.

Despite the desire of the COSs, supported by Hankey, to restore friendly relations with Italy, especially after Hitler's re-occupation of the Rhineland in March 1936, the termination of sanctions did not lead to a rapid improvement. Nor was progress towards a solution helped by King Edward VIII's tour round the Mediterranean in the yacht *Nahlin* in September 1936. Though we now know that he had no purpose beyond his desire to be with Mrs Ernest Simpson, and completely failed to appreciate the political effects of his presence and conduct,[5] his visit to the Dalmatian coast aroused great hostility in Italy, while his talks with Kemal Ataturk in Istanbul produced sus-

[1] JDC. 319 of 19th May. Revised 30th July 1937 to meet Admy. objections to first draft. Also 296th CID meeting of 5th July 1937. Cab. 2/6.

[2] Minute on JDC. 319 (Revised) of 30th July 1937.

[3] See Roskill, *War at Sea*, II, pp. 57–8 and G. W. G. Simpson, *Periscope View* (Macmillan, 1972), pp. 122–3.

[4] Sir Charles Bonham Carter to Colonial Sec. 19th Jan. 1938. Adm. 116/4061. Also JDC. 374 of 11th Feb. 1938.

[5] See Frances Donaldson, *Edward VIII* (Weidenfeld and Nicolson, 1974), pp. 211–14.

picions in Berlin.[1] Certainly the King had not helped the diplomacy of his own government.

In November the Foreign Office telegraphed their ideas for a settlement with Italy to Sir Eric Drummond, the ambassador in Rome. The chief points were that Italy should stop the spate of virulent anti-British propaganda, adhere to the Montreux Convention[2] and the London Treaty of 1936 (to be discussed in the next chapter), and if possible return to the League. On our part there could be no acceptance of new commitments in the Mediterranean, nor would we limit the size and disposition of our forces or recognise the conquest of Abyssinia; but we would perhaps reduce our representation in Addis Ababa to that of Consul-General. Such terms were not likely to appeal to a dictator flushed with his recent successful defiance of the League. In that same month the Admiralty wrote to the Foreign Office stressing that they desired 'to emphasise the importance on general strategic grounds of securing some easement in our relations with Italy'. They gave their reactions to the recent exchange of telegrams with Drummond,[3] and declared that 'any limitation on British naval strength in the Mediterranean would be totally unacceptable' from their point of view. Nor did they attach great importance to early acceptance of the London Treaty; since what they wanted was 'to reach an agreement with her'.[4] These arguments became a constant refrain in the thinking of the Naval Staff and the Board during the next three years—not out of any affection for Mussolini but because we simply did not have the strength to fight all three dictatorships; and Germany, being the nearest to the homeland, was considered the greater threat.

The successful conclusion of an alliance with Egypt was, from the

[1] Adm. 116/3302 contains reports on Italian and German reactions.

[2] On the Montreux Conference of 1936, convened to replace the Lausanne agreement of 1923, see *Gathorne-Hardy*, pp. 421–4. The Admiralty papers on this conference are in Adm. 116/3656A. Broadly speaking the outcome was that control of the Straits was in effect returned to Turkey but the Black Sea powers were accorded substantial advantages.

[3] FO to Drummond no. 428 of 14th Nov. and his no. 695 of 17th Nov. 1936 in reply. Copies in Adm. 116/3302.

[4] Admy. to FO. M. 05225/36 of 21st Nov. 1936. Adm. 116/3302. On the proposed 'Gentleman's Agreement' of this time see Vansittart's minute of 9th Nov. 1936 and draft telegram no. 705 to Rome. Vansittart's reaction to Mussolini's conditions was cautious in the extreme. The agreement he thought reasonable was to be made '. . . at a future date. That date, however, would have to be carefully chosen . . . with mature reflection' and would be the outcome of '. . . a series of considerations—joint, tripartite [i.e. with France included] and multi-lateral . . .' FO. 371/19160.

Admiralty's point of view, a much happier story than the attempt to reach an accord with Italy. The 1930 negotiations to settle the long-vexed question of the clash between Egyptian nationalist aspirations and British interests in the Middle East had ended in failure, but in February 1936 the Foreign Office raised the possibility of an alliance in telegrams to Sir Miles Lampson, the British High Commissioner in Egypt;[1] and preliminary talks began in the following month. In April an inter-departmental meeting took place in the Foreign Office to consider which military bases we might give up. The War Office, though prepared to make some concessions, insisted that troops must remain at Alexandria and in the Canal Zone, and without time limit;[2] and the COSs supported that view.[3] The Foreign Office then presented a gloomy picture to the Cabinet regarding the likely effects of such a stand.[4] Next Eden proposed to the Admiralty a tactfully worded clause that Egypt should 'take all steps necessary for the maintenance of the security of and freedom of navigation in the said Canal',[5] and the CID agreed that this was acceptable.[6] On 27th April the Dominions were represented at a CID meeting, with the Prime Minister in the chair, and the conclusion reached was that, provided we could keep troops in Alexandria and in the Canal Zone, the Cairo garrison could be withdrawn. The question of the 'time limit' was reserved for decision by the Cabinet.[7]

In May Lampson reported that, although Nahas Pasha, the Egyptian Premier, was insistent on putting an end to the indignity of our military occupation he was prepared to concede us the right to send in reinforcements 'in the case of apprehended emergency'.[8] In the following month a series of meetings took place with Lampson present at which the proposal received from Nahas for 'a perpetual treaty of alliance' was discussed. Nahas appeared to be 'prepared and even anxious' to enter into such an alliance—provided that we did not adhere to the 'no time limit' proviso regarding the stationing of troops

---

[1] FO telegrams nos. 94 and 95 of 21st Feb. 1936 to Lampson approved the proposed programme for conversations. Adm. 116/3588.

[2] Record of conference of 20th April 1936. Adm. 116/3590.

[3] COS. 458 of 9th April 1936. Cab. 53/27.

[4] CP. 131(36). Cab. 24/262.

[5] Eden to Admy. 24th April 1936. Adm. 116/3590.

[6] CID. 1232B. Cab. 4/24.

[7] 277th CID meeting on 27th April 1936. Cab. 2/6.

[8] Lampson to FO nos. 472 and 473 of 26th May and FO to Admy. 25th June 1936. *ibid.*

in Egypt.[1] The Naval Staff remarked that this 'puts a totally fresh complexion on the matter' and was hopeful of an agreement on those lines;[2] but in July optimism was shaken by Lampson reporting that Nahas's colleagues 'had proved very difficult'. The Foreign Office for their part considered that we had gone as far as possible in making concessions (such as giving up our telecommunications system, building or improving various roads and accepting that military personnel should wear plain clothes when out of barracks), and ordered Lampson to stand firm.[3]

None the less in that same month meetings of the full British and Egyptian delegations, led respectively by Lampson and Nahas, took place, and on 17th July the High Commissioner telegraphed home the draft Military Articles proposed for inclusion in the treaty. They provided that the occupation would be terminated and an alliance established when the treaty was signed.[4] Though many difficulties still had to be surmounted, the greatest of which was the Egyptian desire to station their own troops in the Sudan and our desire to keep them out,[5] the Admiralty made no difficulty about the Egyptians manning the Alexandria coast defence guns—provided that we had a garrison there.[6] In May there was an adjournment in the talks during the Egyptian elections (in which the Wafd, or Nationalist party scored a sweeping victory), but when they were resumed good progress was made and on 11th August the Admiralty told the C-in-C, Mediterranean that the treaty would probably be initialled next day.[7] That was done, and Nahas came to London for the formal signature on 26th August.[8] From the Admiralty's point of view the outcome was satisfactory, since both the use of Alexandria and control of the Suez Canal were secured for 20 years.

Publication of the treaty produced some grumbles in Parliament— notably about the cost to the British taxpayer of building new roads

[1] Record of meetings in Adm. 116/3590.

[2] Minute of 8th June 1936. *ibid.*

[3] FO to Lampson no. 416R of 8th July 1936. *ibid.*

[4] Lampson to FO no. 846 of 17th July 1936. *ibid.*

[5] Lampson to FO no. 24 of 12th March and no. 273 of 6th April 1936. Adm. 116/3589.

[6] CID. 1220B and 275th meeting of 26th March 1936. Cab. 4/24 and 2/6.

[7] AM. 1020 of 11th Aug. 1936. Adm. 116/3589.

[8] Cmd. 5270 is the Treaty. Ratification was approved by Parliament on 24th Nov. 1936. Parl. Deb., Commons, vol. 1079, cols. 251–339, and Ratifications were exchanged in Cairo on 22nd Dec. 1936. Cmd. 5360.

($£9$ millions);[1] and before the debate on the treaty took place on 24th November the Admiralty prepared a brief for the Prime Minister's use. In it they wrote that 'The solution which has been evolved, namely a perpetual alliance, is undoubtedly the next best arrangement' to the 'ideal' one of Britain being 'recognised as the international authority charged with the duty of the defence of the Suez Canal'.[2]

With the treaty at last out of the way the Admiralty returned to the question of the defence of the canal and control of traffic through it in war. The original plan, made in 1935, provided for closure of the canal except to our ships. By the end of 1936 a European war was obviously more likely than one against Japan, and the plan was reconsidered. But in fact it underwent no fundamental change, though a final review was carried out in July 1938 to deal with the possibility of a European war (presumably between Germany and Russia) in which Britain and Egypt were neutral.[3]

If, as seems likely, Italian aggression in Abyssinia and the failure of sanctions contributed to the comparative ease with which the Anglo-Egyptian treaty was brought to a successful conclusion the same factors unquestionably produced deliberations on whether reform of the League Covenant was desirable or possible. Hoare, now First Lord, consulted senior members of the Naval Staff, because the issue was likely to go to the COS Committee in the first instance. The views of Admiral James, the DCNS were perhaps the most cogent. 'Our naval forces', he wrote, 'being limited and *the relative strength to other naval forces being exactly known* our course of action has always seemed to me to be quite plain. Firstly—to be *honest*, and cease to enter into a maze of collective security pacts which we have no intention of honouring if the security of *our own people* is simultaneously threatened [by several powers]. Secondly—to be *sanely selfish*, by subduing the modern day passion to intrude into every two-halfpenny quarrel from the Vosges to the Great Wall [of China], be always sure that we can safeguard that quarter of the globe painted Red on our maps (another colour presumably on Russian maps!). Shorn of trimmings this memorandum approaches these simple ideas' (his italics throughout).[4]

---

[1] There are many references to and questions about the Anglo-Egyptian treaty in Hansard for the 1935–36 and 1936–37 Sessions of Parliament.

[2] Memo., undated but c. 18th Nov. 1936. Adm. 116/3589.

[3] Adm. 116/3656B, 3657 and 3658 contain many papers on the defence of the Suez Canal 1935–38.

[4] Memo. by DCNS of 7th Aug. 1936. Adm. 116/3691.

A week later the Admiralty produced its views in more official form. The revision of the Covenant, they declared, 'affects the Admiralty very closely', and from the earliest days the department had been 'much concerned with the commitments involved in our adherence to it'. They had often pointed out that in any League dispute the burden of upholding the actions of the League 'would be likely to fall on the British Navy'; and recent events had 'proved the truth of this forecast . . .' The conclusion reached was that in the prevailing conditions 'we can expect very little support from other members of the League' in a war started through its actions. From 'the military point of view' they would like to be 'relieved of all commitments under Article 16', but if that was impossible they urged that such commitments 'should be limited to a Western European Pact'; and they strongly disliked any proposal that League decisions should be 'reached by a two-thirds majority'. In other words the Admiralty wished to be relieved of any obligation to restrain Japan—because they knew they did not possess the strength to do so.[1] The discussion went on until the end of 1937 when the Cabinet decided 'to approve generally . . . that when the question of Reform of the League was brought up . . . the UK representative should not make any pronouncement until he had to do so'. But if he found himself obliged to make a statement 'he should be authorised to take a middle course and to suggest that membership of the League should involve a general obligation to consult and an additional obligation to take coercive action when, but only when, consultation between members of the League indicated that coercion might properly be employed . . .'; which was a tortuous way of saying that the government was not prepared to throw the League system publicly overboard but would only give very conditional support to any future application of Article 16.[2] Discussion on reform of the Covenant and on repudiation of the 'Optional Clause' of the Statute of the Permanent International Court of Justice continued,[3] and in December 1938 the CID recommended denouncement of the General Act of the same Statute before 15th February 1939.[4] Except

---

[1] Admy. memo. of 15th Aug. 1936. *ibid.*

[2] Cabinet 48(37) of 22nd Dec. 1937. Cab. 23/90A.

[3] The clause of Article 36 of the Statute of the Permanent Court of Justice obliging the submission of disputes to that Court. See *Gathorne-Hardy*, pp. 178–9.

[4] CID. 1492B of 9th Dec. 1938. Cab. 4/29. Release from the Optional Clause could not be legally obtained before Feb. 1940.

for accumulating a mountain of paper nothing had been accomplished on these issues when war put an end to the discussion.

While the Abyssinian crisis was in progress, and most of the fleet was on a war footing, the Admiralty had to continue the normal peace-time practice of preparing the estimates and building programme for the 1936–37 Financial Year. It will therefore be appropriate to end this chapter with an account of those negotiations. In August 1935 the Staff summarised for the First Sea Lord the situation which had arisen since the reconstitution of the DRC and the creation of the new Ministerial Defence Policy and Requirements (DPR) Committee to co-ordinate defence policy and review the DRC's proposals. The DRC's brief was 'to work out . . . programmes on the assumption that by the end of the financial year 1938–39 each of the Defence Services should have advanced its state of readiness to the widest necessary extent in relation to the military needs of national defence and within the limits of practicability'.[1]

Accordingly the Staff produced a Naval Deficiency Programme up to 1942, and asked the Admiralty departments to produce new proposals for the first year of the accelerated programme under the headings of Deficiencies, Personnel, Fleet Air Arm and New Construction.[2] Early in 1936 the Board considered the Sketch Estimates, which had been prepared 'on the assumption that a considerable increase would be accepted to put the Navy into a thoroughly sound condition within a period of years'. They came out at £80.5 millions before imposition of any 'Shadow Cut', and included increases of 36,148 in personnel and of £1.6 millions for the FAA.[3] However in the next month the Admiralty was told that the estimates 'should be presented on the basis of existing policy', and Supplementary Estimates presented after a new Defence White Paper had been considered by Parliament.[4] Monsell objected strongly to what he described as a policy which 'diverges so widely from what I had conceived to be the intentions of the government'. He also disliked the prospect of having three debates on the Navy Estimates—the normal one in March and others on Deficiencies and Supplementaries in April and May. He considered that a meeting with the Chancellor would be futile, so sent the whole correspondence to Baldwin. The Prime Minister however

[1] DRC. 27. Cab. 16/112.
[2] D of P memo. of 6th Aug. 1935. Adm. 116/3437.
[3] Board Minute 3329 of 3rd Jan. 1936. Adm. 167/94.
[4] Chamberlain to Monsell 14th Jan. 1936. Adm. 116/3394.

supported the Chancellor, so Monsell gave way and the estimates were revised accordingly.[1] They now came out at just under £70 millions after application of the 'Shadow Cut' of over £2 millions, and the Chancellor accepted that figure.[2] Lord Stanley, the Parliamentary Secretary, presented the estimates to Parliament on 16th March, and although they showed an increase over the previous year of nearly £10 millions he had little difficulty in dealing with the Opposition.[3] On 20th April Chamberlain, the Chancellor, also approved the Supplementary Estimate of £10.3 millions already mentioned.[4]

As to the building programme, at the end of November 1935 the Board learnt that the DRC had accepted the Staff's proposals;[5] but no provision for the programme was included in the original estimates. By the first Supplementary Estimate of 28th April 1936 funds were provided to start two capital ships, five cruisers, nine *Tribal* class destroyers, one aircraft carrier, four submarines, six sloops and some lesser vessels. This substantial programme was increased by a second Supplementary Estimate on 7th July. The two capital ships (*King George V* and *Prince of Wales*) remained unchanged, but the cruisers were increased to seven (two 'improved *Southamptons*' and five *Didos*), the destroyers were doubled by bringing in the J class flotilla, the carriers were increased to two (*Illustrious* and *Victorious*), and the submarines were doubled. Nor did Monsell or his successor from 6th June Sir Samuel Hoare experience any serious difficulty over getting Parliamentary approval for the Supplementaries, though the Opposition always introduced an amendment seeking to reduce them.[6]

Between January and April 1936 the Sea Lords and then the full Board devoted a lot of time to the design of the ships included in the new building programme. Thus at the end of February Chatfield stressed that more small cruisers were needed, and that we should therefore build no more big ones after the two 'improved *Southamptons*'.[7] Thence arose the final decision to build five *Didos*. In April

[1] Monsell to Baldwin 15th Jan. and reply by latter of 17th Jan. 1936. *ibid.*

[2] Board Minute 3335 of 13th Feb. 1936. Adm. 167/94 and Adm. 116/3402.

[3] Parl. Deb., Commons, vol. 310, cols. 55–192 and Cmd. 5105 of Feb. 1936. The draft of the First Lord's statement is in Adm. 116/3394.

[4] Adm. 116/3402.

[5] Board Minute 3315 of 28th Nov. 1935 and Adm. 1/9037–114/36.

[6] See for example the motion introduced on 20th July 1936 Parl. Deb., Commons, vol. 315, cols. 193–6. A. V. Alexander moved to reduce the Supplementary by £100.

[7] Board Minute 3352 of 5th March 1936. Adm. 167/94.

the legend of the new battleships (known initially as 'Design 14 O') were exhaustively discussed, and the conclusion reached was that ten 14-inch guns rather than twelve, a speed of 29¼ knots and good protection offered the best compromise within the permitted displacement of 35,000 tons.[1] The design of the new armoured deck carriers has already been described.[2] In June the Board considered measures to increase and accelerate the building programme, about which the First Lord had written to the DPR Committee. The outcome was the Supplementary Estimate of July mentioned above, but in addition the Board intended to advance the three battleships of the 1937 programme by six months, and to start increased recruiting forthwith so as to reach a total of 130,000 men by 1940.[3]

Early in 1937 the US Naval Attaché reported home on the foregoing proposals which, he wrote, 'would be prosecuted with even more vigour' but for shortage of building ways, berthing and yard capacity, skilled labour and draftsmen—all of which was perfectly true and a legacy of the years of financial stringency.[4] As to the US Navy itself, although good progress was being made with the ships for which funds were provided by New Deal agencies in 1933–34, and the first Vinson Act had provided authority to build up to full treaty strength, only a dozen destroyers and six submarines were started in 1936. Early in the following year Roosevelt emphasised the need to speed up building, and Swanson circulated the instruction to all authorities, stressing the importance of avoiding delays by altering ships' characteristics.[5] But it was not until a year after the Royal Navy had begun to rearm in earnest that the USA followed suit.

As to the other naval powers, in 1936 Germany authorised another battleship (which finally became the *Tirpitz*), two cruisers, ten destroyers or torpedo-boats and fifteen submarines. The latter followed on the two dozen of the 1935 programme, which had in fact been built secretly in sections since 1934. France had already begun the *Richelieu* and *Jean Bart* but only added three destroyers and two submarines in

[1] Board Minutes 3357 and 3373 of 3rd April and 28th May 1936. *ibid.* The legend and approval for the ships' names by the King were formally accepted by Minute 3405 of 15th Oct. 1936. *ibid.* They were laid down on 1st Jan. 1937. Adm. 1/9106–96/1937.

[2] See pp. 223–4.

[3] Board Minute 3380 of 24th June 1936. Adm. 167/94.

[4] Report of 12th Jan. 1937. USNA, RG. 80.

[5] GB. 420–2, serial 1744 of 18th Feb. 1937.

1936; while Italy started work in that year on 28 destroyers or torpedo-boats and ten submarines. Japan was of course progressing her big First and Second 'Replenishment Programmes' of 1931–35 and 1934–37 already referred to, and the first ships of the former were completed in 1936. Plainly competitive building, with each country trying to meet what it regarded as its own special needs, was beginning in earnest—even before the new Naval Conference long since arranged for 1935 had been convened.

To return to the Royal Navy, the years 1935–36 were a period of extraordinarily heavy strain on senior officers. The shock of Invergordon was still felt, the previous excellent relations between officers and men had been shaken if not shattered, and among those on whom a measure of blame was held to fall were some very promising officers. Now that the fleet was expanding again, and war had become a distinct possibility, it was plain that more senior officers would be needed, and that the best of them would soon have to be picked out for command of squadrons and as potential Cs-in-C and Sea Lords. Chatfield's correspondence shows that he was deeply conscious of his responsibilities in this matter, and he often discussed the rising genera-tion of admirals or potential admirals with his contemporaries. At or near the very top we saw earlier how Admiral Dreyer was never liked or trusted, even by his closest associates in Whitehall or in the fleet; and he was one of those at whom criticism had been directed over the Invergordon mutiny. Chatfield was well aware of this feeling, and admitted that he did not think he 'would ever make a C-in-C' because 'with all his brains he definitely fails in some respects. He is too much of a paper man'.[1] It can therefore have come as no surprise to Dreyer to be told by Chatfield that his appointment in China would be ex-tended by four months but after giving up that command there was little likelihood of further employment for him.[2]

In 1935 doubts clouded the future of two of the ablest young Rear-Admirals—Geoffrey Blake and Bertram Ramsay. The former was offered command of a cruiser squadron that year but had to decline it

[1] Chatfield to Kelly 20th Feb. 1932. Holograph. Kelly papers, KEL/110. Dreyer was of course appointed C-in-C China in 1933. Possibly Chatfield meant that he would never make a C-in-C of the two major commands—Home and Mediterranean Fleets—which was then regarded as an essential prerequisite to holding the office of First Sea Lord.

[2] Chatfield to Dreyer 31st May 1935. Chatfield papers, CHT/4/4.

on account of his wife's ill health.[1] He did however return to service in command of the Battle Cruiser Squadron in the following year— only to be overtaken by an accident which resulted in his being invalided.[2]

Ramsay's was a sadder story—but had a far happier ending. In August 1935 he was appointed Chief of Staff to Sir Roger Backhouse when he succeeded Lord Cork as C-in-C, Home Fleet. Backhouse was a man of impressive presence, some 6 foot 4 inches tall, and of un-questionable ability. But he, like a good many senior officers of his day, had never learnt to use a staff properly, and absolutely refused to dele-gate any of his authority to his Chief of Staff or anyone else. This method of work produced a crisis between him and Ramsay, and after the latter had tried to come to a *modus vivendi* and failed he resigned his appointment and retired from the Navy a short time later. Chatfield took Backhouse's side in this unfortunate quarrel, telling Tyrwhitt, who had pleaded that Ramsay 'had not had quite a fair deal' that he had 'failed very badly in *Nelson*'.[3] The outcome was that, after four very happy and restful years with his family, Ramsay took up the Dover command in 1939 completely fit, rested and refreshed; and in World War II no British naval officer distinguished himself more—by the evacuation from Dunkirk, and by planning the great amphibious assaults of 1942-44. Backhouse on the other hand continued to centralise and overwork; and the ultimate result was inevitable. Though Sir John Kelly's criticisms and his commendations of his col-leagues were both of them sometimes laid on too heavily, he is en-titled to be heard on the subject of who should be the next First Sea Lord because he had placed the whole navy in his debt for his part in remedying the damage done by the Invergordon mutiny. On receiving an opening from Chatfield to give his views he replied that although he used to look on Backhouse 'as a possibility' he had become 'con-vinced that he is too weak: too fearful of accepting responsibility'. 'Dudley Pound', he continued, 'would not be a success . . . In the first place he suffers from not being *quite* a gentleman', which he con-sidered 'a disastrous *lacuna* in a First Sea Lord'; furthermore Kelly

[1] *ibid.*

[2] Chatfield to Pound 2nd July 1937. Chatfield papers, CHT/4/10.

[3] Tyrwhitt to Chatfield 22nd Feb. and reply by latter of 24th Feb. 1936. Chatfield papers, CHT/4/1. See W. S. Chalmers, *Full Cycle. The Biography of Admiral Sir Bertram Ramsay* (Hodder and Stoughton 1959) ch. v for a full account of Ramsay's clash with Backhouse.

considered him 'too pig-headed; too unwilling to recognise that there *may* be another side to a question'.[1] If at the end of 1936 signs were not lacking that the navy was going to be very short of first class men at or near the top of the promotion ladder, the next two years were to make matters far worse.

[1] Kelly to Chatfield 30th July 1936. Chatfield papers, CHT/4/6.

CHAPTER X

The Second London Naval
Conference
1935-1936

WHEREAS THE preliminaries to the London Naval Conference of
1930 only took about three months[1] those for the next conference
were extremely protracted, and to follow them we must go back to the
closing months of 1933 when Norman Davis, the American President's
chief negotiator on disarmament problems, met the General Board
onboard the SS *President Roosevelt* for a discussion. The policy arrived
at included 'balanced reduction of the components of the fleet'; but the
Board considered the future of the submarine to be 'the real key'.
Comparisons were made of the American view with those likely to be
held by Britain and Japan, and three alternative plans were sketched
out to deal with various eventualities.[2] Interesting points in the notes
taken of Davis's views were that 'Feeling against Japan is growing in
England', and 'that, very confidentially, the President sees that we
must keep up to Treaty strength'.[3] Early in the New Year H. L.
Roosevelt, Acting Secretary of the Navy, asked the Chairman of the
General Board, Admiral R. H. Leigh, 'to submit recommendations . . .
as to the attitude the United States should take in this forthcoming
conference'.[4] The General Board passed the question to Admiral D. F.
Sellers, the C-in-C, US Fleet; but after he had replied that he had
neither the time nor the knowledge to tackle the problem Admiral

[1] See pp. 38-57.
[2] Memo. for the Chairman, General Board dated 16th Nov. 1933. GB. 438-1.
[3] 'Notes on talk of [sic] Mr. Norman Davis' dated 18th Nov. 1933. *ibid.*
[4] USNA, RG. 80, serial 1640. Letter of 8th Jan. 1934.

J. M. Reeves, the Commander, Battle Force took on the job.[1] Expectedly he took a very hard line, urging 'the strongest possible attitude', that the navy's air force was 'the strongest factor we possess', and that it should be expanded 'as a strategical move in the Treaty negotiations'.[2] Leigh found these views 'certainly sound and strong', as he did those submitted by the President of the Naval War College,[3] and he sent them on to Secretary Swanson.[4]

In March 1934 Ramsay MacDonald met Davis, who had recently come to London to take soundings, at the American embassy. Davis was then 'quite emphatic' that the USA would not agree to Japan being allowed parity with herself, and 'almost as emphatic' against allowing her any increase above the Washington Treaty ratio.[5] On 6th Davis sent the President a full account of this meeting. He remarked shrewdly on the personalities he met—for example 'Simon does not hate the United States . . . one of his faults is that he does not hate some things he ought to hate'; and he reported that Eden had told him he 'is satisfied that Hitler now is most desirous of reaching a disarmament agreement and of mollifying France'.[6] A few days later Judge Robert W. Bingham, the American ambassador in London, sent Roosevelt an account of a meeting over lunch with Monsell. He and the First Lord were, he wrote, 'agreed that we ought to be able to carry out our naval programmes along the lines best suited to our countries, without suspicion, competition or hostility'.[7] Next, back in Washington, a report from the Naval Attaché, Tokyo emphasised that Japan would insist on parity and that *only* naval questions should be discussed at the conference—by which of course they meant exclusion of all discussion of their actions in China.[8] On 7th March Davis went to Sweden, where he evidently had some business to do for the President in connection with the Kreuger scandal,[9] but returned to London a fortnight later.

[1] GB. 438–1, General Board to C-in-C, 26th Jan. and reply by latter of 27th Feb. 1934.
[2] Reeves to Chairman, General Board 14th March 1934. *ibid.*
[3] Leigh to Reeves 20th March 1934. *ibid.*
[4] Leigh to Swanson. *ibid.*
[5] Record of meeting on 2nd March 1934. Cab. 29/149. The American record of this meeting is in Roosevelt papers, PSF, Box 56, Folder 1.
[6] Davis to FDR from Claridge's Hotel, 6th March 1934. Roosevelt papers, PSF, London Naval Conference file.
[7] Bingham to FDR 8th March 1934. Roosevelt papers, *loc. cit.*
[8] NA Tokyo no. 89 of 22nd March 1934. *ibid.*
[9] Ivar Kreuger (1880–1932) built up a vast monopolistic match manufacturing

On 23rd he sent Roosevelt another interesting letter about British policy and politicians. On Monsell, for example, he went further than Bingham, stating that the First Lord 'thought co-operation between our governments in dealing with the Japanese was essential'. He also reported that the Prince of Wales (soon to be King Edward VIII) had called at the embassy, and had said that 'there must be a change in conditions here, and a correction of social injustices . . .' What Britain needed, in the Prince's view, was leadership such as Roosevelt was giving the USA; all of which was, to put it mildly, a strange intervention by the heir to the throne.[1]

While these informal discussions were in progress in London, and in Washington the General Board was busy preparing a monumental brief for the US delegates,[2] the Admiralty was not idle. In March Chatfield produced a paper stating Britain's 'Strategic Requirements', which gave priority to the need to provide in the Far East 'a force of sufficient strength to ensure security for the Empire and its essential interests . . .', while at the same time being able to keep 'sufficient forces in European waters and the Atlantic to give us security against the strongest European naval power'. Such a policy, he stressed, meant a return to the Two Power Standard established in 1889,[3] which we were nowhere near possessing. As to duration of a new treaty, Chatfield thought that a period of ten years would be advantageous, since most of the fleet would, he hoped, be modernised by 1945.

In Parts III to VIII of his compendious paper Chatfield reviewed British needs in each class of ship. For capital ships he preferred a qualitative limitation of 25,000 tons and 12-inch guns, but would be prepared to settle for 28,000 tons—partly in deference to the American preference for big ships. The 70 cruisers required (fifteen 8-inch, ten M class, and forty-five smaller 6-inch ships) totalled nearly 562,000 tons—which was a big increase on the existing tonnage and likely to arouse strong American opposition. Turning to aircraft carriers, a limit of 22,000 tons per ship and a total of 110,000 tons was proposed.

---

empire. In March 1932 he shot himself in a Paris hotel, and it was discovered later that for many years he had been forging documents and falsifying returns.

[1] Davis to FDR 23rd April 1934. Roosevelt papers, *loc. cit.* On the habit of Edward, Prince of Wales, making unexpected, and even improper interventions in political questions see Frances Donaldson, *Edward VIII* (Weidenfeld and Nicolson, 1974), pp. 194–6 and *passim*.

[2] GB. 438–1, serial 1640 of 1st Oct. 1934. Also in USNA, RG. 80.

[3] See Arthur J. Marder, *The Anatomy of British Sea Power* (Knopf, 1940), p. 17 and *passim*.

If submarines could not be abolished he wanted them kept down to 250 tons. Destroyer tonnage depended on the decision taken over the submarine. If abolished we could accept 100,000 tons, but if retained double that figure would be necessary; and in either case the present qualitative limitation of 1,850 tons and 5.1-inch guns should be retained. Though prepared to allow Japan 65% of our destroyer tonnage Chatfield wanted the Washington Treaty 5:5:3 ratio for capital ships and carriers to be continued.[1] This paper was discussed with Vansittart and R. L. Craigie, the head of the Western Department of the Foreign Office, and became the first of the many memoranda circulated to the Ministerial Committee formed under the Prime Minister's chairmanship to consider departmental views and provide the Cabinet with recommendations on the line to be taken at the conference. On 23rd March Chatfield and Vansittart circulated their joint views as an Annex to this paper. The Foreign Office considered that a shorter period than ten years for the duration of the treaty had something to be said for it; and they were against declaring at an early stage that we intended to have 70 cruisers. As to destroyers, they considered 200,000 tons could not be justified because in the 1930 London Treaty we had accepted 150,000 tons in relation to a parity figure of 52,700 tons of submarines. Finally they considered that 'some advance will have to be made to meet Japan on the question of [the] ratio if an agreement is to be concluded'; but they accepted the Admiralty's premise regarding the provision of a fleet for the Far East, because the Cabinet had as yet given no clear ruling on whether it should be 'capable of engaging the Japanese fleet'.[2] The implication that it would be strategically sound to send out a fleet which was incapable of doing so certainly seems a little odd.

Also in April 1934 the Naval Staff produced an 'Appreciation of Requirements for the 1935 Naval Conference';[3] but as it was not circulated until early October we will defer consideration of it for the present. In the same month the Ministerial Committee met for the first time.[4] The principal item on the agenda was Chatfield's paper and

[1] Memo. of 14th March 1934. Adm. 116/2999. Became NCM(35)1.

[2] Cab. 29/148.

[3] Proof copies dated April 1934 in Adm. 116/3373 and 1/8802-39/35.

[4] The other members were Baldwin (Lord President), Simon (Foreign Secretary), J. H. Thomas (Dominion Affairs), Monsell (First Lord) and Neville Chamberlain (Chancellor of Exchequer). Baldwin sometimes took the chair in place of MacDonald, whose health was visibly deteriorating, and after he and MacDonald exchanged offices in June 1935 he became the regular chairman. Cab. 29/147.

the Foreign Office remarks on it. Admiral Little, the DCNS, and Craigie reported on the informal conversations held with Bingham and Ray Atherton, Counsellor in the US embassy, which had gone very well. MacDonald supported Chatfield's desire to achieve lower qualitative limitations for capital ships and to maintain the Washington Treaty ratios; but he was doubtful whether the Americans would come as low as 22,000 tons for such ships, and confident that Japan would demand some increase in her ratio—as in all probability would France and Italy. Chamberlain expressed the view that, even if the conference broke down, the British people would welcome an agreement with Japan, and he wanted to aim at achieving 'something definite and something new' with that country. He also believed that 'some arrangement' with her about China could be reached. Such views corresponded of course to those expressed by the DRC in their report of the previous February;[1] while Monsell suggested that 'we might try and allay American objections by saying that we should be in a position to exercise influence with Japan'. On 19th April Sir Warren Fisher, Permanent Secretary of the Treasury, circulated what the editor of *Documents on British Foreign Policy* describes as his 'boldly worded' paper on the broad issues before the Ministerial Committee. It made it plain that he too wanted to achieve 'a thorough and lasting accommodation with the Japanese'.[2] Chatfield's views on trying to get agreement for limitation of capital ships by numbers rather than by tonnage or, failing that, acceptance of total tonnage limitation were agreed; but his strong desire to start capital ship replacement in 1937 was merely 'noted'.[3]

The discussion continued at the next two meetings of the Ministerial Committee, when Chatfield pressed hard for approval of his 70 cruisers —which MacDonald feared would produce 'political repercussions'. Chatfield preferred no agreement on cruisers to acceptance of less than 70 and declared, very optimistically, that he believed 'Japan could not afford to build much further'. The Foreign Office preferred a six year naval building programme to the Admiralty's ten year plan, which

[1] See pp. 168–72.

[2] NCM(35)3 of 19th April 1934. It is printed in full in DBFP, 2nd series, vol. XIII, appendix I, but on p. VI of the Preface it is misdated 29th April. Unless otherwise stated all references to DBFP in this chapter are to that volume, full particulars of which will not be repeated. Chatfield replied to Fisher's paper on 29th May. NCM(35)6. Cab. 29/148.

[3] NCM(35)1 and 2 of 23rd April and minutes of first meeting of Ministerial Committee on 16th April 1934. Cab. 29/148 and 147 respectively.

would mean building 152,000 tons of new cruisers, and the two departments were told to confer together on the subject. Chatfield's proposals that no more 8-inch cruisers should be built, that large 6-inch cruisers should be limited on the basis of the Washington Treaty ratios, that a qualitative limit of 7,000 tons and 6.1-inch guns for such ships should be sought, and that we would accept no quantitative limitation on future cruiser building were agreed to. The discussion on cruiser limitation was continued at the next meeting, when Monsell and MacDonald came into conflict over the Admiralty's 70 cruiser figure—chiefly because it would force the Americans to embark on a big building programme if they were to achieve their declared policy of 'parity' with Britain. The decision taken was to aim for 60 under-age and ten over-age (i.e. over twenty year old) ships, but accept 50 of the former if necessary. The 60 figure was, however, to be put to the Americans at the first informal discussion. Only in return for 'some substantial *quid pro quo*' would we agree to an increase in the Japanese cruiser ratio. Chatfield's proposals regarding aircraft carriers, destroyers and submarines had an easy passage.[1] We can skip the fourth meeting, when telegrams telling the Tokyo embassy of our intentions were discussed. At the fifth one the committee reverted to the size and armament of capital ships, and Craigie said he feared that American insistence on bigger ships would force us to accept 31,000 tons and 14-inch guns at a cost of some £6 millions each. Chatfield commented that, as a result of 'realistic tests', he was confident that such ships could 'withstand the air menace'.[2] The committee decided to try for the 25,000-ton 12-inch ship in the talks with the Americans, to maintain the Washington ratios, and not to accept postponement of the replacement programme.[3]

The Ministerial Committee had the draft of its report, on the foregoing lines, ready in early June;[4] but its circulation produced a protest from Lord Londonderry, the Secretary of State for Air, about his Ministry not having been consulted. Although the issues were, he admitted, 'primarily a naval matter' the navy alone could not defend its bases against air attack, and he therefore asked that he should be kept

[1] Third meeting of same on 23rd April 1934. *ibid.*

[2] Chatfield referred in particular to A-A firings against wireless-controlled 'Queen Bee' aircraft, but probably also had the tests against the 'Job 74' float (see p. 222) in mind. He certainly had an exaggerated idea of the effectiveness of the A-A gunfire.

[3] Fifth meeting of Ministerial Committee on 31st May 1934. Cab. 29/147.

[4] NCM(35)12 of 11th June 1934. Cab. 29/148.

'in close touch' with the development of policy.[1] It certainly appears odd that copies of Chatfield's and the Naval Staff's papers on the preparations for the conference should not have been sent to the Air Ministry; but the two departments did meet together a few weeks later, and a letter from Chatfield to Ellington suggests that the Air Ministry's concern was not only with the defence of naval bases but with the old issue of their dislike of the aircraft carrier.[2]

As the Ministerial Committee did not meet between the end of May and the middle of October 1934 we will now turn to the preliminary talks with the Americans and Japanese. The informal meeting between MacDonald and Davis in March referred to earlier, was followed by a series of high-level meetings in June when the British proposals for smaller capital ships and for more cruisers were discussed.[3] The former aroused no enthusiasm at all in American breasts, and the latter, involving some half million tons of cruisers, provoked Davis to say that his country 'had never dreamt of the increases Great Britain envisaged', that American public opinion demanded 'further all-round reductions', and his government would 'not permit negotiations on the basis of such a large increase in numbers' of cruisers. Nor was he prepared to accept so low a limit as 25,000 tons and 12-inch guns for capital ships.[4] Though these reactions corresponded to British expectations they did not augur well for the outcome of the conference. On 27th June the President confirmed his delegate's firm line by cabling to him that he wanted the Washington and London treaties renewed for at least ten years and a 20% reduction in strength achieved during that period.[5] Davis replied that the dominant 'Baldwin group'

[1] Londonderry to Monsell 24th Oct. 1934. Adm. 116/3618.

[2] Admy. and Air Min. meeting of 14th Nov. and Chatfield to Ellington 7th Dec. 1934 telling him that we proposed to reduce the total permissible carrier tonnage from the Washington figure of 135,000 tons to 110,000, so giving us five 22,000-ton ships. *ibid.*

[3] NC(USA) First, second, third and fourth between 18th and 27th June 1934. Cab. 29/149. Rear-Admiral R. H. Leigh, the Chairman of the General Board and leading American naval delegate kept a diary giving the record of the naval conversations. It corresponds closely to the British official records. GB. 438–1.

[4] NC(USA) Fourth meeting of 27th June 1934. Cab. 29/149. Evidently MacDonald had communicated the British proposals to Davis at the second meeting. Admiral Leigh's diary records that on 20th June Davis told MacDonald and Monsell 'that the British programme advanced in the morning was a great shock to him', and on 22nd Davis said that 'continuance of the negotiations on [the] basis of their programme would be fruitless'. GB. 438–1.

[5] FDR to Davis no. 270 of 26th June 1934. Roosevelt papers, PSF, Box 56, Folder 1.

had stressed that they now had a European as well as a Far East commitment, and as they could not rely on American co-operation in the
Pacific 'they are thus confronted with the problem of dealing with the
Japanese alone'.[1] Next day he cabled that the British would not accept
renewal of the London Treaty 'without important modifications'; but
the President held to his view that the size of capital ships should be
reduced, and also the number of submarines by 20%. He would be
'delighted to reduce 10, 20 or 30% if risks were reduced in similar
proportion'.[2] This reply was perhaps not very helpful to his delegate,
and hardly accorded with the President's warm support of the Vinson
Act and of other efforts to increase his country's naval strength. Moreover who was to decide if the risks had been reduced?

On 2nd July Hankey circulated a note on the decisions reached in the
first two Anglo-American meetings which were, in his view, so secret
that they were not incorporated in the record. At the first meeting
Davis had proposed that 'both sides should undertake that in no
circumstances would either country agree to any increase in the
Japanese ratio of naval strength'—though MacDonald had preferred
less rigid wording. At the second meeting it was decided that if agreement between Britain and the USA proved impossible a naval race
between them was to be avoided 'at almost any cost', and both countries
would 'regulate their respective naval construction' up or down according to what other countries did.[3] If these conclusions were somewhat
amorphous they did at least show that the British and American
delegates were determined not to quarrel, and would stand together in
face of Japanese demands.

Meanwhile the two countries' 'experts' had been trying to eliminate
some of the differences between them; and it is fortunate that Admirals
Little and Leigh seem to have got on as well together as did Chatfield
and Standley.[4] Admiral Leigh held out firmly for 35,000-ton capital
ships with guns at least as large as 14-inch; but he was satisfied to have
only the eighteen 8-inch cruisers permitted by the 1930 treaty. He
expressed understanding about the British need for large numbers of
smaller cruisers, and was prepared to accept a qualitative limitation
of 6–7,000 tons for 6-inch ships after the nine big *Brooklyn* class had

[1] Davis to FDR no. 363 of 27th June 1934. *ibid.* See also FRUS, 1934, vol. I, p. 279.
[2] Same to same no. 367 of 28th June and reply by FDR of 29th June 1934. *ibid.*
[3] NCM(35)14 of 2nd July 1934. Cab. 29/149.
[4] Little-Leigh meetings of 21st June, 4th and 7th July 1934. Cab. 29/149 and Leigh
diary. Also memo. by Little of 28th June 1934. Adm. 1/8803.

been completed. No difficulties arose over destroyers and submarines.

Anglo-Japanese conversations were taking place concurrently with the Anglo-American ones. On 18th June MacDonald met Tsuneo Matsudaira, the Japanese ambassador, to whom he gave an outline of what had passed in the talks with the Americans. Whereas the British wanted the conference to begin in January 1935 Matsudaira pressed for a postponement until April and stalled over putting forward proposals until the arrival of Admiral Isoruku Yamamoto, who was expected in mid-October and would be bringing the Japanese proposals with him.[1]

At the end of June Craigie met Roger Cambon, Counsellor at the French embassy, who asked what line the British intended to take at the conference, our views on the strength to be allowed to Germany, and whether we would be prepared to return to the principle of 'global' limitation (i.e. a total overall naval tonnage). Craigie gave an outline of the British proposals on capital ships and cruisers but described the concept of global limitation as 'retrograde'.[2] The first formal Anglo-French meeting took place on 9th July when Monsell and François Piétri, the Minister of Marine, outlined their positions. Piétri enlarged on the great value to France of the submarine, and stressed that what really mattered to his country was its strength relative to that of Italy and Germany.[3] The talks then moved to Foreign Ministers' level, and Simon met Louis Barthou on 10th. On the question of an approach to Germany Simon then said that such a move would of course 'be entirely subject to the reservation of all rights under the Treaty of Versailles on the part of France and other countries'[4]—a statement which the British government certainly did not adhere to a year later. Admirals Little and Decoux simultaneously considered the strength we proposed to allow to Germany. It comprised five capital ships (including three *Deutschlands*), one carrier, seven light cruisers, 25 destroyers and 5,000 tons of submarines—which far exceeded the tonnage allowed by the Versailles Treaty, as Decoux pointed out. The French accepted the British view on smaller capital ships and said they would approach the Americans on the subject; but they adhered firmly to the 96,000 tons of submarines permitted by the 'Statut Naval' of December 1924, and still hankered after global limitation—with France allowed a

[1] Adm. 116/3373.
[2] Meeting of 28th June 1934. Cab. 29/149.
[3] NC(F) 1st meeting on 9th July 1934. *ibid.*
[4] NC(F) 2nd meeting on 10th July 1934. *ibid.*

tonnage greater than that of Italy and Germany combined.[1] In August the talks were transferred to Paris; but the French showed no sign of modifying their attitude over submarines, and insisted that if Italy built two 35,000-ton battleships they would do the same.[2] As for the Italians, at the end of July Craigie met Admiral Count Raineri-Biscia, and found him 'adamant' about building the two big battleships and refusing to abolish the submarine. Though Biscia was more accommodating on the cruiser question his statement that 'Italy could not retreat from the policy on which she had settled' showed a degree of rigidity which was highly unwelcome to the British.[3] In that same month the British embassy in Rome reported that the Italians wanted the Washington ratios to be perpetuated, Tokyo telegraphed that the Japanese wanted the conversations 'to touch on all naval questions—including that of ratio'; while Washington reported that the administration was 'considerably disappointed' by the British insistence on 70 cruisers and other increases.[4] The British proposal for the small capital ship was ignored by them all and was plainly moribund.

Although it was clear by the end of July that the first round of conversations had produced formidable obstacles there was one hopeful sign. On 26th Craigie sent Atherton a paper, known among the Americans as 'the Craigie Memorandum', setting out the British position on the cruiser question with convincing clarity and pointing out how 'incorrect and misleading' it was to suggest that whereas the USA stood for naval reductions Britain stood for increases. It seems likely that this paper strengthened the hands of those Americans who wished to reach an accord with Britain.[5]

From the end of July to early October 1934 there was a lull, and it is interesting to find that the British 'Naval Staff Appreciation' which had been drafted in April and the American General Board's statement of their view of the needs of the USA, together with the brief they wanted Davis to use when the discussions were resumed, were circulated in their own countries almost simultaneously.[6] The brief for

[1] NC(F) 4th and 5th meetings on 11th and 12th July 1934. Cab. 29/149.

[2] NC(I) 1st meeting on 30th July. *ibid.*

[3] NC(F) 6th, 7th and 8th meetings, Captain Danckwerts-Admiral Abrial. *ibid.*

[4] Rome to FO no. 204 of 17th July; Tokyo to FO no. 112 of 9th July and Washington to FO no. 237 of 17th July 1934. Adm. 116/2998.

[5] NCM(35)16 of 25th July 1934. Circulated on 2nd Aug. Printed in full in DBFP, no. 2 and in FRUS, 1934, vol. I, pp. 299–303. Original in Cab. 29/148.

[6] The Staff Appreciation on 3rd Oct. (Adm. 116/3373) and the General Board's long memorandum to the Secretary of the Navy on 1st Oct. 1934. (GB. 438–1,

Davis stated that 'the preponderating value of the battleship. . . is its power of survival in a naval campaign'—a view with which Chatfield was, as we have seen, in full accord. The General Board was strongly opposed to the British proposal to reduce the displacement of battleships or the calibre of their guns.

On 3rd October the Foreign Office and Admiralty circulated a paper about preparations for the conference. They summarised the position regarding the ratios, and said that the expected Japanese claim to parity was unacceptable both to the Americans and to ourselves. A slight decrease in capital ship displacement to 32,500 tons and of their guns to 14-inch was all we could expect to achieve regarding that class. The British desire to let the 8-inch cruiser die out and to restrict numbers of big 6-inch cruisers was likely to be accepted by the Americans; but the large increase in the total tonnage in that class sought by us had been an unpleasant surprise to them and was likely to cause trouble. As for aircraft carriers, reduction from the Washington limit of 27,000 tons to 22,000 and of the total tonnage permitted to Britain and USA from 135,000 to 110,000 tons seemed likely to prove acceptable. The French Ministry of Marine had 'proved unexpectedly conciliatory and helpful', and might be willing, on some conditions, to reduce their submarine tonnage to 80,000 or even less. The qualitative limits placed on destroyers by the London Treaty (1,850 tons and 5.1-inch guns) were likely to remain; but we had been given no inkling of American views on quantitative limitation—except for the overall 20% reduction proposed by Roosevelt. All three of the countries consulted favoured ten years for the duration of the treaty, and the general desire was for the conference to take place in London.[1]

Meanwhile Davis had returned home in order to brief the President on the progress made and difficulties encountered in the preliminary talks. Early in October Roosevelt asked him to go back to London for the next round, and gave him his own ideas on the line to be taken. 'I cannot approve', wrote the President, 'nor would I be willing to submit to the Senate . . . any new Treaty calling for larger navies'.[2] At the end of that month Davis wrote to the President that Matsudaira had told him that Japan 'definitely confirmed' her decision to denounce the Washington Treaty by the end of 1935, and that he was satisfied that

---

serial 1640). The General Board's brief for Davis of 1st Oct. 1934 is also in GB. 438-1.

[1] Adm. 116/3373.

[2] FDR to Davis 5th Oct. 1934. Roosevelt papers, PSF, Box 56, File 1. Davis drafted the instructions to himself and Cordell Hull vetted them.

the 'cardinal policy' of Britain was 'to co-operate as closely as possible with us'.[1] The only jarring note from across the Atlantic at this time was in a paper which Admiral F. H. Schofield, recently a member of the General Board, sent to Standley. In it he wrote that 'British naval policy is supremacy of the seas . . . confronted with rivals she seeks alliances with the most powerful', and 'when war comes we shall find ourselves alone'.[2] Swanson sent this polemic on to Roosevelt, who made no comment on it; but it shows that anglophobia of the W. S. Benson style still existed among some high-ranking American officers.[3]

By October 1934 Chatfield was utterly pessimistic about the conference succeeding. 'I think we shall have no treaty', he told a former holder of his office; 'The Japanese proposals are likely to be unacceptable to the USA. I think the sparks will be flying in a fortnight's time'.[4] Yamamoto and his staff arrived in the Cunard liner *Berengaria* in the middle of that month. Though the Japanese government had nominated Matsudaira as chief delegate it did not augur well that an Admiral of known 'hard-line' views should be a full delegate—not merely an 'expert adviser' as were the British and American admirals. Davis and the American delegation arrived in the liner *Manhattan* at about the same time.

The first meeting between the British and Japanese took place at 10 Downing Street on 23rd October, and Yamamoto then put forward his proposal for a 'Common Upper Limit' in naval strength. In reply to MacDonald's request for a definition of the term he said that it represented 'a figure which the country feeling most vulnerable deemed necessary for herself'; which of course meant no limitation at all. Yamamoto also proposed the abolition of 'offensive weapons' and acceptance of the principle of 'non-aggression and non-menace'. Aircraft carriers, capital ships and heavy cruisers, stated in that order, were all classed by him as 'offensive' weapons.[5] The discussion was continued three days later, when the Japanese said that if offensive weapons were not abolished they wanted to see them substantially reduced; and they proposed 'global' limitation of defensive vessels as well. Monsell accepted the abolition of heavy cruisers on behalf of the British.[6]

[1] Davis to FDR 31st Oct. 1934. *ibid.*
[2] Schofield to Standley 5th Oct. 1934. Copy in *ibid.*
[3] See vol. i, pp. 54, 62–4 and 134.
[4] To Admiral Sir Charles Madden 4th Oct. 1934. Chatfield papers, CHT/3/2.
[5] NC(J) 1st meeting. Cab. 29/149.
[6] NC(J) 2nd meeting on 26th Oct. 1934. *ibid.*

Chatfield, supported by Little, met Yamamoto that same day; but the latter merely reiterated his earlier proposals.[1] The British admirals would probably have agreed with the telegram sent by the American delegation that 'the rigidity of the Japanese position . . . is diminishing the agreement possibilities'.[2]

The Anglo-Japanese talks, usually with Chatfield and Yamamoto acting as leading counsel for their countries, continued throughout the autumn of 1934; but a compromise proposed by Simon to give the Japanese 'equality of prestige and of security' produced no response;[3] and Chatfield described the level for the common upper limit proposed by Yamamoto as 'quite impossible'.[4] Nor were the American-Japanese meetings held at about the same time any more fruitful, and after two months of patient negotiation it was plain that no modification of the Japanese demands had been achieved.[5]

While these abortive discussions were in progress Sir Warren Fisher was watching developments from the side-lines, and in October he wrote to Simon stressing that Germany would 'at some future date . . . once more fight for the domination of Europe', and asking what would happen 'if on her next venture . . . she could find England distracted with a hostile Japan?'[6] Fisher evidently received, or at any rate claimed to have received, some support from Chatfield, since in the same week he wrote to Neville Chamberlain to that effect;[7] but in truth

---

[1] NC(J) 3rd meeting on 26th Oct. 1934. *ibid.*

[2] Telegram of 26th Oct. 1934 to State Dept. Copy in USN Operational Archives.

[3] NC(J) 4th meeting on 7th Nov. 1934. Cab. 29/149. The draft of Simon's compromise proposal is in DBFP, no. 41.

[4] NC(J) 10th meeting on 28th Dec. 1934. Cab. 29/149. A good summary of the Anglo-Japanese conversations is in NCM(35)22 of 27th Oct. 1934. DBFP, no. 37.

[5] GB papers, series XIII. Record of conversations with Japanese on 24th, 29th and 31st Oct. 1934.

[6] Fisher to Simon 30th Oct. 1934. Copy in Chatfield papers, CHT/3/2. On 1st Nov. Fisher wrote to Chatfield in similar vein. *ibid.*

[7] Fisher to Chamberlain 12th Nov. 1934. Fisher described Chatfield as 'a man of exquisite restraint' and claimed that he had called the record of recent talks with the Americans 'a piece of damned impertinence on the part of Mr. Craigie'. Copy in Chatfield papers, CHT/3/1. In fact the Craigie-Davis conversation had only dealt with the need to negotiate a new treaty if *one* of the signatories denounced that signed at Washington in 1922, and with the desirability of having informal talks between the American and British naval experts. As Chatfield was at the time working very closely and cordially with Craigie it seems unlikely that he expressed himself as crudely as Fisher said. The record of the talk is in NC(M)(35)26 of 8th Nov. Cab. 29/148.

Chatfield and the Admiralty, though they would probably have been glad to reduce their commitments by reaching an agreement with Japan, were certainly not prepared to do so at the price of alienating the USA.

Towards the end of October 1934 Davis said that though 'willing to be very patient indeed' he found it difficult to carry on with bi-lateral conversations, and wanted the Japanese to be brought into the Anglo-American talks. MacDonald and Simon were strongly opposed to this idea—at any rate at the stage then reached. Though Davis assured the British that 'the last thing' he and the President wanted was for 'England to be weakened and that she should be incapable of coping with her problems', he still hankered after the 20% reduction given in his brief. MacDonald spoke firmly on British naval needs, especially in the Far East.[1] On the last day of the month Davis wrote to the President reporting the Japanese decision to denounce the Washington Treaty, and urged the need to be 'patient and wise'; but a week later he reported that Japanese intransigence had virtually eliminated the possibility of an Anglo-Japanese deal, and that the British would not agree to an increase in the Japanese ratio. He was sure that the 'cardinal policy' of the British was 'to co-operate as closely as possible with us'.[2] At about the same time the President wrote to Admiral Reeves, the C-in-C, US Fleet, 'Frankly I gravely doubt a successful outcome, but Admiral Standley and Mr. Davis seem to be succeeding in getting the British in line with us'.[3]

Davis's letter of 6th November must have crossed with one from the President telling him that 'Simon and a few other Tories [*sic*. Simon was a Liberal National] must be constantly impressed with the simple fact that if Great Britain is even suspected of preferring to play with Japan to playing with us' he would 'be compelled . . . to approach public sentiment' in the British Dominions to make them 'understand clearly that their future security is linked with us'.[4] This was strong stuff, but if it got to British ears, it would have seemed more convincing if the President had not been still holding to his proposal for an all

[1] NC(USA) 5th meeting on 29th Oct. 1934. Cab. 29/149.

[2] Davis to FDR 31st Oct. and 6th Nov. 1934. Roosevelt papers, PSF, Box 56, File 1.

[3] FDR to Reeves 8th Nov. 1934. *ibid.* OF 18.

[4] Roosevelt to Davis 9th Nov. 1934. William Phillips, Under-Secretary of State, minuted on this telegram that it was important to send such messages by letter as 'we must assume that the British decypher everything that we send by code'. Perhaps he recalled that we had decyphered all Colonel House's telegrams to President Wilson in World War I. See Roskill, *Hankey*, I, pp. 246–7.

round 20% reduction in naval strength. In fact on 6th November MacDonald came to the firm decision that the Japanese proposals were unacceptable, and told them so.[1]

Rumours about an Anglo-Japanese understanding, and leaks to the Press, probably produced an exaggerated and alarmist impression of British plans and purposes in America. But the reaction to any such idea was universally and intensely hostile. For example Hull tele-graphed to Davis that 'any Anglo-Japanese agreement no matter how negative in form would be used by the Japanese . . . as an indication of an Anglo-Japanese partnership'.[2] In the *New York Times* Arthur Krock, the influential columnist, wrote that 'Patience wanes as British dicker with Japan', followed by a strong attack on Simon's foreign policy;[3] while Low's cartoon in the London *Evening Standard* was captioned 'Rule Japonica' and showed the Japanese equivalent to Britannia sitting in the centre place on a see-saw and saying 'Very nice Yes?—So long as honourable foreign ladies [Britannia and her American counterpart] continue to sit apart'.[4] In fact the Admiralty would not even counten-ance a compromise such as the two countries having equal building programmes.[5]

Towards the end of November Davis wrote to Roosevelt, quite correctly, that 'the small, wilful group that favoured playing with Japan . . . have been losing ground', and that in consequence he was much more hopeful. MacDonald, Baldwin and Simon, he said, agreed with the American delegates on that question, while Neville Chamber-lain 'has been the leader of that group in the Cabinet that favoured conciliating Japan'.[6] However Davis's misgivings were not yet wholly allayed. In mid-December he wrote again, declaring that British business interests planned to divide the China trade between them-selves and the Japanese; but British fear of a German-Japanese alliance was, he said, increasing, and as the British could not get from the USA 'a binding agreement for co-operation' they 'do not feel like casting Japan aside'. He was sure enough of the trend not to pass on to the

[1] Adm. 116/3373. The General Board papers, series XIII, section 5, contain a report of the statement by MacDonald of 14th Nov. that 'Our eyes are primarily on the Pacific'.

[2] Davis to Hull no. 266 of 9th Nov. 1934. Roosevelt papers, PSF, Box 51, File 1.

[3] Hull to Davis no. 26 of 17th Nov. 1934. *ibid.*

[4] *NY Times* 21st Nov. 1934, and London *Evening Standard* of same date.

[5] Minutes by Little and Chatfield of 24th and 26th Nov. 1934. Adm. 116/3373.

[6] Davis to FDR 27th Nov. 1934. Roosevelt papers, PSF, London Naval Conference file.

British Roosevelt's threat to incite feeling in the Dominions, referred to above.[1]

In November, while the Americans were still worrying about the possibility of an Anglo-Japanese rapprochement, the British Dominions were brought into the picture for the first time. Simon told the High Commissioners about the Japanese proposals and our attempt to find a compromise through granting 'equality of status' and all parties openly declaring their building programmes. Chatfield reported the results of his talks with Yamamoto, and how the Japanese admiral had said that if the treaties 'went by the board' his country would not agree to any qualitative limitation but would build the ships 'best suited for her own defence'. Simon, having come off the fence, declared that 'friendship with the USA [was] a *sine quâ non*', but then climbed on to it again by asking whether we could rely on the probability that the USA 'would always be there when the British wanted her help'.[2] At the second meeting Monsell reported on his talks with Yamamoto and Standley, which had gone better than expected despite the American lack of detailed instructions from their government—which was a cause of frequent British complaints. 'The Admiralty', said the First Lord, 'were most anxious to come to some agreement', and feared, that if we failed in that purpose 'Japan would take the bit between her teeth'. Special importance was attached to qualitative limitation, and 'the Battle Fleet should . . . be able to proceed to the Far East where the centre of gravity of the British Commonwealth lay'. These views were accepted by the Dominions' representatives, and that was the last meeting with them for almost a year.[3]

As 1934 drew to a close it was plainer than ever that no progress had been made towards the limitation of naval armaments by agreement, and further talks between Standley and Yamamoto in December did nothing to break the deadlock.[4] On the other hand British-American relations had been excellent on all levels, and once the ghost of an Anglo-Japanese agreement had been laid, there was every reason to expect co-operation to continue and to be extended. For this ac-

[1] Same to same 14th Dec. 1934. *ibid.*

[2] NC(D) 1st meeting on 13th Nov. 1934. Cab. 29/151. See DBFP, no. 55. The Dominion representatives were G. H. Fergusson (Canada), S. M. Bruce (Australia), Sir James Parr (New Zealand), J. C. Smuts and H. T. Andrews (South Africa), J. W. Dulanty (Irish Free State), plus Sir H. Wheeler (for the Indian Empire). J. H. Thomas (Secretary of State for the Dominions) took the chair at these meetings.

[3] NC(D) 2nd meeting on 18th Dec. 1934. *ibid.*

[4] On 3rd and 31st Dec. 1934. GB records, section XIII, 5.

complishment much was owed to the patience and good sense of Chatfield and Standley.

Early in the New Year a detailed exposition of 'The Minimum British Naval Strength Necessary for Security' was given to the Japanese delegation; but as the strategic arguments on which those needs were based and the actual figures for each class of warship, including the need for 70 cruisers and the desire to abolish the submarine, have already been recounted there is no need to recapitulate them here.[1] At the same time the Foreign Office and Admiralty produced a 'Survey of the Present Position of [the] Naval Conversations and Recommendations as to Future Procedure'.[2] The 'General Conclusions' were that the USA was certain to insist on maintaining parity with Britain and superiority to Japan; but hopes were entertained that the Japanese would so far modify their stand as to accept the compromise we had put forward. The French should, it was suggested, be invited to send representatives to London to receive our report on the recent conversations and our suggestions regarding future procedure; the compromise proposal would, we hoped, be put by the French to the Italians, who would be told of what passed between the French and ourselves; and, finally, if the French and Italians 'do not raise serious objections' the German government should be invited to start discussions on their 'requirements for a building programme'. If this survey was too optimistic in tone it did show that British patience had not been exhausted and that efforts to reach an agreement would continue.

Towards the end of January 1935 Simon reviewed the line to be taken when talks began with the French. Of the various possible alternatives his preference was to table immediately the concrete results we hoped to achieve—namely abrogation of Part V of the Versailles Treaty (the armaments clauses) as soon as Germany had agreed to the new provisions regarding her armaments 'on a basis of equality and free negotiation' and had cancelled her withdrawal from the League.[3] Such an idea certainly showed little understanding of Hitler's purposes and methods, since even in 1935 it was plain that he intended to get rid of the 'shackles' of Versailles by unilateral action if necessary; and he had

---

[1] NCM(35)45 of 17th Jan. 1935. Cab. 21/148. DBFP, no. 110.

[2] NCM(35)46 of 17th Jan. 1935. *ibid.* DBFP, no. 111. The draft of this paper is in Adm. 116/3373.

[3] FO note of 23rd Jan. 1935 and minute by Simon of same date. Cab. 29/146.

shown his contempt for the League too often to allow himself to be lured back into it.

The Anglo-French preliminary talks led naturally to consideration of the maximum naval strength Germany should be allowed, and in January a paper was circulated to the Cabinet setting out the British view. It stated that the first objects were a general settlement, the return of Germany to the League and the signing of an 'Armaments Convention', which might include 'Supervision', 'Budgetary publicity' and control of the trade in and manufacture of armaments. Limitation should if possible be on a qualitative basis, and the German note of 16th April 1934 could be taken as the starting point for the negotiations.[1] As to the size of the German navy, the British proposals of July 1934 have already been given, and the Germans had then expressed a preference for a fixed percentage of British strength. It was now suggested that the Germans should be asked what their intended building programme was for the years 1937–42 'without prejudice to the present validity of the naval clauses of the Treaty of Versailles'—which they must by this time have realised we would not strive to perpetuate.[2]

The talks between MacDonald, Baldwin, Simon and Eden on the British side and Pierre-Etienne Flandin and Pierre Laval, respectively Premier and Foreign Minister, on the French side began on 1st February, and it quickly became clear that the French wanted to link cancellation of Part V of the Versailles Treaty with the signature of an Air Pact, often referred to as an 'Air Locarno', whereby the western powers would agree to use their air forces to assist any victim of 'aerial aggression'—a euphemism for the bombing of cities.[3] Such a pact held no appeal to Hankey or to Ellington, the CAS. The former saw little difference between such a pact and 'a direct alliance with France', and exerted all his considerable skill to get it killed.[4] On 9th March Hitler made his attitude towards the Versailles Treaty abundantly clear by announcing the existence of the Air Force which it had prohibited.

During the long interval before invitations to the London Conference

[1] See Cmd. 4559. Misc. no. 5 (1934), *Further Memoranda on Disarmament Feb. 14th to April 17th 1934*, p. 18.

[2] CP. 23(35) of 25th Jan. 1935. Cab. 24/253. Copy in Cab. 29/146 (Anglo-French conversations of Jan.–Feb. 1935).

[3] See DBFP, nos. 259 and 263 (Annex) regarding the German views on the Air Pact.

[4] See Roskill, *Hankey*, III, pp. 155–64.

were actually issued important developments took place in the Anglo-German field. There can be little doubt that the Wilhelmstrasse (German Foreign Office) and Ministry of Marine had been watching the prolonged negotiations and the manœuvres of the chief powers with lively interest and, in all probability, with awareness of the fact that they might well be turned to German advantage; for the reasons why Britain was anxious to restore friendly relations with Japan and Italy can hardly have escaped their attention. As early as April 1934 the British Naval Attaché in Berlin gave the ambassador Sir Eric Phipps the gist of a talk with the Chief of Staff to Admiral Raeder, the C-in-C of the German Navy since 1928. The Attaché reported how, on a previous occasion, 'Admiral Raeder, had assured me that Germany had not the slightest intention of building a navy against England . . . or, for that matter, against France or anyone else in the world'; but, Raeder continued, 'Germany was entitled to security in the Baltic . . .', and Russia was rebuilding her navy.[1] The sincerity of Raeder's protestations must surely be called in doubt, because he certainly knew all about the secret U-boat building which had been going on for years in defiance of the Versailles Treaty, and the plans made for the rapid expansion of that arm.

In addition to the announcement by Hitler of the existence of the German Air Force the month of March 1935 saw the doubling by France of her period of National Service, and the German decree introducing conscription. The League Council did no more than pass a critical Resolution.[2] But in that same month Simon suggested to Hitler that talks should take place in London on Anglo-German naval questions, and the offer was accepted.[3] Because of the possible effects on Italy and France of taking such a step on the eve of the Stresa Conference action was postponed,[4] and not until 18th April was Phipps told to issue an invitation to start the talks on 1st May or as soon afterwards as was convenient to the German government.[5] The Foreign Secretary and First Lord circulated the proposed agenda on 3rd June,[6] and next day Admiral Little met Admiral K. G. Schuster, the leading German naval delegate informally.

The Germans were all sweet reasonableness during the preliminaries.

---

[1] Captain G. C. Muirhead-Gould to Sir Eric Phipps 9th April 1934. Circulated as NCM(35)6 of 7th May. Cab. 29/148.

[2] See *Gathorne-Hardy*, pp. 392–3.   [3] See DBFP, 2nd series, vol. XII, no. 651.

[4] *ibid.*, nos. 685, 686 and 708.   [5] *ibid.*, vol. XIII, no. 121.

[6] NCM(35)42. Cab. 29/150. DBFP, no. 282.

They supported qualitative limitation, a maximum for capital ships of 25,000 tons with 12-inch guns and of 22,000 tons for carriers; they were prepared to accept a 'holiday' in the building of 8-inch cruisers, and to limit 6-inch cruisers to 7,000 tons and destroyers to 1,850—all of which corresponded closely to the British *desiderata*. They even went so far as to support the British over abolition of the submarine. Schuster tabled the intended German building programme for 1934–36, which included the two *Scharnhorst* class battle-cruisers (allegedly of 26,000 tons with nine 11-inch guns but actually displacing about 32,000 tons); but he forecast construction of one, and perhaps two 35,000-ton 15-inch gun battleships if the French built their two *Richelieus*. Hitler was, reported Schuster, 'unilaterally determined' that the proposed 35% ratio should be achieved by 1942; but he gilded the pill by giving an assurance that his country would adhere to the 'cruiser rules' regarding submarine warfare on merchant shipping incorporated in Part IV of the 1930 London Treaty.[1] The Germans certainly baited their hook attractively, since the Admiralty was, as they surely must have realised, very hard pressed to meet current needs in the Mediterranean, and deeply conscious of the thunder clouds gathering on the Far Eastern horizon.

Compared to the tortoise-like progress of the preliminary negotiations for the main London Conference the rapidity of decision and of action shown by the Germans must have seemed a refreshing change to the British delegates. But it is now plain that they were in fact rushed into an agreement with somewhat unseemly haste, since at the very first formal meeting Ribbentrop took an extremely intransigent line, insisting that the British must 'recognise the 35% ratio as fixed and unalterable' if the conversations were to proceed.[2]

On 5th June the Naval Staff produced their reactions to the German proposals. They were favourable to the point of warmth, and ended with the remark that 'From the point of view of general limitation . . . it would be greatly to our advantage to recognise the decision of the German Government *lest the demand should be increased*' (italics supplied).[3] The italicised sentence certainly suggests that something like blackmail on the part of the Germans was in train—as indeed Ribbentrop had indicated in his opening speech, quoted above. Next day Simon told the Cabinet that the German proposals 'might stop un-

---

[1] Record of Little-Schuster talks dated 23rd June 1935. Adm. 116/3373.

[2] NC(G) 1st meeting of 4th June 1935. Cab. 29/150. DBFP, no. 289.

[3] NCM(35)50 of 5th June 1935. Cab. 29/149. DBFP, no. 305, Annex.

limited building and if not accepted immediately Hitler might increase his demands'.[1] On 6th the Ministerial Committee, which had not met for nearly seven months, was reconvened with Baldwin in the chair to consider the German proposals, and Simon again welcomed the offer of the 35% ratio as 'final and permanent'. Monsell also favoured accepting it; but Chatfield was more cautious and wanted it to be 'precisely stated what the 35% ratio implied', lest the German interpretation of it should differ from our own. Hoare was nervous about French reactions,[2] while Monsell described the issue whether an agreement with the Germans would constitute a breach of the Versailles Treaty as 'a purely academic question'. The decisions taken were to keep the naval talks separate from the proposed Air Pact, to tell the Germans we were prepared to continue discussions on the basis of the 35% ratio, and to inform the other naval powers about what was in train.[3]

By the time the fourth and fifth meetings with the German delegates took place on 6th and 7th June it was clear that the Air Ministry had no objections to the German proposals, and that the American and Japanese governments were also agreeable to them.[4] The Italians wanted the negotiations to be widened to include all aspects of naval limitation—which may well have been a delaying manoeuvre;[5] but the French reaction, about which more will be said shortly, was very different. The Ministerial Committee, however, had approved the broad lines which the British delegates should follow on the day the talks began, with the result that progress was very rapid. At the sixth Anglo-German meeting on 15th the draft of an agreement was tabled and discussed.[6]

Meanwhile Craigie had reported to the Ministerial Committee that he had told the Americans about the talks, and that they had 'noted with particular satisfaction' that the Germans accepted the principle of limiting tonnage by categories of warships (i.e. capital ships, carriers, etc.). The Americans were also prepared to accept that a British-German ratio should, once agreed, be regarded as final—no matter what building was put in hand by 'third powers'. They also accepted that, as Britain was more intimately concerned in the strength of European

---

[1] Cabinet 32(35) of 5th June 1935. Cab. 23/81.

[2] Hoare replaced Simon as Foreign Secretary on 7th June, Simon moving to the Home Office.

[3] 11th meeting of Ministerial Committee on 6th June 1935. Cab. 29/149.

[4] NCM(35) 51 and 52. Cab. 29/148.   [5] NCM(35)54 of 17th June 1935. *ibid.*

[6] NC(G) 6th meeting of 15th June 1935. *ibid.* Also DBFP, no. 337.

navies than themselves, the actual ratio decided on was 'primarily one for British decision'.[1]

Between 4th and 18th June seven Anglo-German meetings took place. The chief difficulty arose from the German desire to include a 'transfer' clause whereby if tonnage in one category of warship was under-used another category could be increased correspondingly. In the end a compromise was reached whereby the principle of transfer was accepted but 'the manner and degree' of its application would be left open for discussion between the two powers 'in the light of the Naval situation then existing'.[2] At the seventh meeting (18th June) Hoare told Ribbentrop that the British government not only accepted the ratio of 35% of her total tonnage for Germany (45% for submarines) but agreed that Germany should have the right to build up to 100% of British submarine tonnage 'in the event of a situation arising which, *in their opinion* [italics supplied] makes it necessary for Germany to avail herself of her right'.[3] The agreement was to come into force on 1st January 1937 or on such later date as might be applicable to the new naval treaty, and its duration was to be six years.[4] After the signature of the agreement a number of notes were exchanged in order to clarify points such as the precise meaning of the 35% ratio and the age at which capital ships could be replaced.[5] No difficulties arose during this process.

Three more formal and two informal meetings took place between 18th and 22nd June.[6] Their chief purpose was to settle the two powers' building programmes. On 18th Schuster said that if abolition of submarines was rejected at the main conference (as indeed was virtually certain) he preferred a qualitative limitation of 500–600 tons, and intended to give that type priority after the current programme of small 250-ton boats had been completed. Twelve of the latter had, he reported, already been laid down and twelve more would be added in 1935. Thus was the Admiralty, though they probably already knew it,

[1] NCM(35)51 of 12th June 1935. DBFP, no. 325 and FRUS, 1935, vol. I, pp. 164–5.

[2] NC(G) 4th and 5th meetings on 6th and 7th June 1935. Cab. 29/150. DBFP, nos. 311 and 318. Appendix to the latter gives the compromise on 'transfer' of tonnage.

[3] NC(G) 7th meeting. Cab. 29/150. DBFP, no. 348. Hoare was speaking to the terms agreed by the Ministerial Committee and the Admiralty. See NCM(35)50. DBFP, no. 305.

[4] Cmd. 4930 and 4953 of 18th June 1935.

[5] Adm. 116/3377. The notes are printed in Cmd. 4930.

[6] NC(G) 8th to 12th meetings. Cab. 29/150.

made aware officially of the fact that revival of the U-boat arm had already gone a long way.

At the meeting on 19th Ribbentrop reiterated a point he had stressed earlier—'that Germany intended to have her fleet as soon as possible'.[1] The Admiralty and Foreign Office certainly were worried about the pace of the German *surface ship* building programme, and their anxiety plainly arose from the possibility of German building leaving us inferior in home waters if a fleet had to be sent to the Far East. At the same meeting Schuster admitted that Germany had two 750-ton submarines under construction 'as an experiment'. These were of course the prototypes of the famous 'Type VII' class, of which over 700 were ultimately built in various models.[2] The threat to shipping far out in the broad oceans inherent in such boats should surely have been appreciated by the British Naval Staff; but the records contain no hint of any enquiry regarding the performance of these 'experimental' boats.

Next day, 20th, the Germans tabled their building programme up to 1942. It comprised six capital ships, 44,000 tons of carriers, eighteen cruisers, 37,500 tons of destroyers and 17,500 tons of submarines. Admiral Little produced the British programme for the same period, with which the reader is already familiar. He remarked, rather mildly, that the German proposals 'would come as a shock to other powers'. Little and Craigie asked, not very emphatically, for a slower rate of construction up to the agreed ratios; but their request had no perceptible effect.[3] The fact that so many important points were discussed *after* the signature of the agreement surely confirms the view that the Germans adopted rush tactics—and very successfully too.

In Parliament however unease had become evident, and Monsell found himself under fire. On 25th June, in answer to a question about German intentions regarding submarine warfare, he said that by acceding to Part IV of the London Treaty of 1930 'Germany has agreed never again to resort to what was known during the war as unrestricted warfare'. His confidence was no doubt based in part on the view frequently expressed by the Admiralty that the Asdic had reduced the submarine threat almost to extinction. Aneurin Bevan challenged the First Lord's confidence by asking whether he really

---

[1] NC(G) 9th meeting on 19th June 1935. *ibid.*

[2] The figure of 700 includes Types VII B to VII F. The later boats were much larger than the earlier ones and had heavier armaments and longer endurance.

[3] NC(G) 10th meeting on 20th June 1935. Cab. 29/150.

thought 'that, if a nation is on the verge of defeat and victory can be obtained by violating that convention it will stick to it?' To which Monsell riposted that such a view was 'a policy of despair'.[1]

In late June and early July the British delegates reported progress to the Ministerial Committee.[2] They claimed that, with only minor variations, they had followed the instructions given to them on 6th June; but in truth it was the Germans who had set the pace throughout the negotiations.

To turn to the French reactions to the Anglo-German agreement, on 21st June Eden, the Minister for League Affairs met Laval, now Premier as well as Foreign Minister and Piétri the Minister of Marine, in Paris.[3] Sir George Clerk, the British ambassador, reported that the talks were 'distinctly difficult', and that the Premier was 'clearly troubled'.[4] Eden however strongly defended our acceptance of the 35% ratio against the charge that it condoned a breach of both the Versailles Treaty and the 'Stresa front'. Though he admitted that 'from the strictly juridical point of view' the French case 'might be strong', he argued that practical considerations should take precedence, notably that Britain 'wished to make peace with Germany'—provided she would make peace 'with everyone else'. Laval finally accepted the ratio but refused to send experts to London to discuss details because 'it would give the appearance of acquiescence'.[5] The talks then turned to the proposed Air Pact and air limitation agreement between the five Locarno powers, which fall outside the scope of this history.[6]

In July Hoare sent the ambassador in Paris a detailed refutation of the French complaints against the naval agreement. Although it was

---

[1] Parl. Deb., Commons, vol. 303, cols. 948–50. Also in answer to a statement by Lloyd George, cols. 1867–8.

[2] NCM(35) 55 and 56 of 29th June and 4th July 1935. Cab. 29/150.

[3] Laval formed a Ministry on 6th June—at the second attempt. He continued as Foreign Minister and held both offices until 22nd Jan. 1936.

[4] Sir G. Clerk to FO nos. 128–129 of 21st June 1935. DBFP, no. 362. For Eden's account of this interview see Lord Avon, *The Eden Memoirs*, vol. I, *Facing the Dictators* (Cassell, 1962), pp. 230–2.

[5] As much of the astringency of the official French reply to the above telegrams is lost in translation the ending of it is quoted in the original language. It said '*Le Gouvernement de la République, aimerait savoir si le Gouvernement de Sa Majesté a mesuré comme lui ces conséquences inévitables de la revendication allemande*'. (The Government of the Republic would like to know whether His Majesty's Government has assessed, as they have done, the inevitable consequences of the German demand.) NCM(35)54 of 17th June 1935. Cab. 29/148.

[6] See DBFP nos. 363–9 and Roskill, *Hankey*, III, pp. 155–64 and 169–70.

well argued it still leaves an uncomfortable feeling that by our rapid acceptance of the German proposals we did not play entirely straight with the French.[1] Sir George Clerk certainly appears to have felt that way, since he told Vansittart that the agitation had died down and he was reluctant to revive it by passing on Hoare's self-exculpatory despatch.[2] Charles Corbin, the French ambassador in London, evidently agreed with Clerk, since he told Hoare that there was still 'an aftermath of disquiet' in his country—especially since the German building programme had become known.[3]

In the following month Captain Danckwerts, the Admiralty's Director of Plans, went to Paris to try and 'break the ice'.[4] He met Admiral Abrial, the French Deputy Chief of Naval Staff on 6th and 7th August, and at the first meeting Abrial expressed his country's 'great anxiety' over the rate of German building; but he accepted with good grace that the British could not give him details of the German programme for 1936–42 because they had been communicated to them in confidence. The French did not give vent to overt recriminations about the Anglo-German agreement, and the talks centred on the questions which might be discussed if they sent representatives to London in September to prepare for the main conference. They did however make it clear that if Italy built two 35,000-ton 15-inch battleships they would do the same.[5]

In September Craigie met Corbin who admitted that French hostility had died down but declared 'that Germany would violate the agreement as soon as it suited her'—a justifiably cynical view with which Craigie expressed disagreement.[6] Next month the Ministerial Committee was given a summary of the negotiations and prepared a report for the Cabinet. The principal recommendations were to adhere to qualitative limitation, to produce a formula for declaration of building programmes for the next six years, and to issue invitations to the Naval Conference to open on 2nd December. Monsell considered that, with a General Election in the offing, it would be 'politically ad-

---

[1] NCM(35)59 of 19th July 1935. Cab. 29/148. Hoare to Clerk 1356 of same date.

[2] Clerk to Vansittart 23rd July 1935. Adm. 116/3377.

[3] NCM(35)57 of 23rd July 1935. Cab. 29/148.

[4] 'Memo. on the Course of the Naval Negotiations', para. 4. Adm. 116/3374.

[5] NC(F), 6th, 7th and 8th meetings of 6th and 7th Aug. 1935. Cab. 29/149. DBFP, no. 461.

[6] Adm. 116/3374 and Cab. 29/149.

vantageous' to call the conference that year.[1] Approval of the committee's recommendations was quickly given by the Cabinet.[2]

Despite the confidence in German good faith shown by the British delegates during the London talks leading up to signature of the agreement doubts soon began to be expressed—by the Foreign Office rather than the Admiralty. In February 1936 a report reached the latter that keels for two aircraft carriers and a 10,000-ton cruiser had been laid in the Germania yard at Kiel; but the DNI declared that Admiral Raeder had quite recently 'categorically denied that Germany is violating' the recently signed agreement.[3] In May 1936 Monsell and Craigie met Ribbentrop, who was in London again, and objected to the German proposal to build five 10,000-ton cruisers—even though it did not breach the agreement. Ribbentrop claimed that the Franco-Soviet pact, signed on 2nd May, 'had altered the whole situation and made it essential for Germany to build up to her full treaty tonnage'; and he went on with a lengthy digression in justification of the re-occupation of the Rhineland. When asked by Craigie if Germany would 'eschew the use of force in future' he 'became evasive'; and on the cruiser question Craigie admitted that he 'made no perceptible impression', despite describing himself as 'one of the Englishmen whose confidence needs some restoring'.[4] Surprisingly the Naval Staff found the German attitude 'very satisfactory'; but Chatfield was more cautious and dubiously minuted 'all right so far'.[5] It is therefore clear that some doubts about the wisdom and permanence of the agreement were felt within a year of it being signed.

We must now retrace our steps to the summer of 1935 and continue with the preparations for the London Conference proper. At the end of July 1935 Hoare gave Bingham, who was about to return to USA, a copy of the 'Memorandum on the Course of the Naval Negotiations' which had been sent to the French and Italian governments.[6] The British view was that, while we adhered to our quantitative proposals, agreement on qualitative limits appeared to be 'of

---

[1] NCM(35)72 of 11th Oct. 1935. Cab. 29/148. 12th and last meeting of Ministerial Committee (Baldwin in chair) on 21st Oct. 1935. Cab. 29/147.

[2] Cabinet 48(35), Conclusion 9. Cab. 23/82.

[3] Adm. 116/3377.

[4] Adm. 116/3376.

[5] Record by Craigie of conversations of 29th May 1936, with minutes by Director of Plans and Chatfield. Adm. 116/3377.

[6] Hoare to Lindsay 29th July 1935. Cab. 29/149.

more immediate importance'.[1] The French and Italian replies were on
the whole sympathetic; but Atherton complained that we were trying
to secure a European agreement in order to form a united front on
proposals 'which must be unacceptable to the United States Government'. Craigie refuted this charge, and he and Atherton accordingly
met towards the end of September in an endeavour to clear up the mis-
understanding. The discussion centred on the size and gun calibre of
battleships, and it was again apparent that, although the Americans
might accept the 14-inch gun if other powers did so, they were very
unlikely to come down appreciably on the Washington Treaty figure
of 35,000 tons. Nor would they accept any reduction of the same
treaty's limits on cruisers (10,000 tons and 8-inch guns).[2] Next the
Japanese were consulted, but adhered stubbornly to the 'common
upper limit' and would not even agree to voluntary declaration of
building programmes unless their chief demand was conceded.[3]
Interchanges also took place on whether the conference should take
place in 1935, and if so where. In July the Foreign Office and Admiralty
put forward the arguments for holding it, and MacDonald minuted 'I
favour the attempt'—because he wanted the onus of rejection to be
placed on others.[4] In America the General Board was prepared to
agree to advance notification of building programmes, but in all other
respects they stood fast on the principle to 'maintain the [Washington
and London] Treaties'.[5] Swanson was totally opposed to calling a
conference which would be 'purely *pro forma* in character', and agreed
with the President that advance notification of building was 'the
minimum requirement'.[6]

---

[1] The qualitative limitations which at this stage the British government believed
likely to prove acceptable were:
Capital ships 25,000 tons and 12-inch guns.
Aircraft carriers 22,000 tons and 6.1-inch guns
Heavy cruisers 10,000 tons and 8-inch guns (but we hoped no more would be built)
Light cruisers 7,600 tons and 6.1-inch guns
Destroyers 1,850 tons and 5.1-inch guns
Submarines 2,000 tons and 5.1-inch guns
NCM(35)61 of 30th July 1935. Cab. 29/149.

[2] These discussions are summarised in the 'Memorandum on the Course of Naval
Negotiations' of 22nd Oct. 1935, paras. 7–11. Adm. 116/3374.

[3] *ibid.*, paras. 12–15.

[4] Memo. of 18th July 1935. Circulated as NCM(35)58 of 1st Aug. with minute by
MacDonald. Adm. 116/3332. DBFP, no. 415.

[5] GB. 438–1, serial 1693 of 1st Aug. 1935.

[6] Swanson to FDR 5th Aug. 1935. Roosevelt papers, PSF, Dept. Corresp., Box 28.

Though the prospect of achieving any appreciable reduction of naval armaments had become very dim indeed, on 23rd October the Cabinet decided to go ahead and issue invitations. They were prepared to accept the 35,000-ton 14-inch battleship and the other qualitative limitations set out above 'if found to be the best obtainable'; they would propose 'limiting construction by means of unilateral declarations for six years'; they accepted that no quantitative limitation was likely, and wanted the responsibility for failing to achieve it to be placed firmly where it belonged—namely on Japan, Italy and France. Finally they proposed that continuation of the Washington 'non-fortification' clause should be left for 'separate treatment between the interested powers'. Invitations were to be sent for the opening of the conference on 2nd December, soon amended to 5th.[1]

In mid-November the Dominion representatives, who had not been brought into the conversations or put into the picture regarding their progress—except informally—for nearly a year, were called to a meeting. Craigie then outlined the result of the preliminary talks with the French, Italians and Japanese, but made no mention of the Anglo-German agreement, about which the Dominions had not in fact been consulted. Chatfield said that, in the matter of qualitative limitation of battleships and cruisers the USA had been 'the culprit'; while the question of treating the Dominion Navies separately from the Royal Navy had, according to Craigie, caused 'a terrific outburst' in USA. Perhaps the most sensible comment came from S. M. Bruce of Australia, who remarked that he could not 'see any successful outcome'.[2] The next steps were to create the necessary organisation to run the conference, and to draft the Prime Minister's opening speech.[3] It should be remarked that Hankey, who had acted as Secretary-General of almost every international conference since 1918, declined to take any active part in this one. Almost certainly the reasons were, firstly that he was very much involved in the British rearmament programme, and secondly that, like Bruce, he saw little likelihood of anything useful being achieved.

In America Roosevelt had some trouble with Bingham, who wanted to represent his country at the conference; but the Navy Department preferred Norman Davis as chief delegate, and the President therefore sent his ambassador a tactful letter explaining why he had

[1] Conclusions to memo. of 22nd Oct. 1935. Adm. 116/3374.
[2] NC(D) 3rd meeting on 13th Nov. 1935. Cab. 29/151.
[3] Minutes of meeting in FO on 4th Nov. 1935. Adm. 116/3374.

to take a back seat.[1] It is interesting to find that Harold Laski sent to Roosevelt through his principal private secretary a note urging that the American delegates should 'come with an agreed and dramatic programme for drastic reduction', in order, so he hoped, to 'rally British opinion and force the government on to the side of disarmament'.[2] Thus did the Left-Wing pacifist 'intellectuals' help to prepare their country to face the dictators—despite recent events in China, Abyssinia and the Rhineland. What they did do, or helped to do, was to slow the pace of rearmament by making the government cautious over coming into the open and declaring that, if the worst came to the worst, the people must be prepared to fight for their freedom.

While the Anglo-German negotiations, and the repercussions produced by the agreement, were demanding most of the attention of the Admiralty and Foreign Office, in Washington Swanson asked the General Board for a new study to be made of the policy to be adopted when conversations were renewed or the conference was called.[3] The General Board replied that the most important development had been Japan's announcement of her intention to terminate the Washington Treaty, her claim for a common upper limit and her proposal to abolish 'offensive weapons'. The Board found 'no basis for belief that a conference in 1935 will accept a treaty along the broad lines of the Washington and London treaties'; but they believed that a conference would none the less be convened, and that the British would try to secure both agreement on qualitative limitation and the 'practical continuance' of the treaty system 'through announced building programmes'—which was an accurate summary of British intentions.[4] The Board's reply continued with an analysis of British and Japanese aims and purposes. As regards the British demand for 70 cruisers they admitted that it had 'a more logical foundation' than the Japanese claim to a 50% increase in submarine tonnage; but they considered that the two proposals 'can hardly be accorded different treatment', and proposed that the USA should be granted 'compensating increases' in carriers, heavy cruisers and destroyers. They put forward a complicated formula, reminiscent of the notorious 'yardstick' of the 1930 conference,[5] whereby those increases might be calculated (e.g. that 'three tons of destoyers is equivalent to one ton of submarines'), and

---

[1] Roosevelt to Bingham 23rd Nov. 1935. Roosevelt papers, Official File 18, Box 2A
[2] Laski to Miss Le Hand 5th Nov. 1935. Roosevelt papers, Official File 18.
[3] Swanson to General Board 9th Aug. 1935. USN Operational Archives.
[4] GB. 438-1, serial 1696 of 4th Oct. 1935.   [5] See pp. 39-46 and 62-3.

rules to govern the transfer of tonnage between different categories—excluding capital ships. Regarding future ships of that class the General Board adhered strongly to its previously expressed view[1] that any reduction of tonnage or of characteristics *'made without reference to all other elements* of naval power' would be *'an irrecoverable step backward in national security'* (italics in original). This paper and its predecessor of October 1934 certainly outlined with clarity the policy which the more conservative elements in the Navy Department wished to see adopted; but it is noteworthy that in the second of them account seems to have been taken of the excellent understanding reached between the British and American delegates in London, and it contains no hint of the earlier rivalry and anglophobia, such as Admiral Schofield had recently given vent to.

In November 1935 President Roosevelt called the American delegates to the White House to discuss their instructions for the conference. Davis's view was that a quantitative agreement had been made extremely unlikely by Japan's demand for parity. He therefore sought permission to join with the British in seeking a limited agreement 'which will prevent a naval race' and defeat an effort 'to alter the *status quo*' until the times were more propitious.[2] Though Roosevelt urged that the search for a quantitative agreement should continue, and Davis agreed to make the attempt, the President accepted that, if the Japanese withdrew from the conference, the Americans should try and negotiate a tripartite qualitative agreement. It should however include an 'escape clause' designed to allow a signatory to meet 'undue construction by a non-contracting party'.[3] In effect therefore Roosevelt came round to the British compromise proposal—despite the long-standing insistence of the General Board and of the State Department on maintenance of the Washington ratio system.

At about the same time the Japanese were also considering the instructions to be given to their delegates; but the big navy interests were now in complete control and insisted that there was to be no settlement with the USA on any basis except parity. The delegates were however given latitude to vary the level of the common upper limit with some countries; and the hope evidently was that the negotiations would be so conducted as to produce a rift between Britain and the USA.[4]

On 8th November the British and American delegates met informally in London to confirm their joint opposition to the common upper

[1] See GB. 438–1, serial 1640 of 1st Oct. 1934, pp. 286 and 293–5 above.
[2] FRUS, 1935, I, pp. 144–9.   [3] *Pelz*, p. 159.   [4] *ibid.*

limit. They also agreed that neither qualitative restrictions nor the British claim to possess more cruisers should be allowed to breach their united front. The first Plenary Session of the eleven nations taking part was held at the Foreign Office next day,[1] and Baldwin, now Prime Minister, gave warning that 'the evolution of new types and sizes [of warship] . . . [is] the most expensive and dangerous of all types of naval competition'.[2] But Admiral Osami Nagano, the Japanese Navy Minister and chief delegate, riposted with the old claim for the common upper limit in order 'to ensure mutual security'. The main work of the conference was then delegated to a First Committee of the whole conference, which met sixteen times between 10th December 1935 and 21st March 1936.[3]

At the next three meetings of that body Admiral Nagano developed the Japanese proposals fully, arguing for a great reduction in tonnage by the abolition of aircraft carriers and battleships as 'offensive weapons' and a low common upper limit which would be applicable only to the USA, Britain and Japan. The other European powers should, Nagano proposed, make their own settlement within that limit. Qualitative limitations would, he insisted, not be entertained without a quantitative agreement. In their replies the British and Americans repeated the arguments used in the preliminary negotiations. Monsell stressed with growing impatience the absurdity of a proposal whereby the three major naval powers would be allowed only small fleets while the lesser powers were to be allowed to build up to parity with them; and Chatfield argued that the low common upper limit would produce an Anglo-Japanese ratio of 2:2, but as Britain was a Pacific as well as a European power it should be 4:2.[4] The Italian and French delegates protested against their exclusion from the common upper limit, and joined with the British in seeking continuation of qualitative limitations. Within a few days the conference had plainly reached a deadlock,

---

[1] These were USA, Britain, France, Italy, Japan, Australia, Canada, New Zealand, Irish Free State, South Africa and India.

[2] LNC(35). Stenographic notes of Plenary Sessions. Cab. 29/152.

[3] Full records of the Plenary Sessions and First Committee meetings are in *Documents of the London Naval Conference December 1935–March 1936* (HMSO, 1936).

[4] First and second British-Japanese meetings on 13th and 16th Dec. 1935. The third meeting was between the British and American delegates. LNC(35) (UK 1, 2 and 3). DBFP 580, 583 and 586. Also in Adm. 116/3312. The British and Japanese delegates also met on 5th Dec. and the British and Americans on 8th; but no British record of those meetings exists in the Foreign Office or Admiralty archives. On the meeting of 8th Dec. see FRUS, 1935. vol. 1, pp. 156–8.

and although Craigie and Chatfield continued to show unshakable patience that of Monsell and Davis was near breaking point. Nor did informal meetings between the British and Japanese achieve any progress towards a compromise, since Nagano merely reiterated that 'the realisation of parity is basic to our demands', while Davis gave warning that if the Japanese tried to disturb the present relative strength 'the USA and Great Britain will outbuild her whatever she does'. Davis and Standley once again flatly rejected the Japanese demand for parity.

To avoid, or at least postpone a final confrontation on the parity issue the British next brought out the compromise plan for voluntary limitation of construction over a period and notification of building programmes. The Americans and French supported the proposal, but Nagano would have none of it. On 19th and 20th December he resurrected the proposal made by Yamamoto during the preliminaries —that Japan would accept exchange of building programmes if granted parity. He claimed that the British compromise would merely continue the ratio system in a disguised form—in which there was in fact a good deal of truth.

If Davis and Standley had entertained any doubts about a renewal of some form of Anglo-Japanese understanding before they left Washington they were evidently quickly eliminated; for while the above negotiations were in progress Davis telegraphed to the President that 'the pro-Japanese group here, who were routed last year, have been unable to mobilise their forces again', and that 'British co-operation has been 100%'.[1]

The Commonwealth countries were now kept informed regarding all aspects of the negotiations, and between 11th December 1935 and 6th March 1936 they met eight times with the British delegates.[2] At the second meeting they were told that the Japanese 'recognised the British Empire's need for special naval strength', and had even proposed a higher upper limit for Britain and Japan than for the USA. Such suggestions were probably part of the Japanese plan to divide the British from the Americans; but the bait was not taken. A recess took place over Christmas and discussions were renewed on 6th January.

Eden, who had replaced Hoare at the Foreign Office on 23rd December, had now taken over as President of the conference. That same day the British ambassador in Tokyo telegraphed home con-

[1] Davis to FDR 10th Dec. 1936. Roosevelt papers, PSF, Box 56, folder 2.
[2] LNC(35)(BC) series. Cab. 29/158 and Adm. 116/3313.

firming what the British delegates very well knew—that the Japanese navy 'are absolutely determined to have a free hand and will accept no compromise to their own proposal of [a] Common Upper Limit'.[1] When the fourth meeting of the Commonwealth delegates took place on 10th Monsell told them that a critical stage had been reached because the Japanese had also refused to discuss exchange of information about programmes unless the common upper limit was conceded.[2] Actually Nagano had announced the intention of the Japanese to withdraw if their conditions were not accepted at a meeting presided over by Eden on the previous day; and the Foreign Secretary's attempt to reduce the temperature did not appear to have succeeded.[3] On 13th January, Nagano received instructions to withdraw from the conference if the Japanese claim was not met, and after careful deliberation by the other delegates regarding the method by which the break should come with the least damage it was decided to discuss and reject the proposal for a common upper limit.[4] The crucial debate took place on 15th, and when Nagano received no support from any quarter he acted according to his instructions. All the other delegations were willing to continue the conference, and the Japanese left behind two 'observers' who would be able to report on its proceedings. Negotiations now continued steadily, interrupted only by the death of King George V on 20th January.

The Japanese withdrawal simplified some of the issues on which a settlement might be based, notably agreement on qualitative limitation and on the advance notification of building programmes; but new, and in some cases unexpected difficulties soon arose.

On 17th January the First Committee set up a Technical Sub-Committee under Craigie's chairmanship to work out a scheme in accordance with the view 'that exchange of information is an essential feature of any agreement for limitation of armaments, and advance notification most desirable'.[5] On the last day of January a Sub-Committee on Qualitative Limitation was set up under Chatfield 'to prepare a report on the definitions of the various categories of vessels, the standard displacement of naval combatant vessels, the age limits to be applied to such vessels and the Qualitative Limitations to be included

[1] Sir R. Clive to Eden 6th Jan. 1936. DBFP, no. 598. Adm. 116/3312.
[2] LNC(35)(BC) 4th meeting on 10th Jan. 1936. Cab. 29/158.
[3] Meeting of 9th Jan. 1936. Adm. 116/3312.
[4] LNC(35)(UK)13 of 14th Jan. 1936. Cab. 39/157. DBFP, no. 617.
[5] LNC(35)AN series. Cab. 29/156.

in the Treaty'.[1] At the first meeting of the Craigie Committee the Italians tabled a proposal that programmes should be announced yearly within four months of 1st January, and that at least four months should elapse before keels were laid. Once declared a programme was not to be exceeded in any category within the period of the programme. This came very near to the British compromise proposal put forward earlier, which had been rejected by the Japanese. It was included in the Craigie Committee's report with only minor alterations, was adopted by the First Committee, and was ultimately included in the Treaty (Part III).[2]

The Chatfield committee had a more difficult task, since the Americans had become reluctant to hold to the qualitative limitations which had been agreed during the preliminary conversations. The principal points at issue were the reduction of capital ships' guns from 16-inch to 14-inch, the construction of no more 'Washington Treaty' cruisers, and limitation of future 6-inch cruisers to 8,000 tons. In the end a complicated compromise was reached whereby the 8,000-ton limitation was accepted but the USA was allowed, under certain circumstances, to start building 10,000-ton 8-inch ships again.[3] This satisfied the British because they could reach the total of 60 under-age cruisers required much more economically with 8,000-ton than with 10,000-ton ships.

Strong but unsuccessful efforts were made by the European powers in late January and early February to persuade the Americans to improve on the qualitative limits of 35,000 tons and 14-inch guns for battleships. But the Americans only accepted the 14-inch limitation subject to a proviso that it was also accepted by the other signatories of the Washington Treaty *before* the new naval treaty came into force;[4] and that of course was most unlikely with regard to Japan. It is on this insistence on the big gun battleship that the hand of the General Board is, perhaps, most clearly to be detected; but it should be mentioned that the Admiralty did not believe that a satisfactory 16-inch gun ship could be built on 35,000 tons displacement, and considered that if that calibre of gun had to be accepted the qualitative limit should be raised to 40,000 tons.

As regards aircraft carriers, no difficulty was experienced in getting

[1] LNC(35)QL series. Cab. 29/153.   [2] Cmd. 5136.

[3] The compromise is given in NCM(35)86 of 19th May 1936, para. 9. Cab. 29/148 and Adm. 116/3376.

[4] LNC(35)(UK)21 of 23rd Jan. 1936. DBFP, no. 632.

a reduction from 27,000 to 23,000 tons agreed. But the British proposal to abolish submarines was flatly, if expectedly, rejected by the French; so the only limitation remained at the 1930 treaty figure of 2,000 tons. On the other hand a 'non-construction zone' for surface vessels between 8,000 and 17,000 tons was agreed; and although that did not go as far as the original British proposal (8,000 to 22,000 tons) it did prevent advantage being taken of the cruiser limitations to build small battleships. As the British had always viewed the commerce-raiding capabilities of the German 'pocket battleships' with grave concern this agreement must have been a source of satisfaction to them.

After the Japanese withdrawal the British put out feelers regarding the inclusion of Germany, the USSR and other nations in the final phase of the conference with a view to obtaining their acceptance of the agreed limitations. But the French government objected to the inclusion of the USSR on the grounds that it would antagonise Japan, and flatly refused to send representatives to sit at the same table as the Germans because it would be tantamount to condoning a German infringement of the Versailles Treaty, and would prejudice her rights relating to land and air armaments. The change of front by the French provoked the British delegation into remarking 'We are, in fact, suddenly faced with a revival of the traditional French contention about the interdependence of all armaments'.[1] If there was some logic in that contention it was irrelevant to the accomplishment of the purpose of the conference, which was and always had been to reach a *naval* limitation agreement. The most that could be achieved was to send the draft of the treaty to the Germans and await an opportunity to open bilateral conversations with the USSR.[2]

If the French change of front was abrupt, and perhaps influenced by residual resentment over the Anglo-German naval agreement and by the internal political situation, the Italian change of front in mid-February was worse; since whereas a compromise was reached to enable the French to sign the treaty the Italians refused altogether to sign. The reason given was that they were dissatisfied with the capital ship limitations and the non-construction zone; but there are several statements in the British records that she would not sign while League sanctions were still—theoretically—in force against her; and they were

[1] NC(M)84 of 21st Feb. 1936, para. 12. Cab. 29/157.
[2] Meeting of UK delegates on 11th Feb. 1936. LNC(35)(UK)31, annex 1. DBFP, no. 646.

not cancelled until 15th July.[1] Then came a final flurry with the Americans, who suddenly became nervous about the possibility that, in the absence of any quantitative limitation, the British would go back on the earlier agreement on 'parity', as provided in the Washington and London treaties. This dangerous rumour, probably started by the big navy and anti-British lobbies, had to be scotched quickly by an exchange of letters between Davis and Eden on 24th and 25th March.[2] Finally the Irish Free State and South Africa declined to sign the treaty on the grounds that they were not naval powers and so not interested in its provisions. One wonders why they had ever agreed to take part in the conference.

On 10th February Cordell Hull wrote to Roosevelt outlining the main points on which agreement had been reached in London.[3] The draft treaty reached Washington about the middle of March, and on 19th the State Department sent it to the President with a covering note saying that they considered it acceptable. Roosevelt only made one suggestion—that the right to make up any deficiencies which might arise between signature and ratification should be included.[4] The draft was circulated in London on 20th March, and the Admiralty had no criticisms or suggestions to offer.[5]

The second and final Plenary Session took place on 25th March 1936, and the treaty was signed that day at St. James's Palace by Britain, the USA, France, Canada, Australia, New Zealand and India. Accession to it by Japan and Italy was left open, and in April 1938 the latter announced her intention to do so.[6] Between 1936 and 1938 prolonged correspondence took place with the Scandinavian countries, and Finland, Denmark, Norway and Sweden finally came into the fold at the end of 1938. In July and August 1936 negotiations took place between Britain and the USSR for a bilateral agreement whereby the latter would accede to the treaty.[7] The Soviets accepted an 8,000-ton

---

[1] Director of Plans minute of 14th July 1936, Craigie-Drummond exchange of that month and Drummond to FO no. 695 of 17th Nov. 1936. Adm. 116/3376. The Italian instrument of accession reached the Foreign Office on 2nd Dec. 1938.

[2] Printed as annex I and II of NCM(35)86. Cab. 29/148. DBFP, nos. 716 and 717.

[3] Hull to FDR. Roosevelt papers, Official File 18, Box 3.

[4] Same to same, 19th March 1936. *ibid.*

[5] LNC(35)11. Copy in Adm. 116/3376.   [6] Adm. 116/3950.

[7] The Admiralty's papers on these negotiations are in Adm. 116/3369 and 4053. Progress in the negotiations can most easily be followed in the 'Statements by the First Lord on the Navy Estimates' for 1937, 1938 and 1939, Cmd. 5385, 5680 and 5952, under the sections headed 'Naval Treaties'.

limit for cruisers, of which they proposed to build seven; and they gave notice of their intentions to lay down two battleships with 15-inch or 16-inch guns before 1943. These first stirrings of Russia's re-entry into the field of naval power caused apprehensions in London and Washington. The General Board expressed strong views against such a development, and was suspicious of the motives of the British in encouraging Soviet accession to the treaty.[1]

In October 1936 the Naval Staff considered whether to advise ratification of the treaty, and concluded unenthusiastically that on the whole they favoured doing so.[2] It was ratified by France in June and by the USA in October 1936 and actually came into force on 29th July 1937.[3]

As regards the prohibition of unrestricted submarine warfare against merchant ships, which had always been one of the Admiralty's principal *desiderata*, shortly before the expiration of the 1930 London Treaty at the end of 1936 the clauses embodied in that treaty were made the subject of a special Protocol, which was ratified by Britain, the USA, Japan, France and Italy.[4] Germany and the USSR acceded to the Protocol in 1936, and by the time war broke out in 1939 over 40 states, including all the chief maritime powers, had either ratified the Protocol or acceded to it. The value of those signatures may be regarded as justification for cynicism about attempts to 'humanise' war.

It is difficult for the historian who has waded through the mountain of paper accumulated in course of the negotiations described in this chapter not to come to the conclusion that the whole proceedings were a colossal waste of time and effort, since the treaty finally signed did not in fact have any significant success in achieving the naval limitation for which the conference was convened. But one has to remember that the treaties of 1922 and 1930 made it mandatory to create a new instrument by the end of 1936—if a free-for-all building race was to be avoided; and the fact that such a race did in fact ensue does not surely render invalidate the reasons for calling the conference. There are, however, several items which can reasonably be placed on the credit side of the scales to counterbalance the failures—such as the rejection of any quantitative agreement or reduction of the displacement of battleships. First among the credit items must surely be placed the improvement in Anglo-American relations; and for that accomplishment the credit must go chiefly to Norman Davis and Admiral Standley on the

---

[1] GB. 438-1, serial 1728 of 25th Aug. 1936.
[2] Minute by Director of Plans of 30th Oct. 1936. Adm. 116/3332.
[3] League of Nations document 180 of 9th Oct. 1937.   [4] Cmd. 5302.

American side and to Craigie and Chatfield on the British side. Indeed the most outstanding feature of the negotiations is perhaps the inexhaustible patience and skill in negotiation of Craigie and Chatfield. Moreover if the Japanese withdrawal augured ill for the future peace of the world, and the Anglo-German agreement was entered into too hastily and in too trustworthy a spirit, excessive trust is surely preferable to suspicion which, even with a Hitler, might have proved unjustified. Moreover the treaty did at least leave it open to the two great democracies to rearm if the world situation continued to deteriorate or our trust in German intentions proved misplaced; and for that benefit we should be thankful. From the British Navy's point of view the outstanding figure was without doubt Chatfield; and while it is true to say that he was supported by the strongest Board of Admiralty since the Bridgeman-Beatty combination of the 1920s, one cannot but marvel at the stamina he displayed and the way he was able, day after day, to stand the strain of conducting intricate negotiations on several different fronts, and at the same time prepare for a great and rapid expansion of his service, for the production of a vast amount of new material, and also keep a watchful eye on the morale and spirit of its officers and men. The next chapters will therefore be devoted to the harvesting of the first fruits of his labours.

CHAPTER XI

The Beginning of Rearmament

1936-1937

◆

THE SIGNATURE of the London Treaty on 25th March 1936 marked a watershed in the naval policy of the democratic nations, since the protracted negotiations and the withdrawal of Japan had shown beyond doubt that the era of naval limitation by agreement, initiated at Washington in 1921–22 had come to an end.

We have already seen how the British 1936 building programme was initially received with a very cold douche by the Chancellor, and that the Prime Minister supported him. None the less the estimates for 1936–37, together with the three supplementary estimates presented to Parliament later, produced a final total of £81.3 millions, which was an increase of over £20 millions on the previous year and enabled a start to be made on what was by far the biggest building programme since 1918.[1] The ships were to be laid down at various dates between May 1936 and March 1937, and the whole programme completed by 1940.[2] Thus in the final outcome the Admiralty virtually won that battle.

In order to expedite execution of the programme a Treasury-Inter Service committee was set up in March to establish which of the deficiencies listed by the DRC in its final report were the most urgent, and to authorise departure from the normal procedure for placing

[1] Adm. 116/3402 contains details of the 1936–37 Estimates and correspondence concerning them.

[2] Adm. 116/3394. The programme originally put forward was considerably changed before the 1st and 2nd Supplementary Estimates were presented on 28th April and 7th July 1936. See pp. 278–9 for its final form.

contracts in order to make them good. Its creation was certainly a significant departure from the time honoured principle of strict Treasury control over all expenditure.[1] At the end of that year the Treasury told the Admiralty that authority was to be sought from Parliament to borrow £400 millions for defence expenditure over the five years ending in March 1942, that £80 millions was to be asked for in the 1937 Financial Year, and that the Navy and Army were each to get £27 millions and the RAF £26 millions out of that sum. This foreknowledge was obviously a great help to the departments in framing their estimates for the next year.[2] Early in 1937 Chatfield, in commenting on the draft of the first Defence Loans Act, told Hoare the First Lord, that the new arrangements would 'facilitate enormously the provision of adequate money for a speedy building up of the fleet'.[3]

A few days later, when he was considering the presentation of the 1937 estimates, Chatfield complained that except for Craigie no one in the Foreign Office had taken much interest lately in the recently achieved naval agreements. 'I think the Anglo-German Treaty', he wrote, 'is of the greatest benefit not only from a military standpoint but from a political and international one'. Any reference in speeches 'to the great moral and military value of this remarkable agreement, unique in world history, would have I believe, a most valuable effect generally';[4] all of which shows that his confidence in German good faith was not yet shaken—as Craigie's undoubtedly had been.

At the time when preparation of the 1937 estimates was occupying much of the attention of the Board of Admiralty British foreign policy was undergoing a period of heart-searching, provoked in part by a paper entitled 'The World Situation—British Rearmament' circulated by Vansittart. Hankey and Chatfield both saw it in draft form, and both of them sent Vansittart their reactions.[5] As Chatfield's influence in the CID, the COS Committee and the Admiralty was so strong, and unquestionably permeated from those bodies both to individual Ministers and to the Cabinet collectively, it will be of interest to record the salient features of the carefully considered answer he sent to

[1] Admy. Office Memo. 15 of 14th March and Secret Office Memo. C of 22nd April 1936. Adm. 1/9042–126/36.

[2] Adm. 116/3596. The First Defence Loans Act did not actually receive Royal Assent until 19th March 1937. 1 Edw. 8 and 1 Geo. 6. ch. 13.

[3] Chatfield to Hoare 4th Jan. 1937. Adm. 167/97.

[4] Memo. of 8th Jan. 1937. Adm. 116/3596.

[5] The paper was dated 21st Dec. 1936. For Hankey's views on it see Roskill, *Hankey*, III, pp. 237–8.

Vansittart. 'We all agree—we want peace', he wrote; 'But . . . we do not want a false peace; we do not want to buy off the aggressors if it means that we are only to fall later on to their increased power'. He agreed with Hankey that France was 'an unreliable ally'; and because Britain now had 'no friend we can trust', he continued, 'we have to stand more or less alone and unsupported in both hemispheres'. War simultaneously in the east and west would in his view be fatal; and therefore 'it must not happen'. Hence, he concluded, it was essential 'to make an agreement in one area or the other' which would give us greater security during the dangerous period when we were rearming. 'An understanding with Japan' was therefore in his view 'the first essential'—though he admitted that it would be difficult to attain. He urged that it would be 'wrong and dangerous' to allow ourselves to be drawn into a continental war against Germany, and wanted her to be given 'reasonable satisfaction . . . *as part of a general settlement*' (his italics) in substitution for the penal clauses of the Versailles Treaty. Such an agreement would include restoration of 'some of the oversea territories that were taken away from her'—a proposal to which Hankey was totally opposed. Finally Chatfield wanted to 'rid ourselves of any League responsibilities which might involve us in war'.[1] There is plenty of evidence in the Admiralty's and COS papers that such views were widely held in those quarters at the time when our rearmament had only just begun.

To return to the 1937 estimates, the Board began to consider them, as was usual, in the autumn of the previous year. To man the ships to be built under the new programme some 11,000 more officers and men would be needed each year until 1940, and as a start the Board therefore decided to ask for Vote A (personnel) to be increased to 106,577 in 1937–38 as compared with 99,755 in the previous year.[2] As regards money, the DRC had forecast a figure of £89 millions, but Hoare pointed out to Chamberlain that the changes made in the building programme and the increase of the Fleet Air Arm forced him to ask for nearly £19 millions more for 1937–38.[3] This seems to have been a bad guess, since only a few days later the Board revised its figures downwards;[4] nor did the Board demur seriously to a request from the

[1] Chatfield to Vansittart 5th Jan. 1937. Chatfield papers, CHT/6/2.
[2] Board Minute 3426 of 14th Dec. 1936. Adm. 167/94.
[3] Hoare to Chamberlain 12th Jan. 1937. Adm. 167/97.
[4] Board Minute 3435 of 14th Jan. 1937 reduced the Sketch Estimates by over £1 million. Adm. 167/96.

Chancellor to cut the estimates by a further £2 millions and to eliminate several ships from the 1937 building programme.[1] The 1937 estimates were finally circulated by Hoare on 26th February. They totalled just over £105 millions, including the £27 millions from the Consolidated Fund under the Loans Act already mentioned.[2] The debate on them took place on 11th March and Hoare's defence of the battleship building programme only came under somewhat desultory fire from A. V. Alexander, the former Labour First Lord.[3] Indeed Churchill, who followed Alexander at the despatch box, admitted that his opponent's speech had left him 'in a very considerable state of mystification as to what is his point of view'. Perhaps the most important point made by Churchill was his insistence that 'the Fleet must have absolute control in all its integrity of all the aeroplanes . . . which start from ships of war or aircraft carriers'. Though Churchill was critical of the government for having wasted a whole year over the promised inquiry into the control of naval aviation, and challenged the extreme proponents of air power over the exaggerated claims made for the effectiveness of bombing, his general tone was of support for all that the Admiralty was doing or trying to do.[4] The opposition did not seriously challenge the need for the large sum of money asked for, but concentrated instead on improvement of the welfare organisation under the new system introduced in 1932, on the disadvantages of the thirteen-year-old cadet entry to Dartmouth, and on the need to widen the class from which the navy drew its potential officers.[5] Lord Stanley, the Parliamentary Secretary of the Admiralty, who wound up the debate for the government, had no difficulty in disposing of such criticisms of his department as had been made, and the government's motion was approved by a large majority.

It is relevant to mention here that the British Admiralty was by no means the only naval authority to obtain a large increase of money at this time. A comparison of all the major powers' expenditure in 1935–36 with that of 1937–38 produces the following results:—

1. *Britain.* Increase from £60 to £105 millions (including grant from Consolidated Fund under 1937 Defence Loans Act). Percentage increase 70.

2. *USA.* Increase from $477 to $556 millions (including 'Emergency Appropriation' but excluding funds appropriated for New Deal

---

[1] Board Minutes 3444 and 3449 of 4th and 12th Feb. 1937. *ibid.*

[2] Cmd. 5385.   [3] Parl. Deb., Commons, vol. 321, cols. 1367–1483.

[4] *ibid.*, cols. 1307–1407.   [5] *ibid.*, cols. 1424–1440.

agencies). Sterling equivalents approximately £97.9 to £114.2 millions. Percentage increase 16.6.

3. *France.* 2,903 to 3,395 million Francs. Sterling equivalents approximately £23.4 to £27.4 millions. Percentage increase 16.9.

4. *Italy.* 1,265 to 1,793 million Lire. Sterling equivalents approximately £13.5 to £19.1 millions. Percentage increase 41.7.

5. *Germany.* 695.1 to 1,478 million Rentenmarks. Sterling equivalents approximately £57 to £121 millions. Percentage increase 112.6.

6. *Japan*, for whom expenditure on new construction only is available, 72,983 to 206,342 million Yen. Sterling equivalents approximately £43.2 to £122.1 millions. Percentage increase 182.7.

It is therefore plain that by 1937–38 the three dictatorships were increasing their naval armaments far faster than the democracies.[1]

Having got the 1937–38 estimates out of the way, in April 1937 the Board of Admiralty began to consider the draft of a paper setting out what came to be known as the 'New Standard of Naval Strength'. It was planned to meet the broad strategic requirements stated by the DRC and accepted in principle by the Ministerial Committee which took its final report – namely that we should be able to send a strong enough fleet to the Far East to provide 'cover' against the Japanese Fleet, and at the same time retain enough forces in home waters 'to prevent the strongest European Naval Power from obtaining control of our vital home terminal areas'.[2] In May the Permanent Secretary of the Admiralty had an informal talk with Treasury officials about the financial implications of this proposal. Sir Archibald Carter reported that, not surprisingly, they had shown 'considerable distress at the size of the figures revealed', and that the Chancellor would probably be unwilling 'to take even a provisional decision before the [1937] Imperial

---

[1] The sources for these figures are:
Britain and USA. See Appendices D and E.
France. From *Flottes de Combat* (Paris). Yearly figures.
Italy. From *Ministero della Marina* (Rome). Yearly figures.
Germany. From Jost Düffler, *Weimar, Hitler und die Marine* (Düsseldorf, 1975), p. 563.
Japan. From American Japanese Monographs *Outline of Naval Armament and Preparations for War* (Department of the Army, Washington, n.d.), part I, p. 36 and part II, p. 3. The rates of exchange used for conversion to sterling are average figures for 1935 as published in *The Times*.

[2] DPR (DR9) of 12th Feb. 1936, para. 8. The same principle was put to the Ministerial Committee which handled preparatons for the London Naval Conference. NCM(35)12 of 11th June 1934. Cab. 29/148. See also CID. 1215B of 2nd March 1936.

Conference'.[1] This of course was not much help to the Admiralty in preparing next year's estimates and building programme; and in June there were further indications that all would not be as plain sailing as had appeared likely six months earlier; for the Cabinet gave its assent to a hedging proposal by Sir John Simon[2] 'approving generally' his proposals on defence expenditure 'subject to reconsideration by the Chancellor of the Exchequer in consultation with the Prime Minister and Minister for Co-ordination of Defence'.[3]

The proposal for the 'New Standard of Naval Strength' was accordingly sent by Hoare to the Defence Plans (Policy) Committee of the Cabinet on 29th April.[4] After quoting those parts of the DRC's final report and those of the Ministerial Committee which had reviewed its recommendations, the Admiralty explained at length the circumstances which had made a new standard essential. They emphasised that, chiefly because naval rearmament was bound to be a slow process— especially after a long period of stringent economy—an early decision was essential. The size of the 'New Standard Navy' was perhaps somewhat breathtaking, at any rate in Treasury eyes. It consisted of 20 capital ships, fifteen aircraft carriers three of which would be kept at long notice in peace time and so require no aircraft, 100 cruisers, 22 flotillas of destroyers (some 198 boats), 82 submarines and 'the usual proportion of smaller vessels'. The total cost was estimated at £104 millions per annum over and above normal Navy Votes, and it might total £800 millions during the seven years over which the expansion would be spread. But the Admiralty was prepared to accept the elimination of certain ships and to effect other economies, such as allowing a longer 'effective life' for some classes, so bringing the yearly cost down to £97 millions. If an agreement were reached with Japan and Germany (additional to the Anglo-German naval agreement of 1935) some further reduction would, they continued, be possible; but they declared that even if such agreements were made 'no reduction below the total of 20 capital ships' could be recommended because 'ultimately our sea power depends on our battle fleets'.[5] As the digestion of this large meal took a long time and did not take place until after the period covered by this chapter we will now return to the 1937 building programme.

---

[1] Carter to First Lord and First Sea Lord 7th May 1937. Adm. 116/3631.

[2] Simon succeeded Chamberlain as Chancellor of the Exchequer on 28th May 1937.

[3] Cabinet 27(37) of 30th June 1937. Simon's proposals are in CP. 165(37) Cab. 24/270.

[4] DP(P)3 of 29th April 1937. Cab. 16/182.   [5] *ibid.* paras. 32–42.

Early in 1936 the staff examined in detail the characteristics of the 1937 programme battleships. They insisted that it was essential to build three, but as they would have to be laid down before they knew whether a qualitative limitation of the main armament had been accepted it was extremely difficult to decide on the calibre of their guns.[1] In the end the staff rejected 15-inch weapons because, if adequate A-A armaments were to be fitted and the desired high speed of 29 knots attained, the displacement could not be kept down to the 35,000-ton treaty limitation. Thus only two alternatives appeared possible—namely nine 14-inch guns combined with the desired speed or twelve 14-inch with the speed reduced to 27 knots. In both cases strong long- and close-range A-A armaments were considered mandatory.[2] In the end a compromise was reached, as is usual in a debate on ship characteristics, and it was decided that the *Duke of York*, *Anson* and *Howe* should be similar to the 1936 programme ships (ten 14-inch guns),[3] though many improvements were to be incorporated. The Board, however, appears to have had misgivings about accepting the 14-inch gun, since at about this time they called for designs to be prepared with eight or nine 16-inch; but it proved impossible to fit the heavier weapons if the treaty displacement was adhered to and the other important characteristics maintained.[4]

As late as July 1936 the staff still entertained hopes that Japan would agree to the 14-inch qualitative limitation,[5] and Chatfield therefore put off coming to a final decision for the moment and suggested to the First Lord that he should see the American Ambassador and stress our anxiety to avoid 'a new race in battleship construction'—especially as Germany intended to build two 15-inch and Russia two 16-inch ships.[6] Then reports came in that the Americans also intended to build 16-inch ships, which in effect meant that Britain alone was left with the 14-inch

---

[1] Plans Division minute of 3rd July 1936. Adm. 116/3382.

[2] Tactical Division memo. of 12th Feb. 1936. The 14-inch designs were known as 14-N and 14-O and the rejected 15-inch design as 15-C. Adm. 1/8867-41.

[3] The *Duke of York* was originally to have been named *Anson*, the *Anson* named *Jellicoe* and the *Howe* named *Beatty*. No record has been found to explain why the names of the two Grand Fleet Cs-in-C of World War I were dropped in favour of those of great leaders of earlier times, but Lady Jellicoe wrote to the First Lord in protest.

[4] These designs were known as 16A-38 and 16G-38 (both with nine 16-inch) but the latter had the higher speed. However its displacement came out at 43,000 tons. Adm. 1/9421 and 9434.　　[5] Plans Division minute of 3rd July 1936. Adm. 116/3382.

[6] Minute of 24th July 1936. *ibid.*

design. Henderson, the Controller, wrote that if we changed to 15-inch for the new ships eighteen months' delay would result, while if we adopted a modified *Nelson* type of 16-inch gun the displacement would go up by 10,000 tons.[1] As regards Japanese intentions Henderson forecast that if they went for ships with nine 16-inch they would displace 44,000 tons; but rumours (which were actually correct) had been received that they were designing an 18-inch gun,[2] which complicated the problem still more. Henderson, whose influence on such issues was paramount as it was he who had to produce the guns and mountings, finally said that he was prepared to accept what he called 'the gamble' of giving the 1937 ships 14-inch guns, and in October Chatfield and Hoare agreed to go ahead with them.[3] Though more telegrams passed between London and Tokyo in the endeavour to persuade the Japanese to accept a lower limitation they were fruitless.[4] Such in brief outline was the chain of events which resulted in the newest British battleships being given lighter armaments than the corresponding ships of any other naval power—a matter about which Churchill was to complain bitterly—if somewhat unfairly—later.

The reader will recall that a committee had been set up in 1936 to report on the 'Vulnerability of Capital Ships' and another, known initially as the 'Sub-Committee of Assessors on Bomb versus Battleship Experiments', to report on the effectiveness of bombing and A-A gunfire.[5] Inevitably the work of the two bodies was complementary, and their papers show that there was a good deal of overlapping between them.[6] Though neither inquiry produced any firm and final conclusions before the outbreak of war put all such arguments to the test the ABE Committee did render three valuable Interim Reports to the CID.[7] In the second of them the Chairman, General Sir Hugh Elles, remarked with unquestionable accuracy that 'the controversy had indeed been carried out on the basis of aspirations rather than actuals'; and it is plain that both parties tried to bend such statistical

---

[1] Minute of 4th Sept. 1936. *ibid.*

[2] Tokyo telegram no. 236 of 26th Aug. 1936. *ibid.*

[3] Minutes of 11th and 16th Oct. 1936. *ibid.*   [4] Copies in *ibid.*

[5] This latter body was renamed the 'Sub-Committee on Bombing and A-A Gunfire Experiments' in March 1938, short title 'ABE Committee'.

[6] For example ABE. 2 of 8th March 1937 consists of a number of papers produced for the VCS Committee (VCS. 7, 18 and 27); and some of the latter were in addition printed for the CID (VCS. 27 became CID. 1258B). Cab. 16/178.

[7] ABE. 24 of 18th Oct. 1937 and ABE. 47 of 21st Feb. 1938. Cab. 16/178. ABE. 63 of 30th Jan. 1939. Cab. 16/179.

results as did become available to prove the case which they wished to support.[1] Churchill very naturally took a lively interest in the progress of the experiments, and evidently received these committees' papers. In May 1936 Chatfield told him that he did not suggest that our battleships could not be sunk, but did argue that they must be able to sink the enemy's; to which Churchill replied 'You ought to be able to prove . . . that you can build battleships that you would not be afraid . . . to send readily to sea in the teeth of mine, torpedo or aeroplane';[2] and that was the very thing which of course the Admiralty could not prove.

At the end of 1936 the Staff considered the implications of building up carrier strength to fourteen ships by 1943 as part of the New Naval Standard; but the DCNS (Admiral W. M. James) thought that the shortage of aircrews was so acute that it would prove impossible to man and operate such a large number of ships.[3] However the Plans Division pointed out that the number of carriers had been based on war with Japan *and* Germany, and that if we were not at war with the former three or four ships could be dropped. 'Thus', they remarked, 'the hypothesis of war with Japan is considered to control our aircraft carrier needs'. As reduction of the capital ship programme was, they considered, out of the question the issue therefore was whether we should build more carriers at the expense of cruisers;[4] but as the New Standard was as yet no more than an aspiration no decision was taken at that time.

The Board next turned to the design of the 1937 carriers (to become *Formidable* and *Indomitable*) and those of the following two years (to become *Implacable* and *Indefatigable*).[5] The first two were to be repeti-

---

[1] The Admiralty's copies of the VCS Committee papers are in Adm. 116/3732, 3733 and 4324. See also CID. 1258B. The ABE Committee's are in Cab. 16/177, 178 and 179. The author of this history had to represent the Admiralty's A-A Gunnery interest on this body in 1939 and, having had five years' sea experience with the latest A-A weapons, was deeply disturbed to find how falsely optimistic a view of its effectiveness had been presented. A letter to the author of 7th Jan. 1975 from Commander D. W. Waters, a former FAA pilot, now Deputy Director of the National Maritime Museum, gives interesting recollections of the false statistical basis on which the bombing results of RAF squadrons were assessed in the 1930s.

[2] Chatfield to Churchill 5th May and reply by latter of 10th May 1936. Chatfield papers, CHT/4/3.

[3] Minute by DCNS of 10th Dec. 1936. Adm. 116/3376.

[4] Minute by D of P. *ibid.*

[5] Adm. 1/9426 and Board Minute 3587 of 17th Nov. 1938.

tions of the *Illustrious* class of 1936, which only had one hangar;[1] but the other two were bigger ships (26,000 tons), capable of operating 72 aircraft and with the considerably higher engine power needed to make them capable of 32 knots. The deck armour remained as in the earlier ships; while the hangar height was increased to accommodate the new types of aircraft (Albacore TSRs and Skua Fighter-Dive-Bombers). Thus did the Royal Navy recover equality with, and in at least one respect (the armoured flight deck) superiority to the Americans and Japanese in aircraft carrier design—an art in which we had led the world in the first war.

The design of the cruisers which were to become the *Dido* class was approved in June 1936 and Chatfield was euphoric about it.[2] 'I congratulate DNC and Controller', he wrote, 'on what appears to be a beautiful design. Eight of these ships will be of inestimable value in the fleet and, as they age, for convoy work also . . .';[3] and they were in fact to prove very valuable, especially in the famous 15th Cruiser Squadron in the Mediterranean in World War II.[4] One can understand why, taking account of the conditions which had prevailed since he became First Sea Lord in 1933, Chatfield should have been annoyed by a sweeping attack made by Churchill on the Admiralty's cruiser policy in general and the *Dido* class in particular. 'It is perhaps natural', he wrote, 'that Mr. Churchill's active mind should be always worrying about the wisdom of the Admiralty, and as his technical knowledge is very slight he lets himself run [? away] rather frequently in his criticisms and anxieties'.[5]

In mid-1936 the Admiralty began to consider the design of the 1937

---

[1] Adm. 1/9426, 9431 and 9433. The *Illustrious* class had three shafts and could develop 110,000 horse power. The *Indefatigables* had four shafts and could develop 148,000 horse power. The design of the 1938 carriers was approved by Board Minute 3587 of 17th Nov. 1938. For a full account of the design and development of the armoured flight deck carrier see J. H. B. Chapman, *The Development of the Aircraft Carrier*, Transactions of The Royal Institution of Naval Architects, vol. 102, no. 4 (Oct. 1960).

[2] Board Minute 3383 of 24th June 1936. Adm. 1/9396.

[3] Minute of 18th June 1936. *ibid.*

[4] See for example Roskill, *War at Sea*, vol. II, pp. 51–5 and Sir Philip Vian, *Action This Day* (Muller, 1960, chs. 8 and 9). Eleven ships of this class comprised the first group (1936–38 programmes) and five the second group (1939 and later). The second group had four instead of five twin 5.25-inch guns and larger close-range A-A armaments. Their displacement went up to 5,770 tons.

[5] Minutes by Chatfield of 14th and 26th May 1937, and Minute by Hoare of 27th May 1937 on above. Adm. 1/9427.

programme cruisers, and seven alternatives were produced with various armaments, speed and protection on a displacement of about 8,000 tons. Though Henderson favoured the design with fourteen 5.25-inch guns in twin mountings,[1] the one finally selected had twelve 6-inch in triple mountings, fairly good A-A armaments and two triple torpedo tubes, and was capable of 31 knots.[2] These were the *Fiji* or 'Colony' class, of which eleven were built starting with the five in the 1937 programme.[3]

To turn to destroyers the J and K classes of the 1936 and '37 programmes had six 4.7-inch twin gun mountings, as compared with the *Tribals* eight, but were given two quintuple torpedo tubes compared with one quadruple in the *Tribals*. With the L class (1937) and M class (1938) the gun armaments were made dual purpose (HA/LA). Taken as a whole the British destroyer building programme of the 1930s may be classed as a success—as is evidenced by their remarkable war record.

Early in 1937 Henderson very sensibly wanted to combine 'the three types of sloop into one type which could be rapidly produced in numbers if required';[4] and he put forward proposals for what sort of a ship she should be. In the Estimates for that year we find that the convoy sloops have been renamed 'Escort Vessels' and the coastal sloops 'Patrol Vessels', though their functions still remained undefined.[5]

Seven submarines (T class of 1,090 tons surface displacement and ten torpedo tubes—the largest armament of any British submarines), four minesweepers (improved repetition of the class begun as sloop-minesweepers in 1932), a destroyer and a submarine depot ship designed to facilitate storing and upkeep on foreign stations, ten motor torpedo-boats and a variety of other small craft completed the 1937 programme. Bearing in mind the broad strategic purpose for which the new fleet was being built, referred to above, and the limited funds made available, it is difficult to find serious fault with the priority given to the various classes—except for the comparative paucity of trade defence vessels.

In 1936–37 the rapidly improving performance of aircraft, and perhaps the deliberations of the ABE Committee, stimulated the

---

[1] Minute of 22nd Oct. 1936. Adm. 1/9402.

[2] *ibid.* for particulars of the designs offered.

[3] Three of the later ships (*Ceylon, Uganda* and *Newfoundland*) had the superimposed after turret removed and heavier A-A armaments fitted. Their displacement went up to 8,800 tons. Board Minute 3483 of 8th July 1937 modified the design for the 1938 and later ships.

[4] Minute of 30th Jan. 1937. Adm. 1/9410.   [5] Cmd. 5385.

Admiralty to great activity in A-A defence measures. Though the fairly regular successes achieved in shooting down the wireless-controlled 'Queen Bee' target aircraft produced confidence that the threat of the high-level bomber would be countered such confidence was soon shown to be much exaggerated.[1] Furthermore by 1936 Admiral Fisher, the C-in-C, Mediterranean, recognised that the navy had no effective defence against the dive-bomber.[2] In May 1937 the Board was fully aware of the fact that a great deal needed to be done to improve A-A defence, and tried, not very successfully, to establish an order of priority for new weapons and control systems.[3] Then came an eye-opener when a Queen Bee circled the Home Fleet for two-and-a-half hours in the presence of the ABE Committee and members of the Board, and not a shot went near it. Chatfield described the 'profound alarm' that this caused to the Parliamentary Secretary (Geoffrey Shakespeare); but his account suggests that it was the Admirals who were really alarmed. 'Our present system of H-A control', wrote Chatfield 'is very imperfect'.[4]

The truth was that as long ago as the late 1920s the Admiralty had gone for the wrong sort of control system—one in which enemy aircraft movements were in effect guessed instead of being actually *measured* and the measured results used to provide the required control data. This latter, called a 'tachymetric system',[5] was the proper answer and in the letter already quoted Chatfield said that he realised that this was so. The Admiralty's Director of Scientific Research C. S. (later Sir Charles) Wright was strongly of the same opinion, and in 1937 he circulated a damning critique of the existing long-range control system.[6] But the plain truth was that the earlier mistake could not be rectified quickly, and that British designers and the light engineering industry had fallen far behind foreign countries in this respect. By 1938 the DSR was describing the current state of affairs as 'wholly unsatisfactory' and the existing system as 'a menace to the service'.[7] Nor could the Naval Ordnance Department, which was responsible for it, produce a convincing rebuttal of such statements.[8]

---

[1] See for example Fisher to Chatfield 30th May 1933 and Backhouse to Chatfield 27th March 1936. Chatfield papers, CHT/4/5 and 4/1.

[2] Quoted Backhouse to Chatfield 27th March 1936. CHT/4/1.

[3] Board Minute 3468 of 5th May 1937. Adm. 167/96. Memos. in Adm. 167/97.

[4] Chatfield to Backhouse 8th Oct. 1937. Chatfield papers, CHT/4/1.

[5] From 'tachometer', an instrument for measuring velocity. OED.

[6] SRE. 1496/37. Adm. 1/10848.

[7] *ibid.*   [8] Minute of 3rd Dec. 1938 by the DNO. *ibid.*

It thus came to pass that the Germans and Americans both produced efficient tachymetric control systems, while the Royal Navy had to make do with the inefficient alternative which was by 1937 in quantity production. The lessons to be derived from this failure are that British specialist officers were not properly trained in scientific design and armament engineering, and that they were far too slow to seek advice from those who were so trained. The Gunnery branch undoubtedly indulged in a great deal of self-deception and wishful thinking on these matters—notably in Chatfield's optimistic prophecy to Churchill of 1936 about the air defence of merchant ships already quoted.[1] The story is a sad one, and the conclusion is inescapable that the severe losses suffered from bombing attacks, especially when ships were operating in coastal waters, would have been mitigated if greater foresight and less confidence had been shown, and better use made of the scientific skill and knowledge available.

The strengthening of the fleet's A-A defences was, very naturally, linked with the question whether aircraft would be used to extend the enforcement of 'Belligerent Rights' against neutral merchant ships suspected of carrying contraband, and whether unrestricted bombing attacks on the merchant ships of a belligerent were likely. The former was a very old issue, going back to the early 1920s, and international jurists had never been able to agree on the principle involved. At the end of 1936, when the defence of trade was once again taking a prominent place in the Admiralty's deliberations, the matter was reopened.[2] In mid-1937 the Admiralty brought the subject up to the CID, which instructed the unwilling Air Ministry to draw up draft rules governing the conduct of air warfare against shipping.[3] The ruthless use of bombers against all sorts of targets at Shanghai and elsewhere by the Japanese, and the experiences of the Spanish Civil War, to be discussed in the next chapter, lent urgency to the discussion, and a long interchange of memoranda followed. Expectedly the Admiralty and Air Ministry took opposite views, the former wanting restrictions on bombing in some form, while the latter considered it quite impossible to enforce them even if, as was highly improbable, an international agreement was reached.[4] None the less in November 1937 Duff Cooper, now First Lord, took the matter up with Sir Thomas Inskip, who had been appointed Minister for Co-ordination of

---

[1] See p. 227. [2] Memo. of 3rd Dec. 1936 by Secretariat. Adm. 116/4155.
[3] 284th CID meeting. Cab. 2/6.
[4] Minute by DCNS of 11th Oct. 1937. Adm. 116/4155.

Defence in March 1936 as a result of a Parliamentary and Press campaign against leaving defence issues to be handled solely by the CID and its numerous subordinate bodies.[1] Discussion continued between Inskip, the service departments and the Foreign Office throughout 1937 and well into the following year, when a specially appointed committee produced its final report on 'the Humanisation of Aerial Warfare'—which reflected the grave anxiety felt in Britain over the effects of bombing on the civilian population (estimated by the Air Staff as 1.8 million casualties in a 60-day offensive in 1937). Today the whole issue seems highly academic, and the draft rules governing air bombardment were in fact still circulating on the outbreak of war.

While air defence of the fleet was proving such an intractable problem study of the related though in many ways dissimilar problem of trade defence was placed under the aegis of the Shipping Defence Advisory Committee, formed by the Admiralty in February 1937.[2] Though differences of outlook and of purposes between, for example, the Admiralty, the Board of Trade, Lloyds and the Shipping Federation (representing the shipowners) quickly became apparent it was certainly advantageous to have all the interested parties represented on a committee which met regularly under the same chairman. Chatfield himself opened the first meeting on 10th March 1937, presumably to impress on the 28 senior officials present the importance which the Admiralty attached to the committee's work. He then turned the chairmanship over to the DCNS, Admiral James, who claims to have been the originator of the idea of the SDAC.[3] At the first meeting a number of sub-committees (ultimately seven) were set up to produce recommendations on every aspect of trade defence, from creating the machinery for communicating confidential advice to owners and ship masters, and providing the Admiralty with up-to-date information about the distribution of the whole merchant navy, to the defensive arming of ships and training their crews in the use of the weapons which were to be kept in store at selected depots all over the world and fitted when an emergency arose.[4] All these sub-committees tabled their initial recommendations at a meeting of the parent body in July 1937.

At the second meeting of the SDAC Admiral James made the

[1] See Roskill, *Hankey*, III, ch. 5 regarding the campaign against Hankey and the CID and the appointment of Inskip.
[2] AL of 5th Feb. 1937. Adm. 116/3635.
[3] Letters to the author of 2nd March 1968 and 21st May 1969.
[4] Terms of Reference of SDAC Sub-Committees A to G. Adm. 116/3978.

important pronouncement 'that the convoy system is considered by the Admiralty to be the most effective form of protection against surface, submarine or air attack', that plans had been prepared to introduce it in 'possible war areas', and that steps had been taken 'to ensure that there will be available for convoy work sufficient escorts' in whatever areas convoy 'may be deemed necessary'.[1] If the assurance of a sufficiency of escort vessels was much too optimistic the firm declaration about the efficacy of convoy was wholly justified—though doubtless unpopular with ship owners and masters of merchant ships, who have always exhibited a strong antipathy towards the naval compulsions inherent in the operation of the convoy system. It is interesting to find that, early in the following year, the US Naval Attaché in London reported, quite correctly, that if war came the Admiralty intended to introduce convoy. He wrote enthusiastically about the 'gratifyingly far advanced' measures taken by the British for trade protection and, a few months later, about the Merchant Navy defence courses being conducted at British ports.[2]

At the end of July 1937 the SDAC circulated an Interim Report setting out the progress made by the sub-committees. It slowly percolated upwards, and reached the Cabinet in October.[3] Approval was then given to the government carrying the cost of stiffening merchant ships selected by the Admiralty to enable guns to be mounted on them; but the question whether powers existed, or should be sought, to compel owners to strengthen future ships was referred back to the Board of Trade and Admiralty for investigation and report.[4] This was typical of the problems which arose in connection with the control and operation by the Admiralty of a huge privately owned mercantile marine. Since the work of the SDAC assumed steadily increasing importance as the international situation darkened we will revert to it in a later chapter.

In the autumn of 1937 the CID reverted to the Protection of Seaborne Trade, which it had reviewed comprehensively a year earlier under the title of 'Food Supply in Time of War'. The Joint Planners had then produced a long report for the COSs on that subject, and it is a fair assumption that it probably contributed to the formation of the

[1] Minutes of 2nd meeting of SDAC on 14th July 1937.
[2] Reports of 23rd March and 7th July 1938. USNA, RG. 38.
[3] The Sub-Committees' recommendations are summarised in Adm. 1/9182.
[4] Cabinet 35(37)12. Cab. 23/89.

SDAC.[1] Every form of attack on shipping and the counter-measures were then considered, including the possible renewal of unrestricted submarine warfare. Though the Naval Staff admitted that, if this took place, 'heavy losses may be anticipated' they regarded the problem as far less serious than it had been in World War I because of the Asdic development. They declared that when the policy of fitting all small ships with it was completed, as would be the case shortly, 'the submarine should never again be able to present us with the problem we were faced with in 1917', and that war experience would show that submarine attacks on ships in convoy 'can be made unprofitable'.

As regards air attacks they admitted the vulnerability of our commercial ports to bombing but were doubtful whether, taking account of all military demands for aircraft, sufficient strength would be available to achieve a decision by this means. The Air Staff on the other hand, while admitting that a proportion of our air strength should consist of fighters, which they described as 'a strategically defensive type', insisted that 'the largest possible proportion' should be devoted to 'strategically offensive tasks'—by which they meant of course bombing in accordance with the Trenchard gospel. The Naval Staff held that if air attacks took place at sea the best defence was convoy combined with 'adequate A-A armament . . . and the maintenance of fighter formations over the convoy'; but as demands for fighters would be heavy the 'A-A artillery of the escorts and close-range weapons in the merchant ships themselves would have to be the chief defence'. To that thesis the Air Staff riposted that the effect of A-A gunfire was over-estimated and that of bombing under-estimated.[2] The Naval Staff summarised all the measures for the protection of merchant shipping which had been or would be put in hand, and although they accepted that 'aircraft are fundamentally offensive weapons' there was a wide divergence of opinion on 'the provision of specialised aircraft detailed solely for operations over the sea'. This was of course the heart of the problem, and the Air Staff would not accept that such aircraft were necessary. The bombers in their view came first all the time, and shore-based maritime aircraft a very poor second.

When the matter was reopened in November 1937 the specific case of war against Germany or Japan or both of them was considered, and 'a vigorous offensive against our trade in the Atlantic and possibly elsewhere' was anticipated. As regards attack by surface raiders the

[1] FS. 9 of 2nd July 1936. Also cos. 488. Cab. 53/28.
[2] *ibid.*, paras. 40, 74, 79 and 83.

COSs believed that our superiority over Germany would eventually defeat the threat; and they did not expect 'any major offensive operations against British trade' in the Far East because of 'Japan's strategic position'. They reiterated the confidence expressed a year earlier over the decline of the submarine menace, and set out the number of shore-based aircraft needed for trade protection in both the cases under review. The number was 339, including 165 for convoy escort, in a war with Germany and 393 in a war with Japan—which far exceeded the numbers available or projected for the home and overseas RAF commands concerned.[1] The Admiralty was in sum fairly satisfied that our naval forces, whose intended dispositions and duties the Joint Planners had set out in full detail, would prove adequate for trade protection, but far from satisfied that the RAF was capable of providing the necessary maritime air co-operation, or indeed intended to do so. The Air Staff was moreover sceptical of the value of convoy, which they considered likely to provide the enemy with easier targets than independently routed ships. This time however a satisfactory agreement was reached—perhaps because the deteriorating international situation had made it essential to put an end to the protracted inter-service bickering. The Joint Planners, and after them the COSs, accepted that unrestricted submarine and air attacks were likely, while the Air Staff dropped their opposition to convoy and their claim to divert Coastal Command aircraft to other duties—a possibility which had long caused the Admiralty concern. When the matter came before the CID Chatfield reported that the earlier differences 'had now all been resolved', and Lord Swinton the Secretary of State for Air, described the recommendations presented to the committee as 'an admirable piece of Combined Staff work'. The report was approved, and everything was sweetness and light.[2] The termination of this long debate is an example of the CID system, working through the Joint Planning and COS Committees, at its most effective. Every aspect of the problem was discussed, needs and intentions were set out clearly, differences of opinion were not glossed over, and a solution satisfactory to both parties was in the end achieved.

An important development of this period in the Admiralty concerned the War Registry, which had been formed under the Permanent Secretary in 1914 and was responsible for the distribution of all incoming and outgoing signal traffic throughout World War I. Soon

[1] COS. 640 of 26th Nov. 1937. Cab. 53/34. Also CID. 1368B. Cab. 4/26.
[2] 303rd CID meeting of 2nd Dec. 1937. Cab. 2/7.

after the Armistice it was reduced to a skeleton staff which worked only on a 'single watch' (i.e. eight hours a day) basis instead of the war-time three watch system; and so it remained until 1934 when a small expansion took place to improve the speed with which signals were handled.[1] In 1937 more staff were added,[2] and at the time of the Munich crisis a full twelve-hour watch was being kept in daytime with a skeleton staff on duty at night. Both the staff, which then numbered about 30, and the accommodation, which was in two rooms in the Admiralty's old building, proved quite inadequate to cope with the flood of signal traffic produced by the crisis. A great and rapid expansion was obviously essential, and men were recruited from the Ministry of Education and other civil departments. By the spring of 1939 a 24-hour continuous watch was being kept, and the Registry had moved to protected but still unsuitable quarters in the basement of the Admiralty. Not until completion of the 'Citadel' in 1940 was it properly accommodated, and in that year the staff reached a total of some 500. Incidentally a conflict soon took place over whether the Registry should remain a civilian organisation or be transferred to the Naval Staff and manned by naval officers and ratings; but the outcome was that it remained civilian.[3] Though it would be an exaggeration to suggest that no mistakes were ever made in the handling of the vast flow of signals and messages which passed daily through the War Registry's hands, there can be no question that it provided a highly efficient service—as is evidenced by the fact that Churchill continued to use the naval communications system for his personal traffic after he had left the Admiralty for Downing Street in 1940.[4]

The 1937 Combined Fleet Exercises took place at the beginning of March. The original plan had been to carry them out in the Mediterranean; but at the end of February they were transferred to the Atlantic in order to avoid the risk of ships getting involved in the Spanish Civil War, which had broken out in July 1936. The exercises, in which ten capital ships, two carriers, three cruiser squadrons, five flotillas of

[1] Minute by Murray of 15th June 1934. Adm. 1/8778–184/1934.

[2] Office Memo. G of 15th Dec. 1937.

[3] I am indebted to Sir Richard Powell, Mr. F. W. Mottershead and Sir John Lang who were successively Head of War Registry from 1939 for valuable recollections of the build-up and working of the organisation. Unfortunately practically all pre-war papers about the War Registry have been destroyed during the departmental process known as 'weeding' the records.

[4] Interview with Sir John Lang, Head of War Registry 1940 and Permanent Secretary of Admiralty 1947–61 on 26th Nov. 1974.

destroyers and a number of submarines took part, were of a tactical nature designed 'to make a thorough test of the full fleet action W/T organisation', including 'enemy' jamming of wireless traffic. We now know that the Germans were at this time making an intensive study of 'British wireless signals and their vocabulary and routines', and that 'the outcome of long years of effort' in this field contributed to the later success of their highly skilled cryptanalysts in breaking British naval codes and cyphers.[1] It is interesting to remark that we too were engaged in 'traffic analysis' of German and Italian communication systems, but we must await publication of the history of the British Intelligence effort in World War II before we can say exactly how and when our successes were accomplished.[2] It is however a fair guess that the German 'B-Dienst' or Wireless Intelligence Service benefited from the 1937 British exercises. They lasted for a week and included submarine attacks on the Mediterranean Fleet, long-range air reconnaissance and striking force attacks, night attacks by destroyers, testing the cruising disposition of the fleet when under air attack, and a torpedo-bomber attack on a battle fleet 'before there is time to engage them with gunfire'. Though the new arm of seaborne air power was certainly given an important place, the emphasis of the whole series remained concentrated on the old idea of attack on and defence of the battle fleet; and no shore-based aircraft appear to have taken part.[3] Apart from the torpedo-bomber attacks the 1937 exercises do not seem to have contributed anything significant to preparing the navy for war in the new era which had plainly begun.

The great expansion of the fleet which began with the 1936 programme inevitably produced difficult personnel problems. One such problem concerned the steep rise in foreign service, brought about by

[1] Letter of 27th Jan. 1975 to the author from Captain Heinz Bonatz, who served in the German wireless intelligence service 1927–44 except for breaks in other appointments and became its Director in 1934.

[2] At the time of going to press this history of the work of the Government Code and Cypher School at Bletchley Park in World War II is in course of preparation in the Cabinet Office under the direction of Professor F. H. Hinsley who served in the GCCS. It is understood that this work (probably two volumes) will form an addition to the British Military History Series of the Second World War.

[3] Adm. 116/3873. It is noteworthy that, perhaps as a result of this author's complaint about the destruction of the records of earlier fleet exercises in the first volume of this work, the records of the 1937, 1938 and 1939 Combined Fleet Exercises have been preserved.

the increase in size of the China Fleet and the Abyssinian crisis.[1] The effect on morale of long separations from wives and families was disturbing; but there was not much the Board could do about it as long as the government demanded a strong naval presence in foreign waters, though they did bring ships home to give leave as soon as an opportunity arose—for example towards the end of the Abyssinian crisis.

A second, and equally worrying trouble was the shortage of officers —a remarkably sudden reversal of the drastic measures taken in the early 1930s to 'clear the lists' of surplus officers. The problem resurrected the old dispute between what may be called the 'Intellectual' school, who believed that officers should be given a broad and fairly long education, not only in professional subjects, and the 'Blue Water' school, who argued that education should take second place to gaining sea experience at the earliest possible age. The most vocal advocate of the 'Intellectuals' was, expectedly, Admiral Sir Herbert Richmond, Vere Harmsworth Professor of Naval History at Cambridge University 1934–36, who had recently published a critical analysis of the methods of entering and training officers;[2] but he enjoyed the support of Admiral Sir Reginald Drax, the C-in-C, Plymouth, and of Admiral James the DCNS. The latter appears to have been the only member of the Board of those days who was in sympathy with the 'Intellectuals'. At any rate the committee appointed by the Board in July 1937 to report on the training of junior officers found Richmond's proposals 'of a revolutionary nature' and 'unacceptable to the Admiralty.'[3] In fact the educational course for Sub-Lieutenants at Greenwich was first reduced and then abolished 'until the shortage of Lieutenants had been

[1] In May 1937 the Director of Personal Services (DPS) told the Board that 36.4% of the navy's personnel was on foreign service as compared with 19.6% in 1921. Adm. 1/9181.

[2] H. W. Richmond, *Naval Training* (Oxford UP, 1933). Richmond had written the first draft of this book when Director of Training in the Admiralty in 1918. The 1933 proposals included abolition of the 13-year-old cadet entry and substitution of selection by competitive examination at 16–18 years. The subjects set would, he proposed, comprise 'a compulsory datum' of general education and a number of optional papers. Headmasters' reports on candidates would be used to help assess their potential qualities as leaders. These proposals were very badly received by the Admiralty at the time, but were in general adopted after World War II.

[3] This was the committee initially under Admiral R. Leatham appointed on 21st July 1937. Leatham was succeeded by Admiral B. C. Watson on 13th Sept. Adm. 16/3673. Admiral Sir Louis Hamilton's papers contain interesting views collected for the above committee in 1938. HTN/229. NMM.

remedied';[1] and if the reason for doing so is, in the circumstances prevailing at the time, understandable it does also illustrate the generally anti-intellectual attitude of senior naval officers in the 1930s.

In its final report the Watson Committee dealt with the training of specialist officers, and evidently felt that this was too extended. They recommended reducing the Gunnery, Torpedo and Signals courses arbitrarily to one year.[2] This amounted only to a very minor change, and it does not appear to have had appreciable effect on specialist training before war broke out.

While the foregoing inquiry was in progress the attention of the Board was turned to the shortage of candidates from the lower deck for promotion to Sub-Lieutenant under the scheme introduced in 1933 to replace the earlier 'Mate Scheme'.[3] An interesting discussion ensued, revealing that, to take only one ship the *Hood*, no more than two suitable candidates had been found during her last commission out of a ship's company of some 2,000. Apparently candidates for commissions were 'regarded with suspicion' on the lower deck, and so were discouraged from attempting what was still a formidable hurdle. On the other hand a good number of men 'of a very fine type' were applying for promotion to Warrant Officer.[4] In a thoughtful minute Admiral James suggested that the best solution might well lie in promoting Warrant Officers earlier to the rank of Lieutenant, which he considered 'by far the most natural and suitable way for the majority' of men to gain commissioned rank.[5] However the proposal was turned down after discussion by the Sea Lords, and only minor changes were made to the existing system.[6] It may here be remarked that many Warrant Officers were promoted to Lieutenant, and even to higher ranks, during the war and gave splendid service.

While these matters were being discussed in Whitehall the Admiralty asked all Commanders-in-Chief for their views on how a greater number of suitable candidates could be obtained from the lower deck. As might be expected their views by no means coincided. For example Drax from Plymouth wanted selection to be made much earlier and special training given to candidates; but E. R. G. R. Evans, C-in-C,

[1] Board Minute 3453 of 16th March 1937. Adm. 167/96.

[2] Final report of above committee dated 30th June 1938. Adm. 116/3764.

[3] See pp. 31–2 and 191–2.

[4] Adm. 1/9092–67/1937. The discussion was initiated by Admiral Sir Martin Dunbar-Nasmith on 19th Feb. 1937.

[5] Minute of 19th Feb. 1937. *ibid.*

[6] On 30th July 1937. *ibid.*

Nore, a tough destroyer man who had served with Scott in the Antarctic,[1] wanted later selection and then more rapid promotion; while Fisher, now in the Portsmouth Command, remarked on the lack of really suitable candidates, who should in his view be of 'good appearance, physique and parentage' and 'sufficiently intelligent'.[2] Nor were the reports from the Cs-in-C Home and Mediterranean Fleets any more helpful. Once again Admiral James put his finger on the correct point when he told the Board that they should 'satisfy a perfectly healthy ambition . . . by erecting a new ladder to the Quarter Deck which will be of an easier gradient and will produce a body of officers for whom there is a definite need'.[3] But few senior officers were as broad-minded as James, and that snobbish distinctions did still play a part in the selection of officers is shown by a complaint emanating at this time from the Captain of the *Excellent*, the gunnery school at Portsmouth, that many of the young officers who had come in under the Direct Entry scheme at eighteen instead of going to Dartmouth College at thirteen 'have so pronounced an accent that they cannot be said to be capable of speaking "the King's English" '. Lord Cork, the C-in-C, Portsmouth, did not regard the matter very seriously, commenting that the Interview Board was 'fully alive to the importance of a boy's speech', and that he would 'be sorry to see too much importance attached to this particular handicap' which, he believed, would quickly disappear when the boys came into the proper environment. When the correspondence reached Chatfield he remarked that he had heard similar complaints before. 'The ability [to speak the King's English] should', he wrote, 'be an essential quality for a boy who is to become an executive cadet;'[4] and there the matter was left.

To summarise the problems involved in the selection, education and training of young naval officers in the last years of peace it is certainly true to say that the 'Intellectuals' did not win the battle, that selection was still on a restricted though slowly widening basis, and that specialist training continued to dominate officers of Lieutenant's rank—because

[1] See Reginald Pound, *Evans of the Broke* (OUP, 1963).

[2] Reports of 20th March (Plymouth), 19th March (The Nore) and 11th March 1937 (Portsmouth). Also from C-in-C, Mediterranean (Pound) of 21st March 1937. Adm. 1/9082–54/1937.

[3] Memo. of 19th Feb. 1937. Adm. 167/97.

[4] Report by Captain H. M. Burrough of 10th Nov., covering letter by Lord Cork to Second Sea Lord of 17th Nov. and minute by Chatfield of 24th Nov. 1937. Adm. 116/3989. In fact the last list of candidates interviewed included the son of a blacksmith and the son of a former naval signalman.

the Post Captain's and Flag Lists showed all too clearly that specialisation was the golden road to promotion. Only in the furnace of war did the qualities of the 'salt horse' officers, who had served nearly all their time in small ships, come into their own; while 'Intellectuals' were then in strong demand for staff and inter-service posts.

Early in 1937 a new body was set up to take over from the Man Power Committee of the CID all the complex issues which would arise if National Service were introduced.[1] It threw off a number of subordinate bodies to deal with such matters as the numbers of men required under various schemes of mobilisation, the reservation of skilled labour, and Women's Reserves—on all of which the Admiralty was represented. The only serious troubles that arose concerned the Admiralty's desire to call up merchant seamen aged between 18 and 25, which infuriated ship owners; but the Admiralty also wanted to take large numbers of fishermen, whom the Ministry of Agriculture and Fisheries insisted should be reserved. Though a good deal of heat seems to have been generated by these issues all such problems were shelved—temporarily—by the government's decision not to establish a National Register in peace time.[2] The Admiralty, believing that they would only need 'a moderate number of men' in the first few months of a war, was not seriously perturbed by the decision and reached an amicable agreement with the Shipping Federation about the number of merchant seamen they would take.[3]

At the end of June 1937 the reconstructed and rearmed battleship *Warspite*, which was to be Admiral Pound's flagship in the Mediterranean, completed modernisation and commissioned to full complement at Portsmouth with a Chatham crew—an arrangement which, though sometimes unavoidable, was always unpopular and could easily lead to trouble over leave. In this case the trouble was serious enough for the Admiralty to order an inquiry, as a result of which three officers were relieved, three ratings were discharged from the service and half a score were drafted to other ships.[4] The Admiralty, whose sensitiveness over any reports of indiscipline had been acute ever since the Invergordon mutiny, evidently regarded this incident as a warning that

[1] NS. 71 of 11th March 1937. Copy in Adm. 116/3600.

[2] 290th CID meeting of 11th March 1937. Cab. 2/6. CID. 1341B of 15th July 1937. Cab. 4/26. The Admiralty papers on the discussions of 1936–37 are in Adm. 116/3600.

[3] In 1936 the Royal Naval Reserve totalled 7,680 including men who had joined the Patrol Service; but only 2,566 would be taken for the RN and fishermen would be excluded. Adm. 116/3600.

[4] See Roskill, *H.M.S. Warspite* (Collins, 1957 and Futura Books, 1974), pp. 168–9.

renewed 'Mass Indiscipline' (a euphemism for mutiny) was possible, and in September they sent a long confidential letter to all Cs-in-C setting out the most likely causes of such trouble, outlining how it could be forestalled by timely action, and describing how it should be handled if it did occur. Its contents were to be communicated to all officers of Lieutenant's rank and above.

It is perhaps of greatest interest to the social historian, because it sets out the Admiralty's views on relations between officers and men at that time—though many officers who read it may well have felt that such views were far removed from reality. For example, after making the platitudinous remark that discipline 'must be based on mutual confidence and respect between officers and men', the letter went on to say that discipline 'will only be achieved if officers regarded their men as human beings with ambitions, hopes and fears, who have private lives and private troubles'. Those with long experience as Divisional Officers, who knew all their men and learnt about their private problems and troubles through almost daily contact with them, may well have read that statement with astonishment. As regards the Petty Officers, the Admiralty totally rejected the opinion expressed by Sir John Kelly after Invergordon that they had failed badly on that occasion and that their loyalty was suspect[1]—in which view the Admiralty was certainly right. The letter ended with a number of 'principles governing the action' of officers if 'mass indiscipline' should occur. These principles were in essence sensible enough in establishing guide lines, though the variabilities were so great that, as the Admiralty admitted, 'hard and fast rules which will meet every incident' could hardly be established.[2] But the letter ignored what in this historian's view was the basic trouble, namely the vast gulf—in pay, prospects, living conditions, food and privileges—between the quarter deck and the lower deck. It was to take another war, and a social revolution, to narrow that gap appreciably.

In 1937 the first Imperial Conference to be held since 1930 took place in London. Before the arrival of the Commonwealth delegates Inskip, assisted by Hankey and the COSs, produced a full 'Review of Imperial Defence'. The first draft was revised to meet criticisms from the Foreign Office, which held that it did not take sufficient account of recent political developments such as 'the close reciprocal relationship which had recently grown up between Rome and Berlin' (presumably

---

[1] See pp. 123–4.

[2] AL NL. 2938/37 of 23rd Sept. 1937. Sir Louis Hamilton papers, HTN/227A. NMM.

the Rome-Berlin Axis of November 1936), and the consequential threat to France.[1] As was to be expected the review dealt chiefly with the rising threat from Germany at home and the aggressive actions of the Japanese in the Far East. As regards naval policy, the report referred to the need for the 'New Naval Standard', and gave as the chief 'military liabilities' the security of Imperial communications, the safety of the British Isles against German aggression, the maintenance of 'Empire interests' in the Far East, the Mediterranean and Middle East, and the defence of India against Soviet aggression—in that order of priority. However the COSs did not expect Japan 'to challenge us directly unless we are already at war in Europe', and hoped for the restoration of 'a certain degree of Anglo-Italian co-operation' as a result of the recent conversations, which had produced the somewhat inappropriately named 'Gentleman's Agreement' of 2nd January 1937.[2] As regards the antipodean Dominions and India the COSs reaffirmed that their security 'hinges on the retention of Singapore as a base for the fleet', and that 'the despatch of a Fleet to the Far East remains the operation upon which the security of the eastern half of the Empire depends'.[3] In an Annex to their review the COSs set out the 'Possible forms of Dominion Co-operation' in war. For Australia and New Zealand 'general naval co-operation' and the provision of land and air reinforcements for Singapore were named as *desiderata*; from Canada (which still only possessed small naval forces) no more than the use of port facilities on both coasts was looked for; South Africa, the COSs hoped, would take on the defence of her own bases and allow the British Fleet to use them; while India's primary role was to provide reinforcements for Singapore. If these proposals did not amount to much in terms of warships they did involve very important strategic considerations.

Conversations with the Commonwealth delegates began in May,[4]

---

[1] CID. 1305B of 22nd Feb. 1937. Cab. 4/25. The original paper was taken at the 288th CID meeting on 11th Feb., and the chief critics were Vansittart, Chamberlain, Malcolm MacDonald and Ormsby Gore. The remarks quoted were by Vansittart. The revised report was taken at the 289th CID meeting on 25th Feb. and approved with only minor qualifications. Cab. 2/6.

[2] See *Gathorne-Hardy*, p. 434 regarding this agreement.

[3] CID. 1305B, paras. 14 and 85.

[4] These were Sir R. Archibald Parkhill (Minister of Defence, Australia), and Mr. Michael J. Savage and Mr. Walter Nash (respectively Prime Minister and Minister of Finance, New Zealand). General Sir William H. Bartholomew, Chief of General Staff, India, represented the Indian Empire.

and it quickly became apparent that there was considerable scepticism, and even mistrust, about whether the repeatedly promised 'Main Fleet to Singapore' would in fact materialise if and when the need arose. In Australia there was at the time a strong movement to concentrate on the land and air defences of the homeland rather than make a contribution to the fleets of the Empire and Commonwealth, which would in any case not be very substantial. The penetrating questionnaires produced by the Australian and New Zealand delegates after the end of the main conference were probably influenced by such views.[1] For our purposes the most important request then made was for 'a clear definition of the strategical object of the Empire forces in a war with Japan or with Japan and another first class naval power'. The answer given was categorical, namely that in either case 'the basis of our strategy lies in the establishment of our Fleet at Singapore at the earliest possible moment...'; and even if Italy or the USSR intervened on the side of our enemies 'our policy must be governed by the principle that no anxieties or risks ... can be allowed to interfere with the despatch of a fleet to the Far East'. Whilst making every allowance for the many difficulties the COSs had to cope with it is difficult not to feel that they, and especially the Admiralty, were less than honest to the Commonwealth delegates in these discussions, and that the concept of the 'Main Fleet to Singapore' had, perhaps through constant repetition, assumed something of the inviolable sanctity of Holy Writ.[2]

Discussions on naval issues between Parkhill, the Australian Minister of Defence, and senior members of the Board of Admiralty, took place in mid-June, when eight papers were brought forward for consideration. They varied from important strategic issues such as the type of squadron best suited to the Australian station and how far that country could be regarded as a source of supply in war, to administrative matters such as the constitution of the Commonwealth's Navy Board, and personnel problems such as British appointments to the ACNB and to command of the Australian squadron. A full brief was prepared for Duff Cooper, probably by the Permanent Secretary, in which he

[1] The questionnaires and the British answers are in cos. 593 of 4th June (Cab. 53/32) and CID. 450 and 451C of 15th June 1937. Cab. 5/8. The latter were taken at the 294th CID meeting on 17th June and merely noted. Cab. 2/6.

[2] This view is developed at length in B. N. Primrose's unpublished doctoral thesis *Australian Naval Policy, 1919–1942. A Case Study in Empire Relations*. (Australian National University, 1974.) See also Roskill, *Hankey*, III, pp. 275–84.

was urged to keep off finance because the Admiralty held that Australia ought to pay for facilities such as wireless stations at Port Darwin and Canberra, and their government was decidedly reluctant to accept the commitment. As to the RAN squadron, the Naval Staff naturally supported the idea that Australia should build destroyers, and would have liked a capital ship to replace its two fairly modern cruisers. They also wanted oil storage at Fremantle to be increased to at least 24,000 tons; but again the question who should pay for it would arise. There was evidently trouble over the top naval appointments. Admiral Sir George Hyde, the First Naval Member of the Board, had evidently got at odds with Parkhill, who was very much opposed to any extension of his appointment; and the Admiralty was of the same opinion. The Australians also wanted to get rid of Admiral R. H. O. Lane-Poole who commanded the sea-going squadron; but the Admiralty considered his recall quite unacceptable. Such conflicts of personality were all too liable to arise when British officers were appointed to senior posts in Dominion navies, which understandably wanted them for their own people;[1] and one has to admit that a certain type of Englishman would never go down well with the Australians. However the naval discussions evidently went fairly smoothly, and the real difficulties were those faced by the COSs and CID.

After the end of the Imperial Conference a high-level meeting took place in the Admiralty to review the strategic issues which had been brought up. The record shows that the department was not unaware of the contradictions in which they had become enmeshed; for it states that 'The Dominions were shown the Far East Appreciation [of which more later] and it is quite clear to them that unless a new standard [of Naval Strength] is worked to, we could not, as the German navy rises, live up to the assurances we have given them'.[2] Chatfield himself virtually admitted the validity of this pessimistic prognostication when, at the end of the year, he told Admiral Pound, the C-in-C, Mediterranean, that the whole position was 'very uncertain', and that the situation at Singapore 'left much to be desired'. 'The Fleet you will have to take out', he wrote, 'is not very satisfactory', and because the Germans would be able to send out their three pocket battleships on commerce raiding we must keep substantial strength at home.[3] Doubt-

[1] Adm. 1/9134–132/37.

[2] The discussion was on the New Naval Standard paper DP(P)3 of 29th April 1937, but it is not clear who took the notes on it. Adm. 116/3631.

[3] Chatfield to Pound 30th Dec. 1937. Chatfield papers, CHT/1/3. AM. 1630 of 1st

less Parkhill, Savage and their colleagues returned home with very much the same thoughts in mind. Though it is futile to speculate on what might have happened had we told the Australians and New Zealanders outright that the Eastern Fleet might never materialise, it is fair to mention that none of the Commonwealth countries contributed anything approaching the British *per caput* expenditure on defence,[1] and that their vehement insistence on their equal and independent status made it extremely difficult to frame a co-ordinated Empire strategy. Yet it none the less remains a regrettable fact that wishful thinking on the part of the COSs and Admiralty came near to crossing the border line into outright deception in the summer of 1937.

Perhaps the most satisfactory outcome of a conference whose deliberations Lord Casey has stigmatised as having been 'far removed from reality'[2] was that Australia and New Zealand made no difficulties about placing their warships at the general disposal of the Admiralty in the event of war. Canada had at the time little to offer, and in any case it was doubtful whether she or South Africa would come to the aid of the Mother Country; while India made difficulties about placing control of the RIN sloops under the British C-in-C, East Indies, but finally agreed to do so.[3]

The abdication of King Edward VIII on 10th December 1936 had no significant influence on naval policy though his personal popularity in the fleet was never in doubt, and was strikingly demonstrated when, only a month earlier, he had visited Home Fleet ships at Portsmouth accompanied by Hoare and Chatfield.[4] The Proclamation of his brother as King was signalled to the fleet on 12th December and was immediately followed by a personal message in which the new monarch recalled 'with pride that . . . I received my early training in the Royal Navy'.[5]

In May 1937, while the Commonwealth delegates were in London for the Imperial Conference, another Naval Review was held at

---

Nov. told the C-in-C, Mediterranean that he would take over command in the Far East from the C-in-C, China. Adm. 116/9767.

[1] See vol. I, pp. 406 and 465-6.

[2] Letter to the author of 27th July 1970.

[3] Correspondence between Admiralty and India Office and between Lord Zetland, the Secretary of State for India, and Simon the Chancellor of the Exchequer 1937. Adm. 116/3593. The Royal Indian Marine was renamed the Royal Indian Navy on 6th Sept. 1934.

[4] See Frances Donaldson, *Edward VIII* (Weidenfeld and Nicolson, 1974), pp. 234-5.

[5] Adm. 1/9045-142/36.

Spithead as part of the celebrations organised to mark the coronation of George VI. Most of the Mediterranean Fleet, except the ships involved in the patrols necessitated by the Spanish Civil War, came home for it, the Reserve Fleet was again commissioned, and by 20th 141 British and Dominion warships and 127 liners and passenger vessels had assembled in the historic anchorage. The organisation followed closely that of 1935 and earlier occasions, but this time eighteen foreign warships were present to represent their countries and to do honour to the new monarch. At the head of the line of foreign warships and parallel to the flagships of the Home and Mediterranean Fleets was the USS *New York*, which had been Admiral Hugh Rodman's flagship when the American 6th Battle Squadron joined the Grand Fleet in 1917. The initial happy inspiration of choosing the *New York* and inviting Rodman to rehoist his flag in her was evidently Admiral Leahy's, though Swanson gave definite approval to the proposal.[1] France was represented by the new battle-cruiser *Dunkerque* and Germany by the pocket-battleship *Graf von Spee*, whose smartness and very evident power made a great impression on the vast crowds which visited the fleet. But the significance of the Americans occupying the place of honour at the head of the line was probably not appreciated by the Germans. No modern British battleship took part, but there were two of the new *Southampton* class cruisers, and this time four aircraft carriers were present and fourteen squadrons of Fleet Air Arm aircraft took part in the fly past.[2] Yet the great majority of the British ships were still of World War I vintage, and must have taken part in several earlier pageants of this nature. As in 1935 the weather was good, and this time everything seems to have gone smoothly—except for the BBC commentary in the evening which was 'faded out' after four minutes because it was deemed 'unsatisfactory'.[3] On 22nd, after the

[1] Leahy to FDR 1st March and Swanson to same 10th April 1937. Roosevelt papers, OF 18, Box 3A.

[2] *The Times* of 18th–22nd May devoted great space to the review.

[3] *The Times*, 20th May. At the 1935 review there had been a complete breakdown of the catering for the Admiralty's official guests on board the hospital ship *Maine*, which produced protests in Parliament and apologies from the First Lord. In 1937 the BBC commentator Lieut.-Cmdr. Woodroffe evidently met too many friends before starting his commentary on the illumination of the fleet from the *Nelson*. To the best of this author's recollection Woodroffe began 'The fleet's lit up. We're all lit up . . .'; after which he was 'faded out'. The incident caused great amusement in the fleet at the time. The Admiralty docket on the subject (Adm. 178/140) is still 'closed' as being 'personally sensitive'!

King had visited many ships, the concourse began to disperse; and as no exercises and firings took place as in 1935 the anxiety then felt about the results was not repeated. Though the occasion was in the main cere-monial the mobilisation of the Reserve Fleet was again rehearsed, and the general tuning up of the Navy for war was thus carried a stage further—amid all the gun salutes, displays of bunting, cheering to order and fireworks. But it is worth recalling that only some three weeks before the review the little Spanish town of Guernica had been destroyed by German bombers.

While the Imperial Conference was deliberating on the Far Eastern situation in London a new crisis blew up in the threatened area. The conflict referred to euphemistically by the Japanese as the 'China Incident' began on the night of 7th–8th July 1937 when their troops clashed with Chinese on the Marco Polo bridge near Pekin. The significance of the event lay in the fact that the Japanese were now plainly not restricting their military intervention to Manchuria,[1] where a semi-independent, colonial régime might ultimately have been accepted by China, but were set on a vastly wider scheme of conquest. At about the time when this dangerous development became plain a long exchange of telegrams between the Foreign Office and the Tokyo embassy came to an end with a flat refusal by the Japanese to consider either the 35,000-ton or the 14-inch gun qualitative limitations for capital ships; and news of their ominous intransigence was at once passed to all the Dominions.[2]

In June the Chiefs of Staff circulated their revised 'Appreciation of the Situation in the Far East'.[3] It considered in full detail the conditions which would influence our strategy against Japan in two different circumstances. The first was when we were at peace with Germany but had to keep enough strength in home waters to neutralise her fleet; while the second assumed that we were already at war with Germany in alliance with France, when war broke out against Japan. The conclusions were in the main depressing. As to the time which would elapse before the main fleet could reach Singapore, the minimum was still assessed at 28 days if it used the most direct route via the Suez

[1] See James B. Crowley, *Japan's Quest for Autonomy* (Princeton UP, 1966) and W. Roger Louis, *British Strategy in the Far East 1919–1939* (OUP, 1971), pp. 241ff or full accounts of the Japanese and British sides of this story.

[2] Circular Telegram B33 of 31st March 1937. Adm. 116/3382 which also contains copies of all the telegrams on the subject.

[3] COS. 596 of 14th June 1937. Cab. 53/32.

Canal and the Malacca Strait; but preliminary preparations and fuelling delays made 53 days a more realistic estimate. Use of the Sunda Strait between Java and Sumatra, which would avoid constricted waters where the danger from mines and submarines would be serious, would add two days to the time on passage. If however the fleet went out by the Cape of Good Hope the total time, including preparations and fuelling, rose to 70 days to Singapore or 90 days to Hong Kong. Bearing in mind the relative proximity of the bases from which the Japanese could launch an expedition (some 2,600 miles) the COSs concluded that 'the time factor is very much against us in the initial stages'.[1]

Their general conclusions were, firstly, that we would have to rely mainly on economic pressure to defeat Japan, a process which would take at least two years; secondly that an earlier decision could only be obtained by 'a successful fleet action'; and the Japanese could easily 'deny us the opportunity' by holding their fleet back; and thirdly that the war 'will make full demand on our naval reserves', but 'will not require the employment of army or air forces on a national scale'.[2] Though the precise meaning of 'a national scale' is not clear the misjudgement over the type and scale of the forces needed to defend our interests in the Far East remains staggering. Other sections of this appreciation show that confidence in the ability of the fixed defences of Singapore, together with the planned land and air reinforcements, to hold out until the fleet arrived remained as sanguine as ever. As regards Hong Kong, the Air Staff considered it 'not tenable or usable as a base', and the COSs agreed that it could not be reinforced once war had broken out with Japan. However they considered that, although its loss would be a serious blow to our prestige it would not prove fatal.[3] The COSs did not believe that intervention by the USSR on our side 'would introduce any serious change in our policy for war in the Far East' (as regards Europe their views on this matter were, as will be told later, very different); but the intervention of Italy 'would at once impose conflicting demands on our fleet'.[4] Yet a few weeks later they gave Australia and New Zealand the categorical assurance, already mentioned, that Mediterranean problems would not be allowed to interfere with the despatch of a sufficient fleet to the east or with the defence of Singapore.

Re-studying this important paper today it is clear that the COSs

[1] *ibid.*, paras. 45–49.   [2] *ibid.*, para. 109.
[3] *ibid.*, para. 313.   [4] *ibid.*, para. 126.

The Silver Jubilee review at Spithead, 16th July 1935. Centre—*Resolution, Iron Duke, Hood, Renown* (capital ships); *Courageous, Furious* (aircraft carriers); *Orion, Neptune, Achilles, Leander* (light cruisers); *Kempenfelt* (flotilla leader) and destroyers of 'C' class. Left hand line destroyers of 'E' class. Right hand line seven destroyers of 'B' class, *Faulknor* (flotilla leader) and destroyers of 'F' class.

Destroyers leaving Sliema harbour, Malta c.1937. *Whitshed* (D 71) and *Volunteer* (D 77) leading. Probably 1st Flotilla.

The destroyer *Watchman*
(launched 1917)
in a heavy sea. c.1935.

did recognise the danger of 'maintaining remote garrisons at the end of a long sea line of communication', and that 'the total of British and Dominion air strength in the East is greatly inferior to that of Japan'. Yet those factors were not given their due weight; and the conclusions finally reached show not only sublime confidence in British sea power and naval efficiency but a good deal of wishful thinking about what was in fact practicable in the Far East. To reconcile unquestionable weakness with the need and the desire to uphold Imperial interests was to attempt to square the circle. In the same month that this paper was circulated the COSs reviewed the reinforcement of Malaya from India with the Australian and New Zealand representatives present. Though the General Staff of the Indian Army declined to accept a categorical commitment, its chief, General Sir William Bartholemew, did make clear that the importance of Singapore to the whole British position in the Far East was fully recognised.[1]

In August the Japanese aggression was extended to Shanghai and the Yangtse valley, and incident soon piled on incident. Admiral Little, now C-in-C, China went to Shanghai and recommended the evacuation of women and children—which was done.[2] Presumably it was to test his countrymen's reaction to a more forward policy in China that President Roosevelt made his famous 'quarantine speech' at Chicago on 5th October; but if that is so the howl of rage that went up from the isolationist Press must have convinced him that he would have to move very slowly and cautiously. In London the feeling was strengthened that, as Chamberlain put it, 'It is always best and safest to count on nothing from the Americans but words'.[3]

In December British and American Yangtse river gunboats were bombed, and the American *Panay* was sunk.[4] When Swanson sent to the President the reports on this and other incidents received from Admiral H. E. Yarnell, commander of the US Asiatic Fleet, he commented on the fact that whereas the Japanese were exhibiting violent anti-British feelings their conduct towards the Americans was 'very

[1] 211th COS meeting on 7th June 1937. Cab. 53/7.

[2] C-in-C, China R of P, 1937. By 6th Sept. the China Fleet had evacuated 3,351 persons of British nationality from Shanghai and the final total was 4,159. Adm. 116/3682.

[3] See Keith Feiling, *Life of Neville Chamberlain* (Macmillan, 1946), p. 325.

[4] Admiral Leahy, the CNO, sent the President a summary of Admiral Yarnell's messages about this incident on 20th Dec. Roosevelt papers, PSF, Dept. Corresp. For a study of Yarnell's role in the China crisis see James H. Herzog, *Closing the Open Door. American-Japanese Diplomatic Negotiations 1936–1941* (Annapolis, 1973).

conciliatory'.[1] Obviously the Japanese were trying to keep the chief powers with interests in the Far East divided; and their apologies for the *Panay* incident certainly sufficed to prevent any serious rise in American temperatures. Admiral Yarnell even urged that the Japanese Admiral Hasegawa should not be made a scapegoat for the sinking of the *Panay* 'as he is friendly towards the United States'.[2]

On the British side Admiral Little's letters show strong resentment of Japanese ruthlessness, and sympathy with the Chinese; but he described them both as 'these inferior yellow races', and seems chiefly to have regretted that the conflict between them should be proving so disruptive to British trade and interests.[3]

From about this time until the autumn of 1938 the general line taken by the British was that a firm but conciliatory policy might restrain Japan's aggressiveness.[4] The futility of all such ideas did not become apparent until Japanese policy, plans and purposes could be thoroughly examined after World War II. As the COSs remarked in their Far East Appreciation of June 1937 it was virtually impossible to obtain accurate information about the extent of Japanese militarisation;[5] and in fact neither we nor the Americans obtained any reliable information about their 'Third Replenishment Programme', for which funds were appropriated in 1937. It actually consisted of the two giant battleships *Yamato* and *Musashi* (laid down November 1937 and March 1938), two large aircraft carriers (*Shokaku* and *Zuikaku* of 25,675 tons and capable of operating 84 aircraft), eighteen large destroyers, fourteen submarines and a large number of minesweepers, minelayers, gunboats and lesser vessels—all of which were to be completed by 1942.[6]

To turn to developments among the European powers, this was a period which saw the attempt to mend our shattered relations with Italy—initially welcomed by Mussolini's Foreign Minister Count Ciano.[7] Such moves appealed strongly to the Admiralty, and the American Naval Attaché in Rome was correct in reporting to Washington that his British colleague had volunteered the information that his country's three services 'had represented to their government their anxiety to compose their differences with Italy', since only then would

---

[1] Swanson to FDR 8th Dec. 1937. Roosevelt papers, *loc. cit.*   [2] *ibid.*

[3] Reports of Proceedings of C-in-C, China of 14th Sept. and 8th Oct. 1937.

[4] W. Roger Louis, *op. cit.*, pp. 247–54.

[5] COS. 596, para. 48.   [6] See *Pelz*, pp. 196–7.

[7] Rome to FO no. 727 of 6th Dec. 1926 and later telegrams. Copies in **Adm.** 116/3376.

they be free 'to deal with the Far East menace'.[1] But the Admiralty was sore about Italy's insistence on arming her new battleships with 15-inch guns, and still anxious about the vulnerability of Malta and the lack of any reasonably equipped alternative base. In November Chatfield told Pound that the development of a base in Cyprus was 'out of the question for the immediate needs of the moment', as it would take ten years and cost £20 millions.[2] As regards Malta, in 1934 the CID had admitted that this 'centre of British naval power in the Mediterranean' was virtually defenceless, but little was done because it was not until February 1937 that the Cabinet admitted that 'Italy cannot be counted on as a reliable friend' though 'in present circumstances she need not be regarded as a probable enemy'—doubtless a reference to the diplomatic negotiations referred to above.[3] Although at a time when so much cried out to be done to improve our defences a scheme of priorities obviously had to be established, the papers of the CID show very plainly that Singapore was regarded as the next priority after home defence, and in consequence Malta came off badly.[4] Early in 1938 the Governor reported what he had been able to carry out; but the improvements did not include the bomb-proof shelters for submarines and MTBs which had been under discussion for over a year.[5]

As regards Germany, the confidence of Chatfield and the naval staff in the value of the Naval Agreement signed in June 1935 remained unshaken well into 1938.[6] But shortly after Duff Cooper replaced Hoare as First Lord in May 1937 he wrote 'I think Germany will scrap the agreement as soon as she is in a position to do so with advantage to herself'.[7] Actually the Germans ostensibly played to the

[1] Report of 4th Nov. 1937. USNA, RG. 80, Box 171.

[2] Chatfield to Pound 23rd Nov. 1937. Chatfield papers, CHT/4/10.

[3] CID. 441C of 25th Feb. 1937. Taken at 290th meeting on 11th March when Cabinet approval was noted. Cab. 2/6.

[4] JDC. 319 of 19th May, revised 30th July 1937.

[5] Bonham Carter's despatch to Secretary of State for Colonies of 19th Jan. 1938. Adm. 116/4061. See also Bonham Carter papers, Churchill College, Cambridge.

[6] Minute by Director of Plans of 11th Jan. 1938 'The Anglo-German Naval Treaty is probably the most valuable factor that we have today in the whole realm of defence, and what our naval problem would be if it did not exist or is denounced is difficult to contemplate.' Adm. 116/3929. Chatfield several times expressed exactly the same view (e.g. to First Lord 10th Nov. 1937. Adm. 116/3631); and he and Hankey were evidently in complete accord over the need to reach a political agreement with Germany (see Chatfield to Vansittart 5th Jan. 1937. Chatfield papers, CHT/6/2).

[7] Holograph minute of 7th Aug. 1937. Adm. 116/3377.

rules of the agreement over notification of building programmes throughout the period covered by this chapter,[1] though reports which reached the DNI about large submarines being built for Turkey and Roumania were disturbing—because identical ones were being built for the German navy.[2] None the less the DNI considered it improbable that Germany would again resort to unrestricted submarine warfare —partly because she would not have enough boats to make it 'immediately effective', and partly because 'progress in anti-submarine measures may have rendered submarine warfare less effective . . .'[3] This was of course a reaffirmation of the Admiralty's oft repeated confidence in the Asdic.

With France relations remained distant if not positively chilly at this time. The Admiralty disliked her decision to build 15-inch gun battleships, though they placed the greater blame on Italy and the USA; and when towards the end of 1936 Admiral Durand-Viel, the French Chief of Naval Staff, raised informally the question of closer collaboration 'to facilitate concerted action between our fleets in case of emergency' the British Naval Staff was strongly opposed to re-opening the conversations which had not proved at all fruitful at the time of the Rhineland crisis. Chatfield supported the despatch of a very cool answer, on the grounds that we were working for a western European pact which would include Germany; and such an idea was of course anathema to the French.[4] About a year later the Foreign Office raised the same question, and the Chiefs of Staff were as cool as the Admiralty had been on the previous occasion.[5] This attitude of course stemmed partly from fear that closer liaison with the French would lead to our involvement in another costly continental war of attrition, and partly from the desire to reach a lasting accord with Germany.

In May 1937 Chatfield wrote to the First Lord suggesting that he should retire when he had completed five years as First Sea Lord early in 1938. He proposed that his successor should be either Fisher or

[1] Adm. 116/3368 contains the German notifications. The British ones are in Adm. 116/3929.

[2] Reports of 6th and 22nd July 1937. Adm. 1/9074-38/1937. The drawings received make it plain that we had an agent in the drawing office of the Germaniawerft at Kiel.

[3] Draft NID report on Germany dated 29th Aug. 1936. Adm. 1/9074-38/1937. The report was finally printed as CB. 1818 and gives a clear and accurate account of the German navy at that date.

[4] Report by Naval Attaché, Paris of 21st Nov. 1936 and minutes by Director of Plans and First Sea Lord. Adm. 116/3379.

[5] Eden raised the issue on 16th Dec. 1937. See Roskill, *Hankey*, III, pp. 310-11.

Backhouse. As to Pound, he remarked that both Fisher and Backhouse were senior to him, and he doubted whether Pound's claims were such as to justify passing them over.[1] Hoare passed the problem on to Duff Cooper who was about to succeed him at the Admiralty, saying that he preferred Backhouse—chiefly in order to 'maintain continuity'.[2] The problem was resolved, quite unexpectedly, by the sudden death of Admiral Fisher after a short illness on 24th June, at the age of only 62. Chatfield was deeply distressed by the loss of an outstanding figure and his former second-in-command at such a difficult time, and had to recast his plans for the top naval appointments.[3] In December he wrote again to the First Lord, offering to leave in favour of Backhouse early in the New Year; but Cooper was understandably reluctant to lose so able and experienced an adviser; he dismissed a recent attack on Chatfield in Parliament as having 'drawn strong protests', and said he had told Baldwin that Chatfield would stay on until September 1938.[4] The decision was, in the circumstances prevailing at the time, certainly a wise one. As to the very important post of Controller, Henderson unselfishly decided to sacrifice his chance of a higher appointment by staying on for five or six years, and so making the task of 'rebuilding the Navy' his life's work.[5] When in 1938 Chatfield told Pound that Backhouse was to be his successor the latter replied that he was not at all disappointed and was 'in no way envious'. In August of that year Chatfield told him that he was to have the Portsmouth Command on his return from the Mediterranean.[6]

In the autumn of 1937 the Admiralty began, as was their wont, to consider the following year's estimates; but with Inskip now installed as the Minister responsible for co-ordinating the proposals of all three defence departments the matter was handled differently from earlier times. In October Inskip presented a summary of the departments' forecasts to the Cabinet;[7] but Simon, the Chancellor, adopted a stalling

[1] Chatfield to Hoare 24th May 1937. Chatfield papers, CHT/1/3.

[2] Hoare to Cooper 28th May 1937. *ibid.*

[3] Chatfield to Pound 2nd July 1937. *ibid.*, CHT/4/10. For an appreciation of Fisher see Sir William James, *Admiral Sir William Fisher* (Macmillan, 1943). Lord Cork was given the Portsmouth command in Fisher's place.

[4] Chatfield to Cooper 7th Dec. and reply by latter of 8th Dec. 1937. CHT/1/3. Commander R. T. Fletcher, a Labour MP (later Lord Winster), made a strong attack on the further extension of Chatfield's appointment on 10th Feb. 1938. Parl. Deb., Commons, vol. 331, col. 1253. I have been unable to find in Hansard an earlier attack, such as Chatfield referred to in Dec. 1937.

[5] Chatfield to Pound 5th Aug. 1937. Chatfield papers, CHT/4/10.

[6] Same to same 3rd Aug. 1938. *ibid.*   [7] CP. 256(37). Cab. 24/272.

policy by referring the forecasts back to Inskip and giving him a panel of experts, including Hankey and Sir Horace Wilson, to review them in concert with the Service Departments.[1] Having met four times the panel produced a detailed 'Review of the Navy Estimates' in the following month,[2] and soon followed it up with a more far-ranging 'Review of Defence Expenditure in Future Years' in which the whole history of the financing of rearmament was first recapitulated and the gravity of the economic problems involved was stressed.[3]

It then turned to the issue which the Admiralty had previously pressed—namely that in the long run Britain could only provide herself with adequate defences if her foreign policy were adjusted so as to change 'the present assumptions as to those nations which we must consider our potential enemies'.[4] This of course meant coming to an agreement with at least one of the dictatorships. In December the Board produced Sketch Estimates for 1938–39 totalling just over £130 millions—an increase of some £25 millions over the previous year. The number of personnel (Vote A) was to be increased from 112,000 to 119,000 by the end of the new financial year, and as most of the cost of the Fleet Air Arm previously borne by the Air Ministry would, by the government's decision of July 1937, to be referred to later, now fall on the Admiralty some further increase would plainly be necessary.[5] These figures were, from the Treasury's point of view alarming, and by the end of 1937 it was plain that the Admiralty was going to have a very hard fight to get the 'New Standard of Naval Strength' accepted.

Hankey now added his weight to those who held that Germany was 'by far the most formidable of our possible enemies', since she alone was 'capable of dealing our country and empire a decisive blow at the heart'.[6] He therefore placed air defence of the homeland first in order of priority and naval needs second—which was a fundamental shift of opinion on his part. One cannot but remark also the divergences between the strong advocacy of the Anglo-German agreement of 1935 frequently expressed by the Admiralty and by Hankey and the view eighteen months later that Germany was the most dangerous enemy.

[1] Cabinet 39(37) of 27th Oct. 1937. Cab. 23/90A.
[2] Dated 12th Nov. 1937. Adm. 116/3631.
[3] CP. 316(37) of 15th Dec. 1937. Cab. 24/273.
[4] Minute on above by Director of Plans dated 21st Dec. 1937. Adm. 116/3631.
[5] Board Minute 3508 of 15th Dec. 1937. Adm. 167/96.
[6] Memo. of 23rd Nov. 1937. Cab. 21/531.

The new building programme approved by the Board at the end of 1937 comprised two battleships, two carriers, seven cruisers, one destroyer flotilla, seven submarines, a destroyer and a submarine depot ship and a wide variety of smaller vessels. An interesting point is that 'in certain circumstances' (not specified) the Board proposed to substitute two 'small trade route aircraft carriers' for part of the cruiser programme; but that was not in fact done. The total cost of the building programme was estimated at £61½ millions spread over the years 1938–42.[1]

To cross the Atlantic and review the events which took place in the USA during the period covered by this chapter, the election of Franklin Roosevelt for his second term as President in the autumn of 1936, and by an even more decisive majority than he had obtained in 1932,[2] enabled him to pursue his purposes with greater confidence—though he still had to move cautiously for fear of arousing a new wave of isolationism and providing the anti-British lobby with ammunition. Perusal of the Roosevelt papers leaves one in no doubt regarding his constant interest in the strength and welfare of the navy; and he often turned his attention to the *minutiae* of naval administration as well as intervening on matters of policy. Yet it is none the less plain that he was fully aware of the fact that, until he had educated the American people in the responsibilities of being a world power—largely by his famous 'fireside chats' on the radio—he could never move faster than public opinion allowed.

A case in point which arose early in his second term was revision of the Neutrality Acts of 1935 and 1936 in order to eliminate, or at any rate reduce, the assistance which they afforded to the dictatorships.[3]

[1] Board Minute 3503 of 9th Dec. 1937. Adm. 167/96. The documents relating to this programme are in Adm. 167/98.

[2] In the popular vote Roosevelt received 27,476,673 votes as against the Republican candidate's 16,679,583. Even more decisive was the fact that he carried all but two of the states (Vermont and Maine) in the electoral college election.

[3] The Neutrality Act of 1935, at the time of the Italian aggression against Abyssinia, finally became a Resolution empowering the President to prohibit arms shipments. Roosevelt only signed it reluctantly, on the grounds that it could 'drag us into war instead of keeping us out'. The Act of 1935 was extended on 25th Feb. 1936 and forbade the grant of loans or credits to belligerents. Again Roosevelt pointed out its dangers. The Spanish Civil War, starting on 18th July 1936, was not covered by the 1936 Act and new legislation was necessary. The new Act (6th Jan. 1937) enabled Roosevelt to embargo export of munitions to both sides; but as it worked to the disadvantage of the lawful Spanish government a new and more flexible measure was substituted for it on 1st May 1937. But that Act in turn was proved ineffective

Shortly before the elections the DPR Committee in London considered whether, in the event of Roosevelt's re-election, an approach should be made to the President 'in order to bring home to him that their neutrality laws would, in the event of war, tend to place a premium on aggression'.[1] Early in 1937 Eden telegraphed to Sir Ronald Lindsay, the ambassador in Washington, giving him an account of a talk with Judge Robert Bingham in which the American ambassador in London had told the Foreign Secretary that Roosevelt was dissatisfied with the neutrality legislation as it stood and hoped to get it amended by Congress at a propitious moment.[2] In fact several amendments were discussed in America, and in March Lindsay reported that a Resolution permitting a belligerent to buy warlike stores and ship them herself on a 'cash and carry' basis had passed both Houses by large majorities.[3]

Much discussion ensued between the Foreign Office and the Admiralty on the question whether the new Neutrality Act, enacted at the end of April, and described by the *New York Times* as 'the high tide of isolationist sentiment', was so prejudicial to the democracies that we should try and persuade the American administration to get it altered.[4] However the Foreign Office considered that we might thereby merely irritate an administration which was basically sympathetic to and well aware of British views, and the Admiralty accordingly dropped the idea. In October, however, the Admiralty asked for a thorough investigation of the effects of the American legislation by the CID's Advisory Committee on Trade Questions in Time of War;[5] but Inskip was dubious of the value of such an investigation, and when it was carried out the conclusion amounted to no more than a decision to leave things alone, while endeavouring 'to enlist as far as possible the sympathies of the US government and people'.[6] There the matter remained until the spring of 1939.

In the same month that the review of the American Neutrality Acts took place in London a Press campaign was started in USA to create a

---

when the 'China Incident' started on 7th July. See Robert A. Divine, *The Illusion of Neutrality* (Chicago UP, 1962) for a full discussion of the various Neutrality Acts.

[1] 28th meeting of DPR Committee on 22nd Oct. 1936. Copy of minutes in Adm. 116/4102.

[2] Telegram Eden to Lindsay of 18th Jan. 1937. Copy in *ibid.*

[3] Letter Lindsay to Eden of 3rd Feb. and telegram of 19th March 1937. *ibid.*

[4] AL to FO of 3rd June and reply by latter of 29th June 1937. *ibid.* On the Neutrality Act of May 1937 see Divine, *op. cit.*, ch. 6.

[5] AL of 12th Oct. 1937 to Sec., CID. *ibid.*

[6] ATB (EPG)38 of 7th Sept. 1938. Copy in *ibid.*

'Navy General Staff',[1] and a Bill was actually introduced in Congress to do so.[2] This proposal aroused the wrath of Josephus Daniels, Roosevelt's former chief as Secretary of the Navy 1913–21, now ambassador in Mexico, and of the President himself.[3] He told Swanson that it would be 'a good idea to pass the word down the line . . . that anybody caught lobbying for a General Staff will be sent to Guam'[4]—an amusing example of Roosevelt's confidence in his own judgement on naval affairs, and moreover a case in which he was wrong; for it was actually left to Admiral E. J. King as CNO and C-in-C, US Fleet in World War II to introduce a staff similar to that which the Admiralty had accepted, albeit reluctantly, in 1917.[5] Until that happened the Chiefs of Bureaux in the Navy Department remained the most influential authorities.

We must now briefly survey the US Navy Department's action to continue the process of building the fleet up to the strength authorised by the first Vinson Act of 1934, and to meet the threat of virtually unrestricted Japanese building inherent in their withdrawal from the London Conference. The General Board was satisfied with 'the material change in the naval situation' brought about by the authorisations under the NIRA and the 1935 Appropriations Act, and at last saw the achievement of 'treaty strength' on the horizon. Accordingly for the 1936 Fiscal Year they only recommended adding one carrier, two 6-inch cruisers, fifteen destroyers and six submarines.[6] But to fund the start of those ships as well as continue the substantial number of ships already building required a large increase in the Construction Budget. The Navy Department asked for $140 millions for that purpose, and Congress actually authorised $127 millions—which, like

[1] See *New York Times* of 17th Oct. 1937.

[2] The Bill (HR. 8843) 'To promote the efficiency of the Navy by establishing a General Staff . . .' was introduced by Congressman Melvin J. Maas of Minnesota. It was referred to the Naval Affairs Committee, which declined to support it.

[3] Daniels to FDR 27th Oct. and reply by latter of 5th Nov. 1937. Roosevelt papers, PSF, Dept. Corresp., Box 28.

[4] FDR to Swanson 5th Nov. 1937. *ibid.*

[5] By the President's Executive Order no. 9096 of 12th March 1942 the CNO was given the legal authority 'for which the office had been striving since its establishment 27 years before'—including authority over the Bureaux. See Julius A. Furer, *Administration of the Navy Department in World War II* (Washington, 1959) for a study of the evolution of the increased powers of the CNO.

[6] GB. 420–2, serial 1659 of 9th May 1934.

the total naval expenditure of $436 millions, was a very large increase over the previous year.[1]

Important changes took place in the upper hierarchy of the US Navy Department in 1936. In February H. L. Roosevelt, Assistant Secretary since March 1933, died in office, but the post was not immediately filled. In the following September the President suggested Charles Edison, a son of Thomas A. Edison the famous inventor, to Swanson, and the latter replied that he was sure he would make 'a most excellent Assistant Secretary'.[2] Edison actually took up office on 18th January 1937, and as Swanson himself was increasingly unfit and the pace of rearmament was soon to accelerate, he had to carry a heavy load. Early in 1938 the British C-in-C, America and West Indies, who had just visited Washington, reported that Swanson 'has seen better days and talks and walks with difficulty now',[3] and he actually died in office on 7th July 1939. As Edison himself was seriously ill earlier that year,[4] the US Navy does not seem to have been fortunate in getting fit men for the top civilian posts. It was more fortunate in the choice of the top naval men. At the end of 1936 Admiral Standley retired from the post of Chief of Naval Operations. He had made many friends in London during the Naval Conference, and was given a warm-hearted farewell by his British opposite number Chatfield at the end of it. His own service's farewell to him was also 'a grand occasion'.[5] As with his predecessor Admiral Pratt the British and American navies both owed a great deal to Standley. His successor

[1] Excluding the money provided by New Deal agencies only $33½ millions were authorised for new construction in the 1935 Fiscal Year. On 30th June 1936 the most important ships building were two carriers, two heavy and nine 'light' (i.e. 6-inch gun) cruisers, 51 destroyers and twelve submarines. Op.-09B91R of 5th May 1965. See Appendix E for total annual expenditure on the US Navy.

[2] FDR to Swanson 12th Sept. and reply by latter of 29th Sept. 1936. Roosevelt papers, PSF, Dept. Corresp., Box 28. Roosevelt pointed out that Edison had been 'in the original NRA set up' as one advantage of his going to the Navy Dept., and in view of the heavy involvement of the department with New Deal agencies this was probably the case.

[3] Admiral Meyrick to Chatfield 4th April 1938. Chatfield papers, CHT/3/1. See also p. 159.

[4] Edison to FDR 16th May 1939. 'It has been a long drag but I am gradually getting there.' He hoped to be back on duty in June. Roosevelt papers, Dept. Corresp., Box 28. Edison succeeded Swanson as Secretary of the Navy in Jan. 1940 but resigned in the following June.

[5] Naval Aide to President to FDR 31st Dec. 1936. Roosevelt papers, Official File 18, Box 3.

Admiral William D. Leahy was, according to the British C-in-C on that side of the Atlantic, 'most forthcoming', and, he believed, 'genuinely pro-British'[1]—an opinion which was to be substantiated on the Combined Chiefs of Staff Committee of World War II.

To return to the expansion of the American Fleet, early in 1937 Roosevelt gave instructions to start work on the two new battleships authorised under the 1936 Appropriation Act,[2] and a few weeks later Swanson circulated all authorities, in accordance with the President's wishes, emphasising the need to speed up construction by avoiding alterations to 'characteristics'.[3] Next Roosevelt enquired what additional building slips and workshops were required at all the major Navy Yards to enable auxiliary war vessels to be built 'if found desirable by Administration policy'. Obviously he had a further, and major expansion in mind. Edison replied that by mid-1939 all existing building facilities would be in use or fully committed.[4]

In April 1937 lengthy negotiations took place between Edison and Leahy for the Navy Department on the one side and the Director of the Bureau of the Budget on the other side about appropriations to build 48 auxiliary vessels, modernising the carriers *Lexington* and *Saratoga* and five battleships, and 'public works proposals' (i.e. shore facilities). Though the Navy Department had to accept fairly substantial reductions in all three categories they stood firm on the modernisation of the two big carriers, and the reduced appropriations were presented to Congress at the end of the month.[5] Two months later the Secretary asked the President to urge on Carl Vinson, the author of the famous 1934 Act, the need to expedite the passage of the proposed Auxiliary Building Programme through Congress, and Roosevelt did so. This measure became the second Vinson Act of 1938, to which we will revert later.[6]

Approval of the new battleships brought to a head the question of the calibre of their main armament. In May 1937 Admiral J. M. Reeves, who had recently been C-in-C, US Fleet, wrote a long letter

[1] Meyrick to Chatfield 4th April 1938. Chatfield papers, *loc. cit.*

[2] On 11th Jan. 1937. Roosevelt papers, Official File 18, Box 27.

[3] GB. 420–2, serial 1744 of 18th Feb. 1937.

[4] FDR to Edison 17th July 1937. Roosevelt papers, PSF, Dept. Corresp., Box 25. Also in OF 18, Box 27.

[5] Director, Bureau of Budget to FDR 13th April 1937 and subsequent correspondence. Roosevelt papers, OF 18, Box 3. The Appropriations Bill in question became HR. 5232 of 27th April 1937.

[6] Swanson to FDR 2nd June and FDR to Vinson 8th June 1937. *ibid.*

to the President insisting that, thanks to the availability of air spotting, gunnery efficiency at very long ranges had increased substantially; and long-range fire gave a better chance of penetrating a ship's vitals. Thus, he argued, if the US Navy accepted the 14-inch gun (favoured by the British of course) it would sacrifice a great advantage.[1] It seems likely that the views of Reeves, who was no anglophile, stiffened opinion in the General Board and Navy Department over adhering to the 16-inch gun for the new ships.

In that same month the General Board reviewed the known building programmes of all the naval powers and produced their proposals both for immediate expansion and for a long-term programme spread over the next ten years.[2] The former was fairly modest (an increase of one battleship, twelve destroyers and six submarines). Although the inclusion of the first two battleships caused the Construction Budget to leap up to $168½ millions for 1937 Congress authorised virtually the whole sum.[3] It is interesting to find that, exactly as in Britain, the chief difficulty in carrying out the naval expansion was in the manufacture of heavy guns and of armour plate.[4] In September 1937 Leahy answered a list of questions from the President about stocks of mines, net defences, Sonar (Asdic) development and the supply of the new torpedo-bomber aircraft to carriers. In general the CNO was satisfied with the position except for production of torpedoes, of which there was 'a most critical' shortage and only one factory was producing them.[5] Steps were taken early in 1938 to increase production.[6]

The US Navy, like the British, had at this time not only to get approval for increased personnel—from 112,313 in 1935 to 123,540 in 1936 and 131,840 in 1937—but to form Naval and Marine Corps Reserves. After a conference had been held on the latter subject in the Navy Department the draft of a Naval Reserve Act was submitted to the President. It became law in June 1938.[7]

[1] *ibid.*, PSF, Dept. Corresp., Box 25.

[2] GB. 420-2, serial 1741 of 8th May 1937.

[3] Op. 09B91R of 5th May 1965. The total expenditure in the 1936–37 Fiscal Year was $529 millions.

[4] GB. 420-2, serial 1741 of 8th May 1937.

[5] Leahy to FDR 18th Sept. 1937. Roosevelt papers, PSF, Dept. Corresp., Box 28.

[6] Letters Swanson to FDR 8th April 1937 and Chief of Bureau of Ordnance to same 5th Jan. 1938. *ibid.*, Boxes 28 and 25 respectively.

[7] HR. 10594, 75th Congress, 3rd Session. Enacted 25th June 1938. Correspondence on it is in Roosevelt papers, Official File 18, Boxes 3 and 3A.

Towards the end of that year Admiral H. E. Yarnell, the C-in-C, US Asiatic Fleet sent Leahy an outline plan for a maritime war against Japan which would avoid deployment of huge land forces. He believed that Japan could be 'strangled' by economic pressure and blockade, and attacked the concept that victory could only be achieved by a 'battle fleet action'. There was of course nothing particularly original in Yarnell's appreciation, but it is interesting to find it put forward by a Flag Officer at a time when, in the American as well as the British and Japanese Navies, the battle fleet concept was still dominant. Leahy thought it important enough to send on to the President, who replied 'Yarnell talks a lot of sense' and gave the CNO his own thoughts on the matter. They included the conversion of oil-fired long-endurance merchant ships for use in the 'Fleet Train' of supply vessels, each fitted with about ten scout planes and a dual purpose A-A armament. To that idea Leahy replied that his plans provided for conversion of a dozen such vessels to seaplane tenders and another dozen to aircraft carriers; but the latter had to be capable of 20 knots, and the USA only possessed ten ships which met that need. Thus the concept of 'mobile support', later known as the Fleet Train, though certainly favoured by the Navy Department, made little progress towards fulfilment in the 1930s.[1]

As regards the official American joint services' war plan, at about the time when Yarnell's views were being discussed a new 'Orange Plan' for war against Japan was prepared. Its primary object was to hold the 'strategic triangle' formed by joining Alaska to Hawaii and Panama; but the navy still adhered to their concept of an offensive strategy mentioned earlier. The outcome was a not very satisfactory compromise reached early in 1938 by which maritime control was to be extended westwards as fast as possible, while attacks on Japan's sea communications and economic pressure would, it was hoped, combine to weaken the expected southward drive by her forces. The fact that the Philippines could not be held was now tacitly admitted.[2]

The reader will recall that British policy with regard to exchange of information with the Americans was discussed in 1936, and that the Admiralty view was then distinctly cool. In mid-1937 the US Naval

[1] Yarnell's report of 15th Oct. 1937 and correspondence between FDR and Leahy on it. Roosevelt papers, PSF, Dept. Corresp., Box 25.

[2] Louis Morton, *The War in the Pacific: Strategy and Command: The First Two Years* (Washington, 1962) which is vol. I of the American official military history of World War II, has the best account of the pre-war evolution of the plans here outlined.

Attaché in London reopened the issue with the DNI, and as the proposal circulated around the Admiralty it became evident that the Naval Staff favoured a wider exchange of information but the supply and technical departments, with the noteworthy exception of the Director of Scientific Research, were against it on the grounds that they stood to gain little or nothing thereby. The issue went to the Board, and Chatfield wrote, 'I consider that the closer we can get to the US Navy the better', though he agreed with the technical departments' view that we would not gain much by it. Duff Cooper, the First Lord, sensibly remarked that it was futile to enter such negotiations in a bargaining spirit, and reminded his naval colleagues that the American Fleet Air Arm 'is supposed to be the best in the world whereas ours is a source of grave anxiety'. He proposed that a list of subjects 'with regard to which they could teach us something' should be prepared.[1] This proposal finally produced 75 subjects on which the Admiralty was prepared to exchange information 'on a reciprocal basis' and 25 on a 'non-reciprocal basis'. The Board's decision was that 'the US Navy was to be treated exceptionally', and that where information was asked for 'we shall where possible give it', demanding however a *quid pro quo* if there was a different subject on which we might benefit from exchange. Broadly speaking, the Board thus overruled the misgivings and self-confidence of the technical departments, though Chatfield adhered to the view 'that in tactical matters we are superior to them' (the US Navy).[2] A recent naval air mission led by Commander John[3] had, the ACNS pointed out, revealed that 'we have little or nothing to learn from the USA on the *operational* side', and although there was much 'we would like to copy' on the *training* side the current division of responsibility between the Admiralty and Air Ministry made it difficult.[4] It will thus be seen that by early 1938 there had been a considerable change in the Admiralty's outlook; and the change was emphasised by the arrival in London of Captain Royal E. Ingersoll for talks with the Director of Plans (Captain T. S. V.

[1] Minutes by Chatfield and Duff Cooper of 8th and 12th March 1938. Adm. 116/4302. An example of the opposition from technical departments was the DNC's view that nothing should be given about Damage Control or Boom Defence of harbours.

[2] Board Minute 3547 of 7th May and Memo. of 12th May 1938. Adm. 167/101 and 167/100.

[3] Later Admiral of the Fleet Sir Caspar John, First Sea Lord 1960–63.

[4] Minute of 15th June 1938 by Admiral J. H. D. Cunningham. Adm. 116/4302.

Phillips) on a very wide field of policy and operational matters.[1]

On the American side the background to the Ingersoll-Phillips talks may be traced to Roosevelt's idea of instituting a distant blockade of Japan jointly with the British, about which he had first given a public hint in his notorious 'quarantine speech' of 5th October 1937. Though the very unfavourable reception accorded to it had prevented him from developing the idea further it seems to have remained in the back of his mind, and the sinking of the *Panay* and other acts of Japanese aggression in December of that year produced the opportunity desired by the President.[2] Broadly speaking his idea was that the Americans would 'look after everything up to the Philippines and Great Britain the western section' of the Pacific, with the object of cutting off Japan's supply of raw materials.[3] The US Navy Department linked this concept with their current building programme, and Ingersoll was instructed to seek British agreement to waiving the 35,000-ton limit for the projected new battleships. He arrived in London on the last day of the year and was met by, among others, Eden the Foreign Secretary— which shows the importance he attached to the conversations.[4]

On the British side the detailed discussions, which started on 3rd January, were left in the hands of Captain Phillips, but Chatfield and James (DCNS) took an intimate interest in their progress. Phillips at once outlined the plan to send to Singapore a formidable force, including nine capital ships, three aircraft carriers, nineteen cruisers and large numbers of lesser vessels; but he did make it plain that these optimistic proposals would have to be considerably reduced if a general European war broke out. On the American side Ingersoll gave warning that his department was wholly opposed to any strong steps being taken until the fleet already in commission 'is brought up to 100 per cent full complement and prepared in all respects for war'; but he revealed that the submarines and aircraft on the Pacific coast were in fact fully manned, that the 'advanced force' was being completed to full complement, and that most of the important units on the west side of the continent were 85% manned. He also reported a modification of the President's original 'distant blockade' plan, whereby the

[1] Adm. 1/9822.

[2] See article by John McV. Haight, *Franklin D. Roosevelt and a Naval Quarantine of Japan*. Pacific Historical Review, vol. XL, no. 2 (May 1971).

[3] Sir Ronald Lindsay's report of meeting with Roosevelt and Hull on 16th Dec. 1937. FO. 371/20961 (1937).

[4] Lord Avon, *Facing the Dictators* (Cassell, 1962), pp. 619–20.

British should cover a line from Singapore through the southern Philippines at least as far as the new Hebrides, and the Americans extend the line eastwards through Fiji, Samoa and Hawaii. The final agreement was that the US Navy would assume responsibility for the entire west coast of North and South America, including the defence of Canada and the Panama Canal.[1]

The talks lasted from 3rd to 14th January, and the 'agreed record' covered a very wide range of subjects such as the 'Composition, state of readiness and initial movement of Fleets', and 'General Policy', which included the synchronisation of the arrival of the British Fleet at Singapore and the US Fleet at Honolulu. The effects of German or Italian intervention in the event of an Anglo-American war with Japan were also covered. 'Arrangements for inter-communication' between the two fleets, and the use of each other's codes and cyphers were agreed, as was 'Interchange of Communication Personnel' to familiarise them with the other navy's procedures. Finally Chatfield made not the slightest objection to the increase of battleship tonnage desired by the Americans. The formal and informal records make it plain that the talks went very well, and one cannot but contrast the open-handedness shown by the Admiralty towards the Americans with the extreme caution shown over the question of staff talks with the French. The difference must surely have arisen from British reluctance to accept a 'Continental commitment'.

[1] Record of Ingersoll-Phillips conversations. Adm. 1/10012, copy in US Naval History Division. Also 'Notes on Conversations with Admiralty' by Ingersoll's assistant Captain Russell Wilson. Records of US Naval War Plans Division.

CHAPTER XII

The Spanish Civil War

1936-1939

THOUGH THE terrible civil strife which tore Spain to pieces in the 1930s had greater influence on international politics and, in the field of the fighting services, on air and land warfare than on naval policy, no history of any aspect of the period can possibly ignore it; and it did bring to the fore a number of important features of maritime war.

The end of the dictatorship of Primo de Rivera in January 1930, followed by the abdication of King Alfonso XIII in April 1931, initiated a long period of political turmoil in Spain. Though army officers had for the most part taken the oath of loyalty to the new Republic many of them had no intention of keeping it. The situation was complicated by strong separatist movements in the Basque provinces in the north-west and in Catalonia in the north-east; but from 1931–33 the predominantly socialist government of Manuel Azaña was able to hold a fairly even balance, and to keep extremists of the right and left in check. In 1934 however widespread industrial strife broke out in the mining region of Asturias, and was savagely repressed by military forces partly brought from Spanish Morocco under General Francisco Franco. For his part in these events he was 'exiled' to the Canary Islands.[1]

In the elections of February 1936 the 'Popular Front' government of Azaña was returned by a large majority; but plotting against it among the military none the less continued. On 12th July an aircraft chartered in England for cleverly disguised purposes flew to Casablanca and then on to Las Palmas on Grand Canary, where it arrived on 15th. During

---

[1] This brief summary of a very involved story depends heavily on Hugh Thomas, *The Spanish Civil War* (Revised Ed., Penguin Books, 1965). Henceforth cited as *Thomas*.

the following night Franco reached Las Palmas by boat from Tenerife, and on 18th he issued a manifesto establishing military government throughout the Canaries. Meanwhile revolts had broken out in Spanish Morocco and in Andalusia, and on 19th the first troops of the Army of Africa, which consisted of the Foreign Legion and Moorish regulars, were ferried by a destroyer to Cadiz. That day Franco landed in the chartered aircraft at Tetuan, and took charge of the revolt in Morocco.

The division of the Spanish Navy between the government and the supporters of the rising began on 18th July when the officers of three destroyers sent from Cartagena to Melilla were overwhelmed by their crews, who refused to act in support of the revolt. In nearly all the warships the officers refused to accept the orders of José Giral, the Minister of Marine, who thereupon dismissed them and delegated their authority to ratings. This led to widespread slaughter of the officers, with the result that the sea power which the government should have been able to wield by virtue of its possession of the greater part of the fleet was rendered ineffective at the crucial moment. The Republic's warships were ordered south from Vigo and Ferrol with the object of commanding the Gibraltar Straits; but at Ferrol fierce fighting ended with the surrender to the rebels of the old battleship *España* and the modern light cruiser *Almirante Cervera*. The acquisition of the naval bases on the Atlantic coast by the Nationalists also brought them the new heavy cruisers *Canarias* and *Baleares*, which had been laid down at Ferrol in 1928 and were almost completed. Those ports now became the principal Nationalist (or rebel) naval bases, and it was to Ferrol and Corunna that the Germans sent arms and supplies by sea when, as will be told shortly, they decided to support Franco.

From the early days the Republican government controlled the battleship *Jaime Primero*, three cruisers, fifteen destroyers and about ten submarines, which should have been enough to secure local command of the sea in the Straits of Gibraltar—had not discipline completely broken down as a result of lower deck committees taking over control—with the connivance of the Madrid government.

As the only reliable troops available to the rebels were the Foreign Legion and Moorish regulars (about 32,000 strong) transport from Morocco to the mainland was the first crucial issue; and because local maritime control could not be relied on air transport became essential. It was Germany who supplied an air lift for some 1,500 troops to Seville in late July and early August. The withdrawal of the government's warships to Cartagena and Barcelona marked the failure to carry out what should have been their primary task; and the fact that the revolt was not crushed in the early stages must be attributed largely to that cause. Early in August the Nationalists were able to ferry men and supplies across the Straits to Algeciras in Gibraltar Bay virtually unhindered. Later that month the Italian heavy cruiser *Gorizia* was badly damaged by a petrol explosion while at Tangier. She was towed to Gibraltar and docked, and 'careful measurements' revealed that, as had long been suspected, her displacement was at least 10% higher than the 10,000 tons permitted by the Washington Treaty. When this fact was reported home the CID considered making a protest in some form or other; but the Committee was anxious not to do anything which might vitiate the current attempt to achieve a rapprochement with Italy, and to obtain her accession to the 1936 London Naval Treaty. After a great deal of talk nothing at all had been done by the end of October 1937, and the matter was then apparently dropped.[1]

In the Balearic Islands the important harbour of Port Mahon, Minorca, was secured for the government; but an expedition sent to Majorca early in August ended in fiasco. The 7,000 government troops put ashore simply were not trained to carry out that most difficult of maritime undertakings, a combined operation, and were put to flight by a small number of Italian aircraft and a contingent of soldiers from Africa. Thenceforth Majorca remained in Nationalist hands, and was to play an important part in later events.

Both sides in the conflict were quick to seek foreign aid. The air transport from Morocco supplied by the Germans in July 1936, already mentioned, was the first occasion on which it was of vital importance to the Nationalists; but on the other side the French soon provided the Republican government with naval technicians and with air pilots. The first German merchant ship carrying munitions for the Nationalists left Hamburg early in August at a time when the Republicans were negotiating to buy arms from the same source. The Germans also organised a 'tourist group' to provide pilots and technicians to Franco; while in Italy Ciano, the Foreign Minister, set up a special department to handle aid to the same side.

The second crucial intervention in the civil war took place in November 1936, when Soviet Russia's aid and the arrival of the International Brigades probably saved Madrid; but that result was offset by the massive German and Italian supplies sent to the Nation-

[1] CID. 1326B and 1348B of 24th May and 18th Aug. 1937. Cab. 4/26. Taken at 294th, 299th and 300th CID meetings of 17th June, 14th and 18th Oct. 1937. Cab. 2/6.

alists early in 1937, so helping to restore their morale, which had been badly shaken by the failure to take the capital. Though the French Popular Front government of Léon Blum was very sympathetic to the government cause, the Franco-Spanish frontier was only opened for the transit of volunteers and supplies for comparatively brief periods.[1]

The concept of 'Non-Intervention' in the civil war is certainly attributable to Blum's government; but it was British pressure to make that policy effective which limited French aid and caused the closures of the frontier. On the German and Russian sides there was a remarkable affinity between Hitler's and Stalin's aims. Both wanted to prevent the defeat of the side they supported, but both were markedly reluctant to provide assistance on such a large scale that a general European war would result. The 50,000 Italian troops sent to Spain were numerically much the largest contingent on the Nationalist side, but were not enough to achieve victory; and it is likely that if a comparable number of German or Russian soldiers had been sent the conflict would have spread. The reluctance of Germany and Russia to accept that risk was among the causes that prolonged the civil war.

The initial strategy of the Nationalists was to drive north from Seville in order to cut the country in two and secure the industrial areas of the north, while other columns struck eastwards to relieve the besieged rebel pockets in southern Spain. The Basque provinces of Guipuzcoa (capital San Sebastian) and Vizcaya (capital Bilbao) were unhappily placed. Though strongly Catholic they threw in their lot with the government because it had promised to respect their strong desire for a large measure of autonomy. Their conquest thus became a primary object of the Nationalists, who sent many of their warships to blockade and bombard the seaports. It was a misfortune for the government that, in addition to coping with the military revolt, it should have been weakened by the separatist tendencies and differing ideologies of Catalonia and the Basque provinces.

As the Nationalists closed in on Bilbao in the spring of 1937 the transport of foodstuffs and medical supplies by sea in British ships (which carried no military equipment) became an issue which aroused very strong feelings in Britain—especially after the destruction of

[1] *Thomas*, p. 768 gives as the periods when the French frontier was open as 17th July to 8th Aug. 1936, about 20th Oct. 1937 to Jan. 1938, 16th March to 13th June 1938, and finally from January 1939.

Guernica by German bombers on 26th April, an act of barbarity immortalised by Picasso.[1]

We must now turn to the influence of these events on British naval policy. The sudden and heavy demands for the presence of warships which arose so soon after the conclusion of the Abyssinian crisis in June 1936, while many ships were still concentrated in the eastern Mediterranean or on passage home, must have been highly unwelcome to the Admiralty. For they wanted to give long overdue leave to ships' companies and to resume the heavy training programme necessitated by the expansion of the fleet. Thus there was an instinctively favourable reaction in Whitehall towards the idea of 'Non-Intervention'. None the less as soon as the civil war broke out ships were diverted to Spain, and by 22nd July 1936 fifteen had arrived in the major ports. The broad dispositions were that the Home Fleet looked after the northern sector, keeping one or two capital ships or heavy cruisers and about half a destroyer flotilla off that coast, while the Mediterranean Fleet, based generally on Gibraltar, assumed responsibility for protecting British interests on the east coast of Spain.

At the outbreak of the revolt the British embassy under Sir Henry Chilton was at its summer residence at San Sebastian, then in Republican hands. However it soon moved first to Hendaye just over the French frontier and then to St. Jean de Luz, where it was not well placed to receive rapid, accurate and impartial reports on events inside Spain. The function of the British warships was to rescue refugees of many nationalities, including summer visitors to Spanish seaside resorts, from military attacks or air raids by either side. It was difficult, as well as frequently harrowing work; but it was discharged with tact and diplomacy.[2] The arrival of the German pocket battleship *Deutschland* off San Sebastian in July introduced new complications, and the German Admiral Carls was with some difficulty dissuaded by a British destroyer from sending a landing party ashore.[3]

---

[1] Arising out of a review by Professor Hugh Thomas of Herbert R. Southworth's book *La Destruction de Guernica* in the *Times Literary Supplement* of 11th April 1975 a long controversy ensued in the correspondence columns regarding whether the Germans or the Basques themselves had destroyed Guernica. But the outcome was conclusive reaffirmation of the fact that it was done, deliberately, by the Germans.

[2] Adm. 116/3677 has a contemporary narrative of the activities of the British Navy in the Spanish Civil War. Reports of Proceedings of individual ships and squadrons and copies of the many signals which passed between London and them are in Adm. 116/3678 and 3679.

[3] R of P *Veteran*. Adm. 116/3678.

The first meeting of the 'International Committee for the Application of the Agreement regarding Non-Intervention', to give its full title, took place in London on 9th September 1936. The chair was taken by W. S. Morrison, Financial Secretary to the Treasury, but at subsequent meetings he was replaced by Lord Plymouth, Under-Secretary for Foreign Affairs.[1] Progress in making the concept of Non-Intervention effective was however very slow, and it was not until Observers (many of whom were retired naval officers) were placed on board ships bound for Spanish ports early in 1937 that the agreement began to assume some reality.

On 15th August 1936 the British government prohibited the export of war material to Spain, and an informal French approach by Admiral François Darlan, the Chief of Naval Staff, to Chatfield made it plain that there was no possibility of overt British assistance being given to the Republican cause, and that it was no use trying to use Hankey as the channel to further that purpose. Doubtless the murder of so many Spanish naval officers had not created a favourable impression of the Republicans in the eyes of Chatfield, and indeed of the British navy as a whole. Though it continued to act with impartiality in such matters as the rescue of refugees, its views, and sometimes its reports (notably regarding the blockade of Bilbao, to be referred to shortly) were in general pro-Franco.

On 23rd August the USSR and next day Germany signed decrees forbidding the export of arms to Spain—without the slightest intention of observing them. As Professor Thomas has remarked 'Russian double-dealing was closely matched by Germany', and the Non-Intervention Committee thus graduated 'from equivocation to hypocrisy and humiliation'.[2] In all 28 nations took part in these farcical proceedings,[3] and study of the Committee's deliberations makes it seem astonishing that so many flagrant abuses could have

---

[1] The papers dealing with this subject are in the EAC (Economic Advisory Council) series. The reason apparently is that Mr. Francis Hemming was secretary to both the EAC and the Non-Intervention Committee, and found it administratively convenient to treat the two activities together. The papers are now in the Cab. 62 class in the PRO and the related Foreign Office papers in FO. 849. The surviving records of the International Board, which operated the Non-Intervention Committee's 'Observation Plan' and organised 'Neutrality Observers' to take passage in ships bound for Spanish ports were placed in Corpus Christi College, Oxford by Mr. Hemming.

[2] *Thomas*, pp. 337-8.

[3] Cmd. 5300 of 3rd Nov. 1936. Mexico was the only country which openly sent arms and supplies to the Republicans.

been disregarded and so much bland duplicity condoned. Nor does the USA, though not a signatory of the agreement, come out of the story with any better credit. The Neutrality Act of May 1935 made it illegal to sell arms to a belligerent once the President had proclaimed the existence of a state of war. But Cordell Hull, the Secretary of State, was strongly in favour of the Anglo-French Non-Intervention concept; and as the President could not invoke the Neutrality Act because it did not cover civil wars, all that was done was to announce a 'moral embargo' on the export of arms to Spain on 7th August. This of course proved futile, and in fact favoured the Nationalists.[1]

Towards the end of August 1936 the British COSs placed their views on these intricate problems before the CID at the request of the Foreign Office. They expressed strong concern about the possible occupation by Italy of any part of Spain, including the Balearic and Canary islands and Spanish Morocco; and they declared that our interest lay in maintaining 'the territorial integrity of Spain and her possessions' and in ensuring her 'benevolent neutrality . . . in the event of our being engaged in a European war'. At the same time they regarded it as 'most important to avoid any measures which, 'while failing to achieve our object, merely tend to further alienate Italy'. Finally they wanted to press ahead with the conclusion of a 'Non-Intervention pact by all the principal powers'.[2] On the same day that the Cabinet took this paper they had before it one by Eden in which, in a circumlocutory way, he proposed to give Italy a warning that 'any alteration of the *status quo* in the western Mediterranean must be a matter of the closest concern to HM Government'.[3]

Late in September the Cabinet considered what policy should be adopted with regard to evacuation of refugees, and it is evident that the chief anxiety was to preserve strict neutrality by not allowing partisans of either side to use British warships.[4] The Admiralty very reasonably asked for latitude to be allowed to Captains of warships in deciding who could be evacuated, and that was agreed to.

In November Eden brought up the question of granting Belligerent Rights to Franco. Hoare, the First Lord, and Runciman (Board of Trade) favoured doing so because British ships were known to be

---

[1] See p. 359 *note* regarding the replacement of the 1935 Neutrality Act later.

[2] COS. 509 of 24th Aug. 1936. Became CID. 1259B. Cab. 2/6. Taken by Cabinet on 31st Aug. as CP. 234(36). Cab. 24/264.

[3] CP. 233(36) of 31st Aug. 1936. *ibid.*

[4] CP. 252(36) of 29th Sept. 1936. Cab. 24/264.

carrying arms from Russia to Barcelona, and Franco had expressed the intention to stop this traffic by blockading the port.[1]

Though powers existed to prohibit the export of arms from Britain new legislation would be needed to stop British registered ships from carrying such cargoes from any other country to Spain, and the government proposed to tell both sides that they intended to introduce it. Meanwhile the policy of Non-Intervention was to continue.[2] In retrospect it does seem strange that any British government should have been prepared to acquiesce in the stopping of its merchant ships on the high seas, and in their being searched for contraband. But it was known that large numbers of foreign ships, especially Greek-owned vessels, were being transferred to British register in order to partake in the highly lucrative arms traffic to Spain; and it was natural to try and prevent such abuses of the British flag. In August 1937 the Naval Staff commented that such reports emphasised 'the scandalous nature of these so-called British ships', and declared that 'it is monstrous that this state of affairs should be allowed to continue'. Action by the Foreign Office had however so far been 'disappointing'.[3]

Having decided to take action to stop the carriage of arms from all countries the Cabinet ordered the 'Carriage of Munitions to Spain Bill' to be drafted, and Eden said that he would watch for 'a favourable opportunity to confer Belligerent Rights on both sides'. He mentioned the fall of Madrid, which at the time appeared imminent, as the moment when it might be done.[4] In the following month the Foreign Secretary asked what action should be taken about the large quantity of German and Italian arms being landed in Majorca; but no decision was reached.[5]

Early in 1937 Eden drew attention to the large number of 'volunteers' serving on the Nationalist side and produced a complicated plan to use the British Fleet 'to supervise by sea all approaches to Spanish ports'.

[1] *Thomas*, Appendix 3 shows that out of 164 merchant ships which sailed from Black Sea ports to Spain between Sept. 1936 and March 1938, 39 were British, 34 Soviet and 71 Spanish, but as shipowners changed the registry of their ships in order to enjoy the fruits of this highly profitable traffic it is impossible to feel confidence in such statistics—which in any case are of German origin.

[2] CP. 312(36) of 22nd Nov. 1936. Cab. 24/264.

[3] Minutes by DOD and D of P on report of Captain, 4th Destroyer Flotilla 20th Aug. 1937. Adm. 116/3678.

[4] Cabinet 27(36) of 25th Nov. 1936. Cab. 23/86.

[5] CP. 335(36) of 14th Dec. 1936. Cab. 24/265. Taken by Cabinet on 16th Dec. Cab. 23/86.

When the Cabinet discussed it Hoare, the First Lord, understandably expressed opposition to what would in effect be a blockade of the whole Spanish coast; and one does feel that the Foreign Office showed remarkably little understanding of what such an undertaking would entail. As Hoare said, mobilisation of the Home and Mediterranean Fleets would be necessary, and even so success could not be guaranteed.[1] The outcome was that Eden threw the responsibility for working out how the principle involved in his idea should be implemented on to the Non-Intervention Committee, a body which was not likely to produce an effective answer.[2] More to the point was the question he raised in March about what should be done regarding the seizure by the Nationalists of the products of British mining enterprises—notably those of the Rio Tinto and Tharsis companies. In fact Franco was using their products to finance his purchases of German arms.[3] Again one feels that the Foreign Office was out of touch with realities since, as Hoare pointed out, although we could legally intercept British ships, to take such action against foreign ships could be regarded as a *casus belli*.[4] The outcome was that Eden had in effect to withdraw an idea which, as most of the cargoes in question were carried in German or Italian ships, certainly contained dangerous possibilities.[5]

In London a 'Committee on the Protection of British Shipping' was formed and met for the first time under the chairmanship of Lord Hailsham, the Lord Chancellor on 7th April.[6] Three more meetings with Simon in the chair took place before the end of the month;[7] but the intricacies of the situation were such that no firm decisions emerged.

In April 1937, at about the time of the destruction of Guernica, the blockade of Bilbao became an important international issue. As the Nationalist land forces closed in on the port they naturally tried to prevent all supplies, including foodstuffs, being carried in by sea. British warships advised merchantmen not to enter north Spanish ports but to go to St. Jean de Luz and await developments. A number of cargo ships, though anxious to enter Bilbao, complied with this

[1] CP. 6(37) of 8th Jan. 1937. Cab. 24/267. SS(37) 1st meeting of same day. Cab. 23/87. (SS papers recorded special Cabinet meetings. Also in Cab. 27/628.)
[2] SS(37) 2nd meeting on 9th Jan. 1939. Cab. 24/267.   [3] *Thomas*, p. 351.
[4] CP. 80(37) of 1st March. Cab. 24/268. Taken by Cabinet with First Lord's memo. CP. 82(37) on 3rd March 1937.
[5] Cabinet 10(37) of 3rd March 1937. Cab. 23/87.
[6] MRS(37) series. Cab. 27/639.
[7] On 16th, 21st and 28th April 1937. Cab. 27/639.

advice. The Nationalist attempt to blockade Bilbao and other ports raised many intricate legal problems, such as exactly where the limit of territorial waters ended. We only recognised the limit as three miles, but the Nationalists claimed six miles; and it was uncertain whether the line ran from headland to headland or followed coastal indentations. There was also the tricky question of whether a warship which was outside territorial waters could legally seize a merchant ship which was inside that limit.

Here Commander Harry Pursey, whom we last encountered on board the *Hood* at the time of the Invergordon mutiny, appears once more on the scene. He had recently retired from the Navy, taken up journalism and become active in Labour party politics. He argued vigorously that the blockade of Bilbao announced by the Nationalists was largely bluff and was incapable of enforcement. A 'Committee of Investigation into the Working of the Non-Intervention Agreement' invited him to go out to Bilbao and ascertain whether the blockade was effective and so legal in International Law—which argument had been the justification for the advice given to British merchantmen not to enter the port.

In fact reports on the effectiveness of the blockade sent by the senior officer of the British destroyer patrol[1] and from the embassy at St. Jean de Luz were almost certainly Nationalist inspired. Pursey was able to show that the mines laid off Bilbao (actually of World War 1 origin and often defective) had been swept up, and that the coast defence guns, which were of British manufacture and modern, could and would defend ships against Nationalist interference within the three mile limit. Thus all that was needed was for the British Navy to exercise its normal function of protecting merchant shipping on the high seas. Pursey represented that state of affairs vigorously to his political leaders at home.[2]

Meanwhile feeling was rising in Parliament and the Press regarding the aid reaching the Nationalists, the British government's inertia when Republican interests were at stake, and the ineffectiveness of Non-Intervention. On 14th April Attlee moved a motion of censure in the Commons and launched a bitter attack deploring the government's

[1] Captain (later Vice-Admiral) C. Caslon of the *Blanche*. See Rs of P in Adm. 116/3678 and 3679.

[2] Pursey to the author 18th July 1975. See G. L. Steer, *The Tree of Gernika* (Hodder and Stoughton, 1938) regarding Pursey's part in the breaking of the blockade of Bilbao and, later, the rescue of Basque refugees from Santander.

failure 'to give protection to British merchant ships on their lawful occasions'—with recent events at Bilbao very much in mind. Simon (Home Secretary) and Eden defended the policy of Non-Intervention, which had been signed as long ago as 28th August 1936 but which had so far failed signally to produce the desired results. Their speeches were not very convincing; while some ruminative remarks by Churchill did not help much. The debate was notable for the constant interruption of the speakers, and although Attlee's motion was heavily defeated (345 to 130) the embarrassment on the government benches was very evident.[1] Six days later the Opposition returned to the attack on an Adjournment Motion proposed by A. V. Alexander, the former Labour First Lord, who strongly criticised the government for failing to protect British shipping outside Spanish territorial waters and for discouraging, if not actually preventing ships carrying foodstuffs from entering the allegedly blockaded port of Bilbao. Alexander read out telegrams recently received from Bilbao, and declared that the blockade was a fiction. Hoare, the First Lord, replied for the government, and claimed that the sources of the information received about the blockade were reliable. Once again the debate generated a great deal of heat, and although the government majority was again large (119 to 49) it was plain that there was widespread concern over the treatment of the Basques.[2] It is however noteworthy that speakers on both sides made no criticism of the Navy, which they realised was doing a very difficult job with great tact and patience.

The first challenge to the so-called blockade was made by the British merchantman *Seven Seas Spray* with a cargo of foodstuffs embarked at Valencia, whence she had sailed to St. Jean de Luz. She had on board the owner to take responsibility for the consequences of ignoring warnings about entering the port—and also the Captain's 20-year-old daughter Fifi, who apparently 'slept like a top' during the passage.[3] The ship was not interfered with on the high seas, and by her safe arrival on 20th gave a highly practical demonstration of the fact that the blockade was not effective. Next day the Admiralty signalled to the senior officer, one imagines with some embarrassment, asking for particulars about the state of affairs at Bilbao.[4] On 22nd three

---

[1] Parl. Deb., Commons, vol. 322, cols. 1020–1142.   [2] *ibid.* cols. 1651–62.

[3] A. V. Alexander read this story, which actually was included in one of the telegrams sent by G. L. Steer, correspondent of *The Times*, in the House on 20th April. See Steer, *op. cit.*, pp. 202–5 and Parl. Deb., Commons, vol. 322, cols. 1656–7.

[4] AMS. 2030 and 2130 of 21st April 1937. Copies in Cab. 27/639.

British ships successfully ran the 'blockade', thanks in large measure to the *Hood* preventing interference by the *Cervera*. Though there were some tense moments the firm hand and steady nerve of Admiral Geoffrey Blake paid off. Two more British ships followed in on 25th, one on 26th ('Guernica Day'), and four more on 29th. The fiction of the 'blockade' of Bilbao was thus completely exposed.

At the time when the campaign in northern Spain was moving to its climax the Naval Staff reviewed the broad issue of the effects of the civil war. Though the Director of Plans deplored the adoption of a policy which appeared likely to antagonise 'that side . . . which it seems may eventually make Spain strong' (i.e. the Nationalists)[1] Admiral James, the DCNS, considered that whichever side won 'Spain will be weak for a generation'.[2] Chatfield was more forthright. 'A friendly Spain', he wrote, 'is of the greatest importance to this country', and 'when we return to the Foreign Policy of 'Keeping Our Friends' we shall be on safer ground'.[3]

Early in July Backhouse, the C-in-C, Home Fleet, wrote to Chatfield expressing the view that 'it would be much better to grant both sides Belligerent Rights and let them get on with the war'. We 'had done our utmost', he continued, 'in the cause of humanity, but we certainly cannot evacuate refugees indefinitely'.[4] He considered that we had acted in a 'very definitely pro-Government manner, especially in the North', and he defended the Nationalists against the charge of murdering women and children. He concluded with the revealing remark that Franco 'does restore order quickly'.[5] Chatfield replied that 'the Spanish situation remains perplexing and uncertain', and considered that we were 'at the crossways' and that 'an important decision', presumably about Belligerent Rights, 'must be taken this week'. He had refused, he continued, to accept 'a combination of Naval Patrol and Belligerent Rights' to prevent supplies reaching both sides, because 'it would only

[1] Minute of 28th May 1937. Adm. 116/3917.
[2] Minute by DCNS of 31st May 1937. *ibid.*
[3] Minute by Chatfield of 20th June 1937. *ibid.*
[4] On the earlier attitude of the Admiralty to the maintenance of the British claim to exercise Belligerent Rights in wartime see vol. I, pp. 549–51. Hankey was always a strong opponent to any relaxation of the claim. See Roskill, *Hankey*, II, pp. 451–9.
[5] Backhouse to Chatfield 4th July 1937. Chatfield papers, CHT/4/1. Backhouse is obviously here referring to evacuation of refugees from the ports of southern Spain and the Balearic Islands. British warships had stopped evacuating refugees from the northern ports in May.

ead to incidents'. 'If we are going to grant Belligerent Rights (as I hope we are)', he wrote, 'it will have to be combined with a system of observers in the Spanish ports'; but he doubted whether either side would accept that idea. He wanted to see a settlement made, even if it only lasted for a few months, because it would be important in calming the international situation, which is now very dangerous'.[1]

On 30th April the defenders of Bilbao gained a fillip by the sinking of the Nationalist battleship *España* by a mine off Santander. But despite the gallant fight put up by the Basques, Nationalist superiority on land was overwhelming, and German and Italian aid, especially in the air, was decisive. On 14th June, by which time shells were falling in the outskirts of the town, the last of the British merchant ships was ordered to leave the port. That evening (9.45 p.m.) the Basque President ordered the evacuation of women and children, and harrowing scenes ensued. During the night thousands of refugees left by sea for Santander, and perhaps 200,000 more made their way there by road during the next four days. About half the population of the city was evacuated. At sea British refugee ships were given naval protection, and the senior officer, now Admiral C. G. Ramsey, disobeyed orders by extending it to Spanish ships when the Nationalists tried to seize them.[2] On 19th the port fell, and so ended Basque hopes of freedom. One benefit to Britain was that the iron mines and foundries were found intact, and export of the high grade Spanish ore, which was an important element in our rearmament programme, began again almost at once.

The campaign next moved westwards, and as the Nationalists now had fewer ports to watch they were able to make their blockade more effective. Pursey moved to Santander and, there being no British Consul, he took on the consular functions on his own initiative in order to help in the evacuation of the thousands of Basque and Republican refugees. Though there were more tense encounters between British and Nationalist warships the tact and patience of the former and what British officers regarded as forbearance by the latter prevailed; but there were cases of British ships being arrested within territorial waters by Nationalist warships, and of firing on others from outside that limit. Italian forces entered Santander on 25th August. Pursey had collected a small party the previous night and escaped in a motorboat. They were picked up by a British destroyer. A mass exodus in small

---

[1] Chatfield to Backhouse 12th July 1937. *ibid.*
[2] R of P *Royal Oak.* Adm. 116/3678 and narrative in Adm. 116/3677.

boats followed and the sea was soon strewn with helpless craft. Fortunately a British merchant ship arrived and rescued many of them.[1]

In mid-September Chatfield wrote to Backhouse 'I shall be very relieved, and I am sure you will also [be], when the North coast of Spain is finally cleared up by the Insurgents and you can take away all your ships from there before winter'.[2] That somewhat myopic wish was fulfilled when in October Gijon and Aviles fell to the Nationalists and the campaign in northern Spain came to an end.

The Nationalists were now able to transfer all their warships to the south and their troops to other fronts, and we must therefore follow the former to the Mediterranean, which we left at the time when the first units of the Army of Africa were transported to the Spanish mainland.

In February 1937 the Nationalists eliminated the Republican pocket centred on the town of Malaga on the south-east coast. The Italians gave much help on land while the *Canarias* and *Baleares* bombarded the town from the sea and the German pocket battleship *Graf Spee* lay in the offing—presumably to lend the support of her presence to the Nationalists. The slaughter which followed on the capture of the town was, despite Admiral Backhouse's denial of such atrocities, mentioned above, horrible.

On 13th May 1937 the destroyer *Hunter* was mined off Almeria and suffered 17 casualties, including 8 killed. She was towed to Gibraltar for repairs, and a claim for compensation from the Nationalists amounting to £127,054 was prepared. Not surprisingly none of it was ever paid.[3] A fortnight later the *Graf Spee*'s sister ship the *Deutschland* was off Ibiza, a Nationalist stronghold in the Balearic Islands—presumably for the same reason that the *Spee* had been off Malaga. On the evening of 29th she was attacked by two aircraft—which approached out of the setting sun and caught her by surprise. One bomb exploded in the seamen's mess, causing 31 deaths and nearly 100 injured. After coming to Gibraltar to land her wounded she took the vengeful and vicious step of bombarding the town of Almeria, killing nineteen innocent people and destroying a large number of buildings. One must presume this was done with the approval of the

---

[1] Pursey claims (letter to the author of 12th June 1974) that but for his efforts evacuation of refugees in British ships would have ceased after the fall of Bilbao, and that he was instrumental in saving 60,000 persons. Steer (*op. cit.*, p. 379) gives the figure of 50,000 rescued.

[2] Letter of 17th Sept. 1937. Chatfield papers, CHT/4/1.   [3] Adm. 116/11594.

German government; but it can hardly have endeared the Nazis to the Spanish people.[1]

Early in August 1937 the Nationalists reported to Rome that very large supplies were about to be sent by the Soviets, and on 11th the Republican tanker *Campeador* was sunk in the Malta Channel by Italian destroyers in a most inhuman manner. Next day the Admiralty told the C-in-C, Mediterranean that a submarine campaign would start shortly. This intelligence, which was quickly proved correct, derived from our having broken the Italian naval cypher; but in fact Admiral Pound, the C-in-C, Mediterranean, had anticipated such attacks as long ago as the previous June, after torpedoes had been fired at the German cruiser *Leipzig* off Oran, and had already prepared plans and instructions for dealing with such an eventuality.[2] A French ship was sunk off Tunis on 13th August, and two days later the campaign was extended to the Aegean, where a Spanish ship was sunk off Tenedos. Italy not being at war these attacks were flagrant acts of piracy. On 17th the Admiralty authorised counter-attacks against any submarine which attacked a British merchant ship, and next day the C-in-C gave his command somewhat complicated rules for carrying out that permissive instruction.[3] On the last day of August a torpedo narrowly missed the destroyer *Havock*, which was on passage in the western Mediterranean. She obtained Asdic contact but failed to hold it. Other destroyers came to the scene, and after a prolonged search a deliberate attack was carried out. We now know that the target was the Italian submarine *Iride* and that, although shaken, she escaped. This comparative failure of the Asdic does not appear to have shaken British confidence in its effectiveness. Ciano, we may note, complained in his diary at this time that while 'the Army does its job' and 'the [Fascist] Militia is enthusiastic' the 'Spanish enterprise is constantly opposed by a policy of passive resistance on the part of the Navy'.[4] Evidently that service did not relish playing the part of pirates.

In London a meeting of Ministers took place early in September to discuss the developments in the Mediterranean and frame recommen-

[1] It is curious that Professor Thomas (*op. cit.* pp. 564–5) gives considerable space to the bombing of the *Deutschland* but does not mention the mining of the *Hunter* in the same month.

[2] C-in-C, Med. to Admy. no. 374 of 24th June 1937. Adm. 116/3522.

[3] AM. 2236 of 17th Aug. to C-in-C, Med. and general message 1708 of 18th Aug. 1937 by latter. *ibid.*

[4] *Ciano's Diary 1937–1938*, Trans. A. Mayor (Methuen, 1952), p. 6. Entry for 28th Aug. 1937.

dations regarding what should be done for consideration by the Cabinet.[1] Eden was prepared to go as far as to use the British Fleet to sink the *Canarias*, which would of course have been a plain act of war. Such an idea aroused understandable apprehension in the Admiralty, where the Naval Staff considered various alternatives. Their conclusion was that the only practicable measure was to conduct intensive anti-submarine operations in the areas where Italian submarines were known to be operating. They expected that searches by Asdic-fitted ships would be an effective deterrent, but if that did not prove to be the case the sinking of even one submarine would suffice to end the piracy.[2] Admiral Pound considered that the only alternative to searching for and attacking the submarines was to institute convoy, and although he was reluctant to adopt such a measure the necessary preliminary measures were put in hand.[3] Convoy would of course have involved assuming full naval control of merchant shipping, which was not a step to be undertaken lightly in time of peace. The Ministerial meeting agreed to recommend that the destroyer strength available in the Mediterranean should be increased, and that further urgent representations should be made to the Italian government. On 2nd September a British tanker, recently transferred from Greek registry, was sunk without warning off Valencia. Then Nationalist aircraft joined in the game, and ships of many nationalities were bombed indiscriminately.

On 7th September 1937 the Russians protested vigorously to Rome about the sinking of their ships, claiming that they had 'indisputable proof' that it had been done by Italian warships; but the Foreign Office, which had telegraphed two days earlier to all European embassies and legations proposing a meeting on 10th to consult about 'the intolerable situation which has arisen',[4] tried to mollify the Italians by urging that 'the conference is to discuss the future', and that they should not 'be influenced by past events'. The Italians rejected the Russian protest, while the Germans recalled that we had failed to take any action when Spanish government aircraft had bombed their own warships.[5] Mean-

---

[1] CP. 208(37) of 3rd Sept. Cab. 24/271. Taken by Cabinet on 8th Sept. 1937. Cabinet 34(37). Cab. 23/89.

[2] Minute by D of P of 1st Sept. 1937. Adm. 116/3522.

[3] C-in-C, Med. to Admy. 2318 of 26th Aug., 0018 of 5th Sept. and 2218 of 8th Sept. 1937. The second signal (no. 757) was made in three parts, but the various alternatives are in the first of them. *ibid.*

[4] Telegram of 5th Sept. and Consular Telegram no. 82 of 6th Sept. 1937 to Dominions. Copies in Adm. 116/3522.

[5] Rome and Berlin embassies to FO 9th Sept. 1937. *ibid.*

Japanese destroyers *Mochitsuki* and *Mikatsuki* (launched 1926-27) in the Whangpoo river, Shanghai August 1937. Probably a sister ship in left background.

Coronation illuminations, Hong Kong 12th May 1937, showing part of the China fleet in the harbour.

Chatfield (left) with Hore-Belisha and Kingsley Wood (Secretaries of State for War and Air) arrive at 10 Downing Street for a Cabinet meeting.
18th March 1939.

Inspection by Sir Bolton Eyres-Monsell, First Lord, at Devonport.
12th October 1934.

while Eden and Yvon Delbos, the French Foreign Minister, had been in disagreement about which nations should be invited to the conference. In the end Russia and the Black Sea states were invited, as well as all nations with Mediterranean coastlines. On 9th the Admiralty told Pound that the conference would go ahead despite the absence of Italy and Germany, and that Chatfield and Eden were leaving at once for Paris and Nyon.[1]

Things now moved very fast and on 11th September Chatfield was able to tell Pound that it seemed likely that four areas of responsibility would be established, and that the British ones would be the Malta Channel and western Mediterranean.[2] Late on 14th the agreement was signed, and the naval measures were to come into force on 20th. The British were to be responsible for the waters around Gibraltar, Malta and Cyprus and for part of the Aegean; the French for the Tunis area and Gulf of Hammamet, and Greece for the Gulf of Corinth. The Tyrrhenian Sea would be allocated to the Italians—if they came in—and the main routes which all ships were to follow were agreed.[3] But in truth there was an element of farce in these proceedings, since London knew from decyphers that the Italians had already called off their submarine operations, and the Admiralty had informed Eden and Chatfield accordingly.[4] Thus the British delegates were well aware that the purpose of the conference had been fulfilled long before the agreement was signed. Perhaps the most satisfactory feature was the cordiality of Anglo-French naval co-operation, which was markedly different from the extreme coolness shown at the time of the Abyssinian crisis, and included the use of each other's bases. Eden justifiably described the conference as a success, and telegraphed home that the French 'had played up much better than any of us had expected'. The only 'fly in the ointment' was, he continued, the Italian attitude.[5]

By the time the Nyon patrols came into force no less than 36 British destroyers were disposed in the areas of our responsibility. Two RAF flying-boat squadrons were sent out to provide air co-operation and worked from Arzeu near Oran. But the lack of shore support for them necessitated a naval depot ship being provided; and the slowness

[1] AM. 1530 of 9th Sept. 1937. *ibid.*   [2] Telegram 1700 of 11th Sept. 1937. *ibid.*
[3] Telegram 2130 of 14th Sept. and 1600 of 15th Sept. 1937. *ibid.*
[4] Ciano's diary says that he gave the order to stop the submarine operations on 4th Sept. *op. cit.*, p. 9.
[5] Telegram no. 32 to FO of 15th Sept. 1937. Copy in *ibid.*

with which the flying-boats arrived and took up their task aroused
good deal of naval sarcasm. Pound justifiably insisted that they mus
be placed under his operational control.[1] There is no need to go int
the details of the patrol arrangements, but it should be mentioned tha
the French provided 28 destroyers and also some air patrols.

After the main Nyon agreement was signed discussions continue
on three questions raised by Chatfield. They concerned the verificatio
of flags flown by merchant ships at sea, action to deal with air attack
and measures in the event of surface ship attacks. Probably with th
Campeador incident in mind, and contrary to Chatfield's desire, th
French insisted that strong measures should be taken in the event o
any repetition of such attacks. The Supplementary Agreement wa
signed on 17th September.[2] These accords were of course highl
unpopular with the Spanish Nationalists, who could thenceforth onl
use their submarines inside territorial waters, and had to rely o
surface ships to blockade Republican ports. It should also be remarke
that throughout the negotiations the French took a tougher line toward
the Nationalists than the British.

On 27th September staff talks began in Paris to try and settle th
detailed working of the Nyon Agreement, but quickly ran into diffi
culties. The Russians wanted a through-Mediterranean route whic
would ensure their ships not meeting Italian patrols; the Turks an
Greeks refused to allow Italian warships to use their ports; while th
Italians for their part insisted on recognition of their equality of statu
with the other powers before they would play. None the less anothe
supplementary agreement was signed on the last day of the month
but it was not until 30th October, and after further tricky negotiation
that the three Cs-in-C (Admirals Pound, Esteva and Bernotti) met a
Bizerta. Pound reported that the encounter was 'very satisfactory an
pleasant', agreement was reached on the zones to be taken over by th
Italians, and the date when their patrols would start was decided
Thus did the chief pirates join the Excise Men—or the principal poache
the gamekeepers; but the truth was that the ex-pirates' new activitie

[1] AM. 1335 of 16th Sept. 1937 to C-in-C, Med. Adm. 116/3525. The arrangemen
for depot ships for the flying-boats are in Adm. 116/3527.

[2] Copy in Adm. 116/3526.

[3] The chief delegates to the Paris talks were Vice-Admiral James (Britain, th
DCNS), Rear-Admiral Godfroy (France) and Vice-Admiral Pini (Italy). Adn
116/3530.

[4] C-in-C, Med. 2033 of 30th Oct. and 0243 of 11th Nov. Adm. 116/3525.

were superfluous because all the Italian submarines except the four 'Legionary' boats lent to Franco were inactive by that time.

The British flag officers and destroyer flotilla commanders were meanwhile becoming worried about the heavy wear and tear on machinery imposed by the patrols, and as everything remained quiet they wanted to reduce them. It was however difficult to do this just when the Italians had joined in. Early in December the Foreign Office agreed that the two flying-boat squadrons should return home and on 11th, after consulting Paris, that the naval patrols should be reduced.[1] On New Year's Day 1938 the Admiralty told the Cs-in-C that only minimum patrols need be continued—subject to quick reintroduction if necessary.[2] Then, on the last day of the month, a British ship was sunk (actually by a Nationalist, not an Italian submarine) off Valencia; and so the movement towards relaxing the patrols was checked. Not until the end of March was further reduction authorised, and even then the C-in-C, Mediterranean, was told to keep them 'adequate'. The British government was at the time very anxious to avoid any more 'incidents' in the Mediterranean because, in the Admiralty's words 'a delicate phase of international negotiations [with Italy] has now been entered'.[3] Compared with the futile and ineffective arrangements made by the Non-Intervention Committee the Nyon agreement and the patrol system developed out of it were outstandingly successful.

In the small hours of 6th March the most important naval action of the war took place off Cape Palos, the promontory just east of Cartagena. A convoy from Sicily escorted by three Nationalist cruisers suddenly encountered a Republican force of two cruisers and destroyers on an opposite course. Surprise was apparently complete on both sides, but a torpedo hit was scored on the *Baleares* and caused a heavy explosion. It was left to British destroyers on Nyon patrol duty in the vicinity to rescue survivors, 470 of whom were picked up under very difficult conditions.[4] That was the last success achieved by the Republican navy.

In the spring of 1938 there was a good deal of German naval activity in the western Mediterranean. No less than five U-boats were reported

---

[1] Phipps (Paris) to FO of 17th Dec. 1937 and other telegrams. Adm. 116/3530.

[2] AM. 1621 of 1st Jan. 1938. *ibid*.

[3] AM. 1156 of 1st March 1938. *ibid*. Many Cabinet papers on the Anglo-Italian conversations of Feb.–March 1938 are in Cab. 24/275.

[4] Narrative in Adm. 116/3677.

passing through the Gibraltar Straits and calling at Tangier or Ceuta, and in May the pocket battleship *Admiral Scheer* was lying in the latter port. Though the purpose of these visits must have been to show support for the Nationalists there was never any evidence that German submarines joined in the piratical Italian campaign. Though the Admiralty remained anxious about these activities they had no cause for trying to interfere with them.[1]

The piratical Italian submarine campaign in the Mediterranean and the movements of German surface warships and U-boats to support the Nationalists brought the Admiralty an uncovenanted benefit which was to yield immensely important fruits in World War II. In 1936 Admiral James, the DCNS, who had been in charge of Admiral Sir Reginald Hall's famous cryptographic organisation in World War I known as 'Room 40 OB', proposed that an Operational Intelligence Centre (OIC) should be formed in the Admiralty. In the following year a tiny nucleus was established under Paymaster Lieutenant-Commander N. E. Denning,[2] and his first task was to track and identify the Italian submarines. The experience gained emphasised the need to build more direction-finding wireless stations, of which there were at the time only three; and that was done. The DNI of the period (Admiral J. A. G. Troup) also initiated the organisation for the promulgation of Intelligence to the fleet, and took care to organise proper co-ordination between Intelligence and Operations—the lack of which had caused serious failures in World War I, notably by contributing to the escape of the German High Seas Fleet on the night after the Battle of Jutland.[3] The experience gained during the Spanish Civil War led to a steady expansion of the OIC, and by August 1939 its staff had expanded to about thirty and had been properly accommodated. After the outbreak of war a further great expansion took place, and subsections were formed to handle all aspects of enemy activity. Captain Rodger Winn, RNVR, a barrister by profession,[4] then became head of the Submarine Tracking Room, while Denning dealt with enemy surface ship activities. The contri-

[1] Between March–July U.28, 29, 31, 35 and 37 were all reported in the Gibraltar area. All were Type VII A, displacement 626/745 tons. Adm. 116/3530.

[2] Later Admiral Sir Norman Denning. He became the last DNI on the old model 1959–64 and the first Deputy Chief of Defence Staff (Intelligence) in the new organisation 1964–65.

[3] See A. J. Marder, *From the Dreadnought to Scapa Flow*, vol. III (Oxford UP, 1966), ch. IV.

[4] Later Lord Justice Winn.

bution made by the OIC to victory in the Atlantic Battle was vital.[1] It may therefore be no exaggeration to say that the totally unscrupulous activities of the Axis navies in the Spanish Civil War ultimately contributed to their own defeat.

To return to the Mediterranean and mid-1938, in that year foreign aid twice produced important, perhaps decisive, results—and for opposite sides in Spain. The opening of the French frontier from March to June and the flow of Russian supplies staved off defeat for the Republicans after the successful Nationalist campaign in Aragon. Then in the autumn the exchange by Franco of the largely British-owned mining rights mentioned earlier for German arms enabled the 'Condor Legion' to be re-equipped and the successful campaign to be fought in Catalonia.[2]

As 1938 advanced and the international situation became more threatening so did the impatience of the Admiralty and the naval Cs-in-C to be rid of the Nyon patrols increase. Though they had been chiefly planned to deal with submarine attacks it was in fact the bombing of British ships off the east coast of Spain and in government-controlled ports which caused them to be continued, though on a declining scale. In June Lord Halifax, now Foreign Secretary, wrote to Chamberlain about what he called 'this wretched Spanish bombing' of our ships. He could not see his way to granting Franco Belligerent Rights as the price for stopping such attacks.[3]

The Anglo-Italian agreement which had made the British government tread so warily in March was signed on 16th April 1938; but the British had always considered cessation of intervention in Spain an essential condition for bringing it into force, and by October the Nationalist successes had progressed so far that Halifax told the Cabinet that he believed 'we shall never again have as good an opportunity' to do so.[4] In November, following on Anglo-French conversations, the

---

[1] Roskill, *The War at Sea*, vol. 1 (HMSO, 1954), pp. 18–22 describes the organisation of the OIC, and its work constantly appears in the later volumes of that series. For a more detailed account see Donald McLachlan, *Room 39* (Weidenfeld and Nicolson, 1968). In 1975–76 three admirable articles, revealing for the first time part of the story of the British cryptographic contribution, by Patrick Beesly, who served in the OIC throughout World War II, were published in *The Naval Review* (private circulation journal).

[2] See *Thomas*, pp. 766–9 and Appendix 3.

[3] Halifax to Chamberlain 9th June 1938. Premier 1/360.

[4] CP. 231(38) of 21st Oct. 1938. Cab. 24/279. For a concise account of the Anglo-Italian agreement see *Gathorne-Hardy*, pp. 453–8.

old question of granting the Nationalists Belligerent Rights came up again in Cabinet, since Franco had rejected the Non-Intervention Committee's proposals for the withdrawal of 'volunteers' unless he was granted such rights—which would of course make it possible for him to blockade the last ports in Republican hands effectively.[1] In fact however the Nationalist victory on land rendered such a step unnecessary, and Belligerent Rights never were granted.

In the final phase of this terrible war British warships were employed almost exclusively on rescuing refugees. In February 1939 large numbers were carried from Majorca, where the garrison was still Republican but a Nationalist attack or coup was expected, to Marseilles, and in the following month members of the Spanish government were rescued from Valencia after the fall of Madrid on 27th March. In mid-February Halifax again raised in Cabinet the question of recognising the Franco government.[2] The Cabinet decided that 'it was desirable' to take that step 'in the near future',[3] and on 22nd, French agreement having been obtained, they went ahead.[4]

After it was all over the major powers tried to draw military lessons from the long war fought at the expense of the unfortunate Spaniards. The French and Russians drew the wrong lessons regarding tank warfare; but the German General who commanded a tank unit and later achieved high command called the conflict 'the European Aldershot' for what it had taught.[5] The British COS Committee deliberated the same issues, and no less than six reports were prepared on the influence of air power on land and sea warfare.[6] It is interesting to find that all of them were sent to Churchill by Kingsley Wood, the Secretary of State for Air. The one which concerns us most is the report by the JIC on 'Air Attack on Ships'. Those made on warships had totalled 80 and although no ships were sunk seventeen were damaged. The percentage of 'successful attacks' was calculated as 15.6. As regards merchant ships 81 attacks were reported, six ships were sunk and 29 damaged.[7] The COSs did not attempt to draw any

[1] Cabinet 36(38) of 22nd Nov. 1938. Cab. 23/96.
[2] CP. 46(39) of 13th Feb. 1939. Cab. 24/283.
[3] Cabinet 7(39) of 15th Feb. 1939. Cab. 23/97.
[4] Cabinet 8(39) and 9(39) of 22nd Feb. and 2nd March 1939. *ibid.* The actual date of recognition was 27th Feb. The USA followed suit on 1st April.
[5] General von Thoma. See *Thomas*, pp. 769–70.
[6] COS. 622(JIC), 624(JIC), 716(JIC), 728 and 734(JIC). Copies in Air 19/25 (Kingsley Wood Papers).
[7] COS. 685(JIC) of 17th Feb. 1938. Cab. 53/38.

conclusions from these figures—probably because the ABE Committee was still considering such questions, and every endeavour was already being made to improve the A-A armament of warships and to procure light A-A guns for merchant ships. But the Spanish war statistics certainly showed that air attack could be a very serious threat to ships—at any rate when the defences were weak.

On 20th April 1939 the Non-Intervention Committee, which had not met since July 1938, dissolved itself, and by the end of June the withdrawal of German and Italian forces was complete. The cost to Spain can only be roughly guessed, but Professor Thomas gives it as about ½ million deaths, of whom perhaps 100,000 were murdered or summarily executed. The Nationalist estimate of the financial cost put it at £3,000 millions, and several years of acute privation followed for the Spanish people.[1] It is futile to argue whether stronger British and French support for the Republican government would have resulted in Franco's defeat. It does however seem likely that it would have involved us in a general European war when our rearmament had not progressed very far—since it is hard to believe that Hitler and Mussolini would have stood by and let their protégé go down.

[1] *Thomas*, pp. 758–9.

CHAPTER XIII

The Naval Aviation Controversy Resolved

1936-1939

◆

AT THE beginning of the period covered by this chapter the Admiralty was still plagued by the shortage of volunteers to specialise in both Pilot and Observer duties in the Fleet Air Arm. We have already seen how the Air Ministry repeatedly refused proposals to train naval ratings as pilots, and under the terms of the Trenchard-Keyes agreement of July 1924 there was nothing the Admiralty could do to get what they wanted. But, illogical though it was, they were free to train whoever they liked as Observers, and accordingly at the end of 1935 they took steps to introduce a new class of rating for training as 'Observers' Mates' who could be promoted to Warrant Rank as Boatswains (O). Treasury approval was obtained fairly easily and the new rank and ratings were actually introduced in 1935–36.[1]

In the autumn of 1935 the Naval Staff prepared and sent to the Air Ministry a paper setting out 'Requirements of Aircraft for Protection of Trade and for Coastal Operations' as a basis for discussion on the number and type of aircraft needed to provide 'reasonable security to our trade routes and operations in coastal waters'. The choice between flying-boats and carrier-borne aircraft was closely investigated, and although use of the former was not ruled out the latter were preferred as being 'the more economical and mobile provision'—a view which was amply borne out by the long delay over getting flying-boats out to the Mediterranean during the Abyssinian crisis,

[1] Observers' Mates by Order-in-Council of 13th Aug. 1935 and Boatswains (O) by Order-in-Council of 3rd July 1936. Adm. 178/169.

and which was to be repeated during the Spanish Civil War.[1] A curious feature of this paper is the preference expressed in it for evasive routing of merchant ships in between focal areas. Only if this policy 'should prove ineffective', it stated, 'convoy must be introduced'; but the value of aircraft searching ahead of a convoy and so forcing submarines to submerge was also stressed. Though the requirements for a war against Germany and Japan differed the staff estimated that one medium size carrier with 30 small amphibian aircraft, four small trade protection carriers each with fifteen amphibians, and 81 coastal reconnaissance aircraft at home and 36 at Singapore was a reasonable forecast of the needs. The naval staff did not expect that unrestricted submarine warfare would be employed immediately, but was anxious 'that enemy submarines should be given a decided check as soon as possible after the outbreak of war' so that 'his belief in the submarine may be shaken'.[2]

Early in 1936 the Air Staff circulated their reply. Expectedly they described 'offensive action against the enemy's submarine bases and building yards' as 'the most effective use of aircraft in meeting the menace of submarine attack against shipping'; and the same principle applied in their view to dealing with air attacks on shipping by a 'counter-offensive against the sources of his air power'. These opinions were of course a reiteration of the long-held Trenchard gospel on strategic bombing.[3] In short this inter-departmental exchange produced no progress on the contribution of aircraft to trade defence.

After Hankey, who had been present throughout the renewed discussions on the provision of naval air crews, had written to Monsell at the end of 1935 that 'it was impossible to make any progress as [the] matter stood',[4] the First Lord suggested that Sir Warren Fisher might be invited 'as a perfectly impartial person . . . to enquire into the working of the Balfour agreement' of 1923.[5] But Hankey replied that if this meant 'a re-opening of the general question' of control of the Fleet Air Arm, as of course it did, Cunliffe-Lister (soon to be Lord

[1] A staff paper of 17th Dec. 1936 drew attention to the very poor record of RAF flying-boats as regards 'mobility' on numerous occasions in that year—especially by comparison with the performance of American naval flying-boats. Adm. 116/3722.

[2] Memo. by ACNS of 28th Oct. 1935. Adm. 116/3724. The number of aircraft for trade protection in home waters was to be increased from 81 to 162 on the outbreak of war.

[3] Air Staff memo. of 4th Jan. and Naval Staff reply of 11th Feb. 1936. *ibid.*

[4] Letter of 6th Dec. 1935. Quoted in Adm. 116/3721.

[5] See vol. I, pp. 373-7.

Swinton), the Secretary of State for Air, would not agree to such a proposal.[1] Having been blocked on that front Monsell wrote to Inskip, who had just been appointed Minister for Co-ordination of Defence, asking him 'to carry out an enquiry into the whole problem of the Fleet Air Arm', which 'if there is any single question vitally affecting our defence and security shrieks for co-ordination'.[2] Inskip however replied that although 'a reopening of the fundamental question of control at the present time' would require a Cabinet decision,[3] he would do his best 'to find or suggest solutions' to the prevailing difficulties 'without prejudice to the examination of the fundamental issues at a later date'.[4] Monsell, who was about to give up office, next wrote to Inskip that, 'having lived with this subject for more than four years' he could not leave him 'in any doubt as to the very strong views of my colleagues and I as to the inefficiency of the present arrangements'.[5] In May Churchill wrote to Chatfield that he intended 'to press continually in the House of Commons' for the transfer of control of the Fleet Air Arm to the Admiralty, and Chatfield replied that he had no doubt 'that the Fleet Air Arm injustices will now be investigated by Sir Thomas Inskip, and he realises the urgency of the whole matter. As you say weak compromises cannot be accepted'.[6]

Such was the background to the first Inskip Inquiry, which took place in the latter half of July 1936 and was restricted to the provision of personnel for the FAA, the period of service by RAF officers in it, and the creation of adequate reserves of pilots and observers. In June Chatfield expressed concern about the narrowness of the inquiry. Though he found Inskip 'very sympathetic', the Minister was anxious to avoid having to obtain a Cabinet ruling seeking 'permission for him to reopen' the fundamental question of control. He believed such a decision 'might be adverse [to the Admiralty] at the moment'; so Chatfield saw 'great difficulty in tackling it except bit by bit'.[7] On 12th July he wrote to a brother officer that he was taking a short rest

[1] Hankey to Monsell 24th Jan. 1936. Quoted in Adm. 116/3721. See also Monsell's memo. of 17th Feb. 1936 to the Board which sums up the whole problem. Adm 167/94.

[2] Monsell to Inskip 21st April 1936. Cab. 16/151.

[3] See Roskill, *Hankey*, III, pp. 210–11 and 252–3.

[4] Inskip to Monsell 1st May 1936. Adm. 1/9034.

[5] Monsell to Inskip 4th June 1936. Quoted in Adm. 116/3721.

[6] Churchill to Chatfield 5th May and reply by latter of 26th May 1936. Chatfield papers, CHT/4/3 and 3/1.

[7] Chatfield to Backhouse 17th June 1936. Chatfield papers, CHT/4/1.

in the country 'before my greatest battle';[1] and there is no doubt that he intended to get the scope of the inquiry widened far beyond Inskip's original intentions.

As was always the case with these inquiries they produced a mountain of paper. Early in 1936 the Naval Staff, believing that 'the absence of a settled policy . . . has been due as much to the lack of a clearly defined statement of the problem as a whole as to lack of experience' set itself the task of remedying the deficiency. The result was a two-part volume dealing with 'The Operation of Fleet Aircraft' and 'The Provision of Aircraft to implement this policy'—including carrier-borne and catapult aircraft. Appendices gave statistics for the rate of hitting by capital ships' guns with and without air spotting, the percentage of hits with bombs and torpedoes obtainable by carrier-borne aircraft, their probable losses to A-A gunfire, and a lot of other technical data.[2] This weighty document does not appear to have been circulated outside the Admiralty, but it was probably used in producing six papers for the Inskip Inquiry between May and July. After the inevitable recapitulation of past history in the first of them, the others continued with factual statements regarding the organisation of RAF units for naval work, the Admiralty's views on the personnel problems discussed above, and answers to specific questions posed by Inskip.[3] The Air Ministry of course riposted with their version of the controversy and criticisms of the Admiralty's statements on efficiency.[4]

From the Admiralty's point of view it probably was a misfortune that Hoare took over as First Lord just before this inquiry began; for he had been Secretary of State for Air from November 1922 to June 1929 except during the brief interval of the first Labour government January-November 1924), and he was therefore fully familiar with the other side's viewpoint and with their version of the controversy. At any rate one quickly finds a cooling off of the temperature in the Admiralty after Hoare took over. To give only two examples, within a fortnight of taking office Hoare agreed to a suggestion from Inskip that the paragraphs in the Admiralty's statement about control of the FAA 'that seemed to prejudice your decision' should be deleted,[5] and in August we find him questioning the Captain of the *Glorious* very

---

[1] Chatfield to Kelly 12th July 1936. Kelly papers, KEL/110.
[2] *Naval Air Policy*, vol. 1 dated 26th March 1936. Adm. 116/3724.
[3] Papers FAA. 1–6 of 20th May to 4th June 1936. Adm. 116/3721.
[4] Papers FAA. 7–9 of May to July 1936. *ibid.*
[5] Hoare to Inskip 18th June 1936. Adm. 116/3721.

closely on 'what were the main difficulties in connection with the present organisation', and exhibiting a marked lack of enthusiasm for changing it.[1]

On 9th October Inskip sent Hoare the draft of his report with a covering note saying that it represented the views he had formed 'on the particular questions' on which he had been asked to arbitrate, but he was asking the COSs to check statements of fact before the report was issued in its final form.[2] Ten days later Chatfield produced 'a note of certain points I am hoping to raise orally with him [Inskip]';[3] but on 5th November Inskip sent his report virtually unamended to the Prime Minister with a long covering letter in which, ominously for the Admiralty, he recalled Baldwin's refusal of July 1935 to allow the issue of control of the FAA to be reopened. On the other hand although Inskip expressed the hope that his recommendations would eliminate 'some difficulties' he admitted that they were 'only a first step', that 'the real heart of the controversy' remained unsolved, that 'the constitutional question of control . . . is as acute as ever', and that 'the absence of common ground between the services is very disquieting'.[4] As a whole this important letter, though worded with lawyer-like circumspection, could be read as an offer to renew the inquiry on widened terms of reference.

If Inskip's carefully chosen words were intended to produce that effect on Baldwin they certainly did not do so on Chatfield, who evidently felt that the time had come to abandon tactful persuasion and adopt a tougher line; for he wrote that 'the Report offers no adequate solution of the problems confronting the Admiralty', that 'the vital point is that the "Efficiency of the Navy" is at stake, no less', and that except for the slender olive branch of the Air Ministry's offer to train 12–15 naval ratings as pilots 'as an experiment', it gave the Navy 'no more than [was] conceded 13 years ago' by the Balfour Committee. He pointed out that 'If ever the Fleet's Air Units fail under the test of war . . . responsibility for its failure will be laid not upon the RAF but upon the Royal Navy', and added that the Navy 'ought not to be asked to shoulder this vital responsibility, without full

[1] 'Notes on a talk with the First Lord concerning the Fleet Air Arm', 30th Aug. 1936 by Captain B. A. Fraser (later Admiral of the Fleet Lord Fraser, First Sea Lord 1948–51). Chatfield papers, CHT/4/10.

[2] Inskip to Hoare 9th Oct. 1936. Adm. 116/3721.

[3] Chatfield to Hoare 19th Oct. 1936. *ibid.*

[4] Inskip to Baldwin 5th Nov. 1936. Premier 1/282. Copy in Adm. 116/3721.

and undivided powers'. He therefore urged that the Prime Minister should be made aware of the dangers he apprehended, and concluded with the claim that full control and responsibility for the FAA should therefore 'be transferred to the Admiralty at the earliest possible date'.[1] At any rate the real object for which Chatfield and his colleagues were working, and which Baldwin and Inskip had been trying to avoid facing, was now brought into the open. Hoare immediately sent Chatfield's protest on to Baldwin, with a copy to Inskip, saying that he was 'convinced that the views expressed in it represent the view of the Navy as a whole . . . It cuts deeply into the life of the Fleet', and feelings were probably more 'deeply stirred' there than in Whitehall.[2] Plainly Hoare had decided to give his unequivocal support to the department of which he was now head.

While the first Inskip Inquiry was in progress a conflict over policy with regard to fitting catapults in capital ships and cruisers developed inside the Admiralty. The staff wanted to build more carriers, fit more A-A guns in major warships and abandon catapults. 'It is upon this [A-A] armament', they declared, 'that the security of the vessels against air attack for their final offensive must rest'.[3] For trade protection they favoured developing a floatplane capable of landing in a moderate swell, and autogyros (the forerunner of the helicopter, developed by the Spaniard De La Cierva).[4] Henderson, the Controller, strongly disagreed with these proposals, which he considered exaggerated the weakness of catapult aircraft and played down their advantages—such as spotting for gunfire. Chatfield was 'very disturbed', and remarked that for years he had been urged to fit catapults in all large warships, but now he was being asked to take them out. He therefore decided that the views of the Cs-in-C of the main fleets should be obtained, and another meeting held when they had been received.

Chatfield's dilemma was, unfortunately, not resolved by the Cs-in-C, since Backhouse (Home Fleet) wanted 'carriers from which to operate aircraft', while Pound (Mediterranean) wanted capital ships to be 'self-contained' with spotting aircraft and also a fighter to deal with enemy

[1] Chatfield to Hoare 16th Nov. 1936. Adm. 116/3721.
[2] Hoare to Baldwin 19th Nov. 1936. *ibid.*
[3] Record of staff meeting on 26th May 1936. Adm. 1/9088–63/1937.
[4] Juan De La Cierva y Codorniu, Spanish engineer (1896–1936). The first auto-gyro flight took place in 1923 but success in hovering while stationary was not achieved until 1934. Two years later Cierva was killed in an air accident on leaving Croydon.

spotting aircraft. The First Sea Lord came down predominantly in Pound's favour and decided that capital ships should be given two TSR aircraft, and that the development of the autogyro was 'all important' as it came closest to meeting trade protection needs. He deprecated sole reliance on carriers because they might become detached from the fleet;[1] and that accordingly became the Admiralty's policy until war experience proved that catapult aircraft were rarely of use and could be a danger to their parent ships; while the autogyro was not sufficiently developed to play an important part in trade defence until long after the war. The disagreements of 1936–37 are of interest in showing how extraordinarily difficult it was to frame sound policy as long as experience was confined to theoretical argument backed only by the sometimes dubiously valid experience of peacetime exercises.

To return to the main controversy over control of the FAA, after the result of the first Inskip Inquiry had been given to Parliament the usual flood of letters from retired officers, 'our special correspondent', and various experts appeared in *The Times* under the heading 'Dualism in the Air Services'.[2] Though most participants in the argument adhered to their previously committed views it is noteworthy that Admiral Keyes, the co-author with Trenchard of the 1924 agreement, had come round to favouring the complete transfer of control of the FAA to the Admiralty.[3] Early in 1937 he wrote at length to Hoare and to Chatfield explaining the background to the 1924 decision and why it could now reasonably be regarded as out of date.[4] In April Keyes followed up this recantation by sending Chatfield the result of 'a great deal of talk and argument' on the subject with Churchill, which the latter had sent to Inskip. Churchill had come out in favour of transfer, and Chatfield naturally found his views 'very helpful'.[5] Keyes, who always plunged into controversy with all the vigour expected of the leader of the Zeebrugge raid of 1918, kept up the pressure to the end, and in July 1937 we find him writing direct to the Prime Minister (now Chamberlain) stressing that he held 'the strongest possible views on the

[1] Conclusions dated 23rd June 1937. Adm. 1/9088–63/1937.

[2] Lord Trenchard 23rd Nov., 'Your Naval Correspondent' (actually Admiral H. G. Thursfield) 24th Nov., Marshal of the RAF Sir John Salmond and Admiral Richmond 30th Nov. 1936 all published letters in *The Times*.

[3] See letter in *The Times* of 25th Nov. 1936.

[4] Letters of 5th and 6th Jan. 1937. Adm. 116/3722.

[5] Keyes to Chatfield 22nd April and reply by latter of 27th April 1937. Adm. 116/3725.

urgency and importance of developing Naval aviation . . .';[1] but one may doubt whether his influence in getting the issue settled was appreciable. What is plain is that both in the Press and in Parliament the general tenor of the debate was far more sympathetic to the Admiralty's views than on former occasions;[2] and that change may be attributed, at any rate in part to the very evident patience they had shown, and to the fact that, under Chatfield, the Sea Lords had not indulged in backstairs lobbying and intrigue—as they unquestionably had done in the 1920s.[3]

We have seen how the debate revolved around control of shore-based maritime aircraft as well as carrier aircraft, and the Admiralty was particularly worried by the poor performance of the RAF's flying-boats, and the doubt whether they would be available to the navy for reconnaissance work in war. At the end of 1936 Chatfield wrote to Hoare about what he called the Air Ministry's 'anomalous flying-boat position' and his concern over the fact that they 'do NOT consult the Admiralty about them'; 'nor have we indeed', he continued, 'any guarantee that in war they will be placed at our operational disposal'.[4] But that issue was not resolved until the end of the following year.

Early in 1937 the controversy was renewed. Swinton expectedly told Hoare that the Air Ministry was prepared to accept the report by Inskip;[5] but the Admiralty maintained its pressure for a new inquiry with wider terms of reference, including the fundamental issue of control of the FAA. In February Baldwin told Swinton that such a measure was 'politically necessary', and enclosed the draft Terms of Reference which had been drawn up with Hankey's help.[6] Swinton's reply was that he regarded such a proposal 'with great surprise and concern'; and he protested over the work which it would involve his department in at a time when its main effort was devoted to expansion

[1] Keyes to Chamberlain 23rd July and reply by latter of 29th July 1937. Premier 1/221.

[2] For example on 27th Nov. 1936 the *Manchester Guardian* published a long letter describing the dual control of the FAA as 'an astonishing system'.

[3] See vol. I, pp. 377–82.

[4] Chatfield to Hoare 14th Dec. 1936. Adm. 116/3722. Chatfield was referring to Inskip's answers to Parliamentary Questions about whether the Admiralty was consulted about the design of flying-boats and shore-based reconnaissance aircraft. See Parl. Deb., Commons, vol. 318, cols. 1258 and 2815.

[5] Swinton to Hoare 1st Jan. 1937. Air 19/23 (Swinton papers in PRO).

[6] Baldwin to Swinton 16th Feb. and Inskip to Swinton 24th Feb. 1937. *ibid.*

of the RAF. He also warned the Prime Minister that Lord Weir, who was acting as unofficial adviser on air matters and to whose 'unique experience and constant help' he attached enormous importance, would 'not continue to give his co-operation if the general question [of control] is to be reopened'.[1] This threat certainly had more than a hint of blackmail in it, and may well have hardened Baldwin's resolve to get the issue settled one way or another.

On the other side at the end of January Hoare wrote to Baldwin foretelling that, with the debates on the service estimates drawing near, 'it will be quite impossible to hold the present position . . . unless we can say that an enquiry has been started'. Moreover Inskip had given him the impression 'that he thought an investigation into the whole question was inevitable'; and Hoare himself felt that such a step 'might be forced upon us from the outside if we do not take the initiative ourselves'.[2] This was a clever line to take with as astute a politician as Baldwin, and may have helped to counter-balance Swinton's opposition and Weir's threat. A fortnight later Chatfield apparently saw Baldwin. Though the brief he prepared for himself is unsigned and much amended the draft in Chatfield's papers and a letter to Backhouse make it plain that the interview did take place.[3] Chatfield apparently then explained how 'The Fleet feels that having loyally made every attempt for 13 years to make the Balfour scheme work, and having represented that it will *not* work, they should not be compelled to continue it unheard'; and he said that this state of affairs was being blamed on his own 'personal failure'. Though he had 'always acted constitutionally' and had discouraged attempts 'to raise this matter in the Press and in Parliament' he ended by saying that 'unless an immediate inquiry is held I shall lose the confidence of the service'. The hint that two could play the resignation gambit was plain.[4]

It was presumably thanks to the efforts of Hoare and Chatfield that

[1] Swinton to Baldwin 17th Feb. 1937. For Weir's side of this story see W. J. Reader, *Architect of Air Power* (Collins, 1968) pp. 269–86. There is also much correspondence on it in the Weir and Swinton papers at Churchill College, Cambridge.

[2] Hoare to Baldwin 28th Jan. 1937. Adm. 116/3722.

[3] Dated 16th Feb. 1937. CHT/4/1. The copy in the Chatfield papers is dated 11th Feb. CHT/1/3. Chatfield wrote that he had told Baldwin that 'I must have a decision. He has promised me an early inquiry and I only hope he will not change his mind during the next few days'. It seems likely that the second sentence refers to the effect of Weir's threat.

[4] Memo. of 11th Feb. 1937. Unsigned but obviously by Chatfield. Adm. 116/3725.

at the end of February Inskip was able to send Swinton the draft Terms of Reference for a new and widened inquiry by a Cabinet Committee,[1] and on 1st March the Board of Admiralty discussed this development. Hoare was away ill, but Chatfield reported that he had written to express the wish that the Admiralty's case should be discussed by the Board before it went to the Cabinet Committee 'with a view to seeing that the claims made did not go too far in certain directions such as control of the shore-based aircraft and in questions of supply . . .' In other words the Sea Lords were warned not to open their mouths too wide.[2] Within three days the voluminous Admiralty case, on which a lot of work had of course been done earlier, and which Hoare described as 'formidable', was sent to Inskip. It was in four parts titled—'History', 'Basic Considerations governing Naval Air Work and General Observations on the Nature of the Problem', 'Sketch of the Existing Organisation', and 'Defects of the Existing System'.[3] Then, to Chatfield's consternation, Baldwin changed his mind 'at the last hour . . . owing to the threat of Lord Weir to resign all his government posts'.[4] When Inskip wrote to say that the inquiry was to be held on the level of the COS Committee Chatfield was subjected to heavy pressure from the Prime Minister and his advisers, notably Horace Wilson and Hankey, to accept such a proposition; but he refused to yield unless Inskip himself would take the chair.[5] That the Minister agreed to do, and in consequence the COSs met three times between 9th April and 13th May.[6] They had before them long papers prepared by both parties, but as the main arguments will already be familiar to the reader it need only be remarked that the Admiralty based their case chiefly on the specialised nature of air work over the sea, particularly from carriers, on the great expansion of the FAA in progress, and on the shortage of personnel, while the Air Ministry pressed the somewhat abstract concept of 'the indivisibility of air power'.[7] Expectedly no agreed recommendations emerged, and Inskip therefore told Chatfield that he intended to make his own

[1] Inskip to Swinton 24th Feb. 1937. Air 19/23.

[2] Minutes of meeting of 1st March 1937. Adm. 116/3722.

[3] Copy in *ibid.*

[4] Chatfield to Hoare 12th March 1937. Endorsed by Hoare 'This is what I am going to discuss with the First Sea Lord on Tuesday 14th. S.H.'. *ibid.*

[5] *ibid.*

[6] 202nd, 205th and 206th meetings on 9th April, 6th and 18th May 1937. Cab. 53/7.

[7] COS. 571 and 572 both of 20th April 1937 are respectively the Admiralty's and Air Ministry's statement of their cases. Cab. 53/31.

'appreciation of the situation' for the information of Lord Halifax and Oliver Stanley whom the Cabinet had nominated for that purpose.[1]

At the end of May Alfred Duff Cooper succeeded Hoare as First Lord and Neville Chamberlain took over from Baldwin as Prime Minister. Though the new First Lord was promptly and fully briefed on the Fleet Air Arm controversy by the Admiralty's secretariat[2] one can readily understand that Chamberlain could not at once devote a large amount of time to it; and that may, at any rate in part, account for the further delay which took place. It is however interesting to find that Hoare, who had moved to the Home Office but was still a member of the Cabinet, continued to interest himself in the matter after he had left the Admiralty. Early in July he wrote to Chatfield warning him that 'the Air Ministry have a very strong argumentative case', and that it would not be shaken unless the Admiralty could show convincingly that new conditions had recently arisen, that the air was now 'immensely more important to the fleet', and that the RAF was 'no longer struggling for its existence' as had been the case in the early 1920s.[3] Though this support was no doubt encouraging one may doubt whether Chatfield needed advice on the handling of the Admiralty's case.

On 10th June Inskip wrote to Cooper that he would do all he could 'to expedite a decision', and on 23rd he wrote again saying that the inquiry by Halifax, Stanley and himself would take place on 2nd, 6th and 13th July.[4] Chatfield must now have felt that he was approaching the last fence when, on 25th, a telephone message came from Inskip asking for his letter of 23rd to be withdrawn. No reasons were given, and one can only guess at the behind-the-scenes pressures which brought about this *volte-face*; but to Chatfield it was evidently the last straw. Three days later, having obviously thought the matter over carefully, he wrote to Cooper in unusually forceful terms. He pointed out that whereas he and his department had shown exemplary patience ('my critics will no doubt feel that I have been unduly so') the Air Ministry 'has continually worked against an Enquiry'. A point had been reached, he continued, where 'I can no longer endure the position

[1] The Lord President of the Council and the President of the Board of Trade respectively, whom the Cabinet had nominated to assist Inskip in the inquiry on a Ministerial level.

[2] On 4th June H. V. Markham of the secretariat sent Cooper all the more important of the vast accumulation of papers. Adm. 116/3727.

[3] Hoare to Chatfield 11th July 1937. Chatfield papers, CHT/1/3.

[4] Adm. 116/3721. No. 28.

in which I have been placed'; and he therefore informed the First Lord that 'unless this Enquiry can be immediately held and completed before the House rises it is no longer justifiable for me to continue as First Sea Lord.'[1] The cards were now on the table face upwards, and Chamberlain had to decide whether to go against Swinton and Ellington, the CAS, and probably lose Lord Weir's services, or whether to allow Chatfield to resign—which would certainly have produced an outcry against the government. On 2nd July Chatfield wrote to Pound that 'the Fleet Air Arm controversy is now at boiling point. Both the new First Lord and I are determined to have it settled before the summer holidays and there is every prospect that this will be achieved'.[2]

What in fact happened was that Cooper and Swinton met Chamberlain and Inskip shortly after Chatfield had issued his ultimatum, and although no record of the talks has survived the outcome was that Inskip agreed to produce the report for the Cabinet himself, without the help of Halifax and Stanley.[3] This compromise was readily acceptable to the First Lord and First Sea Lord; for Chatfield had earlier expressed his 'complete confidence' in the impartiality of Inskip;[4] and as he had already received the big Admiralty dossier on their case further delay should be avoided. None the less by 20th July nothing had happened, so Chatfield again wrote to Inskip stressing the importance of a decision by the Cabinet before the House rose for the long summer recess.[5]

In fact Inskip's report was by that time ready, and he sent it to the Prime Minister next day. Though it is too long a document to summarise with fairness the conclusions must be stated. The first was 'that when so much that concerns the air units depends upon the Naval element in the ship and in the Fleet, the Admiralty should be responsible for selecting and training the personnel, and generally for the organisation of the Fleet Air Arm'; and the second was that 'I have come to the conclusion that the Admiralty's claim with regard to shore-based aircraft [of Coastal Command] ought not to be admitted'.[6]

[1] Chatfield to Cooper 28th June 1937. Adm. 116/3725. Copy in Chatfield papers, CHT/3/1.

[2] Chatfield papers, CHT/4/10.

[3] This meeting appears as Item 31 in the Admiralty's record of the negotiations on the Fleet Air Arm, but no actual date is given. Adm. 116/3721.

[4] To Duff Cooper 28th June 1937. Adm. 116/3725.

[5] Chatfield to Inskip 20th July 1937.

[6] CP. 199(37) of 21st July 1937, paras. 21 and 27. Cab. 24/270. Copy in Air 19/23.

On 26th Inskip forwarded a Supplementary Report, evidently pro-voked by the strong reaction of Swinton and the Air Staff to the first recommendation in the main report. Inskip, however, after studying the Air Ministry's dossier and interviewing the CAS, decided that 'I see no reason for altering my recommendation'.[1] Three days later both reports came before the Cabinet, when Inskip developed his case at some length. Cooper's reaction was that 'although the decision on shore-based aircraft was not what the Admiralty had hoped for, they were willing to accept it'. However Swinton for the Air Ministry produced a whole string of objections to Inskip's proposals, and ended by asking the Cabinet 'not to agree in principle to a scheme that no-one had seen and which, therefore, no-one could appraise'.[2] Hoare, with experience of both sides' cases, argued that the position was now quite different from what it had been in 1923 when the Balfour Report was accepted, and that in his view 'the Royal Air Force ought to be glad to be quit of these Naval units which must be a nuisance to them'; and Simon, the Chancellor of the Exchequer, even agreed that if extra expenditure was involved, he would accept it. The remarks of other members of the Cabinet strongly favoured acceptance of the report and Swinton finally said that 'though he did not think the decision a right one he was not one of those who favoured the formal recording of dissent'. Accordingly the Cabinet agreed that the Prime Minister should make a formal statement on these matters on 30th July, and asked Inskip to prepare the draft. That was done, and Chamberlain gave the broad decisions in answer to a Private Notice Question by Attlee. Though some MPs expressed a desire to debate the issue the Prime Minister's statement was on the whole well received.[3]

No time was lost by the departments in initiating measures for the transfer. On 6th August Sir Cyril Newall, who was about to take over as CAS from Ellington, wrote to Chatfield that his predecessor had suggested that it would be 'more convenient' if he at once took over the arrangements for carrying out the Cabinet decision, and asked the Admiralty to prepare an outline scheme.[4] This proposal was

---

[1] CP. 199–A(37) of 26th July 1937. *ibid.*

[2] Cabinet 33(37) of 29th July 1937. Cab. 23/89. When the author interviewed Lord Swinton on this matter in 1968—before the Cabinet records were available—he gave a totally different version of his attitude at this Cabinet meeting; which only shows how unreliable memory is. See Roskill, *Hankey* III, pp. 292–3.

[3] Parl. Deb., Commons, vol. 326, cols. 3512–16.

[4] Newall to Chatfield 6th Aug. 1937. Adm. 116/3725.

accepted, and after informal discussions had taken place Chatfield sent Newall proposals which, he suggested, should form the basis for 'the preparation of a comprehensive and agreed plan'.[1] His representative was to be Admiral J. H. D. Cunningham, the ACNS (Air), while that of the Air Ministry was to be Air Vice-Marshal W. L. Welsh, the member of the Air Council for Supply and Organisation. The correspondence thereafter continued on a cordial note,[2] an Admiralty committee under Cunningham was formed to handle all the details,[3] and in November a new Air Branch was added to the secretariat to handle administration.[4] None the less some difficulties which had to go to Inskip for arbitration arose. The chief ones were whether the Admiralty should take over responsibility for all training in FAA work, including flying training, and how many shore air stations should be handed over to them.[5]

Towards the end of November the two parties placed their case before Inskip, who recommended that 'greater flexibility and economy in manpower and establishments' would be achieved if the training of naval personnel were carried out 'in schools controlled by the Air Ministry'.[6] Chatfield refused to accept a decision which he described as 'a serious blow to the FAA now at last being restored to confidence after years of depression and anxiety',[7] and Cooper therefore took the matter up with Inskip, from whom it reached the Prime Minister in January 1938. Chamberlain supported Inskip's refusal to modify his decision, and the Board of Admiralty reluctantly accepted that intermediate flying training should be done in RAF schools.[8]

While this trouble was still simmering the Board had before it comprehensive proposals from the committee they had set up to

---

[1] Reply by Chatfield of 27th Sept. 1937. *ibid.*

[2] Newall to Chatfield 5th Oct. with endorsement by Chatfield to Cunningham 'This is helpful. Please discuss with me', and reply to Newall of 8th Oct. 1937. Also later correspondence in same file. *ibid.*

[3] Office Acquaint no. 235 of 18th Oct. 1937. Adm. 1/9174–178/37.

[4] Meetings of FAA Personnel Sub-Committee of 9th and 26th Nov. 1937. Adm. 116/4036.

[5] Cunningham's note on a meeting in the Air Ministry of 17th Nov. 1937. The Air Ministry agreed to hand over Ford, Donibristle, Lee-on-Solent, Worthy Down, Lympne and possibly Eastchurch but refused to hand over Thorney Island or Gosport. *ibid.*   [6] Memo. by Inskip of 7th Dec. 1937. *ibid.*

[7] Chatfield to First Lord 9th and 14th Dec. 1937. The former note, though unsigned, is obviously by the ACNS. *ibid.*

[8] Chamberlain to Cooper of ? Jan. 1938 (date not clear) and Board Minute 3520 of 3rd Feb. 1938. *ibid.*

deal with the transfer of the FAA. The first part dealt with building up the necessary organisation within the Admiralty. A new Air Division of the Naval Staff was to be created (as had existed briefly in 1918[1]), and new Departments were to be set up to handle Air Personnel, Air Material and Aircraft Maintenance and Repair.[2] The member of the Board generally responsible was to remain the ACNS (Air); but in fact that arrangement did not last long, and early in July 1938 a Fifth Sea Lord was appointed—again a reversion to the World War I organisation.[3] As regards the personnel required, schemes had been prepared to introduce Short Service Commissions for the FAA, an Air Branch of the RNVR, and Warrant Officer Pilots and Observers. Furthermore ratings were to be accepted for training in the two latter capacities, and special new ratings were to be introduced for maintenance duties.[4] In sum these two Board Minutes may be described as the charter for the new Fleet Air Arm—though a great many difficult problems, chiefly brought about by the acute shortage of trained personnel, remained to be resolved. Moreover opinion within the FAA itself was divided on some issues—notably whether the dual function Pilot-Observer scheme recommended by the Danby Committee in 1934, should be persevered with.[5]

Though the provision of adequate shore bases was of course essential to the efficient build-up of the FAA, and in August 1938 Cooper again took up with Inskip the urgent need for the Navy to take over Thorney Island and Gosport,[6] personnel questions were really the crux of the whole problem of the transfer and of the date when it could be made effective. Those problems were of course the result of the accumulated arrears of years. A stream of Fleet Orders calling for volunteers for the new ranks and ratings was issued early in 1938;[7]

[1] See Roskill, (Ed.) *Documents Relating to the Naval Air Service*, vol. 1 (Navy Records Society, 1969), Doc. 216.

[2] Board Minute 3512 of 23rd Dec. 1937. Adm. 167/96. Henderson, the Controller disagreed on the need for the Air Material Department.

[3] Roskill, *op. cit.* Docs. 146, 152, 153 and 154 all of 1916–17. The first Fifth Sea Lord under the new scheme was Admiral The Hon. Sir Alexander Ramsay.

[4] Board Minute 3513 of 23rd Dec. 1937. Adm. 167/96.

[5] See pp. 208–9 and minutes of 14th May by DNAD and 30th May by Controller. Adm. 116/3726 and 3728.

[6] Holograph letter from Inskip to Ramsay (Fifth Sea Lord) of 14th July, note by Ramsay to Chatfield of 21st July and letter from Cooper to Inskip of 2nd Aug. 1938. Adm. 116/3726.

[7] AFOs. 381, 457, 458 and 459/38 dealt respectively with Short Service Commissions in the FAA; transfers from the RAF to the RN; training of Pilots, and Rating Pilots.

but it was one thing to call for volunteers, and quite another thing to get them properly trained—whether as Pilots, Observers or maintenance ratings.

In March a committee appointed three months earlier to examine the needs for technical officers came before the Board, and the only solution found was to ask the Air Ministry for the permanent transfer of suitably qualified officers.[1] The correspondence between the two departments on this and similar subjects was perfectly amicable, and it is obvious that the Air Ministry, which had all along foreseen that the chief difficulties would be in the field of technical personnel, did its best to help; yet the Admiralty came up against the harsh fact that no powers existed to compel men to transfer from the RAF to the Navy, and it was hopeless to look to the government to find time to get legislation through Parliament to make it possible—even if they were convinced of its necessity. It was now that the navy felt most acutely the loss of nearly all its aviation officers of middle seniority when they had turned over to the new-born RAF in 1918. The second serious shortage was in the field of technical officers, and in May 1938 the Admiralty decided to ask for the help of the Air Ministry to fill both gaps.[2] The reply was discouraging; for Welsh pointed out how impossible it was for his service to supply the navy's needs when it was faced by an expansion of the Home Defence Air Force from 500 aircraft in 1935 to 2,370 by 1940.[3]

By May the Admiralty had received applications from 116 RAF officers to transfer to the FAA; but not one of them was of higher rank than Flight-Lieutenant.[4] Welsh suggested that suitable candidates should be sought from among the 294 officers trained by the RAF as pilots or observers between 1926 and 1937 but whom the Admiralty was no longer employing on flying duties; and that the Admiralty was very willing to do—provided that reports showed them to be suited to senior and responsible appointments. Other measures were to seek transfers from the RAF's Reserve of officers, and extend the employment of officers who had been passed over for promotion

---

[1] Board Minutes 3536 of 31st March and 3543 of 7th April 1938. Adm. 167/100. See also Adm. 116/4436.

[2] J. H. D. Cunningham to Welsh 12th April 1938. Adm. 178/183.

[3] Welsh to Cunningham 24th May 1938. Adm. 178/183 and 116/3726. The latter file contains the complete correspondence between the Fifth Sea Lord and AMP in 1938-39.

[4] Adm. 178/183.

to Commander or Captain.[1] Both measures were put in hand, though they did savour rather of scraping the bottom of the barrel, since at any rate some candidates from such sources were not likely to be of the highest quality. The next step was to try and get the Treasury to approve the permitted totals of Commanders and Captains to be increased, since otherwise the older branches would suffer from the arrival of the new 'A Branch' officers of those ranks. Though the Treasury refused to increase the total number of Captains above the long-standing figure of 275 they did in the end agree to increase the number of Commanders by ten, and a Fleet Order calling for volunteers was accordingly issued.[2] With those few crumbs of comfort the Admiralty had to be content—for the time being.

In July 1938 the Board once again considered the dual-purpose Pilot-Observer scheme put forward by the Danby Committee of 1934. They agreed that, although it remained 'an ultimate goal', and they stuck to the opinion that every aircraft should be commanded by an officer, there was no possibility of introducing it for the time being because of lack of training facilities and shortage of officers;[3] nor was it a success when it was finally introduced during the war.[4] The well-informed US Naval Attaché was right on the mark when, in reviewing these problems in April 1938, he reported to Washington that it would be 'a long haul' to build the FAA 'into a force comparable in effectiveness with the rest of the British Navy'.[5] At any rate by the middle of 1938 the Admiralty was able to report that the first 40 officers of the new Air Branch had been selected, the first Rating Pilots were about to start their training, and a Selection Board was interviewing serving and retired RAF officers who had volunteered to serve in the navy.[6] During the latter half of the year the personnel problems went up to the Ministerial level; but the replacement of Lord Swinton by Sir Kingsley Wood at the Air Ministry in May and of Duff Cooper by Lord Stanhope at the Admiralty in October introduced two new actors

[1] There were at the time two 'Over-Zone' Commanders and 14 'Over-Zone' Lieut.-Commanders with pilot or observer qualifications. Adm. 178/183.

[2] Adm. 178/183 and AFO. 3002/38.

[3] Board Minute 3573 of 25th July 1938. Adm. 167/100.

[4] These became known as (F) Officers, but those with pilot's qualifications disliked being required to fly in the 'back seat'. In fact they were so highly qualified that they were mostly employed in staff appointments.

[5] Report of 11th April 1938. USNA, RG. 80.

[6] 22nd Progress Report of Naval Deficiency Programme, dated 12th May 1938. Adm. 167/101.

into the leading parts of a complicated play—which did not make the settlement of disagreements easier.[1]

In June the squabble over the transfer of Thorney Island and Gosport air stations to the navy went to Inskip, who decided that the former should remain with the RAF but that accommodation for disembarked naval units should be provided at the latter. 'Whatever conclusions I might reach', remarked the unhappy Minister, 'will be bound to react seriously on the efficiency of one or the other of the two services'.[2] In July Admiral Ramsay, the recently appointed Fifth Sea Lord, reviewed the issue again, and expressed the fear that unless the navy took over Thorney Island the number of torpedo-bomber pilots needed for the new carriers simply could not be trained.[3] The First Lord himself entered the fray,[4] but nothing had been done by the time mobilisation of the navy for the Munich crisis took priority over everything else.

When that useful rehearsal for war was over and Cooper had resigned from the government in protest over the Munich agreement, the Board took stock of 'Air Requirements in War'. They estimated that within the first two years the number of 'embarked aircraft' would increase from the 1938 figure of 360 to 700, and that the number of pilots and observers needed would total 1,127; and of course maintenance officers and ratings would have to increase proportionately. In short this piece of crystal gazing made it clear how much time the FAA needed to prepare for war.[5] At the end of the year a high-level meeting on personnel took place in the Air Ministry to review the 'considerable' needs set out in a recent Admiralty letter. Nothing of comfort to the Admiralty emerged except for agreement that each FAA unit should only be transferred to the Admiralty when half its personnel came from the navy, and that the two services would have to 'dilute' equally with short service and semi-trained officers.[6]

Early in 1939 things looked rather better. Some 300 short service (A)

[1] Kingsley Wood—Stanhope correspondence of Nov. 1938 is in Adm. 116/3728.

[2] Memo. of 1st June 1938 by Inskip. Adm. 116/3726.

[3] Memo. of 21st July to First Sea Lord. Ramsay had evidently taken the matter up personally with Inskip as the latter's holograph and non-committal reply of 14th July is in this file. Adm. 116/3726.

[4] Cooper to Inskip 2nd Aug. 1938. *ibid.*

[5] Memo. of 20th Sept. 1938. Discussed by Sea Lords 5th Oct. and reviewed by James (DCNS) and Chatfield on 6th Oct. 1938. Adm. 116/3726.

[6] Admy. letter to Air Min. of 12th Dec. and record of meeting on 22nd Dec. 1938. Air 19/23.

officers had been entered, a start had been made with the RNVR (A) Branch, and 27 Rating Pilots had been granted their 'Wings' by the Air Ministry. The new 'Skua' (Fighter/Dive-bomber) had undergone preliminary deck-landing trials, the first 'Albacore' torpedo-bomber was doing flight trials at the manufacturers, and the first 'Roc' fighter had come off the production line.[1]

With the setting up of the Cabinet Sub-Committee on the Acceleration of Defence Programmes under Chatfield in March 1939 the pace quickened.[2] As a first step the Admiralty was asked to produce lists showing short term projects concerning the FAA which could be quickly fulfilled, and longer term projects which should be initiated as soon as possible.[3] The reply was that under the first heading came the extension of the air station at Hatston in the Orkneys near the Home Fleet's main base in Scapa Flow, the improvement of Donibristle on the Firth of Forth, the transfer to the Admiralty of land held by the Air Ministry at Eastleigh near Southampton where a supply base was to be established, and the improvement and extension of facilities in the training establishment *Impregnable* at Devonport to enable it to cope with increased lower deck entries. Longer term projects included the take-over of three air stations and improvements to three other. and a depot.[4] Though the Cabinet criticised the shore accommodation asked for as being on a 'lavish scale' the Treasury accepted it as necessary and agreed to provide £5.8 millions for the purpose.[5] The FAA could now dispose 46½ squadrons at various shore stations.

Personnel problems continued to prove intractable, but at the end of March 1939 the Board approved the introduction of a new substantive branch for the whole Navy—comparable to the Seaman Engineer, Supply and other existing branches—to include all FAA ratings including pilots, observers, air gunners etc. This was a big leap as it placed the FAA wholly on a level with the older specialisa-

[1] 26th Report on Naval Deficiency Programme of Feb. 1939. Adm. 167/104. In fact neither the Albacore nor the Roc were successful aircraft.

[2] This committee's papers are in the DP(39) series. It met for the first time on 20th March 1939. Cab. 27/657.

[3] Secretary, CID to Admy. 21st March 1939. Adm. 1/9773.

[4] Board Minute 3597 of 1st Dec. 1938 had originally contained these proposals The stations at Ford, Lee-on-Solent and Worthy Down and the depot at Bedenham were to be transferred to the Admiralty but required improvements. The three additional stations required were Arbroath, Crail and Yeovilton. Adm. 1/9773.

[5] Treasury letter to Admy. of 28th April 1939. *ibid.*

tions.[1] By early May the Board was ready to take over administrative control of the FAA and with it six shore stations, and informed the Air Ministry accordingly.[2] The change took place accordingly on 24th May, and a little later a Flag Officer was appointed to take command of all Naval Air Stations in home waters, flying his flag at Lee-on-Solent.[3]

In July, when it seemed likely that mobilisation would be ordered in the near future, the Board was still worried about the shortage of pilots, which could only be mitigated by the establishment of a new Flying Training School. The matter had been fully discussed with the Air Ministry but, as they were faced with similar problems, they could not help.[4] This trouble, together with the need for additional maintenance ratings, was therefore raised on the level of the COS Committee, and early in August a cut-and-thrust debate took place between Admiral Pound, who had taken over as First Sea Lord in succession to the ailing Backhouse on 15th June, and Sir Cyril Newall the CAS. Pound's concern was to find trained aircrews for the Reserve Fleet carriers if mobilisation was ordered, and he pressed the vital importance of trade defence. Newall however challenged the view expressed by the Admiralty to the Shipping Defence Advisory Committee that 'nothing would paralyse our supply system and seaborne trade so certainly and immediately as successful attack by seaborne raiders', and insisted that an onslaught by enemy bombers on our terminal ports could prove more dangerous. Hence he had to consider the air defence of the country as a whole, and must resist 'further inroads into a Metropolitan Air Force which would be very hard put to it to carry out its responsibilities in war'. No agreement having been reached the issue was shelved 'pending a comprehensive review of our air requirements';[5] and that is where matters stood on the outbreak of war.

[1] Board Minutes 3621 and 3624 of 24th Feb. and 30th March 1939. Adm. 167/103. The full memo. on this subject is by Second and Fourth Sea Lords undated but marked in Ms. 23rd Feb. 1939. Adm. 167/104.

[2] Board Minute 3634 of 4th May 1939, Adm. 167/103, and memo. of same date in Adm. 167/104.

[3] 28th Progress Report on Naval Deficiency Programme of June 1939. Adm. 167/104.

[4] Board Minute 3649 of 12th July 1939, Adm. 167/103, and memo. by Fifth Sea Lord B.101 in Adm. 167/105.

[5] COS. 953 and 310th COS meeting of 2nd Aug. 1939. Cab. 53/53 and 53/11 respectively.

On the day after war was declared the Fifth Sea Lord circulated a paper showing the state of the FAA.[1] In the six aircraft carriers and one seaplane carrier in service, and in ships fitted with catapults there were 147 TSRs, 41 Amphibians and 30 Fleet Fighters; and 192 more aircraft of various types were employed on shore training. An Immediate Reserve of 100% of First Line aircraft was available, and a War Reserve of about 50% more; but manning the aircraft in the ship-borne squadrons and ancillary services had absorbed all the available Pilots and Observers, which totalled 395 and 190 respectively. The output from training establishments should raise the totals to 570 Pilots and 375 Observers by March 1940, by which date Admiral Ramsay hoped that 'it may be possible to return some pilots to the RAF'. The situation regarding maintenance personnel was, thanks to loans from the RAF, fairly satisfactory; but the supply of stores and equipment left very much to be desired. For trade protection purposes new air stations were needed at Kingston (Jamaica), Sierra Leone, Gibraltar and Halifax, and steps were being taken to provide them. As regards the six new carriers building, the first of them (*Illustrious*) would complete in May 1940; and to man their squadrons a balance was required in the provision of aircrews, maintenance personnel, stores and equipment. It was the current shortage of 100 Pilots and of stores which caused most anxiety.

Looking back today at the twenty-year controversy over control of the FAA it is difficult not to feel that the Air Staff was unjustifiably rigid in their 'indivisibility of Air Power' argument, and that the government ought to have grasped the nettle resolutely at least two years earlier—at the time when the DRC rendered its third and final report (November 1935). A share of the blame for this not being done must be placed on Hankey, who was very influential in defence matters and resolutely resisted attempts to reopen the debate.[2] On the other hand it was he who first put forward the compromise ultimately accepted by Inskip and the Cabinet.[3] When the issue was dumped into Inskip's lap he handled it with lawyer-like thoroughness and tact, and obviously grasped even the *minutiae* of both sides' arguments. It took courage on his part to find a solution to a problem which had bedevilled inter-Service relations for two decades, and was certain not to please everyone. On the Admiralty's side Chatfield played the chief part under Hoare, Duff Cooper and Stanhope, showing immense patience

[1] Memo. by Admiral Ramsay of 4th Sept. 1939. Adm. 116/3722. The total of pilots included 50 who had transferred from the RAF.

[2] See Roskill, *Hankey*, III, pp. 290-3.   [3] *ibid.*

in pressing his case and only using the threat of resignation as a very last resort. On the Air Ministry's side they accepted the decision that the FAA should be transferred with reasonably good grace, and did their best to make it a success. For example by February 1939 no less than 1,340 maintenance ratings had turned over to the navy.[1] Finally the difficulty experienced in providing personnel and shore facilities for a Naval Air Service of less than 50 squadrons makes it plain that the Admiralty could not possibly have taken over at the same time the shore-based Coastal Command squadrons—at any rate without the compulsory transfer of personnel from one service to the other being accepted by Parliament. Thus although the naval take-over of the ship-borne squadrons should have been made a good deal earlier it is hard to fault the findings of the Inskip Inquiry when it did at last take place.

To turn to Japanese and American developments in naval aviation in 1938–39 we knew very little about the former at the time, though the enormous 'Third Replenishment Programme' was in progress and included the two big carriers *Shokaku* and *Zuikaku*; but the general under-estimate of Japanese naval skill and efficiency was without doubt extended to their naval air branch, and no one in the Admiralty seems even to have considered the possibility that they might produce better carrier-aircraft and just as skilled pilots as our own. It is the more difficult to understand this error because the efficiency with which the Japanese had conducted amphibious operations at Shanghai in 1937 certainly was noticed by the staff, and probably contributed to increased interest in building the specialised craft needed.[2]

As regards the US Navy's air arm the British estimate of its strength at the beginning of this period was 475 ship-borne and 231 shore-based aircraft—the latter being mostly flying-boats; and the Admiralty was, not without reason, confident that the American flying-boats were far better equipped than our own to carry out reconnaissance work for the fleet.[3] When the General Board considered its recommended programme for the 1939 Fiscal Year there were three aircraft carriers building and no more were included for the time being.[4] Rather oddly

---

[1] Newall mentioned this figure at 310th COS meeting on 2nd Aug. 1939.

[2] Adm. 116/3682 contains full reports, photographs and diagrams of the Japanese landing craft.

[3] 'Comparison of British and US Naval Air Services' of 17th Dec. 1936. Adm. 116/3722.

[4] GB. 420-2, serial 1741 of 8th May 1937, para. 7.

at about the same time there was a revival of interest in rigid airships, Edison telling the President that he was very reluctant to accept that the German-designed *Los Angeles* should not be replaced.[1] The President however was unenthusiastic; he considered that the idea was being pushed by 'a very powerful lobby conducted by the rubber company which is seeking to salvage a fairly heavy speculative investment';[2] and he would do no more than approve an appropriation for plans to be made for a much smaller training airship.[3] The Navy Department did not want to build any such craft.[4]

In their recommendations for the 1940 Fiscal Year the General Board remarked with satisfaction on the approaching completion of the *Yorktown*, *Enterprise* and *Wasp*. An authorisation Bill was before Congress asking approval for two more carriers of 20,000 tons or possibly three of about 13,300 tons; but the Board asserted that 'experience and information' regarding the new ships should be awaited before they committed themselves to the type of future carriers. They therefore again proposed to omit any ships of that class from the 1940 programme, but intended to include two in the following year;[5] which shows how dominant the 'battleship school' still was in that body at so late a date—three 45,000-ton ships of that class being included in the programme. However when in April 1939 the programme for the 1941 Fiscal Year was presented the Board did include one 20,000-ton carrier.[6]

When in July 1938 the Secretary of the Navy made his annual report on 'Naval Activities' to the President he stated that 'procurement of new and replacement planes' out of the 2,050 aircraft included in the Vinson-Trammel Act of 1934 was satisfactory, and that $10 millions was available from WPA funds 'for improvement of Air Station facilities'. More would be needed when the total of naval aircraft increased to 3,000 in a year's time.[7] In the following November Edison wrote to Roosevelt 'in connection with your current plans for strengthening our aviation arms', and pressed for more shore facilities in accordance with a recent study made by Admiral Hepburn's

[1] Edison to FDR 4th June and 21st Sept. 1938. Roosevelt papers, OF 18, Box 4. See vol. I, pp. 250 and 365 regarding the *Los Angeles*.

[2] FDR to Secretary of Navy 10th Sept. 1938. *ibid.*

[3] Authorised by Act of 17th May 1938. *ibid.*

[4] Note to FDR of 25th April 1938. *ibid.* Box 27.

[5] GB. 420-2, serial 1790 of 3rd May 1938.

[6] GB. 420-2, serial 1828 of 26th April 1939.

[7] Memo. for the President, dated July 1938. Roosevelt papers, PSF, Nav. 9 file.

Statutory Board. Edison reported that the Regular Navy and Marine Corps had 'on hand' 1,997 planes out of the approved total of 3,000, with 212 more in 'Aviation Reserve'. The yearly procurement of planes was running at 350 and Edison proposed to increase it by 230 more at a cost of $124½ millions. The chief trouble was over providing adequate shore facilities, for which purpose Edison asked for $120 millions.[1] These figures make the British Fleet Air Arm seem very small beer indeed. The truth seems to be that, as regards air expansion, until about 1938 the US Navy owed less to the General Board than to the comparatively small band of far-sighted naval men who followed Admiral Moffett as Chief of the Bureau of Aeronautics or served in the seagoing fleet at the time when the concept of the carrier task force was born.[2] But President Roosevelt's frequently astringent notes to the Secretary of the Navy or the CNO make it abundantly plain that, though he could be highly critical, one of his greatest interests was the navy, and it was lucky to have him at the helm at such a time.

[1] Edison to Roosevelt 25th Nov. 1938. Roosevelt papers, PSF, Dept. Corresp., Box 25.

[2] On Moffett's work and death in 1933, see vol. 1, pp. 57–8. His successors as Chief of the Bureau of Aeronautics were Admirals E. J. King (June 1933–June 1936), A. B. Cook (June 1936–June 1939) and J. H. Towers (June 1939–Oct. 1942).

CHAPTER XIV

The Road to War

1938-1939

◆

BY THE last months of 1937 the auguries for the future had become markedly more ominous. On 6th November Italy joined the 'Anti-Comintern Pact' signed a year earlier by Germany and Japan,[1] and although we did not know it at the time there took place almost simultaneously the meeting between Hitler and his military chiefs which resulted in the production of the famous 'Hossbach Memorandum'. In it Hitler roundly declared his intention to swallow up Austria and Czechoslovakia as a first step to winning the desired 'Lebensraum'.[2] On 18th Hitler and Mussolini, as though to cement and publicise their new accord, recognised General Franco's Spanish government in almost identical terms.[3] From the point of view of the British Chiefs of Staff, and especially of the Admiralty, the danger signals about which they had been so apprehensive for the previous four years were now flying for all to see. Yet at the beginning of 1938 Chatfield felt obliged to send his colleagues on the COS Committee a paper on 'Military Preparations in relation to Imperial Defence Policy' in which he expressed the gravest concern about what appeared to him to be a 'marked swing of the pendulum' against expenditure on rearmament in the last few months.[4] The CIGS and CAS shared Chatfield's anxieties, but as they all realised that the cuts in defence spending which were in the air were the result of Inskip's recent review,

[1] See Alan Bullock, *Hitler. A Study in Tyranny* (Odhams Press, 1952), pp. 324, 328 and 331.

[2] The memo. is named after Colonel Friedrich Hossbach who kept the record of the meeting. See Joachim Fest, *Hitler* (Weidenfeld and Nicolson, 1973), pp. 539-40; *Mowat*, p. 596; *Gathorne-Hardy*, pp. 336-8.

[3] *Gathorne-Hardy*, p. 433.

[4] Memo. of 17th Jan. Taken at 227th COS meeting on 19th Jan. 1938. Cab. 53/8.

and it was therefore already on a Ministerial level, there was not much that they could do about it except ask Hankey to represent their views to the Minister. That he did on a number of occasions, though not perhaps with very great vigour.[1] Though Hankey felt no enthusiasm for the 'rationing plan' which Chamberlain had brought before the Cabinet in April 1936 with the object of re-establishing strict Treasury control over the escalating cost of the rearmament programme[2] he did appreciate better than the COSs that, as the Chancellor had constantly stressed, finance was the nation's 'fourth arm' of defence and its purse was certainly not limitless. The outcome was that the ration was fixed at a total of £1,500 millions spread over five years, of which £400 millions were to be borrowed.[3] Yet in February 1938 Inskip told the Cabinet that *excluding* the New Naval Standard the total cost would rise to £1,962 millions and if the New Standard was approved it would be £1,968 millions.[4] Small wonder that the Treasury was worried.

Chatfield quickly followed up the COSs' discussion of 19th January 1938 with a note to Cooper, the First Lord, in which he repeated his opinion that there were in reality only two alternatives for the government to consider. One was to alter our foreign policy 'so as to reduce our enemies', while the other was to obtain more money for re-armament 'at the cost of the social services';[5] but the issue was so obviously a political one that, after discussion with Hankey, the COSs agreed to expunge all reference to it from the minutes. Instead a letter which Chatfield had sent to Inskip on the previous day was to be taken as representing their joint views on the matter.[6] In his letter Chatfield urged that the vital need was for the leaders of 'the various political parties to come into secret conference in order that the alternatives might be put squarely before them', and the decision taken should be a truly national one—'not a party question'. Cooper, however, endorsed Hankey's note 'I fear . . . it would not be possible to persuade the opposition that there are only two alternatives'—in which he was almost certainly right. Yet it is difficult not to feel that an issue of such

[1] See for example Hankey to Inskip 16th May 1938. Cab. 21/531.

[2] Meeting of 11th April 1936. Cab. 23/86.

[3] CP. 165(37) of 25th June 1937. Cab. 24/270. Sir Richard Hopkins of the Treasury was the chief author of this plan.

[4] CP. 24(38) of 8th Feb. 1938. Cab. 24/274.

[5] Chatfield to First Lord 26th Jan. 1938 with holograph note by latter. Chatfield papers, CHT/6/2.

[6] Chatfield to Inskip 25th Jan. 1938. *ibid.*

import ought to have been made a national one, and that the government should at least have attempted to make it so.

On 11th March Hitler's troops marched into Austria, so fulfilling the first stage of expansion outlined in the Hossbach Memorandum, and completely outflanking the main Czechoslovak defences which ran along the frontier with Germany. Two days later Cooper wrote to the Prime Minister expressing his grave concern over expansion of the RAF being given priority over the naval building programme. He reasoned that 'nothing we can do in the air is going to alarm Germany', that if we had to fight her again 'blockade must be our principal weapon', and that although 'our superiority over Germany and Japan is very narrow and will diminish, so long as we retain naval superiority we cannot be defeated.'[1] At the end of that month Cooper circulated officially a paper on Defence Expenditure and Naval Policy, in which he outlined the story of Anglo-Japanese and Anglo-German relations, stressed the need to adopt the New Standard, and told how the Admiralty had until the end of 1937 been carrying out what they believed to be the policy of the government—namely 'that no financial considerations were to be allowed to interfere with or delay the task of rebuilding the Fleet'. He went on to attack the decision to cut the 1938 building programme by a third after 'grave exception was taken to it by the Treasury', and pointed out that the decision meant that not only would the New Standard be ruled out but even the previous standard (i.e. the 'DRC fleet' of their final report[2]) would be endangered. He said that he had become convinced 'that the system of rationing the Service Departments is impossible to defend', and asked the Cabinet to request the Defence Plans Policy (DPP) Committee (a Ministerial body) 'to examine without delay the role of the Navy' in order to establish 'a definite standard for the guidance of the Admiralty'.[3] In view of Chatfield's recent remarks in the COS Com-

---

[1] Cooper to Chamberlain, 13th March 1938. Holograph. Premier 1/346.

[2] The main units of the so-called 'DRC fleet' frequently referred to at this time were fifteen capital ships, 70 cruisers, sixteen flotillas of destroyers and 55 submarines. See DRC. 33 of 9th Oct. 1935. Cab. 16/112 and Chatfield's memo. of same date on that paper. Adm. 116/3437. The omission of aircraft carriers from the DRC fleet is explained by the fact that, with six carriers completed, a deficiency could hardly be said to exist in that class.

[3] CP. 104(38) of 28th April 1938. Cab. 24/276. The copy in Premier 1/346 has many marginal notes in manuscript which appear to have emanated from the Treasury.

mittee it is surely safe to detect his hand in this paper. At any rate it produced a furious reaction from the Treasury, who declared it 'to be outrageous in its misstatements', recalled the Cabinet decision of June 1937 whereby rationing had been imposed, and proposed that the Chancellor should see the First Lord 'and persuade him of the error of his ways'.[1] Obviously the Admiralty had a tough fight ahead of it; and while the fate of the New Naval Standard hung in the balance all that they could do was to design the ships of the 1938 programme and hope that they would be allowed to build the numbers which they believed necessary. It will therefore be logical to review the Board's plans for each class of ship in turn.

We have already seen how, late in 1937, the Board had doubts about the wisdom of continuing the 35,000-ton 14-inch capital ships, and how such doubts were enhanced by rumours that the Japanese were building more heavily gunned ships of far bigger displacement. The Admiralty's initial reaction was to propose to the CID that we should protest to Japan (though she was not a signatory of the 1936 London Treaty), and if that produced no result, threaten to invoke the escalator clause in the treaty and to use our greater capacity to outbuild her.[2] The Americans and French were consulted, but the former did not want to invoke the escalator clause—presumably because it might well lead to a free-for-all race in battleship building. After a lot of telegrams had passed between the Foreign Office and the ambassador in Tokyo, and the latter had made it plain that there was not the slightest chance of moving the Japanese,[3] a Protocol to the 1936 Treaty was signed by Britain, the USA and France on 30th June 1938 increasing the permissible displacement of capital ships to 45,000 tons but leaving the 16-inch gun limit unaltered.[4]

With the displacement limit at last modified the way was clear for the Admiralty to take action on the lines they had come round to wanting, and in May the Board approved going ahead with the design

---

[1] Minute on above by Sir Richard Hopkins of 28th April 1938. Premier 1/346.

[2] CID. 1387B and 1389B. Cab. 4/27. Taken at 306th CID meeting on 13th Jan. 1938. Cab. 2/7.

[3] Adm. 116/3735 contains copies of all the telegrams on this subject.

[4] Cmd. 5781. However the Admiralty decided not to go above 40,000 tons 'for the present'—presumably as a measure of economy. In effect there thus came into being three different limitations for capital ships—45,000 tons for USA, 40,000 tons for Britain and 35,000 tons for France and Italy; and the USSR had announced construction of a ship of 44,190 tons. The final state of capital ship qualitative limitation was thus chaotic. Adm. 116/3369.

of a 40,000-ton ship with nine 16-inch guns and improved protection.[1] That design was used for the four ships of the *Lion* class, all of which were cancelled in 1940 because they were unlikely to be completed in time to take part in the war. Throughout the long controversy over capital ship design the Admiralty was handicapped not only by treaty limitations but by the acute shortage of manufacturing capacity for heavy guns and mountings and for armour plate. In 1937 a good deal of the armour needed for the new ships was ordered from the Skoda works in Czechoslovakia; but little had been delivered before the German invasion of Poland cut us off from that source of supply.

At about the time when the Admiralty got their way over building bigger battleships to match those of other powers the deliberations of the ABE Committee began to cast serious doubts on whether such ships would not in fact be obsolete before they could possibly be finished. In February that body rendered its Second Interim Report, which was non-commital about the effects of A-A gunfire because analysis of all results had not yet been completed; but they remarked only too truly on 'the very serious lack of facilities for the research into and for design and development of [A-A] fire control instruments'.[2] It will be convenient here to carry on the story of its deliberations to the end. A Third Interim Report was circulated in January 1939.[3] It commented on the efficacy of the tachymetric close-range system developed for the Army by Colonel A. V. Kerrison; but the navy's problem was of course far more difficult since some form of stabilisation would be essential to compensate for the ships' movements.

The Committee's conclusions on bombing made unpleasant reading in the Admiralty, since they estimated that two hits would be scored on every aircraft carrier or one on every cruiser *for each bomber shot down by gunfire*, and that destroyers were 'virtually defenceless against air attack'. A weakness of this reasoning was of course that it ignored the possible effects of the presence of ship-borne or shore-based fighter protection; but the Committee was on sound ground in declaring that 'the problem of the protection of merchant shipping from air attack is at present unsolved'. The CID took this remark very seriously, and

[1] These designs were known as 16A–38 and 16G–38. Both had nine 16-inch guns, but the latter had the higher speed. Adm. 1/9421, 1/9434, 1/9441 and Board Minute 3575 of 25th July 1938.

[2] This report became CID. 1406B. Cab. 4/27 and was taken at the 312th CID meeting on 4th March 1938. Cab. 2/7. The original papers are in Cab. 16/178.

[3] ABE. 63 of 30th Jan. 1939. Cab. 16/179. It became CID. 1518B. Cab. 4/29.

told the Admiralty and Air Ministry to get busy with doing something about it.[1] The outcome was the decision to order 500 of the Swiss 20 mm. Oerlikon gun, and to buy rights to manufacture the weapon in Britain. The Oerlikon 20 mm. and Bofors (Swedish) 40 mm. guns had proved by far the most efficient light and medium close-range A-A weapons in comparative trials carried out on the Eastney range near Portsmouth and at sea against Queen Bee targets;[2] and although it was to be a very long time before a sufficiency of either weapon became available war experience amply supported the belated decision, taken in the spring of 1939 in the teeth of stubborn opposition from the Admiralty's supply departments and of British manufacturers, to order foreign weapons.[3] But decisions taken many years earlier had the result that British ships of all types and classes entered the war with close-range A-A weapons which were inferior to comparable foreign weapons. The ABE Committee was still deliberating when war broke out. Though its work was inconclusive it did show that scientific analysis could produce the best answer to technical problems, and it did put its finger on several points on which the Admiralty was far too complacent.[4] In retrospect one cannot but regret that it was not set up several years earlier; but the Admiralty of those days always resisted with the utmost tenacity any attempt by outside bodies to investigate issues which they regarded as their own affair; and the mere idea of ordering weapons abroad was anathema to them.

Just as the refusal of the government to approve the New Naval Standard, or even build up to the full DRC fleet of 1935, prevented any funds being made available for capital ships in the 1938 programme, so was the Admiralty forced to restrict its aircraft carrier construction to one ship—finally the *Implacable*—whose characteristics have already been described.[5]

To turn to cruisers, of which class the Naval Staff had aimed at

---

[1] 349th CID meeting on 22nd March 1939. Cab. 2/8.

[2] The author of this history was the Naval Staff representative at these trials. On the ordering of the Oerlikon see Adm. 1/10291. The licence to manufacture in Britain was finally signed, after a great deal of haggling, on 3rd Oct. 1939. It was later manufactured on a very big scale in USA—as was the 40 mm. Bofors gun.

[3] Other weapons tried were the Danish Madsen 20 mm., the Hispano-Suiza 20 mm., and various British and American weapons. The Vickers 2-pounder and 0.5-inch machine gun both came badly out of these trials.

[4] The last paper circulated to it was ABE. 72 of 30th Aug. 1939. Cab. 16/179.

[5] Board Minute 3538 of 10th March 1938 and Memo. for Controller by DNC on new carrier design. Adm. 167/100 and 167/101 respectively.

100 under the New Standard but was prepared to accept 88 if the cost proved too high (as of course it did), in August 1938 the situation was reviewed yet again. The position at the time was that the Empire had 42 reasonably modern large ships[1] and fourteen small ones built or building[2]—which fell far below the estimated needs. Although there was among the staff a division of opinion about the functions of cruisers and whether more small ships should be built, everyone was agreed that we had nowhere near enough to fight a two-ocean war.[3] In the end seven cruisers (four improved *Fiji* class and three *Dido* class) were included in the 1938 programme, but early in the following year Chatfield asked for sketch designs of a ship with nine 6-inch guns in triple turrets, a powerful A-A armament and a speed of $32\frac{1}{2}$ knots.[4] The DNC pointed out, perhaps a little sarcastically, that he had prepared such a design as long ago as 1936.[5] In truth we were committed to the modified *Fiji* class and the small *Dido* class and had to make do with them throughout the war.[6] The conversion of the first two of the small C class light cruisers of World War I design to A-A ships had in the meanwhile begun.[7] This pouring of new wine into very old bottles proved useful for convoy protection work, especially after short-wave radar sets had greatly increased the efficiency of their armaments. In March 1938 Admiral Leahy sent Roosevelt particulars of these conversions—presumably supplied to the Navy Department under the new agreement for interchange of information referred to earlier. The CNO evidently thought well of them, though he was not wholly right to say that the purpose for which they were designed was 'as base defence vessels rather than as components of the mobile fleet'.[8]

Chatfield had originally intended to include two destroyer flotillas in the 1938 building programme, but the drastic reductions right across

[1] Fifteen 'Washington Treaty' 8-inch ships, nine *Fiji* class, ten *Southampton* class, and eight *Leander* class. The three *Hawkins* and two E class were included in this category but were in fact of World War I design.

[2] Ten *Dido* class and four *Arethusa* class.

[3] For differing views on cruisers see minutes by ACNS, DCNS and Controller of 16th Nov., 18th Nov. and 23rd Dec. 1938. Adm. 1/9442.

[4] Minute by Chatfield of 2nd Jan. 1939. *ibid.*   [5] *ibid.*

[6] The *Minotaur* class, of which only three were completed as cruisers during the war, were in design similar to the modified *Fiji* class and like them mounted nine 6-inch guns in triple turrets.

[7] The *Coventry* and *Curlew* were the first two conversions and the *Curacoa* of the same class was the third. Four of the similar *Cape Town* class were also converted to A-A ships.

[8] Leahy to FDR 3rd March 1938. Roosevelt papers, PSF, Dept. Corresp., Box 2 5

the board necessitated by the imposition of the 'rationing' system forced him to omit one flotilla—as well as a capital ship, a carrier and four submarines. Then the one flotilla of destroyers was cut out by the Cabinet for financial reasons; and so the extraordinary situation arose whereby no destroyers at all were included—an omission which brought unfair criticism on Chatfield's head later.[1]

The Sketch Estimates for 1938 had originally come out at just over £130 millions;[2] but early in February Simon, the Chancellor of the Exchequer, wrote to Cooper that the provision of such a sum would 'seriously prejudice' the Review of Defence Expenditure then being carried out by Inskip, and asked for a reduction to £124.6 millions.[3] On the same day the Board discussed the future of the 1938 programme; for Simon had refused to agree to 'a programme on anything like the scale proposed', claiming that the Admiralty was trying to telescope the seven year DRC programme into three years in carriers, destroyers and submarines. He asked for 'a very much smaller programme' which kept wholly within the DRC's recommended standard.[4] Cooper valiantly refused to accept such a proposal without the specific sanction of the Cabinet, and informed Simon and Inskip accordingly. A week later, and after further exchanges with the Chancellor, Cooper told the Board that he had been forced to accept a figure of just under £124 millions at the price of 'deliberately slowing down the speed of our rearmament';[5] and towards the end of that month he told his colleagues that, as a result of Inskip's review, the Chancellor had asked that the provision for new construction should be reduced from £70 to £36 millions. In the end a figure of £47 millions was agreed;

---

[1] The Admiralty did obtain three fast minelayers (*Abdiel* class) in the 1938 programme, and it appears that they gave the minelayers priority over the destroyers—knowing they could not get both. See letter signed 'Rowland' (Paymaster Captain R. C. Jerram, Chatfield's former secretary) to Chatfield of 4th March 1942. Chatfield papers, CHT/3/1. In a speech in support of 'Warship Week' at Retford on 2nd Feb. 1942 Randolph Churchill made an intemperate attack on Chatfield for, among other things, not ordering any destroyers in 1938. It was rebutted by Sir Warren Fisher and, more effectively, by C. G. Ammon, formerly Labour Parliamentary Secretary of the Admiralty, who described Randolph Churchill's statements as 'an ill-founded and inaccurate attack on a distinguished admiral who enjoys the affection and respect of the whole Navy'. See *The Times* of 2nd and 4th Feb., and 3rd, 4th and 5th March 1942.

[2] Board Minute 3508 of 15th Dec. 1937. Adm. 167/98.

[3] Board Minute 3517 of 3rd Feb. 1938. Adm. 167/100.

[4] Board Minute 3518. *ibid.*

[5] Board Minute 3526 of 10th Feb. 1938. *ibid.*

but that was by no means the end of the fight over the 1938 programme.[1]

Three days after the figure for new construction had been agreed Cooper presented the 1938 estimates to Parliament. He asked for a total of £123.7 millions, an increase of £18.6 millions over the previous year; but £30 millions were to come from the Consolidated Fund under the Defence Loans Act.[2] For reasons which the reader, who has been taken behind the scenes of the stage on which the battle over the 1938 programme was waged, will readily understand Cooper did not ask Parliament to vote any money for new construction; but in March, when the Annual Statement Relating to Defence was published, the government foretold that the total expenditure on the Defence Services for the five years 1937–41 would probably exceed the £1,500 millions asked for a year earlier;[3] and in May the First Lord presented the expected Supplementary Estimate. It amounted to £2.4 millions to start the 1938 programme and included provision of the long awaited Marriage Allowance for officers.[4]

Meanwhile Cooper was continuing his campaign for a bigger programme, and he and Chatfield produced another paper attacking the rationing system and the cuts made in the 1938 programme.[5] On 9th May Cooper met Simon to discuss this paper, and reported despairingly to his colleagues that 'the result of my conversation with the Chancellor . . . was, as I anticipated, Nil'.[6] That same day Simon wrote to the First Lord in true Treasury style that the cost of the DRC fleet as given in July 1937 had been £534 millions, and that in February 1938 the Admiralty had revised it upwards to £625 millions. 'It is obvious', he wrote, 'that the increase cannot be all due to increases in the rates of wages: presumably other items have been added in . . .[7] To which suggestion of subterfuge the First Lord replied with exem-

---

[1] Board Minute 3530 of 25th Feb. 1938. *ibid.* At this stage the 1938 programme comprised two battleships, one carrier, seven cruisers (four *Fiji* and three *Dido* class), three minelayers, depot ships for destroyers and submarines and the usual miscellany of small craft. The destroyer flotilla had already been dropped.

[2] Cmd. 5680 of 28th Feb. 1938.

[3] Cmd. 5682. Statement Relating to Defence of March 1938.

[4] Cmd. 5746 of May 1938. See vol. I, pp. 118, 337 and *passim* regarding the long battle to obtain a Marriage Allowance for naval officers comparable to that paid to Army and Air Force officers.

[5] The draft of this paper is undated, but it was obviously produced in late April or early May 1938. Amendments and the whole of the final paragraph are in Cooper's hand. Adm. 116/3631.

[6] *ibid.*   [7] Simon to Cooper 9th May 1938. Adm. 167/101.

plary patience and at great length, pointing out for example that the whole cost of the Fleet Air Arm now fell on the Admiralty, and ending with the warning that, since the DRC fleet had been conceived, the international situation had deteriorated and 'Germany has grown more powerful and Japan less friendly'. He pleaded once again for review by the DP(P) Committee, stressed the urgent need for a decision, and sent copies of the letter to Inskip and the Prime Minister.[1]

In July Inskip circulated to the Cabinet a paper in which he pointed out that there were three courses to choose from. The first was to approve the New Naval Standard and find compensatory savings elsewhere; the second was to change our foreign policy so as to eliminate the possibility of the two-ocean war which the New Standard fleet was designed to cope with; while the third was to leave the policy unchanged but try to carry it out 'with more slender resources that those deemed adequate by the Naval experts'.[2] Chatfield considered the issues raised by this paper 'so great and the decisions that may be taken by the Cabinet so momentous' that he sent the First Lord his full and detailed remarks. He insisted that the vital question of priority as between Air and Naval needs had never been properly considered, and should be referred to a body like the DP(P) Committee or the DRC. Moreover it was in his view 'unsound in principle to give the maintaining of *bomber* parity with Germany priority over our vital needs for sea power'. As to seeking an accord other than the 1935 Naval Agreement with Germany or Japan he did not believe that any such measure could 'justify the Government in exposing Great Britain, and her vital sea communications, to sudden attack by a superior power'; and he drew cogent attention to the commitment we had made to Australia and New Zealand at the 1937 Imperial Conference. Lastly the risks of leaving the policy unchanged but trying to carry it out with less strength were in his view obvious; but Chatfield urged the importance of what ships we possessed being modern, and that Parliament should at least be told 'that the Naval Programme *must* be reduced and delayed on account of the Air Programme'.[3] Small wonder that in August he wrote to Pound that he was 'having great difficulties during my last month [as First Sea Lord] over money for the Navy'; but he told how, despite Inskip having rather gone over to the Treasury side, he believed 'the Cabinet were somewhat shaken by

---

[1] Reply by Cooper of 28th May 1938. *ibid.*

[2] CP. 170(38) paras. 56 and 57. Cab. 24/278.

[3] Chatfield to Cooper 16th July 1938. Chatfield papers, CHT/3/1. Italics in original.

the fight the Admiralty put up', and he had succeeded in getting £60 millions more for the Navy spread over the years 1939–41 than Inskip had recommended.[1]

At the end of July the Secretary of the Admiralty circulated, for departmental use only, a 'Very Confidential' paper on the purposes to which the £410 millions finally allocated to the navy for the three years 1939 to 1941 should be devoted. The proposed new construction comprised four battleships, three carriers, twelve large cruisers, three destroyer flotillas and twelve submarines; but only eight escort vessels and sixteen minesweepers were included—a notably small proportion of a large programme. As to other expenditure, the Secretary proposed adopting the somewhat empirical basis of striking a mean between the needs of the DRC and New Standard fleets—which was probably as good a guess as could be made.[2] Though the conclusions reached fell far short of the expansion which Cooper and Chatfield had striven to achieve it none the less represented a substantial success for the Admiralty, and when in the following November the latter handed over to Sir Roger Backhouse he must surely have felt reasonably satisfied with what had been accomplished.

Chatfield was allowed hardly any rest, and left almost at once for India as head of a Commission 'to reorganise the principles of Indian defence and connect it up in a more virile way with our Imperial responsibilities'.[3] Though it falls outside the scope of this work, it may be mentioned that the Commission worked fast and their report was signed at Delhi on 30th January 1939. It recommended the provision by Britain of £30 millions to modernise the Indian defence forces, and that four new escort vessels should be built for the RIN.[4]

More germane to the subject of this history is the fact that in December Lord Linlithgow, the Viceroy of India, wrote to Baldwin 'Chatfield is here in Calcutta. The more I see him the more I think of his qualities. I should like to see him try his hand at co-ordination of defence at home';[5] and that may have given Baldwin the idea that Chatfield should succeed Inskip, which he did at the end of January 1939—

---

[1] Chatfield to Pound 3rd Aug. 1938. *ibid*. CHT/4/10.

[2] Memo. of 29th July 1938 by Sir Archibald Carter. Adm. 116/3631.

[3] Chatfield to Pound 3rd Aug. 1938. Chatfield papers, CHT/4/10.

[4] Copy in *ibid*. CHT/5/1. See also CID. 198D. Cab. 6/6. The other members of the Commission were Lieut.-General Sir Bertram Sergison-Brooke, Air Vice-Marshal C. L. Courtney and Major-General C. J. E. Auchinleck. The naval side of the funding of the modernisation of the RIN is in Adm. 116/3593.

[5] Linlithgow to Baldwin, 20th Dec. 1938. Baldwin papers, vol. 107.

almost immediately after his return from India. What is indisputable is that Chatfield stood head and shoulders above not only all the other naval men of the period but those of the other services as well. If his eyes were sometimes too focused on the naval side of defence problems, the fact that he took over as First Sea Lord at a time of psychological uncertainty and material neglect, and in less than six years wholly restored morale and initiated the construction of the fleet which was to distinguish itself in World War II surely explains his occasionally excessive single-mindedness. The debt owed to him by the British Empire and the people of the free world was immense—and has yet to be properly acknowledged.

In the sea-going fleets, the first nine months of 1938 were very active as regards training and exercising, while in the Admiralty a great deal of thought was expended on preparing for war and establishing the principle on which our forces should conduct it. A new 'Naval War Manual' was written, chiefly by Captain John Cresswell at the Staff College, and in it much attention was devoted to trade defence problems.[1] The responsibility for translating the agreed principles into action rested mainly with the Shipping Defence Advisory Committee established in 1936, whose early deliberations have already been described. In January 1938 the full committee met for the third time and reviewed the progress made. It is interesting to find that no less than 1,922 Merchant Navy officers had by that time been through the special Defence Course organised for them, and that by May the total had risen to 4,616.[2] Plainly the shipowners were playing their part by releasing officers for this purpose. In July a Progress Report covering the first six months of the year was circulated by the SDAC, as was the draft of a handbook for shipowners entitled 'The Defence of Merchant Shipping'.[3] The fourth full meeting took place in October and was attended by Backhouse, the new First Sea Lord. He thanked all members for what they had accomplished, but stressed that their task

---

[1] No copy of this important book appears to have survived, but I am grateful to Captain John Cresswell for letting me have his copy of the final typescript. It is now preserved in the Churchill College Archive Centre. The preparations made from 1936 onwards for the defence of merchant shipping are fully described in the Naval Staff Monograph entitled 'The Organisation necessary for the Protection of Merchant Shipping in Time of War'. Again I have to thank Captain Cresswell for his typescript copy and for many valuable letters on the subject.

[2] 3rd meeting of SDAC on 12th Jan. 1938. Adm. 116/3635.

[3] SDA. 10 of 15th July 1938. *ibid.*

was far from completed. The principal resolutions then adopted concerned the stiffening of merchant ships to take defensive armaments and the need to expedite the supply of A-A guns and ammunition. We have already seen how the Swiss 20 mm. Oerlikon gun was originally ordered to meet that need. By the fifth and final meeting of the full SDAC in April 1939 the Defensively Equipped Merchant Ship (DEMS) handbook was finished and being distributed, as were the necessary signalling instructions.[2] In sum the SDAC was a remarkably successful example of the co-ordination of many departments and interests, and its work certainly played a great part in preparing the Merchant Navy for the terrible ordeal it was to undergo.

In 1938 Paymaster Rear-Admiral Sir Eldon Manisty, who had played a key part in the operation of the convoy system in 1917–18, made a tour of all convoy assembly ports to instruct the Naval Control Service Officers (NCSOs) and their staffs in their duties and generally supervise the creation of the whole vast and intricate convoy organisation.[3] Finally the necessary legal steps were taken to introduce War Risks Shipping Insurance, on which subject the committee drew heavily on the experiences of 1914–18,[4] and for the Admiralty to assume control of all British merchant shipping—some 5,500 vessels in all. Though most of the work of the SDAC and its subordinate bodies appears in retrospect to have been admirable there was one aspect of trade protection which it seems to have neglected. This was the provision and organisation of Rescue Tugs, which was not tackled until just before war was declared.[5] An acute shortage of vessels capable of carrying out that important duty then became apparent.

Despite the authoritative pronouncements of 1937–38 on the convoy system being the lynch-pin of trade defence measures an extraordinary ambivalence, and even contradiction, between the acceptance of that principle and the employment of striking forces or hunting groups is evident. For example in June 1938 the Tactical Division produced a paper advocating the stationing of anti-submarine striking forces 'around the British Isles' consisting of groups of about five ships

[1] 4th meeting of SDAC on 19th Oct. 1938. Adm. 116/3978.

[2] On 19th April 1939. Adm. 116/3635.

[3] Adm. 1/9767 and letter Admiral James to the author 21st May 1969.

[4] CID. 1511B of 26th Jan. 1939. Cab. 4/29. The committee paid great attention to the report of 28th Feb. 1923 (CID. 400B) setting out World War I experience on this subject.

[5] The Tug Distribution Committee's first recorded meeting was on 1st Sept. 1939. Adm. 1/9765.

working with reconnaissance aircraft; and it was sent to all sea-going authorities and to the Air Ministry.[1] Such was the confidence in the Asdic that the chances of detecting a submarine were assessed at 80%. The Rear-Admiral, Aircraft Carriers, was critical of this proposal, but the Admiralty described it as only 'a basis for the study of the best means of sea-air co-operation', and not 'as executive instructions for such operations'.[2] Admiral Pound the C-in-C, Mediterranean, declared that in a war with Italy 'it will be important to carry out a vigorous offensive against enemy submarines at the earliest possible moment'; and therein one may find the explanation for his addiction to hunting groups later as First Sea Lord—in which purpose he was strongly supported by Churchill as First Lord.[3] The Admiralty however replied that 'generally speaking' they considered that security of shipping was best effected 'by providing escorts for all movements likely to be menaced by submarine attack' except in narrow waters like the Straits of Dover and of Gibraltar, and that it was necessary 'to adopt a strategically defensive policy in this matter in the initial stages'. The fallacy of the hunting group was to prove enduring—and costly; and if the convoy system was strategically defensive it was, tactically speaking, highly offensive; since submarines had to approach close in order to attack a convoy, and that gave the escorts the chance to strike back.

On 1st September 1939 the US State Department telephoned to Admiral Leahy a report just received from London that 'The Admiralty expects and is prepared for unrestricted submarine warfare'[5]—which was perfectly true, though final confirmation that their prognosis was correct was not received until the Donaldson liner *Athenia* was sunk without warning (actually through her identity being mistaken by the U-boat for an Armed Merchant Cruiser) on the day war was declared.[6]

While preparations for the control of merchant shipping and for its defence were being pressed ahead comparable measures were put in hand to institute blockade measures through the interception of cargoes destined for enemy countries. This was in fact a repetition of the

---

[1] Memo. of June 1938. Adm. 1/12141. The same view appeared in CB. 3024 *Manual of Anti-Submarine Warfare* and CB. 1870 *Anti-Submarine Manual*, vol. 3.

[2] RA(A) letter of 16th Sept. 1938 and Admy. reply. Adm. 1/12141.

[3] C-in-C, Med. letter of 7th Dec. 1938. *ibid.* See for example Churchill's minute to First Sea Lord of 20th Nov. 1939, *The Second World War*, vol. I, pp. 589–90.

[4] *ibid.*   [5] USNA, RG. 80, Box 171.

[6] Roskill, *The War at Sea*, I, p. 103.

practices used, in the end very effectively, in World War I.[1] In April 1938 the Naval Staff raised the issue of establishing Prize Courts at the most important centres of trade throughout the Empire. As regards the Crown Colonies this was a simple matter, but with the Dominions and Mandated Territories it produced great difficulties because it could be regarded as an infringement of the independence of the former under the Statute of Westminster, and the application of British law in the latter was not established. In June the Dominions Office reported that there was 'not the smallest chance' of South Africa or Canada accepting British administration of Prize Courts in those countries on the same lines as was done by the British and Colonial courts under the Acts of 1874 and 1925. Much correspondence ensued, but as the crisis deepened the Dominions became more co-operative, agreeing to introduce the necessary legislation themselves if they felt unable to have British courts in their territories.[2] Finally just before war was declared sufficient agreement had been reached for Prize Courts to be brought into operation by Order-in-Council in all Colonies, Protectorates, Mandated Territories and Dominions except South Africa, which considered it 'inexpedient'.[3]

Parallel action was taken to set up Contraband Control Bases at British or British-controlled ports all over the world. In the Dominions they were to be operated and administered by their own governments, but uniform instructions prepared by the Admiralty were accepted and provision of the vessels needed to intercept and bring in shipping was arranged.[4] Patrols were to start as soon as war broke out, and measures were taken to delay innocent neutral shipping as little as possible by authorising Control Stations to issue 'Clearance Forms' which gave ships immunity as far as the next station.

Fleet exercises became more frequent and more realistic as the threat of war came closer and its probable nature clearer. For example in July 1938 a joint Navy-RAF exercise took place in the North Sea 'to exercise General Reconnaissance squadrons in tracking and locating vessels [i.e. surface raiders breaking out into the Atlantic] and coast defences in warding off raids'. The attacking forces were under the

---

[1] See M. W. W. P. Consett, *The Triumph of Unarmed Forces 1914–1918* (Williams and Norgate, 1923).

[2] Adm. 1/9446 has all the correspondence on this intricate legal problem.

[3] Order-in-Council of 2nd Sept. 1939. Adm. 1/9756.

[4] The instructions were in CB. 1993 *Contraband Control Service Manual*, but were several times revised in 1939. Adm. 1/9800 contains the various instructions and amendments to them.

C-in-C, Home Fleet.[1] The Combined Fleet Exercises of March 1938 have already been described. Those for 1939 took place almost exactly a year later, once again in the Atlantic to the west of Gibraltar. Though 'Blue' (the Mediterranean Fleet) planned to attack the merchant shipping which 'Red' (the Home Fleet) was trying to protect, and day and night attacks by destroyers, submarines and aircraft all found a place in the exercises, the climax still was the 'Battle Fleet action', which took place late on 1st March. Plainly the principle that sea warfare would be decided by such means was far from dead on the eve of World War II.[2] The *Fleet Tactical Instructions* issued in March 1939 fully confirm that view, the whole emphasis being on the handling and defence of a battle fleet of up to a dozen ships;[3] and exactly the same principles will be found in the new edition of the *Fighting Instructions*, also issued over the signatures of Admirals Forbes and Pound in March 1939.[4] Truly the memories of Jutland died hard; and if much of the thought put into Trade Defence, as evidenced by the new *War Manual* mentioned above, was soundly based it did not penetrate far into the training of our main fleets, and most senior officers remained wedded to the theories propagated by Captain A. T. Mahan.[5]

As regards the Mediterranean Fleet, in June 1939 Admiral Pound handed over to Cunningham a thoroughly efficient and well-tuned instrument of war, which the latter was to exploit to great advantage; and Cunningham was justified in writing that 'in the spring and summer of 1939 the Mediterranean Fleet as a whole carried out more intensive gunnery training and practices than have ever been accomplished in peace'.[6] The weaknesses of the fleet's weapon training (e.g. in A-A gunnery, minesweeping and defence of slow mercantile convoys) have already been discussed.

[1] The US Naval Attaché, London, sent home a report on this exercise on 27th July 1938—presumably as part of the fruits of the new agreement on exchange of information. USNA, RG. 38.

[2] For the full report on the 1939 Combined Fleet Exercises see Adm. 116/3873.

[3] *Fleet Tactical Instructions* were issued jointly by the Cs-in-C, Home and Mediterranean Fleets (Admirals Sir Charles Forbes and Sir Dudley Pound) on 15th March 1939. *Home Fleet Tactical Training Memoranda* and *Gunnery and Torpedo Orders* of 1936 will be found under the same reference. Adm. 116/4204.

[4] Roskill, *The War at Sea*, vol. III, part II (HMSO, 1961), pp. 406–7 and vol. I of this work pp. 535–7.

[5] See *The Influence of Sea Power on History* (Sampson, Low, Marston and Co., 1890).   [6] Report dated 9th Dec. 1939. Adm. 1/10280.

In the Far East large scale exercises, involving 25 warships and some 10,000 troops, took place early in 1938 to test the defences of Singapore —the problem which had cropped up again and again ever since the decision to build the naval base there had been taken in 1921.[1] As regards Far Eastern Strategy, it remained as stated in the Joint Staff Appreciation of June 1937,[2] with only minor variations such as the Flag appointments which would come into force if a 'main fleet' went out.[3] Everyone at home realised that, as regards land reinforcements, the defence of Malaya and Singapore, and of a great deal more, depended very largely on India, and in May 1938 a strong Army and RAF Committee was sent out to review what should be done;[4] but as it did not deal with naval problems it need not detain us. What the Admiralty and the local naval authorities were worried about was how to get the reinforcements under discussion safely to their destination; since British maritime control of the Indian Ocean was by no means assured, and to the east of Singapore it was virtually certain to be lost. At the end of 1938 Backhouse wrote, realistically, that '1939 will be a bad year' with only ten capital ships available. 'The fact of the matter is', he continued, 'that we cannot be strong everywhere. Things have been allowed to go back too far . . . Things will be very different at the end of 1941 . . .'[5]

One place where we were definitely not strong in 1938–39 was in the Far East as a whole and in North China in particular. The Japanese were well aware of this, and in consequence began to apply increasing and humiliating pressure against the British concession in Tientsin.[6]

[1] Adm. 1/9903 has reports on the combined exercises of 2nd–5th Feb. 1938.

[2] COS. 596. See pp. 351–3.

[3] The C-in-C, Mediterranean, if he went out, was to fly his flag afloat as C-in-C, Eastern Fleet. The C-in-C, China was to become Second-in-Command and fly his flag ashore at Singapore, a Rear-Admiral being appointed to command the China Fleet's 5th Cruiser Squadron in his place. The C-in-C, East Indies was to stay afloat. Approved by First Lord 27th March 1939. Adm. 1/9767.

[4] Under Major-General H. R. Pownall. See CID. 198D of Aug. 1938. Cab. 6/6. The Pownall Committee's report was taken by a strong Cabinet Committee under Inskip, which made drastic recommendations for strengthening and modernising the Indian Army and the RAF in India. This in turn led to the despatch of the Chatfield Commission later that year. See p. 426.

[5] Backhouse to Somerville 5th Dec. 1938. Adm. 1/9767.

[6] On the 'Tientsin Incident' see W. Roger Louis, *British Strategy in the Far East 1919–1939* (Oxford UP, 1971), pp. 260–7, and article by Aron Shai, *Was There a Far Eastern Munich?* Journal of Contemporary History, vol. 9, no. 3 (July 1974). For the COSs' view see COS. 928 and 931. Cab. 53/50.

The Americans were naturally watching the situation closely, and Admiral H. E. Yarnell, the C-in-C, Asiatic Fleet, was undoubtedly right to report that the Japanese were well aware that British and French commitments in Europe made their concerted action in the Far East unlikely, that Japanese agitation was directed mainly against the British, and that they would continue to show what he called 'studied friendship' towards the USA, avoiding further incidents like the sinking of the *Panay* which were likely to inflame public opinion in America.[1] Incidentally it is interesting to find Leahy assuring the President at this time that if the Japanese Fleet moved south *'we believe we will know at once'* (his italics)[2]—which was presumably a guarded reference to the Americans having broken the Japanese naval cypher. It should also be remarked that, whereas the Admiralty still greatly under-rated Japanese naval skill and efficiency, assessing it at no more than 80% of our own, Yarnell reported that their navy was 'highly trained and efficient', that their material was 'equal if not superior to that of the United States', and that in aviation they had 'made great strides in the last two years'.[3]

Meanwhile there was little the Admiralty could do except keep their plans up to date and hope that the need to implement them would not arise—at any rate until our rearmament had progressed much further. Such, in effect, was the Naval Staff's policy when, arising out of the Tientsin Incident they proposed to tell all naval authorities that we could not produce three fleets, that the home theatre was the vital one, that if a fleet went east 'it must be of sufficient strength', that a choice between the Far East and Mediterranean 'must depend on circumstances', and that the idea of a 'flying squadron' for the Far East had nothing to commend it. These proposals were approved by the First Sea Lord; who ordered the *Naval War Memoranda* to be amended accordingly.[4] It is ironical that when in 1941 the situation long apprehended arose we adopted the very measures which were condemned in 1939.

In 1938 the activities of the large number of Japanese officers accredited to their embassy in London aroused the DNI's misgivings.

[1] Report to Sec. Nav. of 20th July 1939. (A16-3(190)). Copy in Pratt papers. See also report of 17th Nov. 1939 by ONI to CNO on the Japanese attitude towards the USA. Roosevelt papers, PSF, Dept. Corresp., Box 28.

[2] Leahy to FDR 20th April 1939. Roosevelt papers, *ibid*.

[3] Yarnell, *op. cit*. On the British view of Japanese efficiency see discussion of June–July 1939 in Adm. 1/9767.

[4] Minute by Director of Plans 2nd Feb. Approved 22nd July 1939. Adm. 1/9767.

He had earlier pointed out that, whereas we had only eight or nine officers in Japan (including those studying the language) the Japanese had 30 in Britain, that their headquarters at Broadway Court were 'a centre of espionage', and that visits were constantly being made to firms engaged on armaments production.[1] Matters came to a head in February 1938 when two Japanese officers paid visits to Portsmouth and Plymouth without observing any of the customary courtesies or formalities. The Admiralty drew the attention of the Foreign Office to this incident, with the result that Eden proposed to expel the guilty parties.[2] However when the Japanese ambassador called on the Foreign Secretary, expressed his regrets and argued mendaciously that the two officers had acted in ignorance of the normal formalities, the expulsion order was withdrawn—presumably as an act of 'appeasement' towards Japan. Yet there is not the slightest doubt that from the breakdown of the London Conference in 1935 onwards the Japanese carried out intensive espionage—not only in Britain but in Singapore and Malaya, and indeed all over the Far East.

To return to British war plans, negotiations with the antipodean Dominions continued in 1938–39, and although they were generally co-operative uncertainty whether the RAN and the NZ Division warships would actually be placed under full Admiralty control finally resulted in the Naval Staff excluding them from the proposed dispositions.[4] Furthermore the Australians were unwilling to shift the boundary of the Australian station so that Port Darwin in the Northern Territory came within the command area of the C-in-C, Eastern Fleet; and Darwin's position on the Timor Sea facing Java and the islands of the Eastern Archipelago made its strategic importance second only to that of Singapore. However agreement was reached that an Intelligence Centre should be established there, and that Reporting Officers in the Solomon Islands, the New Hebrides and other islands in the archipelago should send their reports through Darwin.[5]

The Czechoslovak crisis of the autumn of 1938, and the resultant British naval concentration in the eastern Mediterranean, revived the anxieties expressed at the Imperial Conference of the previous year.

[1] Minute by DNI of 23rd April 1934. Adm. 178/178.
[2] Admy. to FO 7th Feb. and reply by Eden of 17th Feb. 1938. *ibid.*
[3] FO letter of 22nd March 1938. *ibid.*
[4] Minute of 22nd April 1938. Adm. 1/9530.
[5] Minute by DNI of 8th July 1938. *ibid.*

In March 1939 Admiral Colvin, the First Naval Member of the Australian Naval Board, telegraphed to the Admiralty that S. M. Bruce, the Australian High Commissioner in London, had told the Commonwealth government that in his opinion Britain would not be able to send 'capital ship forces' to Singapore in the event of a war with Japan occurring when we were already at war in Europe. Colvin said he was vigorously refuting such a heretical view, but hoped to use Bruce's case as an argument for Australia to provide increased naval forces. As this obviously could not be done before 1943 he asked whether the Admiralty could lend the Commonwealth a capital ship in the near future and keep another in eastern waters. He suggested that Australia might buy a third one. Colvin's anxiety stemmed from the danger of 'Australia turning to military self-dependence' which, although he considered it 'illusory and impossible' was 'attractive to uninstructed public opinion'.[1] Backhouse minuted that Bruce 'was being a bit fractious', though 'in view of what he was told here [at the 1937 Imperial Conference presumably]' he did not know why he should be. On the other hand Stanhope, the First Lord, wrote that Bruce felt doubtful 'as I do as to whether a UK government when it comes to the point would leave Egypt and its neighbours defenceless...'[2] Though this was a breath of honest reasoning the reply sent to Colvin was that '... there has never been any doubt that a force of capital ships would have to be sent east in [the] event of war with Japan', that a firm commitment about its composition could not be given, and that the situation would improve after 1939 which 'is a very difficult year for us'.[3]

The next expression of such anxieties came from New Zealand, which proposed that a fairly high level Pacific Defence Conference should take place in Wellington in April. It was duly convened, and the various possible courses of action open to the Japanese were considered. Note was also taken of 'the firm intention of His Majesty's Government in the United Kingdom ... to defend Singapore as one of the two keystones on which the survival of the British Empire depended'—the other one being of course the home country.[4] Con-

[1] ACNB telegram 1700 of 14th March 1939. Adm. 1/9831.

[2] Minute dated 15th March 1939. *ibid.*

[3] Admy. to ACNB 17th March 1939. *ibid.*

[4] Section I, para. 2 of final report of conference, 26th April 1939. Adm. 116/3803. The chairman of the conference was Viscount Galway, Governor-General of New Zealand. The chief naval delegate was Admiral Sir Ragnar Colvin, First Naval Member, Australian Commonwealth Navy Board.

siderable discussion took place on the size of the fleet which would come east, and on the period that would elapse between the outbreak of war and its arrival; and although the conference accepted that the uncertainties were too great to justify a firm numerical commitment it was made clear that these uncertainties 'did not alter the intention of the United Kingdom Government to despatch a portion of the British fleet to the Far East immediately on the entry of Japan into the war...', and that it would be strong enough 'to give a measure of cover to Australia and New Zealand'.[1] Though there is a plain note of anxiety in most paragraphs of the report, notably regarding the multiplicity of objectives open to Japan, the conference correctly appreciated that Port Moresby in New Guinea and Suva in the Fiji group were the most suitable advanced bases for them to try and seize; but the broad conclusion was that, given the reinforcements promised from India, 'Singapore would be in a position to resist capture'.[2] As regards naval forces and supplies, the conference recommended that New Zealand should provide a third cruiser, two escort vessels, increase oil storage and modernise the dockyard at Auckland; while Australia was asked to add two 6-inch cruisers, two *Tribal* class destroyers, two escort vessels and a dozen MTBs to its sea-going forces, as well as take responsibility for five Armed Merchant Cruisers and improve many naval shore facilities. It is a tribute to the loyal support of the two Dominions that this programme was in general finally carried out, and in some respects greatly exceeded.[3]

The reader will recall that Anglo-French co-operation in the Mediterranean had been excellent during the Spanish Civil War, and that the iciness shown towards France at the time of the Abyssinian crisis had to some extent thawed by 1938. In May 1939 the COSs, in accordance with the new policy recently adopted, told the top authorities of all the services in the Far East to convene a conference at Singapore at which the French would be strongly represented.[4] It met from 22nd to 27th June and rendered a massive report. From our point of view the most important features were that it was now recognised that Singapore was not 'a fortress' which could withstand a

---

[1] *ibid.*, para. 4.   [2] *ibid.*, paras. 7, 8 and 21.

[3] *ibid.*, paras. 86 and 89. Sir Harry Batterbee, Permanent Secretary of the Dominions Office, made a personal report to Inskip on this conference, a copy of which is in this file; but it adds little to the apprehensions expressed and the improvements urged by the main conference.

[4] See cos. 903 of 12th May 1939. Cab. 53/49.

long siege, but that its defence depended on holding the greater part of the Malay peninsula, and especially the airfields in the north-east.[1] The hypothetical 'period before relief' was increased from 70 to 90 days by the COSs at about the same time. On the outbreak of war there were sizeable British and Indian Army and RAF forces in the theatre;[2] but they were totally insufficient to hold the whole peninsula, and their training and equipment left a very great deal to be desired. Yet in November 1939, when the antipodean Dominions again asked the same question as they had been asking for about four years, Churchill as First Lord promised them that, if it came to a choice, the Far East would be given priority over the Mediterranean, that Singapore would be held, and that Britain would not allow a serious attack to develop against either Dominion.[3]

We must now return nearer home and retrace our steps to February 1938 when the question of initiating staff conversations with the French and Belgians came up once more—before the COS Committee and CID in the first place,[4] and then before the Cabinet. The COSs were opposed to such conversations—at any rate on a more 'generous interpretation' than had governed the fruitless and futile conversations of 1936. The CID considered the problem in February 1938,[5] but nothing was done until April when, after a very long discussion, the issue was passed to the Cabinet with the COSs' recommendations.[6] The chief decisions were that the extent of the proposed conversations would be communicated to the French on a Ministerial level, and that the basic assumption should be that we had been called on to honour our guarantee to France under the Locarno Treaty. The Mediterranean theatre was to be excluded because 'satisfactory progress' was being made in the talks with Italy, and the government wanted to avoid upsetting them.[7] The military background was not to be 'a repetition

---

[1] Dated 27th June 1939. Copy in Adm. 116/3767.

[2] They totalled nine battalions, four of which were Indian and one Malay, and eight RAF squadrons totalling 90 aircraft—but no fighters. See S. W. Kirby, *The War Against Japan*, vol. I, p.21.

[3] S. W. Kirby, *op. cit.*, ch. II. cf. Churchill, *The Second World War*, vol. I, pp. 326–7.

[4] COS. 680 of 4th Feb. 1938. Became CID. 1394B. Cab. 4/27.

[5] 309th and 310th meetings of 10th and 17th Feb. 1938. Cab. 2/7.

[6] 319th CID meeting on 11th April 1938. *ibid.*

[7] The attempt to improve relations with Italy culminated in the visit by Chamberlain and Halifax to Rome in January 1939. See Lord Birkenhead, *Halifax* (Hamish Hamilton, 1965), pp. 428–30. Over lunch in the British Embassy in Washington in 1944, at which the author was present, Lord Halifax gave a vivid description of this

of 1914' (i.e. unlimited war with a large BEF) but was to be based on the expectation of an attempted 'knock-out blow' (i.e. limited war). Naval conversations were not to take place 'at present' because, with Japan and Italy not involved, no redistribution of the British or French Fleets was called for, and such plans 'could be concerted very quickly' later if the need arose. Furthermore the government was anxious lest news of naval conversations should reach the Germans, and so perhaps vitiate the Anglo-German agreement of 1935 'to the maintenance of which the Admiralty attach great importance'.[1] Such was the somewhat chilly atmosphere between London and Paris when, in the summer of 1938 the Czechoslovak crisis blew up.

On 23rd August, by which date Lord Runciman's mission to Prague was in progress,[2] and the likelihood of war, stimulated by Hitler's venomous attack on the Czechs of 12th, appeared great, Admiral Pound, the C-in-C, Mediterranean, telegraphed home to ask the Admiralty to clarify the command organisation between himself and the Gibraltar squadron. He also asked for enlightenment on the French dispositions and the arrangements for liaison with them. If the German threat in the Atlantic subsided he wanted the Gibraltar capital ships to join him 'to safeguard [the Suez] Canal and discourage intervention by Mediterranean and Far East powers'; he also asked for more destroyers to strengthen the anti-submarine patrols in the Gibraltar Straits, and for RAF flying-boats to be sent to Gibraltar, Dakar and, if possible, Oporto for reconnaissance purposes.[3]

The reply was that liaison officers were to be exchanged with the French, and that their naval dispositions were 'most secret' but particulars would be telegraphed. The Admiralty said that the broad strategy decided was that we would accept responsibility for the Gibraltar Straits and the French for the whole of the western Mediterranean. No more light forces could be spared from home, but the seaplane carrier *Albatross* was being sent to Freetown, and the Air

---

encounter, and how the organised shouting of the crowd for 'Tunisia, Corsica, Nice' swelled and declined, presumably by means of a bell pressed by Mussolini, according to whether the talks were going well or badly. Halifax ended his description with the ruminative remark 'And to think that that man had his son-in-law [Ciano] shot', which was revealing regarding his own standard of what constituted criminal conduct.

[1] 319th CID meeting. Cab. 2/7.

[2] Runciman arrived in Prague on 4th Aug. and left on 15th Sept. See *Mowat*, pp. 606–9 for a concise account of his mission.

[3] C-in-C, Med., to Admy. 1848 of 23rd Aug. and reply 1450 of 27th Aug. 1938. Adm. 1/9543.

Ministry had been told about the request for flying-boats. On 1st September a telegram was sent to the Cs-in-C of both main fleets about the 'dispositions and intentions for French naval forces in event of war with Germany'. Broadly speaking we were to be responsible for the North Sea and its exits to the Atlantic and the French for 'general control of Mediterranean'. Cover for French troop transports from North Africa would be given priority over trade protection in the early stages, but we hoped that the French battle-cruisers (*Dunkerque* and *Strasbourg*), then at Brest, would help with Atlantic trade defence. The particulars of the French forces at Brest, Oran and in the 'Toulon-Bizerta' area were extremely sketchy.[1] Obviously the staff discussions had not so far produced anything resembling close co-ordination.

On 9th September the Cabinet considered making what Cooper called 'a symbolic act' to show the dictators that we meant business, and which the First Lord considered 'might speak more effectively than words'. Three days later, when Cooper was absent, Chatfield was brought in to describe what the First Lord had in mind.[2] He told the Cabinet that four reserve fleet destroyer-minelayers had been put in full commission, and that the First Minesweeping Flotilla had been brought up to full complement and placed under the C-in-C, Home Fleet. Both these measures had been announced in the Press, and they had produced a visit by the German Naval Attaché, Captain Siemens, to the DNI to enquire what they signified. Admiral Troup had made no bones about telling Siemens that 'everybody in England knew that if France were involved in war, we should be likewise'; which forthright statement had 'greatly shaken' Siemens, who described himself as 'being overwhelmed', and that he 'had never thought until now that such a position could come about'. Siemens apparently communicated what Troup told him to the German Foreign Office and Admiralty, and to Nazi headquarters at Nüremberg, where Hitler was about to make one of his notorious speeches at the Party Rally. On 11th Cooper proposed a further step—to bring a reserve destroyer flotilla up to full complement; but the Cabinet considered this would be of too 'offensive' a character, and withheld approval.[3] Chamberlain had however evidently taken in the effects of the plain warning given by Troup to Siemens, who, he said, had evidently 'detected that our ships were at their war stations, and that he would report home accordingly'.

[1] AM of 1st Sept. 1938. Adm. 1/9543.
[2] Cabinet 37(38) of 12th Sept. 1938. Cab. 23/95.   [3] *ibid.*

At the next Cabinet, on 14th, there was a very long discussion on whether Chamberlain should make a final appeal and go and see Hitler.[1] Cooper said that 'in his view the choice was not between war and a plebiscite [in the Sudeten districts of Czechoslovakia] but between war now and war later'. He had come intending 'to propose mobilisation of the Fleet', but now considered that 'out of the question', and preferred the visit to Hitler which had been discussed earlier in Cabinet and was known as 'Plan Z'. It is likely that Cooper's switch from the tough line he had taken on 12th to expressing a preference for Plan Z two days later arose from the fact that Chamberlain had already preempted Cabinet approval for the latter in messages sent to Sir Nevile Henderson, the ambassador in Berlin, and to Hitler on 13th.

So much has already been written about Chamberlain's visits to Hitler that it is unnecessary to go over that well-trodden ground again; but it should be noted that at the first of them at Berchtesgaden on 15th Hitler said in answer to a question by Chamberlain, that he would 'denounce the [Anglo-German Naval] Treaty before we went to war with him'.[2]

In London the COS Secretariat started a special series of papers on the Czechoslovak crisis, and the first two dealt with 'Measures to improve the degree of preparedness of the three Services' and 'Naval measures to impress Germany'.[3] The Prime Minister himself took the chair for the latter discussions, and again on 13th when further 'measures to improve preparedness for war' were approved. There was then a pause during which the services pressed ahead with such preparatory measures as had been allowed, and on 25th the COSs met to discuss the situation. The main points that emerged were that the Reserve Fleet was at fourteen days' notice, and without it the Navy 'cannot be ready to carry out all the duties required of it'. Thus 'nothing short of full mobilisation of the Fleet will really enable us to get ahead with our preparations', though various secondary measures, such as the shortening of the notice at which ships stood and the despatch of Coastal Command squadrons to their war stations for North Sea reconnaissance

---

[1] Cabinet 38(38) of 14th Sept. 1938. Cab. 23/95.

[2] Cabinet 39(38) of 17th Sept. 1938. Cab. 23/95. For a succinct account of these discussions in Cabinet see Ian Colvin, *The Chamberlain Cabinet* (Gollancz, 1971), ch. XIII.

[3] CZ. 1 and 2 of 8th and 9th Sept. 1938. Adm. 116/3671 and 3672. Also CID. 1473B. Appendix A to CZ. 1 contains a statement of 'the steps already taken'—for example the despatch of the *Hood* and a destroyer flotilla to Gibraltar.

purposes, could be put in hand. The COSs considered it 'essential to refrain from any provocative action, such as bombing Germany until we are ready both to defend ourselves and to strike effectively'.[1] This report was no doubt a dampener on taking a serious risk of war over Czechoslovakia, especially as the COSs considered that the Home Fleet 'would run a considerable risk' (presumably from submarines) if it moved north to Scapa Flow by the east coast route, and it was therefore diverted to the western route. They also stressed that the defensive booms at the northern bases were still at two to five weeks' notice.[2] It is however interesting to find the American Naval Attaché reporting at this time the outcome of the visit made by his German colleague Captain Siemens to the DNI, and that when Siemens expressed the view that 'no-one in Germany believed that Great Britain would intervene in a war between Germany and Czecho-slovakia' Troup had replied that he was 'apparently making the same mistake which was made in 1914'.[3] Two big American cruisers arrived in the Thames in the middle of the month—ostensibly to prepare for the evacuation of American civilians; but the significance of their presence as 'a gesture of support' for Britain appears to have made no impression on the Germans.[4]

On 27th Chamberlain took the chair at a conference of Ministers at which it was decided that mobilisation of the Navy should take place next morning after the necessary meeting of the Privy Council had been held. It was not however to be taken as signifying the start of the 'precautionary period' which, according to the War Book, should follow automatically on such a decision. On 28th Leahy, quite correctly, told Roosevelt that 'the British Navy has been fully mobilised'.[5]

At home the call-up of Reservists evidently produced some muddles and confusion but, as regards the Mediterranean Fleet, the mobilisation went very smoothly.[6] The big Cunard liner *Aquitania* had been chartered in good time and was ordered to Marseilles, while the officers and men needed to bring the fleet up to full war complement travelled out overland. The *Aquitania* reached Alexandria on 5th October—

---

[1] COS. 770 of 23rd Sept. 1938. Cab. 53/41. Also DP(P)33.   [2] *ibid.*

[3] Report of 20th Sept. 1938. USNA, RG. 38. Troup passed on to the American Attaché the gist of his talk with Siemens.

[4] *ibid.* The cruisers were the *Nashville* and *Honolulu.*

[5] Roosevelt papers, PSF., Dept. Corresp., Box 25.

[6] CZ. 10 of 27th Sept. 1938. Adm. 116/3671 and 3672. For particulars of the muddles in the home ports see notes on discussion dated 25th Oct. 1938 on the lessons of the crisis at the RN Staff College, paras. 14–26. Staff College papers.

after the crisis was actually over; but it was a valuable rehearsal to
have the fleet fully manned within a few hours of her arrival.[1] Pound
wrote to Chatfield that 'the mobilisation went off extremely well and
was a wonderful experience for everybody'; and from the Home Fleet
Forbes also expressed his satisfaction, though he described communications at Scapa as 'shocking'.[2]

On the day before the Munich Conference the Mediterranean Fleet
made its final preparations for war. All shell were got up on deck and
fused, and the preliminary preparations for action were put in hand.
The atmosphere was of perfectly calm acceptance of the inevitable
and morale was obviously very high. Late that night a conference took
place in the Admiral's chart house of the flagship.[3] If Italy joined her
Axis partner, as was thought probable, the fleet would sail at dawn,
sweep the whole eastern Mediterranean and bombard Tobruk on the
way back. No-one in the fleet flagship got much sleep that night,
and when the news of the Munich agreement was received the feeling
was not so much of relief as of anti-climax. No-one had wanted war
but the Navy had got tired of the recurring alarms and was fully
prepared this time to see it through.

Rivers of ink have been spilt, and much malice has been displayed
towards Chamberlain and his colleagues by some historians over the
policy of 'appeasement' and its climax in the Munich agreement
signed on 29th September. It is not proposed here to continue that
particular argument, since our concern lies only with the naval measures
taken to meet the crisis and their effects; but a few relevant points may
none the less be made. The first is that, as Chatfield and Backhouse both
repeatedly represented, the crisis arose at the worst possible time from
the naval point of view, when a large number of major warships were
undergoing big refits or modernisation and none of the 1937 programme
had yet entered service.[4] The second is that South Africa would
certainly not have gone to war over Czechoslovakia in 1938 and it is
improbable that Canada would have done so;[5] while in Australia the

---

[1] Personal experience of author while serving as First Lieutenant of the *Warspite*
Mediterranean Fleet flagship. It was a tribute to the efficiency of the drafting officers at
the home ports that she received exactly the right number of men with the right
qualifications.

[2] Pound to Chatfield 11th Oct. and Forbes to same 8th Oct. 1938. Adm. 205/3.

[3] The author was there.

[4] See Appendix A to CZ. 1 of 2nd Sept. 1938, para. 1. Adm. 116/3671. Also Backhouse to Somerville 5th Dec. 1938. Adm. 1/9767.

[5] On 3rd Nov. 1938 Admiral D'Oyly Lyon, C-in-C South Africa station, reported

Labour Party was against intervention. Serious difficulties in fact arose with both South Africa and Canada over the calling up of British Reservists resident in those Dominions, which appear to have regarded the Admiralty's claim to call on them as an infringement of their independent status under the Statute of Westminster. The Admiralty's secretariat put its finger on the point when they wrote 'It is well known that the Union Government is particularly touchy about war preparations, and especially about advance arrangements for co-operation', and proposed that the department should not insist on a right which, though in British eyes perfectly legal, could be disputed.[1] In the end the issue was not pressed, but the Reservists in question responded for the most part to the call from the Mother Country as individuals rather than under the duress of the Royal Proclamation.

The last point in defence of the Chamberlain Cabinet that may be mentioned here, even though not of strict naval relevance, is that in September 1938 hardly any of the eight-gun all-metal fighters had entered service in the RAF. Bearing the above facts in mind it is at the least arguable that an attempt to save Czechoslovakia by force of arms in 1938 would have been as great a failure as the guarantee to Poland of the following year, and would have had more serious long-term consequences.

The run-down after the climacteric of 29th September was not rapid. On 3rd October a conference of Ministers took place under Inskip, who reported that Chamberlain was against relaxing our preparations 'until it was clear that Germany had applied a measure of demobilisation of her land and air forces'. Accordingly the Reserve Fleet ships were held in full commission to carry out much needed training, and only those Reservists not required for immediate duty

a conversation with the Governor-General Sir Patrick Duncan during which the latter stated 'that he thought there would have been a revolution in the country if the Union Government decided to enter the war . . .' Oswald Pirow, the Minister of Defence, had been very difficult about the Proclamation calling up Reservists, and declared he would not recommend the Governor-General to sign it. Adm. 1/9827. On 9th Sept. the SNO, Simonstown, reported the 'extreme acuteness of the political situation', and that 'the whole Defence Department [in Pretoria] is in a state of chaos through legal difficulty of the Union Defence Act'. J. V. Woolford's article *South Africa and the War* in History Today, vol. XXIV, no. 7 (July 1974) gives the story of that Dominion's attitude in detail. On Mackenzie King and the Canadian government see Keith Feiling, *Life of Neville Chamberlain* (Macmillan, 1946), pp. 361–2.

[1] Minute of 22nd March 1939 by Military Branch. Adm. 1/9827, which contains much correspondence on this subject of calling up Reservists in the Dominions 1938–39.

were released.[1] Not until 27th October was the decision taken to end the state of emergency on 12th November.[2]

On 3rd October, just before Parliament met again and the debate on the Munich agreement took place in a highly-charged atmosphere, Duff Cooper resigned from the office of First Lord in protest against the government's policy and action.[3] From the navy's point of view it would scarcely have been possible to choose a worse moment to change both the top offices in the Admiralty than the autumn of 1938. Not only had Cooper proved a doughty warrior in the perennial battles with the Treasury but his successor Lord Stanhope, though he had previous experience of naval administration as Civil Lord 1924-29 and as Parliamentary Secretary for a few weeks in 1931, suffered from the serious disability of being a Peer and so not sitting in the House of Commons. This change and the loss of Chatfield's long experience made it certain that the Board was weakened just at the time when the 1939 estimates were being deliberated.

During the months following on the signature of the Munich agreement a great deal of the time and effort of the Board, the staff and the supply departments was in fact taken up by a prolonged *post mortem* on the lessons to be learnt from the mobilisation of the navy. It revealed a division of opinion on whether the existing high command system had proved satisfactory or whether a Minister of Defence served by a Combined Staff was needed. The latter was of course Churchill's opinion, and it may well have been reflected in that of some senior officers; but the majority view appears to have been that the well-tried CID system had worked well and was capable of the desired 'instant decisions'. As to the naval command system, apprehensions, which were to prove justified, were expressed about confusion arising through several Cs-in-C being concerned with operations in the same area, and the Admiralty exercising an undefined measure of direct control in home waters. Co-operation with Coastal Command left a good deal to be desired, because the 'Area Combined Headquarters' were in fact merely RAF Operational Headquarters.[4] The need for naval and RAF officers to be closely integrated in the same room was stressed, and was in fact achieved before war broke out. A

---

[1] CZ. 13 of 3rd Oct. 1938. Adm. 116/3671.   [2] 336th CID meeting. Cab. 2/8.

[3] Duff Cooper's resignation did not take effect until the new Board Patent was 'read' on 27th Oct.

[4] ACHQs were established at Plymouth, Chatham and Rosyth in 1939. See Roskill, *The War at Sea*, I, Map I.

good many failures of telephone and teleprinter systems were reported
—and blamed on the General Post Office; but many reports praised
the efficiency and keenness' of the seamen Reservists. Those belonging
to the engineer and other technical branches were less satisfactory,
partly because they had, very naturally, become unfamiliar with the
new equipment provided.

On the whole the mobilisation had gone well, though there were
complaints about excessive medical examinations, which some RNVR
ratings apparently underwent no less than five times; and because the
manning depots did not know the war stations of ships special clothing
was sometimes not supplied.[1] Here it is relevant to mention that in
1938 the proposal was made that all RNVR Divisions should provide
trained and complete 'Anti-Aircraft Units' to ships. The scheme was
finally approved in February 1939 and although the exigencies of war
resulted in most units being soon broken up it did give the RNVR a
particular and specialised task.[2]

The Admiralty also made a full survey of the deficiencies in material
revealed by what had proved to be a test mobilisation, and were
probably justified in blaming them in the main on the 'rationing'
system introduced in June 1937. The sum needed to rectify them came
to the substantial total of £65½ millions, which of course was additional
to the navy's share of the 'ration'.[3]

The security of the fleets' bases at home and overseas had been a
recurrent anxiety during our period; but financial stringency prevented much being done, except to establish the needs on paper, until
1937 when the Board made a comprehensive survey of what equipment was required and the state of readiness to be aimed at in every
theatre. A programme had been included under 'deficiencies' in the
DRC's reports, but little could be provided until the purse strings were
loosened. In May 1937 the Board estimated that £4¾ millions were
needed to provide anti-submarine booms, anti-torpedo baffles, indicator
loops and so on, and the matter was frequently raised to the Overseas
Defence Committee of the CID.[4] In the summer of 1938 a survey of

[1] Report on conference of Admiralty and Staff College officers held at Greenwich
25th Oct. 1938. Staff College papers. On 20th Oct. the Admiralty prepared four
papers for the CID summarising the lessons of the crisis. Adm. 167/100.

[2] Board Minute 3612 of 2nd Feb. 1939. Adm. 167/103 and 116/3982.

[3] Board Minute 3581 of 17th Nov. 1938. Adm. 167/100. About £45½ millions
could, the Admiralty calculated, be met within the naval 'ration' of £410 millions
for the three years 1939–41.

[4] Board Minute 3473 of 27th May 1937. Adm. 167/96. Apart from the defence of

Scapa raised serious anxiety about the vulnerability of the various entrances to the anchorage, and some blockships were placed to close them—though incompletely—in March 1939. The local naval authorities continued to press for better defences and in June the C-in-C, Home Fleet, represented that 'unless these channels are effectively blocked' he could not 'be free from constant anxiety as to the safety of his ships'.[1] More blockships were therefore purchased but progress in placing them was leisurely. After the sinking of the *Royal Oak* inside the Flow by U.47 on 14th October 1939 Chatfield was asked to investigate and report on how this disaster came about.[2] His conclusion was that the installation of defences had not been pressed ahead 'with adequate vigour', largely because of the illness of the First Sea Lord and Controller in 1939. 'It is difficult to avoid the conclusion', he wrote, 'that the main responsibility was that of the Admiralty'.[3]

Rosyth dockyard had fulfilled an important need in World War I because the Firth of Forth was far better placed than Scapa to get major units of the fleet quickly to the probable area of action in the central North Sea; but in 1928 it was placed at twelve months' notice as a measure of economy—which meant that, as regards modernisation of equipment, stagnation ensued. In 1938 the Naval Staff declared that this state of affairs was 'not acceptable unless a war with Germany can be ruled out'.[4] The matter was referred to the CID, but shortage of material and of skilled men prevented appreciable progress being made before war broke out.

At about the same time as the future of Rosyth was being considered negotiations with the Irish Free State government took place over the British right to the use of bases at Berehaven, Queenstown and Lough Swilly—which we had retained under the 1921 Treaty. The Admiralty view was that, although retention of the bases was strategically desirable,

---

Singapore, which was under virtually continuous consideration, CID. 1409B of 11th March 1938 dealt with Alexandria, 402C of 1st Oct. 1934 with Malta, 419C of 13th March 1936 and 455C of 4th Dec. 1937 with South African bases, 441C of 25th Feb. 1937 with Mediterranean and Red Sea bases, 447C of 4th May 1937 with Cyprus, 471C of 15th July 1938 with Hong Kong, 489C, 491C of Jan.–April 1939 with Mediterranean bases etc.

[1] C-in-C, Home Fleet, to Admy. 28th June 1939. Adm. 116/3831, which contains the whole story of the defence (or non-defence) of Scapa.

[2] See Roskill, *The War at Sea*, I, pp. 73–75. Also Map 6 for the actual defences of Scapa 1940–41.

[3] Chatfield to Chamberlain 18th and 20th Nov. 1939. Chatfield papers, CHT/6/1.

[4] Memo. of 30th May 1938. Adm. 167/101.

hey would not be much use if they had to be garrisoned against a
hostile population. As the Irish certainly would not have welcomed the
presence of British troops, and the Army could ill afford to provide
them, the Admiralty considered that the bases were likely to prove
more of a liability than an asset, and preferred to give them up rather
than risk Irish territory being used by an enemy. The COSs accordingly
raised no serious objections to the rights being surrendered at the end
of the year, the Cabinet approved and the agreement was signed on
25th April 1938.[1] Churchill strongly attacked this decision in Parliament, and has described it as 'this improvident example of appeasement';[2] and Chatfield's defence of it does not now read very convincingly because the mere continuation of our rights potentially
enabled protection of our convoys to be extended some 150–200 miles
further out into the Atlantic.[3] Though Churchill's pejorative use of the
word 'appeasement' in this context is perhaps too harsh, the arguments
in favour of maintaining the rights do now appear to have been given
insufficient weight by the Admiralty; for the pressure to surrender
them was not heavy and their value had been amply proved in 1917–18.

Taking the whole problem of providing adequate and secure bases
for the fleets at home and overseas, and making every allowance for
the long period of financial stringency, it is difficult to avoid the
conclusion that far too little was done until the Munich crisis showed
that war with two, and perhaps three of the dictatorships was all too
likely; and even then there was inadequate drive behind the effort to
provide what was needed.

Shortly after Munich a close scrutiny of the organisation and
working of the Naval Staff was undertaken by a committee under
Admiral T. H. Binney.[4] The outcome was a recommendation that
the ACNS, who had not been a member of the Board since 1929,
should resume his former position as a Lord Commissioner of the
Admiralty in order that he might reduce the load on the CNS and
DCNS. New divisions responsible for Local Defence and for Trade,
which had only been sections of Plans Division for nearly 20 years,
should be created, and they and the Training and Staff Duties Division

---

[1] Cmd. 5728. The Cabinet conclusions are in Cabinet 48(37) of 22nd Dec. 1937,
2(38) of 26th Jan. 1938 and 10(38). Cab. 23/90A and 23/92. The Admiralty papers on
he subject are in Adm. 116/3659.
[2] *The Second World War*, vol. I, pp. 216–17.
[3] See Lord Chatfield, *It Might Happen Again* (Heinemann, 1947), ch. XVIII.
[4] Memo. by First Sea Lord of 6th Oct. 1938. Adm. 116/4194.

would be placed under the ACNS.[1] The reorganisation was finally approved in May 1939.[2] Shortly after the outbreak of war Mine-sweeping and Anti-Submarine Warfare were separated from Local Defence and made into separate Divisions.[3] These changes and the all-important creation of the Operational Intelligence Centre under the DNI mentioned earlier completed the organisation of the Naval Staff which was, *mutatis mutandis*, to direct the British maritime effort from 1939 to 1945.

The threat from the air was taken so seriously in 1938 that plans were made to evacuate from London all except the 'nucleus staff' essential to the conduct of operations and to carry out wartime administration.[4] 'Permanent War Quarters', including refuge accommodation, were to be provided for the Plans, Operations, Trade and other essential Divisions as well as for the OIC; and therein lies the origin of the concrete abortion, officially known as The Citadel but more collo-quially as Lenin's Tomb, which still insults the dignity of London's Mall and Horseguards Parade.[5] However when completed in 1940 it served the purpose for which it was intended admirably. The rest of the Admiralty was to move to a 'selected site' outside London, and the choice finally fell on the lovely Georgian city of Bath, which received all the Supply Departments in September 1939—initially in requisitioned hotels and schools. Later a conglomeration of hideous hutments was built on the hills overlooking the city; and there the Supply Departments have remained to this day.

At the end of 1938 the Admiralty, or at any rate those of its staff who had supported so strongly the Anglo-German Naval Agreement of June 1935, received a nasty shock when the Foreign Office sent across a note delivered by the German ambassador Dr. von Dircksen stating that his government intended to exercise their right under the treaty to build up to 100% of British submarine tonnage, and that their two latest cruisers would be armed with 8-inch guns in reply to Soviet construction of similar ships. The ambassador said that his government hoped 'that these measures, which they had been com-

---

[1] Binney Committee's report of 26th Oct. 1938. *ibid.*

[2] AL CE. 3692/39 of 23rd May 1939. *ibid.*

[3] Minutes by First Sea Lord and First Lord of 26th Sept. 1939. *ibid.*

[4] The matter was first raised by the ACNS on 24th May 1938. Adm. 1/9457. The first idea was to move the nucleus staff itself to a protected 'nerve centre', but the difficulties were so great that it was dropped.

[5] Meeting under First Sea Lord of 8th Nov. 1938. Adm. 1/9538.

pelled to take, would not impair the spirit of the Naval Agreement'.[1] The reply sent was icy. It pointed out that the agreement in question provided for 'friendly discussion' before such a measure as the increase in submarine tonnage was adopted; and that, as regards the cruisers, our information was that the USSR had not laid down the seven large cruisers which they had at one time projected.[2] The Germans did however agree to discussions taking place—in Berlin—and the Admiralty accordingly nominated a delegation under the DCNS, Admiral A. B. Cunningham.[3] The Foreign Office wisely gave the delegates highly restrictive terms on which the consideration of a proposal 'which if carried out cannot but have an adverse effect on Anglo-German relations' should take place.[4] The discussions took place on 30th December, but as the Germans maintained that 'it was quite impossible for them to reconsider their decision on submarine tonnage', and also refused to accept the British proposal to limit capital ship displacement to 40,000 tons they got nowhere at all.[5] An agreed text of the discussions was signed by both parties at the end of March 1939. Coming so soon after the dreadful atrocities against the Jews of the notorious 'Kristallnacht' (9th–10th November 1938) the realities of Nazi rule and diplomacy should surely no longer have been in doubt. On 27th April 1939 Hitler made a speech denouncing both the 1935 Agreement and the Protocol of July 1937 on exchange of information;[6] and so Duff Cooper's prophecy that Germany would do precisely that as soon as it suited her came true.[7]

---

[1] FO to Admy. 12th Dec. 1938. Adm. 116/3765.

[2] Dated 14th Dec. 1938. *ibid.*

[3] Plans Division to FO 22nd Dec. 1938. *ibid.* The Admiralty's brief for its delegates is in Adm. 116/3369.

[4] Memo. of 28th Dec. 1938. *ibid.*

[5] Berlin embassy telegram to FO of 30th Dec. 1938. *ibid.*

[6] The same action is in the German Ambassador's memorandum delivered to Lord Halifax on 27th April 1939. FO. A3092/1/45. Halifax's reply is in FO. A4372/1/45 of 23rd June 1939. Copies of both in Adm. 116/3369.

[7] See p. 355.

CHAPTER XV

The Last Months of Peace

1939

◆

WHILE THE lessons of the Munich crisis were still being digested the Board of Admiralty had to turn its attention to preparing the Sketch Estimates for the 1939 Financial Year. The preliminary deliberations at once revealed that there was a gap of some £36 millions between the navy's share of 'the ration' of £410 millions for the three years 1939–41 and the sum needed to continue even the reduced programme which they had been forced to accept for 1938 and make good the deficiencies already mentioned. In mid-December the Finance Committee produced Sketch Estimates totalling £162.7 millions and told the Board that nothing short of a change of policy on the ration or 'drastically restricting [the naval] services' would bring such a figure within reach.[1] At about the same time the Board considered the building programme for 1939 and decided to ask for two battleships, one carrier, four large cruisers, two flotillas of destroyers, 23 escort vessels, four submarines and a dozen MTBs. A new proposal was that twelve trawlers should be bought and converted for minesweeping. This programme would, if accepted, have provided a fairly large slice of the New Naval Standard which the Board had been vainly trying to get accepted in principle for two years; but they remarked that, as that proposal was in abeyance, they still remained without an established standard at which to aim.[2]

Meanwhile the Public Accounts Committee, which was the Parliamentary watchdog on all departmental expenditure, had criticised the Admiralty for over-spending on various items in the 1938 estimates. So a new committee on Financial Control was appointed to investigate the complaint just when preparations for war were what really

[1] Report to Board by Finance Committee of 14th Dec. 1938. Adm. 167/101.
[2] Board Minute 3604 of 15th Dec. 1938. Adm. 167/100.

mattered. The futility of such proceedings is nicely illustrated by the fact that when, after holding ten meetings, the committee rendered its report it commented that it was 'a matter for surprise not that the occasions for complaint are so numerous but that they are so limited'.[1] The truth surely was that by continuing normal peace-time procedure regarding financial control right up to the eleventh hour a democracy must suffer from a grave self-imposed handicap.

The argument and the correspondence continued until early February 1939 when the Board, by a little more cheese-paring got the estimates down to £149.5 millions, which Simon finally accepted—subject to all sorts of hedging conditions.[2] The building programme underwent considerable reductions. The battleships were cut out and the cruisers reduced from four to two; but the two destroyer flotillas (M and N classes) remained, and for the first time heavy emphasis was placed on convoy escorts by including two score escort destroyers ('Hunt' class) and 56 of the new, easily built 'Whalecatcher type' corvettes ('Flower' class).[3]

We have seen how the making good of 'Deficiencies' was, from the time of the first report of the DRC Committee, kept separate from new requirements—despite the fact that the two frequently overlapped. The reason for the adoption of this double-harnessed coach appears to be that, because the listing and costing of deficiencies had begun in 1934 it was administratively simpler to continue that practice rather than bring all naval requirements and expenditure under one umbrella. At any rate Progress Reports on the Naval Deficiency Programme continued to be forwarded to the DPR Sub-Committee of the CID about every two months, and they do give a clear picture of the progress of rearmament.[4]

[1] Office Acquaint of 28th July 1938 and report by Financial Control Committee of 2nd Aug. 1939. Adm. 116/3988.

[2] Report by Finance Committee of 2nd Feb. 1939. Adm. 167/103. First Lord to Simon 4th Feb. and reply by latter of 12th Feb. 1939. Adm. 167/104.

[3] These figures exclude the First War Emergency Programme of Aug. 1939. The design of the corvettes was based on that of whalecatchers built, mainly for Norwegian firms, by Smith's Docks, North Shields. They had a single screw and reciprocating engines and the simplicity of their equipment made rapid production possible. Though the early ones were very wet ships and taxed their crews most severely in Atlantic weather, the design was steadily improved and, taken as a whole, the class played a vital part in the Atlantic Battle. Over 100 were built in British yards and many more in Canada.

[4] The 20th to 25th Progress Reports on the Naval Deficiency Programme cover 1938 and are in Adm. 167/101.

In September 1938 Backhouse raised to the Permanent Secretary the question of how much money the Admiralty could expect to receive after the expiry of the five years covered by the DRC's final report (1936–41). Both the Admiralty and the Treasury were anxious to arrive at an agreed 'stable figure' for naval expenditure—whether we finally built the DRC fleet or the New Naval Standard fleet. Backhouse and Carter investigated the problem together, and came to the conclusion that for the DRC fleet a 'stable figure' of £88 millions annually might be achieved by 1946 and for the New Standard fleet £104 millions (in both cases plus or minus £5 millions).[1] Though the outbreak of war rendered all such crystal gazing obsolete it is of interest as showing the figures at which the Admiralty hoped to stabilise expenditure—if one or other of the new fleets was actually built.

More significant for our purpose was the Committee on Defence Programmes and Acceleration formed by the Cabinet under Inskip on 26th October 1938.[2] The Terms of Reference were 'to consider proposals for extending the scope of Defence Programmes and measures designed to accelerate production . . .',[3] and the committee was extremely active from the beginning. For example in the first paper to come before it the Admiralty drew attention to the fact that the Munich crisis had revealed that 'the number of destroyers and escort vessels is inadequate for all duties including trade protection', and proposed accordingly to build the new types referred to above. A shortage of minesweepers and anti-submarine vessels was also reported, and proposals made to ameliorate it.[4] It thus appears true to say that the Munich crisis drove home for the first time the fact that large numbers of escort vessels and minesweepers would be needed, and that it was in the autumn of 1938 that the Admiralty first gave construction of those classes of ship high priority. The provision of Asdic sets for destroyers and convoy escorts was at this time reasonably satisfactory— thanks to the decision taken as far back as 1932 to fit not only all new destroyers but also the old ones earmarked for escort duties with the device, and to build up a reserve of sets for vessels which would be requisitioned and employed on the same service. The result was that on the outbreak of war over 100 modern destroyers, about 45 sloops

[1] Backhouse to Carter 5th Sept. and reply by latter of 12th Sept. 1938, with tables of expenditure 1938–46. Adm. 1/9672.

[2] Cabinet 50(38) Conclusion 4. Cab. 23/96.

[3] CP. 247(38) of 3rd Nov. 1938. Cab. 24/280.

[4] Paper D(38)1. This became CP. 247(38) above.

and old destroyers and some two score trawlers were Asdic fitted. Though experience was to prove that this provision was far from sufficient for convoy escort purposes it went some way in the right direction; and incidentally it provides an example of a technical development in which we were ahead of the US Navy.

It will be relevant to mention here that in the last year of peace three major warships were fitted with the first air warning radar sets. Though clumsy in this form the development was by far the most promising step towards improving the air defence of the fleet.[1] In the German Navy a set originally designed for coast defence (known as 'Seetakt') had been sent to sea earlier in the pocket battleship *Graf Spee* and the cruiser *Königsberg*; but that was a gunnery ranging and not an air warning set. The US Navy had tried out a set (known as XAF) in the 1938 exercises in the Caribbean, and on finding it very successful for air warning and gunnery purposes they put it into production in the autumn of 1939. If there was little to choose between the progress made in the radar field by the British, Americans and Germans, the Japanese were far behind in this respect, as were the French and Italians.

At the end of January 1939 Chatfield, on whom a very well deserved Peerage had been conferred in 1937 shortly before he left the office of First Sea Lord, succeeded Inskip as Minister for Co-ordination of Defence, and it was as chairman of the Committee on the Acceleration of Defence Programmes that he performed what was to prove the last, and perhaps the greatest of his services to the country. In March the Board produced for it a comprehensive review of the naval measures needed. The first priority was, they wrote, to speed up ship building, and the second to add to the approved programme. Next came the possibility of building a 15-inch-gun battleship instead of one of the projected 16-inch *Lion* class, using the spare guns and mountings of the *Queen Elizabeth* and *Revenge* classes and so circumventing the bottleneck in manufacturing heavy guns and mountings of new design; but as that ship (ultimately HMS *Vanguard*) was not completed until after the war she falls outside the scope of this history. The fourth priority was to increase the capacity for gun and mounting manu-

---

[1] The ships in question were the battleship *Rodney* and the cruiser *Sheffield*. The A-A cruiser *Curlew* was fitted a little later. The set fitted in *Curlew* (Type 792) was an improvement on that fitted in the first two ships and could pick up aircraft flying at 20,000 feet at 90 miles range. This set was put into production in Aug. 1939 and was the progenitor of all the many radar sets produced during the war.

facture, which was plainly falling far behind the construction of new cruisers and destroyers, and the fifth concerned the expansion of the Fleet Air Arm.[1] The additional cost of these measures was estimated at £30 millions.

The health of Admiral Henderson, the Controller, had unfortunately broken down as a result of nearly four years of unremitting toil in that most taxing of offices, and in March he was succeeded by Admiral B. A. Fraser. He produced detailed proposals covering the whole vast range of measures required to produce what was needed, and urged the importation of skilled and semi-skilled labour, of which the shortage was acute; while Admiral H. M. Burrough, the ACNS, reported that only the Swiss 20 mm. Oerlikon gun could meet the need for some 2,000 close-range A-A weapons for merchant ships and for the increased programme of small warships.[2] The Board considered these far-reaching measures at the end of March,[3] and within a week they had been sent to the Treasury; but despite Hitler's seizure of the rump of Czechoslovakia in that month, only about two thirds of them were approved.[4] On 27th March the second Defence Loans Act, authorising the borrowing of another £400 millions, received Royal Assent.[5] Next month the Admiralty set about dividing the items to be accelerated into 'short term' and 'long term' proposals—since it was plainly impossible to fulfill them all;[6] and in June another statement of the needs of the Navy was prepared for Chatfield's committee.[7] These protracted and somewhat hectic negotiations, instituted when the fateful day plainly could not be long deferred, made it clear that a nation-wide system of priorities had to be established. In April the Cabinet accordingly approved the creation of a Ministerial Priority Committee,[8] and in July Chatfield circulated his proposals for a number of sub-committees to deal with Materials, Production and Labour, on which all departments concerned would be represented.[9]

[1] Memo. for Board of 29th March 1939. Adm. 1/9773.

[2] Memos. by Controller and ACNS of 28th March 1939. *ibid.*

[3] Board Minute 3627 of 30th and 31st March 1939. Adm. 167/103.

[4] Admy. to Treasury 3rd April 1939. Simon's letters of 5th and 9th May 1939 to First Lord. *ibid.*

[5] 2 and 3 Geo. 6. Ch. 8.

[6] DP(39)3 of 25th April and DP(39)8 of 20th June 1939. Cab. 27/657.

[7] Board Minute 3646 of 15th June 1939. Adm. 167/103. The full memo. (B. 100) is in 167/104.

[8] Cabinet 21(39) Conclusion 11 of 19th April 1939. Cab. 23/98.

[9] Adm. 1/9790.

This scheme was approved by the CID on 3rd August, though it was agreed that if war came the CID's functions in this respect should be taken over by a Central Priority Committee—as indeed happened on 19th October.[1]

We have here dealt in brief outline with only the naval needs which came before the Committee on the Acceleration of Defence Programmes during the last months of peace, which may give a false picture of the scope and scale of its deliberations because in fact it dealt simultaneously with the needs of the other two services as well. Taken as a whole its accomplishments were remarkable in planning what could and should be done at top priority. Though it is of course true that few tangible results had been achieved before war broke out the acceleration of delivery of many ships and much equipment of the War Emergency Programmes of 1939–40 can be attributed, at any rate in part, to the work of that body.

While the expansion of the fleet and its preparation for war occupied most of the Admiralty's efforts, early in 1939 the old question of the 'main fleet for Singapore' was revived. Towards the end of 1938 the British Minister in Bangkok had raised the possibility of sending a powerful squadron to Singapore to bolster the shaky British prestige in the Far East. If it came home via the Panama Canal and US ports it could, the Minister represented, help in co-ordinating British and American naval plans.[2] Craigie, now ambassador in Tokyo, strongly supported the idea, but wanted the squadron to stay at Singapore as a deterrent to further Japanese aggression.[3] This appears to be the first time that the concept of a naval 'deterrent' force, as opposed to a balanced fleet capable of fighting the Japanese, was suggested. The Admiralty's reply was that such a force simply could not be produced while the situation in Europe remained so threatening.[4]

In February 1939 Chatfield emphasised to the CID the importance of the guarantees repeatedly given to the Dominions regarding the strength of the fleet which would be sent out;[5] but Backhouse felt that the current weakness of the fleet, with three capital ships refitting, had made all such plans obsolete, and that it was more realistic to build

---

[1] 373rd CID meeting of 3rd Aug. 1939. Cab. 2/9. Also Adm. 1/9796.

[2] Sir Josiah Crosby to Halifax 7th Nov. 1938. Copy in Adm. 1/9909.

[3] Craigie to Halifax 14th Dec. 1938. DBFP, 3rd series, vol. VIII, pp. 320–2.

[4] Minute by Backhouse of 18th March 1939. Adm. 1/9909. Also Adm. to FO 29th March 1939 replying to FO memorandum on this subject. DBFP, *op. cit.*, Appendix I.

[5] 348th meeting of CID on 24th Feb. 1939. Cab. 2/8.

up a modest force capable only of maintaining control of the Indian Ocean.[1] Here we find the first clash between the idea of a deterrent force in the Far East and that of a covering force in the Indian Ocean, which was to come to a head in the autumn of 1941.[2] Backhouse's view received support from Admiral Drax, whom he had brought to the Admiralty to advise on war planning as an independent authority,[3] and in retrospect it certainly seems that Chatfield held too rigidly to a strategic principle which had been repeated so often that it had come to assume the authority of a dogma.

In March 1939, while this issue was being debated, Churchill sent Chamberlain a 'Memorandum on Sea Power 1939'.[4] Though far too optimistic in some respects such as 'The submarine has been mastered' and 'an air attack upon British warships, armed and protected as they now are, will not prevent full exercise of their superior sea power', we may here remark Churchill's obsession with the Mediterranean, which he described as 'England's first battlefield . . . British domination of the Mediterranean will inflict inevitably injuries upon Italy which may be fatal to her power of continuing the war'. As regards the Far East Churchill saw no hope of protecting our interests in North China—'on this tableau we must bear the losses and punishment, awaiting the final result of the struggle'. 'The farthest point we can hold in the conditions imagined', he continued, 'is Singapore'; and that 'should be easy' for what he described as 'a fortress of this character'. 'Consider how vain is the menace that Japan will send a fleet and army to conquer Singapore', he wrote; and he was confident that 'One can take it as quite certain that Japan would not run such a risk'. He went on to press for an offensive against Germany in the Baltic, which had been a favourite project of his as First Lord in 1914–15.[5] 'Here', he declared, 'is the sole great offensive against Germany of British sea power'; and it is surely justifiable to see in that statement the genesis of the operation known as 'Catherine' for which he pressed very strongly after his return to the Admiralty in September 1939.[6]

---

[1] First Sea Lord's paper SAC. 4 of 28th Feb. 1939 and minutes of meeting of Strategic Appreciation Committee on 1st March. Cab. 16/209.

[2] Roskill, *The War at Sea*, vol. 1, pp. 554–9.

[3] Backhouse to Drax 15th Oct. 1938, and his report of 15th March 1939. Drax papers, Churchill College, Cambridge 2/10 and 2/9. See also Adm. 1/9897.

[4] Churchill to Chamberlain, 'Private and Personal' 27th March 1939. Premier 1/345.

[5] *The World Crisis*, vol. II (Thornton Butterworth, 1923), ch. 11.

[6] *The Second World War*, vol. 1 (Cassell, 1948), pp. 364–5 and 434–5.

The Last Months of Peace

Much that happened after the outbreak of war, and many of Churchill's strategic ideas become more comprehensible in the light of this paper. Chamberlain sent it on to Chatfield, whose reply was cautious. He regarded the Baltic ideas as impracticable until after we had 'settled the Mediterranean problem' and the situation in the Far East had become clearer.[1] Though Churchill and Chatfield were evidently on reasonably good terms during the last months of peace, as soon as the former achieved power he ruthlessly brushed aside one of those who had done most to further rearmament, leaving him nothing to do 'except the job of awarding George Medals'.[2] This action deprived the navy, and the country, of the services of by far the ablest naval officer of his generation—and at a time when there was an acute shortage of first-class brains in the top ranks. But Churchill felt an unreasoning, and sometimes unfair prejudice against those who had served in Chamberlain's cabinet; and, probably because he had never forgotten or forgiven 'Jacky' Fisher's part in his downfall in May 1915, he surely did not want to have a man of strong character and powerful intellect in the First Sea Lord's chair.

We have so far dealt only with the material and financial aspects of the last years of peace; but personnel problems also loomed large in the deliberations of the Board at that time. A special committee was formed under the Second Sea Lord to carry out the 'Review of Service Conditions' which had been established in 1932 in place of the earlier and unsuccessful Welfare Conferences but had been postponed because of the Abyssinian crisis. Over 4,000 requests had accumulated, and a stream of Fleet Orders was issued in 1937–39 promulgating the decisions reached on them.[3] In the autumn of 1938 the First Sea Lord and Permanent Secretary circulated a joint report on the results. They came to the unsurprising conclusion that 'there cannot be the least doubt that pay is the largest factor in the life of the vast majority of the men]', and that 'leave and food come second and third';[4] but no fundamental changes had been introduced before the outbreak of war, and the crews of warships served loyally throughout that struggle under conditions which today seem astonishingly outmoded.

[1] Note by Chatfield of 29th March 1939. Premier 1/345.
[2] Lady Chatfield to the author, writing on behalf of her husband, 30th March 1966. hatfield File, Churchill College Archive Centre.
[3] Adm. 116/3748–3751. The sixteen Fleet Orders began with AFO. 274/37 and ended ith AFO. 1423/39.
[4] Dated 10th Oct. (Backhouse) and 14th Nov. 1938 (Carter). Adm. 167/101.

In 1936–38 the number of volunteers for naval service assumed the proportions of a flood, and the problem of how best to utilise them became acute.[1] In September 1938 the eight RNVR divisions were allowed to expand, and in the following year three new Divisions were formed; but it was plain that more far-reaching measures were essential if the keenness and patriotism of the volunteers were to be adequately used. Admiral A. B. Cunningham, the DCNS, was the leader in this campaign and he finally succeeded in getting the First Lord to put before the Cabinet a proposal to form Naval Brigades on the World War I model.[2] The Cabinet approved the proposal, but the passing of the Military Training Bill in May 1939 caused it to be shelved because it would obviously have cut across the whole scheme of National Service, which would be administered by a new Ministry.[3]

Early in 1939 the Admiralty was faced by a serious shortage of junior Executive officers for the expanding fleet, and in February the Board considered various ways of meeting the deficiency—such as promoting young Warrant officers early and accepting RNVR or RNVSR officers for extended service. Increasing the cadet entry would not help, because it would take at least four years to have effect.[4] Some 240 officers had, the Second Sea Lord reported, already transferred from the RNR, and the Admiralty had powers to retain them;[5] but they had no comparable powers with regard to Volunteer Reserve officers, and looked covetously at the 1,500 yachtsmen or 'gentlemen of means with nautical experience' who had joined the RNVSR as a result of the earlier appeal, and many of whom already held Board of Trade Masters' Certificates or their equivalent. The outcome was an application to the Treasury for powers to retain selected officers from that source for up to three years. Approval in principle was obtained fairly easily, though there was some rather trivial niggling about whether they should receive a gratuity at the end of their service, as did ex-RNR officers. None the less the necessary Fleet Order was

---

[1] Memo. by DCNS of Jan. 1938. Adm. 116/3870.

[2] CID. 1484B. Cab. 4/29. Taken at 339th CID meeting on 24th Nov. 1938. Cab. 2/8 Became CP. 183(38) of 21st July 1938. Cab. 24/278.

[3] Adm. 116/3870 has the whole story of the abortive Naval Brigades. The Military Training Bill 1939 was discussed by the Board on 25th April 1939. Minute 3632 Adm. 167/103. The Ministry of Labour became the Ministry of Labour and National Service on 3rd Sept. 1939.

[4] Board Minute 3622 of Feb. 1939. Copy in Adm. 178/189.

[5] Memo. of 23rd Feb. 1939. *ibid.*

issued in March and an Order-in-Council was signed in May.[1] The RNVR and RNVSR officers performed admirable service during the war and some rose to command their own ships; but the shortage of junior officers persisted, and indeed greatly increased as soon as war broke out, when the Admiralty assessed it at 700. They were forced to insist on extensive 'dilution' of fully trained regulars by part-trained new entrants—much to the discomfiture of the C-in-C, Home Fleet.[2] Such were the consequences of the drastic reduction in the number of junior officers forced on the Admiralty in the early 1930s.[3]

As regards the regular personnel of the Navy, at the end of 1938 the First Sea Lord asked for Vote A to be increased from 119,000 to 131,000, plus 10,000 for the Fleet Air Arm, for the 1939–40 Financial Year. Although Stanhope, the First Lord, thought that greater dependence might be placed on conscripts, his naval colleagues declared, with good reason, that 'our long service system is the envy of foreigners'.[4] The number approved finally rose to 178,000. The introduction of National Service, however, produced new problems, since by August 1939 19,000 men who had registered had expressed a preference for service in the navy. It was therefore decided to restrict normal recruitment in the event of war in order to make use of these conscripts (soon to be called 'Hostilities Only' ratings), and recruitment for the RN Special Reserve was also stopped.[5] On 5th September the Butlin's holiday camp at Skegness was requisitioned as a training school for HO ratings.[6]

The selection and reservation from call-up of scientists and engineers required for naval research establishments was organised by the Technical Sub-Committee of the CID's Man Power Committee, and seems to have gone fairly smoothly except that demands soon far outran the supply, and special measures to train additional men had to be instituted.[7] Over the Women's Reserves the Admiralty showed much less imagination, and initially visualised them being employed only in clerical and domestic capacities and as motor drivers. As late as May 1938 their view was that no steps were necessary for recruiting

[1] AFO. 612/39 and O-in-C of 5th May 1939. *ibid.*

[2] AL of 15th Jan. 1940 to C-in-C, Home Fleet.   [3] See p. 32.

[4] Minutes by First Sea Lord of 3rd Dec. 1938 and by First Lord of 27th Feb. 1939. Adm. 1/9798.

[5] Memo. by DNR of 22nd Aug. 1939. Adm. 1/9817.   [6] *ibid.*

[7] Adm. 116/3704 has the whole story of the Admiralty's side of the Technical Sub-Committee's work. It met almost continuously throughout 1938–39, and produced 27 papers in the NS(T) series by July 1939.

and training women in peacetime, and the total requirement envisaged was only 3,000.[1] Not until after the outbreak of war was recruitment for the WRNS started, and it was some time before the navy appreciated the vast scope and skills which the 'Wrens' could bring to it.

To turn to relations with potential allies, we have seen how the Phillips-Ingersoll conversations marked a new era of co-operation with the USA, though Roosevelt was deterred by Congress and by public opinion from taking any steps which would have decreased British anxieties and perhaps checked Japanese aggression in the Far East. Nothing short of moving the main US Pacific Fleet to Singapore could have done that; and such a step was out of the question—for internal political reasons among others. By March 1938 Staff talks with the French were at last making some progress, and a year later a comprehensive paper on British policy and strategy was ready for use by the British delegates. As however the reader will already be familiar with the principles and purposes involved there is no need to recapitulate them here.[2] None the less as late as May 1938 the COSs were still against raising the level on which the talks were being conducted higher than that of Directors of Staff Divisions.[3] Not until the following November, after the Munich crisis, is a change noticeable;[4] and it seems to have been inspired chiefly by the desire to gain the help of the two *Dunkerque* class battle-cruisers in the Atlantic.[5] In February 1939 the scope was at last widened, at the instigation of the Cabinet's Foreign Policy Committee,[6] and in July three stages were established, starting with the 'general strategic conception of a war' with Germany and Italy, continuing with 'formulation of broad outline plans', and ending with 'preparations by each of the services of detailed joint plans'.[7] In June telegrams were sent to the Cs-in-C of all services in the Far East to arrange the conversations mentioned earlier,[8] and finally on 8th September 1939 the Supreme Command organisation in France

[1] Minutes of meeting on 11th May and Board Minute 3572 of 25th July 1938. Adm. 116/3701.

[2] See AFC. 1 of 20th March 1939. Cab. 29/159. The minutes of Anglo-French meetings are in Cab. 29/160.

[3] COS. 727 of 20th May 1938. Cab. 53/38.

[4] COS. 795 of 18th Nov. 1938. Cab. 53/42 and CID. 1486B. Cab. 4/29. Also Cab. 29/159.

[5] COS. 799 of 21st Nov. 1938. *ibid.* and CID. 1478B. *ibid.*

[6] FP(36)77 of 25th Jan. 1939. Approved by Cabinet 3(39) of 2nd Feb. 1939. Cab. 23/97.

[7] AFC. 30 of 14th July 1939. Cab. 29/159.   [8] AFC. 31 of 28th June 1939. *ibid.*

was set up.[1] On the British side the whole saga of the Anglo-French conversations indicates a marked reluctance to accept a new 'Continental Commitment', and contrasts markedly with the cordiality of approach and rapidity of results shown in the Anglo-American talks. None the less in the spring of 1939 a series of joint staff meetings with the French on trade protection did produce a full and frank statement of British plans and intentions, in the Mediterranean as well as the Atlantic, and particulars of our equipment, including Radar and Asdic, were supplied to the French.[2]

With the renewal in the spring of 1939 of the central European crisis the Admiralty brought its Operational Intelligence Centre, with its linked Surface Ship Plot and Submarine Tracking Room, to a state of full readiness. An additional Deputy to the DNI was appointed to take charge of it, and the teams to run each section were organised and trained. The OIC was by this time provided with direct teleprinter lines to all the Wireless Interception and Direction Finding stations in the country, and to the cryptographic section known as the Government Code and Cypher School soon to be moved to Bletchley Park in Buckinghamshire. The OIC was in truth the nerve centre of the whole naval war, in it took place many of the discussions which produced crucial decisions, and to and from it flowed via the War Registry mentioned earlier the whole of the vast communications traffic produced by a world-wide maritime war.[3]

Despite British misgivings over the Russian intention to build very large battleships and heavy cruisers,[4] and mistrust of Soviet military capacity consequential on the Stalinist purge of most senior officers, when in March 1939 the question was raised whether it would be more advantageous to Britain to form an alliance with the USSR or with Poland the COSs had no hesitation in recommending the former.[5]

---

[1] AFC. 35 of 8th Sept. 1939. *ibid.*

[2] Six meetings of Staffs took place in London and one in Paris between 30th March and 3rd May 1939. Conclusions are in AFC(J)74 of 8th May 1939. Cab. 29/160.

[3] Unfortunately the OIC War Diary, which had been kept on a continuous basis from the first to the last day of the war, was destroyed soon after it ended, thereby depriving historians of what must have been by far the most valuable source on the conduct of the conflict. Later that grave mistake was compounded by destroying most of the daily bundles of 'In' and 'Out' signals.

[4] See minutes by Plans Division of 19th Sept. and 28th Nov. 1938. Adm. 116/4053.

[5] 282nd and 283rd COS meetings of 18th March 1939. Also 285th meeting of 28th March on implications of the Anglo-French guarantee to Poland and Roumania. Cab. 53/10. The whole question of the choice between alliance with Poland or the

Unfortunately Chatfield, who had been in the chair as Minister for Co-ordination of Defence at three meetings, failed to make the COSs' recommendation clear to the Cabinet, and indeed expressed an entirely contrary view regarding the relative merits of alliance with the two eastern countries.[1] The only rational explanation seems to be that Chatfield was still obsessed by fear of what the Japanese reaction to an Anglo-Soviet alliance might be; but it is only fair to record that by mid-May he had come round to the view of the COSs, and argued forcefully that 'we should . . . reinsure by doing everything in our power to bring Russia in on our side'.[2] Hoare and Stanley supported Chatfield, but the majority of the Cabinet were against them. A week later Chamberlain came round to accepting the principle of a pact with Russia; but the chance of a military alliance which would have forced Germany to fight on two fronts was destroyed by those hesitations.

We saw earlier how in the mid-1930s there were indications that the Royal Navy was going to be very short of senior officers of first-class ability and outstanding character in years to come. Admiral B. H. Ramsay's retirement after his clash with Backhouse as C-in-C, Home Fleet, at the end of 1935 was one serious loss although, in the long term, the outcome was fortunate. The loss of the services of Admiral Geoffrey Blake, whom Chatfield had noted as a possible future First Sea Lord, has already been mentioned, as has the sudden death of Sir William Fisher in 1937—described by Chatfield as 'a very great blow'.[3] Worse was to happen in 1939. The choice of Backhouse to succeed Chatfield, though readily understandable after Fisher's death, was not a happy one. Admiral James has described Backhouse as 'possessing a passion for centralising',[4] and his conduct towards Ramsay certainly supports that view, as do his numerous long and detailed letters and minutes. Moreover in October 1935 he had been involved in an air crash, suffered quite serious injuries but refused to allow himself sufficient rest to recover properly.[5] It seems doubtful whether he was really fit physically when in November 1938 he took over from Chatfield;[6]

USSR is fully discussed by Robert Manne in *The Journal of Contemporary History*, vol. 9, no. 3 (July 1974).

[1] FP(36) 38th meeting of 27th March 1939. Cab. 27/624.

[2] FP(36) 47th meeting of 16th May 1939. Cab. 27/625.

[3] Chatfield to Backhouse 12th July, 1937. Chatfield papers, CHT/4/1.

[4] Letters to the author of 6th April 1964 and 2nd March 1968.

[5] See W. S. Chalmers, *Full Cycle* (Hodder and Stoughton, 1959), p. 45.

[6] See Hugh L'Etang, *The Pathology of Leadership* (Heinemann Medical Books, 1969), p. 125.

and in the Admiralty he certainly continued his centralising habits. The result was, inevitably, a breakdown in health soon followed by death (15th July 1939). Henderson, the Controller, having been forced by ill health to resign a few months earlier a double change thus had to be made on the Board at a most critical time; and the choice was extremely restricted. Another grievous loss occurred that same year when James Somerville was invalided due to traces of tuberculosis, though he, like Ramsay, made a splendid comeback during the war.[1]

Though Chatfield had intended that Pound should stay in the Mediterranean command until about May, 1940, and he had agreed to do so, Backhouse's illness upset all such plans.[2] Pound was the obvious heir to the office of First Sea Lord; but he too was not a fully fit man as he suffered from 'a long-standing osteo-arthritis of the left hip with consequent shortening of the left thigh', which the Medical Director-General described as 'a painful condition and one which prevents comfortable sleep and rest'.[3] Pound too was addicted to extreme centralisation;[4] he constantly drafted Admiralty signals in his own hand, and interfered repeatedly in the conduct of operations by the Home Fleet in 1939–42.[5] That was the reason why Admiral Horton declined to take over command of that fleet when Pound decided that Forbes should be relieved prematurely.[6] Pound had no intellectual

[1] See Donald Macintyre, *Fighting Admiral* (Evans, 1961), pp. 42–5.

[2] Chatfield to Lord Cork (C-in-C, Portsmouth) 16th Nov. 1938. Adm. 205/3.

[3] Letter by MDG to the author 1st Sept. 1952. See also H. L'Etang, *op. cit.*, pp. 125–7, where the author states that after his death on 21st Oct. 1943 Pound was found to have been suffering from a tumour of the brain. We do not know at what date either the tumour or the dangerously high blood pressure from which Pound was found to be suffering in 1943 first became evident; but as L'Etang remarks 'it is only natural to wonder over what period of time, and to what degree, the tumour accounted for the fatigue and drowsiness which were noticed by lay observers as early as 1940'.

[4] Letters from Admiral Sir Ralph Edwards to the author of 28th July and 4th Aug. 1954; also one from Admiral Sir William Davis of Oct. 1961. Admiral J. H. Godfrey in his memoirs (private circulation) makes very similar remarks on Pound as First Sea Lord, and expanded on them in many letters to the author. Admiral of the Fleet Sir Algernon Willis, who was Chief of Staff to Pound as C-in-C, Mediterranean in 1939, has described to the author how he used to come into his office, go through his papers and draft replies to signals in his own hand. Interview, 12th Sept. 1975.

[5] The climax of Pound's interference in operations came with the disaster to Convoy PQ17 in the Arctic in July 1942. See Roskill, *The War at Sea*, II, pp. 134–45.

[6] See W. S. Chalmers, *Max Horton and the Western Approaches* (Hodder and

interests or social graces; his whole life was bound up with the navy, and his only recreations were fishing and shooting. Admiral James writes that he was 'hard working and efficient at his job, but he failed to evoke wholehearted response from his subordinates', and that he 'loved schedules and Courts of Enquiry'[1] an opinion with which this historian, who served under him for five consecutive years in the Mediterranean Fleet Flagship and the Admiralty 1937–41, fully agrees. He had little or no sense of humour, and lacked the dignified presence and charisma of William Fisher, who though sometimes pompous often showed great humanity as well as a nice sense of humour—even against himself.[2] Nor did Pound possess any quality as impressive as Chatfield's mastery of every aspect of his profession combined with great patience and resolution and complete integrity of character. Certainly Pound kept the Mediterranean Fleet at a high pitch of fighting efficiency as C-in-C 1936–39, and handed over to Andrew Cunningham as fine an instrument of war as he had inherited from Fisher and Fisher from Chatfield; but he was a driver rather than a

---

Stoughton, 1954), pp. 100–2. The author prints in full Horton's letter of 10th Oct. 1940 to A. V. Alexander, declining the appointment and stating his reasons.

[1] Letter to the author 6th April 1964. One example of Pound's addiction to enquiries is the despatch of Lord Cork to Gibraltar in Nov. 1940 to investigate Admiral Somerville's action in breaking off pursuit of the Italian Fleet in order to protect a through-Mediterranean convoy (Roskill, *The War at Sea*, I, pp. 301–4); but Churchill almost certainly had a hand in that decision. A more clear-cut case is Pound's proposal that Admiral Wake-Walker, Commander of 1st Cruiser Squadron, and Captain Leach, Captain of the *Prince of Wales*, should be tried by Court Martial for not re-engaging the *Bismarck* after the *Hood* had been sunk by her on 24th May 1941. Also the trial by Court Martial of the Captain and two officers of the *Manchester* for scuttling her after she had been seriously damaged close off the north African coast in the 'Pedestal' convoy to Malta of Aug. 1942. The former proposal was defeated by Admiral Tovey, the C-in-C, Home Fleet. I did not mention this in *The War at Sea*, vol. I, because it did not affect the operations, but I gave my correspondence with Lord Tovey about it to Ludovic Kennedy who used it in his excellent account of the *Bismarck* operation *Pursuit* (Collins, 1974, p. 226). The latter incident I mentioned briefly in *The War at Sea* (vol. II, p. 306). Pound minuted on the account of the scuttling of the ship that there could be no excuse for such a step as long as a single gun remained in action—so pre-judging the findings of the Court before the defence had even been heard.

[2] Based on the author's service for two commissions under Fisher in the Mediterranean 1930–33 and 1935–36, and on personal friendship with the Fisher family. There are many stories of Fisher's human touch as C-in-C, Mediterranean, some of which are told by Admiral James in his biography *Admiral Sir William Fisher* (Macmillan, 1943).

leader of men, and never impressed his personality on the fleet as a whole as did his two predecessors.[1] His lack of the right touch was shown when he addressed the ship's company of the newly arrived flagship the *Warspite* in 1937. The disciplinary trouble experienced in that ship before she sailed from Portsmouth has already been recounted, as has the fact that the officers who were held to have failed were relieved, while the men deemed to have been involved were discharged from the service or drafted to other ships. Yet in his inaugural speech Pound described the ship's company as having been 'mutinous' —and at a time when his fleet had been trying to obliterate memories of Invergordon 1931. In fact no one involved in the trouble at Portsmouth was still in the ship; and moreover the trouble had, at any rate in part, been caused by Pound himself, who had insisted on the Admiralty's choice for the key job of Executive Officer and second-in-command being replaced by his own nominee—who had previously been his Flag Lieutenant. Such a change, made in the final stage of commissioning a new ship was bound to be unsettling.[2] The indignation produced forward and aft by Pound's speech was such that the Flag Captain was moved to protest to him about its likely effects; yet a few weeks later he wrote a somewhat self-satisfied letter to Chatfield about the speech, evidently in complete unawareness of the damage he had done.[3]

[1] Lower deck nicknames given to senior officers are often both witty and shrewd. Pound was known as 'Twenty-four ounces to the pound'!

[2] That the change was made on Pound's insistence is confirmed by Admiral Sir Victor Crutchley, VC, Captain of *Warspite* 1937-40. Letter to the author of 29th April 1975. Lady Andrewes, widow of the officer who was relieved confirms this. Letter to the author of 20th April 1975.

[3] Dated 7th Feb. 1938. Chatfield papers, CHT/4/10. For a different view of Pound see Arthur J. Marder, *From the Dardanelles to Oran* (Oxford UP, 1974), ch. 4. In support of his claim to know better than I what I did when serving on the Naval Staff in 1939-40 Marder declares that I was 'nowhere near the top échelon' of that organisation —a status which, it is scarcely necessary to say, I have never claimed to have occupied (*op. cit.*, p. 173). He cites the recollections of what A. J. P. Taylor aptly described as 'Admirals . . . enough to sink a battleship' (*The Observer*, 1st Dec. 1974). But a glance at a Navy List for 1939 would have shown Marder how misleading this 'evidence' is, since of the 21 officers whose memories of some 35 years ago he has sought no less than nine were *at that time* of Commander's rank—the same as I held; eight were Captains (one rank higher than me) and only four were Admirals, and of the latter only two (Rear-Admirals Burrough and Godfrey) were on the Naval Staff. The one full Admiral on Marder's list is Sir William James, who was C-in-C, Portsmouth, not in the Admiralty. Moreover the many letters received from Admirals James and

The reader is entitled to ask who other than Pound could have taken Backhouse's place—at rather short notice—and done better by way of preparing the navy for the war which, in the spring of 1939, was all too plainly imminent. In this historian's opinion by far the best decision would have been to recall Chatfield to the post which he had given up only seven months earlier. True he was some four years older than Pound, but he was a very fit man (he lived to be 94); he was wholly familiar with the problems facing the Admiralty and the fleet, and was well known to the political leaders of the time. As his period as First Sea Lord had been nearly two years shorter than Beatty's time in the same office there was a precedent for an outstanding officer to hold the appointment for an unusually long period. Though he could still have undertaken the mission to India mentioned earlier he could not of course have continued as Minister for Co-ordination of Defence; but he could surely have carried on with the Committee on the Acceleration of Defence Programmes, on which he did indispensable work.[1] The only other possible candidate for the office of First Sea Lord was Sir Charles Forbes, and one officer who held many important staff and seagoing appointments during the war and afterwards has expressed the view that things might have gone more smoothly had he been appointed.[2] Certainly Forbes showed a clear-sighted grasp of the strategy to defeat the invasion threat of 1940 and of the priorities of naval defence, and on at least one occasion converted Churchill to his views.[3] It is of course impossible to say how Chatfield would have got on with Churchill as First Lord, but up to 1939 their relations had been friendly. Not until much later did Churchill blame Chatfield for the deficiencies from which the navy suffered—notably the 14-inch battleships—and for not having included any destroyer flotillas in the 1938 programme.[4] Indeed as recently as March 1938 Churchill had praised Chatfield in the House of Commons in the most glowing

---

Godfrey by the author on this subject show that they were both fully in agreement with my view and not with Marder's—as the use by the latter of their names (*op. cit.*, p. 105) may reasonably be held to imply.

[1] Ian Colvin in *The Chamberlain Government* (Gollancz, 1971), ch. XVIII pays warm tribute to Chatfield's work on 'this remarkable Committee', which is the more impressive as he is highly critical of much that the government did (or did not do) at that time.

[2] Admiral Sir William Davis to the author 29th April 1975.

[3] Roskill, *The War at Sea 1939–1945*, I, pp. 80–1.

[4] Churchill to Chatfield 4th March and reply by latter of 10th March 1942. Chatfield papers, CHT/4/3.

erms.[1] In sum those two great men would surely have made an incomparable team during the difficult years 1939–42, after which Admiral Cunningham would have been available and wholly qualified to take over. Furthermore the recall of Chatfield would have achieved the important need for 'continuity in naval policy', which Churchill had stressed so strongly in his speech referred to above.

The question of the appointment to the office of First Sea Lord in 1939 is of much more than academic interest because, in the opinion of this historian, if the Admiralty had been more strongly represented at the top some of the worst naval disasters of the war (notably the despatch of the *Prince of Wales* and *Repulse* to Singapore without air cover in the autumn of 1941 and the scattering of the Arctic convoy PQ17 in July 1942) might well have been averted.[2] Moreover a stronger fight for more long-range aircraft for the Atlantic Battle in 1942 could well have produced victory in that crucial struggle some six months earlier, so saving perhaps four million tons of shipping, and thereby advancing the date when the great combined operations of 1943–45 could have been carried out; for it was always shortage of shipping that cramped and restricted Allied Grand Strategy in those years.[3] It may even not go too far to suggest that the duration of the war would have been shortened by some six months had the Admiralty been represented on the COS and Defence Committees by a more effective team than A. V. Alexander and Admiral Pound.[4]

In fairness to Pound it should be mentioned that, as this historian has made plain elsewhere,[5] he became a pastmaster at what may be called 'playing out time' when some of Churchill's wilder schemes, such as the forcible occupation of islands like Pantelleria which were doing us no harm but would be difficult and costly to supply and defend, were under discussion; but he did so at the price of causing his staff immense frustration through having to waste time planning operations which they knew would never take place. It is also to Pound's credit that in the matter of loyalty towards Churchill and A. V. Alexander he proved a paragon, even taking the blame himself

[1] Parl. Deb., Commons, vol. 333, cols. 656–7.

[2] See Roskill, *The War at Sea*, vol. I, ch. XXVI and vol. II, pp. 134–44.

[3] *op. cit.*, vol. II, chs. VII, XI and XVII.

[4] Admiral Sir William Davis (letter to the author of Oct. 1961) expresses the view that 'the war lasted certainly 8 or 9 months longer than it needed'—for this reason; but, he adds, Churchill 'might well have lost it earlier if he (Pound) had allowed some of his projects to go through'.

[5] See *The Sunday Telegraph*, article 'Churchill and his Admirals' of Feb. 18th 1962.

when it really lay with the political leaders; but one may doubt whether loyalty, when carried to such extremes, is beneficial because it can all too easily descend into weakness on vital issues—as some of Pound's staff certainly felt to be the case in 1941–42.[1]

While the Admiralty was struggling to cope with the implications of the darkening international scene the US Navy Department was thinking on very similar lines—but, until about the middle of 1938, with considerably less urgency. As completion of the big programmes financed in 1934 and 1935 from NIRA funds and from 'Emergency Relief and Public Works' approached,[2] the problem of manning the fleet loomed larger on the American than on the British horizon; since the RN had never experienced in recent years the acute manning difficulties which beset the US Navy. Between the wars the average manning of that service's major units (excluding submarines and aircraft) was 80 to 85% of their full war complements, the proportion allowed being based on what was considered a reasonable share of the total personnel authorised by Congress. In the case of the less important vessels the average of manning fell as low as 65%, and in the 1930s many ships had to operate with even less than their prescribed allowance actually on board—a state of affairs which was not conducive to preparedness for war.[3] The legislation, finally approved in June 1938 to establish Naval and Marine Corps reserves has already been mentioned,[4] and at about the same time discussion took place between the Navy Department, the Bureau of the Budget and the President on legislation to improve 'the distribution, promotion and retirement' of Line (i.e. Executive) Officers, of whom more would plainly be needed. The proportion of Line Officers had always been fixed by Congress, and Roosevelt disliked increasing it from $4\frac{3}{4}$% to 6% of the total personnel, and was also opposed to any tendency to increase promotion by seniority rather than by selection. He was 'much disturbed' by the Reserve Bill which he believed 'is going to ball up the Navy for the next 20 years'.[5] The triangular argument was lengthy but in the end

[1] Paper by Admiral Sir William Davis on 'The Top Admirals in 1939 and After' of 6th Aug. 1975 and letters from Admiral Sir Ralph Edwards mentioned above (p. 463, note). [2] These amounted to $238 and $40.6 millions respectively.

[3] See Admiral James O. Richardson, *Treadmill to Pearl Harbor* (Washington, 1973), pp. 59–64.

[4] HR. 10594. Approved 25th June 1938. This was in fact one of a succession of Reserve Acts, which date back to much earlier times.

[5] FDR to Admiral J. O. Richardson (Chief of Bureau of Navigation, which became Bureau of Personnel in 1942), 21st June 1938. Roosevelt papers, OF 18, Box 4.

the Navy Department got its way with both Bills, though it had to be content with only 5½% of Line Officers.[1]

It is difficult to understand why Roosevelt, who was unquestionably doing all he could to increase the strength of the navy, viewed those two Bills with suspicion, since early in that same year he had sent a Message to Congress asking for authorisation to build additional ships, including an increase in tonnage of combatant vessels of 20% and a wide range of other measures. The cost was estimated at $800 to $1,000 millions spread over a number of years.[2] This was the origin of the Second Vinson Act which, after much debate and many amendments in both Houses, was finally approved on 17th May.[3] It included authorisation of a large additional capital ship tonnage, with a loophole to build bigger ships than the 35,000-ton Treaty tonnage, and also of carriers, cruisers, destroyers and submarines, as well as a very wide range of auxiliary vessels and lesser craft.[4] Roosevelt also asked for a list of yachts suitable for conversion to auxiliary warships to be prepared, and when the Navy Department only chose some three dozen big ones he was critical of them for 'choosing only ideal vessels' and asked for 175 to be selected to a less rigid standard.[5] Once again his intimate interest even in minor naval matters, and his claim to superior knowledge and understanding of what was needed, is to be remarked.

Another step taken at this time, which had far-reaching implications, was the requisitioning of three fast tankers which were building for the Standard Oil Company; and one may therein find the origins of the US Navy's superb mobile organisation for fuelling its fleets.[6] A parallel and contemporary measure was the General Board's issue of 'Instructions for Naval Transportation and US Merchant Vessels in Time of War', which was not only a blueprint for the famous 'Fleet Train' of the future but included plans to give merchant ships defensive armaments and provide them with 'armed guards' analogous to the British DEMS scheme.[7] However it is noteworthy that the General

---

[1] HR. 9997. Approved 23rd June 1938.

[2] Message to Congress of 28th Jan. 1938. Roosevelt papers, OF 18, Box 27.

[3] HR. 9218.

[4] The increases were—capital ships 105,000 tons, carriers 40,000 tons, cruisers 68,754 tons, destroyers 38,000 tons and submarines 13,658 tons, and up to 3,000 'useful aircraft'. *US Statutes at Large*, vol. 52, pp. 401–3.

[5] Roosevelt papers, OF 18, Box 4.   [6] *ibid.*, Box 27.

[7] Whereas the British DEMS scheme relied largely on Merchant Seamen the US Navy's Armed Guards for merchant ships were provided by navy personnel. See *History of the Naval Armed Guard Afloat* (Naval History Division, Washington).

Board evidently regarded convoy with scepticism. It is only mentioned once in these instructions, which refer almost wholly to ships 'operating singly'.[1]

The Second Vinson Act was as much a milestone on the road of expansion of the US Navy as the first one of 1934 had been. The original General Board proposals for the 1939 Appropriations Bill were substantial (two battleships, two cruisers, eight destroyers and six submarines[2]); but the Supplementary Programme in Roosevelt's Message to Congress almost doubled it. In April the Bureaux prepared a joint report for the Secretary of the Navy setting out where the ships would be built if, as they expected, the programme was spread over ten years. Swanson approved it 'as a basis for budgetary planning'.[3]

In May 1938 the General Board put forward what they regarded as the needs for the 1940 Fiscal Year—an enormous programme including three 45,000-ton capital ships (of 53,000 tons 'battle displacement', which made them comparable to the German *Bismarck* class). They also set out the desired characteristics, and proposed that completion of the 1939 programme, and especially of the *Atlanta* class light cruisers, which were similar to though larger than the British *Didos*, should come first, and the battleships second.[4] In the same month Roosevelt endorsed with his laconic 'OK' a wide range of projects for the navy to be financed from WPA and PWA funds,[5] and in June he approved the modernisation of the big carriers *Lexington* and *Saratoga*, for which the Navy Department had long been pressing.[6] With the *Enterprise* completed in July, the *Yorktown* in November and the smaller *Wasp* approaching completion, and plentiful provision having been made for carrier-borne aircraft, the American naval air service was becoming an arm of power and efficiency compared to which the Royal Navy still made a poor showing. In July the General Board produced a vast ten-year building programme for 1939–48, comprising 234 ships in all, including 14 battleships and five fleet carriers,[7] and at the end of the year Roosevelt increased the pressure with a strong complaint to the Secretary about the length of time taken to build the new destroyers. The Navy yards, he wrote impatiently,

[1] GB. 425 of 16th Feb. 1938.   [2] GB. 420–2 of 2nd Feb. 1938.

[3] Dated 5th April 1938. *ibid.*

[4] GB. 420–2, serial 1790 of 3rd May 1938. *ibid.*

[5] Roosevelt papers, OF 18 of 16th May 1938. The same remark appears, for the same purpose, on 16th Jan. 1939. *ibid.*

[6] HR. 7560. Approved 16th June 1938.

[7] GB. 420–2, serial 1802 of 25th July 1938.

'should be ordered—not requested—to put as many people to work on new ships as it is possible to use . . . it is time to get action';[1] and in the same month he pointedly asked Edison 'what would happen if we worked two or three shifts in both Navy yards and private plants?'[2] The aggregate effect of all these measures was that the US Navy ultimately obtained the 'New Naval Standard' necessary to fight a two-ocean war for which the Admiralty had been strongly but vainly pressing since 1937. But the USN was of course fortunate in not being involved in war until the fruits of the great expansion of 1937–40 had started to come to harvest.

The change in outlook of the President who in 1935 had sent his delegates to the London Conference with firm orders to achieve a 20% all round reduction in naval armaments but in 1938 signed the Second Vinson Act and applied constant Congressional and departmental pressure to increase the size and efficiency of the navy is indeed astonishing. Nor can it be doubted that the change arose mainly from the realisation that the dictatorships aimed at world domination, and from a desire to help the democracies withstand their pressures—as far and as fast as Congress would permit him to go. But the distribution to the navy of a substantial share of New Deal largesse also helped Roosevelt's purpose of stimulating industrial activity and reducing unemployment. Thus whereas in Britain, with its weak balance of payments and shaky credit, domestic and foreign policies conflicted—or at least were held to conflict by the Treasury—in the USA they coincided, though the administration did of course often encounter serious difficulties with Congress. Since the money voted for new construction is as good an indicator as any of naval rearmament a few figures may be given.[3] (See overleaf p. 472.)

In April 1939 the General Board produced their proposals for the Fiscal Year 1941. They were identical to the programme framed by Leahy and approved by Swanson shortly before his death except that the battleships were increased by one. The principal units were two battleships (*Missouri* and *Wisconsin*), one carrier (20,000 tons, which became the *Hornet*), two big 6-inch cruisers (*Cleveland* class), eight large destroyers and six submarines.[4] The characteristics of each class were

---

[1] FDR to Swanson and Leahy 28th Dec. 1938. Roosevelt papers, OF, Dept. Corresp., Box 25.

[2] FDR to Edison 1st Dec. 1938. *ibid.*, OF 18, Box 27.

[3] From Navy. Dept. Op–09B91R of May 1965.

[4] GB. 420–2, serial 1828 of 26th April 1939.

Naval Policy Between the Wars

U.S. NAVAL CONSTRUCTION 1939–40.
MONEY VOTED AND SHIPS ORDERED[1]

Year	Navy Budget Request Construction	Ships	Congressional Authorisation	Ships under Construction	Ships in Commission (all types)
1934	$38.8 millions	22	$33.4 millions plus $238 millions from NIRA	46	436
1935	$32.4 millions	22	$33.6 millions plus $40.7 millions from 'Emergency Relief and Public Works'	64	462
1936	$140 millions	77	$126.9 millions	79	491
1937	$168.5 millions	99	$168.5 millions	71	535
1938	$157 millions	121	$130 millions	70	533
1939	$143.7 millions	110	$154.1 millions	77	546
1940	$270 millions	125	$290.1 millions	138	592

[1] Prepared by US Naval Historical Branch. Op-09B91R of May 1965.

stated, but to speed construction the Board proposed taking certain vessels of each class as prototypes for a War Building Programme—if war came.[1] It is curious to find that, at about the time when the General Board's constant pressure for more ships was bearing fruit the abolition of that body should have been discussed—apparently at the instigation of Admiral H. R. Stark, who was to succeed Leahy as CNO in August.[2] The argument presumably was that the functions of the Board could equally well be carried out by the CNO and his staff, and that its existence merely added a fifth wheel to the coach. But in fact it was not abolished until 1951.

In August Edison, who was acting as Secretary since Swanson's death in the previous month, asked the General Board to make a survey of the 'critical deficiencies' from which the navy suffered—which was of course analogous to the much earlier British 'deficiencies' programme. The principal trouble revealed was the old one of shortage of men, which was described as 'critically inadequate'; but the Board also drew attention to the shortage of seaplane tenders and fast tankers, the lack of any properly organised and defended base west of Hawaii, and the need for a patrol plane base on that island. All those needs were to prove vital.[3] Shortly after the outbreak of war the General Board repeated and extended the survey mentioned above, with the result that Admiral Stark asked the President for 145,000 men and 25,000 marines to man the fleet, and to call up Reserve Officers. Some $167 millions were, he wrote, needed as a 'first jump' to carry out that programme.[4] It is noteworthy that, despite its vastly greater industrial capacity the USA suffered from exactly the same shortages as Britain—notably gun, gun mounting and armour plate manufacturing capacity.[5]

As the crisis deepened in 1939 the President asked Congress to pass three Deficiency Acts—corresponding to British Supplementary Estimates;[6] and the purse strings were apparently loosened without

---

[1] *ibid.* serial 1862A.

[2] Callaghan to FDR 26th May 1939. Roosevelt papers, PSF, Dept. Corresp., Box 28.

[3] GB. 425, serial 1868 of 31st Aug. 1939. Subject 'Are We Ready?'

[4] GB. 425, serial 1868 of 9th Sept. 1939 contains requirements additional to those listed in the previous month on 11th Sept. Stark wrote to Admiral Greenslade, a member of the General Board, congratulating him on the August report and telling him about the action he was taking with the President.

[5] Reports of Chiefs of Bureaux of Ordnance, Construction and Engineering to CNO Jan.–Feb. 1938. GB. 420-2, serial 1741 of 8th May 1937.

[6] Roosevelt papers, OF 18, Box 5.

serious difficulty. In June plans to evacuate American nationals from Europe were framed. The total was estimated at 28,638, and a special task force was formed to fetch them from ports stretching from Sweden to Portugal.[1] Two months later the C-in-C, US Fleet (Admiral C. C. Bloch) prepared a comprehensive survey of 'The Readiness of the Naval Establishment'. He was worried about the weakness of the defences of Manila and Guam, and called for anti-submarine booms and nets for all the fleet's bases. Aircraft and air equipment were, he wrote, 'keeping pace with the expansion of the fleet', but shortages of carrier-borne fighters, torpedoes and air-borne depth charges were serious. Most of the aircraft carriers suffered from deficiencies of some sort, but the aviation personnel Bloch described as 'very good'. Fifteen battleships were, he reported, available and twelve of them were in the Pacific, where the navy's main strength had been deployed ever since the Manchurian crisis blew up in 1932.[2] Not until early in 1941 did a major redisposition take place, with the formation of an independent Atlantic Fleet.[3]

The Navy Department's organisation and staff were reviewed at this time, and the Joint Army and Navy Munitions Board reported on shortages of 'strategic and critical materials'.[4] It is interesting to find the Office of Naval Intelligence advocating the creation of a high-level organisation on the lines of the British CID—just after, as we saw earlier, the CID system had come under severe criticism in Britain. The ONI proposed setting up a National Defence Committee and a National Defence College like the British Imperial Defence College.[5] Stark supported these ideas, and although it is the case that the Americans copied British organisation and administration in many respects, especially after studying our war experience of 1939–41 at close quarters, the CID system was not actually extended to Washington until the Combined Chiefs of Staff Committee came into being early in 1942 as a result of the Washington ('Arcadia') Conference.

In the early months of 1939 a large scale American naval exercise took place in the Atlantic and Caribbean, to test 'control of the Atlantic Ocean and South America'. It included the protection of a convoy against air and submarine attack, and the conclusion was that

[1] Roosevelt papers, PSF, Dept. Corresp., Box 28.

[2] Bloch to Chairman, General Board 24th Aug. 1939. GB. 425.

[3] See Monograph by Richard W. Leopold, *Fleet Organisation 1919–1941*. US Navy Dept. Historical Section.

[4] On 15th Nov. 1938.   [5] ONI to CNO 1st Sept. 1939. GB. 425.

those weapons would have great influence, though Bloch was inclined to the view that the results of the exercise might have given an exaggerated impression of their importance compared to that of large surface warships.[1] As in earlier USN exercises the carriers played a dominant part, but it is none the less plain that the Battle Fleet concept was no more dead in the US Navy than in the Royal Navy—or for that matter the Japanese Navy. The 1939 exercises were the last to take place before the outbreak of war in Europe.

At the end of April 1939 the US Joint Planning Committee analysed the world situation, and concluded that a Japanese attack on the Philippines was more likely than German or Italian aggression in the western hemisphere. None the less security of the Caribbean Sea and Panama Canal was in their view vital, and offensive measures against the European Axis powers might therefore be necessary.[2] This plan may be said to mark the genesis of the 'Europe First' or 'Atlantic Strategy' which was to play so great a part in World War II.

The next step was preparation by the Joint Planning Committee of the plans to be adopted in various contingencies such as war alone, with allies, and with one or more enemies. These became known as the 'Rainbow Plans', and replaced the Orange, Red and Black plans of earlier years. No less than five Rainbow Plans were produced, but as they fall outside the scope of this history we need only note their origin.[3]

As the clouds gathered the Neutrality Acts again became a dominant consideration in Anglo-American relations. In August, when Lord Lothian presented his credentials as British Ambassador, he reported that 'There is certainly nothing neutral about the President's attitude towards the conflict between the dictatorships and the democracies'; and Roosevelt had even suggested instituting patrols in the western half of the Atlantic by warships of all the republics of the western hemisphere, which 'he thought would be of great assistance to England and France'.[4] But when in the following month Roosevelt addressed Congress and the ambassador was present the latter noted how passages like 'keeping the United States out of war' and referring to the 'cash

---

[1] Fleet Problem XX, 20–27th Feb. 1939. See also Roosevelt papers, PSF, Dept. Corresp., Box 28.

[2] USNA, RG. 225, Exploratory Studies of 21st April 1939.

[3] See Louis Morton, *The War in the Pacific: The First Two Years* (Washington, 1962), pp. 68–77.

[4] Report by Lothian of 31st Aug. 1939. FO. 371/23904. Copy in Adm. 116/4103.

and carry' clause of the 1937 Neutrality Act were loudly applauded, but that wholesale repeal of the neutrality legislation 'would it seems meet with much opposition'.[1] And so 'cash and carry' it was—until British reserves of cash were almost wholly exhausted and our capacity to 'carry' had been vitiated by serious shipping losses. The Lend Lease Act of December 1940—described by Churchill as a 'glorious conception' and 'the most unsordid act in the history of any nation'[2]—was then passed; and if it saved Britain from bankruptcy it also preserved American prosperity—and profits.[3]

In June 1939 the Admiralty, presumably as a follow-up to the Ingersoll-Phillips conversations of January 1938, sent an officer of the Plans Division to Washington for talks with Admirals Leahy, the CNO, and Ghormley his Director of Plans, on the recent deliberations regarding naval strategy, including the Far East and European War Appreciations prepared for the Strategic Appreciation Committee and approved by the CID.[4] The talks, in which the British Naval Attaché joined, took place on 12th and 14th June, and although no concrete decisions regarding co-operation between the two navies emerged, the Americans did not dissent from British views and intentions. Leahy, though emphasising that he was only expressing a personal opinion, went so far as to envisage a division of strategic responsibility between the Pacific for his country and the Atlantic for Britain. He also indicated that an American force would move to Singapore to join with a British token force of unspecified strength but probably including capital ships.[5] The talks took place in utmost secrecy because both parties realised that a leak to the Press could produce disastrous repercussions. Probably for that reason the Dominions were not told about them, which, though understandable, gives further grounds for the complaint that they were never kept properly informed regarding British plans. A month after the Washing-

---

[1] Report of 21st Sept. 1939. Adm. 116/4103.

[2] *The Second World War*, vol. II, pp. 502–3.

[3] See Warren F. Kimball, *The Most Unsordid Act: Lend Lease, 1939–1941* (Baltimore, 1969) for a balanced account of the origin and passing of this historic measure. A more controversial work is Gabriel Kolko, *The World and United States Foreign Policy 1943–1945* (Random House, NY, 1969). In a review of the latter by Gaddis Smith in the *New York Times* of 13th April 1969 the reviewer wrote that 'The United States did use its economic power to undermine the British Empire during the war, and to advance, often selfishly, American economic interests'.

[4] The officer sent out was Commander T. C. Hampton.

[5] Record of meetings in Adm. 116/3922.

ton talks the 'period before relief' of Singapore was increased, on the initiative of the Admiralty, to 90 days, and the supply of stores and food to withstand a six month siege was approved in principle.[1]

Early in July the British DNI distributed to Consular Reporting Officers and to Lloyds' Agents comprehensive statements to clarify exactly the state of their preparations for war, the instructions they were to follow and the handbooks they should have received.[2] Plainly nothing was left undone to enable those officials to carry out their functions efficiently from the moment the word was given; and as Axis merchant ships were certain to seek the protection of neutral harbours quick reporting of their movements was plainly very important.

A month later the Admiralty sent to all naval authorities at home and afloat all over the world what may be regarded as their final thoughts on the dispositions to be adopted in the event of Japan intervening when we were already at war with Germany and Italy—the development which the COSs had so long striven to avoid and had always viewed with the utmost concern. 'There can be no doubt', the Admiralty now wrote, 'that the intervention of Japan would be a serious threat to our position in the Far East', since it would mean that the Allies were opposed 'by powerful enemy forces in three theatres'. The Home one, they declared 'is the decisive theatre and we must do nothing to endanger our position there'. This meant that we must retain at home six capital ships, including all three battle-cruisers, to deal with the German *Scharnhorsts* and pocket battleships. As to the projected Eastern Fleet, our objectives remained the same as before—namely to make Singapore secure, to defend Australia and New Zealand and to exert economic pressure on Japan. They again assessed Japanese efficiency at 'approximately 80% of our own', and by accepting that dubious premise they arrived at a maximum strength of seven capital ships for the Far East, accompanied by one aircraft carrier, three heavy and five light cruisers, 35 destroyers and two depot ships; but three more heavy and five light cruisers, another carrier, fourteen destroyers and fifteen submarines were allocated additionally to the Persian Gulf and East Indies or to the China station. The Admiralty also hoped for the co-operation of four and two cruisers from Australia and New Zealand respectively, as well as the RAN's five destroyers. On paper these forces looked substantial; but they were required to cover a

[1] 364th CID meeting on 6th July 1939. Cab. 2/9.
[2] AL of 8th July 1939. Adm. 178/192.

vast area stretching from East Africa to the China Sea and southwards through the Eastern Archipelago to Australia and New Zealand; and the likelihood of being able quickly to concentrate all the ships listed was obviously remote.

The Mediterranean was, as before, divided between us and the French, but even so the old conflict 'between our interests in the Eastern Mediterranean and the Far East' had not been resolved. The despatch of the full strength allocated to the Far East would, the Admiralty wrote, 'depend on a variety of circumstances which cannot be decided in advance'—such as the reactions of the USSR and USA to Japanese intervention. The full strength earmarked for the Far East could only be sent out if Italy remained neutral; but the uncertainties and imponderables were so many that it was, the Admiralty wrote, impossible to lay down rigid intentions. If most of the Mediterranean Fleet went east only eleven submarines and some small craft would remain in the eastern basin of that sea; but considerable numbers of cruisers, destroyers and escort vessels were to be kept in the Red Sea to secure the vital traffic from the Cape to Suez, and other cruisers were allocated to trade defence in accordance with the principles set out in earlier letters and manuals. The Admiralty obviously doubted whether the convoy strategy could be adopted quickly, because they wrote that 'we must rely primarily on evasive routing for the protection of trade' until such time as 'large numbers of AMCs [Armed Merchant Cruisers] are available'; and that was not expected to be fulfilled for six to eight months.[1]

Several points in these plans merit attention. The first is that naval strength was obviously still assessed chiefly by capital ship numbers; and the second is that trade defence was regarded from the point of view of the surface raider rather than the submarine, since the cruisers and AMCs allocated for that purpose were useless against the latter. Yet, making due allowance for the effect of the principles of maritime strategy accepted much earlier and only brought under scrutiny by the VCS and ABE Committees in recent years, it is hard to conceive of a better disposition of forces than was set out in this letter. That when hostilities began they were, except as regards the priority given to the Home Fleet, subject to major changes does not necessarily mean that they could have been improved upon at the time they were issued.

The disposition and strength of the Royal Navy on the outbreak of

[1] AL M. 06226/39 of 4th Aug. 1939. Adm. 1/9676.

war have been published in detail elsewhere and need not be repeated in detail here;[1] but it should be mentioned that its chief strength was divided about equally between the Home and Mediterranean Fleets, with detached squadrons, mainly of cruisers and escort vessels, in China, the East and West Indies and the South Atlantic. The Dominion navies were still mainly in their home waters. About 140 ships of all classes of the 1936–39 programmes were building, and three capital ships, three heavy cruisers and about a score of lesser vessels were undergoing major refits and modernisation.

At this time the principal American naval forces were the United States Fleet, based in the eastern Pacific, the Asiatic Fleet, based on the Philippines and China and the Atlantic Squadron organised in the previous January. By far the most powerful was the US Fleet, whose chief units were five carriers with twenty squadrons of aircraft, each of eighteen planes embarked, fifteen battleships (the whole of the service's strength in that class), sixteen heavy and fifteen light cruisers and a large number of destroyers and submarines. Of the five major sub-divisions of the fleet much the strongest was the Battle Force. The Atlantic Squadron consisted only of three battleships and nine destroyers. The 'Operating Force Plan' for 1940 was issued in June 1939 and showed that 368 warships and 1,714 aircraft were to be provided in the 1940 Fiscal Year. As the approved number of enlisted men had risen only by about 6,000 plus 1,000 for the Marine Corps over the previous year's figures the Navy Department's chief anxieties lay in obtaining and training the additional men needed for the 105 ships building on 1st July 1939, and in the unsatisfactory number and state of the auxiliary vessels needed for the support of the fleet. Though Line (Executive) Officers were 700 under the allowed total of 7,562 this caused less anxiety than the shortage of enlisted men, and especially of technicians, who took far longer to train than young officers required to carry out subordinate duties. The quality and morale of all personnel was high, and experience was to show that the peacetime nucleus was, as with the Royal Navy, capable of expanding very rapidly in the event of emergency. In terms of strategy the lack of bases west of Hawaii, mentioned earlier, continued to be a cause of acute anxiety, rendering the accepted concept for an 'Orange War' highly dubious in terms of practicability. In sum although a great deal had been accomplished since the passing of the first Vinson Act in 1934 no American senior officer felt that the correct answers to the General Board's

[1] See Roskill, *The War at Sea*, vol. I, Appendix E.

'Are we Ready' memorandum of August 1939 were affirmative.[1] We now know that all the Axis navies were, comparatively speaking, in a far higher state of readiness at this time.

In mid-July 1939 the Admiralty informed all naval authorities that 'in order to increase the readiness' the greater part of the Reserve Fleet was to be commissioned with Reservists and pensioners, who would be called to report to their depots on the last day of the month. Care was to be taken, they wrote, to avoid any use of the word 'mobilisation' in connection with these measures. Next day details were sent out giving particulars of the officers being recalled for various duties and where they were to go.[2]

In the early weeks of August 1939 the Home and Mediterranean Fleets ostensibly continued to carry out their normal programmes of cruises combined with ship and squadron training; but a great deal of preparatory work went on quietly in the background at the same time, with the object of improving the readiness of the fleets for war. Early in September the Mediterranean Fleet, having called briefly at Malta to complete with stores and ammunition, assembled quietly at Alexandria —exactly as had been done at the time of the Abyssinian crisis. Although as a base Alexandria still left a good deal to be desired the defences had been strengthened and the facilities, though still mainly afloat, improved;[3] and as Malta was still almost defenceless, and the threat of Italian air power was regarded very seriously, there was no alternative but to concentrate in the eastern Mediterranean, leaving the western half of that sea mainly to the French navy.[4]

As regards the Home Fleet mobilisation went smoothly and the main bases at Portsmouth, Devonport and Chatham were in reasonably good order to fulfil their multi-purpose role of operational, manning and repair bases. But the decision once again to adopt the strategy of distant blockade, and the vulnerability of the southern bases

[1] A valuable account of the state of the US Navy in 1939 is in Admiral James O. Richardson's *On the Treadmill to Pearl Harbor* (Washington, 1973).

[2] ALs M. 06551 of 13th July and CW. 13047/39 of 14th July 1939. Adm. 205/1.

[3] Adm. 53/106839 and 106840. Log of *Warspite* (Fleet Flagship) for Sept. and Oct. 1938.

[4] Some notes of (probably unconscious) humour appear in the official records during this critical month. For example on 16th Aug. the Consul-General, Naples, sought Foreign Office approval 'by safe hand' to spend the sum of 202 Lire (about £2.20 at the current rate of exchange) for making and supplying an incinerator for the destruction of confidential documents in accordance with orders already received. FO. 371/23904.

387

OFFICES OF THE CABINET
AND COMMITTEE OF IMPERIAL DEFENCE,
RICHMOND TERRACE,
LONDON, S.W. 1.

Date.....3rd September, 1939.

Time of Despatch......11.15 a.m.

MOST IMMEDIATE.

SECRET.

INSTITUTION OF WAR STAGE.

Sir,

I AM directed by the Prime Minister to inform you that a state of war exists between the United Kingdom and Germany. ~~that His Majesty's Government have decided to declare war against~~ ~~that war has broken out between His Majesty's Government and~~

with effect from 11 a.m. 3rd September, 1939.

2. I am to request that the arrangements laid down in the War Book for the War Stage may be put into operation ~~with effect from~~ forthwith.

3. Please acknowledge the receipt of this letter immediately.

I am,

Sir,

Your obedient Servant,

William Elliot.

to air attack, combined to bring about the decision again to use Scapa Flow in the Orkneys as the Home Fleet's main base; but its defences were very far from satisfactory, and it possessed hardly any repair facilities. Nor was Rosyth dockyard yet restored to anything like its World War I capacity. Thus as regards security of its bases the position of both main fleets was unsatisfactory, and a heavy price was to be exacted before that deficiency was rectified.

On 24th August the Admiralty sent an 'Immediate Telegram', drafted the previous day by the COSs,[1] to all holders signified in the War Book saying that the situation with Germany was 'critical', but the 'Warning Telegram' was not being sent for the present. Cs-in-C were however authorised to increase the state of readiness of their fleets, but were warned to avoid steps that 'cannot be disguised and might have political repercussion'.[2]

On 23rd August the Cabinet set up the Defence Preparedness Committee under Chatfield's chairmanship. It met four times between that date and the outbreak of war, and considered 25 papers in a new series submitted to it.[3] This body in effect put the final touches to naval measures which had long been planned in detail. For example at the first meeting warnings were issued to all merchant ships to keep away from Axis ports; as a result of the second one the arming of the first 25 of the 74 ships which had been earmarked for conversion to Armed Merchant Cruiser was to go ahead, and 35 deep sea trawlers were to be requisitioned for A/S work. At the third meeting it was decided that 5,000 more Reservists were to be called up by personal notification.[4] On 25th the COSs reviewed a paper entitled 'Preparation for the Declaration of War' to decide the earliest date on which a communication likely to result in war should be sent to 'a prospective enemy government'. As regards the naval measures already in hand the conclusion was that issue of an ultimatum need not be delayed by any of those factors, and that if it was not to be issued until all new preparations had been completed 1st September was the earliest possible date.[5] On 25th August the Admiralty gave instructions 'for reporting the movements of British sea-going merchant ships', and instructed

---

[1] COS. 964 of 23rd Aug. 1939. Cab. 53/54.

[2] AM. 1441 of 24th Aug. 1939. FO. 371/23904.

[3] The DM(39) series. Cab. 27/662.

[4] Minutes of 1st, 2nd and 3rd meetings of DM Committee, 23rd–31st Aug. 1939. *ibid.*

[5] COS. 966 (Revise) of 25th Aug. 1939. Cab. 53/54.

MESSAGE.
MOST IMMEDIATE.

To Addressees of W.List 47   Date 3.9.39.

P/L.

___

MOST IMMEDIATE.

From   Admiralty

Special telegram TOTAL GERMANY repetition

TOTAL GERMANY.

1117/3

Head of M.

1st Lord.
1st S.L.
2nd S.L.
3rd S.L.
4th S.L.
5th S.L.
D.C.N.S.
A.C.N.S.
Deputy Controller
Parl. Sec.
Civil Lord.
Sec.
 aval Sec.
C.S.O./1st S.L.
P.A.S.(S)
D.N.I.(3)
O.D.(2)
D. of P.(2)
M. (6)
O.I.C.
I.P.

M.M.

Lloyds to inform all their agents accordingly—which was the first step towards assumption of full control of merchant shipping. Next day telegrams indicated that it was very doubtful whether South Africa or Eire would enter a war with the Mother Country, and the Admiralty became concerned about the possible consequences to British ships calling in South African ports;[1] but in the event, after a political crisis, the Union did declare war on 6th September. The next COS paper surveyed 'measures to be taken in connection with a declaration of war'.[2]

On the last day of August the Colonial Office sent a telegram to the Governor, Straits Settlements, saying that as the government was 'making every endeavour to promote better relations with Japan' he should at once cancel the orders prohibiting Japanese, as well as German and Italian, merchant ships berthing at certain wharves in Singapore.[3] Plainly the spectre of war against all three dictatorships had not been laid.

At the fourth meeting of the Defence Preparedness Committee on 1st September all preparations were reviewed and it was decided that the Precautionary Stage should be instituted and the 'Warning Telegrams' sent, both Germany and Italy being named as potential enemies. General mobilisation of Naval Reserves was to be completed by Royal Proclamation, and a wide range of other preparatory measures put in hand.[4] That same day the Admiralty informed the Foreign Office that the 'Warning Telegram' had been sent to all Cs-in-C and SNOs.[5] At 10.30 a.m. on 3rd the War Book Committee met at Richmond Terrace under the chairmanship of Sir Edward Bridges, the Secretary of the Cabinet, and at 11.13 Bridges 'informed those present that as no answer had been received to the ultimatum, which had been delivered to Germany at 9.0 a.m., he was authorised to say that all departments should at once take steps . . . to institute forthwith the War Stage as laid down in the Government War Book'.[6] The signal to commence hostilities must already have been drafted as it is timed 11.15.

At Alexandria the Mediterranean Fleet War Diary records the

---

[1] FO. 371/23904.   [2] COS. 968 JP. Cab. 53/54.   [3] FO. 371/23904.

[4] 4th Meeting of DM Committee on 1st Sept. 1939. Cab. 27/662. Conclusions in CP. 190(39). Cab. 24/288.

[5] AL M. 08512 of 1st Sept. 1939. FO. 371/23904. Another touch which reads humorously is that the Cabinet conclusions for that day record that the Chancellor of the Exchequer said that the Bank Holiday 'planned on the outbreak of war' should be on Monday 4th Sept. Cabinet 47(39) of 1st Sept. 1939. Cab. 23/100.

[6] K. 323 of 3rd Sept. 1939. FO. 371/23904.

various precautionary stages put in hand between 19th August and 3rd September, and ends with the laconic statement that at 12.51 p.m. (Zone-2) on 3rd September the order was received to start hostilities against Germany.[1] On other foreign stations the signal 'Total Germany' was received at about the same time. The log of the Mediterranean Fleet flagship records that on 1st September 'hands [were] employed preparing regatta boats', and that the First Battle Squadron's regatta began that afternoon and ended next day. Perhaps the C-in-C had in mind Francis Drake's—probably fictitious—remark about finishing the game of bowls on Plymouth Hoe in 1588. For Sunday 3rd the flag-ship's log records that Divine Service took place at 10.10 a.m., but is thereafter a complete blank. That of the Home Fleet flagship the *Nelson* records that she was at sea from 1st to 6th September, that 'Divisions and prayers' took place at 10.40 on 3rd, and that at 11.17 'War [was] declared on Germany'.[2]

Study of the Cabinet and Departmental papers may perhaps give a somewhat misleading impression of the smoothness with which the transition from peace to war was accomplished; but the detailed planning made during the preceding years, especially with regard to completing the War Book, and the rehearsals of 1935 and 1937 undoubtedly paid a very good dividend in August and September 1939. Anyone who saw the Reservists streaming into the barracks in answer to the calls they had received, and the ships steadily coming forward for service, could not fail to be impressed by the quiet resolution with which a democracy, having once decided that the aggression of the dictators had to be stopped no matter what the price, set itself to accomplish the task. And when on 3rd September the Admiralty sent a General Signal 'Winston is back' the navy knew that it had the leader it wanted, and that all the vacillations and frustrations of recent years had come to an abrupt and decisive end. Though officers and men certainly did not expect a quick or easy victory they were imbued with the confidence bred of long tradition, professional competence and familiarity with all the vagaries of 'the unquiet sea with its gifts and its unending menace'.[3] And, perhaps most important of all, was the knowledge that behind them stood a nation united in its detestation of a vile tyranny, whose people looked to them to preserve and perpetuate the heritage of centuries.

[1] Adm. 199/389. [2] Logs *Warspite* and *Nelson*. Adm. 53/111091 and 111092.
[3] Joseph Conrad, *Rescue* (Dent. Ed.), p. 108.

Appendices

British Navy Estimates and Actual Expenditure 1919-39

This reprint replaces the same Appendix in Volume 1 which contained several errors.

Year	Net[1] Estimates in £1,000s	Net Expenditure in £1,000s
1918–19	149,200	334,091
1919–20	157,529	154,084
1920–21	84,372	92,505
1921–22	82,479	75,896
1922–23	64,884	57,492
1923–24	58,000	54,064
1924–25	55,800	55,694
1925–26	60,500	60,005
1926–27	58,100	57,143
1927–28	58,000	58,123
1928–29	57,300	57,139
1929–30	55,865	55,988
1930–31	51,739	52,274
1931–32	51,605	51,015
1932–33	50,476	50,164
1933–34	53,570	53,444
1934–35	56,550	56,616
1935–36	60,050	64,888
1936–37	69,930[2]	80,976
1937–38	78,065[3]	78,259
1938–39	93,707[4]	96,396
1939–40	69,399[5]	99,429

[1] 'Net' Estimates and Expenditure are the gross figures less receipts in the form of 'Appropriations in Aid'.

[2] With 3 Supplementary Estimates increased to 81,289.

[3] The Defence Loans Act of 1937 provided that up to £400 millions from the Consolidated Fund might be spent on naval defence during the five years ending 31st March 1942. In 1937, 1938, and 1939 respectively sums of £27 millions, £30 millions and £80 millions were spent under this act. Such sums were credited to 'Appropriations in Aid' and so did not affect the Net Estimates and Expenditure.

[4] With 2 Supplementary Estimates increased to £96,117.

[5] The large difference between Net Estimates and Net Expenditure in this year was met in part from extra receipts (£1.469 millions) and the balance (£28.561 millions) out of the Vote of Credit of £500 millions provided by Parliament on 1st September 1939 for, *inter alia*, 'Securing the public safety, the Defence of the Realm . . . and the efficient prosecution of any war in which His Majesty may be engaged . . .'

PERSONNEL NUMBERS

Year	Vote A	Average number borne
1918–19	450,000	381,311
1919–20	280,000	176,087
1920–21	136,000	124,009
1921–22	123,700	127,180
1922–23	118,500[1]	107,782
1923–24	99,500	99,107
1924–25	100,500	99,453
1925–26	102,675	100,284
1926–27	102,675	100,791
1927–28	102,275	101,916
1928–29	101,800	100,680
1929–30	99,800	99,300
1930–31	97,050	94,921
1931–32	93,650	92,449
1932–33	91,410	89,667
1933–34	90,300	89,863
1934–35	92,300	91,351
1935–36	94,482[2]	94,259
1936–37	99,095	99,886
1937–38	112,000	107,040
1938–39	119,000[3]	118,167
1939–40	133,000[4]	161,000

[1] From 1922–23 to 1924–25 the original Vote A included Coastguards and Royal Marine Police. From 1925–26 to 1939–40 it included Royal Marine Police only. In all cases the totals for Coastguards and RM Police have been deducted so that the table should show the effective personnel strength of the RN.

[2] Increased by Supplementary Estimate to 101,158.

[3] Increased by Supplementary Estimate to 146,500.

[4] Increased to 178,000 after the outbreak of war.

US Navy Expenditure and Personnel Numbers 1919-39

Fiscal Year	Expenditure in $1,000s	Converted to £1,000s sterling at $4.87 to £1[1]	Personnel
1918	1,278,840	262,595	501,425
1919	2,002,311	411,152	320,978
1920	736,021	151,133	139,010
1921	650,374	133,547	155,817
1922	476,775	97,900	121,444
1923	333,201	68,419	113,768
1924	332,249	68,224	118,516
1925	346,142	71,076	114,708
1926	312,743	64,218	112,458
1927	318,909	65,484	114,114
1928	331,335	68,036	114,822
1929	364,562	74,859	115,913
1930	374,166	76,831	116,270
1931	353,768	72,642	112,089
1932	357,518	73,412	109,945
1933	349,373	71,740	107,298
1934	296,927[2]	60,971	108,673
1935	436,266[3]	89,582	112,313
1936	528,882	108,600	123,540
1937	556,674	114,307	131,840
1938	596,130	122,409	137,441
1939	672,722	138,136	144,634

Authority—Column II *A Statistical Abstract Supplement, Historical Statistics of the United States from Colonial Times to 1957* (US Dept. of Commerce).
Column III *The Army Almanac* (US Govt. Printing Office, 1950).

[1] From 1920–1939 the official dollar-sterling parity rate was $4.87 to £1. The trading rate in 1918 and 1919 was $4.76 and $3.84 respectively and no parity rate is given for those years. Between 1929 and 1934 the trading rate fluctuated considerably between the low point of $3.32 in 1931 and 1932 and the high point of $5.02 in 1933. The official parity rate of $4.87 has been taken as the fairest figure to use throughout this period.

[2] Plus $238,000 from National Industrial Recovery Administration funds for construction of 2 ships.

[3] Plus $40 662 for emergency construction from appropriation for 'Emergency Relief and Public Works'.

Supplement to Bibliography
in Volume I

◆

Author's Note. The number of books dealing with various aspects of the period 1919–1939 has recently become so large that it has proved difficult to keep this Bibliography within reasonable bounds. I have therefore excluded most books which will be familiar to the reader, such as Sir Winston Churchill's own works and the many books about him, and also the memoirs or biographies of most leading politicians of the period. The books here listed are those which I have found most interesting or valuable. This Supplement is divided into the same sections as the Bibliography in Volume I, but where a section only dealt with a subject covered by that book (e.g. Section VI, The Washington Conference 1921–22) it has been omitted here and the numbering of sections carried on as before. This accounts for there being some breaks in the numbering of the sections below. With the object of making this Supplement and the original Bibliography as representative as possible (though not of course approaching completeness) a few books dealing with 1919–1929 which were omitted from Volume I have been added here.

I. BOOKS OF GENERAL INTEREST

Aster, Sidney *The Making of the Second World War* (André Deutsch, 1973)

Barnes, Harry E. *Perpetual War for Perpetual Peace* (Caxton Printers, Idaho, 1953)

Bond, Brian *Chief of Staff. The Diaries of Lieut-General Sir Henry Pownall*, vol. 1 (Leo Cooper, 1972)

Brodie, Bernard *A Guide to Naval Strategy* (New ed. Princeton UP, 1958)
  War and Politics (Cassell, 1974)

Caute, David *The Fellow Travellers* (Weidenfeld and Nicolson, 1973)

Colvin, Ian *The Chamberlain Cabinet* (Gollancz, 1971)

Dilks, David *The Diaries of Sir Alexander Cadogan* (Cassell, 1971)

Documents on British Foreign Policy
  Series 2 (1929–1936) vols. I–XIII published (HMSO, 1946–70)
  Series 3 (1938–1939) vols. I–IX complete (HMSO, 1949–55)

Documents on German Foreign Policy, Series C (1933–36) and D (1937–45), (HMSO, 1949–66)

Donnelly, D. *Struggle for the World* (Collins, 1965)

Evans, Trefor (ed.) *The Killearn Diaries 1934–36* (Sidgwick and Jackson, 1972)

Foot, Michael R. D. (ed.) *War and Society* (Elek, 1973)

493

Gilbert, Martin *The European Powers* (Weidenfeld and Nicolson, 1965)

Harvey, John *The Diplomatic Diaries of Oliver Harvey 1937–1940* (Collins, 1970)

James, Robert R. (ed.) *Chips. The Diaries of Sir Henry Channon* (Weidenfeld an Nicholson, 1967)

Jones, Thomas (ed. Keith Middlemas) *Whitehall Diary* (3 vols. Oxford UP, 196 1971)

Kahn, David *The Codebreakers* (Macmillan, NY, 1957)

Kimball, Warren F. *The Most Unsordid Act: Lend Lease 1939–1941* (Baltimore, 196

L'Etang, Hugh *The Pathology of Leadership* (Heinemann Medical Books, 1969)

Mackintosh, John P. *The British Cabinet* (2nd ed. Methuen, 1968)

Macleod, R. and Kelly D. (eds.) *The Ironside Diaries* (Constable, 1962)

Mallaby, George *Studies of Men in Power* (Leo Cooper, 1972)

Marwick, Arthur *Britain in the Century of Total War* (Bodley Head, 1968)

Middlemas, Keith *Diplomacy of Illusion* (Weidenfeld and Nicolson, 1972)

Mowat, Charles L. *Great Britain Since 1914* (Hodder and Stoughton, 1970)

Naylor, John F. *Labour's International Policy* (Houghton Mifflin, Boston, 1969)

Noguères, Henri *Munich* (Eng. Trans. Weidenfeld and Nicolson, 1965)

Norman, Aaron *The Great Air War* (Macmillan, NY, 1968)

O'Connell, D. P. *The Influence of Law on Sea Power* (Manchester UP, 1975)

Parker, R. A. C. *Europe 1919–1945* (Weidenfeld and Nicolson, 1969)

Robbins, Keith *Munich, 1938* (Cassell, 1968)

Seton-Watson, R. W. *Britain and the Dictators* (Cambridge UP, 1938)

Skidelsky, R. *Politicians and the Slump* (Macmillan, 1967)

Taylor, A. J. P. *The Origins of the Second World War* (Hamish Hamilton, 1961)

Thompson, Neville *The Anti-Appeasers* (Oxford UP, 1971)

Toynbee, A. J. *Survey of International Affairs* (Royal Institute of International Affair yearly 1930–1939)

Watt, Donald C. *Too Serious a Business* (Temple Smith, 1975)

Wheeler-Bennett, John W. *Munich. Prologue to Tragedy* (Macmillan, 1948)

II. BOOKS ON BRITISH DEFENCE POLICY 1918–1939

Blackett, P. M. S. *Studies of War* (Oliver and Boyd, 1962)

Cable, James *Gunboat Diplomacy* (Chatto and Windus, 1971)

Collier, Basil *Barren Victories. Versailles to Suez* (Cassell, 1964)

Cresswell, John *Generals and Admirals. The Story of Amphibious Command* (Longman Green, 1952)

Divine, David *The Blunted Sword* (Hutchinson, 1964)

   The Broken Wing (Hutchinson, 1966)

   Mutiny at Invergordon (Macdonald, 1970)

D'Ombrain, Nicholas *War Machinery and High Policy* (Oxford UP, 1973)

Fuller, J. F. C. *The Conduct of War 1789–1961* (Eyre and Spottiswoode, 1961)

Gooch, John *The Plans of War* (Routledge and Kegan Paul, 1974)

Graham, Gerald S. *The Politics of Naval Supremacy* (Cambridge UP, 1965)

Gretton, Sir Peter *Maritime Strategy* (Cassell, 1965)

Hankey, Lord *The Supreme Command* (2 vols., Allen and Unwin, 1961)

Supplement to Bibliography

Hezlet, Sir Arthur *The Submarine and Sea Power* (Peter Davies, 1967)
   Aircraft and Sea Power (Peter Davies, 1970)
   The Electron and Sea Power (Peter Davies, 1975)
Howard, Michael *Soldiers and Government* (Eyre and Spottiswoode, 1957)
   The Continental Commitment (Temple Smith, 1972)
Hyde, Montgomery *British Air Policy between the Wars* (Heinemann, 1976)
James, William *The Most Formidable Thing* (Hart-Davis, 1965)
Kemp, Peter *History of the Royal Navy* (Arthur Barker, 1969)
Liddell Hart, Basil *The Defence of Great Britain* (Faber, 1939)
Louis, W. Roger *British Strategy in the Far East* (Oxford UP, 1971)
Martin, L. W. *The Sea in Modern Strategy* (Chatto and Windus, 1967)
McLachlan, Donald *Room 39* (Weidenfeld and Nicolson, 1968)
Olson, Mancur *The Economics of the Wartime Shortage* (Duke UP, 1963)
Pack, S. W. C. *Sea Power in the Mediterranean* (Arthur Barker, 1971)
Padfield, Peter *The Battleship Era* (Hart-Davis, 1972)
Reynolds, Clark G. *Command of the Sea* (Morrow, NY, 1974)
Robertson, E. M. (ed.) *The Origins of the Second World War* (Macmillan, 1971)
Roetter, Charles *Psychological Warfare* (Oxford UP, 1974)
Roskill, Stephen *Hankey. Man of Secrets* (3 vols., Collins, 1970, 1972, 1974)
Saunders, Hilary St. G. *Per Ardua. The Rise of British Air Power 1911–1939* (Oxford UP, 1944)
Schofield, B. B. *British Sea Power* (Batsford, 1967)
Schurman, D. M. *The Education of a Navy* (Cassell, 1965)
Slessor, Sir John C. *Air Power and Armies* (Oxford UP, 1944)

III. BOOKS ON AMERICAN DEFENCE POLICY 1918–1939

Beard, Charles A. *American Foreign Policy in the Making 1932–1940* (Yale UP, 1954)
Borg, D. *The United States and the Far Eastern Crisis 1933–1938* (Cambridge, Mass., 1968)
Collier, Basil *The Lion and the Eagle* (MacDonald, 1972)
Current, Richard N. *Secretary Stimson. A Study in Statecraft* (Rutgers UP, 1954)
Davis, Burke *The Billy Mitchell Affair* (Random House, NY, 1968)
Dawes, Charles G. *Journal as Ambassador to Great Britain* (New York, 1939)
Divine, Robert A. *The Illusion of Neutrality* (Chicago UP, 1961)
Langer, W. M. and Gleason S. E. *The Challenge to Isolation 1937–1940* (Harper, 1952)
Melhorn, Charles M. *Two-Block Fox. The Rise of the Aircraft Carrier 1911–1929* (Annapolis, 1974)
Polmar, Norman and others *Aircraft Carriers.* (Doubleday, NY, 1969)
Reynolds, Clark G. *The Fast Carriers* (McGraw Hill, NY, 1968)

V. DISARMAMENT, GENERAL

Carlton, David *MacDonald versus Henderson* (Macmillan, 1970)
League of Nations *Disarmament. Preparations for the General Conference* (Geneva 1931)
  Armaments Year Books 1930–1939 (Geneva, yearly)
Royal Institute of International Affairs *The Future of the League of Nations* (NY, 1936)
  International Sanctions A Report by a Group (Oxford UP, 1938)
Zimmern, A. *The League of Nations and the Rule of Law* (Revised ed., Macmillan, 1939)

VII. THE LONDON NAVAL CONFERENCE 1935–1936

Pelz, Stephen E. *Race to Pearl Harbor* (Harvard UP, 1974)

VIII. BIOGRAPHIES AND AUTOBIOGRAPHIES

(A) BRITISH POLITICAL

Attlee, C. R. *As It Happened* (Heinemann, 1954)
Birkenhead, Lord *Halifax* (Hamish Hamilton, 1965)
Bullock, Alan *The Life and Times of Ernest Bevin* (2 vols., Heinemann, 1960, 1967)
Butler, Lord *The Art of the Possible* (Hamish Hamilton, 1971)
Chamberlain, Neville *The Struggle for Peace* (Hutchinson, N. D.)
Chandos, Lord *Memoirs* (Bodley Head, 1962)
Colvin, Ian *Vansittart in Office* (Gollancz, 1965)
Cooper, Duff *Old Men Forget* (Hart-Davis, 1953)
Dalton, Hugh *Memoirs* (2 vols. Muller, 1953, 1957)
Donoghue, B. and Jones, G. W. *Herbert Morrison. Portrait of a Politician* (Weidenfeld and Nicolson, 1973)
Donaldson, Frances *Edward VIII* (Weidenfeld and Nicolson, 1974)
Hyde, Montgomery *Baldwin* (Hart-Davis MacGibbon, 1973)
James, Robert R. *Memoirs of a Conservative. J. C. C. Davidson's Memoirs and Papers* (Weidenfeld and Nicolson, 1969)
Jenkins, Roy *Mr. Attlee. An Interim Biography* (Heinemann, 1948)
Kilmuir, Lord *Political Adventure* (Weidenfeld and Nicolson, 1964)
Nicolson, Harold *King George V* (Constable, 1952)
Pope-Hennessy, J. W. *Queen Mary* (Allen and Unwin, 1959)
Sparrow, G. *RAB Study of a Statesman* (Odhams, 1965)
Strang, Lord *At Home and Abroad* (André Deutsch, 1956)
Taylor, A. J. P. *Churchill. Four Faces and the Man* (Allen Lane, 1969)
  Beaverbrook (Hamish Hamilton, 1972)
Wheeler-Bennett, J. W. *King George V. His Life and Reign* (Macmillan, 1958)

Supplement to Bibliography

(B) BRITISH NAVAL, MILITARY AND AIR FORCE

Birkenhead, Lord *The Prof. in Two Worlds. The Official Life of Lord Cherwell* (Collins, 1964)

Connell, John *Wavell. Scholar and Soldier* (Collins, 1964)

Clark, Ronald W. *Tizard* (Methuen, 1965)

Douglas, Lord *Years of Command* (Collins 1966)

Ismay, Lord *Memoirs* (Heinemann, 1960)

Liddell Hart, B. *Memoirs*, vol. I (Cassell, 1965)

Pack, S. W. C. *Cunningham the Commander* (Batsford, 1974)

Pound, Reginald *Evans of the Broke* (Oxford UP, 1963)

Reader, W. J. *Architect of Air Power. The Life of 1st Viscount Weir* (Collins, 1968)

Roskill, Stephen (ed.) *Documents Relating to the Naval Air Service, Vol. I, 1908–1918* (Navy Records Society, 1969)

Tedder, Lord *With Prejudice* (Cassell, 1966)

Warner, Oliver *Cunningham of Hyndhope* (Murray, 1967)
   Admiral of the Fleet. The Life of Sir Charles Lambe (Sidgwick and Jackson, 1969)

(C) UNITED STATES. POLITICAL

Barron, Gloria J. *Leadership in Crisis. FDR and the Path to Intervention* (Kennicote Press, USA, 1973)

Baruch, Bernard M. *The Public Years* (Odhams, 1961)

Brogan, Denis W. *Roosevelt and the New Deal* (Oxford UP, 1952)

Burns, James MacG. *Roosevelt. The Lion and the Fox* (Secker and Warburg, 1956)

Dawes, Charles G. *Journal as Ambassador to Great Britain* (New York, 1939)

Foreign Relations of the United States of America (Government Printing Office, Washington)

   Japan 1931–1941 (2 vols., 1943)

   1932, vol. I, *General*, vol. II, *British Commonwealth, Europe etc.*

   1933, vol. I, *General*, vol. II, *British Commonwealth, Europe etc.*

   1934, vol. I, *General and British Commonwealth, Europe etc.*

   1935, vol. II, *British Commonwealth, Europe etc.*

   1936, vol. I, *General, British Commonwealth*, vol. II, *Europe etc.*

   1937, vol. II, *British Commonwealth, Europe etc.*

   1938, vol. II, *British Commonwealth, Europe etc.*

   1939, vol. II, *General British Commonwealth, Europe etc.*

Hull, Cordell, *Memoirs* (Hodder and Stoughton, 2 vols., 1948)

Kennan, George *Memoirs* (Hutchinson, 1968)

Leuchtenburg, William E. *Franklin D. Roosevelt and the New Deal 1932–1940* (Harper and Row, NY, 1963)

Moley, Raymond *After Seven Years* (Harpers, NY, 1939)

Myers, William S. *The Foreign Policies of Herbert Hoover* (Scribners, NY, 1940)

Roosevelt, Eleanor (ed.) *The Roosevelt Letters*, vol. 3, 1928–1945 (Harrap, 1952)

Roosevelt, Elliott (ed.) *The Roosevelt Letters* (Harrap, 1952)
Roosevelt, Franklin D. *Public Papers and Addresses* (vols. 1–5, Random House, NY, 1938. vols. 6 and 7, Macmillan, NY, 1941)
Schlesinger, Arthur M. Jr. *The Age of Roosevelt* (3 vols. Heinemann, 1957–1961)
Stimson, H. L. and Bundy, McGeorge *On Active Service in Peace and War* (Hutchinson, ND)
Rauch, Basil R. *Roosevelt from Munich to Pearl Harbor* (Creative Age, NY, 1950)
Tansill, Charles C. *Back Door to War. The Roosevelt Foreign Policy 1933–1941* (Regnery, NY, 1952)
Tugwell, R. G. *Roosevelt. The Architect of an Era* (Macmillan, NY, 1967)

(D) UNITED STATES, NAVAL, MILITARY AND AIR

Clark, J. J. with Reynolds, Clark G. *Carrier Admiral* (McKay, NY, 1967)
Pogue, Forrest C. and Harrison G. *George C. Marshal. Education of a General 1880–1939* (MacGibbon and Kee, 1964)
Richardson, Admiral James O. *On the Treadmill to Pearl Harbor* (Washington, 1973)
Wheeler, Gerald E. *Admiral William Veazie Pratt* (Washington, 1974)

IX. BRITISH COMMONWEALTH AND EMPIRE

Beloff, Max *Imperial Sunset*, vol. 1 (Methuen, 1969)
Bowle, John *The Imperial Achievement* (Secker and Warburg, 1974)
Hancock, W. K. *Smuts* (2 vols., Cambridge UP 1962, 1968) with 7 vols. of selections from papers.
Perham, Marjorie *Colonial Sequence 1930–1949* (Methuen, 1967)

X. FRANCE

Bury, J. P. T. *France 1814–1940* (New ed. Methuen, 1969)
Chapman, Guy *Why France Collapsed* (Cassell, 1968)
Reynaud, Paul *In the Thick of the Fight* (Eng. trans., Cassell, 1955)
Werth, Alexander *France in Ferment* (Jarrolds, 1934)

XI. GERMANY

Burden, Hamilton J. *The Nüremburg Party Rallies* (Praeger, NY, 1968)
Compton, J. V. *The Swastika and the Eagle* (Houghton, Mifflin, NY, 1968)
Dyck, Harvey L. *Weimar Germany and Soviet Russia* (Chatto and Windus, 1966)
Fest, Joachim *Hitler* (Eng. trans. Weidenfeld and Nicolson, 1973)
Friedländer, S. *Prelude to Downfall. Hitler and the United States* (Knopf., NY, 1968)
Gannon, F. R. *The British Press and Germany* (Oxford UP, 1971)
Irving, David *The Rise and Fall of the Luftwaffe* (Weidenfeld and Nicolson, 1974)

Supplement to Bibliography

O'Neill, Robert J. *The German Army and the Nazi Party 1933–1939* (Heinemann, 1968)

Robertson, E. M. *Hitler's Pre-War Policy and Military Plans 1933–1939* (Citadel Press, 1968)

XII. RUSSIA

Barron, John *KGB The Secret World of Soviet Secret Agents* (Hodder and Stoughton, 1974)

Dinerstein, H. S. *War and the Soviet Union* (Praeger, NY, 1959)

Erickson, J. *The Soviet High Command* (London, 1962)

Hyde, Montgomery *Stalin. The History of a Dictator* (Hart-Davis, 1971)

Mitchell, Donald W. *A History of Russian and Soviet Sea Power* (Deutsch, 1974)

Saunders, M. G. *The Soviet Navy* (Weidenfeld and Nicolson, 1958)

XIV. THE SPANISH CIVIL WAR

Crozier, Brian *Franco. A Biographical History* (Eyre and Spottiswoode, 1967)

Kemp, Peter *Mine Were of Trouble* (Cassell, 1957)

Steer, G. L. *The Tree of Gernika* (Hodder and Stoughton, 1938)

Thomas, Hugh *The Spanish Civil War* (New ed., Penguin, 1965)

Wintringham, Tom *English Captain* (Faber, 1939)

XV. JAPAN AND CHINA

Borg, Dorothy and Okamoto, Shumpei *Pearl Harbor as History* (Columbia UP, 1973)

Grew, J. C. *Ten Years in Japan* (Hammond, NY, 1944)

Hornbeck, S. K. *The United States in the Far East* (Boston, 1942)

Iriye, A. *After Imperialism* (Cambridge, Mass., 1965)
  Across the Pacific (New York, 1967)

Morley, J. (ed.) *Dilemmas of Growth in Pre-War Japan* (Princeton UP, 1971)

Ogata, S. N. *Defiance in Manchuria* (Berkeley UP, 1964)

Potter, John D. *Admiral of the Pacific. The Life of Yamamoto* (Heinemann, 1965)

Shigemitsu, M. *Japan and Her Destiny. My Struggle for Peace* (Hutchinson, 1958)

Stimson, H. L. *The Far Eastern Crisis* (Harper, NY, 1936)

Thorne, Christopher *The Limits of Foreign Policy. The West, The League and the Far Eastern Crisis of 1931–1933* (Hamish Hamilton, 1972)

Tuleja, Thaddeus V. *Statesmen and Admirals. The Quest for a Far Eastern Naval Policy* (Norton, NY, 1963)

XVI. ITALY

Carsten, F. L. *The Rise of Fascism* (California UP, 1968)
Ciano, Galeazzo *Ciano's Diary 1937–1938* (ed. M. Muggeridge) (Methuen, 1952)
  Diplomatic Papers (ed. M. Muggeridge) (Odhams, 1948)
Pini, Giorgio *The Official Life of Benito Mussolini* (Hutchison, ND)

XVII. ARTICLES IN PERIODICALS

NOTE. This list is by no means exhaustive, particularly with regard to articles which have appeared in *The Proceedings of the United States Naval Institute* (Annapolis), *The Journal of the Royal United Service Institution* (London) and *The Naval Review* (London). Between them those three journals contain scores of interesting articles concerned with the subject of this history—far too many to be listed here. However a complete Author and Subject Index of the RUSI Journal 1857–1963, edited by Robin Higham, is now available from University Microfilms, Ann Arbor, Michigan, and is of great value to students. Each annual volume of *The Naval Review* contains an Index, but circulation of the journal is restricted to members. Complete sets are available to approved students in the Royal United Services Institute for Defence Studies and in the Naval Library, London. The list below only cites articles which I have found especially valuable, or which contain information which is not easily found elsewhere.

Akagi, R. *Japan's Economic Relations with China* (Pacific Affairs, June 1971)
Birn, Donald S. *The League of Nations and Collective Security* (Journal of Contemporary History, vol. 9, no. 2, July 1974)
Burns, R. D. *Inspection of Mandates 1919–1941* (Pacific Historical Review, vol. XVIII, 1968)
Butterworth, Susan B. *Daladier and the Munich Crisis. A Reappraisal* (Journal of Contemporary History, vol. 9, no. 2, 1974)
Current, R. N. *The Stimson Doctrine and the Hoover Doctrine* (American Historical Review, vol. LIX, 1953–54)
Glover, Richard *War and Civilian Historians* (Journal of the History of Ideas, vol. XVIII, no. 1, Jan. 1957)
Goldman, Aaron L. *Sir Robert Vansittart's Search for Italian Co-operation against Hitler* (Journal of Contemporary History, vol. 9, no. 2, July 1974)
Gretton, Peter W. *The Royal Navy in the Spanish Civil War* (Naval Review, London, vol. LXII, nos. 1, 2 and 3, Jan., April and July, 1974)
Haight, John McV. *Franklin D. Roosevelt and a Naval Quarantine of Japan* (Pacific Historical Review, vol. XL, no. 2, May, 1971)
Howard, Michael (ed.) *Empire to Commonwealth 1910–1970* (The Round Table Diamond Jubilee Number, no. 240, July 1970)
Manne, Robert *The British Decision for Alliance with Russia, May 1939* (Journal of Contemporary History, vol. 9, no. 2, July 1974)

Supplement to Bibliography

Mansergh, P. N. S. *Studies in British Commonwealth Affairs. The Commonwealth and the Nations* (Royal Institute of Commonwealth Affairs, 1948)
 Survey of British Commonwealth Affairs. Problems of External Policy 1931–1939 (*ibid.,* 1952)

Marder, A. *The Royal Navy and the Ethiopian Crisis* (American Historical Review, vol. LXXV no. 5, 1970)

Okumiya, M. *For Sugar Boats or Submarines?* (US Naval Institute Proceedings, vol. 94, no. 8, Aug. 1968)

Overy, Richard J. *Transportation and Rearmament in the Third Reich* (The Historical Journal, vol. 16, no. 2, June 1973)

Pratt, L. *The Anglo-American Conversations of January 1938* (International Affairs, vol. 47, no. 4, 1971)

Ray, Thomas W. *The Bureaus Go On For Ever* (US Naval Institute Proceedings, vol. 94, no. 1, Jan. 1968)

Royal Institute of International Affairs, *Survey of British Commonwealth Affairs. Problems of External Policy 1931–1939* (Royal Institute, 1952)

Shai, Aaron *Was there a Far Eastern Munich?* (Journal of Contemporary History, vol. 9, no. 2, July 1974)

Thorne, C. G. *The Shanghai Crisis of 1932. The Basis of British Policy* (American Historical Review, vol. LXXV, no. 6, 1970)

Toynbee, A. J. *Survey of International Affairs* (International Affairs, yearly 1930–39)

Wilds, Thomas *How Japan Fortified the Mandated Islands* (US Naval Institute Proceedings, vol. 81, no. 4, April, 1955)

XVIII. COMMAND PAPERS 1930–1939

NOTE. *Some titles have been slightly abbreviated.*

First Lord's Statement Explanatory of the Navy Estimates 1929–30	Cmd. 3283
Fleets (Great Britain and Foreign Countries) 1929–30	Cmd. 3464
Memorandum of Position of HM Government at the London Naval Conference 1930	Cmd. 3485
See also Cmd. 3547, 3597, 5137	
First Lord's Statement Explanatory of the Navy Estimates 1929–30	Cmd. 3506
International Treaty for the Limitation of Naval Armaments (April 1930) [First London Treaty]	Cmd. 3556
Protocol for the Prohibition of the use of Poison Gas and Bacteriological Warfare	Cmd. 3604
Statement Explanatory of the Naval Construction Programme for 1930	Cmd. 3620
First Lord's Statement Explanatory of the Navy Estimates 1930–31	Cmd. 3799
Fleets (Great Britain and Foreign Countries) 1930–31	Cmd. 3805
Report of National Economy (May) Committee	Cmd. 3920
Fleets (Great Britain and Foreign Countries) 1931–32	Cmd. 4005
First Lord's Statement Explanatory of the Navy Estimates 1931–32	Cmd. 4024

XIX. UNPUBLISHED THESES

Fagan, George V. *Anglo-American Relations 1927–1937* (University of Pennsylvania, 1954)

Supplement to Bibliography

Levine, Robert H. *The Politics of American Naval Rearmament 1930–1938* (Harvard University, 1972)

Primrose, B. N. *Australian Naval Policy 1919–1942. A Case Study in Imperial Relations* (Australian National University, 1974)

Shay, Robert P. *When the Devil Drives. The Economic and Political Restraints on Britain's Rearmament Policy 1932–1939* (Columbia University, 1974)

Index

Index

Index

Index

Index

Index

Index

Hall, Admiral Sir Reginald W. (1870-1943), Director of Naval Intelligence, 388

Hamaguchi, Usachi (1870-1931), Japanese Prime Minister, 64; assassinated, 67

Hankey, Rt. Hon. Sir Maurice (Baron 1938) (1877-1963), Secretary to Cabinet and CID; his constant insistence on retention of Belligerent Rights, 44, 48, 69, 79, 87; Secretary General of First London Naval Conference, 57, 65; dislike of Ten Year Rule, 74, 144, 145-6; Chairman of Foreign Policy and Defence Sub-Committee for Imperial Conference of 1930, 76; his tribute to Alexander, 119; his attitude towards air bombardment, 143, Singapore Base, 149; and Disarmament Conference, 155, 171; alarmed at actions of Japan and Germany, 167; Chairman of DRC 168, 169; Empire tour of, 173, 184; his views on Naval-Aviation Controversy, 209-10, 393, 399, 401; prepares Defence White Paper of 1935, 214-15; campaigns for retention of private manufacture of arms, 246; opposed to sanctions against Italy, 252, 256; his close relations with Chatfield, 261, 271; desire to revive good relations with Italy, 272; and Second London Naval Conference, 291; reaction to Anglo-German Naval Agreement, 301, 358; views on France and Japan, 323, 324; at Imperial Conference of 1937, 345; his services to COS Committee, 417; Mentioned 182, 257

Harding, Warren G. (1865-1923), 29th President of USA, 38

Hasegawa, Kiyoshi (b. 1883), Japanese Admiral, 354

Hawaii, US base in, 23, 83, 173, 174 n2, 176, 180, 234, 365, 368, 479

Henderson, Rt. Hon. Arthur (1863-1935), Foreign Secretary, 51 n3, 56, 59, 62, 68, 78, 84, 134-5, 145, 155

Henderson, Rt. Hon. Sir Neville (1882-1942), British ambassador in Berlin, 440

Henderson, Rear-Admiral (later Admiral Sir Reginald E. H.) (1881-1939), successively commanding Aircraft Carriers, Controller and Third Sea Lord, his general brilliance and support of naval aviation, 188-9, 199-200, 202, 223-4; his work on gunnery design and other reforms, 225, 329, 332, 357, 397; collapse of health leads to resignation, 454, 463

Hepburn, Admiral A. J. (1877-1964), USN, 141, 142, 414

Hindenburg, Field-Marshal Paul von Benckendorff und (1842-1934), German President, 152

Hirota, K. (1878-1948), Japanese Foreign Minister, 180

Hitler, Adolf (1889-1945), German Chancellor and President, appointed Chancellor, 138, 152; withdraws from League of Nations, 164; denounces Treaty of Versailles, 184; introduces conscription, 216, 250; occupies Rhineland, 235, 272; intentions deceive Simon, 285, 300; announces existence of German Air Force, 301; agrees to Anglo-German Naval Agreement, 302, 303, 304, 321; his intervention in Spanish Civil War, 372; his designs on Austria and Czechoslovakia, 416; invades Austria, 418; his attitude during Czechoslovak Crisis, 438, 439, 440; denounces Agreement of 1935 and Protocol of 1937, 449; seizes rest of Czechoslovakia, 454; Mentioned 32 n4, 119, 131, 155 n1, 156

Hoare, Rt. Hon. Sir Samuel J. G. (1st Viscount Templewood 1944) (1880-1959), on Admiralty, 105; on Abyssinian war, 250-1, 257; relations with Chatfield, 261; Laval Pact, 257, 264; succeeds Monsell, 269, 279; and League Covenant, 276; wins Supplementary Estimates, 279; appointed Foreign Secretary, 304 n2; on German naval negotiations, 304-8; and Second London Naval Conference, 309; Eden succeeds, 315; and 1937-38 Estimates, 324-5; on battleship building programme, 325, 329; and 'New Standard Navy', 327; replaced by Duff Cooper, 355, 357, 402; on Chatfield's successor, 357; on blockade of Spain, 377, 379; on control of Fleet Air Arm, 395-404, 412; on Soviet alliance, 462

Hodges, Admiral Sir Michael H. (1874-1951), Second Sea Lord, 31-2, 70; C-in-C Atlantic Fleet, 93-4, 95, 105

Hong Kong, defence problems of, 80, 144-5, 185, 236, 238, 352

Hood, HMS, built in 1918, 45; involved in Invergordon Mutiny, 94, 96, 98, 99, 101-2, 103, 104, 107, 108, 109, 112, 114, 120 n2, 129, 130; rumour of trouble in, 239; at Gibraltar, 267 n4; activities in Spanish Civil War, 378, 380

Hoover, Herbert C. (1874-1936), 31st President of USA, assumes Presidency, 21; and decline of battleship, 24; and arms limitation, 37, 39, 139-41; talks with Macdonald, 45-9, 52, 69; and London Naval Conference, 53, 64; opposes Adams over naval appropriations, 67 n3; proposals at Geneva Disarmament Conference, 140-1

Horton, Admiral Sir Max Kennedy (1883-1951), 463

Hossbach, Col. Friedrich, memorandum, 416, 418

Index

Index

Index

Index

Index

Index

Index